The Supreme Court under
Earl Warren, 1953–1969

CHIEF JUSTICESHIPS
OF THE UNITED STATES SUPREME COURT

Herbert A. Johnson, Series Editor

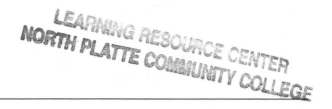

The Supreme Court under Earl Warren, 1953–1969

Michal R. Belknap

University of South Carolina Press

© 2005 University of South Carolina

Published in Columbia, South Carolina,
by the University of South Carolina Press

Manufactured in the United States of America

09 08 07 06 05   5 4 3 2 1

Library of Congress Cataloging-in-Publication Data

Belknap, Michal R.
  The Supreme Court under Earl Warren, 1953–1969 / Michal R. Belknap.
    p. cm.—(Chief justiceships of the United States Supreme Court)
  Includes bibliographical references and index.
  ISBN 1-57003-563-6 (cloth : alk. paper)
    1. United States. Supreme Court–History–20th century. 2. Political questions and judicial
  power–United States–History–20th century. 3. Warren, Earl, 1891–1974. I. Warren, Earl,
  1891–1974. II. Title. III. Series.
  KF8742.B427 2004
  347.73'26'09–dc22

                                                                                            2004019056

This book is dedicated to the memory of my father, Professor Robert H. Belknap (1917–1999). I promised you I would finish it, Dad, and, by the grace of God, I finally have.

Contents

Illustrations

Series Editor's Preface

Three decades ago retired chief justice Earl Warren died in Washington, D.C.; an era passed and a legend began. Part of a historian's task is to differentiate fact from legend, and an even more difficult task is to explain why things in the past occurred and happened as they did. Biographers struggle with these intellectual challenges as well, but they also do their best to remain objective despite close interaction and identification with the documentary record left by their subjects. Legal historians, a hybrid group of lawyer-historians, have struggled for the past forty years to write a definitive technical history of the law and its development on the one hand and on the other to explain the dynamic relationship between law and the society that both shapes law and is shaped by it. Professor Michal R. Belknap has faced all of these challenges in researching and writing this book, and the final product now emerges as an outstanding example of biographical art and legal history.

In keeping with the goal of this series, this volume, like its predecessors, is designed to provide the reader with a relatively brief but comprehensive discussion of the work of the United States Supreme Court during the leadership of one or more of the chief justices. The very magnitude and complexity of the Warren Court's achievements have dictated that this be a longer book than earlier titles in the series, and the meticulous research in extensive archival materials justifies the expanded size of this volume. To achieve economies of space while preserving valuable annotation, we have decided to place the notes at the end of the volume where they will be available for scholars wishing to benefit from Professor Belknap's exhaustive research. In addition, we have used a system of alphabetical coding to identify the most frequently used sources, and a guide to those abbreviations precedes the endnotes.

This is a very special book in two ways. First, it deals with the Warren Court, which played a critical role in the lifetime of an entire generation of lawyers and historians. Many, like the writer, remember the decision day of *Brown v. Board of Education* (1954), and some had the challenging task, as first-year law students, of writing a classroom exercise over whether the implementation of that decision should be gradual or immediate. Others will recall the decision in *Baker v. Carr* (1962) and their amazement that the Court had abandoned the "political question" doctrine after so many years of seeking its theoretical protection in this vital area of voting rights and equal protection. Those of us who taught constitutional history in the 1960s will never forget the demanding task of keeping up with Supreme Court opinions that "federalized" criminal justice and made frequently confusing (and amusing) attempts to define obscenity. We have lived through an era in which the justices led the nation in re-defining the nature of federalism and the right of federal citizens to due process and equal protection. Those imperatives drew the Court into more active involvement in the political life of the United States, as evidenced most recently by the revolu-tionary decision of *Bush v. Gore* (2000). These are the long shadows cast by the Warren Court—in the recollections of many, and in the historical memory of many more younger citizens and scholars.

This legal and constitutional history monograph is special for another reason as well: the background against which this volume, undoubtedly one of the best War-ren Court studies to appear in print, was prepared. Professor Belknap has persevered over a period of several years that have been marked by family death and illness, and more recently by his own serious illnesses and lengthy rehabilitation. The quality and craftsmanship of the book speaks for itself, but those of us involved in writing U.S. Supreme Court history have been greatly enriched and inspired by his scholarship, his dedication, and his courage.

Every book begins to be obsolescent on the day it is published, and this study despite its high quality will not be exempt from this fate. Others will follow Professor Belknap into Warren Court history, and their work may well modify a few of his find-ings and conclusions. Yet he has laid out for us a rich body of material that raises questions concerning the legendary Warren Court that only time will resolve. He has traced the marked alteration of the Warren Court's jurisprudence after the 1961 term and the departure of Justice Felix Frankfurter. In many ways those changes—in the Court's decision making, in its definition of its role in American life and politics, and in its sense of responsibility to provide legal and constitutional underpinnings for the achievement of the American dream—are still in process today. The driving force and energy of the Supreme Court under Earl Warren is not a matter of the past, but very much a dynamic component part of the living Constitution of the United States at the start of the twenty-first century.

Herbert A. Johnson

Acknowledgments

I am indebted to many individuals who assisted me in numerous ways during the ten years it took to write this book. I owe an especially large debt of gratitude to Herbert Johnson. After I had completed a draft, but while the manuscript still needed a great deal of revision, I nearly died from a brain abscess. It left me for many months barely able to read, let alone write a book. Herb wound up doing a great deal more work on my manuscript than series editors generally do. Alex Moore, my editor at the University of South Carolina Press, also went above and beyond the call of duty, even documenting the impact of my health problems on this project for some medical malpractice litigation.

My graduate school mentor, Stanley Kutler, and my University of California, San Diego, colleague, Michael Parrish, read and commented on the whole manuscript. Laureance A. Benner of the California Western School of Law and Josephine Gittler of the University of Iowa both provided detailed critiques of the criminal justice chapter. I would also like to thank the staff of the California Western Law Library, especially Linda Weathers and Bill Bookheim, without whose assistance writing this book would have been impossible.

It also could not have been written without immense assistance from a series of wonderful student research assistants. Particularly valuable were the contributions of Thomas LaVaut, who transcribed hundreds of handwritten justices' notes, and Charles Coleman, who compiled data documenting changes in the types of cases the Warren Court was deciding. Johanna Canlas, Theresa Conley, Brendan McHugh, and Noel Warner also made major contributions to *The Supreme Court under Earl Warren*.

So did my wife Patricia, who lovingly prodded me to keep working during some dark days when I thought the brain abscess had ended my career as a historian. I owe her a debt I can never fully repay.

Introduction

The Supreme Court over which Chief Justice Earl Warren presided from 1953 to 1969 occupies "a unique place in American law," as even such a sharp critic of its work as Judge Robert Bork acknowledges. Bork would not dispute legal historian Bernard Schwartz, an unabashed fan of the Warren Court, who contends that it carried out a judge-made revolution. Friend and foe alike recognize that the decisions of Chief Justice Warren and his colleagues profoundly altered numerous areas of the law, recasting everything from criminal procedure to the relationship between the government and religion. Perhaps equally important, they revolutionized the role of the Supreme Court in American life. As Morton Horwitz observes, the Warren Court "regularly handed down opinions that . . . transformed American constitutional doctrine and, in turn, profoundly affected American society."[1]

The nature of the changes it effected were as unusual as their magnitude. Traditionally, the Supreme Court had been a conservative body, often employing judicial power to protect property rights and resist the advances of democracy and egalitarianism. The Warren Court broke that mold. Aligning itself with the forces of political liberalism, it sought to make constitutional law an instrument for the reform of American government and society. The Court that Warren led often ignored the self-imposed limitations on judicial power that its more cautious predecessors had used to avoid conflict with the states and with the legislative and executive branches of the federal government. Its rampant activism made 1953–69 a creative and productive period. Only during the Marshall era did the Supreme Court produce so many significant decisions.

Many of these rulings were quite controversial when they were handed down, and some of them remain controversial today. More than four decades after Warren retired as chief justice, debate over the legacy of his Court rages on. As Mark Tushnet notes, "The Warren Court's definition of the Supreme Court's role in government remains prominent in contemporary political discussion." To conservatives, the tribunal Warren headed represents everything the Supreme Court should not be and should not do. Liberals, in contrast, long for a return to what they view as the "true course" that the Court charted during the Warren era.[2]

Their "nostalgia for the Warren Court is necessarily," as Lucas A. Power Jr. astutely observes, "a nostalgia for the 1960s."[3] Most of the decisions that aroused the admiration of its army of loyal supporters and the animosity of its legions of bitter foes were products of the political and social ferment of that turbulent decade. Not all were, to be sure. The Warren Court's best-known and most honored ruling, *Brown v. Board of Education,* was handed down in 1954, and decisions that it rendered in 1956 and 1957 thwarting a variety of anti-Communist initiatives ignited a political firestorm. Like the landmark cases of the 1960s, these earlier ones reflected changes in society and the body politic that were transforming much more than constitutional law. When the Warren Court held school segregation unconstitutional in *Brown,* it joined a struggle to win equal rights for African Americans that had begun at least as early as the 1930s. Its controversial decisions in 1956 and 1957 reflected a decline in hysterical anti-Communism that had begun with the armistice that ended the Korean War in 1953 and had manifested itself in the 1954 Senate censure of the man who gave his name to hysteria-inspired abuses of civil liberties, Senator Joseph R. McCarthy of Wisconsin. Confronted with intense congressional reaction against those decisions, the Court staged a strategic retreat under fire that highlighted the extent to which it followed rather than created political trends.

The trend that was gaining force in the country when the Eisenhower administration relinquished power in early 1961 was a liberal one, and by the time the assassination of John F. Kennedy thrust Lyndon Johnson into the presidency in November 1963, liberalism dominated the political landscape. Liberal causes, such as equal rights for African Americans, enjoyed widespread support. A surging egalitarianism made unacceptable the malapportionment of state legislatures, which subjected rapidly growing cities and suburbs to domination by more lightly populated small towns and rural areas. It also inspired public and private efforts to improve the lot of the poor and even generated interest in the plight of prisoners and those accused of crimes. Along with expanding support for political and social democracy came a sexual revolution. During the 1960s the advent of birth control pills allowed women to be sexually active without becoming pregnant, and sexual attitudes and practices changed dramatically.

The Warren Court responded sympathetically to the changes taking place around it. In 1962 Justice Felix Frankfurter, the leading proponent of the idea that the judiciary should leave reform to the political branches of the government, retired. The Court came under the control of liberal activists, who saw nothing wrong with judges using the power of their offices to improve life in America. During its last seven terms the Warren Court rendered decision after decision that advanced the liberal agenda.

The results were stunning. The Court forced the reapportionment of state legislatures, holding that the Constitution mandated "one person, one vote." It responded to America's increasing religious diversity with rulings intended to ensure governmental neutrality toward religion by banishing prayer and Bible reading from the public schools. It gave consistent support to the movement for racial equality, handing down decisions prohibiting segregation in a variety of contexts, protecting civil rights activists from harassment by southern police and judges, and affirming the constitutionality of congressional civil rights legislation. The Warren Court also responded to the egalitarianism of the era by revolutionizing the criminal justice system. Bent on making that system more fair and eliminating discrimination against defendants who were black, poor, or both, the Court constitutionalized much of the law of criminal procedure. It transformed what had been a field of law left largely to the states, incorporating most provisions of the Fourth, Fifth, Sixth, and Eighth Amendments into the Due Process Clause of the Fourteenth Amendment, and thereby requiring state and local police and prosecutors to observe the same rules as their federal counterparts. At the same time, the Court significantly expanded the rights of all those accused of crimes. Warren and his colleagues also interpreted the First Amendment in ways that expanded freedom of speech, not only for those who wished to express their political views but also for those who wanted to write and speak more openly and explicitly about sex. They extended constitutional protection to a good deal of material that earlier generations would have condemned as obscene, while also creating a right of privacy that protected marital intimacy from governmental intrusion.

These decisions were unpopular in many circles. The Warren Court's criminal justice rulings outraged police, prosecutors, and many ordinary Americans concerned about the country's rapidly rising crime rate. Warren's Court also angered southern segregationists by supporting African American civil rights, national security alarmists by limiting anti-Communist initiatives, state politicians by reapportioning some of them out of their jobs, church leaders by "banning God from the schools," and prudes by giving constitutional protection to sexually explicit books, magazines, and movies. The "Impeach Earl Warren" billboards that came to dot the landscape offered highly visible evidence of how much some people hated Warren and his Court.

That Court staggered to an ignominious end in 1969, amid scandal and controversy. Although gone, it is not forgotten. Nor is it ever likely to be. The Supreme Court that Earl Warren headed fundamentally transformed too many areas of the law for the mere passage of time and the addition of a few hundred new cases to the *United States Reports* to extinguish its significance. "The Warren Court," as Powe reminds us, "created the image of the Supreme Court as a revolutionary body, a powerful force for social change." That image is, he insists, not entirely accurate. It is, however, one to which many lawyers and lay people cling. The belief that Warren and his colleagues used constitutional law to transform American government and society makes the Warren Court a powerful symbol, not only to those disturbed by the changes for which it is often blamed, but even more to those who long for a new wave of liberal reform. The Warren Court's symbolic significance and the sheer magnitude of the changes that it wrought in the corpus of constitutional law ensure that it will always occupy a preeminent place in American legal history.[4]

The Supreme Court under
Earl Warren, 1953–1969

1

ARRIVAL OF THE SUPER CHIEF

"The day of my induction as Chief Justice of the United States was for me at once the most awesome and the loneliest day of my public career," Earl Warren recalled years later. Warren had served three terms as governor of California and had been the Republican Party's nominee for vice president in 1948. But when President Dwight Eisenhower nominated him to replace Chief Justice Fred Vinson, following Vinson's sudden death from a heart attack on September 8, 1953, Warren had not been in a courtroom for years. He approached his new position "with profound recognition of my unpreparedness to assume its obligations in such an abrupt manner." So suddenly had Warren been thrust into the nation's highest judicial office that there had not even been time to make him one of the robes that judges traditionally wear on the bench. When the justices of the Supreme Court gathered in their conference room on October 5 to administer the constitutional oath of office to the new chief in a private ceremony and to dress for the public session of the Court that afternoon, Warren had to don a robe that someone had scrounged up somewhere in the building. It was too long for the six-foot-one chief justice, and he stepped on the hem while walking to his seat. "I literally stumbled onto the bench," he recalled years later. The justices marched to their seats in reverse order of seniority, with the most junior, Tom Clark, in the lead, and the most senior, Hugo Black, next to last. "In accordance with tradition," Warren noted, "I brought up the rear."[1]

Not for long would he march behind the other members of what would soon become famous (and in some circles infamous) as "the Warren Court." Warren would quickly demonstrate a capacity for leadership that would prompt observers to rank him—along with John Marshall, Roger Taney, and Charles Evans Hughes—as one of the four most influential chief justices in the history of the Supreme Court. His sixteen-year term would be remembered as one of the most creative in the annals American public law, rivaled only by the formative era when Marshall headed the Court.[2] As Morton Horwitz observes, "From 1953, when Earl Warren became Chief Justice, to 1969 when Warren stepped down as Chief Justice, a constitutional revolution occurred."[3] That revolution made the Warren Court "the best known Supreme Court in history, and probably the most controversial."[4]

Under Warren's leadership the Court moved to the center of the national political stage, injecting itself into a host of public policy controversies generated by the profound social and political changes that the United States underwent during the decades after World War II. In 1953 America was experiencing a baby boom, its suburbs were exploding, and its cities, while burgeoning, were beginning to show signs of decay. Racial, generational, and religious tensions that would unravel the social fabric in the 1960s were simmering just below the surface, waiting to trigger political controversies in which the Warren Court would play a major role.

When Warren assumed the chief justiceship, however, the national political stage was dominated by Senator Joseph R. McCarthy (R-Wisc.), an accomplished demagogue who had effectively exploited concerns about Communism that had reached hysterical proportions during the recently concluded Korean War. Although a July 27, 1953, armistice had ended fighting with the Communist North Koreans and Chinese, Americans remained fearful of the Soviet Union, a Communist superpower with a massive army and atomic weapons, which they erroneously assumed was bent on world conquest. In order to contain Soviet expansionism, the United States had made diplomatic and military commitments throughout the world and had embarked upon a massive program of rearmament. The Cold War with the USSR fueled fears of Communist subversion at home; investigations conducted by a number of Republican-controlled congressional committees fanned these fears into a full-blown Red Scare. Mounting public concern about Communism compelled the administration of Democratic president Harry Truman to initiate a loyalty-security program for federal employees and to prosecute the leaders of the American Communist Party for sedition. These initiatives, like the congressional investigations, engendered numerous invasions of individual rights. They failed, however, to save the Democrats from defeat in the 1952 presidential election, in which a military hero, General Dwight D. Eisenhower, exploited popular concerns about Communism, Korea, and corruption to capture the presidency. Even with a fellow Republican in the White House, McCarthy continued to make wild charges about Communist influences in the executive branch of the federal government. His tactics inspired mounting opposition, and by December 1954 his Senate colleagues would find the political courage to censure formally the Wisconsin demagogue.

When Warren assumed the chief justiceship, however, Americans remained preoccupied with Communism and the Cold War. These issues had pushed into the background perhaps the most serious social problem confronting the United States: the long-standing segregation and subordination of the country's African American minority. Truman had created a presidential commission to study this "American dilemma," but its 1947 report, *To Secure These Rights,* had outraged white residents of the South, where separation of the races was required by law. The opposition of its southern members kept Congress from enacting the proposals Truman made to implement the commission's recommendations. Numerous states adopted legislation forbidding employers to discriminate on the basis of race, but Truman found himself limited to actions he could take without congressional authorization. In 1948 he issued executive orders abolishing segregation in federal employment and calling for the integration of the armed forces. During his administration the Justice Department also began filing amicus curiae briefs with the Supreme Court, supporting private litigants who were attacking segregation.[5] One case in which the department had intervened, *Brown v. Board of Education*, would present Chief Justice Warren with his first great challenge.

The man who would have to lead the Supreme Court to a resolution of that divisive dispute had never before decided a case. He came to the chief justiceship devoid of judicial experience, having spent most of his life in politics. Sixty-two at the time of his appointment, Warren had been born in Los Angeles on March 19, 1891. The son of immigrant parents (his father was from Norway and his mother from Sweden), he grew up in a working-class family. His father, a railroad car repairman and inspector, was blacklisted for participating in the 1894 Pullman Strike, forcing him to move the family to San Bernadino, and then on to the Bakersfield area, where he found employment with Southern Pacific. While in high school Earl too worked for the railroad. His observations of the Southern Pacific equipped him with an understanding of the costs of economic dependency and bred both sympathy for working men and antagonism toward giant corporations. "I saw that [company's] power exercised and the hardship that followed in its wake," he recalled years later. Warren remembered with distaste the callous way the railroad had treated workers injured on the job, habitually laid off employees at the end of the fiscal year so it could pay a higher dividend, and exploited the members of the minority groups it imported to provide cheap labor. During his youth in the wide-open frontier town of Bakersfield, Warren also acquired a lifelong antipathy for prostitution, gambling, and other forms of vice, as well as for the corruption of public officials that allowed these vices to flourish.[6]

In 1908 he left Bakersfield for Berkeley to attend the University of California. Warren studied law but did not distinguish himself academically. After receiving a B.A. in 1912 and a law degree in 1914, he was admitted to practice on motion of a Berkeley professor. The new attorney's first job was in the law department of the Associated Oil Company in San Francisco. He left after a year to take a position with the Oakland firm of Robinson and Robinson. In April 1917, while Warren and some of his Berkeley classmates were preparing to join one of the firm's senior members in creating a new partnership, the United States entered World War I. Warren promptly applied for officer training. He was not accepted, but volunteered to be drafted and was recommended for Officers' Training Camp after serving for a time as sergeant. After receiving his commission, he trained replacement troops in Virginia and served as a bayonet instructor at Camp McArthur, Texas.

Following his discharge in early December of 1918, Warren returned to California to embark upon a career in politics and public service. During his student days at Berkeley, he had offered his services to popular prosecutor Hiram Johnson, and when Johnson ran successfully for governor in 1910 as a Republican, Warren enthusiastically supported him. After becoming thoroughly enamored with the Progressivism that Johnson championed, he remained devoted to the political values associated with it throughout his own career in public life. That career began when a former associate at Robinson and Robinson and Leon Gray, a college fraternity brother who had just been elected to the California legislature, secured him a temporary position as the clerk of the assembly judiciary committee. After the 1919 legislative session ended, Gray got Warren a job with the Oakland city attorney, and they also engaged in some private practice together.

In 1920 Gray's efforts to get his fraternity brother a job with the Alameda County district attorney's office finally bore fruit. Warren prosecuted criminal cases, defended civil and criminal actions against county officers, counseled boards of education on their potential civil liability, and acted as legal adviser to the board of supervisors. He performed so well that within less than four years he had become one of District Attorney Ezra Decoto's two top assistants. When Decoto resigned in 1925, the supervisors gave Warren his job. The following year, he won a four-year term at the polls. By the time his term ended in 1930, the Depression had begun, making a return to private practice economically impossible. Serving as district attorney for thirteen years, Warren ran his office like a Progressive reformer, crusading against crime, vice, and corruption, while also campaigning to professionalize California law enforcement by making it more efficient and more responsive to public opinion and by ensuring its independence from partisan politics and pressure groups. A 1931 poll of district attorneys rated Warren one of the best in the country. The longer he served, the more interested he became in governmental affairs. Desiring a continuing public career, Warren set his sights on the post of attorney general. He launched a successful campaign to amend the California Constitution to expand the powers and increase the salary of that office and also broadened his political base, becoming chairman of the Republican State Central Committee, yet maintaining good relations with Democrats. When Warren ran for attorney general in 1938, he secured the nominations of both parties under California's cross-filing system. After winning election to the state's highest legal position, he used it to attack gambling, prostitution, and speakeasies and to continue to combat organized crime as he had done in Alameda County.[7]

Warren would have been content to remain attorney general, but Governor Culbert Olson provoked him into running for higher office. Olson, a Democrat, viewed Warren as a potential rival, and by treating him as a Republican partisan, managed to make him one. The governor bypassed the attorney general on legal matters, set aside plans and programs that he had developed in law enforcement, civil defense, and other areas, and vetoed an appropriation for his office. Olson further angered Warren by pardoning some union men he had convicted of murder while serving as Alameda County district attorney. Frustrated that no other substantial candidate was willing to challenge the incumbent, Warren decided to run for governor in 1942. Cross-filing again, he not only won the GOP nomination, but came within one hundred thousand votes of capturing the Democratic one as well. In the general election Warren got 57 percent of the vote. He was reelected in 1946, and in 1950 he became the first California governor ever elected for a third term.

Viewing himself as a Progressive crusader for nonpartisan, open, and honest government, Warren, who had been a rather orthodox Republican in the 1920s and a critic of New Deal policies in the 1930s, compiled a surprisingly liberal record as governor. He secured enactment of legislation to create a modern hospital system, improve prisons and the corrections system, improve old age pensions and unemployment benefits, and reorganize the bureaucracy. Governor Warren even urged the creation of a comprehensive state health-insurance system. By 1950 he could be characterized as a moderate supporter of affirmative government, which placed him at odds with conservative Republicans in his own state.

Yet Warren had become a power in the national GOP. In 1944 he was the keynote speaker at the Republican National Convention, and the party's presidential nominee, Governor Thomas Dewey of New York, tried unsuccessfully to persuade him to become his running mate. When the party renominated Dewey in 1948, he asked again, and this time Warren agreed to run for vice president. He did not really want the job, did not enjoy the campaign, and did not hide his relief when he lost. Warren had developed aspirations for national office, though, and on November 14, 1951, he announced his candidacy for president. An operation for abdominal cancer damaged his chances for the nomination, which suffered a fatal blow when the immensely popular Eisenhower announced two months later that he was running.

Although Warren's bid for the presidency failed, his prominence in the Republican Party enabled him to become chief justice. Contrary to rumors that circulated at the time, he did not receive a seat on the Supreme Court as a quid pro quo for helping Eisenhower secure the presidential nomination. Warren did facilitate the general's victory over Senator Robert Taft of Ohio, because the California delegation, which Warren controlled, voted with Eisenhower's forces to bar challenged pro-Taft delegations from voting on other credentials challenges following their own seating. But even after Warren finished third on a first ballot, which brought Ike within nine votes of the nomination, Warren refused to release his delegates. It was Harold Stassen of Minnesota who delivered the twelve votes that put Eisenhower over the top. "I owed Governor Warren nothing," the president insisted. That was something of an overstatement. Warren directed the California campaign for the Republican ticket, and after its prospects had been dimmed by September revelations that Ike's running mate, Senator Richard Nixon, had been the beneficiary of a secret slush fund, he made a television appearance and numerous speeches on behalf of the GOP nominees. Eisenhower's overwhelming victory in November elicited hearty congratulations from the governor, which were reciprocated with a warm note of appreciation from the president-elect. Although the two men had not had much personal contact, Eisenhower greatly respected Warren and was clearly in his debt.[8]

Indeed, during the convention, his trusted adviser, Lucius Clay, had, without Ike's knowledge, offered Warren any federal position he wanted if he would stay in the race, and thus keep Taft from picking up California delegates. Clay and Herbert Brownell, who had managed the Eisenhower campaign, tried to satisfy the governor with the Interior Department. Citing financial considerations, he rejected the offer. In December, with selection of cabinet members being completed, according to Brownell, "Out of the blue, Ike told me that he thought Warren would make a fine Supreme Court justice." Eisenhower then telephoned Warren to spring the idea on him. It was only 7:00 A.M. in Sacramento, and he caught the governor reading in bed. Eisenhower told Warren that although he had received serious consideration for attorney general, that job was going to Brownell, leaving no place for him in the cabinet. "But I want you to know," Ike assured the governor, "that I intend to offer you the first vacancy on the Supreme Court." Although the president claimed later that he was not "definitely committed to any appointment," he apparently conveyed exactly the opposite impression to Warren.[9]

The place that Eisenhower had somewhat impulsively promised him was not an ideal one for a man who had never been a judge and had not even actively practiced law for many years. By the spring of 1953, the president himself apparently had recognized that Warren needed some "fresh legal experience" before joining the Supreme Court. Brownell was having difficulty finding a solicitor general, and Eisenhower suggested that position could provide the governor with a needed refresher course. While Warren and his wife were passing through Washington on the way to the June 2, 1953, coronation of Queen Elizabeth II in England, Brownell discussed the idea with him. Warren told the attorney general that he had decided to announce his retirement from the governorship as soon as he got back to California, but he expressed doubts about whether his family's financial situation would permit him to become solicitor general. Brownell urged him to think it over. He also arranged for the Warrens to pay a social call on the president and Mrs. Eisenhower at the White House. After the coronation, Warren, who had to return to Sacramento to sign some bills before joining his wife and daughters on a tour of Scandinavia, stopped over in Washington, where he had a "delightful luncheon" with the president. Ike probed Warren about his views and came away convinced the Californian was "a man of big ideals and common sense." Warren still had made no commitment to either the president or Brownell, but after pondering their offer as he traveled through Northern Europe, on August 3 he wired the attorney general from Stockholm. Using a code they had devised, he informed Brownell that if the president appointed him solicitor general, he would accept. Soon after his return from Europe in late August, Warren announced that he would not be a candidate for a fourth term as governor.[10]

When he left Sacramento, however, he did so to become chief justice rather than solicitor general. Five days after Warren's September 3 announcement, Fred Vinson died suddenly in the middle of the night. When the president had made his offer of the first vacancy on the Supreme Court, nobody had been thinking about the chief justiceship. Not believing he was obligated to give that job to Warren, Eisenhower asked Brownell to check out two or three other individuals, whom he thought should be considered for it. The only Republican then on the Court, Harold Burton, had a well-deserved reputation for mediocrity that kept him from receiving serious consideration. The president emphasized that partisan political considerations should not determine the identity of a Supreme Court nominee, and Brownell greatly admired Justice Robert Jackson, a Democrat. He reluctantly concluded, however, that the senatorial hostility Jackson had aroused by taking a leave of absence from the Court to prosecute Nazi war criminals at Nuremberg and the support he had given President Roosevelt's 1937 plan to "pack" the Supreme Court disqualified him. An obvious choice was Chief Justice Arthur Vanderbilt of New Jersey, one of America's most distinguished state judges and, like Brownell, a close political ally of Tom Dewey. Vanderbilt, however, had suffered a heart attack. Two members of the federal appellate bench, Chief Judge John J. Parker of the Fourth Circuit (who had been nominated for the Court by Herbert Hoover, but rejected by the Senate) and Judge Orie Philips of the Tenth Circuit were both eliminated because Eisenhower, anxious to avoid naming someone who might soon be replaced by a "New Deal" president, did not want anyone older than sixty-two. Age also weighed against Secretary of State John Foster Dulles, but Eisenhower offered the job to the sixty-five-year-old corporate lawyer anyhow. Happy in his present position, Dulles "eliminated himself instantly and unequivocally."[11]

That left Warren. He satisfied the president's criteria. At the beginning of his administration, Eisenhower had informed Brownell that he wanted his judicial nominees to have "character and ability," common sense, and no association with extreme legal or philosophic views. Because the chief justice, as head of the Judicial Conference of the United States, was increasingly involved in matters of organization and administration, the president felt that position required someone of demonstrated administrative ability who could provide leadership and promote efficiency. Eisenhower thought a "political figure" who satisfied these criteria could "with propriety" be appointed. To the president, Warren seemed like the leading prospect, but he wanted to get more information about his public record and achievements as a lawyer and also determine whether the governor would prefer to go directly onto the Court, or still wanted to be solicitor general first.[12]

Hence Eisenhower dispatched Brownell to California to meet with Warren. The attorney general managed to reach the governor, who was deer hunting on Santa Rosa Island, by ship-to-shore radio, and they eventually arranged to confer on a Sunday at McClellan Air Force Base in Sacramento. During this meeting Warren made it clear that he wanted to be appointed to the Supreme Court and that he considered the opening created by Vinson's death the "next vacancy." He did acknowledge, however, that the president could fulfill his commitment either by making him chief justice or by elevating an associate justice and giving him the vacated seat. Brownell questioned Warren about some charges that had been leveled at him by his political opponents. He also informed the governor that Eisenhower desired to make an interim appointment. Because a full bench was needed to handle some extremely important cases that were on the calendar for the beginning of the Court's next term, the president wanted a nominee willing to take office when that term commenced on October 4. Although noting that such a hasty departure would be a poor way to end eleven years as governor, Warren said he could take office then. Brownell reported his findings to the president, and the following day Eisenhower chose Warren. Before making a formal announcement, he tried to test reaction to his choice by having the attorney general float the governor's name to a small group of reporters. Brownell did such a poor job of leaking, however, that they immediately wrote stories saying Warren would be the nominee. He and Ike promptly telephoned Warren to tell him the president was about to announce his nomination. As soon as Eisenhower did so at his September 30 press conference, Warren "gratefully and humbly" accepted.[13]

Reaction to the president's choice was mixed. The California legislature adopted a concurrent resolution applauding it. Justice Burton wrote Eisenhower to express his approval, as did the nominee's old friend, Senate Majority Leader William F.

Knowland (R-Calif.), and the president's younger brother, Milton. Mail received by the White House ran nearly three to one against the Warren nomination, however. The most frequently expressed complaint was that the nominee lacked judicial experience. Many disparaging letters came from lawyers. Some conservatives also voiced disapproval. Among them was the president's older brother Edgar.[14]

The chairman of the Senate Judiciary Committee, William Langer (R-N.D.), allegedly unhappy at the White House for ignoring him when appointing North Dakota postmasters, allowed opponents of the nomination the widest possible latitude to express their views. He also sent investigators to California to look into an array of anonymous and rather absurd charges against Warren. One member of Langer's committee, Senator Olin Johnston (D-S.C.) demanded a full FBI investigation of the nominee prior to any vote on his confirmation. Others denounced the charges against Warren as "tommyrot" and "rubbish." The State Bar of California's Board of Governors "unanimously and without reservation" endorsed him, and the American Bar Association's Standing Committee on the Federal Judiciary rated him well qualified and urged confirmation. To demonstrate the administration's continued support for its nominee, Brownell held a reception for him at the Justice Department, and the president took the unusual step of making a personal appearance when Warren took his seat on the Court. On March 1, 1954, the nominee's backers finally prevailed, as the Senate confirmed him on a voice vote.[15]

A career politician had won his last battle in the political arena. In the future Warren would sometimes be mentioned as a possible Republican presidential nominee, especially after Eisenhower's 1955 heart attack, but he quashed all rumors of another run for office. His appointment to the Supreme Court, he assured his son, was "absolutely the end of my political life." The president was gratified "to know that the weighty problems of your office will be attacked with all the energy and determination of a strong man who has enthusiastically devoted his remaining years . . . to the single purpose of upholding justice in the land."[16]

Although abandoning politics for the judicial arena, Warren would need all of his political skill in his new position. He was assuming leadership of a fractious and rather ineffective Supreme Court, torn by ideological and personal conflict. Dominated intellectually by four Franklin Roosevelt appointees, its senior member was the sixty-six-year-old Hugo Black, who had taken his seat in 1937. Like Warren's, his background was political. Black had developed a keen interest in politics as a boy in rural Clay County, Alabama, where his father operated a general merchandise store. Also fascinated by trials at the county courthouse, he resisted his mother's wishes that he become a doctor and enrolled at the University of Alabama Law School. Ranked near the top of his class when he graduated in 1906, Black tried unsuccessfully to practice in his hometown of Ashland, then moved to Birmingham, where within a decade he had become one of the city's most successful litigators. Except for one insurance company, his clientele rarely included corporations. It consisted mainly of middle- and lower-class individuals, whom he represented primarily in personal injury cases, as well as several labor unions. Working mostly for contingent fees, Black won regularly enough to earn a higher income than most other Birmingham lawyers. His most controversial success came when he secured the acquittal of Edwin R. Stephenson, a Methodist minister charged with killing a Catholic priest who had married his daughter to a Puerto Rican.

While building his private practice, in 1912 Black took a part-time position as a police court judge. His next foray into public service came in 1914 when he surprised the Birmingham establishment by successfully challenging the incumbent Jefferson County solicitor, Harrington Heflin, a member of one of Alabama's most politically prominent families. As a prosecutor, Black attacked the county's corrupt fee system, prosecuted coal companies for unfair wage practices, and initiated a grand jury investigation of ruthless police interrogation tactics. Successfully exploiting ambiguities in the state constitution, his opponents filed a lawsuit that deprived him of the authority to hire his own staff. Disgusted, Black resigned to enter World War I military service.

After rising to the rank of captain without ever leaving the United States, he returned to private practice in 1919. In 1923 the politically ambitious Black joined the Ku Klux Klan. Two years later, he launched a campaign for the U.S. Senate. Backed by the Klan, Black waged a vigorous campaign that emphasized populist themes. He defeated two better-known opponents in 1926, and having made no further effort to court the Klan, was reelected in 1932. As a senator, Black sponsored legislation to limit the workweek to thirty hours and conducted investigations of shipping firms, commercial airlines, and public utilities holding companies. He supported legislation beneficial to farmers and labor, as well as higher taxes on corporate profits, but joined other southern Democrats in filibustering antilynching legislation.

Black broke with other senators from his region to champion Roosevelt's 1937 court-packing plan. It failed, but when the retirement of Justice Willis Van Decanter created a Supreme Court vacancy, the president, still anxious to create a pro–New Deal bench, nominated Black. Revelation of his earlier membership in the Klan made the nomination controversial, but the nominee defended himself ably in a nationwide radio broadcast, in which he denied being an enemy of minorities and attacked religious bigotry. Public opinion swung in Black's favor, and the Senate confirmed him by a vote of sixty-three to sixteen.[17]

Black's great rival on the Court, seventy-year-old Felix Frankfurter, also aroused controversy prior to his appointment. An Austrian-born Jew, Frankfurter had immigrated to New York City as a boy. A brilliant student, he graduated third in his class from City College of New York at nineteen. After briefly attending two local law schools at night and working for the city's tenement house commission, Frankfurter enrolled at Harvard Law School, where he led his class academically for three years and earned a position on the law review. Anti-Semitism hindered his quest for employment, however, and only an unusually strong recommendation from Dean James Barr Ames got him a job with a New York law firm.

Frankfurter soon became bored with private practice and, along with a number of other top-ranked recent law school graduates, went to work for United States

Attorney Henry Stimson. When Stimson moved from New York to Washington to become secretary of war, Frankfurter, fired with idealism about public service, went along, becoming a legal adviser in the War Department's Bureau of Insular Affairs. When a change of administration forced his mentor out of office, Frankfurter accepted a teaching position at Harvard. He returned to government service during World War I, acting as a legal adviser to the President's Mediation Commission, chairing the War Labor Policies Board, investigating the Bisbee deportation and the Tom Mooney case, participating in a diplomatic mission to Turkey, and attending the Versailles peace talks.

Frankfurter returned to Harvard in the fall of 1919 to teach for two decades. He established a reputation as a leading academic authority on the Supreme Court and was awarded an endowed chair in administrative law. The commitment to Progressive reform that had inspired his government service and motivated him to defend state wages and hours laws in court before the war continued to animate him, and (with secret financial assistance from Supreme Court justice Louis Brandeis) he immersed himself in a variety of causes outside the classroom. Frankfurter was an active Zionist. He also represented alien radicals arrested during the Red Scare, signed a report attacking the conduct of the United States Department of Justice during the Palmer Raids, and both censured the trial of Sacco and Vanzetti in print and engaged in behind-the-scenes efforts to save the condemned anarchists from execution. Conservative Harvard alumni demanded he be fired for his alleged radicalism. Frankfurter's commitment, however, was to the integrity of the legal system, rather than to radical causes.

Politically, he was a Progressive who became a New Dealer. Frankfurter met Franklin Roosevelt in 1906 and began actively cultivating his friendship after FDR was elected governor of New York in 1928. When Roosevelt became president, he offered to make his friend solicitor general, but after consulting Justices Brandeis and Oliver Wendell Holmes Jr., Frankfurter declined. He continued to advise the president, however, and although never quite as influential as his enemies claimed, did draft important legislation and channel young Harvard graduates to Washington to work for the New Deal. In 1938, after intense lobbying by his many supporters, Roosevelt rewarded him with a seat on the Supreme Court.[18]

There was widespread expectation, especially in liberal circles, that because of his intellectual abilities and familiarity with the Court's work, Frankfurter would become the leader of a progressive bloc of Roosevelt appointees. He had been on intimate terms with several distinguished justices and had corresponded regularly with Chief Justices William Howard Taft and Charles Evans Hughes. At Justice Harlan Stone's urging, he had endeavored, even before his own appointment, to instruct Black on how to do his job. His arrogance, however, soon alienated both Black and another Roosevelt appointee, William O. Douglas.[19]

Like Black and Frankfurter, the sixty-five-year-old Douglas, who joined the Court less than three months after Frankfurter, had climbed to high judicial office from humble origins. Born in Minnesota, he was raised in Yakima, Washington, by an impoverished single mother after his father, a Presbyterian minister, died when he was six. As a boy, Douglas washed windows, swept floors, and picked fruit alongside itinerant laborers. A sickly youth, who later claimed to have survived a bout with polio, he built up his body by hiking in the mountains. Douglas excelled in the class-room, earning a scholarship to Whitman College. There he served in the Student Army Training Corps during World War I. After graduation Douglas taught high school English for two years. Then, bent on becoming a lawyer, he headed east for Columbia Law School with seventy-five dollars in his pocket, riding freight cars and helping to pay for the trip by tending two thousand sheep. His wife's teaching job and the money he earned tutoring financed his legal education.

After earning a position on the law review and graduating second in his class (despite a C in constitutional law), Douglas went to work for the prestigious Cravath firm in New York, where he specialized in securities regulation and corporate bank-ruptcy and reorganization. He tried practicing in Yakima, only to return to Cravath after a few months. Then in 1927 Douglas accepted a teaching position at Columbia Law School. Caught up in a nasty fight over the deanship and proposals for funda-mentally restructuring the curriculum, in which he sided with some of the founding fathers of Legal Realism, he left after one year to join the faculty at Yale.

Douglas remained there until 1934 when President Roosevelt appointed him to the Securities and Exchange Commission. Three years later, despite having aroused the ire of the Wall Street establishment with devastating reports cataloguing the excesses of the New York Stock Exchange and its officers, he became the chairman of the SEC. A sociable individual who partied well, Douglas developed friendships with a number of prominent New Dealers, even playing poker regularly with the president. He acquired sufficient political stature to entertain presidential ambitions and in the 1940s received serious consideration for a place on the Democratic ticket. By then he was on the Supreme Court, having become the youngest appointee ever when Roosevelt, after being lobbied by Douglas's friends and looking for someone who was both a loyal New Dealer and a Westerner, nominated him in 1939.[20]

Douglas became an ally of Black and an opponent of Frankfurter, who for sup-port increasingly looked to another Roosevelt appointee, Robert Jackson. Sixty-one at the time of Warren's appointment, Jackson had been born on a Pennsylvania farm. He attended, but never graduated from, little Albany Law School, acquiring most of his legal education in the nineteenth century manner, by "reading" law in the offices of an attorney in the small town of Jamestown, New York. Jackson developed a suc-cessful practice in Jamestown, representing businessmen, labor unions, and farmers. Also active in politics, he served as an adviser to Roosevelt when FDR was governor of New York and worked in his 1932 presidential campaign. In 1934 Jackson went to Washington himself, becoming general counsel to the Bureau of Internal Revenue. After pressing a successful tax evasion action against former secretary of the treasury Andrew Mellon and winning a Supreme Court ruling upholding the constitutional-ity of the Public Utility Holding Company Act while on special assignment to the SEC, he moved on to the Justice Department in 1936. There Jackson headed the tax and antitrust divisions and served as solicitor general before becoming attorney general in 1940. When Chief Justice Hughes retired in 1941, Roosevelt replaced him with the senior associate justice, Harlan Stone, and gave Stone's seat to Jackson.[21]

Jackson joined a Court that included another former member of Roosevelt's Justice Department, Stanley Reed. A Kentuckian educated at Kentucky Wesleyan and Yale, Reed nevertheless completed his legal training by reading law in the office of a Kentucky practitioner. Reed then built a successful law practice in Maysville, Kentucky, that relied heavily on several wealthy corporate clients. He also dabbled in politics as a Wilsonian Progressive, serving a term in the state legislature. Reed entered government service during the Hoover administration as counsel to the Federal Farm Board. In 1932 he became head of the Reconstruction Finance Corporation. Retaining that post when Roosevelt replaced Hoover, he later became FDR's solicitor general. His reward for loyally but futilely defending the constitutionality of New Deal legislation was a 1938 appointment to the Supreme Court. When Warren joined him there, Reed was sixty-nine.[22]

Although far less impressive than the other Roosevelt justices, Reed was at least the equal of the mediocrities Harry Truman had appointed. In addition to Vinson, President Truman had nominated Harold Burton, Tom C. Clark, and Sherman Minton. The sixty-five-year-old Burton, the son of an MIT dean, had attended Bowdoin College and Harvard Law School before migrating to Cleveland, where he remained, except for a brief period when he headed the legal department of a Salt Lake City power company and the World War I years when he served as an army officer in France. Burton practiced corporate law and taught the subject at Case Western Reserve University. Active in politics and government, he won election to the East Cleveland school board and the Ohio House of Representatives and served for several years as Cleveland's chief legal officer. In 1934 Burton was elected mayor of Cleveland. After winning reelection in 1937 and 1939, he ran successfully for the U.S. Senate in 1940. There Burton, a Republican, served on the committee to investigate the national defense program, chaired by Democrat Harry Truman. In 1945 President Truman, needing to fill a Supreme Court vacancy and under pressure to restore some political balance to a heavily Democratic Court, offered the job to his friend.[23]

Sherman Minton had also been a buddy of Truman's in the Senate, where the two men sat next to each other. Born on an Indiana farm, Minton compiled an outstanding academic record at Indiana University and Yale Law School and also studied briefly at the Sorbonne while on World War I army duty in France. After engaging in private practice in New Albany, Indiana until 1933, he entered government service as counselor to the Indiana Public Service Commission. The following year Minton ran successfully for the Senate. A loyal New Dealer, he vigorously defended the Court-packing plan. Roosevelt seriously considered him for the Supreme Court appointment that went to Black. Instead, after Minton was defeated for reelection in 1940, FDR rewarded his loyalty with a seat on the United States Court of Appeals for the Seventh Circuit. As a judge, Minton proved to be a supporter of labor unions and a critic of big business. He also remained friendly with Truman, and when Justice

Wiley Rutledge died in 1949, Minton reportedly asked him for the seat. Some critics questioned his competence, but the Senate eventually confirmed him by a vote of forty-eight to sixteen.[24]

Sixty-three when Warren became chief justice, Minton was nine years older than Tom C. Clark, who had been serving two months longer. A Texan, Clark had earned his B.A. and LL.B. degrees from the University of Texas, then joined his father's Dallas law firm in 1922. After serving as civil district attorney of Dallas County from 1927 to 1933, he returned to full-time private practice, earning substantial fees representing Texas oilmen. In 1937, through the influence of Senator Tom Connally (D-Tex.), Clark obtained a job with the Justice Department. He started out trying cases in the Bureau of War Risk Litigation and rose through the ranks, becoming head of the Antitrust Division's wages and hours unit and then its New Orleans field office. During World War II he handled the legal aspects of the internment of Japanese-Americans, then took over the war frauds unit of the Antitrust Division, where he worked closely with Senator Truman. In 1944 Clark became the assistant attorney general in charge of the Antitrust Division, and the following year he took over the Criminal Division. After Truman became president, he made his friend attorney general. As head of the Justice Department, Clark promoted civil rights, but also played a key role in the development of the administration's repressive loyalty-security program. Following the 1949 death of Justice Frank Murphy, a noted civil libertarian, Truman appointed Clark to Murphy's seat, a move that horrified liberals. His performance on the bench did not reassure them. The president later called Justice Clark "a dumb son of a bitch" and "my biggest mistake."[25]

When Warren joined Clark and his colleagues in 1953, he found a Supreme Court split by jurisprudential disputes and personal enmity. At the core of the conflict that divided them lay a fundamental disagreement about the role that judges should play in a democratic system of government. Although often characterized as a battle between the forces of judicial activism, led by Black, and the forces of judicial self-restraint, commanded by Frankfurter, the controversy was more complex than that. Jackson, who generally sided with Frankfurter, endorsed a limited form of activism, and the most irrepressible activist on the Court was actually Douglas. Black and Frankfurter disagreed less about the need to restrain judicial power than about how to do it. They agreed with one another, and with the other members of the Court, about a great deal. Seven of the justices were New Deal Democrats, and even the lone Republican, Burton, favored the affirmative use of governmental power to accomplish such objectives as the protection of workers and the prevention of monopoly. All eight were paternalists, who thought that government should actively promote equal economic opportunity, efficiency, humanitarianism, and equality before the law. In short, all were committed to the values associated with mid-twentieth-century political liberalism.[26]

What they disagreed about was the role that the judiciary should play in the realization of liberal aspirations. Those G. Edward White characterizes as "substantive liberals," most notably Black and Douglas, saw nothing inherently wrong with the use of judicial power to promote liberal values. "Process liberals," such as Frankfurter, on the other hand, thought that the goals of liberalism should be attained through action by the people's elected representatives. They condemned judicial intervention in the framing of public policy as inherently undemocratic. While a student at Harvard, Frankfurter had been captivated by the writings of Professor James Bradley Thayer. Upset by the way judges were utilizing their power to enforce the Constitution for the purpose of invalidating economic regulatory and social welfare legislation they disliked, Thayer argued for strict limitations on judicial authority in the areas of social policy and constitutional litigation. According to him, only "when those who have the right to make laws have not merely made a mistake but have made a very clear one—so clear that it is not open to rational question"—were judges justified in invalidating their enactments. Justices Holmes and Brandeis, heroes and personal friends of Frankfurter, echoed these sentiments in a number of opinions, most notably Holmes's famous dissent in *Lochner v. New York* (1905). Frankfurter believed in judicial enforcement of very specific constitutional limitations on governmental power, but he was also committed to empowering government at all levels so that it could experiment with innovative solutions to economic and social problems. As he watched the conservative Supreme Court of the 1920s and early 1930s invalidate reform legislation because it supposedly violated the vague Due Process Clauses of the Fifth and Fourteenth Amendments or exceeded the ill-defined boundaries of congressional authority to regulate interstate commerce, he grew ever more firmly committed to "judicial self-restraint." Frankfurter became convinced that when it was passing judgment on the constitutionality of legislation, the Supreme Court should "put on the sack cloth and ashes of deferring humility." It should strike down statutes as violations of due process only when they were "so outside the limits of a supportable judgment . . . as to constitute that disregard of reason we call an arbitrary judgment."[27]

Any doubt about the validity of a statute "must be resolved in favor of constitutionality." The reason was that "due regard for the process of constitutional adjudication" required it. Frankfurter espoused the "process jurisprudence" that dominated academic legal writing during the 1950s. Its proponents insisted that what justified a judicial decision was the methodology used to reach it. Judges must decide cases according to neutral principles, employing analysis and reasoning that transcended the facts of the case before them. Unless they adhered strictly to reason and refrained from allowing personal biases to influence adjudication, Frankfurter insisted, jurists would become "covert little Hitlers." Developed as a counterweight to the implicit moral relativism of Legal Realism, process theory regarded method as more important than results. Because they sought to confine lawmaking by judges, its proponents emphasized the institutional incapacity of the judiciary to resolve many kinds of problems. They applauded judicial passivity, insisting that often the best decision was no decision at all. Process liberals like Frankfurter championed doctrines that judges could invoke to avoid resolving disputes. "More often than not," according to Melvin Urofsky, "Frankfurter tried to get the Court to avoid deciding cases."[28]

Although often aligned with him, Jackson was no fan of those doctrines (such as ripeness, mootness, and standing) that Frankfurter employed to accomplish that objective. Nor did he share Frankfurter's reluctance to enforce constitutional limitations on governmental power, such as the First Amendment. Although disagreeing with Black and Douglas, who contended that the Court had an obligation to render decisions that would aid the disadvantaged, Jackson also did not believe that judges should avoid entirely involvement in the development of public policy. He conceded to the judiciary an "intermediate power to interpret open-ended constitutional concepts," such as due process, commerce, and the equal protection of the laws. Appellate judges could make law, he believed, but only if in the process they conveyed their ultimate subordination to it. This was particularly true in the area of economic regulation.[29]

While Jackson was less committed to judicial restraint than Frankfurter, Douglas rejected the idea entirely, along with virtually every other tenet of process jurisprudence. For him what mattered was doing justice in individual cases and writing good social policy and moral principles into law. A Realist who dismissed doctrinal analysis as rationalization, Douglas wasted little energy explaining himself, demonstrating a persistent unwillingness to utilize the conventional analytical techniques employed by other twentieth- century justices to justify their decisions. He ignored precedent and, even when purportedly interpreting the text of the Constitution or a statute, eschewed extensive textual exegesis. If no established doctrine justified a result Douglas desired, he invented a new one. He cared little about process, confronted rather than deferred to legislatures, and was temperamentally incapable of practicing judicial self-restraint. Consequently, Douglas generally supported Black in his conflicts with Frankfurter.[30]

His ally had far more reservations about judicial power than he did. Black was committed to the liberal ideal of a paternalistic state, responsive to the plight of the common man, but he had brought with him from rural Alabama a populist mistrust of big government. He recognized that while promoting community welfare, the liberal state could destroy individual rights. Black did not, however, assign the same primacy to protecting liberty that Douglas did. He endeavored to balance personal freedom and community welfare. Black recognized that judicial enforcement of individual rights inevitably meant the imposition of limitations on governmental authority, and that in a democracy this entailed restricting the power of the people to govern themselves. He also understood that, like other governmental officials, the judges who enforced rights could abuse their authority. Like Frankfurter, Black condemned judicial lawmaking, which he too viewed as an affront to majoritarian democracy. Unlike his adversary, he did not believe courts should always refuse to impose limits on the other branches of government. Black considered judicial activism justified when it served to enforce the commands of the Constitution. Although aware that these were often not self-explanatory, that their language and history had to be interpreted, and that there was room for disagreement about their meaning, he was a positivist. Black advocated complete fidelity to the literal meaning of the Constitution and disputed the legitimacy of judicial rulings that rested on any foundation other than its text. For him textual literalism served the same purpose that self-restraint did for Frankfurter. Black's approach to constraining judges, as White explains, "by-passed questions about the proper allocation of power among governing institutions by simply asserting that if the Constitution had declared rights against the government, the judiciary had an obligation to enforce them."[31]

Black—and for that matter all other New Deal justices—agreed with Frankfurter that judges should practice restraint when reviewing economic regulatory legislation. Whether dealing with challenges to federal statutes under the Commerce Clause or attacks on state laws based on the Due Process Clause, they should defer to the policy judgments of legislators. Frankfurter insisted courts should exercise similar restraint in cases involving legislation that allegedly violated the Bill of Rights, but Black strongly disagreed. When government was doing something to the people rather than for them, he believed, judges should act vigorously to guarantee their constitutionally protected rights. Frankfurter condemned the notion that some rights (such as those secured by the First Amendment, about which Black and Douglas cared passionately) occupied a "preferred position" that justified heightened judicial activism on their behalf. While believing in civil liberties, he insisted the people themselves, led by enlightened legislators and executive officials, must defend them.[32]

Black disagreed with Frankfurter, not only about the need for judicial activism to implement the Bill of Rights, but also about the nature of its guarantees. In 1952 he told his clerks, "The Bill of Rights means what it says and there are absolutes in it."[33] Foremost among these were the guarantees of freedom of expression in the First Amendment. By the early 1950s Black had concluded that these should be read literally. When the framers of the First Amendment wrote "Congress shall make no law . . . abridging the freedom of speech," he believed, they intended to place expression entirely beyond the reach of legislation. The First Amendment protected all speech and protected it completely. Douglas came to adhere even more strongly than Black to this absolutist reading. Frankfurter wrote opinions disputing it and was even more critical in private.[34]

He also challenged Black's contention that the Supreme Court should enforce the Bill of Rights against the states. In a dissenting opinion in *Adamson v. California* (1947), Black had marshaled evidence from the legislative history of the Fourteenth Amendment to show that those responsible for its adoption intended to make the Bill of Rights applicable to the states. His historical scholarship was questionable, but he continued to press his "incorporation" theory because he was determined to cabin the Due Process Clause. Following the approach first articulated by Justice Benjamin Cardozo in *Palko v. Connecticut* (1937), however, the Court took the position that only those rights that were "fundamental principles of liberty and justice" and "implicit in the concept of ordered liberty" applied to the states. That was so, Frankfurter believed, because of their historical significance and inherent importance, rather than because they happened to be in the Bill of Rights. Not everything it contained was also in the Due Process Clause, nor was something that satisfied Cardozo's criteria excluded merely because it had been omitted from the Bill of Rights. To Frankfurter due process meant fundamental fairness, and he considered judges (because of their expertise in the law) ideally suited to explicate the evolving meaning of that concept. Black objected that this approach allowed judges to enforce their personal values. Holding that the Due Process Clause mandated state compliance with the Bill of Rights would eliminate subjective decision making and the judicial discretion that he viewed as a threat to democracy. Although widely identified with the cause of restraining judicial power, on this issue Frankfurter was the activist, while Black was the one whose approach restricted federal judges, limiting the grounds on which they could declare states' actions unconstitutional. At the same time, however, Black's approach would enhance their authority by expanding the reach of constitutional provisions they interpreted and administered. The "total incorporation" Black advocated would require the states to comply with all the rules for trying and punishing persons accused of crimes spelled out in the Fourth, Fifth, Sixth, and Eighth Amendments. Frankfurter, on the other hand, insisted that, in order to preserve federalism, the Due Process Clause should be read as imposing upon them nothing beyond those fundamental standards of decency widely recognized in Anglo-American jurisprudence.[35]

On this and most of the other issues that divided the Court in 1953, Frankfurter was in the ascendancy. Black's only consistent ally was Douglas. Until 1949 they could generally count on the support of Wiley Rutledge and Frank Murphy, who accepted Black's incorporation argument and voted with them in most civil liberties cases. When Clark and Minton replaced Rutledge and Murphy, however, the Frankfurter bloc gained two votes. It already had those of Reed and Burton, who were extremely deferential toward the former Harvard professor. Jackson, who had endorsed the preferred freedom position, only to abandon it later, and had characterized Bill of Rights guarantees as absolutes, only to accept restrictions on them imposed for what he regarded as sufficiently important reasons, was extremely unpredictable. Because he objected to judges seizing the initiative in policy formulation and tended to defer to state authority, however, he usually sided with Frankfurter. Outnumbered, Black and Douglas generally expressed their views in dissenting opinions.[36]

Personality conflicts and personal disputes exacerbated tensions arising from ongoing intellectual combat. Despite the strength of his convictions, Black made an effort to be diplomatic in his dealings with his colleagues. Frankfurter, on the other hand, demonstrated a remarkable capacity for alienating other justices. A man who loved disputation, he often seemed to forget that he was no longer a professor. During oral argument Frankfurter subjected lawyers to the sort of argumentative and intimidating questioning often utilized in law school classrooms, and in the Court's closed conferences he treated his colleagues as if they were Harvard students. Many justices resented his lectures and his arrogance, but if any resisted his leadership, Frankfurter took offense. He heaped flattery on potential allies, such as Burton, but if they ultimately failed to support his positions, he pronounced them enemies. Frankfurter personalized issues, and those who disagreed with him became the targets of bitter invective and emotional outbursts.[37] "I thought Felix was going to hit me today, he got so mad," Black told his son after one heated conference.[38] Relations between the two intellectual rivals deteriorated hopelessly during the 1940s. They improved after Frankfurter reached out in friendship to a grieving Black following the death of his wife in 1951. Personal animosity between Frankfurter and Douglas persisted, however. Frankfurter carped about his colleague's political activity and ambitions, while Douglas complained about his antagonist's pontificating and insolence. When particularly bored with one of Frankfurter's lectures, Douglas would leave the conference table, either stretching out on a couch and ignoring him or leaving the room until he finished. Frankfurter labeled Douglas "narrow minded," "malignant," and "amoral," while Douglas called Frankfurter "Der Fuhrer" and the "little bastard"— among other things.[39]

Getting along with Douglas was not easy, even for justices much better at interpersonal relations than Frankfurter. Although he was a genius with a genuinely original judicial mind, Douglas was temperamentally unsuited to service on the Supreme Court. A loner and a doer who traveled his own path, he had little use for such essential aspects of appellate judging as collegial discourse and the forging of collective positions. Maintaining good relations with his colleagues was not a high priority. Douglas often threatened them with public disclosure of some irregularity in internal Court procedure and repeatedly infuriated them by leaving for his vacation home in Goose Prairie, Washington, before the end of the term. He was not really close to any of his colleagues and got along well only with Black. Their backgrounds and values were similar, and, unlike Frankfurter, Black respected Douglas's need for intellectual space. He became something of a father figure to him.[40]

Black's relationship with Jackson was far less amiable. They had clashed in 1945 over Black's failure to disqualify himself from a case in which his former law partner represented one of the litigants. When Chief Justice Stone died in 1946, Jackson, who was in Europe serving as chief American prosecutor at the Nuremberg war crimes trials, coveted his position. Former chief justice Hughes recommended him, and he believed he was entitled to the appointment. Columnists in Washington reported, however, that Black had gone to Truman, threatening that he and Douglas would resign if Jackson were elevated. After the president nominated Vinson, Jackson released to the press a communication to the chairmen of the congressional judiciary committees, in which he attacked Black, castigated his conduct in the 1945 case, and gave a full account of the conference debate on that issue. After his return from Nuremberg, the two men resumed an outwardly civil relationship, but they grew further apart on matters of constitutional interpretation.[41]

The Jackson-Black feud helped make the Vinson Court extremely fractious and ineffective. So did the weakness and incompetence of its chief justice. Vinson proved inept at conducting the weekly conferences where the justices debated and decided cases, and he possessed what other members of the Court regarded as a second-rate legal mind. Associate justices openly displayed their contempt for his abilities and even discussed in his presence the idea of making the chief justiceship a rotating position. The challenge of unifying such a badly divided Court was simply beyond Vinson's abilities.[42]

Under his nonleadership, the Court did not even appear to be working very hard. By 1950 the docket was the smallest it had been since the early 1930s. Yet Frankfurter complained constantly that the Court was accepting too many important cases. Douglas, who required about half as much time as his pedantic colleague to write an opinion, insisted it should be taking more. Academic commentators agreed, excoriating the Court for avoiding constitutional issues and seemingly spending less time resolving cases than deciding which ones it would not decide.[43]

Earl Warren, an almost instinctive activist, was temperamentally unsuited to the sort of passivity that had become the norm for the Vinson Court. Nor was he likely to adopt readily the deference to legislative authority advocated by Frankfurter. Warren believed in the autonomy of each of the three branches within its own domain, and as governor he had repeatedly pitted his own principles against those of lawmakers with different views. He also did not share Frankfurter's conviction that the Supreme Court should dodge controversial issues. "Every man who has sat on the Court must have known at the time he took office that there always has been and in all probability always will be controversy surrounding that body," Warren wrote later.[44]

Although his views were at odds with those that had prevailed on the Vinson Court, this was not readily apparent when he took his seat, for his record on many issues was ambiguous. One of these was civil rights. Warren had played a leading role in the forced removal of Japanese Americans from their homes in California to inland concentration camps, an action he himself came to recognize as "wrong" and "deeply regretted." But he insisted he was not prejudiced, even against persons of Japanese ancestry, and as governor pushed for the creation of a state fair-employment practices commission. A similar ambiguity characterized his record on criminal justice. In the controversial *Point Lobos* case, District Attorney Warren's office subjected the defendants to detrimental pretrial publicity and used against them both evidence secured by surreptitious electronic eavesdropping and a confession obtained through police intimidation of a suspect interrogated in the absence of counsel. When Warren ran for attorney general, he had the support not only of other prosecutors but of sheriffs and police chiefs as well. Yet, as district attorney he had fought to get the Alameda County charter amended to provide for a public defender to represent indigents accused of crimes. Warren's record also raised doubts about whether he would find acceptable the Court's failure to defend civil liberties against the ravages of McCarthyism. On the one hand, he had opposed the adoption of a loyalty oath for professors at the University of California. On the other, he had once denied that civil rights afforded any protection to members of the Communist Party and had exploited the Communist issue in political campaigns from 1942 through 1952.[45]

Although his record was ambiguous, Warren did have some firmly held beliefs. He claimed to be neither a liberal nor a conservative, and Eisenhower seems clearly to have erred in classifying him as a "middle of the road" (i.e., moderately conservative) Republican like himself. While campaigning against Culbert Olson, Warren attacked the New Deal and advocated states' rights, but by 1953 he had endorsed Social Security and proposed state-supported health insurance, positions well to the left of center in the GOP. Brownell understood him better than Eisenhower. Asked later if Warren had become more liberal after joining the Supreme Court, he replied that "many of his rulings could have been anticipated because of his prior experience as a moderate if not a progressive Republican." That is how Warren viewed himself; his commitment, he claimed, was to the Progressivism of Hiram Johnson. His biographer, G. Edward White, agrees with that self-assessment, picturing him as possessing the Progressive generation's perspective on social issues and committed to the Progressive values of morality, patriotism, and progress. Warren retained the Progressives' hostility toward special interests and their commitment to honest and open government that served the public rather than special interest groups. Like the reformers of the early twentieth century he believed in the perfectibility of man, and from one strand of California Progressivism he drew a belief in the need for affirmative governmental action to assist the disadvantaged. His governorship had been "a progressive administration." Yet, Warren had less confidence than some Progressives in the inherent benevolence of government officials. By 1953 he had also shed most of the nativism associated with California Progressivism; Warren now viewed majoritarian government as the protector of minority rights and equality of opportunity. In short, he was a Progressive in the process of becoming a liberal.[46]

That made him ideologically compatible with the New Deal Democrats who dominated the Supreme Court. What set Warren apart from most of his new colleagues was his penchant for activism and his tendency to energize any office that he held and make it an instrument for the promotion of progress. He was still a politician without a well-developed philosophy of judging. Soon, however, Warren would translate the Progressive notion that government should be responsive to the people at large into a vision of an energetic Supreme Court protecting the rights of all Americans.[47]

He did not immediately embrace that conception of the Court's role, however, for the new chief justice was the object of vigorous proselytizing by Frankfurter. Courting him furiously, the champion of judicial restraint welcomed the Warrens to Washington and helped them look for housing. He fawned and flattered and assisted "the Chief" (as his new colleagues nicknamed Warren) with his speeches. Professor Frankfurter also set out, as he had earlier with Black and Burton, to instruct the neophyte on how to do his job. Three days after Warren was sworn in, Frankfurter sent him his 1927 book, *The Business of the Supreme Court.* Numerous other books, articles, memoranda, and short notes followed, offering guidance on matters ranging from the day-to-day work of the chief justice, through jurisdictional problems, to the Due Process Clause. At first Warren appreciated the assistance, and Frankfurter waxed enthusiastic about his new boss. As the Chief grew more comfortable in his position, he felt less need for guidance and became more resistant to Frankfurter's efforts to "educate" him. When that happened, their relationship cooled. Warren became closer to Black, who capitalized on the developing friction between his old rival and the new chief, visiting regularly with Warren and developing a real camaraderie with him. The Chief came to view Frankfurter as manipulative and untrustworthy, a perception that drove him to develop a theory of judging that contrasted starkly with the one championed by his would-be mentor. By late 1956, Warren had become a wholehearted advocate of judicial activism.[48]

"The Court sits to decide cases, not to avoid decision," he concluded, "and while it must recognize the constitutional powers of the [other] branches of government, it must decide every issue properly placed before it." Warren rejected the doctrine of neutral principles as a "fantasy . . . used more to avoid responsibilities than to meet them." He became convinced that, as the defender of the Constitution, the Supreme Court could not be neutral; it had an obligation to rule in favor of litigants making morally correct claims. His job was to find the ethical imperative in a case, then persuade others to join him in effecting it. Only results mattered—not doctrine, process, or institutions. Warren went out of his way to render decisions that protected minorities, individual workers, and institutions, such as the family, about which he cared deeply. Fairness became his polestar; in resolving a case, Warren believed, his overriding concern should be reaching the result that was fair and just. That would, of course, also be the one that was constitutional, for the Constitution, he believed, embodied his own strongly held values. It spoke directly to him, and as a Supreme Court justice, he came to believe, he had both the power and the duty to implement its imperatives.[49]

Rendering the decision demanded by fairness, morality, and the Constitution mattered far more to Warren than did the opinion that justified a ruling. He was indifferent to the standards by which proponents of process theory measured judicial craftsmanship. Warren cared little for reasoned elaboration or careful acknowledgment of the sources on which a decision rested. Not a legal scholar and uninterested in research, he generally left the drafting of opinions largely to his clerks. He would outline in general terms what he wanted to say, then give them substantial discretion with respect to details.[50]

Frankfurter's many disciples in legal academia carped constantly about the ineptitude of Warren's opinions, but his colleagues, while recognizing that the Chief was not the ex-professor's intellectual equal, soon recognized that he brought to the Court leadership skills it had long needed. Although Warren was sensitive to slights and somewhat quick tempered, he managed to maintain warm relations with all of the associate justices except Frankfurter. This was largely because he did not allow disagreements over issues to become personalized, but also because of his considerate treatment of colleagues. When the newly appointed justice Potter Stewart and his wife arrived in Washington, the Chief greeted them at the train station. He also took his colleagues and their wives to the Army-Navy football game in Philadelphia, making all of the arrangements and paying all of the expenses himself. Warren, who made a concerted effort to meet everyone who worked in the building soon after his arrival, dealt with the Supreme Court's other employees in the same friendly and unpretentious manner that he displayed toward the justices.[51]

There was, however, no doubt about who was in charge. "He was the leader," recalled Justice Thurgood Marshall, who joined the Court in the 1960s. Warren took care to learn something about judging and the way the Supreme Court operated before asserting his authority. He retained Vinson's secretary and clerks, and on his first day at the Court visited Black to get a briefing on the procedures followed in the conference room. Warren asked Black, who was the senior associate justice, to preside over the Court's weekly conferences until he could familiarize himself with the way things were done. Black agreed (he also assumed responsibility for assigning opinions during the conferences over which he presided). Although the new chief justice was cautious in picking up the reins of power, within hours after he arrived at the Court, his energy and dynamism had transformed the atmosphere.[52]

The routine changed too. When Warren arrived, the Court met at noon, recessed for thirty minutes at 2:00 P.M., then sat again until 4:30 P.M. It heard cases Monday through Friday, then assembled on Saturday morning to discuss and vote on them. The backbreaking schedule, among other factors, forced the chief justice to deal with his many administrative responsibilities in the morning. Warren, who carried briefs and other reading material home with him practically every night, was a hard worker, but he recognized the inefficiency of this arrangement. He suggested that the Supreme Court commence its sessions at 10:00 A.M., like practically every other court in the country, and adjourn in mid-afternoon. Some of his colleagues resisted this break with tradition, but eventually they agreed to a schedule that allowed him to take care of administrative matters after adjournment. Warren soon determined that by adding one week of argument in the fall and about two in the spring, the Court could hear all of its cases between Monday and Thursday, enabling it to hold its conferences on Friday and eliminating the need to assemble on Saturday. The others agreed to this idea, which the Chief implemented at the beginning of the October 1955 term.

Besides changing the meeting time of the conference, Warren made it much more efficient and productive. When he joined the Court, the established procedure was for the chief justice to summarize a case and state how he was inclined to resolve it. The associate justices would then express their views, speaking in order of seniority. After the case had been fully discussed, they would vote in reverse order of seniority, with the chief justice voting last. The format apparently became somewhat less formal while Warren was in charge, but conferences did not degenerate into the sort of disorderly seminars they had often become during Stone's tenure. Warren did not debate his colleagues, as Stone had done, and always let each one have his full say. Yet, because of his thorough knowledge of the cases and the simple but effective way in which he framed the issue each presented, he generally managed to steer the discussion where he wanted it to go. Warren almost always set forth his own position clearly, unambiguously, and very firmly, but while his powers of persuasion were formidable, his colleagues did not resent his firm leadership. They praised the efficiency with which he managed conferences. The other justices developed the habit of assembling before Warren arrived, then rising when he entered the conference room.[53] "He was an instinctive leader whom you respected and for whom you had an affection," Stewart recalled years later. "As the presiding member of our conference, he was just ideal."[54]

Effective leadership was precisely what the Supreme Court needed when Earl Warren joined it in 1953. He did not possess a great legal mind, but the Court had more than enough of those already. The task that confronted the new chief justice was more political than judicial, so it was perhaps fortunate that he came to it from a career in politics. What the Court needed was someone with the skill to persuade a group of judges who disagreed about fundamental issues, and some of whom despised each other, to work together as an effective agency of government. It was a job for a super chief. Warren would have to prove almost immediately that he was one. When he took his seat, the Court had already heard oral arguments in one of the most important and controversial cases in its history, *Brown v. Board of Education.*

2

THE SCHOOL DESEGREGATION CASES

The Supreme Court that Earl Warren took charge of in 1953 was on a collision course with destiny. Already on the docket were five cases that would require the Court to confront what Swedish sociologist Gunnar Myrdal had called "an American dilemma": the segregation and subordination of African Americans. Warren's first challenge as chief justice was to lead his colleagues to a politically acceptable and legally defensible resolution of those school segregation cases. *Brown v. Board of Education* would be his Court's most important decision. Because the Court proved too cautious to enforce vigorously a decision that school segregation violated the Fourteenth Amendment, *Brown* would do little to integrate public education in the South. Its political and constitutional impact would be tremendous, however. As Morton Horwitz has pointed out, *Brown* began a gradual abandonment of judicial self-restraint by liberals and the legal system. It raised questions about whether government could passively acquiesce in an unequal society and articulated the "central theme" of the Court Warren would lead for sixteen years.[1] While wrestling with the school segregation cases, the Warren Court would find a mission and establish an identity as a champion of the underdog.

Those cases were the most recent in a series brought to the Court by the National Association for the Advancement of Colored People (NAACP), which by 1953 had already elicited rulings casting a constitutional cloud over segregated education. Since 1933 the NAACP had been waging a litigation campaign directed at making school segregation prohibitively expensive for southern states. From 1935 to 1950 its principal targets were segregated universities and differing pay scales for white and African American teachers. NAACP lawyers argued that both violated the "separate but equal" doctrine the Court had announced in *Plessy v. Ferguson* (1896), under which segregation did not violate the Equal Protection Clause of the Fourteenth Amendment if both races were afforded similar treatment. In 1938 the NAACP persuaded the Supreme Court that the University of Missouri had violated that principle by refusing to admit an African American to its law school, even though Missouri was willing to pay the tuition of qualified African Americans who wished to attend law school in other states and had announced its intention to open a law school at all-black Lincoln University. In *Missouri ex rel. Gaines v. Canada* the Court took the position that so long as a state afforded whites something it denied to African Americans because of their race, it was violating the Equal Protection Clause.[2]

24

Gaines was a precursor to *Sweatt v. Painter* (1950) and *McLaurin v. Oklahoma State Regents* (1950), in which the Supreme Court held that neither a brand-new law school for black students, which Texas had created after an African American applied for admission to the all-white school at the University of Texas, nor an education graduate program at the University of Oklahoma, which admitted a black man but segregated him within the school, satisfied the demands of the Fourteenth Amendment. By the time the Court decided those cases, Americans had fought a war against a racist regime in Germany that forced them to ponder the similarities between the enemy's policies toward Jews and America's treatment of her black minority. Outside the South the climate of opinion was increasingly inhospitable to segregation. The consensus among liberal intellectuals was that Myrdal had been correct when he characterized America's version of apartheid as oppressive and incompatible with democracy.[3]

Members of the Supreme Court shared these negative attitudes about segregation. All of them had been appointed by liberal Democrats Franklin Roosevelt and Harry Truman, and African Americans were an important element of the New Deal coalition that supported those presidents. Truman had solicited black votes in 1948 by ordering the desegregation of the armed forces and proposing civil rights legislation. Like him, Supreme Court justices were increasingly inclined to regard African Americans as one of their constituencies. Part of a political and intellectual elite that was hostile to segregation and sensitive to the relationship between racism and totalitarianism, exemplified by Hitler's Germany, they tended to support the kinds of claims advanced by the NAACP. Indeed, Frankfurter, who hired the Court's first black clerk, William Coleman, had once been a member of the NAACP's National Legal Committee. Black, of course, was a former Klansman, who had voted against antilynching legislation in the Senate and believed deeply in the traditions of the white South. But as a prosecutor and state judge in Alabama, he had treated African Americans fairly, and as a justice he had (with the exception of the World War II Japanese cases) compiled an exemplary voting record in litigation involving the civil rights and liberties of racial minorities. Even the Court's lone Republican, Harold Burton, had aided a black choir in Cleveland and, as a senator, had supported creation of a permanent fair employment practices commission and abolition of the poll tax. Although most justices probably would have preferred to see Congress take the lead in attacking segregation, they realized that southern control of key leadership positions on Capitol Hill made enactment of civil rights legislation unlikely. Hence, they were willing to contemplate judicial action to advance the cause.[4]

The executive branch of the federal government repeatedly encouraged the Supreme Court to act. The Justice Department filed an amicus curiae brief in *Shelley v. Kraemer* (1948), supporting the NAACP in its successful attack on state judicial enforcement of racially restrictive covenants in real estate deeds. The solicitor general also filed briefs supporting the NAACP's position in *Sweatt* and *McLaurin*. The Court was receptive to such arguments against segregation, for among its members only Stanley Reed, a white Kentuckian, supported the separate-but-equal doctrine. When NAACP attorney Thurgood Marshall, who had previously demanded only that separate facilities be truly equal, mounted a frontal assault on the constitutionality of segregation during oral argument in *Sweatt,* however, the justices resisted his plea to rule that the separation of the races in and of itself violated the Equal Protection Clause. Instead, in that case and in *McLaurin,* the Court held that the Fourteenth Amendment had been violated because the education Texas and Oklahoma were offering African Americans was unequal in certain intangible ways to that which they afforded white students. In the words of Mark Tushnet, during the years just before Warren became its chief justice, the Supreme Court "marched to the edge of overruling the [separate-but-equal] doctrine and said, 'not yet.'"[5]

Two years after *Sweatt* and *McLaurin,* Marshall was back, urging the Court to take that final step, and to do so in five cases challenging public school segregation. One was *Briggs v. Elliot,* in which a three-judge panel had found that South Carolina's schools for African Americans were inferior to those for whites, but had held that under *Plessy* the state's separate school law was constitutional. *Brown v. Board of Education* came from Topeka, Kansas. Kansas law permitted, but did not require, cities with populations over 15,000 to segregate their elementary schools, something Topeka had done with the lower grades. A three-judge district court had held its white and black schools were substantially equal. Although critical of the separate-but-equal rule, that court too felt bound by *Plessy;* consequently, it declined to invalidate the Kansas statutes. *Davis v. County School Board* had begun when African American high school students in Prince Edward County, Virginia, filed suit, alleging that their school was inferior to the white one and demanding that either the two be equalized or the Virginia statutes and constitutional provisions requiring segregated education be declared unconstitutional. The district court had granted the equalization request, but relying on *Plessy,* upheld the segregation laws. In *Gebhart v. Belton* the chancellor of Delaware had found his state's black schools to be inferior to its white ones, and for that reason had enjoined enforcement of its school segregation laws. While expressing the opinion that the separate-but-equal doctrine ought to be rejected, the chancellor noted that the Supreme Court would have to do this. The final case, *Bolling v. Sharpe,* was a challenge to congressional legislation requiring segregated schools in the District of Columbia, which had been dismissed by the trial court and was before the United States Court of Appeals for the District of Columbia Circuit. The Supreme Court reached out to bring this case up for review along with *Briggs, Brown, Davis,* and *Gephardt.*[6]

The issue posed by these five cases troubled and divided the Vinson Court. "Only for those who have not the responsibility of decision is it easy to decide [them]," Frankfurter observed. "This is because they present a legal issue inextricably bound up with deep feeling on sharply conflicting social and political issues."[7] Black and Douglas were anxious to overrule *Plessy,* and two or three other justices were leaning in that direction. Vinson opposed doing so, believing such a ruling would lead to the complete abolition of the public schools in some areas. Reed also favored retaining "separate but equal." Frankfurter and Jackson were ambivalent. Frankfurter strongly opposed segregation, but Jackson, although generally sympathetic to African American interests, was often not enthusiastically supportive, and he had at least some sympathy for the views of one of his clerks, a future chief justice, William Rehnquist, who argued in a 1952 memorandum, prepared at Jackson's request, that *Plessy* had been correctly decided and should be reaffirmed. The Court should not impose its views on the country, Rehnquist asserted. Jackson shared his belief that school segregation was a political issue, and he argued that it ought to be resolved by Congress. Because of Frankfurter's long-standing commitment to judicial restraint, that argument troubled him. He was searching for legally defensible grounds on which to overturn *Plessy*.[8]

In its brief, the NAACP stressed the psychological harm that segregation inflicted on children of the minority race. Lawyers had presented expert testimony on this subject to the trial courts in South Carolina, Virginia, Delaware, and Kansas, and although ruling against the African American plaintiffs, the Kansas court had included in its opinion a finding that public school segregation had a detrimental effect on black children because it engendered feelings of inferiority that retarded their educational and mental development. The NAACP brief pointed to that finding, and also included an appendix, signed by thirty-two eminent social scientists, that summarized recent research on the harm caused by segregation and arrived at similar conclusions. The NAACP had the support of the American Civil Liberties Union—which filed an amicus brief emphasizing the propaganda value of segregation to America's enemies in the Cold War—and of the United States government. Solicitor General Philip Perlman, who thought it was much too early to end segregation in public schools, had refused to file a brief in the case, but when Attorney General J. Howard McGrath was forced out of office by a scandal, Perlman resigned. Acting Solicitor General Robert L. Stern and another attorney in the office, Philip Elman, managed to persuade the new attorney general, James P. McGranery, to enter the case. The brief that Elman filed attacked *Plessy*, but suggested that even if "separate but equal" remained the test, segregated schools could not pass it, because they failed to provide equality.[9]

South Carolina responded with a brief prepared by the country's most experienced Supreme Court advocate, former solicitor general John W. Davis, and an associate. They challenged the NAACP's social science evidence, stressed South Carolina's efforts to eliminate the inequalities between its white and black schools, and argued forcefully that both precedent and the history of the Fourteenth Amendment supported the state's position. While South Carolina and Virginia defended segregation vigorously, Kansas had to be compelled to join them. A new liberal majority on the Topeka school board had voted to eliminate segregation gradually, and the board declined to defend the *Brown* suit. Kansas assistant attorney general Paul Wilson filed a brief supporting his state's segregation laws, but only after essentially being ordered to by the Supreme Court.[10]

Although a reluctant advocate, Wilson impressed Justice Burton, as did Marshall and the venerable Davis. Oral argument opened on December 9, 1952, before a capacity crowd of three hundred (half of them African Americans), with an even larger throng milling about in the corridors, hoping to get in. Although argumentation continued for three days, Robert L. Carter explicated the essence of the NAACP's position on the very first morning, when he abandoned "any claim of any constitutional inequality which comes from anything other than the act of segregation itself." Carter tried to confine *Plessy*, which had involved the segregation of trains, to railroads, insisting the Court had never actually held that segregated schools were constitutional. Seeing that the justices were not buying this argument, Marshall abandoned it. Like Carter, however, he emphasized that the plaintiff's were challenging segregation itself, not merely unequal facilities—although he added that those were an inevitable consequence of separation. Davis denied that contention and claimed South Carolina's recently implemented building program was eliminating all physical disparities between black and white schools. He belittled the social science evidence on which the plaintiffs had relied and insisted both precedent and the history of the Fourteenth Amendment established that the Equal Protection Clause did not prohibit segregation. Although Davis was sure he would win, questioning from the bench suggested that only Reed was truly sympathetic to his position. Vinson appeared skeptical that segregation could be ended immediately and seemed attracted to the idea of equalizing white and black schools. Jackson tried to get Virginia's lawyers to concede that while the Supreme Court could not end segregation, Congress could, using the authority given it by section 5 of the Fourteenth Amendment, but they would have none of that idea. Instead, Attorney General J. Lindsay Almond warned darkly that the invalidation of segregation would lead to the destruction of public education in his state. It was the consequences of any decision the Court might render that worried Frankfurter. His extensive questioning of the lawyers made obvious his concern about how the South might react if ordered to desegregate its schools immediately. Marshall sought to assuage Frankfurter's fears, but he and his associates insisted firmly that the individual rights of their clients could not be sacrificed by delaying desegregation.[11]

Their firmness failed to overcome Frankfurter's preference for gradualism. Elman, who had been his clerk and still talked regularly with him, had learned from Frankfurter about his concerns and those of his colleagues. Vinson had refused to let the Justice Department participate in the oral argument, but an amicus brief that Elman drafted offered Frankfurter what he was seeking: a formula for gradualism. Elman proposed that the Supreme Court hold segregation in public schools unconstitutional but give the courts below time to work out the details of implementation. He considered his own proposal "entirely unprincipled"; to suggest that someone whose personal constitutional rights had been violated could be denied relief was "just plain wrong as a matter of constitutional law." Elman's brief, however, gave Frankfurter something he could use to win the votes of wavering colleagues, and perhaps more important, a solution to his personal dilemma.[12]

Frankfurter was one of those who remained unsure about how to resolve the school segregation cases when the Court discussed them in conference on Saturday, December 13. Not even a tentative vote was taken that day, and the notes and recollections of the participants differ enough to make it uncertain what the precise result would have been had there been a vote. Douglas exhibited no indecision. He considered segregation an easy problem; the Fourteenth Amendment permitted no classifications based on race, and therefore separate schools were clearly unconstitutional.

Minton and Burton agreed that the Constitution did not permit segregation. So did Black, although he worried that there would be violence if the Court so held. Only Reed, who stated he would "uphold segregation as constitutional," seemed strongly committed to preserving the separate-but-equal doctrine. Both Douglas and Frankfurter later said they thought Vinson and Clark also would have voted that way, but the rambling remarks of the chief justice—which combined expressions of concern about the possible abolition of public school systems in the South with musings about the power of Congress and an assertion that "Boldness is essential"—suggested he was still struggling to make up his mind. Clark thought that because the Supreme Court's past decisions had led the states to believe segregation was permissible, the Court should "let them work it out," but he also suggested he might go along with a decision against separate schools that permitted district courts to withhold relief if there were trouble. Jackson also was ambivalent. While stating that in his opinion nothing in the text of the Constitution or the history of the Fourteenth Amendment showed segregation was unconstitutional, and that on the basis of precedent, he would have to say it was allowable, he hinted he might go along with a contrary ruling, if the Court, by employing equitable remedies that could be shaped to meet the needs of the situation, gave southerners time to eliminate it.

Frankfurter also wanted to proceed slowly. He was sure school segregation in the District of Columbia violated the Due Process Clause of the Fifth Amendment, but he did not think the Fourteenth Amendment had been intended to prohibit states from segregating their schools. He was unwilling to rely on sociology to hold that school segregation violated the Equal Protection Clause. Frankfurter's biggest desire seemed to be to avoid deciding anything. He urged his colleagues to set the school segregation cases down for reargument.[13]

Eventually, Frankfurter managed to persuade them to do that. He suggested reargument in March of 1953, then, concluding a longer delay was needed, proposed waiting until the following term. In order to "facilitate consideration" of his proposal, on May 27 he drafted five questions "to which the attention of counsel . . . should be directed." The first two asked about the intent of the framers of the Fourteenth Amendment with respect to school segregation. The third invited argument on the question of whether only Congress could abolish public school segregation or whether the Supreme Court possessed a concurrent power to do so. The last two questions addressed the problem of remedy, asking the parties to discuss whether a court of equity might authorize gradual adjustment to a ruling that segregated schools violated the Fourteenth Amendment. Black objected to the first three questions, while Vinson opposed the last two. Clark suggested the Court say it was asking about remedy only because the government had raised the issue, but Frankfurter rejected that idea. He also beat back Black's objections to another element of his reargument proposal: a request that the attorney general participate. Black feared Brownell's involvement would draw the Court into political controversy, but Frankfurter noted that the new Eisenhower administration would have to carry out any decision the Court might render and contended it ought to be asked now to accept that responsibility. On May 29 the conference agreed to his plan. A euphoric Frankfurter revised his five questions slightly, and on June 8 the Court asked the parties and the government to argue them in the fall. At the request of the Justice Department, Vinson postponed the reargument until December 7.[14]

By then Warren had replaced him as chief justice. Frankfurter reportedly remarked that Vinson's death was the first indication he had ever seen that there was a God. Although he also insisted that other factors were significant in producing the unanimous decision the Court rendered a few months later, the importance of the change in chief justices is undeniable. While Vinson was in charge, the Supreme Court had maintained segregated washrooms, and Reed could force the cancellation of an integrated staff Christmas party for its employees. Despite his deep personal involvement in the wartime relocation of the Japanese Americans, and the fact that black newspapers in California were cool to him because he had gone along with his party's opposition to the creation of a fair employment practices commission with enforcement powers, the new chief justice was far more sensitive to racial discrimination than his predecessor. While recovering from cancer surgery in 1944, Governor Warren had read and been troubled by a book about race in the United States. He frequently discussed the subject with his African American driver, Edgar Patterson, whom he questioned about his youth in segregated Louisiana, how black children were treated there, and how discrimination made them feel. While campaigning for vice president in 1948, Warren refused to speak to a segregated audience in Savannah, Georgia. One of the first opinions he wrote, *Hernandez v. Texas,* overturned a murder conviction because Mexican Americans had been systematically excluded from the jury. While Vinson had struggled with *Brown,* Warren viewed it as a comparatively simple case. To him it was obvious that separate-but-equal educational systems were seldom truly equal and that separating human beings on the basis of their color was unjust.[15]

Warren's appointment affected the outcome of *Brown* far more than did the reargument. Frankfurter apparently hoped that the answers to his questions about the intent of the framers of the Fourteenth Amendment would refute Jackson's contention that a decision against segregated schools could not be justified legally, and thus would have to be political. They did not. Needing only to give the Court plausible grounds to overturn "separate but equal," the NAACP enlisted a group of able historians and constitutional experts (including Howard J. Graham, Alfred H. Kelly, C. Vann Woodward, John Hope Franklin, and Horace Mann Bond) in a massive effort to locate the sort of evidence Frankfurter wanted. Unfortunately, it did not exist. Backers of the Fourteenth Amendment had denied it would prohibit segregated schools. Confronted with this inconvenient evidence, the NAACP worked out an approach that emphasized the egalitarian views the amendment's Radical Republican sponsors had inherited from pre–Civil War abolitionists and downplayed their occasional comments about education as peripheral to their central purpose.[16]

Neither this carefully crafted historical argument nor the more conventional one put forward by the defenders of segregation had much impact on the Court's decision. At Frankfurter's request, one of his clerks, Alexander Bickel, had spent the summer of 1953 doing his own research into the history of the Fourteenth Amendment.

On December 3, four days before reargument was scheduled to begin, Frankfurter circulated to his colleagues a memorandum summarizing Bickel's findings. It indicated, he informed them, "that the legislative history of the Amendment is, in a word, inconclusive, in the sense that the 39th Congress as an enacting body neither manifested that the Amendment outlawed segregation in the public schools or authorized legislation to that end, nor that it manifested the opposite."[17]

The Court would adopt Bickel's conclusion that the historical record was inconclusive. Thus, the lawyers' arguments on that subject were essentially sound and fury signifying nothing. Indeed, according to Elman, "nothing the lawyers said made a difference." Davis insisted the separate-but-equal doctrine was so well entrenched that the Court could not overturn it. Committed as they were to that position, he and his cocounsel were reluctant to discuss remedy. When Frankfurter forced Justin Moore, representing Prince Edward County, Virginia, to address that issue, he responded that the lower courts should be allowed the broadest possible discretion to act along "reasonable lines." Moore made it obvious, however, that the only thing he considered reasonable was the continued separation of the races. When Frankfurter asked Marshall about remedy, he simply reiterated the position the NAACP had staked out a year earlier, conceding only that administrative problems might justify a delay of up to a year in implementing desegregation. Elman thought Marshall might as well have been reciting "Mary had a little lamb."[18]

The only lawyer whose oral argument proved significant was Assistant Attorney General J. Lee Rankin. As early as Eisenhower's inauguration in January, Vinson had told Assistant Attorney General Warren Burger that the Supreme Court would like to have the views of the new administration. When the Court formally requested that it participate in the oral argument, Eisenhower, who considered *Brown* a troublesome political problem, told Attorney General Brownell to decline the invitation. Brownell, who was a good deal more sympathetic to civil rights than the president, responded that as an officer of the Court, he would find it difficult to refuse. Deferring to his attorney general's expertise on legal matters, Eisenhower allowed him to proceed. A policy group, consisting of most of the top officials in the Justice Department, was set up to deal with the case. Aware of Elman's connection to Frankfurter, Brownell deliberately excluded him from its policy discussions, leaving him with the erroneous impression that nothing was being done about *Brown*. Actually, Rankin, who had gotten the task because there was still no solicitor general, was preparing a brief and historical supplement.

Research done under his direction, much of it in a microfilm collection of state records, pointed to the same conclusion Bickel had reached: history provided no conclusive answer to the question of whether the Fourteenth Amendment was intended to prohibit school segregation. Rankin's brief emphasized, however, that the amendment created "a broad constitutional principle of full and complete equality of all persons under the law, and . . . forbade all legal distinctions based on race or color." Thus, the Justice Department supported the NAACP's position. Eisenhower would not let it cooperate at all with civil rights activists in preparing its brief, however. Indeed, the president would not even let the government take a stand on the question of whether public school segregation was unconstitutional. Rankin's brief was silent on the ultimate issue in the case. Pointing out that Rankin would surely be asked this question during oral argument, Brownell told the president it would be disastrous for him not to answer forthrightly, and when Eisenhower asked the attorney general for his opinion on the constitutionality of school segregation, Brownell responded that he thought *Plessy* had been wrongly decided. Again, the president deferred to his legal adviser. When Rankin was asked the question Brownell had anticipated, he responded by stating the attorney general's position.[19]

Although two administrations had now endorsed the contention that school segregation was unconstitutional, the Supreme Court was still not ready to decide the issue. At their December 12 conference, the justices discussed *Brown* extensively but did not vote. Apparently, the new chief justice had suggested this approach, although his colleagues readily agreed. "Realizing that when a person once announces he has reached a conclusion it is more difficult for him to change his thinking, we decided we would dispense with our usual custom of formally expressing our individual views . . . and would confine ourselves for a time to informal discussion of the briefs, the arguments made at the hearing, and our own independent research," Warren recalled later. He made his own position quite clear: the "separate but equal" doctrine rested on the assumption that the black race was inferior, and the NAACP attorneys had refuted that premise. There was simply no way segregation could be justified in 1953. With Warren committed to that position, "separate but equal" education was doomed. Only Reed, who insisted it was based on "racial differences" rather than inferiority, defended segregation. Although Clark expressed concern that holding segregated schools unconstitutional would provoke violence in the South, he stated forthrightly that he did not like school segregation and would vote for its elimination. Douglas remained determined to do the same, as did Black, who although absent because of a family illness, sent word of his position. Burton said he thought the Court had no choice but to act. Minton did not stake out his position quite as clearly, but he reminded his colleagues that "separate but equal" was a lawyers' gloss on an amendment that actually talked about equal rights and indicated he thought *McLaurin* had greatly weakened *Plessy*. Frankfurter's stance was even more difficult to discern, for he talked mostly about the historical record, which he acknowledged was at best inconclusive. Jackson, who added that precedent and custom supported segregation, insisted a decision against it could not be justified as a judicial act. According to Douglas, he declared, "This is a political question." For the Court to decide the matter would be a failure of representative government.[20]

While Jackson invoked the judicial self-restraint Frankfurter had long championed, his frequent ally seemed more concerned about whether a decision against school segregation could be enforced. They were, he reminded his colleagues, being "asked in effect to transform state-wide school systems in nearly a score of states." Frankfurter's reluctance to resolve the constitutional issue arose from anxiety about whether the Court could devise a satisfactory way to do that. Other justices shared his concern about whether they could fashion an acceptable remedy for what almost all of them now agreed was a violation of the Fourteenth Amendment. Soon after the

December 12 conference, Warren, convinced agreement on this issue was the key to achieving a unanimous decision, decided to direct discussion toward implementation. Determined that the Court should avoid direct involvement in the fashioning of social policy in an area so entangled in passions, Frankfurter circulated a memorandum on January 15, 1954, that recommended appointment of a master to gather facts and determine how best to achieve integrated schools. He did not succeed in selling that idea to the other justices, but at their conference the next day, Warren endorsed his contention (which received support from a memorandum written by one of Burton's clerks) that the Supreme Court should minimize its own involvement in the administration of any decision holding segregated schools unconstitutional. Most of their colleagues agreed. The pensive Jackson expressed doubts that they could properly consider anything other than the rights of the African American plaintiffs. He said he thought the Court needed more time to consider the remedial issue and suggested having it reargued. Black and Clark agreed, and the Court adopted his suggestion. With the issues of right and remedy temporarily divorced from one another, Frankfurter felt free to vote against segregation.[21]

The Court was now close to unanimity, and Warren decided to take a vote. His memoirs indicate he did this in early February, but probably it was after the Senate confirmed him on March 1. Some southern senators were threatening to block confirmation because they feared Warren would vote to end school segregation. While the Court had been careful to maintain the highest level of secrecy concerning its *Brown* deliberations, a politician as experienced as Warren would have been unlikely to risk a leak that could endanger his nomination by taking a vote that had already been delayed two months. He was probably also less than candid when he reported that the justices voted "unanimously . . . to declare racially segregated schools unconstitutional." More likely, the tally was eight to one, with Reed (who sometime in February roughed out a handwritten dissent) still in opposition.[22]

Warren and Burton talked informally with the amiable Kentuckian over numerous lunches. Finally, the Chief confronted Reed directly, reminding him that "you are all by yourself in this now" and urging him to do what was best for the country. Concluding that the Court's recent decisions counted for more than history, Reed succumbed to Warren's appeal. Not wanting to provide diehard defenders of segregation with an excuse to cause trouble, he agreed not to dissent publicly, asking in return only that the decision be implemented gradually.[23]

Warren had suggested that a decision holding school segregation unconstitutional might be more palatable to the South if one of the southerners on the Court wrote the opinion, but Black persuaded the Chief he must speak for them on such a momentous matter. Even before they took a formal vote, the justices agreed he should prepare a memorandum on the school segregation cases. Warren worked on it through much of the term. On April 20 he discussed his preliminary thoughts with Burton. Then on the afternoon of May 1 the Chief called in the three clerks he had inherited from Vinson, told them what the Court had decided, enjoined them to the strictest secrecy, and set them to work drafting two opinions, one for the District of Columbia and another for the four state cases. Warren instructed Earl Pollock, to whom he assigned primary responsibility for composing the latter opinion, that he wanted something short, devoid of legalisms, and written in plain English, that the lay public could read and understand. Pollock produced a draft in thirty-six hours. On May 3 Warren discussed with Frankfurter what his clerks had produced, and two days later he read to and discussed a draft of the memorandum with Burton. After revising this "basis for discussion of the segregation cases," Warren hand delivered it to all of his colleagues on May 7.[24]

He had to take Jackson's copy to Doctor's Hospital, where the ambivalent New Yorker had been confined since suffering a heart attack on March 30. Before being stricken, but after it became clear that the Court was prepared to overrule *Plessy*, Jackson had drafted and revised several times what he apparently intended to be a concurring opinion. This document, which he never circulated to his colleagues, manifested the same ambivalence he had displayed throughout the deliberations. Jackson devoted twenty-one pages to his doubts and fears about what the Court was doing and only two to justifying its ruling, causing a clerk who read his memorandum to say it read as if he were embarrassed by the decision. Despite his many reservations, Jackson managed to rationalize voting with the majority, concluding that changes in the role of public education and the social position of African Americans justified changing constitutional doctrine. The opinion prepared by Warren, who clearly wanted the Court to speak with one voice, relied in part on this line of reasoning. Jackson asked a trusted clerk to read it, and he found what the Chief had written acceptable. When Warren returned later in the day, Jackson made a couple of suggestions, then agreed to join the Chief's opinion.[25]

By the time of the conference on Saturday May 15, the absent Jackson had formally agreed to a revised version, which included minor alterations Warren had made at the request of other justices. The Court approved the Chief's opinion and celebrated by dining on a large salmon that Burton had received from Secretary of the Interior Douglas McKay. Determined to avoid any leaks, they decided to announce their decision the following Monday.[26]

Warren informed the attorney general that the ruling was coming down on May 17, but not what it would be. Brownell was in the Supreme Court chamber that afternoon. So was Jackson. Thin and wan, he dragged himself back from the hospital for what he realized would be a momentous event. The afternoon that would define the Warren Court began routinely with the admission of some lawyers to the Supreme Court bar and the reporting of some antitrust and labor decisions. Then at 12:52 P.M., Warren declared in a flat voice, "I have for announcement the opinion of the Court in No. 1—*Oliver Brown et al. v. Board of Education of Topeka.*"[27]

He then began reading what Bernard Schwartz has called "one of the great opinions in judicial history." Warren dispensed with the history of the Fourteenth Amendment in a mere two paragraphs, pronouncing it too "inconclusive" to be of much help in resolving the issue now before the Court. Historical sources offered little guidance because when the amendment was adopted, public education did not yet exist in the South and was rudimentary elsewhere. Determining the constitutionality of separate-but-equal schools in 1954, Warren explained, necessitated a consideration of the place that public education now occupied in the life of the whole nation. It had become so important to a child's development and prospects for success that when a state undertook to provide it, "such an opportunity . . . must be made available to all on equal terms." The issue, then, was, whether "segregation of children in public schools solely on the basis of race, even though the physical facilities and other 'tangible' factors may be equal, deprive[s] the children of the minority group of equal educational opportunity?"[28]

"We believe that it does," Warren declared. The reason was the psychological impact of segregation on African American students. Separating them from other children because of their race generated feelings of inferiority that affected their hearts and minds in ways unlikely ever to be undone, ways that adversely affected their motivation to learn and retarded their intellectual and mental development. To support this conclusion and refute *Plessy*'s assertion that legally required segregation stamped members of the minority as inferior only because they chose to view it that way, Warren inserted footnote 11, in which he cited a number of recent publications by social psychologists, among them Dr. Kenneth Clark (who had testified for the plaintiffs in South Carolina, Virginia, and Delaware), as well as (over the objections of southerners Black and Clark) Myrdal's book *An American Dilemma*. Apparently reluctant to rest the decision on such extralegal authority, he included in the body of his opinion a lengthy quotation from a finding made by the district court in Kansas. Like the writings of the social psychologists, the finding pointed to the conclusion that "separate educational facilities are inherently unequal." "We conclude," wrote Warren, "that in the field of public education the doctrine of 'separate but equal' has no place." If a state segregated its public schools, it violated the Equal Protection Clause.[29]

Much about Warren's opinion provoked criticism. Some commentators, questioning the research of Kenneth Clark and other social psychologists that purported to prove segregation was harmful to African American children, faulted him for resting the Court's holding on such a shaky foundation. In his 1958 Holmes Lectures at Harvard Law School, Judge Learned Hand criticized the opinion's handling of *Plessy*. By distinguishing it (i.e,. saying its rule did not apply to schools in modern America) rather than rejecting it outright on grounds that racial equality was a paramount value that must always prevail against any conflicting interest, the Court had involved itself in choosing between competing values. That kind of policy-making was a job for legislators, and thus in Hand's opinion, *Brown* violated the principle of judicial restraint. Professor Herbert Wechsler of Columbia Law School did not agree with Hand that the Court's decision had turned on its resolution of the factual question of how much school segregation harmed black children. It rested instead, he asserted in a 1959 Holmes lecture, on the view that racial segregation was in principle a denial of equality. What segregation really did, however, was prevent African Americans from associating with Caucasians. Since treating that as a denial of equality deprived whites of their own right *not* to associate with blacks, the Court had failed to meet what Wechsler regarded as its paramount obligation: to decide the case on the basis of a neutral principle. Yale professors Louis H. Pollak and Charles L. Black responded with spirited justifications of *Brown*, but Hand and Wechsler managed to raise serious doubts about its legitimacy in the minds of those steeped in process jurisprudence.[30]

Warren's disposition of the District of Columbia case also provoked criticism. Pollock suggested to him that it "be treated independently in a short, separate opinion accompanying the other one." Unlike *Brown*, the decision in *Bolling v. Sharpe* would have to rest on the Due Process Clause of the Fifth Amendment, because the Fourteenth Amendment did not apply to the national capital. The *Bolling* plaintiffs had argued that school segregation denied them due process by arbitrarily depriving them of a fundamental liberty—the right to an education. For authority they had relied on *Meyer v. Nebraska* (1923), *Pierce v. Society of Sisters* (1925), and *Farrington v. Tokushige* (1927), in which the Court had struck down laws restricting private schools and education in languages other than English. The first draft of Warren's *Bolling* opinion adopted this argument, holding that government imposition of arbitrary restraints on access to education was a denial of due process and maintaining that racial segregation limited liberty far more than had the restrictions at issue in *Meyer, Pierce,* and *Farrington.* Because the decisions on which the Chief relied were part of a body of case law—which utilized a substantive conception of due process to invalidate legislation that conflicted with justices' personal notions of what was reasonable—that Black and Frankfurter had publicly repudiated, one or both of them objected to his draft opinion. He rewrote it, producing one that reached the conclusion that public school segregation in the District of Columbia was unconstitutional by reading an equal protection requirement into the Due Process Clause. No precedent supported his position, and Warren did not bother to explain why, if due process included equal protection, the Fourteenth Amendment included guarantees of both. He simply declared that it would be "unthinkable" for the same Constitution that prohibited the states from maintaining separate schools to "impose a lesser duty on the Federal Government."[31]

Implicit in Warren's *Bolling* and *Brown* opinions, thought Arthur Krock of the *New York Times,* was the notion that even if the Fifth and Fourteenth Amendments had not specifically applied to school segregation, the Constitution would have outlawed it anyhow. The *Times* praised the Supreme Court for restating "a constitutional principle inherent in the Declaration of Independence," and the *Cincinnati Inquirer* commended it for acting "as the conscience of the American nation." Other northern and western newspapers, such as the *Pittsburgh Post-Gazette, Hartford Courant, Chicago Tribune, Minneapolis Tribune, San Francisco Chronicle, Des Moines Register, Boston Herald, Cleveland Plain Dealer, Chicago Daily News,* and *Los Angeles Times,* joined in applauding the school desegregation decisions, as did the *Washington Post and Times-Herald* and the *St. Louis Post-Dispatch,* both published in communities that segregated their schools. The reaction of the *Washington Evening Star, Baltimore Sun,* and *Louisville Courier Journal* was also mildly positive. While the *Jackson* (Miss.) *Daily News* predicted *Brown* would lead to miscegenation and bloodshed, the reaction of such southern papers as the *Atlanta Constitution, Birmingham Post-Herald, Birmingham News, Chattanooga Times, Dallas News, New Orleans Times-Picayune, Houston Chronicle, Memphis Commercial-Appeal, Miami*

Herald, Charlotte (N.C.) *Observer,* Charleston (S.C.) *News & Courier,* Nashville *Tennessean,* Nashville *Banner,* and Jackson *Clarion-Ledger* was one of resignation, coupled in some cases with pleas for calm. "We hope," editorialized the student newspaper at the University of Mississippi, "that the Supreme Court fully realizes the adjustment will be much more difficult than was its decision."[32]

It was not for Topeka, Kansas, where, by the time the Court decided *Brown,* the Topeka school board already had adopted a plan that allowed some African American students to attend previously all-white schools. In February 1955 it voted to complete desegregation. In Delaware and the District of Columbia as well, substantial desegregation took place even before the reargument on remedy.[33]

In Virginia, South Carolina, and the other states of the Deep South, however, nothing happened. The reaction there was not as strong as some justices had feared, mainly because the Court had not ordered immediate implementation of its ruling. When Warren reviewed the six to seven hundred letters about *Brown* that reached his office during the first two months after the decision was announced, he found that approximately half of them supported what the Supreme Court had done. Northerners Frankfurter and Burton also received correspondence praising the school desegregation decisions. The authors included the Court's first African American clerk, a spokesman for the liberal National Students Association, and a Jesuit, who viewed *Brown* as a blow against Communism. Of the hundreds of letters sent to Black by his fellow Alabamans, however, almost all were sharply critical, damning him as a scalawag, a betrayer, a Judas, and worse. Mrs. William Dickinson of Sumter, South Carolina, informed Black bluntly, "We are not going to send our children to non-segregated schools." The North Carolina legislature adopted a resolution endorsing the report of a citizens' advisory committee, which declared that the mixing of the races in the public schools could not be accomplished and should not be attempted. Senator James O. Eastland (D-Miss.) proclaimed that the South, where at least 80 percent of whites opposed ending school segregation, would not abide by what he condemned as the legislative decision of a political court. Most southern politicians were more temperate. While informing Frankfurter that he himself was adopting a moderate stance, however, South Carolina governor James Byrnes (a former justice) also reported that conditions in his state were somewhat "chaotic." The legislature was willing to wait until it saw what the Court did about implementation, but it had activated a committee that was considering abolishing the public school system to prevent integration. That idea also was receiving "more than perfunctory attention" in other southern states, and segregation was being exploited as an issue in some southern primary elections.[34]

The South's animus toward *Brown* was strong enough to delay the confirmation of Eisenhower's second Supreme Court nominee. After Jackson, who had never fully recovered from his heart attack, died on October, 9, 1954, the president nominated another New Yorker, Judge John Marshall Harlan of the U.S. Court of Appeals for the Second Circuit, to replace him. Harlan, who was fifty-four, came from a wealthy and politically prominent family. After graduating from Princeton, he had studied law and jurisprudence at Oxford on a Rhodes scholarship, then completed a two-year course of study at New York Law School in one year, while employed by the prestigious Wall Street law firm of Root, Clark, Buckner and Howland. Harlan left the Root firm temporarily during the 1920s to work for one of its partners, Emory Buckner, who had become U.S. Attorney for the Southern District of New York, and again during World War II to serve as a colonel in the U.S. Army Air Force and in the 1950s to act as general counsel for the New York State Crime Commission. Throughout most of his career, however, he was a corporate lawyer, attaining wealth and prominence by representing clients such as the du Ponts. Harlan was also active in civic and bar association affairs and dabbled in politics. Associated with the Dewey wing of the Republican party, he was a longtime personal friend of Brownell, who had worked with him at Root, Clark. Backed by the attorney general and a group of prominent New York lawyers, Harlan received a nomination from Eisenhower to the Second Circuit in January 1954. After being pressured into making Warren chief justice, the president had told Brownell he "would not thereafter appoint anyone who had not served on a lower federal court or on a state supreme court." Harlan's brief judicial service and distinguished career as a practicing lawyer pleased the president, and also earned him enthusiastic endorsements from the American Bar Association and the Association of the Bar of the City of New York, as well as a recommendation from the Second Circuit's most distinguished jurist, Judge Learned Hand.[35]

Although Hand and the ABA considered Harlan an ideal choice, southerners did not; he was the grandson and namesake of an earlier justice, John Marshall Harlan, best known for his dissent in *Plessy*. Led by Judiciary Committee member Senator Eastland, segregationists fought the nomination. So did conservative Republicans of an isolationist persuasion, who condemned Harlan's receipt of a Rhodes scholarship and his membership in the Citizens Association for the United Nations and the Atlantic Union Committee. Judiciary Committee chair William Langer (R-N.D.), who consistently opposed all Supreme Court nominees not from states, such as his own, that had not had one, also resisted Harlan. After consulting with Solicitor General Simon Sobeloff and members of the Court, the nominee decided to appear personally before the Judiciary Committee. Following the advice of his future colleagues, he answered only general questions and declined to reveal his views on specific legal and constitutional issues. A number of witnesses appeared to testify against him, but most members of the committee seemed uninterested in their charges. On March 9, 1955, the committee voted ten to four to confirm Harlan, and a week later, after three hours of debate, the full Senate endorsed its recommendation seventy-one to eleven.[36]

Eisenhower deplored "the harassment and delay involved in the confirmation." Although it was conservative resistance that had kept Harlan from taking his seat for over four months, he would become the Warren Court's most prominent conservative. Although not opposed to change, Harlan did view skeptically rapid change driven by abstract philosophical visions of how the world should be transformed. His commitment to judicial restraint and the other tenets of process jurisprudence rivaled Frankfurter's. So did his attachment to federalism, which made him a vigorous defender of state autonomy against expanding federal power, especially federal judicial power. A friend of Frankfurter, Harlan quickly became his collaborator, and after Frankfurter's retirement, carried on the fight for their views on an increasingly liberal and unsympathetic Court. Of the 613 opinions Harlan wrote during a sixteen-year career, 296 were dissents.[37]

In the school desegregation cases, however, he marched with the majority. Immediately after his appointment, Harlan contacted Burton, indicating he wanted to visit the Court as soon as possible after his confirmation and to sit with his new colleagues during the December reargument. Warren's reaction was positive. When the Judiciary Committee delayed consideration of the nomination, the Court, far from anxious for the reargument to take place before the fall elections, postponed it indefinitely. Even while he awaited confirmation, Harlan studied the school segregation problem, reading a clerk's analysis of the briefs and a lengthy report that Warren sent him.[38]

That report had been prepared by six clerks, whom the Chief had assigned to do intensive research during the summer of 1954 and make recommendations for the Court's decree. Warren circulated their analysis in November, and the day before the reargument, he sent his colleagues a nine-page memorandum embodying the clerk's recommendations. Like Frankfurter, they advocated gradualism. The clerks agreed with him that these were really class actions, affecting the rights of millions of children and demanding a radical transformation of southern school systems. Frankfurter had argued in January 1954 that the judiciary's duty to promote integrated education could be satisfied by reversing the direction of unconstitutional past policy and uprooting it "with all deliberate speed" (a phrase he borrowed from Justice Oliver Wendell Holmes Jr.). Similarly cautious, all but one clerk deemed immediate desegregation of all grades impractical and likely to trigger resistance. The clerks recommended that the Supreme Court formulate a simple decree and remand the cases to the district courts, charging them with supervising its execution. They divided over how much guidance the Supreme Court should give the lower court judges. Five considered guidelines essential to prevent confusion and unnecessary delay; the sixth favored giving the states maximum flexibility while retaining discretion to reject any approaches they might adopt that denied individuals their rights. Only one clerk saw any need to require local authorities to submit comprehensive school desegregation plans to the district courts.[39]

The brief submitted by Solicitor General Sobeloff, on the other hand, argued that the lower courts should be instructed to require that defendant districts either or admit the black plaintiffs immediately submit effective programs for accomplishing desegregation as promptly as practicable. Like a majority of the clerks, the government urged the Court to lay down standards to guide the judges who would have to supervise desegregation. Its brief also sounded a cautious note, emphasizing the need to devise intelligent, orderly, and effective solutions to the many and varying administrative problems ending segregation would entail and urging that local authorities be allowed to formulate and execute their own programs. The brief's emphasis on complexity and local discretion reflected the wishes of the president. Under pressure from southern political supporters and fearful of school closings and violence, Eisenhower personally inserted language that looked toward delay in the implementation of *Brown*.[40]

Like the president, the reargument, which finally took place April 11–14, 1955, pushed the Court toward gradualism. The NAACP's Thurgood Marshall requested a decree that would require desegregation by a specified date in the near future. The briefs and oral arguments of the defendants and of the attorneys general of Florida, North Carolina, Arkansas, Oklahoma, Maryland, and Texas (who participated at the request of the Court) made it clear, however, that the South remained committed to segregation and that even gradual compliance with *Brown* would be difficult to obtain. South Carolina attorney S. Emory Rogers asked for an "open decree" that would remand the cases without specifying either when or how desegregation was to take place. When Warren pressed him about whether there would be an immediate and honest attempt to comply with the Court's decree, Rogers responded indignantly that if ordered to send white children to Negro schools, the people of South Carolina would not obey. An angry Warren cut him off, and for a moment appeared about to cite Rogers for contempt. The attorney general of North Carolina had a similar message for the Court, however, and his counterpart from Arkansas predicted endless litigation in that state. Florida's attorney general offered a measured plea for gradualism. Even Sobeloff concurred, saying that while the Court should require a prompt start toward desegregation and some "motion" in that direction, it should not tie the hands of the district courts.[41]

On the last day of oral argument, Frankfurter circulated a memorandum to his colleagues, which maintained they had two alternatives: (1) a bare-bones decree permanently enjoining the defendant districts from excluding African American students and returning the cases to the lower courts; or (2) one that would take into account the considerations (including public attitudes and administrative and financial problems) relevant to fashioning a decree and limiting the capacity of judges to enforce it. He clearly favored the latter course. At the conference on April 16, Black endorsed the first option. Certain that the southerners were "going to fight this," he thought the less the Court said the better. The others, including Harlan, all wanted an opinion as well as a decree, and only Douglas supported Black's contention that the relief the Court granted should be limited to the named plaintiffs. The others all viewed these as class suits. Only Burton, however, seemed interested in a decree that would enjoin all school segregation as rapidly as possible. Most of his colleagues apparently agreed with Black that the Court dare not issue what it could not enforce. Several stressed the need for unanimity. In the end the Court followed the lead of its new chief justice, agreeing to issue a bare-bones decree, but one accompanied by an opinion setting forth considerations lower courts should keep in mind in implementing it. At his suggestion they neither set a date for completing desegregation nor required school districts to submit plans for achieving integration.[42]

Warren's colleagues authorized him to draft an opinion. Modified slightly in response to their suggestions, it was issued on May 31, 1955. Only two pages long,

Brown II acknowledged both the progress that had already been made toward achieving desegregation and the existence of problems that would have to be overcome before full implementation could be achieved. Because the courts in which these cases had originated were familiar with local conditions, and because further hearings might be needed, the Supreme Court was leaving to them the fashioning and execution of decrees. In carrying out that responsibility, they might consider a variety of problems related to administration, such as transportation, personnel, the physical condition of school buildings, and the need to revise attendance zones. The Court instructed them to follow equitable principles, which included flexibility in adjusting public and private needs. While they might take into consideration the societal interest in the orderly elimination of the obstacles to full implementation, however, the constitutional principles announced in *Brown I* "could not be allowed to yield simply because of disagreement with them." The lower courts must require the defendants to make "a prompt and reasonable start" toward full compliance. Once that was done, they might grant school districts additional time, but the burden would be on the defendants to establish that any delay was necessary and "consistent with good faith compliance at the earliest practicable date." The Supreme Court remanded the cases to the district courts with instructions to retain jurisdiction and "take such proceedings and enter such orders and decrees consistent with this opinion as are necessary and proper to admit to the public schools on a racially nondiscriminatory basis with all deliberate speed the parties to these cases."[43]

The Court's "all deliberate speed" formula was intended to minimize resistance by standing firm for the principle announced in *Brown I,* while carefully avoiding requiring anyone actually to comply with that decision. Defenders of *Brown II* lauded it as realistic, and even Marshall thought it "a damn good decision." Yet the approach capsulized in the phrase "all deliberate speed" failed miserably. By laying down no timetables, *Brown II* created uncertainty among educational and political officials in the South and left the executive branch convinced it could not enforce desegregation until the lower courts acted. The 1955 decision irritated both Eisenhower, who disliked *Brown I,* and Brownell, who supported it.[44]

Furthermore, although the South's reaction to *Brown II* was favorable, the Court had not appeased whites there. Resentment of its school desegregation decisions propelled southern politics far to the right, rendering moderation on racial issues untenable. By 1956 250,000 southerners had joined White Citizens Councils, organized to hold the line against integration. In March of that year 19 of the South's 22 senators and 82 of its 106 representatives presented Congress with a "Southern Manifesto," which denounced *Brown* as an "unwarranted" abuse of judicial power. They accused the Supreme Court of encroaching on the rights of the states and of creating "chaos and confusion" in their region. The signers of the manifesto pledged to seek reversal of *Brown* and commended "the motives of those States which have declared the intention to resist forced integration by any lawful means." The Southern Manifesto made resistance to the federal courts respectable. Across the South racial moderates went down to defeat in the 1956 elections. As Michael Klarman observes, *Brown* produced a "unification of southern racial intransigence, which became known as massive resistance, [and] propelled politics in virtually every southern state several notches to the right on racial issues."[45]

In the face of growing southern intransigence, the Eisenhower administration maintained a conspicuous silence. Fearful that southerners might close their schools, the president declined to endorse *Brown*. Indeed, when the Republican Party tried to give him credit for the decision in its 1956 platform, Eisenhower insisted it remove that plank. His purpose, he assured South Carolina's governor James Byrnes, was "to provide a moderate approach to a difficult problem and to make haste slowly." Even when Governor Allan Shivers used Texas Rangers to prevent black children from entering an all-white public school in Mansfield, Texas, the Eisenhower administration did nothing. Brownell later attributed its inaction to *Brown II* and the lack of a federal court order requiring Mansfield schools to desegregate. The justices resented Eisenhower's failure to support them, however, and Warren blamed the rising tide of southern resistance on the unwillingness of a popular president to urge compliance with their desegregation decision.[46]

Resistance to *Brown* assumed a variety of forms. Southern legislatures condemned the decision. Mississippi branded it "unconstitutional and of no lawful effect," while legislators in Alabama, Arkansas, Georgia, North Carolina, and Virginia adopted measures purporting to interpose the authority of those states between the federal government and their people and to declare *Brown* null and void. Virginia committed herself to a program of "massive resistance" to desegregation that included creation of a statewide Pupil Placement Board, authorizing the state to take charge of and close schools that attempted to desegregate voluntarily or were ordered to do so by federal courts, and providing tuition grants for parents from such districts who chose to send their children to segregated "private" schools. Other states also adopted pupil placement laws, which purported to meet *Brown*'s requirement for gradual desegregation by establishing ostensibly nonracial criteria for assignment of students. Yet these could be and were administered so as to ensure continued segregation. Several states sought to avoid integration by replacing their public schools with some sort of nominally private ones. There were many ways to fight back, John Temple Graves of Alabama proclaimed, and "The South proposes to use all of them to make resistance." Sometimes, it resorted to violence. The moribund Ku Klux Klan revived, and between January 1, 1955, and January 1, 1959, the South experienced 210 incidents of intimidation attributable to the increased racial tensions generated by *Brown*. During 1956 efforts to desegregate the University of Alabama, Texarkana Junior College, and the public schools of Mansfield, Texas, and Clinton and Nashville, Tennessee, sparked mob violence. Crosses burned in front of the Washington homes of several justices.[47]

Defiance of *Brown* by politicians and mobs in Little Rock, Arkansas, eventually drew a reluctant Supreme Court back into the school desegregation controversy. For more than four years after its landmark 1954 decision, the Court had studiously avoided saying anything on the subject. When a Florida court sought to use *Brown II* as an excuse to delay admitting to a state university law school an African American whose case had been remanded for reconsideration in light of *Brown I,* the Court, over Frankfurter's objections, reversed without hearing argument in the case. Reed's brief per curiam opinion (which simply stated that the "all deliberate speed" formula was inapplicable to graduate education) pleased Black because "it says very little." The Florida Supreme Court continued to sanction delay, but when the applicant again sought review, he fell one vote short of the four needed to secure a writ of certiorari. The Court also declined in 1958 to hear oral argument in a case challenging Alabama's pupil placement law, summarily affirming a decision declining to hold the statute invalid on its face, because the Birmingham school board might have relied on one of its constitutionally permissible criteria in failing to admit the African American plaintiff's daughter. The justices realized such a decision could encourage southern resistance, but only Douglas seemed willing to confront Alabama.[48]

Little Rock forced the Court's hand. In May 1955 the school board there adopted a plan providing for gradual desegregation, beginning in September 1957. African American students challenged it as being too slow. The U.S. District Court for the Eastern District of Arkansas upheld the plan, but retained jurisdiction to ensure its effectuation. The pending desegregation of the Little Rock schools inflamed the 1956 elections, in which Arkansas voters adopted several constitutional amendments to preserve apartheid and reelected Governor Orval Faubus, a moderate who responded to charges that he was soft on segregation by vowing that no school district would be forced integrate. In August 1957, claiming the impending desegregation of Little Rock Central High School might lead to violence, Faubus persuaded the Pulaski County Chancery Court to enjoin implementation of the school board's plan. Federal district judge Ronald Davies responded by issuing an order forbidding interference with the carrying out of his court's decree. When nine African American students tried to attend Central High on September 3, however, Faubus deployed the National Guard to keep them out. Davies ordered him to remove his troops. The nine students managed to enter Central High on September 23, but disturbances in and around the school forced their removal within hours. Brownell then advised the president that he had "the undoubted power, under the Constitution and laws of the United States" to call the Arkansas National Guard into federal service and use it and the armed forces to suppress this "domestic violence, obstruction, and resistance of law." Although reluctant to employ military force, the president acted on his attorney general's advice, and the African American students were soon attending Central High School under the protection of the 101st Airborne Division.[49]

The students suffered constant harassment. Wearying of the continuing turmoil, the superintendent and the school board asked the district court for permission to discontinue desegregation at Central High and postpone it everywhere until 1960. They argued that because of the extreme public hostility engendered by Faubus and the legislature, maintaining a sound educational program at the high school with the black students in attendance would be impossible. On June 21 Judge Harry Lemley granted the school district a two-year delay. The NAACP sought immediate review of his ruling by the Supreme Court. It refused, but in the process pointedly told the Eighth Circuit to resolve the case quickly, so arrangements could be made for the next school year. That court reversed Lemley and directed that desegregation proceed, but it entered a thirty-day stay of its order, leaving his in place. Both parties then asked the Supreme Court to hear the case. Because its regular October term would not begin until after the start of school, Warren convened the Court in a special term on August 28 to receive the NAACP's application to vacate the stay and then again on September 11 to hear arguments on both appeals.[50]

The Court that assembled to consider the Little Rock case was not the same one that had decided *Brown II.* In May of 1956 Sherman Minton, who suffered from severe anemia and was having difficulty walking and concentrating, informed his colleagues that he intended to retire. In order to qualify for a full pension, however, he needed to remain on the Court until October. Minton waited until September 7 to notify the president of his intention to step down on October 15. The delay forced Eisenhower to make a recess appointment in the middle of his own campaign for reelection. The president wanted to demonstrate that he was above partisanship, to please the Conference of Catholic Bishops and New York's Francis Cardinal Spellman (who were unhappy that there had been no Catholic on the Court since Murphy) and to satisfy the Conference of Chief Justices of State Courts (which contended that when dealing with federalism issues, the high tribunal needed the perspective of someone with state judicial experience). By September 29 Eisenhower had settled on William J. Brennan Jr. He was an Irish Catholic, a Democrat, and an associate justice on the New Jersey Supreme Court. New Jersey's chief justice, Arthur Vanderbilt, a prominent Republican, strongly recommended Brennan. Brownell, who had heard him address a conference on judicial administration as a last-minute replacement for Vanderbilt, also thought highly of him, and Brennan received the endorsement of the ABA. Before submitting his name to the president (along with several others), the attorney general read all of his opinions, which he found well reasoned and well written. Before sending Brennan's name to the Senate, Eisenhower had an aide check with his parish priest to verify that he attended mass regularly. The nominee won almost unanimous Senate support. The only vote cast against him on March 19, 1957, came from Wisconsin demagogue Joe McCarthy, who questioned the nominee's commitment to his crusade against Communism.[51]

The target of McCarthy's animosity was the fifty-year-old son of a Newark union leader and politician. After graduating from the University of Pennsylvania's Wharton School in 1928, Brennan had attended Harvard Law School, where he was a solid student but not a star, finishing among the top sixty students in his class. One of his professors was Frankfurter. After graduating from Harvard, Brennan joined the Newark firm of Pitney, Hardin, and Ward, where he built a statewide reputation in labor law (ironically by representing management) and became the first Catholic partner. After serving as an army lawyer in Washington during World War II, he returned to Newark, where he became active in efforts to reform the New Jersey court system. In 1949 Brennan was appointed to the Hudson County Superior Court. In late 1950 he received a promotion to the appellate division, and in March 1952 advanced to the state supreme court. Besides being a rapidly rising judicial star,

Brennan was a liberal activist with a gift for coalition building. He would become Warren's most trusted lieutenant.[52]

His distinguished career on the Supreme Court contrasts starkly with the brief and unsuccessful tenure of Charles Whittaker. In January 1957 Stanley Reed informed Eisenhower that, having reached the age of seventy-two, he intended to retire on February 25. The president wanted a replacement with prior judicial experience, and Whittaker satisfied that criterion; he had been on the Eighth Circuit for nine months and before that had spent three years as a federal district judge. A fifty-six-year-old graduate of the University of Kansas City Law School and formerly a successful Kansas City corporate trial lawyer, Whittaker had the enthusiastic support of Missouri's bench and bar, as well as the state's GOP leadership. In addition, he was a close friend of Ike's brother, Arthur, a Kansas City banker. In nominating him, Eisenhower resisted pressure to choose a southerner, or at least someone who would promise to retreat from *Brown*. Although apparently committed to the principles of the school desegregation decision, Whittaker was more conservative than previous Eisenhower nominees. He also proved incapable of handling the pressures of his new job.[53]

By the summer of 1958 the Supreme Court workload had also begun to tell on Harold Burton, who suffered from Parkinson's disease. Burton hoped to serve one more term, but in June his doctor told him he needed to retire. Because he would reach age seventy and become eligible for a pension on June 22, he decided to step down then. Both Warren and the new attorney general, William Rogers, urged him to stay on, at least until September 30. When Burton explained his physical problems to them, they reluctantly agreed that he should meet with the president. Their meeting, delayed by various crises until July 17, dealt largely with the subject of a successor.[54]

Burton lobbied for the appointment of someone like himself, with congressional experience, but Eisenhower seemed to feel that Warren's appointment had given the Court enough nonjudicial experience. The president's biggest concern was that Burton's successor be sufficiently conservative. The only person they discussed was Judge Potter Stewart of the U.S. Court of Appeals for the Sixth Circuit. Born in Cincinnati in 1915, Stewart had attended Hotchkiss and Yale, then spent a year at Cambridge University on a Henry Fellowship. Following his 1941 graduation with honors from Yale Law School, he accepted a position with the Wall Street firm of Debevoise, Stevenson, Plimpton, and Page. Stewart left New York to serve in the navy as a deck officer during World War II. Returning to his native Cincinnati after the war, he became one of the city's leading lawyers and a partner in the firm of Dinsmore, Stohl, Sawyer, and Dinsmore. He also plunged into Republican politics, was twice elected to the city council, and served one term as vice mayor. In 1954 Eisenhower appointed him to the Sixth Circuit, where his carefully crafted opinions, engaging style, and independent jurisprudence captured the attention of the legal community. Apparently with the understanding that Stewart would be his successor, Burton submitted a resignation that would take effect on October 13. Then he left for Europe.[55]

The Little Rock crisis interrupted his vacation. It also alarmed Eisenhower, Rogers, and Warren, who were wary of launching a Supreme Court nominee into the resulting political tempest. On September 19 the attorney general tried to persuade Burton to postpone his retirement, and a week later, the chief justice had still not informed the rest of the Court of Burton's intention to step down. Their political instincts (which also kept Eisenhower and Rogers from nominating Brownell because he was identified with civil rights) were sound. When Stewart's appointment was announced, southern senators, viewing him as another northern liberal unfriendly to segregation, opposed it. They delayed his confirmation for four months and cast seventeen votes against him. Senator Richard Russell (D-Ga.) claimed the Stewart nomination was part of a Justice Department plot to perpetuate the Court's recent desegregation decisions.[56]

Among those he had in mind was *Cooper v. Aaron*, the last case in which Burton participated. On August 28, after hearing argument on the motion to vacate the Eighth Circuit's stay of its own order, the justices concluded that deciding that issue required consideration of the merits of the decision reversing Judge Lemley. With the opening of school in Little Rock imminent, the Court, over Clark's objections, agreed to hear the board's appeal on an extremely short schedule, requiring it to complete formal application for review by September 8, instructing both parties and the solicitor general to file briefs by September 10, and scheduling oral argument for September 11. In the interim the Arkansas legislature passed a number of laws that gave Faubus the authority to close public schools facing integration and transfer public funds to segregated private ones. Attorney General Rogers, obviously anticipating that the Court would nevertheless order Little Rock to desegregate, wrote to the president of the school board, suggesting he seek an injunction against those who might interfere with the board's efforts to comply. Rogers also communicated with the city manager, telling him the Justice Department intended to increase the number of U.S. marshals in Little Rock and offering to cooperate with local police in preventing disorder and violence.[57]

Oral argument left little doubt that the Supreme Court's ruling would be what Rogers expected. The justices had no questions for Thurgood Marshall, and they asked Solicitor General Rankin only one, but they rigorously interrogated the school board's lawyer, Richard Butler. His brief had emphasized the district's good faith effort to begin desegregation and argued that the risk of future violence justified suspending it. A skeptical Frankfurter, who had already written a memorandum urging his colleagues to reject the board's request for a delay, suggested the cause of Little Rock's problems was the state officials who had incited opposition to desegregation. Warren was also hard on Butler, asserting that even if the board were proceeding in good faith, the State of Arkansas was still responsible for keeping African American students from exercising their constitutional rights. When the lawyer lamented that his clients were caught in the middle between Governor Faubus and the national government, Brennan and Black reminded him that the Supremacy Clause required them to resolve such a conflict in favor of compliance with the Constitution.[58]

Butler could hardly have been surprised when the Court reversed Judge Lemley. At a conference immediately following the June 11 hearing, Warren urged his colleagues to take that action and also to reaffirm the duty of state officials to obey the law as laid down by the Supreme Court. They agreed with him so quickly that the meeting was over in thirty minutes. Because Central High was about to start classes, the justices decided to disclose their ruling on September 12 in a three-paragraph per curiam, drafted by Frankfurter and Harlan, which merely announced the judgment and explained that an opinion would follow later.[59]

Warren assigned the task of writing one to Brennan. Harlan, however, produced an alternative draft, and Clark, who objected to the speed with which the Court was disposing of the case, even composed a handwritten dissent. Other justices disliked sections of Brennan's draft that attempted to define more precisely what "all deliberate speed" meant. Brennan and Black wanted to state specifically that it required not only initiating desegregation but also specifying a completion date for the process. Frankfurter and Burton disagreed, and ultimately Brennan eliminated all discussion of the subject. Harlan wanted him to tone down passages virtually asserting that judicial interpretations of the Constitution were part of the supreme law of the land, but Brennan prevailed on that issue. His colleagues did compel him to accept two other changes proposed by Harlan. One was the addition of a declaration that the three justices appointed since *Brown I* agreed completely with the 1954 decision and that the Court "unanimously reaffirmed" it. Harlan also persuaded his colleagues (including a protesting Douglas) to take the unusual step, first suggested by Frankfurter, of publishing the opinion under the names of all nine justices.[60]

That gesture failed to produce the intended image of solidarity. The reason was Frankfurter's insistence on publishing as a concurring opinion on August 27 a memorandum he had written. His objective in composing it was to encourage moderate southerners to support *Brown*. Frankfurter had earlier tried unsuccessfully to persuade Warren to commend Butler and the school board for resisting Faubus. Now he insisted on writing separately to address moderate southern lawyers, many of whom he had taught at Harvard. Black, who understood, as Frankfurter did not, how isolated and impotent southern moderates were, thought this gesture would be counterproductive. He, Brennan, and the Chief were furious. Other justices attempted to dissuade Frankfurter, but they managed only to deter him from announcing his concurrence when *Cooper v. Aaron* was read from the bench on September 29. Black and Brennan prepared and sought support for a rebuttal, but at the first conference of the fall term, Warren made it clear he did not want other members of the Court airing their animosity toward Frankfurter. Harlan's contention that they were making a mountain of a molehill prevailed, and there was no response to his opinion.[61]

Even with Frankfurter's concurrence appended, *Cooper v. Aaron* was a powerful demand for compliance with *Brown*. The Court did not question the good faith of Little Rock's school board or superintendent, and it acknowledged that all students would be adversely affected by continuation of the conditions that had prevailed at Central High the previous year. It refused, however, to permit African American children to suffer because of "the violence and disorder which have followed upon the actions of the Governor and Legislature." Law and order could not "be preserved by depriving the Negro children of their constitutional rights." The board's problems had been magnified by Arkansas officials, whose conduct constituted state action violating the Fourteenth Amendment. In dicta, the Court went on to attack Faubus and the Arkansas legislature for acting as if they were not bound by *Brown*. Article 6 made the Constitution the supreme law of the land, it reminded them. *Marbury v. Madison* (1803) had established "the basic principle that the federal judiciary is supreme in the exposition of the law of the Constitution." "It follows that the interpretation of the Fourteenth Amendment enunciated by this Court in the Brown Case is the supreme law of the land, and Art. VI of the Constitution makes it binding on the States." No governor could nullify a federal court order, and any legislator, judge, or executive official who failed to comply with *Brown* was violating his obligations under the Supremacy Clause, the Court declared.[62]

For once, it had the support of the president. Eisenhower remained unenthusiastic about *Brown*, wanted integration to proceed slowly, and would not even let Rogers predict publicly that desegregation would be permanent. Nevertheless, he wrote to an old friend in July 1957: "There must be respect for the Constitution—which means the Supreme Court's interpretation of the Constitution—or we shall have chaos." Following *Cooper*, the White House released a statement, which declared: "It is incumbent upon all Americans, public officials and private citizens alike, to recognize their solemn duty to comply with the rulings of the highest court in the land."[63]

The justices themselves, for a time inclined to avoid further confrontation in the South, eventually grew insistent on compliance with *Brown*. When Memphis, Tennessee, argued in a 1963 case that it should be allowed to desegregate its public parks gradually, the Court held that the "all deliberate speed" formula did not apply to public facilities other than schools. The justices added, "It is far from clear that the mandate of the second *Brown* decision, requiring that desegregation proceed with all deliberate speed, would today be fully satisfied by types of plans or programs for desegregation of public schools which eight years ago might have been deemed sufficient." Even in education, Frankfurter's phrase had never been intended to permit infinite delay in eliminating racial barriers, the Court asserted.[64]

By 1963 it was obviously losing patience with the failure of southern states to eliminate segregated schools. In *Goss v. Board of Education* (1963) the Court invalidated a transfer policy that allowed students assigned to schools where their race was in the minority to switch to ones where they would be part of the majority, viewing it as likely to perpetuate segregation. *Griffin v. Prince Edward County Board of Education* (1964) provided an even more dramatic demonstration of the Court's growing impatience. A defendant in the 1954 cases, Prince Edward County had closed its schools for five years, rather than desegregate them. While white students attended nominally private academies, which received financial support from the state, black children were denied an education. The Supreme Court ordered the Prince Edward County schools reopened, ruling that a state could not abolish public education in one county while continuing it elsewhere. Justice Black, who reminded his colleagues that he had urged them a decade earlier to order this district to admit the African American plaintiffs, punctuated his opinion with an emphatic declaration that "the time for mere deliberate speed has run out."[65]

The Court's greater firmness actually did little to desegregate public schools in the South. As late as 1963–64, the last academic year before Congress passed legislation forbidding institutions that received federal funds to discriminate on the basis of race, a mere 1.2 percent of African American students in the eleven southern states attended school with whites, with 60 percent of those who did so living in Texas and Tennessee. The U.S. Commission on Civil Rights viewed these numbers as proof that the all-deliberate-speed approach was a failure. While *Brown II* failed, however, *Brown I* did not. A 1978 review of studies that had examined the impact of desegregation on the achievement test scores of African Americans in the South disclosed that two-thirds had found it produced beneficial effects. "These data indicate that desegregation in the South has resulted in consistently positive outcomes." Although timid enforcement severely restricted the number of African American children actually able to enjoy the kind of equal educational opportunity to which the Supreme Court had held they were entitled, the few who did manage to gain admission to formerly all white schools clearly benefited from that judicially created right.[66]

Furthermore, although *Brown*'s effect on the racial makeup of southern schools was limited, its impact on American constitutional law was profound. Technically, all the Court did in 1954 was hold that the separate-but-equal doctrine did not apply to public education; in all other areas *Plessy* remained good law. It soon became apparent, however, that the Warren Court's repudiation of apartheid was far more sweeping than *Brown* acknowledged. In 1955 the Court affirmed without opinion a Fourth Circuit decision holding that Baltimore could not segregate its public beaches, and also without explanation unanimously reversed a decision upholding the segregation of a municipal golf course in Atlanta. In 1956 it sustained a district court decision that Montgomery, Alabama, had violated the Constitution by segregating its buses. Acting on instructions from Warren, the clerk who wrote that opinion drafted a per curiam simply stating that the decision below was affirmed. It cited the Baltimore and Atlanta decisions and *Brown*, offering no other support for its conclusion that segregated public transportation was unconstitutional. *Plessy* died a silent death, and *Brown* came to stand for the proposition that the segregation of any public facility violated the Equal Protection Clause.[67]

Indeed, *Brown* came to have far greater significance than that. As William Nelson observes, "Equality has been the central issue of American constitutional law in the twentieth century, and *Brown v. Board of Education* has been the central case." In *Brown* the Warren Court took what had been largely an aspirational goal and made it a legally enforceable constitutional right. In this case the Supreme Court accepted and compellingly articulated the proposition that the Constitution entitles everyone, even those whom history and prejudice have consigned to an inferior status, to the benefits of formal equality. One group after another would march into Court demanding judicial recognition of its own right to equal treatment, and the next half century of American constitutional development would be largely an elaboration on the central theme of *Brown v. Board of Education.*[68]

Scholars have heatedly debated the importance of *Brown*, with critics insisting that it did little to integrate public education and actually retarded the movement for African American civil rights. Even the decision's symbolic significance is in dispute.[69] Although *Brown*'s consequences for African Americans are debatable, its significance for the body that rendered the decision is clear. The Warren Court found a mission and defined itself as an institution. As G. Edward White has observed, "*Brown* ushered in a new role for the Supreme Court in the twentieth century, that of an active enforcer of fairness and justice as embodied in the Constitution."[70] Although they did little to integrate the public schools of the South, Warren and his colleagues had spoken out on behalf of America's most persistently victimized minority. Thus, however cautiously, the justices cast themselves in the role of champion of the underdog. *Brown* began a struggle to give constitutional protection to society's losers that would evolve into a veritable crusade, and that would make the Warren Court an object of both veneration and loathing.

3

COLD WAR, COMMUNISM, AND CONFRONTATION

The docket of the early Warren Court was more Red than *Brown*. School desegregation cases grabbed headlines, defined the Court's mission, and shaped both its image and its reputation, but the domestic repercussions of the Soviet-American Cold War absorbed far more judicial time. In 1956 about 40 percent of the cases the justices decided had something to do with Communism or subversion.[1] At first the Warren Court approached such cases warily, emulating the cautious conservatism of its predecessor. By 1957, however, its growing commitment to the protection of underdogs and outcasts had inspired a bevy of rulings restraining McCarthyism. These triggered a political backlash that induced a temporary retreat. By 1963, though, both the Court's composition and the mood of the country had changed substantially. During the last years of Warren's chief justiceship, his Court waged war on internal security measures. By then, however, it was battling ghosts from a bygone era.

The Cold War was much newer and Communism much more menacing when Warren became chief justice. Under Vinson the Supreme Court had decided cases in a crisis atmosphere, engendered by the rapid deterioration of relations between the United States and the Soviet Union following World War II, the "fall" of China to Communism in 1949, and a military conflict with Communist enemies in Korea that began in 1950. Setbacks abroad heightened anxiety at home. Although the Communist Party of the United States of America (CPUSA) was small, lacking in influence, and thoroughly infiltrated by the Federal Bureau of Investigation (FBI), its close ties to the USSR made it seem more menacing than it was. So did highly publicized revelations about Communist espionage committed earlier. Fueled by the Cold War and Korea and fanned by politicians, such as the demagogic Senator Joseph R. McCarthy, smoldering fears of radicalism erupted into a raging Red Scare. Congressional hearings —especially those staged by McCarthy, the House Committee on Un-American Activities (HUAC), and the Senate Internal Security Subcommittee—fed a national obsession with internal security. The Truman administration adopted a loyalty-security program to weed out untrustworthy federal employees, and countless state and local governments followed suit. Meanwhile, Congress endeavored to combat subversion by curtailing individual rights, enacting the McCarran Internal Security Act of 1950, which required "Communist-action" and "Communist-front" organizations to register with the Subversive Activities Control Board (SACB) and authorized during presidentially proclaimed "national security emergencies" the detention of persons believed to pose an espionage or sabotage threat.

Like the McCarran Act, the rulings of the Vinson Court reflected the country's panicky mood. Sacrificing political freedom on the altar of internal security, the Court upheld in *American Communications Association v. Douds* (1950) a provision of the Taft-Hartley Act that required labor union officials to file affidavits disavowing membership in the Communist Party. In *Dennis v. United States* (1951), a decision that "legitimized the rest of the anticommunist crusade," Vinson revised the "clear and present danger" test that the Court had used to protect dissident expression, in order to sustain the Smith Act convictions of eleven party leaders for conspiring to teach and advocate Marxism-Leninism and to organize the CPUSA to provide such instruction. The Vinson Court dealt cautiously with the federal loyalty-security program, ruling in favor of a group that demanded to have its name removed from a list of subversive organizations that the attorney general had published to facilitate the identification of security risks, but only on the narrow ground that the presidential order establishing the program had not authorized the arbitrary designation of a group as subversive. By a four-to-four vote the justices affirmed a lower court decision upholding a loyalty board that had barred a federal employee from government work for three years. Although avoiding the difficult constitutional issues posed by the procedures such boards used, Vinson and his colleagues sanctioned the methods state and local governments adopted to combat disloyalty, sustaining laws requiring candidates for office and government employees to disavow belief in the violent overthrow of the government and membership in seditious organizations. The Vinson Court also upheld New York's controversial Feinberg Law, which barred members of allegedly subversive groups from teaching in the public schools. Only when asked to approve a statute that demanded retroactive disavowal of innocent as well as knowing membership in subversive organizations did the Court balk.[2]

The obsession with Communism and internal security that its rulings reflected began to moderate about the time that Warren became chief justice. Using a combination of threats and diplomacy, Eisenhower obtained an armistice in Korea on July 27, 1953. By ending a conflict that had threatened to expand into Manchuria and even the USSR, the agreement encouraged the new leaders who had assumed power in the Soviet Union following the March death of Joseph Stalin to seek a peaceful resolution of their country's disputes with the United States. Although Secretary of State John Foster Dulles talked about rolling back Communism, the Eisenhower administration also proved more willing than its predecessor to settle for the mere amelioration of international difficulties. By 1955 the president was sitting down with the Soviets at a Geneva summit conference, effectively abandoning the pursuit of military victory in the Cold War and accepting the status quo in Europe and China. The United States and the USSR would continue for years competing for prestige, influence, and allies around the world, and relations between them would occasionally grow extremely tense (particularly during the 1962 Cuban Missile Crisis), but the

Soviet-American conflict had ceased to be an utterly irreconcilable one in which compromise was inconceivable. Ominous confrontation became uneasy coexistence.

As the international climate moderated, so did the mood at home. During 1953 and 1954 the underpinnings of the second Red Scare eroded. The federal government's loyalty-security apparatus began to attract criticism, as journalists such as Edward R. Murrow exposed injustices committed in the program's name, and by 1955 several congressional committees were scrutinizing it skeptically. A number of controversial cases, most notably that of famed physicist J. Robert Oppenheimer, focused critical attention on the program's procedures. In early 1955 Harvey Matusow, a former CPUSA member who testified against suspected Communists in court proceedings and congressional and SACB hearings as a paid expert witness for the Justice Department, admitted that he had committed perjury during a Smith Act trial. When Justice had to fire two other professional witnesses for unreliability, the use of such paid "experts" became politically vulnerable. Meanwhile, concerned that the constitutional right to counsel was being eroded by the inability of indicted Communists to hire lawyers, bar associations in Philadelphia, Cleveland, Denver, and Connecticut stepped forward to assist in the defense of CPUSA members prosecuted under the Smith Act. The most dramatic evidence that the Red Scare was abating was the downfall of the man whose name had become synonymous with the wild charges and violations of civil liberties that it engendered. Senator McCarthy's popularity began to slip, and his televised confrontation with the Department of the Army in the spring of 1954 hastened its decline. On December 2, the Senate voted to censure McCarthy.[3]

That action highlighted the enfeeblement of what Richard Fried has called "the Dracula prowling the mid-century darkness of American politics." According to Fried, it was the Supreme Court "that drove the fatal stake through [the] heart" of McCarthyism.[4] Under Warren's leadership it stepped forward to defend civil liberties. The willingness of his Court to do what Vinson's had not stemmed not only from the waning of hysterical anti-Communism but also from the Warren Court's greater concern for individual rights, which often led it to view skeptically claims that national security required the sacrificing of civil liberties.

That is not to say the Warren Court could never be persuaded to subordinate the rights of a single individual to the needs of national defense. In *Wilson v. Girard* it succumbed to the imperatives of a worldwide deployment of American troops required to occupy defeated World War II enemies and implement a Cold War policy of containing international Communism. Army specialist William Girard, while apparently attempting to frighten away civilian trespassers scavenging expended cartridges on a firing range in Japan, shot and killed a Japanese woman. American officials resolved a nasty diplomatic incident by agreeing, pursuant to a 1953 agreement between the two countries, to turn Girard over to Japan for trial, but a federal district court judge enjoined them from doing so. Anticipating that the case would soon reach the Supreme Court, Warren instructed his clerks to prepare a memorandum on it and, at Frankfurter's suggestion, urged his fellow justices to remain in Washington beyond the end of the term on June 24, 1957. On June 20 the solicitor general personally filed a petition for expedited review with the chief justice. He also expressed to Warren "the belief of the Government that [this] is a matter of paramount importance in foreign relations, not only between this country and Japan, but also as between it and all of the other nations with which we have similar agreements." In the course of this highly improper ex parte communication, Rankin advised the chief justice that the president believed the United States required the ability to waive jurisdiction in cases like Girard's so that other countries would continue to honor their agreements allowing American military courts to punish most offenses committed by persons associated with the U.S. armed forces. The secretaries of state and defense included a similar admonition in a formal statement that they filed with the Court. The justices ruled for the government eight to nothing. Aware that public opinion opposed surrendering an American soldier to another country, Warren persuaded his colleagues to dispose of the case with a brief per curiam opinion. Written by Brennan (who utilized ideas supplied by Frankfurter, Clark, and Burton), the opinion relied on the principle that a sovereign has exclusive power to punish offenses against its laws committed within its borders. There was, Brennan concluded, no constitutional or statutory barrier to the sort of limited waiver of jurisdiction over American military personnel that the United States had accepted in its Status of Forces Agreement with Japan. His opinion did not discuss at all the rights of Specialist Girard, prompting Yale Law School professor Boris Bittker to fault the Court for failing to cope with the issues.[5]

Although its disingenuous disposition of *Girard* showed the Warren Court could be persuaded to subordinate individual rights to the demands of Cold War foreign policy, its resolution of cases challenging the authority of the military to try persons who were not members of the armed forces demonstrated the Court's unwillingness to permit any unnecessary narrowing of constitutionally guaranteed liberties. Dependents and civilian employees accompanied American troops to many of their far-flung foreign duty stations, and Article 2(11) of the Uniform Code of Military Justice (UCMJ) authorized the trial of both by courts-martial. Through status of forces agreements with the United States, a number of nations that hosted U.S. troops had ceded to the American military jurisdiction over offenses committed by such civilians. The Warren Court had to decide whether these arrangements violated the constitutional rights of dependents and employees.

Two women who had been convicted by military tribunals of murdering their husbands (an air force sergeant stationed in England and an army officer serving in Japan) raised this issue, which Clark considered to be one of "immense significance to our Nation in the conduct of present-day international affairs." The United States had more than a quarter of a million dependents and other civilians accompanying its troops overseas, and he thought the future of status of forces agreements depended on how effectively the United States exercised the jurisdiction over its citizens that other nations had ceded. When the justices discussed these cases on May 4, 1956, however, the focus was on the question Reed summarized as "does the Constitution follow the flag?" Warren, Black, and Frankfurter opposed extending military power over civilians abroad, but Minton saw nothing wrong with the use of courts-martial to try them, and Burton insisted Congress had the power to authorize such trials. Although the others were uncertain enough about where they stood that Warren and Douglas recorded their votes differently, four justices apparently wanted to sustain the convictions of the murdering wives, and five wanted to overturn them. The least committed member of the majority was Reed, who on May 14 circulated a memorandum saying he had decided his tentative votes were erroneous. His switch produced a five-to-four majority holding that no constitutional barrier existed to the enactment of Article 2(11).[6]

The victory of its spokesman, Clark, proved only temporary. His opinions disposing of *Reid v. Covert* and *Kinsella v. Krueger* evaded the real issue in the cases, which was whether the power of Congress to make rules for the governance of the land and naval forces entitled it to subject civilians to military trials. Although not dissenting publicly, Frankfurter pointed this out in what he styled a "Reservation" to the Court's opinion, which noted that the Court's earlier decision in *Toth v. Quarles* (1956) made Clark's evasion troublesome. Frankfurter also suggested that, because they had decided these cases during the closing weeks of the term, there had not been enough time to study and reflect upon the difficult issue they raised and the material with which Clark supported his conclusion. In September, counsel for the murdering wives requested a rehearing. Frankfurter and Black circulated dissents they had written earlier, and Harlan, who agreed with Frankfurter, informed the other members of the majority that he had concluded they must confront the congressional power issue. He provided the margin of victory as the Court voted five to four to grant a rehearing and with Frankfurter drafted a per curiam opinion, which asked counsel to discuss the justifications for the exercise of court-martial jurisdiction over civilian dependents abroad, as well as whether the same principles applied to both dependents and civilian employees and to both petty offenses and major crimes.[7]

After reargument the Court rendered a very different decision. Although Burton stressed that the Cold War deployment of the American military around the world meant the safety of the nation was at stake in this case and insisted Congress would not abuse its power over civilians accompanying the armed forces, Warren disagreed. As far as he was concerned, Congress had "no power to put them under military jurisdiction." Black, Douglas, and Brennan supported the Chief. Harlan backed Burton, but with Reed gone, only Clark joined them, and they lost five to three. On June 10 Black read an opinion reversing the convictions and holding that the murdering wives could not constitutionally be tried by military authorities. Only Clark and Burton dissented, but the majority was divided; in concurring opinions Frankfurter and Harlan sought to limit the Court's holding to capital cases.[8]

Other justices persuaded Frankfurter to omit from his concurrence any mention of his disagreement with Black's handling of the government's contention that the law authorizing military trials of dependents living in Great Britain and Japan was a constitutional exercise of the power the Necessary and Proper Clause gave Congress to implement international agreements. Black acknowledged that Article 6 made treaties part of the supreme law of the land and that a treaty, in conjunction with the Necessary and Proper Clause, could empower Congress to enact otherwise unauthorized legislation. He insisted, however, that this authority could not be employed in a way that would violate the Bill of Rights. Frankfurter did not want this issue discussed. Congress was debating the proposed "Bricker Amendment," which if adopted, would render inoperative any provision of a treaty that conflicted with the Constitution and would allow a treaty to become effective as domestic law only if Congress enacted legislation that would be valid in the absence of the treaty. "I need not remind my brethren," Frankfurter wrote to his colleagues, "that the Bricker Amendment is one of the most contentious controversies in the Senate and a matter of the liveliest controversy between the Executive and the Senate." By discussing the treaty-making power, Frankfurter contended, Black was "needlessly fanning the flames of the Bricker amendment controversy."[9]

The two clashed again during the October 1959 term when the Court confronted issues left unresolved by *Reid* and *Kinsella*. Before it were habeas corpus cases arising out of the court-martial convictions of a military wife living in Germany for the noncapital crime of manslaughter and of a civilian employee attached to the army in France for a lesser included offense following a military trial for capital murder, as well as those of civilians working for the army in Germany and the air force in Morocco on noncapital charges of sodomy and of larceny and conspiracy. The Court remained divided and uncertain. Warren and Brennan appeared willing to let the military try civilian employees, but not dependents, while Black argued forcefully that court-martial jurisdiction should not extend beyond uniformed members of the armed forces. Clark insisted "all cases can be brought under military control whether capital or noncapital." Frankfurter retreated into the redoubt of judicial self-restraint, arguing that the Court should defer to the judgment of Congress, whose power to make rules for the governance of the land and naval forces "was not restricted by the Fifth and Sixth Amendment[s]." The justices eventually agreed to prohibit military trials for capital offenses and dependents, to allow them for civilian employees charged with crimes that did not carry the death penalty, and to reserve decision on all other issues. A dismayed Clark could find "no reason in logic nor law why noncapital cases against employees should remain the sole category allowable." He believed the only thing to do was "apply principles of *Reid v. Covert* No. 2 to all prosecutions." With Clark writing opinions doing just that, the Court reversed all four convictions. Harlan and Frankfurter dissented in the two noncapital cases, while Whittaker and Stewart protested the elimination of court-martial jurisdiction over employees.[10]

The willingness of the Warren Court, even by such a narrow margin, to favor Bill of Rights guarantees over what the executive insisted were the imperatives of America's Cold War commitments abroad suggested an inclination to resolve the inevitable tensions between national security and individual rights very differently than had the Vinson Court. This inclination also manifested itself in Cold War–related cases at home. During Vinson's chief justiceship, only Black and Douglas had consistently opposed rulings upholding laws and governmental practices inspired by McCarthyism, but they gained an ally in Warren. His support was somewhat surprising, for earlier in his career the new chief justice had been an outspoken anti-Communist. During the 1930s he exhibited concerns about connections between organized labor and foreign ideologies typical of a California nativist. As Alameda County district attorney, besides vigorously prosecuting the accused murderers of an anti-Communist crewman on the ship *Point Lobos,* Warren repeatedly accused their defenders of being "Communistic." Highly patriotic, he viewed all sorts of "subversives" as threats to California. "As attorney general and governor," writes Edward Long, "Warren was more concerned about policing the activities of Communists than with protecting their civil liberties." Warren even opposed the appointment to the state supreme court of a liberal law professor, Max Radin, who had opposed the state's criminal syndicalism law and supported the *Point Lobos* defendants. Governor Warren did resist adoption of a loyalty oath for University of California professors (apparently because he disliked political tampering with his alma mater), but he signed one that applied to all state employees. "He was," writes G. Edward White, "as militant an anti-Communist as those he associated with McCarthyism." Indeed, Warren himself resorted to tactics associated with Senator McCarthy, using antiradicalism as a political weapon against Culbert Olson during their 1942 gubernatorial contest and (although showing more restraint than many Republicans) joining in the 1952 GOP attack on the Truman administration for allegedly tolerating Communist influences in the federal government.[11]

As chief justice, however, Warren grew increasingly concerned about what anti-Communist hysteria was doing to the Bill of Rights. He did not think that protecting national security required abolishing civil liberties. "But the emotional influences of the times . . . are capable of threatening the basic rights of everyone, unless those emotions are controlled by self-discipline, community spirit and governmental action," he told a St. Louis audience in February 1955. In a speech to the ABA, Warren argued that judicial enforcement of constitutional guarantees, by demonstrating that human rights were living things, would advance the American cause in the Cold War. In November he told readers of *Fortune,* "In the present struggle between our world and Communism, the temptation to imitate totalitarian security methods is a subtle temptation that must be resisted." In his early days as chief justice, Warren stood near the middle of the Court on civil liberties issues, going along with rulings such as one upholding the suspension of a doctor's license for refusing to give HUAC the records of a left-wing organization he headed. During the October 1955 term, however, he moved toward Black and Douglas, beginning to exhibit the concern for individual rights that would become the hallmark of the Warren Court.[12]

Ironically, Frankfurter encouraged this shift. By the summer of 1955 Warren, no longer a neophyte on the Court, was becoming annoyed with his ceaseless tutoring and resentful of his often-patronizing tone. The Chief gravitated toward Black, who, although the senior associate justice, avoided trying to "educate" him. By the end of the 1956 term, Frankfurter regarded Warren as part of the Court's "hard-core liberal wing."[13]

He drove Brennan toward that wing with similar patronizing behavior. Frankfurter courted his former student assiduously, inviting him soon after his appointment to an intimate dinner party with a star-studded guest list. He also gave Brennan lessons on the Court's business. At first the "novice" appreciated this assistance in "getting his feet wet." Soon, however, Brennan tired of being treated like a student. He found Black's passionate but concise arguments in conferences more appealing than Frankfurter's ranting. Brennan, who had earned Senator McCarthy's opposition with two 1954 speeches criticizing recent anti-Communist hearings, probably would have gravitated toward Black and Douglas on civil liberties issues regardless. But Frankfurter's condescending behavior hastened his movement in that direction.[14]

Frankfurter did much better with Harlan, a protégé of his close friend, Emory Buckner. Even before Harlan's appointment, he had developed a personal relationship with the conservative New Yorker. Despite doubts about his capacity and value as an ally, Frankfurter began cultivating him while his nomination was still pending by sending him material on the Court's work. After Harlan took his seat, he bombarded him with correspondence, much of it designed to instruct him on the subtleties of his jurisprudential disputes with Black. Frankfurter monitored Harlan's opinions, alert for any language that might suggest support for his rival's positions on incorporation or the First Amendment. He also fed his new colleague a steady diet of unflattering information about Black and his allies. Despite Frankfurter's machinations, Harlan, who disliked gossip, became friendly with Black. Philosophically, however, he aligned himself with Frankfurter, developing a jurisprudence grounded in convictions that the political process, federalism, and the separation of powers provided more protection for individual liberty than did specific constitutional guarantees. Even when interpreting the Bill of Rights, Harlan became convinced, the Court must keep these other values in mind.[15]

He and Frankfurter found in Whittaker an indecisive and unreliable ally of limited intellectual ability. Having graduated from a night law school and begun his career as an office boy, Whittaker suffered from an inferiority complex and was awed by Frankfurter's vocabulary. Although he never developed anything that could be called a judicial philosophy, his conservative instincts generally inclined him toward positions favored by Frankfurter and Harlan. He found it almost impossible to make up his mind, however, generally agreeing with whoever had spoken most recently and often leaving conferences weeping in agonized indecision.[16]

Nor could either bloc count on Stewart's vote. He shared Frankfurter's conviction that the Court should leave policymaking to the people's elected representatives, but also believed strongly that the duty of a Supreme Court justice was to decide cases and not to promote a particular ideology. Stewart earned a reputation as a pragmatic centrist, committed to narrow, nonanticipatory decision making. Asked to describe his judicial philosophy, he responded, "I like to be thought of as a lawyer." Both Black and Frankfurter cultivated his friendship and his vote, but according to Stewart, "Felix was so unsubtle and obvious that it was counterproductive." Unlike Warren, however, he did not react to Frankfurter's solicitations by moving into the Black-Douglas camp.[17]

That bloc was strengthened by Eisenhower's appointments, however, and even Frankfurter and Harlan came to share their rivals' concerns about the excesses of McCarthyism. In early 1955 correspondence Frankfurter revealed how upsetting he found McCarthy's conduct. He also found disturbing the lower courts' reaction to *Dennis*, which they seemed to view as an authorization to enlist in a Justice Department war on the CPUSA and to treat all Smith Act defendants as presumptively guilty. Among the judges who almost mechanically upheld such convictions was Harlan, whose opinion for the Second Circuit in *United States v. Flynn* bore the unmistakable stamp of Cold War thinking. As a true conservative, however, he found disturbing the reactionary hysteria that was sweeping the country. In a June 15, 1954, address at Brooklyn Law School, Harlan expressed concern about the "false prophets" who were undermining democracy in the guise of fighting Communism. In October 1955 he warned an audience at Brandeis University against falling prey to the notion that to preserve a free society, America must curtail individual liberties. A month later, in reducing the bail of a Smith Act defendant, he cautioned against drawing inferences of guilt from invocations of the Fifth Amendment.[18]

With even Harlan and Frankfurter expressing concern about the impact of McCarthyism on civil liberties, the Warren Court moved to rein in the body responsible for some of the worst excesses. In 1955 it overturned contempt convictions against two witnesses who had refused to answer questions during HUAC hearings into the affairs of a left-wing union. Julius Emspak had based his refusal to respond to sixty-eight questions about his associations and affiliations on the First Amendment, "supplemented by the fifth." Following oral argument in January 1954, Warren urged his colleagues not to condone such behavior. Although several of them wanted congressional committees to stop abusing their power, the Court voted six to two to affirm Emspak's conviction. Black subjected Reed's draft opinion to a blistering critique, however, and supported by Frankfurter and Jackson, he lobbied successfully to have the case argued again in the following term, along with that of Thomas Quinn, who had been held in contempt for refusing to answer questions at the same HUAC hearing. Following reargument, Warren told his colleagues that he had changed his mind, but wanted to rule against the committee without impairing the power of Congress, which he thought an opinion relying on the First Amendment would do. The Chief wrote opinions that focused on HUAC's slipshod method of questioning witnesses, finding the committee guilty of violating the Fifth Amendment rights of Emspak and Quinn. He brushed aside problems posed by the defendants' ambiguous invocation of the privilege against self-incrimination and the probability that responses to some of the questions they had refused to answer could not have incriminated them. Reed and Minton dissented, while Harlan, disturbed about what he regarded as a dangerous extension of the Fifth Amendment, quarreled with part of each decision. Although important to him, the legal grounds for these rulings mattered less than the fact that the Court had finally imposed some limits on HUAC.[19]

Most of the justices remained reluctant to challenge Congress, however, as *Ulmann v. United States* (1956) demonstrated. In that case a six-to-two majority upheld the constitutionality of the Immunity Act of 1954, which provided that witnesses in national security cases might be compelled to testify in return for a guarantee that they could not be prosecuted or otherwise penalized for any transaction they were forced to discuss.[20] However, despite being reluctant to confront the legislative branch, the Court readily rendered narrow rulings invalidating dismissals under the loyalty-security program. For example, in *Peters v. Hobby* (1955), with only Reed and Burton dissenting, it overturned as unauthorized by the executive order that established the program the action of the Loyalty Review Board in barring a Yale Medical School professor from federal employment for three years on the basis of evidence supplied by anonymous informants. In *Cole v. Young* (1956), with only Clark, Reed, and Minton dissenting, the Court overturned the dismissal of a food and drug inspector whom the secretary of Health, Education, and Welfare had fired because of his allegedly close association with reputed Communists. Cole insisted the Veterans' Preference Act gave him a right to appeal his discharge to the Civil Service Commission, and the Court agreed. Harlan held that federal law permitted a nonreviewable dismissal only if there had been a finding that the employee's position was one in which he could adversely affect national security. Since no one had made such a determination in this case, Cole's dismissal violated the Veterans' Preference Act.[21]

Even when passing on the discharge of a local government worker, which it could reverse only on constitutional grounds, the Court adopted a cautious approach. Under the New York City charter, whenever an employee utilized the privilege against self-incrimination to avoid answering a question about his official conduct, his employment terminated immediately. Harry Slochower lost his job as a tenured professor at Brooklyn College for invoking the Fifth Amendment before the Senate Internal Security Subcommittee. Warren wanted to rule that New York had impermissibly burdened the privilege by treating its use as an admission of guilt, but Frankfurter, although outraged by Slochower's termination, favored overturning it on the narrower ground that summarily firing for invoking the Fifth Amendment someone who could only be dismissed for cause was so unreasonable that it violated due process. Warren eventually agreed, and Frankfurter managed to keep a wavering Clark wedded to his approach. Reed, Burton, Minton, and Harlan objected, but with Clark writing the opinion, the Court ruled for Slochower five to four.

The justices exhibited comparable caution in reversing an order of the Subversive Activities Control Board, requiring the CPUSA to register as a "Communist-action organization" in *Communist Party v. Subversive Activities Control Board* (1956). Basing its decision on the government's use of testimony from unreliable witnesses, a badly divided court avoided deciding whether Title I of the Internal Security Act was unconstitutional. That law both required Communist-action organizations to register with the SACB and imposed a variety of sanctions on them and their members. During lengthy conferences on November 18, 1955, and March 8, 1956, Warren contended that the law transgressed the First and Fifth Amendments, while Black condemned it as a bill of attainder that also "violates about all the Bill of Rights except quartering of troops." Minton and Clark countered that the CPUSA was foreign dominated and committed to imposing Communist government on the United States. Further complicating the discussions was the fact that some of the justices, especially Harlan and Burton, saw no problem with the registration requirement, but considered some or all of the sanctions unconstitutional. Reed, and even Warren, indicated a willingness to uphold registration if it could somehow be severed from sanctions. Whether that could be done depended among other things on the effect of a murky severability clause. There was disagreement about whether the sanctions were before the Court at all, and Clark even suggested there were ripeness and standing problems with the whole case.[22]

About the only thing on which there seemed to be agreement was that the court of appeals had erred in refusing to require the SACB to take additional evidence relating to the commission of perjury in other proceedings by three of the principal witnesses against the party. Frankfurter, who was disturbed about the splintered decision that would result if the constitutional issues were addressed, prepared an opinion for what he claimed was a unanimous Court, reversing the registration order and sending the case back to the board so it could determine the truth of the allegations about the three witnesses and, if necessary, eliminate their testimony from the record. Clark objected to shirking "our plain responsibility to pass on [the] constitutional questions," but most of their brethren sided with Frankfurter. His opinion returning the case to the SACB denied that the Court was evading constitutional issues, claiming rather that "the fair administration of justice requires it." Accusing the majority of resorting to pretext, Clark dissented for himself, Reed, and Minton.[23]

Although in some respects a bolder decision than *SACB*, *Pennsylvania v. Nelson* (1956) sought to shift to Congress the onus for thwarting a state anti-Communist initiative. The Court reversed the conviction of Stephen Mesarosh (alias Steve Nelson), a prominent Communist Party leader who had been prosecuted under Pennsylvania's Sedition Act. That law punished sedition against both the state and the United States, and he had been charged with advocating the overthrow of the federal government. The Pennsylvania Supreme Court reversed Nelson's conviction, reasoning that with respect to such conduct, the Smith Act had preempted the Sedition Act. Warren adopted its reasoning, arguing in conference that if the states could prosecute such conduct, they might interfere with federal law enforcement. As a former attorney general, Clark considered sedition against the United States to be FBI business, but he objected to substituting even policy views he shared for those of Congress. In the end he reluctantly joined the Chief's opinion. Only Reed, Burton, and Minton dissented.[24]

The Court handed Steve Nelson another victory the following term in *Mesarosh v. United States* (1956), a Smith Act case. On October 27, 1956, the solicitor general informed the Court that the government had reason to question the truthfulness of testimony one of its principal witnesses, Joseph Mazzei, had given in other proceedings, and during oral argument two weeks later, Rankin acknowledged believing that Mazzei had lied on several occasions. The government wanted *Mesarosh* remanded to the district court for a hearing on the credibility of his testimony, and Frankfurter, Harlan, and Burton favored granting its request. Speaking for the majority, however, Warren, declared emphatically, "This conviction is tainted, and there can be no other result than to accord petitioners a new trial." Although careful to emphasize that it was not deciding the guilt or innocence of the defendants, the Warren Court had done what no other appellate court ever had: overturn Smith Act convictions of Communist Party leaders.[25]

Mesarosh set the tone for a dramatic term, during which the Supreme Court repeatedly restricted federal and state antisubversive initiatives. On May 6, 1957, the Court ruled that the New Mexico Supreme Court had violated Rudolph Schware's rights under the Due Process Clause by allowing the state bar to prevent him from taking its licensing examination on grounds that he lacked good moral character, a determination based on his use of an alias to disguise the fact that he was Jewish, some old arrests for criminal syndicalism and recruiting volunteers to fight in the Spanish civil war, and his membership in the Communist Party from 1932 to 1940. Clark cast the only vote against Schware, and rather than be the sole dissenter, he joined a concurring opinion by Frankfurter. They both dissented in *Konigsberg v. State Bar of California* (1957), as did Harlan. Decided the same day, that case proved more difficult, because the applicant had been excluded from practicing law for failure to prove that he was of good moral character and did not advocate the overthrow of the government by unconstitutional means, at least in part due to his refusal on constitutional grounds to answer questions about his alleged past membership in the Communist Party. In addition, California denied that its supreme court had rejected Konigsberg's constitutional claims, insisting it had ruled against him because of his failure to comply with state procedural rules. Frankfurter, who according to Douglas talked at length in conference "about the restricted role of the Court especially on review of state courts," wanted to decide against Konigsburg on that basis. Speaking for the majority, however, Black held that the constitutional issues he had raised were properly before the Supreme Court, then went on to rule that the record included no evidence providing a rational justification for the bar's finding. Harlan and Clark, who agreed with Frankfurter that the Court lacked jurisdiction, also challenged Black's reading of the record and protested the majority's interference with states' regulation of their own bars.[26]

A week after thwarting efforts to keep radicals from practicing law, the Warren Court used a brief per curiam opinion to reverse convictions of Communists for harboring fugitive Smith Act defendants, granting them a new trial because of the FBI's seizure, following a warrantless search, of all the contents of the cabin where the fugitives had been hiding. Next, the Court pried open the FBI's files. Two of the witnesses against Clinton Jencks, convicted of filing a false non-Communist affidavit with the National Labor Relations Board, had acknowledged supplying information to the Bureau on a regular basis, but the trial judge denied defense motions to require production of their reports. Although the justices discussed the case three times in conference, the only real disagreement among them concerned whether the government should have to turn these reports over to the trial judge for screening or give them directly to the defense. Burton, Harlan, and Clark favored the former, but writing for the majority, Brennan ruled the government must "produce, for the accused's inspection and for admission in evidence, relevant statements or reports in its possession." Failure to do so would result in dismissal of its case. Brennan added that the government might not shift to the trial judge the burden of deciding "whether the public prejudice of allowing the crime to go unpunished is greater than that attendant upon the possible disclosure of state secrets and other confidential information in the Government's possession." "Unless the Congress changes the rule announced by the Court today," Clark fumed in dissent, "those intelligence agencies of our government engaged in law enforcement may as well close up shop." His successor as attorney general, Herbert Brownell, wailed that *Jencks* had created a law enforcement emergency. The decision infuriated not only FBI director J. Edgar Hoover, but also the president.[27]

The Court provoked further presidential outrage when, on June 17, 1957—infamous in anti-Communist circles as "Red Monday"—it handed down four decisions that struck hard at McCarthyism. The least contentious was *Service v. Dulles* (1957), overturning Secretary of State Dean Acheson's dismissal of controversial foreign service officer John Stewart Service, a "China hand," who had been implicated but not indicted in the *Amerasia* case (in which hundreds of classified government documents were found in the offices of a left-leaning Asian affairs journal). The Court held unanimously that because the State Department had not followed its own rules in firing Service, its action was illegal.[28]

Yates v. United States (1957) sparked greater controversy within the Court. Petitioners were fourteen California Communist leaders. Reed, Burton, Minton, and Clark wanted to affirm their Smith Act convictions. Black, who believed the Smith Act promoted political trials, and Douglas contended, as they had in *Dennis*, that the act was unconstitutional. Warren also advocated reversal. He insisted the CPUSA had not been proven to advocate force and violence, denied that each of its members could be held accountable for every bit of Communist dogma, and emphasized the prosecutors' failure to prove any unlawful conduct. Although Frankfurter and Harlan passed when the Court first discussed *Yates* on October 12, 1956, they too found unimpressive the evidence used to obtain and affirm Smith Act convictions. By the summer of 1956 both had clerks researching ways to rein in a war on the CPUSA they believed had gotten out of hand. Harlan advised his clerks "that one of the factors which led to our taking these cases was the feeling of some members of the Court that we should take a new look at these Smith Act conspiracies in light of the accumulated post-*Dennis* experience; particularly . . . the character of the evidence which the lower Courts have come to accept as sufficient to establish *individual* participation in such conspiracies." When the Court formally voted on November 5, Frankfurter and Harlan joined Warren, Black, and Douglas, producing a majority for reversal. By the time the decision was announced, Minton and Reed had retired and Burton had switched sides, leaving Clark to dissent alone.[29]

Harlan spoke for the majority. His complex, scholarly, and painfully dull opinion eviscerated the Smith Act and erected new safeguards for freedom of expression, but avoided an embarrassing reversal of *Dennis* by using statutory interpretation as the rationale. Like the *Dennis* defendants, the California Communists had been charged with conspiring to teach and advocate the violent overthrow of the government and with conspiring to organize the Communist party. The portion of the Smith Act that proscribed organizing could not be used against them, Harlan concluded, because the CPUSA (which dissolved briefly during World War II) had formally reconstituted itself in 1945, and the three-year statute of limitations had already run when they were indicted in 1951. He rejected the government's contention that organizing was an ongoing process that included activities such as establishing new units. Since the trial judge's instructions were such that it was impossible to tell whether the jury had convicted the defendants for conspiring to organize or to advocate, the Court had to set aside the verdicts, Harlan claimed. His interpretation of the organizing section (a dubious one in light of its legislative history) rendered that provision worthless as a tool for prosecuting members of the CPUSA. Harlan also declared that to be punishable under the Smith Act, advocacy had to be of action rather than merely of ideas. Those to whom it was addressed "must be urged to do something, now or in the future, rather than merely to *believe* in something." Lacking evidence of that kind of advocacy, the Justice Department watched helplessly as courts of appeal reversed every Smith Act conspiracy conviction they reviewed after *Yates;* within four years it reluctantly abandoned its Smith Act attack on the CPUSA.[30]

Red Monday rulings thwarted legislative investigators as well as federal prosecutors. In *Watkins v. United States* (1957) the Court reversed the contempt of Congress conviction of a HUAC witness, who had testified freely about his own involvement with Communists in the Farm Equipment Workers Union but had refused to say whether other persons were members of the CPUSA, contending such questions were not relevant to the committee's work. Of the seven justices who participated (Burton disqualified himself because his nephew had represented the government in the case), only Clark favored affirming Watkins's conviction. The others seemed to agree with Warren that this was a good case in which to spell out the limits of Congress's investigative power. For the Chief *Watkins* was above all about the right to be free from governmental intrusions into one's life in the absence of specific and compelling justification. The business of Congress was neither enforcing laws nor conducting trials. It might not expose for exposure's sake; its investigations had to be related to and in furtherance of its legislative function, Warren argued. Although ethical principles resolved the case for him, he based his opinion for the Court on the proposition that Watkins's due process rights had been violated because neither the chair nor HUAC's authorizing resolution had informed him of why the questions he had refused to answer were pertinent to the committee's work. The Chief also asserted that "an investigation is subject to the command that Congress shall make no law abridging freedom of speech or press or assembly" and that "the First Amendment may be invoked against infringement of the protected freedoms by law or by lawmaking." Frankfurter, who was determined to "leave unimpaired the constitutional power of congressional investigations," which he believed had been a force for good during the Progressive era and the 1920s, tried to persuade Warren to alter his opinion to minimize the opportunities for witnesses to thwart such inquiries with "parrotlike" repetition of the phrase "First Amendment." The Chief accepted many of his suggestions, but not enough to prevent a concurring opinion stating that the sole basis of the decision was HUAC's failure to clarify the pertinency of its questions, a view shared by Harlan.[31]

Although Harlan did not join Frankfurter's concurrence in *Watkins,* he did do so in *Sweezy v. New Hampshire* (1957). That ruling overturned a contempt sentence given to a Marxist professor for refusing to answer questions posed by the attorney general of New Hampshire, who, investigating subversive activities for the state legislature, had acted as a one-man legislative committee. Paul Sweezy, a Marxist professor, had declined to discuss the Progressive Party and a lecture he had given at the University of New Hampshire or to say whether he believed in Communism. Warren found the latter question particularly offensive, insisting a legislative committee could not require anyone to reveal his political opinions. Harlan and Brennan agreed. Brennan and Frankfurter thought the queries about the lecture threatened academic freedom, and even Clark and Burton saw problems with some of what Sweezy had been asked. Warren wanted to rule for him on First Amendment grounds, but a canvass of the Court disclosed only an opinion employing the *Watkins* rationale could command a majority. He wrote one that asserted Sweezy's academic freedom and right of political expression had been violated, but held for him on the ground that the legislature's failure to charge the attorney general with sufficient specificity to enable Sweezy to determine the pertinency of questions he had been asked had denied him due process. To the Chief's considerable annoyance, Frankfurter and Harlan would not accept his opinion, which they thought meddled inappropriately in the separation of powers within a state government. Their concurrence, which balanced the harmful effects of New Hampshire's interference with Sweezy's academic freedom and political autonomy against the state's need for the information it sought, relied on First Amendment considerations, but Frankfurter, ever the opponent of incorporation, failed to acknowledge this. Clark and Burton dissented.[32]

Others joined them in criticizing the Court's decisions. "Warren has become a hero of the *Daily Worker,*" declared Senator McCarthy. A congressman branded *Watkins* and *Jencks* the greatest Soviet victories since World War II, and the Texas American Legion accused the Court of paralyzing efforts to curb Communism. Liberal senators and the liberal press applauded *Sweezy* and *Watkins,* and the Gallup Poll found that even after Red Monday the Supreme Court commanded greater public respect than Congress. Nevertheless, its support was eroding. Segregationist senators James O. Eastland (D-Miss.) and Olin Johnson (D-S.C.) proposed amending the Constitution to require that justices be reconfirmed every four years, and Senator Strom Thurmond (D-S.C.), several House members, and the Georgia legislature advocated impeaching members of the Court. In late 1958 the newly organized John Birch Society launched a campaign to remove the Chief for condoning Communism and treason. Its crusade flooded Capitol Hill with malicious mail and blanketed America with "Impeach Earl Warren" billboards.[33]

Although the president did not join the public outcry, he too abhorred the Court's decisions. When the press reported that he had severely criticized the Supreme Court at a private party, Eisenhower wrote to Warren. While denying he was angry, he admitted having expressed "amazement about one decision." Ike asked the attorney general for explanations of both *Nelson* and the bar admission rulings.[34]

Warren informed an agitated Eisenhower, "We must live with what we write and are contented to do so." He reacted less placidly to criticism from the ABA. "Throughout the years of the McCarthy era and the desegregation period, the American Bar Association almost never had a kind word to say for the Court," Warren later recalled bitterly. In 1957 he angrily resigned from the organization. Urged by Frankfurter, Warren had attended its annual meeting in London to represent the Supreme Court at a symbolically significant gathering of lawyers and judges from the United States and Britain. While he was there the ABA's Special Committee on Communist Tactics, Strategy, and Objectives filed a report accusing his Court of aiding the Communist cause with its decisions in fifteen recent cases, and the Individual Rights Affected by National Security Committee censured *Watkins*. Meanwhile, a third committee tabled without discussion a resolution expressing disapproval of inflammatory attacks on the Court. Warren "concluded that I could no longer be a member of an organization of the legal profession which would ask me to lead fifteen thousand of its members overseas on a goodwill mission and then deliberately and trickily contrive to discredit the Supreme Court which I headed."[35] Although it disappointed the chief justice, the ABA did oppose the most extreme aspect of a congressional counterattack on the Court's internal security decisions.

The Justice Department, backed by an outraged press, sent to Capitol Hill a moderate measure to safeguard FBI files, which after being altered to satisfy the concerns of liberals and the Bureau itself, passed Congress in August 1957. The "Jencks Act" ensured that the government would not have to turn over earlier statements made by its witnesses until after they had testified and trial judges had inspected their reports in camera to ensure that the defense was given only the relevant portions. Failure to comply, however, would result in striking of the witnesses' testimony or the declaration of a mistrial. The Senate Judiciary Committee denied this law was designed to limit *Jencks,* and friends of the Warren Court insisted all it really did was codify that decision.[36]

Far more hostile to the Supreme Court was a bill introduced by Senator William Jenner (R-Ind.) in July 1957. His legislation would have eliminated the Supreme Court's appellate jurisdiction in cases involving contempt of Congress, the federal loyalty-security program, bar admissions, state antisubversion statutes, and employment and subversive activities in schools. Jenner's bill enlisted the support of national security alarmists and southern segregationists, but the Justice Department opposed it. So did an array of liberal organizations, most of the press, the deans of the major law schools, and partners in some of the top law firms. Although reserving the right to criticize decisions of the Court, the ABA joined in denouncing Jenner's bill. In an effort to save it, his friend, Senator John Marshall Butler (R-Md.) offered a series of amendments that eliminated all but one of the jurisdiction-stripping provisions and sought to overcome the effects of most rulings by other means. The Judiciary Committee endorsed the renamed Jenner-Butler Bill, but opponents, assisted by Majority Leader Lyndon Johnson (D-Tex.), defeated it on the Senate floor. Congressional critics of the Warren Court did manage, with Justice Department support, to amend the Smith Act so that henceforth the term "organize" would denote an ongoing process, but even that small triumph did not come until 1962.[37]

Although producing little legislation, the furor in Congress caused the Court, led by Frankfurter, to lurch to the right. During the 1956–57 term it had rejected civil liberties claims in only 26 percent of all cases decided by full opinion. In succeeding terms, that figure leaped to 41 percent, then 48.8 percent. The Court demonstrated a growing reluctance even to hear cases raising civil liberties claims.[38]

To be sure, it did not do a complete about-face. For example, the Court reversed several Smith Act convictions after *Yates,* starting with those of some Michigan Communists a week later. In October 1957 it set aside verdicts against Junius Scales and Claude Lightfoot under a clause in the Smith Act that criminalized membership in a group that taught and advocated the violent overthrow of the government. Their cases raised two related issues: whether Congress's enactment of section 4(f) of the Internal Security Act (which provided that belonging to a Communist organization should not constitute per se a violation of any federal law) had repealed this membership clause, and, if it had not, whether the interplay between that provision and the Internal Security Act's registration requirement violated the Fifth Amendment's Self-Incrimination Clause. Four of the seven justices who participated wished to decide the constitutional issue, but Frankfurter, insisting this should not be done by less than a full bench, pronounced himself "a last ditch fighter in avoiding them." The Court set the cases down for reargument. Before that could take place, Solicitor General Rankin conceded that in light of *Jencks,* they should be remanded and the Court reversed both convictions. In May 1958 it freed a *Yates* defendant who had been imprisoned for refusing to identify other persons as Communists.[39]

Besides freeing convicted Smith Act defendants, Warren and his colleagues also held that the Hawaii Supreme Court could not suspend one of their lawyers, Harriet Bouslog-Sawyer, from practice for a year for giving a speech challenging the fairness of the judge in a Honolulu trial. Brennan's opinion held merely that the facts did not support a finding that she had questioned the judge's integrity. In conference, however, Warren and Black, examining what Bouslog-Sawyer had said about the bar's attack on the Court's handling of Communist cases, treated the Hawaiian lawyer's case as an issue of free speech. Brennan's opinion, which suggested he shared their view that lawyers had a First Amendment right to criticize the courts, was unacceptable to Frankfurter, Clark, Harlan, Whittaker, and Stewart, all of whom believed a lawyer's professional role limited what she could say. Denying that attorneys' free speech rights could immunize them from evenhanded discipline for unethical conduct, Stewart concurred separately. The other four dissented.[40]

Frankfurter and Brennan were on the same side when a five-to-four majority ruled the secretary of state had no authority to withhold passports from Communists or persons he believed were going abroad to advance Communist causes. They joined a Douglas opinion in *Kent v. Dulles* (1958), which emphasized that the right to travel was a liberty interest protected by the Due Process Clause of the Fifth Amendment, but declined to reach constitutional issues, holding instead that Congress had not delegated to the secretary the power to refuse to issue passports to Rockwell Kent and Dr. Walter Briehl. Douglas decided *Dayton v. Dulles* (1958) on the basis of *Kent*, dodging discussion of the constitutional question on which the briefs and oral arguments had focused: Had the secretary violated the petitioner's due process rights by denying him a passport because confidential reports allegedly linked him to the Rosenberg espionage ring? Douglas wanted to resolve that issue with a far-reaching opinion, holding that due process required the government to disclose all facts on which it relied in denying a passport, but Whittaker and Frankfurter would not go along. Lacking a majority on the constitutional issue, the Douglas forces decided to avoid it. That satisfied Frankfurter, but Whittaker joined Clark dissents in both *Kent* and *Dayton*.[41]

The Court took a similarly restrained approach when rescuing victims of the federal loyalty-security program. In *Green v. McElroy* (1959) it ruled for a man who had lost his job as an engineer and executive with a defense contractor when the Pentagon revoked his security clearance for past involvement with Communists he claimed were associates of his ex-wife. The Defense Department had acted on the basis of confidential reports from individuals Greene was never permitted to confront or question. From Warren's perspective, the issue was whether people like him might "lose their jobs and . . . be restrained in following their chosen professions on the basis of fact determinations . . . made in proceedings in which they are denied the traditional procedural safeguards of confrontation and cross-examination." His opinion for the Court held that neither the president nor Congress had delegated to the Defense Department authority to bypass these traditional safeguards. Because of pressure from Frankfurter, Warren disclaimed deciding constitutional issues, but upset because he had even mentioned them, Harlan filed a concurring opinion. Clark dissented. Warren yielded to his more cautious colleagues in the companion case of *Taylor v. McElroy*, disposing of it with a per curiam opinion holding the case had become moot when the Defense Department belatedly granted the plaintiff a clearance. In *Vitarelli v. Seaton* (1959) the Chief mustered a narrow five-to-four majority to reinstate a teacher fired by the Interior Department because of his past activities and Communist associations. Although Interior had not followed the procedures for security dismissals mandated by relevant regulations when it dismissed Vitarelli in 1954, the department contended this did not matter because in 1956 the secretary had utilized his undisputed authority to discharge a non–civil service employee for no reason at all when firing him again. The liberal bloc won the support of Harlan, who wrote an opinion holding Interior's failure to follow its own rules made the dismissal unlawful.[42]

The liberal bloc also prevailed in *Shelton v. Tucker* (1960), this time by enlisting Stewart. *Shelton* struck down an Arkansas statute that compelled public school and college teachers, who were hired on a year-to-year basis, to file annually affidavits listing every organization to which they had belonged in the past five years. Speaking for the Court, Stewart acknowledged states might inquire into the fitness and competency of their teachers, but argued, as Warren had in conference, that Arkansas's law was far broader than necessary to achieve its legitimate objectives and impinged unnecessarily on associational freedom. In separate dissents Frankfurter and Harlan argued that a countervailing public interest could override personal liberty. Noting that freedom of expression and association were not absolutes, Harlan asserted: "The controlling inquiry is whether [an action alleged to violate them] is justifiable on the basis of a superior governmental interest to which such individual rights must yield."[43]

Although rejected in *Shelton,* his balancing approach generally prevailed during the four years following Red Monday, a period when Warren, Black, Douglas, and Brennan repeatedly found themselves in the minority. With the Court under fire in Congress and Frankfurter's personal relationship with the Chief deteriorating, he and Harlan deserted the liberals. Abandoning their often carefully camouflaged efforts to constrain McCarthyism, they retreated into deference and balancing, using these rationales to uphold internal security initiatives.[44]

An early manifestation of their growing reluctance to agitate Congress was a per curiam opinion that Frankfurter wrote in 1958 in *Sacher v. United States,* reversing the contempt conviction of a radical lawyer who had refused to answer questions put to him by the Senate Internal Security Subcommittee. Frankfurter spurned Douglas's plea for a full-dress opinion because he did not want to "blow up these cases." He believed "our best hope is to take them in a quiet stride, giving rise to as little rejoinder as possible." Harlan, suggesting "This is not a good time to highlight *Watkins,*" urged Frankfurter to "hold up announcement of the decision pending the present flurry in Congress."[45]

In *Barenblatt v. United States* (1959) the two of them led a full-blown retreat from *Watkins.* With Harlan writing the opinion, the Court upheld the contempt conviction of a Vassar College psychology instructor who had refused to tell HUAC whether he was or ever had been a Communist. In conference Warren contended that *Watkins* was controlling, but Frankfurter, Harlan, and Clark argued successfully that it was not, because Barenblatt had failed to object on pertinency grounds to the questions he had refused to answer. Harlan also rejected Warren's contention that *Watkins* had held the House rule giving HUAC its authority was so vague that the committee could not properly compel testimony from anyone. Finally, and most important, his opinion for the Court declared that the questions Barenblatt had refused to answer did not violate the First Amendment. Harlan employed a balancing-of-interests approach that Warren considered incomprehensible. "Where First Amendment rights are asserted to bar governmental interrogation," he wrote, "resolution of the issue always involves a balancing by the courts of the competing private and public interests at stake in the particular circumstances shown." In this case the great need of Congress to investigate entitled the government to prevail. At Frankfurter's urging, Harlan began his opinion with a preamble highlighting "the far-reaching power of Congress which we are asked to censor." Neither of them wanted to restrict congressional authority to investigate the Communist Party. Because the CPUSA was a threat to national security rather than an ordinary political organization, Harlan insisted, Congress had an interest in probing its efforts to infiltrate educational institutions, and questions about a teacher's membership furthered a legitimate legislative purpose. He denied that HUAC was engaging in exposure for exposure's sake. In a long dissenting opinion, Black, joined by Warren and Douglas, pointed out that while emphasizing the government's need for self-preservation, Harlan had said little about the interest this supposedly outweighed: Barrenblatt's right to remain silent concerning his political activities. Black objected to the very idea "that laws directly abridging First Amendment freedoms can be justified by a congressional or judicial balancing process." Balancing, he argued, made the First Amendment unenforceable, except when enforcing it seemed reasonable to the Supreme Court.[46]

Praising Black's "magnificent" dissent, liberal Washington lawyer Thurman Arnold accused the Court of abandoning *Watkins* in favor of a rule that "the First Amendment should be suspended at any time when a decision upholding it encounter[s] substantial public opposition with influence in Congress." The obeisance to congressional anti-Communism that Arnold found objectionable continued in two 1961 cases, *Wilkinson v. United States* and *Braden v. United States*. Both Wilkinson and Braden had been convicted of contempt for refusing to answer questions during HUAC hearings in Atlanta. The former apparently had been called to testify because of petitions he had circulated advocating legislative action against segregation. The latter claimed he had been subpoenaed because of his involvement in a campaign to abolish HUAC itself. Warren argued that the committee had violated Wilkinson's and Braden's First Amendment right to petition the government for redress of grievances, but Frankfurter and Harlan, who insisted that *Barenblatt* was controlling, prevailed five to four. The liberal bloc did manage to defeat them in *Deutch v. United States* (1961), enlisting Stewart's support for a decision overturning a contempt conviction because of the government's failure to show how the questions the witness had refused to answer about Communism at Cornell University were pertinent to an investigation into Communist activities in the labor field and in the Albany, New York, area.[47]

Frankfurter and Harlan prevailed, however, not only in most cases involving direct challenges to Congress, but also in state ones, such as in *Uphaus v. Wyman* (1959). *Uphaus,* an appeal from a civil-contempt judgment imposed on the executive director of a summer camp for failing to turn over guest lists subpoenaed by the attorney general of New Hampshire in his capacity as a one-man legislative investigating committee, had been vacated and remanded in 1957 for reconsideration in light of *Sweezy.* The Court easily rejected Uphaus's contention that the entire field of subversive activities had been preempted by the Smith Act, an argument even Warren found unpersuasive. It divided badly, however, over whether the demand for the disputed records violated the Constitution. For a majority of five, Clark held that it did not. Succumbing to Harlan's complaint about "the absence of any 'balancing' treatment" in a preliminary circulation of his opinion, he noted in the final version that Uphaus had participated in activities of Communist-front groups and had invited to the camp speakers associated with such organizations and with the CPUSA; consequently, the public's need to determine if there were subversive persons in New Hampshire outweighed his private interests. Dissenting for the liberal bloc, Brennan responded that a report prepared by the attorney general showed the whole point of this investigation had been disclosure for its own sake; hence, there was no valid legislative interest against which to balance Uphaus's rights of expression and association. In another dissent Black maintained that the legislature had violated the constitutional prohibition against bills of attainder. The following year Uphaus was back, arguing that by the time he was interrogated, the legislative authorization for the attorney general's investigation had expired. Douglas saw this as "a new and important question," but Frankfurter argued successfully that it was an issue of state law. With the liberal bloc dissenting, the Court held it lacked jurisdiction.[48]

It also turned a cold shoulder to public employees fired for refusing to answer questions about their alleged Communist affiliations. In *Beilan v. Board of Public Education* (1958) and *Lerner v. Casey,* the Court ruled five to four that, because such a query was relevant to fitness and suitability, a school district could avoid violating the Due Process Clause by dismissing a teacher who refused to answer for incompetence rather than disloyalty, and that the New York Transit Authority could fire a subway conductor who had invoked the Fifth Amendment "because of the doubt created as to his 'reliability' by his refusal to answer a relevant question put by his employer." Two years later, in *Nelson v. County of Los Angeles,* the Court ruled against two social workers who had been fired for refusing to cooperate with HUAC after being ordered by the board of supervisors to answer its questions about their subversive activities.[49]

The Court also ceased protecting would-be lawyers. After *Konigsberg,* the California bar again refused to admit the petitioner, allegedly because his refusal to answer questions about his membership in the Communist Party had obstructed a full investigation into his qualifications. In *Konigsberg v. State Bar* (1961), the Court held its action did not violate the Fourteenth Amendment. It came to a similar conclusion in *In re Anastaplo,* in which an Illinois bar committee, ignoring uncontroverted evidence of the applicant's good moral character, had refused to admit him because he would not answer questions about whether he was a member of the CPUSA. Rejecting Warren's contention that someone could not be excluded from the legal profession because of silence motivated by moral scruples, a five-to-four majority supported Frankfurter, who argued that "those who stand up for their conscience may be disqualified from being lawyers." Harlan, who spoke for the Court in both cases, declared in *Anastaplo* that a state's interest in enforcing a rule requiring applicants to answer all material questions "outweighs any deterrent effect on freedom of speech and association." Dissenting for the liberal bloc, Black excoriated Harlan's balancing and insisted that the First Amendment rights of Konigsberg and Anastaplo had been violated.[50]

Black and his allies suffered another defeat when *Communist Party v. Subversive Activities Control Board* returned to the Court. On June 5, 1961, speaking through Frankfurter, a five-to-four majority denied that the SACB had erroneously construed the Subversive Activities Control Act and that the CPUSA had been prejudiced by its procedural rulings and those of the court of appeals. The Court also rejected the party's constitutional attack on the statute. "This case makes every man face his conception of judicial review & his relationships as a member of the court to the Congress," Frankfurter told his colleagues. He urged them to exercise judicial restraint. Disregarding Black's objections and reservations expressed even by Harlan, he disposed of complaints about the consequences for individual members of requiring

the party to register as a Communist-action organization by holding that consideration of these and of the sections of the act that imposed sanctions was premature.
Frankfurter refused to decide even whether requiring the party to register would compel the officers who had to enroll it to incriminate themselves. He passed only on the
validity of the registration requirement, responding to just three of the CPUSA's five
constitutional arguments against it. Frankfurter denied both that Congress had violated the party's due process rights by making factual determinations essential to the
application of the registration provisions and that these constituted a bill of attainder or violated First Amendment guarantees of freedom of expression and association. Although convinced the Court was ducking issues it should decide, Harlan
sided with his ally. Warren, Brennan, Douglas, and Black dissented. Although considering the statute unconstitutional, the Chief contented himself with highlighting
what he saw as four serious nonconstitutional errors presented by the record. Douglas and Brennan both focused on self-incrimination problems, and Black, who
thought the Subversive Activities Control Act was "intended to hurt people by legislative fiat," branded it a bill of attainder and a violation of the First Amendment and
warned ominously of the threat to critics of the government posed by "the dangerous constitutional doctrine of 'balancing.'" Although censured by his liberal colleagues, Frankfurter's opinion elicited praise from the public. "THANK YOU, SIR!" a
Texan wrote to him. "It is way past time that the high court uphold [sic] the right of
our country to defend itself against the Communist Party."[51]

Many of those who congratulated Frankfurter also praised *Scales v. United States*
(1961). Decided the same day, it was one of the Smith Act "membership clause" cases
the Court had remanded on *Jencks* grounds in 1957. When it returned in 1959, Scales
was represented by Columbia Law School professor and former Nuremberg prosecutor Telford Taylor, who argued that prosecution of any Communist under the
membership clause was barred by section 4(f) of the Internal Security Act. Apparently adopted to safeguard the ISA's registration requirement from attacks based on
the Self-Incrimination Clause, it prohibited using the fact that an individual had
enrolled the party as evidence that he had committed a crime and stipulated that
membership in a Communist organization should not be per se a violation of ISA "or
any other criminal statute." Scales's attorneys also contended that the membership
clause impermissibly imputed guilt by association and infringed the freedoms of
expression and association. So anxious was Frankfurter to avoid confronting Congress that, although one of his clerks had resolved the section 4(f) issue to his satisfaction in 1956, he successfully promoted the idea of having *Scales* reargued in
conjunction with *SACB*. "I have found no case in the history of the Court that has
been on the appellate docket so long or argued so often," Clark protested. Despite
his griping, Frankfurter insisted, the issues demanded "due deliberation" and "mature
reflection," and that like wine, the "judgment of this Court requires seasoning."[52]

Scales continued to age until June 5, 1961, when the Court affirmed the conviction and upheld the membership clause. Brushing aside a legislative history showing
that Congress had been willing to sacrifice that clause in order to ensure the constitutionality of registration, Harlan denied that section 4(f) had effected a *pro tanto*

repeal of the membership clause that precluded prosecuting Communists for violating it. The disputed provision seemed to require only that one belong to the Communist Party with knowledge of its illegal objectives, but Harlan construed it as in effect a conspiracy statute, violation of which also required having the purpose to advance those objectives. As so construed, the membership clause was constitutional on its face; it violated neither the Fifth Amendment by imputing guilt to an individual merely on the basis of his associations and sympathies nor the First Amendment by infringing freedoms of political expression and association. In a portion of his opinion that purported to deal only with the sufficiency of the evidence but really affirmed the constitutionality of the statute as applied, Harlan sought to placate Stewart, who had nearly deserted the majority because he believed *Yates* had overruled *Dennis,* that the First Amendment mandated the *Yates* evidentiary standards, and that those had not been met in *Scales.* Harlan conceded prosecutors had to produce what *Yates* demanded. However, he insisted that they had satisfied this requirement with evidence that illustrated the teaching of forcible overthrow, accompanied by directions as to the type of illegal action to be taken when the time for revolution was ripe, which demonstrated the existence of a contemporary, although legal, course of conduct intended to make productive the illegal undertaking Communists advocated. Harlan pointed to evidence he believed showed the CPUSA endorsed violent revolutionary action, including testimony by Scales himself that in addition established the character of his own membership. The liberal bloc dissented. Douglas insisted Scales's conviction offended the First Amendment, which Black maintained absolutely forbade Congress to outlaw membership in a political association. Along with Warren, they joined a Brennan opinion arguing that section 4(f) barred prosecutions under the membership clause.[53]

Although disputing that contention, even Harlan lacked enthusiasm for Smith Act prosecutions, conceding privately the need to keep a tight rein on them. Having genuflected to Congress in *Scales,* he used his opinion in the companion case of *Noto v. United States* to render the membership clause essentially useless for attacking the CPUSA. Not even Clark (who initially voted to affirm the conviction, still believing *Yates* had been wrongly decided) could find in the *Noto* record the sort of evidence of present advocacy of forcible action that *Yates* required. Speaking for a unanimous Court, Harlan declared that to be valid a conviction under the membership clause had to rest on "some substantial direct or circumstantial evidence of a call to violence now or in the future which is both sufficiently strong and sufficiently pervasive . . . to lend color to . . . otherwise ambiguous theoretical material regarding Communist Party teaching, and to justify the inference that . . . a call to violence may fairly be imputed to the Party as a whole. . . ." Unable to produce what *Noto* demanded, the Justice Department ceased initiating new membership-clause prosecutions. Within two years it had abandoned all pending cases.[54]

The Court was wise to limit the impact of *Scales,* for that decision elicited condemnation from much of the popular press, including such influential organs as the *New York Times* and the *Washington Post,* as well as the censure of most legal commentators. Despite mounting evidence that anti-Communism was losing its grip on the country, throughout the four years following Red Monday, the Court regularly demonstrated obeisance to anti-Communist sentiment in Congress. For example, a 1958 opinion written by Harlan upheld a criminal contempt judgment against two *Dennis* defendants for jumping bail and disappearing in 1951, when they were supposed to report to begin serving their sentences, even though bail jumping was not then a federal crime and the judicial order on which the convictions were based had actually been issued after they failed to appear. Two years later, in *Fleming v. Nestor,* by an identical five-to-four margin, the Court upheld a 1954 federal statute pursuant to which the Health, Education, and Welfare Department had terminated Nestor's Social Security benefits after he was deported for being a member of the CPUSA from 1933 to 1939. The liberal bloc claimed this law was a bill of attainder, but speaking through Harlan, the majority maintained its legislative history did not offer unmistakable evidence that Congress was trying to be punitive.[55]

Although precipitated by the determination of Harlan and Frankfurter to avoid conflict with the legislative branch, the Court's penchant for finding ways to validate governmental actions in national security cases produced rulings against everyone from a notorious Soviet spy to a harmless cafeteria worker. In *Abel v. United States* (1960) the Court affirmed five to four the espionage conviction of Col. Rudolph Ivanovic Abel, rejecting his claim that some of the evidence used against him had been obtained in violation of the Fourth Amendment because it had been seized incident to an administrative arrest by the Immigration and Naturalization Service that was carried out to enable the FBI to get the evidence without a warrant it could not have secured from a judge. The liberal bloc dissented in both Colonel Abel's case and one the following year in which the majority ruled against a civilian cook, employed by a firm that operated the cafeteria on a naval base, who had been barred from that installation because she allegedly failed to meet security requirements. The woman had not been given a hearing or even advised of the specific grounds for her exclusion. Following an oral argument in which he implied that Warren, who thought the employee had been treated unfairly, was distracting counsel from the real issues, Frankfurter led a successful fight for affirmance. Stewart, who provided the crucial fifth vote, wrote an opinion finding statutory and presidential authorization for the exclusion and holding the cook had not been denied procedural due process.[56]

Such opinions were the rule until 1962, when the declining political potency of anti-Communism combined with changes in the composition of the Court to produce a lurch to the left. In April 1962 Whittaker retired and Frankfurter suffered a severe stroke that forced him to leave the Court in August. To replace them President John F. Kennedy selected Deputy Attorney General Byron White and Secretary of Labor Arthur Goldberg. White, who had clerked for Vinson in 1946 and 1947, voted consistently with the conservative bloc in civil liberties cases during his first three terms on the Court and seemed no more inclined than Whittaker had been to thwart anti-Communist initiatives. Goldberg, however, was completely different from Frankfurter. He was no less hostile toward Communism than his predecessor was, having, while he served as the CIO's top lawyer in the late 1940s and early 1950s, supported the expulsion of Communist-dominated unions from the labor movement, the Truman administration's loyalty-security program, and Congress's anti-Communist legislation. But Goldberg had always sought to shelter those he considered innocent from government radical hunters, and by 1954 the CIO was balking at intrusions into civil liberties to ferret out subversives. In addition to substantial skepticism about McCarthyism's methods, he brought to the Court a proclivity for activism. Goldberg quickly joined forces with Warren, Black, Douglas, and Brennan.[57]

Fortified with a fifth vote, they confronted Congress in defense of individual rights. Expatriation cases highlighted the Court's changed posture. In 1957–58 the justices had decided two challenges to provisions of the Nationality Act of 1940, the first American statute making anything other than voluntary change of allegiance grounds for loss of citizenship. One had been brought by Texas-born Clemente Martinez-Perez, whom immigration authorities had deported for going to Mexico in 1944 to evade the draft and then voting in a Mexican election. Albert Trop lost his citizenship when an army court-martial convicted him of desertion. At the May 4, 1957, conference, Warren, animated by a belief that the Court had a duty to protect the fundamental rights of American citizenship, argued passionately that banishment could not be used as a punishment. Frankfurter, a naturalized citizen who believed that in order to enjoy the rights of citizenship one must meet its responsibilities, led the opposition, arguing for deference to Congress. Although convinced that the statute violated the basic spirit and political theory of the Constitution and that the government lacked authority to deprive anyone of citizenship, the Chief based his opinion on the Eighth Amendment's prohibition of cruel and unusual punishment. Brennan, who did not agree with Warren that Congress was wholly without power to provide for the expatriation of citizens, concurred separately, contending revocation of citizenship bore too little relationship to the successful waging of war to be justifiable as an exercise of the congressional power to raise armies, but that when imposed for voting in a foreign election, it was a proper exercise of Congress's authority to regulate foreign affairs. Speaking for the majority in *Perez*, and dissenting in *Trop*, Frankfurter insisted expatriation could constitutionally be imposed in both cases and that the challenged legislation should be upheld out of respect for the politically responsible branches of the government. The Court should exercise its power to invalidate statutes "with the utmost restraint."[58]

That viewpoint no longer predominated after Goldberg replaced Frankfurter. In *Kennedy v. Mendoza-Martinez* (1063) the Court struck down statutes expatriating those who left or remained outside the country in a time of war to evade military service. When the Court first heard *Mendoza-Martinez* in 1959, the vote was five-to-four to uphold section 401(j) of the Nationality Act. The justices remanded the case on a technicality because they could not agree about what the impact would be on *Trop* if the decision were based on the merits, given the difficulty of explaining Whittaker's support of the majority in both cases. *Mendoza-Martinez* returned during the October 1961 term, but the Court divided badly, and Whittaker's retirement left it split four to four in both that case and *Rusk v. Cort*, a challenge to section 349(a) of the Immigration and Nationality Act of 1952, which had superseded 401(j). Warren and Brennan persuaded their colleagues to remand *Cort* on a jurisdictional issue and schedule

both cases for reargument in the next term. By then Goldberg had replaced Frankfurter. With the newcomer writing the opinion, the Court held five to four that sections
401(j) and 349(a) violated the Fifth and Sixth Amendments by imposing punishment
without a grand jury indictment or trial. Brennan agreed, but wrote an opinion of
his own, in part to dispute Stewart, who argued in dissent that the challenged laws
were constitutional because they bore a rational relationship to the congressional
war power. While employing this deferential standard, even he (and apparently the
other three dissenters as well) acknowledged that the authority of Congress to expatriate was not unlimited.[59]

Mendoza-Martinez created a favorable climate for further assaults on expatriation
legislation. A year later (with only Clark, Harlan, and White dissenting) the Court
struck down a provision of the Immigration and Nationality Act that denaturalized
citizens if they resided continuously for three years in their native countries or in others of which they had once been nationals, holding this law violated the Due Process
Clause of the Fifth Amendment because it treated naturalized citizens differently
than native-born ones. At the same time the Court affirmed four to four a court of
appeals decision rejecting a challenge to the expatriation statute by a native-born
American who had served in the Cuban armed forces and as an executioner for the
Castro regime, but only because Brennan recused himself due to his son's involvement as a lawyer in the litigation. Far more representative of the Warren Court's stance
in expatriation cases following Goldberg's appointment was *Afroyim v. Rusk* (1967).
There it set aside the denaturalization of a Polish-born Jew for voting in an Israeli
election. With Black speaking for a five-to-four majority, the Court reversed *Perez v.
Brownell* and held the statute authorizing such expatriations unconstitutional as a violation of the Citizenship Clause of the Fourteenth Amendment. Harlan protested
futilely on behalf of Clark, Stewart, and White that "Justice Frankfurter's opinion for
the Court in *Perez* . . . still proves . . . [this] is within the power of Congress."[60]

The Court no longer displayed the sort of deference to the national legislature
Frankfurter had championed, even in contempt of Congress cases. On May 21, 1962
—with Whittaker gone, Frankfurter not participating, and only Clark and Harlan
dissenting—it threw out the convictions of six witnesses who had refused to answer
questions during hearings conducted by HUAC and the Senate Internal Security
Subcommittee. Essentially ignoring *Barenblatt, Wilkinson,* and *Braden,* the Court held
that in order to be valid, an indictment charging contempt of a congressional committee had to specify the topic of the investigation. It ridiculed the "meandering
statements purporting to identify the subject under inquiry," with which senators had
initiated the hearings that spawned one of these prosecutions. The following year in
Yellen v. United States the Court ruled five to four in favor of a defiant HUAC witness,
faulting the committee for failing to comply with its own rules concerning the handling of a request to testify in executive session. Warren apparently took this tack in
order to avoid having to reconsider *Barenblatt* and similar cases. Neither Goldberg
nor White found his reasoning very persuasive, and while the former finally went along
with it, White dissented for himself, Clark, and Harlan. By 1966 the Court was taking
a more direct approach. In *Gojack v. United States* it threw out a second conviction of

one of the 1962 cases' defendants who had been retried under a properly drawn indictment. A unanimous Court now focused on the lack of any record that HUAC had ever authorized the sort of investigation of Communist Party activities in the labor field that led to this prosecution, as its own rules required. Even had it done so, the Court noted, the committee had not empowered the subcommittee the defendant defied to conduct such an investigation. Without a clear chain of authority extending from the House through the full committee to the subcommittee, whose questions a witness refused to answer with respect to the particular subject matter at issue, the contempt of Congress statute gave the courts no jurisdiction to impose criminal sanctions.[61]

In repudiating the sort of freewheeling investigations by congressional Red-hunters that had epitomized the McCarthy era, the Warren Court merely reflected the changed attitudes of the public, and even of Congress itself. Riotous student protests had greeted HUAC when it held hearings in San Francisco in 1960. Members of Women Strike for Peace, who showed up in force with bouquets and babies to support subpoenaed witnesses, turned the once-feared committee's 1962 probe of that organization into burlesque and subjected HUAC to ridicule. Representative James Roosevelt (D-Cal.) led a movement within Congress to abolish HUAC that produced ninety-six House votes against its appropriation in 1966 and led to a face-saving 1969 name-change to "House Internal Security Committee." Two years later the chairman of the SACB admitted that his organization did "not have enough [to do] to fill our time."[62]

The second Red Scare was already over by the time the Warren Court imposed meaningful limitations on state legislative investigations of Communist activities. In *Gibson v. Florida Legislative Investigating Committee* (1963), with Goldberg providing the crucial fifth vote and writing the opinion, the Supreme Court purported to employ the balancing approach utilized in subversive activities cases since 1958. Now, however, the Court struck the balance in favor of associational freedom, holding that a legislative committee purportedly investigating whether Communists had infiltrated the NAACP was not entitled to require the president of that organization's Miami branch to produce membership records and reveal whether particular individuals belonged. Sensitive to the fact that the target of Florida's inquiry was a civil rights group unpopular in the South, Goldberg announced that the adverse impact of Florida's disclosure demand on the exercise of constitutional rights outweighed the state's limited interest in learning more about a legitimate group that had not been shown to have any subversive connections. He denied what White accurately noted in his dissent: that this decision imposed "a serious limitation . . . upon the right of the legislature to investigate the Communist Party and its activities." The Court further restricted that right in *DeGregory v. Attorney General of New Hampshire* (1966). DeGregory had received a contempt sentence for refusing to discuss any Communist activities in which he might have engaged prior to the 1957 enactment of legislation authorizing the attorney general to investigate and publicize such conduct. With Douglas writing the opinion, the Court held that the state's interest in the information sought was too remote and conjectural to override First Amendment freedoms, which prevented "use of the power to investigate enforced by the contempt power to probe at will and without relation to existing need." Harlan's futile dissent cited *Barenblatt* and pleaded for judicial restraint.[63]

Such arguments had little appeal for an activist majority, whose determination to wipe out the remnants of McCarthyism also inspired rulings limiting what states might do to ensure the loyalty of their employees. Even White and Stewart supported *Baggett v. Bullit* (1966), in which the Court ruled in favor of University of Washington faculty and staff who had challenged two statutes that required them to take a loyalty oath. The Court held these laws void for vagueness. Eschewing reliance on the First Amendment, White nevertheless asserted that "'[t]he vice of unconstitutional vagueness is further aggravated where, as here, the statute in question operates to inhibit the exercise of individual freedoms affirmatively protected by the Constitution.'" He insisted the Court was not questioning the power of the states to safeguard their public services against disloyalty, but *Elfbrandt v. Russell* (1966) clearly did so. With Douglas as its spokesman, a five-to-four majority held that an Arizona public-employees loyalty oath and its accompanying statutory gloss, which penalized knowing membership in organizations that had among their purposes the violent overthrow of the government, violated the First Amendment right to freedom of association because they applied even to adherents who lacked intent to further their groups' illegal aims. "According to unequivocal prior holdings of this Court, a State is entitled to condition public employment upon its employees abstaining from knowing membership in the Communist Party and other organizations advocating the violent overthrow of the government," White protested.[64]

Now, however, even federal anti-Communist initiatives faced invalidation in the Supreme Court. In *United States v. Brown* (1965), for example, the Court declared unconstitutional section 504 of the Labor Management Reporting and Disclosure Act of 1959, which made it a crime for a CPUSA member to serve as an officer or employee of a labor union. The Court also invalidated a section of the Internal Security Act that made it a felony for a member of a group required to register as a Communist organization to apply for, use, or attempt to use a passport. In addition, it struck down a federal law that required postal officials to detain and destroy unsealed mail from foreign countries that was determined to be Communist propaganda, unless the addressee returned a card indicating his desire to receive it.[65] In 1965 the Court vacated and remanded SACB orders requiring the American Committee for the Protection of Foreign Born and the Veterans of the Abraham Lincoln Brigade to register as Communist-front groups because the orders were based primarily on evidence that was a decade old. Douglas, Black, and Harlan dissented only because they thought the Court should address the constitutional issues the cases presented. A majority had agreed in conference to invalidate the registration orders on self-incrimination grounds, but disagreements among them and a desire for unanimity produced a decision that avoided the issue. Early in the following term, though, the Court unleashed the Fifth Amendment in *Albertson v. Subversive Activities Control Board* (1965). It ruled unanimously that orders commanding officers of the Communist Party to register the group with the SACB were unconstitutional because they compelled those individuals to admit violating the membership clause of the Smith Act.[66]

Such a straightforward decision in favor of the leaders of the CPUSA strongly suggested that, at least as far as the Supreme Court was concerned, the Cold War was over. *United States v. Robel* (1967) removed all doubt. In *Robel* the Court held unconstitutional a provision of the Subversive Activities Control Act of 1950 that made employment in a defense facility unlawful for anyone belonging to an organization that the SACB had ordered to register. Robel, a CPUSA member, had been prosecuted after the secretary of defense, acting pursuant to the statute, designated as a "defense facility" the Seattle shipyard that employed him. The government insisted this law was valid under the war power. While conceding the authority of Congress to protect defense plants against espionage, sabotage, and disruption, Warren denied it could do so with a statute that sanctioned all types of association with Communist-action groups; the provision in question imposed too much of a burden on First Amendment rights. The justices had difficulty deciding *Robel,* which had to be reargued after they could not reach agreement in 1966, but their disagreements involved rationale rather than result. The original conference vote was six to two, but Brennan's opinion invalidating the challenged law for violating constitutional standards of definiteness in its delegation of authority to the secretary of defense, won the support of only Black, Douglas, and Warren. The Chief's approach garnered six votes. White and Harlan protested that the Court had no business rejecting the judgment of Congress and the Defense Department that Robel was enough of a threat to national security to warrant making him choose between the CPUSA and a defense plant job. While lauding the Court for seeking to establish "the widest bounds for the exercise of individual liberty consistent with the security of the country," White objected that it had "abrogate[d] to itself an independent judgment of the requirements of national security."[67]

Reacting to *Robel,* the *Dallas Morning News* complained that the Supreme Court seemed "to find every law designed to protect the country from subversion objectionable on one technicality or another." That would have been an absurd charge a few years earlier. For a brief period in the late 1950s the Court had endeavored, often with rather technical and carefully circumscribed rulings, to save civil liberties from the ravages of the international and domestic cold wars. When its initiatives aroused opposition in Congress, though it sought safety in judicial self-restraint. Only after Frankfurter's departure did the Court again render the sort of decisions to which the *Morning News* objected. That even such a conservative newspaper offered only muted criticism of the Supreme Court's rulings showed how little anyone cared. The country had moved on to other issues, and so had the Warren Court.[68]

4

TURNING POINT

Although internal-security and school-desegregation decisions made the early Warren Court a political lightening rod and shaped its public image, these cases were not particularly representative of the Court's work. Until 1962 it played the limited and rather traditional role in the American system of government favored by Justice Frankfurter. Then a stroke drove Frankfurter from the bench, and President Kennedy replaced him with Arthur Goldberg, a liberal activist. That appointment gave Warren and his allies a reliable majority in even the most controversial and politically sensitive cases. The results were a dramatic transformation in the character of the Court and a revolution in constitutional law. The substitution of Goldberg for Frankfurter initiated a second phase in the history of the Warren Court, during which the substantive liberalism espoused by the chief justice, Black, Douglas, and Brennan vanquished the process liberalism Frankfurter had championed. The Court allied itself with liberal Democrats in Congress and the White House, making constitutional law an instrument for the promotion of social and political reform. Its initiatives inspired an abundance of both admiration and animosity, transforming what was merely a controversial tribunal into what Mark Tushnet characterizes as "a cultural phenomenon."[1]

Before 1962 Earl Warren's Supreme Court was not dramatically different from its predecessors. It was, to be sure, somewhat busier. At the beginning of the October 1959 term, the Court found it necessary to add one week to the thirteen already devoted to oral arguments, and by January 1961 the clerk's office was complaining that even this was not enough. In November 1962 the *Harvard Law Review* observed that for the past ten years there had been a steady "increase in the Court's workload insofar as it can be measured in terms of the length of the dockets." During the October 1961 term, an all-time high of 2,570 cases appeared on the combined docket. Up 274 from the previous year, that number represented a 90 percent increase over Warren's first term as chief justice. Although the docket was larger than at any time since passage of the Judiciary Act of 1925, the Court's workload had not actually increased as much as the numbers suggested. The number of cases disposed of with full published opinions rose only from 101 in the 1953 term to 116 in the 1961 one, an increase of just 15 percent. In the most productive term of this entire period (1957), the Court decided only 149 cases with full opinions. As the *Harvard Law Review* pointed out, the caseload was ballooning mainly because of an explosion in the Miscellaneous

Docket, attributable primarily to petitions for certiorari in forma pauperis, the bulk of them from state prisoners. The Court declined to hear most such cases, never granting certiorari in more than 7.5 percent of those on the Miscellaneous Docket, and doing so in only 3.5 percent during the 1961 term. The vast increase in the number of cases disposed of (up from 1,293 in the 1953 term to 2,142 in the 1961 term) was largely accomplished through some form of summary disposition. While the justices' workload did not grow as much as their docket, an increase in the number of cases carried over to the next term, from 160 in 1953 to 428 in 1961, suggests they were having some difficulty keeping up with the higher caseload.[2]

In January 1962, reportedly because of the pressure of business, the justices skipped their annual visit to the Capitol to hear the president's State of the Union address. Stewart complained that a heavy caseload was depriving the Court of adequate time for reflective deliberation, and Harlan urged the legal profession not to burden it with frivolous requests for certiorari and expressed impatience with indigent litigants who were deluging the justices with in forma pauperis petitions. Professor Henry Hart pictured the Court as overburdened, claiming its members did not have enough time for collective deliberation and private study and that the poor quality of their opinions proved they were trying to resolve too many cases. Hart's Harvard Law School colleague Dean Erwin N. Griswold concurred, describing the Court's workload as "staggering."[3]

Judge Thurman Arnold of the Second Circuit dissented. Responding to Hart, he declared, "The plain and simple fact is that they [the justices] are not overworked." Douglas agreed with Arnold. In an April 8, 1960, speech at Cornell Law School, he called the idea that the Court was overworked a myth. Douglas noted that the appellate docket, which comprised about 90 percent of the meritorious cases the Supreme Court was asked to consider, had grown only from 857 in the 1938 term to 886 in 1958. The 116 signed opinions and per curiams (not including mere orders of dismissal, affirmance, etc.) the Court produced in 1958 was less than the total for any term between 1927 and 1948. Douglas also placed in perspective the recent increase in the number of weeks devoted to oral argument. During the 1938 term the Court had heard 296 hours of argument and still managed to adjourn by June 5. In the 1958 term it had heard only 220 hours, yet could not conclude its business until June 29. The reason so many cases were carried over from one term to the next, Douglas argued, was the Court's own rules, which resulted in months of delay while records of proceedings in the lower courts were printed. His statistics established, he claimed, that justices really had fewer oral arguments to hear, fewer opinions to write, and shorter weeks to work. "I do not recall," he said, "any time in my 20 years or more of service on the Court when we had more time for research, deliberation, debate, and meditation."[4]

Although providing impressive data to support his position, Douglas—who insisted that being a Supreme Court justice was a four-day-a-week job—overstated his case. For one thing he ignored the fact that justices did more than just decide cases. The most famous example was Warren's service as chair of the commission that investigated the assassination of President Kennedy. The Chief, aware that his colleagues did not consider such extrajudicial appointments to be in the best interests of the Court, tried to avoid this one. President Lyndon Johnson appealed to his sense of duty, however. Justices Clark, Harlan, and Brennan also took on responsibilities unrelated to deciding cases, but the concerns of their Committee on Space were as trivial as those of the Warren Commission were momentous; it had to ensure not only that each justice had sufficient office space, but also that their wives had a suitably furnished "ladies' dining room" and that the budget contained money to carpet the lawyers' lounge. Clark and Harlan also served with Frankfurter on a committee that Warren appointed in 1958 to study the effect of proposed habeas corpus legislation on the work of the Supreme Court. The Court as a whole had to devote considerable time to supervising the rest of the federal judiciary. In 1961 the conference considered proposed amendments to the Rules of Practice in Admiralty and Maritime Cases, and in 1962 and 1963 it discussed the changes in the Federal Rules of Civil Procedure approved by the Judicial Conference.[5]

Although the justices devoted some of their time to other responsibilities besides judging, they do not appear to have been overworked. Most of the cases they nominally considered received minimal attention. The Court rejected most of the petitions asking it to invoke its discretionary certiorari jurisdiction. Even Frankfurter thought the Court should grant about one in ten of these, but during Warren's first term it acted favorably on only 7.9 percent of such requests. For the 1961 term the figure fell to 7.5 percent, perhaps because, as both Harlan and Dean Griswold suggested, the Court's failure to articulate any consistent criteria for granting and denying cert encouraged lawyers to file futile petitions, hoping lightning would strike in their cases. Besides refusing to hear well over 90 percent of certiorari cases, the Court also disposed quite quickly of most of those within its appeal jurisdiction. Theoretically, it was obligated by statute to decide these, but in fact, as Douglas noted in a 1961 memorandum, "We treat them essentially the same as we treat certioraris, disposing of about 75 percent of them on the motion [to affirm the ruling below]." He objected to the Court's failure even to identify precedents justifying its summary dispositions, noting that during the Vinson era it had "settled into the practice of affirming or dismissing appeals without any citation to authorities."[6]

While giving minimal attention to most of the cases on the docket, the justices relied heavily on the recent graduates of America's top law schools who served them as clerks. The Chief had three of these, and most of the other justices had two, although three of those who were serving when Warren arrived (Douglas, Jackson, and Burton) employed only one. The clerks screened cert petitions and the jurisdictional statements in appeal cases, recommending to their justices which cases the Court should hear. According to Frankfurter, the clerks often discussed the cases among themselves, agreeing on common recommendations. Warren's clerks also had primary responsibility for screening in forma pauperis petitions, searching for the few in vast piles that had real merit. In theory each justice could call up any of these petitions, but in fact they rarely did so; with respect to them the Chief's clerks acted as the Supreme Court. In addition, to a considerable extent, the Court spoke through the clerks. During Vinson's tenure several justices relied on theirs to draft opinions, and by the end of Warren's chief justiceship, all but Douglas did. The extent to which members of the Court delegated responsibility for writing what appeared under their names varied. Warren himself would delineate what he wanted an opinion to say, either orally to the clerk or by dictating an outline to his secretary. He would then review the draft, editing and suggesting changes. Not being a legal scholar and having little interest in research, he tended to leave such matters to the clerk, along with the content of footnotes. Frankfurter was much more scholarly, but even some of his most notable opinions were drafted largely by clerks. As Bernard Schwartz pointed out, "The domain of the clerks was wide enough to give them tremendous influence." How much their views shaped the decisions of the Court became a matter of controversy. In 1957 William Rehnquist, a conservative who had worked for Jackson, charged in *U.S. News & World Report* that liberal clerks made their views the philosophy of the Warren Court. The following year, Senator John Stennis (D-Miss.) proposed that, because of their increasing influence, Supreme Court clerks be required to undergo Senate confirmation.[7]

The clerks were becoming increasingly influential at least in part because of changes in the nature of the Supreme Court and the way it operated. As chief justice, Warren took a number of steps to modernize and make more efficient what had been an old-fashioned and even quaint institution. For example, he replaced the pewter inkwells and goose-quill pens at counsel tables with pencils. The clerk, who was still making docket entries in longhand when Warren arrived, acquired a typewriter. In 1955 the Chief initiated a five-day workweek, moving conferences from Saturday to Friday and making up the lost time by persuading his colleagues to start Court sessions at 10:00 A.M. rather than noon. In 1958, at Clark's urging, Warren ended the tradition of announcing all decisions on Monday and began delivering them whenever the opinions were ready. Conferences, which for some time had been forums for the extended discussion of cases, became under Warren much more meetings in which each justice stated his position so that votes could be counted and opinions assigned. Those were then drafted largely by clerks, working in chambers that communicated through relatively formal letters between justices, most of which were also written by the clerks. Frankfurter, who preferred to deal with his colleagues in a much more personal way, whined about what he viewed as the need to "improve on the means of insuring due deliberation." He also complained about a loss of "collective interchange of views in reaching a collective judgment."[8]

Although the Court was working differently than it had under Warren's predecessors, outside the high-profile areas of race relations and subversive activities, there was no dramatic change in the kind of decisions it handed down. Most of the cases decided during the 1953–61 terms involved neither the sorts of issues that aroused popular passions during the 1950s nor the kind that would sweep the Warren Court into the vortex of cultural conflict and political controversy after 1962. Federal government civil litigation accounted for 36 percent of the total. About four in ten of those cases (15 percent of all decisions) reviewed administrative actions, the largest number of them by the National Labor Relations Board (NLRB) and the Interstate Commerce Commission (ICC). Federal taxation was at issue in 6.8 percent of the cases the Court decided. While only .11 percent arose out of direct enforcement of the Internal Security Act, direct enforcement of the Fair Labor Standards Act accounted for nearly ten times that many. Federal criminal cases generated 17.1 percent of the Court's decisions, but 4.5 percent stemmed from statutory construction issues and 3.9 percent from procedural ones. Only .9 percent involved search and seizure, and just .56 percent self-incrimination problems. State criminal cases, including habeas corpus actions by state prisoners, gave rise to just 7.3 percent of the Court's decisions, with censorship accounting for more than confessions and neither of those producing anywhere near as many as disputes over procedure and the admission of evidence. While dismissals of state employees, often the result of loyalty-security programs, generated .29 percent of the cases the Court decided, claims of intergovernmental tax immunity accounted for 1.1 percent.

The vast majority of decisions during Warren's first nine terms resolved relatively routine and noncontroversial matters. His Court handed down numerous rulings of great legal significance in fields of law that did not much interest the general public, such as immigration. A few cases in that area did produce some controversial rulings in cases implicating Cold War concerns. In *Galvan v. Press* (1954), for example, the Court refused to grant habeas corpus relief to an alien who was expelled for being a member of the Communist Party. Rejecting his contentions that the statute required proof of awareness that the CPUSA advocated the violent overthrow of the government and that it violated the Ex Post Facto, Bill of Attainder, and Due Process Clauses, Frankfurter exhibited his typical deference to Congress. In *Jay v. Boyd* (1955), however, he joined Warren, Black, and Douglas in dissent, as a badly divided Court held that the attorney general might refuse to suspend deportation of an alien for membership in the Communist Party (even though he met the requirements for suspension) because of undisclosed confidential information.[9]

Unlike *Galvan* and *Boyd,* many legally significant immigration decisions resolved obscure and rather technical issues unrelated to the Cold War. For example, in 1955 the Court decided two cases about the extent to which the Administrative Procedure Act applied to immigration proceedings and another that merely held an alien had failed to prove his contention that the attorney general had exerted undue influence over the board that refused to suspend his deportation order. Two 1956 rulings increased procedural protections for subjects of denaturalization proceedings.[10]

Admiralty produced even more legally significant decisions than did immigration and naturalization, but none that implicated national political controversies over civil liberties and civil rights. As the *Harvard Law Review* noted in 1954, more than perhaps any other field of federal law, "the complex of rules regulating maritime activities [were] a judicially molded structure." In this field, where Congress rarely tampered with doctrines the Supreme Court created, it handed down four important rulings during Warren's first term. One conceded that a state court had jurisdiction to order the sale of a tuna boat and divide the proceeds among its nine co-owners, and a second resolved a conflict between the federal Limited Liability Act of 1851 and a Louisiana "direct action" insurance statute. A pair of cases examined the rule that made the owner absolutely liable for injuries to seamen resulting from unseaworthy conditions on a vessel, holding it applicable to both a carpenter who came aboard to make repairs and a stevedore injured by defective equipment belonging to his employer. During the 1956 term the Court twice addressed procedural problems arising under the Limited Liability Act. The 1958 term produced an extremely complex decision holding that a federal court had jurisdiction to hear a personal injury action brought by a Spanish seaman against the Spanish owner of a vessel on which he was injured in Hoboken, New Jersey, but that the seaman had no right of recovery. That term the Court also ruled that federal maritime law, rather than state tort doctrines, determined whether a social guest could recover for injuries suffered on a ship, but that whether recovery could be had for the wrongful death of someone killed while working aboard a vessel in navigable waters depended on state law, and that admiralty practice did not permit a party to defend by setting up a claim arising out of an unrelated transaction, a holding strikingly at odds with the rule in ordinary civil actions. During the 1960 and 1961 terms, the Court sought to ensure that seaman who became disabled were adequately compensated by their employers, holding that the New York Statute of Frauds could not prevent a seaman from recovering on an oral contract that obligated his employer to indemnify him for the consequences of negligent medical care and that an employer could not have what he owed for the maintenance and care of an incapacitated sailor reduced by the amount of any wages the seaman had managed to earn. Other 1962 decisions held that workmen injured on vessels still under construction could recover under the federal Longshoremen's and Harbor Workers' Compensation Act, but that longshoremen overcome by noxious fumes during a freak grain-loading accident could not rely on the unseaworthiness doctrine, which would have made the shipowner absolutely liable for their injuries.[11]

Like admiralty, the federal tax laws generated many important but little-known decisions. Although Frankfurter and Jackson thought that "we only mess up tax law when we take a tax case," in seven of Warren's first nine terms the Court handed down at least one important ruling in this area. Many of these determined whether claimed income-tax deductions were valid. Generally the rulings went against the taxpayer. The Court held that fines imposed on trucking firms for violation of state maximum-weight laws were not deductible business expenses. While allowing deductions for salary and rent expenses incident to an illegal gambling enterprise in a state where there was no sharply defined policy proscribing acts remotely connected with gambling, it refused to permit liquor enterprises to deduct money they spent on publicity aimed at defeating proposed initiatives designed to prohibit or regulate sales of alcoholic beverages. The Court also held that expenditures for food and lodging while one was away from home undergoing medical treatment were not deductible, nor were comparable expenses and transportation costs incurred by construction workers whose jobs required them to work at a series of different locations. When retail corporations owned by the same shareholders merged into a management corporation that they also owned, the Court refused to let that company deduct their net-operating-loss carry-overs. Also held to be nondeductible were the losses incurred by a guarantor who paid the debts of an insolvent corporation.[12]

Besides passing judgment on whether the Internal Revenue Code authorized various claimed deductions, the Court also handed down important rulings on what moneys were subject to the income tax. It broadly defined gross income to include windfall gains from the recovery of "insider profits" under section 16(b) of the Securities Exchange Act and punitive damages for fraud and antitrust violations. The Court also ruled that both stock options and embezzled funds were taxable income. After holding that only "conversions of capital investments" constituted capital gains, it ruled that nonspeculative oil-production payments did not qualify and were taxable as ordinary income.[13]

The Warren Court underscored its distinctly progovernment orientation in income tax cases by holding that the Internal Revenue Service did not abuse its discretion when it retroactively revoked the Auto Club's tax-exempt status. It also interpreted the relevant statute of limitations in a way that allowed IRS to collect back taxes for the period during which the commissioner originally said the Auto Club was exempt. When other types of taxation were involved, the Court was more likely to rule for the taxpayer. For example, it held a documentary stamp tax inapplicable to two instruments used to effect a "private placement" of corporate securities. In estate tax cases it denied a deduction for a conditional bequest to charity and restrictively interpreted the marital deduction, but also ruled that the proceeds of irrevocably assigned life insurance policies did not have to be included in a decedent's gross estate.[14]

Although important to lawyers and estate planners, such rulings were of little interest to the general public. Nor were most of the Court's civil procedure and federal jurisdiction decisions. These involved questions such as whether particular kinds of judicial actions had sufficient finality to satisfy the requirements of 28 U.S.C. section 1291, under which only "final judgments" were appealable. The Court twice wrestled with the question of when the defendant in a civil suit was entitled to a jury trial, holding that in a diversity of citizenship case, this should be determined on the basis of federal rather than state procedural rules and taking the position that in cases involving both legal issues, for which a jury trial was constitutionally required, and equitable ones, for which it was not, the former should generally be tried first. The Court dealt also with a number of problems of jurisdiction and venue. It held, for example, that the ten-thousand-dollar jurisdictional sum requirement for diversity cases was satisfied when an injured worker had sought more than that amount but the administrative award an insurer sought to challenge in federal court was less. The Court clarified when a defendant should be granted a change of venue under section 1404(a) of the Judicial Code and held that by assuming control of the defense in a patent infringement suit, a manufacturer did not thereby waive venue. It also explained when a case should be heard by a three-judge district court. During its first nine terms the Warren Court rendered decisions on such difficult procedural issues as when the corporation should be realigned from defendant to plaintiff in a shareholders' derivative action, whether the statutory prohibition against federal courts staying state court proceedings applied to an action for injunctive relief brought by the United States government, and when individuals who believed their interests were inadequately represented by the parties in a case should be allowed to intervene.[15]

Like its civil procedure and federal jurisdictions decisions, the Court's numerous administrative law rulings often involved arcane issues of limited interest. *Greene v. McElroy* (1959), holding that no authorization existed for the procedures used by the Defense Department to revoke security clearances under its industrial security program, was a high-profile case in an area that concerned the general public. Far more typical, however, were decisions from the 1953 term that elaborated the standard of review to be employed by courts passing on draft board classification decisions, restricted the availability of the Declaratory Judgment Act as a means of obtaining immediate relief from administrative actions, and upheld the authority of the Federal Communications Commission to interpret the Criminal Code while rejecting its interpretation of the particular provision at issue in the case. The early Warren Court also held that the Administrative Procedure Act (APA) authorized the ICC to grant a shipping line a second 180-day temporary permit to operate while it completed action on its application for a permanent certificate of public convenience and necessity, that the Federal Trade Commission (FTC) could require a company to produce file copies of its reports to the U.S. Census Bureau, and that the Federal Power Commission (FPC) could not decide on the merits of a merger application when the merger was being challenged in pending litigation under the antitrust laws. The Supreme Court ruled repeatedly on the extent and nature of judicial review of administrative actions. In two cases during the 1955 term, the Court held that a determination by the ICC that the kinds of products carried by a trucking company were not "agricultural commodities" exempted from its jurisdiction was subject to judicial review and that any ruling of an administrative body falling within the definition of an "agency action" in the APA was a reviewable "final act."[16]

The Court devoted even more attention to statutory interpretation than to esoteric administrative law issues. For example, during Warren's first nine terms it handed down nine important decisions interpreting the Interstate Commerce Act and the Motor Carrier Act (which was absorbed into the ICA in 1957). One of these, *Boynton v. Virginia* (1960), attracted widespread attention because it overturned the trespassing conviction of an African American interstate-bus passenger who had been prosecuted after he refused to move from the "white" to the "colored" side of a terminal restaurant in Richmond, Virginia. The Court held that section 216(d) of the ICA, which prohibited an interstate motor carrier from "subject[ing]" a particular person . . . to any unjust discrimination" and section 203(a)(19), which extended that prohibition to services performed by "facilities . . . operated or controlled by" a carrier, gave him a legal right to remain at the white lunch counter, even though nothing in the record showed it was controlled by an interstate carrier.[17]

By far the most important of the Court's statutory interpretation decisions was *Monroe v. Pape* (1961), construing Title XVIII, section 1983, of the United States Code. Originally part of the Ku Klux Klan Act of 1871, section 1983 authorized civil suits against "every person who, under color of any statute, ordinance, regulation, custom or usage of any state or territory" deprived another of a right, privilege, or immunity secured by the Constitution or federal law. Relying on this old statute, an African American couple sued the City of Chicago and a number of its police officers, who, without a warrant, had invaded and searched their home in the early morning hours, called Mr. Monroe a "nigger" several times, and then hauled him off to the police station to be interrogated for ten hours without being taken before a magistrate or permitted to call his family or an attorney. The defendants argued section 1983 did not apply because the actions of the police violated the constitution and laws of Illinois, which afforded the plaintiffs a remedy, and consequently these actions had not been done "under color of law." Chicago also insisted it could not be held liable under section 1983 because a municipal corporation was not a "person." On the day after oral argument Frankfurter, who recognized that *Monroe* involved important aspects of state-federal relations and was "not an ordinary matter of statutory construction but closely akin to . . . constitutional adjudication," circulated a fifty-three-page memorandum, prepared by one of his clerks, Anthony Amsterdam, that supported the defendants' contentions. To Frankfurter's considerable annoyance, Warren had not read it by the time the justices discussed the case two days later. The Chief had glanced at the conclusions, however, and he made it clear he disagreed with them. Black and Stuart shared Frankfurter's reluctance to hold police liable under federal civil-rights statutes for actions that violated state law, but they concurred with those, including Douglas and Clark, who insisted that earlier cases, particularly *Screws v. United States* (1945), had already answered in the affirmative the question of whether such actions were done "under color of law." On the other hand, although there was considerable uncertainty among the justices as to whether municipal corporations should be considered persons, most of Frankfurter's colleagues seemed to agree with him that they should not be. The Court ruled against the Monroes on that issue, but, with Douglas writing the opinion, held they could sue the police under section 1983. Harlan and Stewart concurred, indicating that they were doing so only because they felt bound by precedent.[18]

Frankfurter dissented. As he predicted, *Monroe v. Pape* proved to be of "far-reaching" importance. The number of civil rights cases filed in federal courts rose from 296 in 1961 to 54,789 for the year ending September 30, 1992, when they accounted for nearly 24 percent of all civil filings. "The net effect of Monroe, and other important cases that have followed it," reports Charles Alan Wright, "is that the door to the federal court is now open to those who think they have been denied federally secured rights by persons acting under state law."[19]

Although of less legal significance than *Monroe v. Pape*, the statutory interpretation cases the Court decided in the exercise of its limited original jurisdiction were of tremendous economic importance. It resolved only twelve original jurisdiction cases during Warren's first nine terms, disposing of ten with memorandum orders, rather than full opinions, and hearing oral argument in only two. One of those, however, was *United States v. Louisiana* (1960), in which the issue was whether the oil and other natural resources under coastal waters in the Gulf of Mexico belonged to the federal government or the states. In 1947 the Vinson Court had rejected California's claim that it owned the three-mile strip immediately adjacent to its coast, and in 1950 it rendered similar rulings concerning the submerged lands in the Gulf of Mexico. Just before leaving office in 1953, President Truman issued an executive order setting aside all submerged lands of the continental shelf as a naval petroleum reserve. The 1952 Republican platform promised to return these lands to the states, and a month after becoming president, Eisenhower announced his support for a joint resolution, sponsored by Senator Spessard Holland (D-Fla.), to do this. Rather than simply setting the seaward boundary for each coastal state, however, Holland's Submerged Lands Act of 1953 purported not to prejudice any state's right to any boundary it claimed before entering the Union that Congress had confirmed. Alabama and Rhode Island tried to get the Supreme Court to declare the Submerged Lands Act unconstitutional, but the Court denied their motions for leave to file complaints, taking the position that Article 4, section 3, clause 2, of the Constitution gave Congress an unlimited power to dispose of property of any kind belonging to the United States. The federal government then sued Louisiana, seeking a declaration that it was entitled to exclusive possession of, and full dominion and power over, all lands, minerals, and other natural resources in the Gulf located more than three miles offshore. The Court broadened the suit to include Texas, Mississippi, Alabama, and Florida. Harlan wrote an opinion during the 1956 term that was never issued, and not until May 31, 1960, did the Court finally decide the case. Speaking through Harlan, it held that Louisiana, Mississippi, and Alabama had no rights in submerged lands lying more than three miles offshore, but that Texas controlled everything out to three marine leagues from her coast, because she had claimed that boundary as an independent republic and it was confirmed by the Annexation Resolution of 1845. In a separate opinion by Black, the Court, over Harlan's objections, held that Florida was entitled to control of a similar strip, because the state's 1868 constitution, which Congress had accepted in readmitting Florida to the Union during Reconstruction, recognized it.[20]

Besides determining who controlled oil-rich submerged lands, the early Warren Court also wrestled with an original jurisdiction case of enormous economic importance to the arid West. In 1952 Arizona filed suit against California, asking the Supreme Court to decide how much of the water from the Colorado River and its tributaries each state could use. Later Nevada, New Mexico, Utah, and the federal government were added as parties. The Court referred the case to a special master for the taking of evidence. After the first one, George Haight, died in 1955, Judge Simon Rifkind took on the assignment. The solicitor general considered this case "so difficult and important" that Rifkind deserved two thousand dollars for the work. He conducted a trial, which lasted from June 14, 1956, until August 28, 1958, taking oral or deposed testimony from 340 witnesses and reviewing thousands of exhibits. Even after Rifkind forwarded 433 pages of findings and conclusions and a recommended decree to the Court on January 16, 1961, the case still had to be briefed and argued twice. The justices debated extensively Douglas's contention that state rather than federal law governed the allocation of much of the water in dispute, and not until June 3, 1963, were they able to hand down a decision. The Court ruled that the Boulder Canyon Project Act had allocated 4.4 million of the first 7.5 million acre-feet of mainstream water to California, 2.8 million to Arizona, and 300,000 to Nevada, and that California and Arizona should share any surplus equally. The decision upheld the federal government's claims to some Colorado River water needed by Indian reservations and also approved settlement of a dispute between Arizona and New Mexico over the Gila River.[21]

Like the Colorado River case, many of the early Warren Court's constitutional decisions dealt with economic problems rather than civil rights or civil liberties. A number involved state regulation and taxation of interstate business activity. For example, during Warren's first term the Court used the "dormant" Commerce Clause to strike down both a Texas tax on a firm that processed natural gas for interstate shipment and a Virginia levy on the Railway Express Agency for the privilege of doing business within Virginia. Similarly, the justices employed the Due Process Clause of the Fourteenth Amendment to invalidate a Maryland requirement that a Delaware retailer collect a use tax on purchases by Maryland residents that they carried home or had delivered to them in Maryland. On the other hand, the Court held that the Due Process Clause did not prevent Nebraska from imposing an apportioned ad valorem tax on the flight equipment of a Texas-based airline. A Texas tax on premiums for insurance not purchased from a state-licensed agent failed due process review, but a new Virginia tax on Railway Express that measured what was owed by apportioned gross receipts passed muster.[22]

In *Bibb v. Navajo Freight Lines, Inc.* (1959), the Court employed the dormant Commerce Clause to invalidate an Illinois statute requiring trucks to use curved mudguards, rather than the straight variety acceptable in at least forty-five other states. The Chief expressed some reluctance to second-guess legislative safety decisions, but he disliked this law, and Frankfurter argued persuasively that it ought to fall because of the burden it placed on interstate commerce. Douglas's opinion for the Court reflected a tension that both of his colleagues seemed to feel between the desirability of deferring to state legislative judgments about highway safety and the need to ensure the free flow of commerce between states. In 1961 the Court again used the Commerce Clause to keep a state from burdening interstate economic activity, invalidating a law that barred from New Jersey courts those corporations that had not obtained certificates authorizing them to do business in the state. The following year, it utilized both the Commerce and Due Process Clauses to keep Pennsylvania from taxing railroad cars habitually operated in New Jersey.[23]

In cases brought under other constitutional provisions, the early Warren Court was less inclined to limit state authority over economic matters. In 1959 it held that taxing imported raw materials that were being stored temporarily before being used in manufacturing did not violate the Export-Import Clause. While holding that Arkansas could not tax equipment bought by a contractor working for the U.S. Navy under a contract that authorized it to act as an agent of the United States in making purchases, the Court rendered two decisions rejecting claims that intergovernmental immunity prevented Michigan communities from taxing property leased from the federal government, even though one of the taxed facilities was producing for the U.S. Army. It spurned a Full Faith and Credit Clause challenge to Arkansas's refusal to use Missouri's workers compensation laws to determine whether a Missouri resident injured while working for a Missouri subcontractor in Arkansas could sue his employer; the Court also rejected a similarly based challenge to Louisiana's application of its direct-action statute in a case brought by a Louisiana resident against an out-of-state insurance company, even though the laws of Massachusetts, where the insurance contract had been entered into, prohibited suing an insurer before establishing the liability of the insured. The early Warren Court did enforce the Full Faith and Credit Clause in *McGee v. International Life Insurance Company* (1957), but the effect of that decision was to require Texas to enforce a California judgment against a Texas insurance company that had sold a policy to a Californian by mail.[24]

Business interests scored a rare victory in *Western Union Telegraph Co. v. Pennsylvania* (1961), where the Court, relying heavily on full-faith-and-credit reasoning, held that in seizing unclaimed telegraphic money orders dispatched from Pennsylvania to destinations elsewhere, Pennsylvania was depriving Western Union of its property without due process. In *Morey v. Doud* (1957), the Court rendered a rare ruling striking down a state economic regulation under the Equal Protection Clause. The invalidated Illinois law imposed certain requirements on currency exchanges as conditions for doing business, but exempted issuers of Western Union, United States Post Office, and American Express money orders. The Court concluded that such a classification scheme, which treated differently entities identified by name rather than characteristics and resulted in differing treatment, was irrational and hence violated equal protection. Although arguing this position in conference, Black confessed to being "on the fence" because he did "not like to strike down state regulation of business."[25]

He and his colleagues manifested a similar reluctance to treat state regulations of private property as violations of the Takings Clause. In its first zoning decision, *Goldblatt v. Town of Hempstead* (1962), the Warren Court upheld an ordinance that prohibited a landowner from excavating below the waterline, thus effectively prohibiting continued use his island property as a sand and gravel quarry. It later ruled, however, that because noise and glare caused by low-level flights of airliners using a county airport had rendered adjacent property unusable for residential purposes, the county had taken an interest in that property for which it must pay just compensation. When the issue was not whether there had been a taking but whether the compensation that had been paid was adequate, the early Warren Court was somewhat inconsistent. It held that when the federal government took riverside real estate in order to build a dam, it had to compensate the holder of a flowage easement for its loss of its right to flood nearby land, but not for the power site value of its property.[26]

Like these Takings-Clause decisions, the Warren Court's separation-of-powers rulings, such as *Wiener v. United States* (1958) (limiting the president's removal power), attracted little attention at the time. Its labor law decisions sparked far more interest. While unions were economically and politically powerful, provisions of the Taft-Hartley Act of 1947 and the Landrum-Griffin Act of 1959 reflected widespread animosity toward them. The decisions of the Warren Court did not. As labor law expert Lee Modjeska notes, the Court "diverted the potential antiunion impact of . . . Taft-Hartley and Landrum-Griffin." Warren, who equated vigorous unions with economic freedom for workers, and his colleagues assigned paramount importance to and consistently supported employee organizational and representational rights. In *Brooks v.*

NLRB (1954), for example, they ruled against an employer who refused to bargain with a union, even though the union had been repudiated by a majority of the workers a week after they chose it as their bargaining agent. Although seemingly rather one-sided, the Warren Court's decisions implemented the basic theory underlying post-1930 American labor legislation: that government action was necessary to equalize the bargaining process by offsetting the inherent advantages of employers.[27]

Because the NLRB was generally more sympathetic to unions than were state courts, a holding that it had exclusive jurisdiction over a matter or that federal law had preempted state authority usually was a victory for labor. The early Warren Court rendered many such decisions. It took the position that states lacked jurisdiction over activity either protected or prohibited by the National Labor Relations Act (NLRA). Even when the NLRB had declined to act for budgetary or other discretionary reasons, states had no authority over matters potentially subject to the act. In *Guss v. Utah Labor Board* (1957), Warren declared that a state might not take jurisdiction over any matter entrusted to the NLRB unless the board formally ceded it pursuant to section 10(a) of the NLRA. Even if the act was silent, the Court might find that a state court lacked jurisdiction because Congress wanted the matter left uncontrolled. It did allow state courts to award contract and tort damages to employees who had been expelled from a union and subjected to harassment, which the NLRB could not do because these remedies would supplement rather than conflict with the board's actions. Usually, however, the early Warren Court construed the authority of the NLRB broadly and read federal legislation as preempting state authority.[28]

Its pro-union leanings produced decisions holding that employers might not prevent organizers from communicating with their company's workers or discriminate against employees who had gone on strike. The Court also required actual negotiation of matters deemed to be subjects of mandatory collective bargaining, condemning "dilatory and evasive tactics, take-it-or-leave-it strategies, and sham bargaining." It also upheld a provision of the Railway Labor Act authorizing union shop agreements. Unwilling to allow crippling blows to unions, the Court read restrictively provisions of the Taft-Hartley Act intended to outlaw the closed shop, and the justices undercut the efforts of authors of that law and Landrum-Griffin to prohibit secondary boycotts.[29]

The Warren Court highlighted its pro-union posture by repeatedly compelling management to accept arbitration. In *Textile Workers v. Lincoln Mills* (1957), it held that section 301 of the Taft-Hartley Act, whose constitutionality Douglas affirmed, had empowered the federal courts to enforce executory agreements to arbitrate grievances and to determine the rights of the parties on the basis of federal rather than state law. Adopting an industrial pluralist model of labor-management dispute resolution, the Court treated such agreements as the quid pro quo for employees' promises not to strike, even implying the existence of a no-strike pledge with respect to matters covered by arbitration provisions. The "Steelworkers Trilogy" of 1960 demonstrated the strength of the Court's commitment to arbitration, which it indicated should be ordered unless there was positive assurance that the arbitration clause in a contract did not cover the dispute in question. Arbitrators, rather than courts, should decide the merits of grievances, Douglas asserted, and judges should not second-guess their awards, of which courts should enforce all but the most outrageous. Some scholars have portrayed these cases as defeats for labor, but the future justice Goldberg, who argued them for the United Steelworkers, had no doubt that unions benefited from reliance on arbitrators.[30]

The Warren Court's commitment to protecting union interests wavered only when freedom of expression was threatened. Then it fractured along lines resembling those in the civil liberties cases spawned by McCarthyism. The Court held in 1956 that a provision of the Railway Labor Act authorizing union shop agreements did not violate the First Amendment, only to be confronted later in *International Association of Machinists v. Street* (1961) with complaints from union-shop employees that their dues were being used to promote political candidates and doctrines they opposed. During the 1959 term Black wrote an opinion, from which Frankfurter and Harlan dissented, accepting the contention that the workers' First Amendment rights had been violated, but because the effect of this decision was to declare a federal statute unconstitutional, and the Justice Department had not been asked participate, the Court set the case down for reargument. It was argued with *Lathrop v. Donohue* (1961), a First Amendment challenge to Wisconsin's integrated bar, brought by a lawyer who objected to having his mandatory bar dues used to oppose legislation he favored. Warren now changed his mind, and the Court splintered hopelessly. Assigned by the Chief to write opinions in both, Brennan sought to dispose of *Street* on purely statutory grounds and to decide *Lathrop* by ruling only on the constitutionality of the integrated bar as such, without reaching the issue of the use of bar dues to support political causes. Initially, he could not win the support of a majority of his colleagues for his approach, but after several months of discussion and numerous position changes, Warren, Clark, Whittaker, and Stewart accepted it. While avoiding the real issue in *Lathrop*, the Court disposed of *Street* by holding that the applicable provision of the Railway Labor Act permitted use of union dues only to support collective bargaining. That disposition of the case satisfied Warren because it left ultimate resolution of the issue of whether mandatory dues could be used for political purposes to Congress. It also avoided what he and Brennan feared most: rulings for lawyers and against unions on the constitutional issue. Black, Douglas, Frankfurter, and Harlan all objected because they wanted to rule on whether the use of compelled dues for political purposes violated the First Amendment; had they been given the opportunity, Black and Douglas would have held that it did, and their frequent foes would have ruled that it did not.[31]

Frankfurter and Harlan sometimes confronted the liberal activists in antitrust cases as well. Like the general public, the Warren Court as a whole was quite supportive of antitrust enforcement. During the 1953–65 terms the Supreme Court held for the Justice Department 92.5 percent of the time, going against it only once in Warren's first nine years as chief. Although ruling against the FTC twice in the 1957 term, the Court sided with the commission in every other case over thirteen years. Even private plaintiffs won antitrust cases 58.3 percent of the time. The Warren Court's opinions reflected a blend of modern economic theory and populism, with the latter particularly evident in its virtual per se prohibition of mergers between firms with substantial market shares. Perhaps its most socially and economically important accomplishment in the antitrust field was fashioning section 7 of the Clayton Act into a potent antimerger weapon. In *Brown Shoe Co. v. United States* (1962), the Warren Court held unlawful the acquisition of a retailer with at most 1.2 percent of national retail shoe sales by a manufacturer producing about 4 percent of the nation's footwear. It also exhibited hostility toward vertical price-fixing, construing narrowly legislation permitting some sellers operating in "fair trade" states to engage in resale price maintenance, and repeatedly rejected arguments for industry-wide exemptions from the antitrust laws.[32]

While the Warren Court consistently supported enforcement of those laws, some of its members were more devoted to them than others. The most committed was Warren, who voted against liability in only 9 of 101 cases decided during his chief justiceship. Determined to combat economic royalism and restore competition, Warren "disliked monopoly." The more he "saw of business and government," he said, "the more committed I became to the theory that the greatest danger to our private enterprise system is monopoly." The Chief cared little for the technical economic aspects of antitrust cases, such as efficiency analysis or market definition. He was animated instead by a populist determination to protect small producers and consumers from the effects of corporate size and power. Black, who matched his 89 percent proliability voting record during the 1953–65 terms, had a similar outlook. In a draft dissent to a denial of certiorari in a Robinson-Patman Act case, he fumed about judgments that made it difficult for "small, independent local compan[ies] to survive against the predatory practices of large and powerful interstate competitors." Brennan and Douglas were also vigorous champions of antitrust enforcement, voting for liability 86 and 85 percent of the time, respectively. Clark, the former head of the Justice Department's Antitrust Division, matched Brennan's 86 percent, and also wrote more opinions for the Court in this field than any other justice. All of Frankfurter's other frequent supporters in civil liberties cases except Reed (81 percent) were well below the average of 74 percent, however. Whittaker (43 percent), Minton (46 percent), Harlan (47 percent), and Jackson (50 percent) all voted against liability at least half of the time. By 1966 Harlan and Stewart (53 percent) established themselves as the Court's most frequent dissenters in antitrust cases. Frankfurter himself cast proliability votes only 52 percent of the time.[33]

Not surprisingly, he and Warren sometimes clashed over antitrust issues. One of these was whether the antitrust laws applied to professional sports. The Court had ruled in 1922 that these laws did not cover baseball. Although he was a passionate fan, Warren disliked this judicially created exemption for what to him was obviously a big business. Soon after the Chief joined the Court, Burton attacked the baseball exemption with a potent dissent in *Toolson v. New York Yankees* (1953). Although the majority followed the 1922 ruling, Warren insisted on adding to his per curiam opinion a sentence saying it was doing so only "so far as that decision determines that Congress had no intention of including the business of baseball within the scope of the federal antitrust laws." Two years later, the Court reversed dismissals, based on the baseball decisions, of antitrust actions against the International Boxing Club and others who promoted championship fights and against the Shubert brothers, who produced theatrical shows and booked them into theaters throughout the country. The Supreme Court held that the Sherman Act applied to both businesses. Warren, who argued forcefully in conference that the 1922 case "covers baseball only," wrote opinions declining to extend that sport's immunity. Frankfurter, contending the unique position of the national pastime was illogical, dissented sharply (although he did delete from his opinion a biting comment that "Judicial law ought not to be a baseball fan"). He and the chief justice clashed again over *Radovich v. National Football League* (1957), in which the Court held that the antitrust laws applied to professional football. Frankfurter managed to persuade Harlan and Brennan, who had joined the Court since *International Boxing Club,* that baseball's unique status made no sense, and Clark was initially sympathetic. He considered overruling *Toolson* unwise, however, and eventually Warren won him over. Clark wrote an opinion for a six-man majority that left elimination of the baseball anomaly to Congress.[34]

Frankfurter and Warren also disagreed concerning industrial giant E. I. du Pont de Nemours and Co. In the so-called Cellophane Case (the Justice Department's only antitrust loss before the early Warren Court), Reed wrote an opinion holding that, although du Pont produced almost 75 percent of U.S. cellophane, it had not violated section 2 of the Sherman Act, because the relevant market was "flexible packaging materials," of which cellophane accounted for about 20 percent. Frankfurter endorsed his rationale, insisting, "Needless disquisition of the difficult subject of single-firm monopoly should be avoided." Warren disagreed. In a powerful dissent, signed by Black and Douglas, he accused the majority of emasculating the Sherman Act. "Only actual competition can assure long-run enjoyment of the goals of a free economy," the Chief concluded.[35]

He and Frankfurter were on opposite sides again in what the press considered the most important antitrust case in years, the government's suit alleging du Pont's ownership of 23 percent of General Motors stock violated section 7 of the Clayton Act because it enabled du Pont to obtain an illegal preference over competitors in the sale of automotive fabrics and finishes to GM. Clark and Harlan had to recuse themselves, the former because the case had originated while he was at Justice and the latter because he had represented the du Pont brothers and their corporate interests in the litigation. In November 1956 their colleagues voted four to two to overturn a district court's dismissal of the case. Frankfurter passed. He subsequently sought to blunt the impact of this decision by urging Brennan to write an opinion that would avoid requiring du Pont to divest itself of its GM stock. Brennan, who also did not favor divestiture, held merely that the government had proved a violation of section 7. Even that stunned the business community. The Court remanded the case to the district judge to determine the appropriate relief. Burton dissented, backed by Frankfurter, who clashed with Warren over whether announcement of the decision should be withheld until after the stock market closed. The case returned to the Supreme Court in 1961. In conference Warren argued strongly that the district judge, who had not ordered du Pont to divest itself of its GM stock, should have done so. Douglas insisted divestiture was the norm. Black, Whittaker, and Brennan supported them.

After passing initially, Frankfurter, prompted by Stewart, launched into a lengthy argument that it was within the discretion of the district judge to decide whether to order divestiture, and unless he had "abused [that] discretion we have no business reversing it." Frankfurter's published dissent (which Stewart and Whittaker joined) mustered legal and policy argument's against the Court's conclusion that du Pont must completely divest itself of its GM stock. He continued to insist that the judgment of the district court should be affirmed because it had not abused its discretion.[36]

As *du Pont* demonstrated, the conflict between Frankfurter and the liberal-activist bloc involved more than just results. It pitted judges primarily concerned with outcomes against a jurist for whom process and procedure, although often used to rationalize conservative results, really mattered much more than they did to his adversaries. Personal tensions exacerbated conflicts over principle. The intensely intellectual Frankfurter had little in common with an avid outdoorsman and sports fan like the Chief, and Warren, a compromiser who liked to get people working together, felt equally uncomfortable with the argumentative academic. "All Frankfurter does is talk, talk, talk," Warren complained. "He drives you crazy." Frankfurter's propensity for writing separately in cases where he agreed with the decision also irritated Warren. As the Chief distanced himself from the professor's principles, the relationship between the two grew increasingly testy. During one heated conference session, Frankfurter screeched at Warren, "Be a judge, god damn it, be a judge!" The strife between them erupted in several heated public exchanges on the bench. After Frankfurter sharply attacked the majority opinion in an otherwise obscure criminal case on April 24, 1961, Warren exploded at him. Likening Frankfurter's comments to a prosecutor's closing argument to a jury, he admonished him that the purpose of delivering opinions orally was to inform the public, not to "degrade . . . this court." Although the friction between the two men lessened during Frankfurter's final term, the relationship was essentially a hostile one.[37]

Nor did Frankfurter get along with Warren's allies. Although he claimed to oppose quarreling, during one conference he accused Douglas of having ulterior motives for supporting some old railroad reorganization decisions. Agitated about "the continuous violent outbursts against me in conference by my Brother Frankfurter," Douglas concluded: "He's an ill man." One of Frankfurter's own clerks thought that by 1961 his fear and distrust of Black had reached something approaching paranoia. His bad relations with his activist colleagues extended even to the affable Brennan, who, as his former student, easily evoked the superciliousness colleagues found so irritating. Unlike Frankfurter, Harlan, who was sensitive to the feelings of others and scrupulously avoided displays of temper, could get along with his jurisprudential rivals. He became a close friend of Black, and Douglas considered his arrival "a fresh breeze into an atmosphere where too much suspicion and distrust prevailed."[38]

Although Harlan befriended colleagues Frankfurter offended and disliked, the two men became allies because they agreed about basic philosophy, and the divisions within the early Warren Court were based more on principle than personality. Frankfurter taught Harlan the arguments with which to answer Warren, Black, Douglas, and Brennan, all of whom were committed to what G. Edward White calls "substantive liberalism." They believed in using their judicial power to implement their humanitarian impulses, promote equality and social justice, and protect the victims of oppression. Such a jurisprudence, charged Judge Learned Hand, a highly respected member of the Second Circuit Court of Appeals, would inevitably turn the Supreme Court into a "third legislative chamber." In February 1958, Hand delivered a celebrated series of lectures at the Harvard Law School in which he spoke disparagingly of the Warren Court's judicial activism. His inspiration, as well as the source of most of his information about the Court's decisions, was Frankfurter, with whom he corresponded regularly, and who campaigned within the Court against departures from the sort of judicial self-restraint that Hand advocated. Warren regarded Frankfurter's espousal of that dogma as hypocritical, noting that when he empathized with one of the parties, he too made decisions on the basis of his human instincts. Harlan, however, found the Hand-Frankfurter creed appealing, in part because it generally produced results that accorded with his conservative political and social values, but also because he embraced the high regard for precedent, separation of powers, and federalism that Frankfurter championed. Shared values made them the consistent core of a shifting restraintist bloc. Assigning great importance to procedure and process, Harlan felt comfortable supporting someone who maintained "that the history of liberty in large measure reflects observance of procedural safeguards" and insisted the Court could not "dispense with the requirements of jurisdiction in order to do justice."[39]

Frankfurter complained that the chief justice seemed to view the Supreme Court as a modern court of chancery, which sat to rectify injustice and ensure fairness and equity in individual cases. He found particularly objectionable Warren's insistence on reviewing cases arising under various statutes protecting workers, such as the Fair Labor Standards Act and the Federal Employers Liability Act (FELA). In Frankfurter's opinion the Court had more important things to do with its time than decide the "frivolous" (mostly factual) issues they raised. Again and again he protested granting certiorari in "FELA-type cases." Unlike Black, who thought "Our rules should make appellate review easier," Frankfurter wanted to make it harder.[40]

He also wanted the Court to resolve those cases it did decide in a more deliberate manner. Noting they were freer than any other branch of government to pursue wisdom in the discharge of their responsibilities, Frankfurter contended, "We could readily improve on the means of insuring due deliberation." At the beginning of each term he circulated a memorandum containing suggestions (many of them repeated year after year) for accomplishing that objective. These included postponing the vote on doubtful cases beyond the Friday following oral argument to allow more time for investigation, consideration, and interchange; delaying the announcement of summary dispositions, the granting of certiorari petitions, and the noting of probable jurisdiction in appeal cases; and letting per curiam orders, even in "clear" cases, lie over for a week or so before handing them down. These changes were needed, Frankfurter insisted, because "undue expedition and premature final adjudication . . . lead to less than attainable excellence." "At the risk of wearisome repetition," and although aware that he might be "mak[ing] a nuisance of myself," he kept promoting them year after year.[41]

He also kept failing year after year to sell his ideas to his colleagues. In October 1957 Frankfurter suggested that the hostile reaction to some of the Court's decisions the previous spring had resulted from "massing" too many of them just before adjournment, and he proposed taking "some steps in the management of our business whereby we will avoid consideration of difficult and far reaching adjudications toward the end of the term." The Chief reacted negatively to what he viewed as criticism of his judicial administration. Contending that "none of the controversy which the Court found itself in" was due to massing big cases at the end of the term, he circulated data showing that large numbers of decisions came down in June because of delays in drafting and circulating opinions. Harlan alone supported Frankfurter, and the only change agreed to by 1961 was delaying for a week the publication of circulated per curiams.[42]

Unable even to persuade his colleagues to change the Court's internal procedures, Frankfurter was an overrated judge who left a very limited judicial legacy. Although an army of former clerks and friends celebrated ceaselessly his supposed greatness, as Michael Parrish notes, "There is now almost a universal consensus that Frankfurter the Justice was a failure." While his long-term influence on constitutional law was minimal, his position in the high-profile cases that attracted the attention of the general public was generally the winning one. This fact made Frankfurter in many respects the preeminent member of the early Warren Court. His views could not prevail without his vote, however, and thus his retirement changed the Court profoundly.[43]

Justice Whittaker's almost simultaneous exit enhanced the impact of Frankfurter's departure. A man whose abilities had never really measured up to the demands of the job, Whittaker regretted almost from the beginning accepting an appointment to the Supreme Court. Unsure of himself and inclined to vacillate, he could easily be won over by a forceful analytical argument. In pursuit of his vote, Frankfurter pressured him relentlessly, subjecting his limited intellect and fragile psyche to more pressure than they could bear. Whittaker's son considered this relentless pounding one of the major causes of the nervous breakdown that sent his father to Walter Reed Army Hospital on March 6, 1962. Ten days later, Warren wrote to President Kennedy, enclosing a certificate of permanent disability and informing him that Whittaker intended to retire on April 1. Whittaker was not really permanently disabled; about ten months later he would contact the chief justice, expressing a desire to return to work on the Eighth Circuit, and skeptical U.S. Army doctors would soon accept his contention that rest and "relief from the constant and arduous pressures of the work of the Supreme Court" had restored his health. Kennedy, never questioning Whittaker's right to a disability retirement, however, granted the purportedly disabled justice's request on March 28.[44]

Eight days later, Frankfurter, who had been in poor health through most of the 1961 term, collapsed in his chambers from a stroke. By April 25 he had suffered a second one. Warren wrote to the other justices that day about what he saw as "the critical condition of our docket," caused by Frankfurter's incapacitation and Whittaker's illness and retirement. The Chief thought "the Court must know at least what the likelihood is of his returning before adjournment." Apparently with the support of the other justices, Warren communicated the Court's need for this information to Frankfurter's physician. The doctor responded that his patient should not return to work during the present term but ought to be able to do so by the next one. The ailing justice, who received visitors ranging from Harlan to President Kennedy while he struggled to regain his strength, intended to do that. In early August he even began reading certiorari petitions. He also had himself driven to the homes of several friends, including Black. Physically unable to leave the car, he conversed cordially with his longtime rival in the back seat. His health remained poor, however. By August 16 Frankfurter's physician had concluded he would never be able to return to the bench and was advising him to retire. Convinced the president should be given time to name a replacement before Congress adjourned, the doctor and Frankfurter's friends had his secretary inform Warren that his retirement was imminent. Harlan and Dean Acheson took on the difficult task of persuading the justice, whose mental faculties had been somewhat impaired by the stroke, that he had to quit. Before the end of the month they had succeeded. On August 28, Frankfurter wrote to Kennedy, "I hereby retire at the close of this day from regular active service as an Associate Justice."[45]

Frankfurter also wrote that day to his former colleagues, making one last plea for the values he had championed. His letter called for "pertinacious pursuit of the processes of Reason in the disposition of the controversies that come before the Court," for "intellectual disinterestedness in the analysis of the factors involved in the issues that call for decision," and for "rigorous self-scrutiny" to achieve that objective. Although Black had vigorously opposed Frankfurter's principles for many years, he was now quite attentive to his fallen antagonist. In December 1964 he wrote to his old adversary that their differences, "which have been many," were only about means, rarely about "the ultimate end desired." Although true, that was beside the point, for to Frankfurter the methods the Court used to accomplish its objectives were crucial. He was not pleased with the men named to take his seat and Whittaker's, who seemed to him to lack the sort of professional background needed to understand their proper role on the Court. When Frankfurter died in February 1965, President Johnson joined all of the justices except Douglas at the small memorial service that marked his passing. Even Black wept when he heard of his old antagonist's death. It was really an anticlimax, though, for most of what Frankfurter represented had perished earlier when President Kennedy chose his successor.[46]

Although urged by Edwin Livingston, chairman of the National Council of Chief Justices, to nominate a state chief justice to replace Frankfurter, Kennedy filled both vacancies with lawyers from his own administration. Forty-one percent of the American people thought presidents should not routinely appoint members of their own party, but JFK does not appear to have seriously considered a Republican.[47]

To replace Whittaker Kennedy chose Deputy Attorney General Byron White. Born in Fort Collins, Colorado, on June 17, 1917, White was one of the most remarkably talented men in America. As an undergraduate at the University of Colorado, which he attended on an academic scholarship, he was elected to Phi Beta Kappa and finished first in his class in the College of Arts and Sciences—while also earning all-conference honors in baseball, basketball, and football. In the latter sport, "Whizzer" White was named an All-American in 1937 and finished second in the balloting for the Heisman Trophy. He played professionally for the Pittsburgh Pirates in 1938, leading the National Football League in rushing, while postponing for a term the start of a Rhodes scholarship at Oxford. During his studies in England, White met John Kennedy, whose father was then serving as U.S. ambassador to Great Britain. Because of the outbreak of war in Europe, the Rhodes scholar left Oxford in the fall of 1939. Enrolling at Yale Law School, he again starred in the classroom. White returned to the gridiron in 1940, playing that season and the next one for the Detroit Lions. He attended Yale in the spring of 1941 and also took law classes at Colorado in the summers of 1940 and 1941. After Pearl Harbor, White joined the navy. Rising to the rank of lieutenant commander, he served as an intelligence officer in the South Pacific, where he renewed his acquaintanceship with Kennedy. In January of 1946, he returned to Yale, graduating at the end of a special summer term. Although unsuccessful in obtaining a clerkship with Justice Douglas, White managed with his help to get one with the new chief justice, Fred Vinson, for the 1946–47 term. In August of 1947 he joined the Denver law firm of Newton, Davis, and Henry. White also became active in Democratic politics, and during the 1960 presidential campaign, he organized a statewide committee that helped deliver a majority of Colorado's votes to Kennedy at the party's national convention, then accepted an offer from JFK's brother and campaign manager, Robert, to head up a group of volunteers, Citizens for Kennedy. After the election Bobby Kennedy became attorney general and made White his deputy. During his brief tenure at Justice, White mobilized and directed a force of four hundred federal marshals that protected civil rights groups from mob violence during May 1961 rioting against Freedom Riders in Montgomery, Alabama.[48]

He was a man of action, and for that reason Attorney General Kennedy doubted that White would want to be a judge. When Whittaker informed the president of his intention to retire, Bobby recommended replacing him with Judge William H. Hastie of the Third Circuit, the first African American to sit on a federal appellate court. The attorney general consulted Warren and Douglas, however, and they objected strenuously to Hastie, complaining that he was not a liberal and would vote with Frankfurter. Numerous White House staffers also opposed Hastie, arguing that naming an African American at this time would look too political. The president himself seems to have worried that it might be too "early" for such a nomination, but what killed Hastie for JFK was an evaluation of his opinions by Assistant Attorney General Nicholas Katzenbach of the Office of Legal Counsel. He found them "pedestrian." Clark Clifford promoted Harvard professor Paul Freund, as did Ted Sorenson and McGeorge Bundy of the White House staff, but Warren and Douglas insisted he, too, would be just another vote for Frankfurter, and with the administration already full of Harvard men, Bobby believed it would be "damn hard to appoint another." Katzenbach, White, and his assistant Joseph Dolan assembled a list of potential nominees, as did Sorenson. Their suggestions included eminent state judges Roger Traynor of California, Stanley Fuld of New York, and Walter Schaefer of Illinois, federal judge Henry J. Friendly, Texas lawyer Leon Jaworski, Edward Levi of the University of Chicago, Secretary of Labor Arthur Goldberg, and even two-time Democratic presidential nominee Adlai Stevenson. The president eliminated Goldberg because he did not think he could spare him from the cabinet. White preferred a sitting judge, but when Dolan contacted Bernard Segal, chair of the ABA committee that evaluated nominees to the federal bench to get his opinion of those under consideration, he spoke highly of the deputy attorney general. According to Dennis Hutchinson, White was also the president's personal favorite. When Dolan and Robert Kennedy met with JFK to discuss those under consideration, they found him anxious to move quickly in order to thwart Senator Richard Russell (D-Ga.), who was pressuring the White House to appoint a conservative. Russell's desires may have kept Jaworski in the running for awhile, but after he made it clear he did not want to leave Texas, the president narrowed the choices to Hastie and White. Despite Bobby's doubts about whether his deputy would want to assume the cloistered role of a judge and his reluctance to lose him from the Justice Department, JFK settled on the former football star. At the president's request, the ABA conducted a perfunctory evaluation by conference call. JFK then telephoned White on March 30 to tell him he would be the nominee. His choice, who had told Bobby earlier that he was not enthusiastic about the idea, hesitated briefly before accepting. Although a reluctant nominee, Kennedy's choice was well received. The press joined the Colorado Bar Association in supporting White, and by April 16 he had been unanimously confirmed and taken his seat.[49]

The president told White House aide Arthur Schlesinger Jr. that in the future "I mean to appoint Freund, Arthur Goldberg, and Bill Hastie." He lived long enough to name only Goldberg to the Court. Born on August 8, 1908, to Jewish immigrants from Ukraine, Kennedy's second nominee had grown up in a working-class section of Chicago with a strong Socialist tradition. The death of his peddler father in 1916 left the family impoverished, but scholarships, financial assistance from six siblings, and hard work at a variety of jobs, ranging from Wrigley Field vendor to union hod carrier, enabled Goldberg to obtain an education. After graduating from high school at sixteen, he attended Crane Junior College and then Northwestern University, where he compiled the best academic record in the history of the law school, was elected editor-in-chief of the law review, and so impressed Dean John Henry Wigmore that Wigmore selected him to assist in revising his famed evidence treatise. Only twenty-one when he received his law degree in 1928, Goldberg had to challenge an Illinois bar rule that forbade the admission of anyone that young before he could begin practicing. Barred by anti-Semitism from Chicago's largest firms, he joined one that had been founded by wealthy German Jews, Pritzger and Pritzger. There, Goldberg handled mainly appeals to the Illinois Supreme Court. Having a small-producer outlook, he found unsatisfying a practice that consisted largely of defending bondholder committees and handling big businesses' bankruptcies. In 1933 he opened his own office, representing small businessmen and doing appellate work for other firms. Through involvement in the Civil Liberties Committee, Goldberg made contacts that enabled him to become a director of the Amalgamated Labor Bank.[50]

That led in turn to an association with Sidney Hillman, president of the Amalgamated Clothing Workers and one of America's preeminent labor leaders. Hillman convinced Goldberg that unions were essential to a sound and egalitarian market economy. In 1939 Van Bittner of the CIO retained him to defend the American Newspaper Guild's right to distribute leaflets during a strike against the Hearst press. Impressed by his work in that litigation, Bittner asked him to represent the Steel Workers Organizing Committee's western region, and as Goldberg demonstrated his ability, Bittner steered his way the legal business of an increasing number of CIO unions. World War II, during which Goldberg served in the OSS, developing intelligence sources within the European trade union movement, only temporarily interrupted his rise as a labor lawyer. In 1948, after a split within the CIO over Cold War issues forced out Communist Lee Pressman, he became general counsel of both the CIO and the United Steelworkers of America (USA). The death of Philip Murray, who headed both organizations, made him the real (although not official) leader of the USA, but disagreements with Walter Reuther, the new CIO president, precipitated Goldberg's departure from that organization's national office. The CIO kept Goldberg's law firm on retainer nevertheless. He negotiated its 1954 merger with the American Federation of Labor and emerged as a major power within the new labor federation.[51]

In response to hearings by the Senate's McClellan Committee, which revealed ties between unions and organized crime, Goldberg sought the expulsion of AFL-CIO affiliates infiltrated by gangsters. This effort brought him into contact with John Kennedy, a member of the committee, and Robert, who was its chief counsel. He collaborated with JFK on the Kennedy-Ives Labor Management Reporting and Disclosure Act and in writing legislation attacking union corruption. They also cooperated in eliminating some of the more obnoxious antilabor features of the Landrum-Griffin Bill. Goldberg was an old friend of Adlai Stevenson, but when Stevenson told him he was not going to enter the Democratic primaries in 1960, he supported Kennedy, becoming JFK's principal liaison to the labor movement. Goldberg hoped to become attorney general, but when Kennedy made it clear that post was going to his brother, he settled for secretary of labor.[52]

Although preferring the Justice Department because it seemed like a better stepping stone to the Supreme Court, Goldberg nevertheless did an excellent job at Labor, playing a key role in implementing administration policies to combat inflation. When Frankfurter retired, he was rewarded. The president again considered Freund. Bobby regarded him as too academic, however, and argued that if the seat were to go to a Harvard professor, it should be Solicitor General Archibald Cox, a man whose ideas he admired and whose work in the campaign he appreciated. Cox also took a job in the administration that Freund refused. Unlike Freund, however, he was not Jewish. Bobby maintained that if the president wanted to continue the tradition of having at least one Jew on the Court, he should give Frankfurter's seat to

Goldberg. JFK offered it to his secretary of labor but, reluctant to lose him as an adviser, apparently hoped he would decline. Goldberg, who had dreamed of the Supreme Court since law school, quickly accepted. The nomination drew praise not only from liberal senators Ralph Yarborough (D-Tex.) and Paul Douglas (D-Ill.), but also from conservative Barry Goldwater (R-Ariz.). Emanuel Celler (D-N.Y.), the Jewish liberal who chaired the House Judiciary Committee, called it "a splendid choice."[53]

Certainly, it was a choice that changed the character of the Warren Court more than had Kennedy's first appointment. Although White was politically well to the left of the erratically conservative Whittaker, his was the kind of liberalism that pervaded Bobby Kennedy's Justice Department. Its most conspicuous feature was egalitarianism, which manifested itself in a strong commitment to African American civil rights and would make him a supporter of legislative reapportionment as well. The Kennedy Justice Department was, however, extremely pragmatic, even in its approach to the struggle for racial justice in the South. Pragmatism characterized its approach to legal rules as well. Because he brought this pragmatic attitude to the Supreme Court, White was likely to resolve cases by looking for the result that would be the most "effective" and to eschew consistent identification with any ideologically defined bloc. Nor was he likely to identify with the antistatist individualism that increasingly characterized the civil liberties opinions of Black, Douglas, Warren, and Brennan. The Kennedy Justice Department fought against organized crime even more fiercely than it fought for black civil rights, and White's sympathies lay with law enforcement, rather than with those who claimed their rights had been violated by the police. As a product of the can-do Justice team, he viewed governmental power as a positive force for justice and social change, rather than as something to be feared. White consistently supported broad-ranging federal authority and vigorous institutions of national government. He did not, however, envision the judiciary as the principal engine of American democracy. He believed, in Allan Ides's words, "that once the legitimate opportunity to participate was established, national, state, and local political institutions should be the primary sources of policymaking." Although not a self-restraint zealot like Frankfurter, White "generally favored legislative solutions and judicial nonintervention." In a private conversation with a college classmate, he criticized the liberal activists for "thinking they have all the answers to social problems . . . and putting them into the Constitution."[54]

Goldberg was different. The two newcomers found themselves on opposite sides in nine of thirteen five-to-four decisions during their first term. Although Goldberg's opinions rarely articulated a conception of the Supreme Court's proper role, his voting pattern soon revealed a clear activist bent. He shared the hostility toward concentrated economic power that animated Warren, Black, and Douglas, and since his days at Northwestern he had believed law's proper function was to provide civil and political equality for all citizens and to eliminate privately organized violence. His years in the labor movement taught him that government could provide a necessary counterweight to corporate power, but he appreciated far better than White its capacity to oppress as well as protect. While still in law school, Goldberg developed a deep intellectual commitment to the protection of civil liberties. As a member of Chicago's

Civil Liberties Committee during the 1930s, he resisted efforts by the mayor's office to censor films and theatrical productions it considered politically offensive or obscene. Although a staunch anti-Communist who helped drive Stalinists from the CIO, Goldberg sought to protect those he considered innocent victims of Justice Department investigations and in 1954 opposed legislation that would have authorized the attorney general to tap the telephones of suspected subversives. During his first term on the Court he voted with a libertarian majority in all ten civil liberties cases decided by five-to-four votes.[55]

The appointment of Goldberg gave Warren and Black a reliable fifth vote, forging a solid liberal majority and opening the most militant chapter in the Court's defense of civil rights and civil liberties. Because of his presence, Harlan replaced Douglas as the Court's leading dissenter. Stewart and Clark took over second and third place. Goldberg aligned himself most frequently with Warren and Brennan and actually voted with White more often than he did with either Black or Douglas. Where the bulk of the Court's business was concerned, the two Kennedy appointees were part of a controlling centrist coalition led by the chief justice. But "when sides were chosen for a showdown," they generally parted company, Goldberg joining the activist bloc and White supporting the conservatives. In the thirty-five cases decided by five-to-four votes during the 1962–64 terms, White dissented 69 percent of the time, Goldberg only 23 percent.[56]

By putting Goldberg on the Court, Kennedy tipped the balance of power in favor of the substantive liberals, creating an activist majority on contentious constitutional issues and initiating a period during which judges transformed the Constitution in order to promote equality and social justice. Although Goldberg's appointment brought into existence what was in many respects a new Warren Court, his departure after only three years on the bench did not significantly alter the Court's innovative nature. The man to whom Lyndon Johnson gave Goldberg's seat was cut from the same cloth. Like him, Abe Fortas was Jewish and the American-born son of Eastern European immigrants. Although he had not grown up in poverty (his father ran a furniture factory and later owned a men's clothing and jewelry store), like his predecessor Fortas began life as an outsider, excluded by religion from the upper echelons of society in his heavily Protestant hometown of Memphis, Tennessee. He sold shoes, played in a band, and gave violin lessons. Like Goldberg, after finishing high school at sixteen, Fortas pursued higher education with the aid of scholarships. He graduated first in his class at tiny Southwestern College in Memphis, then moved on to Yale Law School, where he again starred in the classroom and became editor-in-chief of the *Law Journal.* One of his favorite professors was Douglas.[57]

Like his mentor, Fortas became a government lawyer. While Goldberg moved into the upper echelons of the labor movement through private practice, Fortas worked for a series of New Deal agencies. Although offered a position on the Yale faculty after graduation, he signed on with Jerome Frank at the Agricultural Adjustment Administration. Fortas later worked for Douglas on a study he was conducting for the newly formed Securities and Exchange Commission, while also teaching at Yale. When Douglas became chair of the SEC in 1937, he made Fortas the head of its Public Utilities

Division. In 1939 Fortas moved to the Interior Department, where he served Harold Ickes in several legal capacities before becoming undersecretary in 1942. Press criticism of Ickes's efforts to secure for Fortas an occupational draft deferment during World War II led him to apply for voluntary induction into the U.S. Navy, but he managed for physical reasons to avoid active duty, obtain an honorable discharge, and return to Interior.

In 1945, encouraged by Douglas, Fortas finally entered private practice. Rejecting a full professorship at Yale, he joined another former faculty member, Thurman Arnold, to form the Washington law firm eventually known as Arnold, Fortas, and Porter. It offered clients high-quality legal advice, aggressive litigation, and unusually effective representation before federal regulatory agencies for which members of the firm had once worked. The firm's list of clients soon included Lever Brothers, Federated Department Stores, ABC, Pan American Airways, and Coca Cola. Fortas joined numerous corporate boards of directors. Arnold, Fortas, and Porter became one of Washington's leading law firms, and he became both rich and famous.

Like Goldberg, Fortas was part of the post–World War II power elite. Starting on the margins of society, both men achieved economic success and political influence, partly because of extraordinary ability but also because of the way the New Deal had changed America. It fostered the development of big labor and the administrative state, and these in turn opened roads to wealth and power for men, such as Goldberg and Fortas, clever or lucky enough to seize the new opportunities the New Deal created. As a rich corporate lawyer Fortas no longer preached reform, and he accepted the assumptions of his wealthy clients about what was right. In other ways, however, he remained a New Dealer. Arnold, Fortas, and Porter became famous for its pro bono defense of liberals victimized by the federal loyalty-security program. Like Goldberg, Fortas was a staunch anti-Communist, and his firm would not represent members of the CPUSA, but it devoted up to half of its time to protecting civil liberties from McCarthyism. Fortas also supported civil rights and other social reforms. He was, as Laura Kalman writes, "preoccupied with social justice."

That preoccupation defined not only his political agenda but also his approach to law. Fortas's career mirrored the development of American legal liberalism. Like Fortas himself, this approach was a product of the New Deal. Young lawyers in the Roosevelt administration came to see law as merely a means to an end. Promoting the public good, they became convinced, justified manipulating legal rules and even tossing them aside. New Deal lawyers adopted operating principles that were relativistic, particularistic, and even cynical. It was easy for Fortas to embrace such attitudes, for his thinking had been conditioned by professors, such as Douglas and Arnold, who made Yale a center of Legal Realism during his time there as a student. Such thinking enabled him to support Roosevelt's Court-packing plan in the 1930s and just as readily to adopt novel constitutional doctrines in the 1960s. Both promised to promote liberal economic and social policies, and as Clark Clifford observed, what Fortas cared about most was "the liberal cause." He shared both Goldberg's priorities and his willingness to change the law to promote them. Indeed, Goldberg himself considered Fortas his jurisprudential clone.

The replacement of one with the other really mattered only to Lyndon Johnson. The president and his nominee had been social friends for a quarter of a century, and Fortas did several political favors for LBJ while he was at the Interior Department. In 1948, when Johnson won a senatorial primary by a microscopic margin, amid charges that he owed his victory to vote fraud, Fortas persuaded Justice Black to stay enforcement of a temporary injunction obtained by LBJ's defeated rival, Coke Stevenson, that would have prevented the Texas Democratic Party from placing Johnson's name on the ballot as its nominee. Over the next seventeen years, LBJ regularly sought Fortas's advice on troublesome questions. In 1960 Fortas supported Johnson for the Democratic presidential nomination, and when he was nominated for vice president, took charge of litigation that enabled LBJ to run simultaneously for that office and for reelection to the Senate. One of the first people Johnson called on for help after the Kennedy assassination made him president in November 1963 was Fortas. Later, he tried to make him attorney general, but his friend declined the appointment.

Fortas also resisted appointment to the seat on the Supreme Court that Johnson opened up for him by exploiting the opportunity created by the July 13, 1965, death of Ambassador to the United Nations Adlai Stevenson. The president initially offered Stevenson's job to John Kenneth Galbraith, but wanting no part of the thankless task of defending America's Vietnam policy, Galbraith recommended Goldberg, passing along rumors that he was restless on the Supreme Court. Johnson apparently saw an opportunity to create an opening for Fortas. He telephoned Goldberg to offer him the ambassadorship, appealing to his ego and sense of patriotism by telling him his negotiating skills were needed to resolve a UN funding crisis and end the conflict in Vietnam. Goldberg had no interest in leaving the Court, but he agreed to meet with Johnson at the White House to discuss the matter. So anxious was the president to create a spot for Fortas that his aide, Jack Valenti, asked Goldberg if he would be interested in heading the Department of Health, Education, and Welfare, and LBJ himself suggested that the UN might be a stepping stone to the vice presidency. Finally, as they were returning from Stevenson's funeral on Air Force One, after assurances that Johnson was committed to negotiating a peaceful solution to the Vietnam conflict and that as UN ambassador he would participate in all decision making leading to a settlement, Goldberg bowed to the president's wishes. He believed he was leaving the Court only temporarily, for in his mind LBJ's offer carried with it an implied promise to reappoint him once his UN mission was accomplished. Aware that Warren planned to retire before the next election and would likely recommend him as his successor, Goldberg planned to return as chief justice.[58]

Having eased him out of the way, Johnson telephoned Fortas to offer him Goldberg's seat. Fortas responded on July 19 with a handwritten note declining the appointment. Although he gave other reasons and claimed that his wife, Carol Agger, wanted him to take the job, her opposition appears in fact to have prompted his refusal. Their resistance was motivated mainly by money. A Supreme Court justice's salary fell far below what Fortas was earning in practice, and he and Agger had just purchased an expensive new home, which they were planning to remodel extensively. Fortas had judicial aspirations, but concern about the impact of his departure on

Arnold, Fortas, and Porter reinforced his wife's contention that this was not the time to fulfill them. Three days later, Attorney General Nicholas Katzenbach submitted to the president a list of other possible nominees for the Goldberg seat that consisted of lower court judges and prominent law professors (among them Freund and Soia Mentschikoff of the University of Chicago, whom Katzenbach considered "the only woman worthy of consideration for appointment to the Supreme Court"). Meanwhile, at Johnson's urging and prodded by his own ex-wife, Douglas sought to persuade his former student to accept the nomination. He "received a firm refusal." Johnson kept pressing. Finally, on July 28 he telephoned Fortas and asked him to come to the White House, where he was about to announce the commitment of an additional fifty thousand men to Vietnam. Just as the press conference was about to start, Johnson told Fortas that he was also going to announce his appointment to the Supreme Court; if the fifty thousand men could sacrifice for their country, so could he. As an additional inducement, LBJ apparently told Fortas he would make him chief justice if the opportunity ever arose. Johnson claimed later that the nominee acquiesced; Fortas insisted he never actually said yes. Whether he did or not, the appointment was announced. Kalman questions whether Fortas was as surprised by this turn of events as he and LBJ claimed, but certainly Carol Agger was. When Johnson called to ask the couple to dinner on his yacht, she refused to go. Agger would not talk to the president for two months. The nomination encountered less resistance in the Senate Judiciary Committee (where no member expressed opposition) than it had in the Fortas household. Johnson's nominee, confirmed on August 1, 1965, took his seat on October 4.[59]

Despite the drama and intrigue surrounding Fortas's nomination and Goldberg's resignation, this change in justices was not as important as Goldberg's appointment three years earlier. His nomination marked the end of one era in the history of the Warren Court and the beginning of another. During Warren's first nine terms as chief justice, the Court over which he presided was in many respects less his than Frankfurter's. With the exception of *Brown* and controversial civil liberties cases arising out of the internal-security hysteria inspired by the Cold War, its work was for the most part traditional, technical, and of minimal interest to most Americans. Although not completely conventional, the early Warren Court was far from radically innovative. Warren, Black, Douglas, and Brennan wanted it to promote liberal values and expand the rights of American citizenship, but so long as Frankfurter remained, the Court generally confined itself to the limited role that he considered proper, deferring both to Congress and to the states on issues likely to produce significant institutional conflict. For nine terms activists repeatedly found themselves protesting decisions that valued process over substance. The reason was not Frankfurter's leadership (for he was incapable of leading others), but rather the fact that his jurisprudence promoted a cautious conservatism appealing to a majority of his colleagues, and, for a long time, to most Americans as well. By 1962, though, the Eisenhower era was over. The president and Congress remained cautious, but the country was growing restless. A liberal tide was rising in the land. Had the Court continued to adhere to Frankfurter's jurisprudence, it would have observed this development from the beach. Goldberg, however, lacked his predecessor's reluctance to involve the judiciary in the business of reform. So did Fortas. The liberal surge would eventually sweep along even former Frankfurter allies, such as Stewart and Clark, carrying them to positions he would never have accepted. But the substantive liberals needed only five votes. Once Goldberg took his seat, they had them. The Warren Court changed direction and began a relentless march down the road Frankfurter had blocked.

5

THE MOST IMPORTANT ISSUE

Nothing made the metamorphosis of the Warren Court more obvious than its reapportionment decisions. Nor did anything demonstrate more dramatically the Court's abandonment of judicial restraint in favor of the active promotion of liberal reform. Frankfurter's last battle was over reapportionment—and it was a losing fight. Some of his most cherished principles went down to defeat in *Baker v. Carr* (1962), characterized by Warren as "the most important case of my tenure on the Court." What made *Baker* crucial was that by agreeing to resolve a dispute over legislative apportionment, the Court accepted responsibility for correcting flaws in the political process that prevented true implementation of the will of the people. While Frankfurter thought of democracy in procedural terms, equating it with decision making by politically accountable institutions, Warren paid more attention to results. He realized that representative institutions could fairly define and enforce the rights of citizens only if those institutions were "responsible to all the people." Believing "devoutly that . . . ours is a government of *all* the people, by *all* the people, and for *all* the people," the chief justice became convinced the Supreme Court must square government's performance with that egalitarian ideal. In *Baker* and subsequent cases, he led an unprecedented judicial foray into political territory. These reapportionment decisions converted a simplistic popular conception of political equality into a rule of constitutional law, in the process advancing the reintroduction of political culture into legal thought that Morton Horwitz considers one of the Warren Court's principal achievements. There was, however, an inseparable link between political and social equality. Judicial activism to democratize the electoral process differed only in degree from judicial activism to reform American society. After *Baker* few internal brakes restricted the Court's promotion of humanitarian causes. Reapportionment began the Warren Court's romance with "legal liberalism."[1]

Legalists, like the chief justice, were convinced that most of the flaws in American society could be corrected through legal means. Reform seemed likely to occur, however, only if actively promoted by the judiciary. Numerous structural impediments combined to thwart those who sought to achieve change through the politically accountable institutions on which Frankfurter insisted Americans should rely. Within the electorate a swing toward reform had begun at least as early as November 1958, when the Democratic Party swept to victory in the midterm elections. For eight years after John Kennedy captured the presidency in 1960, liberals controlled the executive branch of the federal government as well. Yet not until after Lyndon Johnson's landslide victory in 1964 did they secure the enactment of legislation designed to end racial injustice and eradicate poverty.[2]

The problems that legislation addressed existed in 1961. Kennedy considered them the most difficult domestic challenges confronting his administration. Racial tensions plagued not only the South, but also the North and West, where suburbs, inhabited mainly by middle-class whites, were exploding. Between 1950 and 1960 the suburban population grew by 46 percent to 60 million, equaling that of central cities. Meanwhile, African Americans, who were moving into the North and West from the South in huge numbers, crowded into poverty-stricken urban ghettos. Economic as well as physical boundaries separated decaying city neighborhoods from the suburbs. Between 1961 and 1965 the United States experienced remarkable economic growth, with the inflation-adjusted gross national product rising 4.5 percent annually. Yet, according to the Council of Economic Advisors, 20 percent of American families lived in poverty. Only about 5 percent of the expanding national income went to the poorest one-fifth of the population. Economic conditions were especially bad in urban slums, the rural South, and Appalachia. Recurrent unemployment and job and wage discrimination forced disproportionate numbers of African Americans, as well as other ethnic minorities and women, to the lowest rungs on the economic ladder.[3]

Despite their national political dominance, liberals could not mobilize government to correct these flaws in American society. One reason was that supposedly representative governmental institutions often poorly represented majority sentiment. Southern states barred most African Americans from voting. As late as 1964 only 32 percent of voting-age blacks were registered in Louisiana, 19 percent in Alabama, and 6 percent in Mississippi. The segregationist and generally conservative whites southern states sent to Congress exercised a disproportionate amount of power in the House and Senate. Rules governing the latter allowed a minority to block legislation with a filibuster, unless two-thirds of their colleagues voted to silence them. In addition, both houses awarded committee chairmanships on the basis of seniority. Because the South was essentially a one-party region, in most parts of which only Democrats were ever elected, it returned incumbents term after term, allowing them to accumulate the years of service that were the keys to power on Capitol Hill. Southern conservatives, such as James Eastland (D-Miss.), chair of the Senate Judiciary Committee, and Howard Smith (D-Va.), head of the powerful House Rules Committee, routinely exploited their positions to bury liberal legislation. The disproportionate power exercised by southerners was one facet of a larger problem. Throughout the country the "safe" constituencies whose senators and congressmen could accumulate sufficient seniority to become committee chairs were mostly rural or small town in nature. Although the country was predominantly urban and suburban, in the Eighty-seventh Congress (1962–63), nine House committee chairs came from rural areas and six from small towns, versus only five from metropolitan areas and one from a lesser city. Predictably, during his first two years in office, Kennedy obtained enactment of little liberal legislation, and Congress weakened the few measures he did manage to pass. He dared not even propose a civil rights law.[4]

Malapportionment magnified the disproportionate power of conservative small towns and rural areas. In the late nineteenth century Congress enacted decennial reapportionment statutes, which set standards for the states that were designed to ensure that House districts would be compact, contiguous, and, as nearly as practicable, equal in population. After 1929, however, it left them free to construct their districts as they chose. By 1962 rural areas had twenty-seven more House seats than their population warranted, while central cities had seven fewer and suburbs twenty less. In Maryland one Congressman represented a rural district with a population of 236,216, while another represented the 634,864 residents of suburban Baltimore County. Reapportionment required by the 1960 census (most of it in states that gained or lost House seats) improved this situation somewhat, but even after that process was completed the total population of the twenty most populous congressional districts (13,941,475) was more than three times that of the twenty least populous (4,500,061).[5]

State legislatures were even more inequitably apportioned than Congress. By 1960 voters living in the most populous urban and suburban districts had less than one-half the representation of those residing in the least populous rural ones. The principal causes of this unequal representation were legislative failure to adjust the allocation of seats to accommodate population shifts and restrictive constitutional provisions, such as those allocating a minimum or maximum number of seats to political subdivisions. In California one state senator spoke for the 6,038,771 residents of Los Angeles County, while another represented the 14,196 inhabitants of mountainous Mono, Inyo, and Alpine counties. As of 1962, only six states had legislatures apportioned in such a way that it took at least 40 percent of the state's population to elect a majority in both houses. Only twenty states had even one house representing as much as 40 percent of the electorate. In thirteen, one-third or less of the population could control both chambers.[6]

Such malapportionment debilitated legislatures. Increasingly, they found themselves ignored by frustrated city dwellers and suburbanites, who sought help from Washington instead. Incapable of acting, state legislatures often abdicated general legislative responsibilities to local governments, thus exacerbating rather than resolving conflicts between cities and their suburbs. Angry urbanites, electing only 25 percent of state legislators but paying 90 percent of state taxes, saw much of the revenue generated in metropolitan areas spent on small towns and farmers. In Tennessee the twenty-five most overrepresented counties received 57.9 percent more state aid than they would have received had it been allocated on a per capita basis. New York City had 46 percent of its state's population, but obtained only 38 percent of the funds distributed to local governments. Overrepresentation of rural areas made state legislatures resistant to liberal policies, especially on race. Because of malapportionment, Tennessee adopted a resolution condemning *Brown* and Maryland added to a public accommodations act exemptions for twelve rural counties. Malapportioned state legislatures also resisted proposals to allocate congressional seats on a more equitable basis.[7]

Although malapportionment distorted the output of republican governments, often keeping them from reflecting the views and serving the needs of their citizens, the political process could not readily correct this flaw in its own operation. In the late nineteenth century, with shifts in population distribution making the elimination of some legislative positions inevitable if representation continued to be based on population, a number of states altered their constitutions to allocate seats on other bases. The rationales they offered for doing so reflected nativist hostility toward the immigrants then streaming into the cities. Even in states that theoretically continued to require population equality, legislative lawlessness often denied metropolitan areas the control their growing size warranted. By 1961 a minimum of seventeen states had at least one house of their legislatures that was invalidly constituted because legislators had failed to comply with provisions of the state constitution requiring periodic reapportionment. Sitting members were unwilling to reallocate seats from lightly populated regions to rapidly growing ones because doing so would deprive some of them of jobs, or at least force them to run against other incumbents. Where reapportionment did occur, it was often merely token and did not satisfy constitutional equal-population requirements. In some states, initiative and referendum could be used to bypass balky legislatures, but proposals to base representation on population did not always pass, and even when they did, legislators could enact laws that rendered them largely ineffective.[8]

Because prospects for obtaining reapportionment through the political process were bleak, those seeking change turned to the judiciary. The refusal of legislatures to enhance the representation of growing cities first became widespread in the years between 1890 and 1910, producing a corresponding flurry of apportionment litigation in state courts. While asserting jurisdiction in reapportionment cases, those courts failed to afford effective relief. When annulling reapportionment statutes that did not comply with state constitutions, they typically revived the preceding ones. Since these were likely to be old and even less favorable to the interests of the challengers, such suits declined significantly after 1910.[9]

Those upset about inequitable apportionment schemes turned to the federal courts, but they fared no better there. A Chicago man contended he should not have to pay income tax because the national government's inaction in the face of the Illinois legislature's failure to reapportion itself between 1901 and 1930 constituted dereliction of its duty under the clause in Article 4, section 4, of the Constitution guaranteeing each state a republican form of government. He had his suit dismissed by a district court; he also lost in the Seventh Circuit and the Supreme Court. In 1932 the high tribunal ruled in *Wood v. Broom* that the compactness, contiguity, and equality of population requirements of a 1911 congressional apportionment act were no longer in effect. It declined to decide whether the issue was a nonjusticiable political question.[10]

Under the so-called political question doctrine, the Court had long treated certain issues as inherently political, and hence best decided by the political branches of the government. That doctrine was a product of *Luther v. Borden*, an 1849 case in which Chief Justice Taney declined, in order to resolve a civil trespass suit, to determine which of two competing groups was the legitimate government of Rhode Island.

The plaintiff sought to invoke the Republican Government Clause, so Taney's ruling consigned responsibility for enforcing that constitutional guarantee to the elected branches of the government. The political question doctrine seemingly doomed attacks on state apportionment schemes.[11]

It defeated one in *Colgrove v. Green* (1946). In that case a Northwestern University political science professor and others attacked Illinois's scheme for apportioning congressional seats, claiming it violated numerous constitutional guarantees, as well as the law unsuccessfully invoked in *Wood*. Frankfurter, speaking also for Reed and Burton, used that precedent to brush aside the plaintiffs' statutory argument. He then declared that what Colgrove was asking the Court to do was "beyond its competence." The Constitution gave Congress the power to correct the evils about which they were complaining, Frankfurter asserted; the Time, Place, and Manner Clause of Article 1, section 4, authorized it to alter state regulations governing House elections. Congressional apportionment was highly political, and "Courts ought not to enter this political thicket." Black dissented for himself, Douglas, and Murphy. Insisting that state legislation that produced glaringly unequal representation violated the Equal Protection Clause, he also disputed the applicability of the political question doctrine. As Black saw it, the petitioners had been denied a right guaranteed by the Constitution, and it had "always been the rule that where a federally protected right has been invaded, the federal courts will provide the remedy." Although concurring in the decision and agreeing with Frankfurter that courts should not adjudicate disputes of this type, Wiley Rutledge thought precedent supported Black's position that the judiciary possessed the power to grant relief in such cases. Thus, only three of seven justices supported Frankfurter's contention that congressional apportionment was a nonjusticiable political question. Nevertheless, *Colgrove* quickly became an obstacle to suits challenging both congressional districting and malapportionment of state legislatures.[12]

Frankfurter's 1960 opinion in *Gomillion v. Lightfoot* undercut somewhat his position that judges should avoid this "political thicket." *Gomillion* was a challenge to a redrawing of the boundaries of Tuskegee, Alabama, that removed from the city all but four or five of its African American voters, while eliminating not a single white one. The fact that this maneuver converted a once-square municipality into "an uncouth twenty-eight sided figure" made the racial motivation behind the redistricting blatantly obvious, and speaking for a unanimous Court, Frankfurter held that it violated the Fifteenth Amendment. In order to reach that conclusion, however, he had to dispose of the contention that *Colgrove* precluded any suit challenging the constitutionality of electoral districts. Frankfurter insisted this case was different because it involved a violation of the Fifteenth Amendment arising out of affirmative action to take away the right to vote for racial reasons, not just to dilute someone's vote. The plaintiffs, however, invoked the Fourteenth Amendment as well as the Fifteenth, and Whittaker, despite his colleague's efforts to persuade him otherwise, insisted this decision should rest on the Equal Protection Clause. If it could, then challenges to electoral districts based on that provision rather than the Guarantee Clause presumably raised no political questions that were nonjusticiable.[13]

To Frankfurter's dismay, the Warren Court took that position in *Baker v. Carr,* a challenge to a Tennessee apportionment statute. Tennessee's constitution actually required, subject to some minor qualifications, that members of both houses of the general assembly be distributed among counties on the basis of the number of qualified voters residing in each. The apportionment statute passed by the general assembly in 1901 did not fulfill this requirement, however, and for the next sixty years the legislature declined to reapportion itself at all. Because of changes in the size and distribution of Tennessee's population, by the 1950s the most populous senatorial district had 131,000 inhabitants, the least populous only 26,204. Voters had no way to rectify this situation, because the state's constitution did not provide for initiative or referendum, and amendments had to be passed by the legislature or adopted by a convention whose agenda the legislature defined. Unable to effect change through the political process, disgruntled Tennesseans filed suit in a Davidson County chancery court. It ruled in their favor, but the Tennessee Supreme Court reversed. A broad coalition, representing the state's largest metropolitan counties, then turned to the federal judiciary, only to have its suit dismissed by a three-judge district court that invoked the political question doctrine.[14]

Seeking to have that decision reversed by the Supreme Court, the coalition enlisted an influential ally: the Department of Justice. The solicitor general's office requested a copy of the transcript, and in the waning months of the Eisenhower administration, Lee Rankin authorized preparation of an amicus curiae brief. Despite lobbying by Tennessee Republicans, the Justice Department remained publicly noncommittal about the case until after the 1960 election. In 1958 Kennedy had vigorously condemned discrimination against city dwellers in the apportionment of state legislatures, and the new attorney general, his brother, Robert, was a college classmate and close friend of Anthony Lewis, author of a *Harvard Law Review* article advocating judicial intervention to redress this outrageous situation. After Tennessee Democrats lobbied Bobby, as well as Byron White and the new solicitor general, Archibald Cox, Cox reaffirmed his predecessor's decision.[15]

He did not expect to win the case, however. Only the minimum four justices voted to hear it. Warren, who as governor of California had opposed reapportionment of that state's legislature, joined Black, Douglas, and Brennan. The Chief now believed that his earlier position was "just wrong" and that judicial deference to legislators who had no incentive to surrender the excessive power that malapportionment gave them made no sense. At the conference following oral argument, on April 20, 1961, he endorsed the solicitor general's contention that the district court should be reversed. Predictably, Frankfurter opposed him, delivering a vigorous four and one-half hour lecture in which he defended *Colgrove* and supported his position by pulling down case reports from the bookshelves and reading from them. Harlan found his arguments persuasive, and Clark also supported him, but Black (who eventually walked out on Frankfurter), Douglas, and Brennan, supported the chief justice. Whittaker apparently became convinced that when confronted with clear violations of constitutional rights, courts had not only the power but the duty to do something about them. Hence, he agreed with the liberals about jurisdiction. Because he did not think *Colgrove* should be rejected by a bare majority, however, Whittaker voted with Frankfurter. Stewart, too, was inclined to follow precedent, but he was, according to Douglas, "not at rest on the issue," and when the time came to vote, he passed. On April 28, at Stewart's urging, the Court agreed to put the case down for reargument in October.[16]

The reargument was unexciting and far less significant than the debate already raging among the justices themselves. Frankfurter was lobbying hard. After the April conference he warned Stewart about the grave implications of accepting jurisdiction in this case. Doing so, he predicted, would stimulate litigation by doctrinaire liberals that would inevitably bring the Court into conflict with political forces. On the eve of the reargument, Frankfurter went to work on Whittaker, endeavoring to convince him that the legislature's failure to comply with the Tennessee Constitution was a matter of state law that should not concern the Supreme Court. One day after the reargument, saying he found it necessary "to state in comprehensive detail the problems involved" in a case that had "far-reaching implications for the well-being of the Court," Frankfurter circulated a sixty-page memorandum to his colleagues. Drafted by his clerk, Anthony Amsterdam, during the 1960 term, it argued that holding *Baker* justiciable would be inconsistent with a uniform course of decisions whose "roots run deep in the Court's adjudicatory history." *Colgrove* and its progeny reflected the need to avoid federal judicial involvement in matters traditionally left to state legislative policymaking, the difficulty of devising judicial standards for determining the proper allocation of political power, and problems of finding appropriate modes of relief. "The present case involves all the elements that have made the Guarantee Clause cases non-justiciable. It is, in effect," wrote Frankfurter, "a Guarantee Clause claim masqueraded under a different label." Cases involving the disfranchisement of African Americans were not inconsistent with his position, he insisted, for with respect to them "the controlling command of the Supreme Law is plain and unequivocal." Here it was not. The Court was being asked to choose among competing bases of representation and to reject one—representation based partly on local geographical division—in favor of another—representation proportionate to population—on the ground that the former, although long and widely used, was so unreasonable as to violate the Equal Protection Clause. Frankfurter sought to play on Stewart's belief that nothing in the Fourteenth Amendment required what Black referred to as the "approximately fair" distribution of votes. "To find such a conception in the broad and unspecific guarantee of equal protection would be a work of making a constitution, not interpreting one," Frankfurter insisted.[17]

Acting as his whip, Harlan solicited the votes of Whittaker and Stewart, which he was sure would be "determinative of the outcome." This case, he told them, was the most important to come before the Court since his appointment; it was comparable in significance to *Brown*. If the Court invalidated state apportionment at the urging of a Democratic administration, it would appear to be doing so because of the political backgrounds and ideologies of its members. Harlan implored Whittaker and

Stewart to stay out of a "political thicket," commending to them the "wise restraint" that had in the past "characterized the court's handling of emotionally-charged popular causes."[18]

Despite intensive lobbying, he and his mentor failed to get Stewart's vote. At the October 13 conference, Frankfurter observed that even principles fundamental to society were not always judicially enforceable and argued that asserting jurisdiction would be fraught with consequences "dangerous to our social system." Harlan argued emotionally that states were entitled to decide for themselves how to constitute organs of their governments, without supervision by the federal judiciary. Even if malapportionment was justiciable, he did not regard it as a denial of equal protection. Clark also supported Frankfurter, pointing out how often in the past the Court had avoided this problem. "Even if there was jurisdiction, I wouldn't exercise it," he said. Whittaker, although still not convinced that the Court lacked power or jurisdiction, also continued to vote with Frankfurter. Arrayed against them were Warren, Black, Douglas, and Brennan. The Chief contended that this case presented a clear violation of equal protection. There was no need to say that state apportionment schemes had to afford absolute equality, he argued; all the Court had to do was find this one arbitrary and capricious, remand the case, and leave the form of the decree to the district court. Black commended Frankfurter for making "a good case for a weak cause," but insisted he had been right in his *Colgrove* dissent. Brennan, who circulated to his colleagues a chart that showed the disparities between Tennessee electoral districts could not be explained on any rational basis, also urged reversal. Douglas, who thought *Gomillion* justified judicial intervention, argued that the "Equal Protection clause [was] not designed just for Negroes" and that the difficulty of resolving the malapportionment problem "can't deter us from doing our job." The last to speak was Stewart. He concluded that this case did not involve a political question and that the district court had jurisdiction to decide it. Stewart also stated, however, that he was not yet prepared to say whether that court could frame appropriate relief. Furthermore, he considered unconstitutional only apportionment systems that were arbitrary and capricious; a "state doesn't have to justify every departure from one man one vote."[19]

Regarding Stewart as weakly committed, Warren contemplated cementing his support by having him write the opinion. Douglas objected to that idea, however, and after discussing the matter with Black, the Chief assigned it to Brennan, "on the theory," as Douglas put it, "that if anyone could convince Stewart, Brennan was the one." A superb judicial tactician, skilled at supplying rationales for decisions Warren wanted and building coalitions that would support them, Brennan was the perfect choice. Although the four liberal activists would have preferred to reach the merits and hold Tennessee's apportionment law unconstitutional, he realized Stewart would not go beyond the jurisdictional issue. Brennan wrote an opinion that stopped "with the holding that the complaint states a justiciable cause of action of a denial of equal protection of the laws." Stewart found his draft entirely satisfactory, even after Brennan made some changes suggested by Douglas. Although Harlan asked him not to cast "the decisive, and . . . fateful vote in this case" before reading a dissent he was preparing,

Stewart stuck with Brennan. To no one's surprise, Frankfurter also circulated as a dissent a slightly revised version of the Amsterdam memorandum. Clark initially found it "unanswerable except by ukase." At Frankfurter's suggestion, he set out to prepare something on the failure of the plaintiffs to exhaust other remedies, only to conclude after checking into the record that there was no practical way for the people of Tennessee to achieve reapportionment "except through the Federal courts." Having come to that conclusion, Clark joined the majority. He wanted to reach the merits, so there were now five votes for the broader decision the activist bloc really wanted. Brennan had made a commitment to Stewart, however, and Warren agreed with him that the majority opinion should not be changed unless Stewart agreed. He would not. Brennan, who earlier had talked Stewart out of saying in a separate opinion that he agreed with Harlan on the merits, now persuaded Clark to style his separate opinion a concurrence, omitting the words "dissenting in part."[20]

Thus, Brennan was able to speak for a six-to-two majority (Whittaker having retired by the time the decision came down). He began by declaring that this dispute was within the subject-matter jurisdiction of the federal courts and that the plaintiffs, as Tennessee voters, had standing to challenge the apportionment of their legislature. Then he took up the decisive issue of justiciability. The mere fact that a suit sought the protection of a political right did not mean it presented a nonjusticiable political question, Brennan insisted. Nor was *Colgrove v. Green* determinative, for this was an equal protection case, not a Guarantee Clause claim. Brennan analyzed the political question doctrine at length; he identified one or more of several elements that he thought distinguished each case in which the doctrine had been applied. None of these, all of which related to the separation of powers, was present here. While suits based on the Guarantee Clause did pose nonjusticiable political questions, not all disputes concerning matters of state governmental organization did so. As proof of that, Brennan pointed to *Gomillion v. Lightfoot.* The complaint's allegations of a denial of equal protection presented "a justiciable cause of action upon which appellants are entitled to a trial and a decision." Furthermore, the right they were asserting was "within the reach of judicial protection under the Fourteenth Amendment."[21]

Brennan announced that Douglas and Stewart joined his opinion, but both of them filed concurrences, as did Clark. Douglas devoted most of his to arguing that, since the judiciary had long protected the right to vote in federal and state elections, this claim was obviously justiciable. He also endorsed Clark's contention that if the plaintiffs could prove their allegations, they were entitled to relief. For his part, Clark echoed Brennan on the question of justiciability, but he objected to his failure to rule on the merits of the plaintiffs claim. Analyzing in depth what he called the state's "crazy quilt" of electoral districts, Clark maintained that no one had "come up with any rational basis for Tennessee's apportionment statute." Hence, it violated the Equal Protection Clause. He would oppose Supreme Court intervention in such a delicate field if there were any other relief available to the people of Tennessee, Clark said, but there was no practical way for them to correct this invidious discrimination. While he was not prepared to say precisely what remedy the federal judiciary should order, he was sure it could fashion an effective decree. Unlike Clark, Stewart emphasized that the Court was ruling only on justiciability, standing, and whether the plaintiffs had stated a claim that could entitle them to relief. It was not, he asserted, deciding what the remedy should be if they won. The Court had not determined whether a state could weight the vote of one county or district more heavily than that of another, and, "Contrary to the suggestion of my brother Harlan, [it] does not say or imply that 'state legislatures must be so structured as to reflect with approximate equality the voice of every voter.'"[22]

Harlan's dissent claimed the majority was doing precisely that. Furthermore, he contended, the Court failed to identify any recognizable constitutional claim asserted by the plaintiffs. The Equal Protection Clause did not demand rigid equality; it required only that any asymmetry be rational. The Tennessee legislature's decision to retain an old allocation of legislative seats in order to maintain governmental stability and promote geographic and demographic balance was within the area the Fourteenth Amendment left to its judgment. Harlan viewed this as a case about the right of a state to choose the legislative structure best suited to its own needs. Unlike Brennan, whose opinion rested on the assumption that the individual was the privileged unit of social action, Harlan's overriding commitment was to federalism and the diversity of local cultures it sanctioned. For him, the fact that the plaintiffs were "unable to obtain political redress of their asserted grievances" did not justify federal judicial intervention in state affairs. The Supreme Court was not "the last refuge for the correction of all inequality or injustice." Preserving the respect on which its authority depended required the "wise exercise of self-restraint."[23]

That was, of course, the gospel according to Frankfurter. In his own dissent the ailing apostle of self-restraint excoriated the Court for disregarding a long course of prior decisions that had established that some controversies simply did not lend themselves to judicial resolution. Like Brennan, Frankfurter reviewed the kinds of disputes the Court had previously placed in this category, but unlike his former student, he concluded that the political question doctrine applied to *Baker*. The Tennessee case had all of the elements that made Guarantee Clause cases nonjusticiable. Fundamentally, the dispute was over an allocation of political power that benefited some groups and disadvantaged others. The plaintiffs' complaint was simply "that Tennessee has adopted a basis of representation with which they are dissatisfied." The one they wanted it to use was not employed in most states. Representation by local geographical division was old and still widespread. By asserting that the Equal Protection Clause required replacing this system with representation proportionate to population, the plaintiffs were seeking to have the Supreme Court decide between competing theories of government. They were raising the sort of political question federal courts were unsuited to resolve and should not attempt to adjudicate.[24]

The *Washington Post* called Frankfurter's dissent a "*tourdeforce*" that far outshone Justice Brennan's "pallid and technical" opinion. Writing in the rival *Washington Evening Star,* William S. White praised both dissenters for "ably and memorably" opposing the rewriting of the Constitution by a Supreme Court guilty of meddling in politics. Frankfurter's former clerk, Alexander Bickel, protested that the Court was "not a fit body to take over from political institutions the necessarily pragmatic business" of apportionment. They spoke for a minority. *Baker v. Carr* was highly popular. President Kennedy promptly endorsed it. So did many Tennessee politicians. Only one of the state's congressmen publicly opposed the decision, while Senator Estes Kefauver, a Democrat, joined Representative Howard Baker, a Republican, in commending it. Tennessee Republican leaders were pleased with a ruling they expected to increase GOP strength in the state, and even rural politicians, whose interests were directly threatened, reacted calmly.[25]

Then, in December 1962, the General Assembly of the States, a group of legislators affiliated with the Council of State Governments, proposed that state legislatures ask Congress to call a convention to consider three constitutional amendments. One would deprive the federal judiciary, including the Supreme Court, of jurisdiction in all cases relating to the apportionment of state legislatures. The others would permit two-thirds of the states to propose a constitutional amendment (thus bypassing Congress in the amending process) and create a "Court of the Union," composed of the chief justices of the state supreme courts, empowered to review decisions of the U.S. Supreme Court in cases involving rights reserved to the states and to the people. Adding fuel to the movement for amendments that *Baker v. Carr* had sparked was southern animosity toward *Brown* and anger over recent rulings on prayer and Bible reading in the public schools, obscenity, and criminal procedure. Concerned about what they viewed as an attack on the Court, Brennan, Goldberg, and Warren spoke out publicly during the spring of 1963. The Chief feared creating a Court of the Union would change "the character of our national institutions and . . . [impinge] upon the Supremacy Clause." Upset that the ABA was not opposing the idea, he chided the legal profession for ignoring the proposed amendments and called on lawyers to serve as "watchmen for the Constitution." Prominent St. Louis attorney Arthur Freund launched a one-man campaign against them, which eventually enlisted the backing of some prominent newspapers. A May Gallup Poll disclosed that 86 percent of Americans opposed the Court of the Union idea, and House Judiciary Committee hearings the following spring demonstrated opposition to overturing the prayer and Bible-reading decisions. By May 1964, although fifteen legislatures had adopted one or more of the proposed amendments, the political attack on *Baker v. Carr* had clearly lost momentum.[26]

What that decision would ultimately mean for the American political system was uncertain, however, for Brennan had set forth no criteria for determining whether a given legislative apportionment satisfied the Equal Protection Clause. *Gray v. Sanders* (1963) suggested what the standard might be. In that case the Court heard a challenge to a version of Georgia's "county unit" system used in primary elections, under which the candidate for nomination to a statewide office who obtained the highest popular vote in a county received two votes for each representative that county had in the lower house of the general assembly. To be nominated for governor or U.S. senator someone had to get a majority of the county unit vote, for any other office a plurality. Because of legislative malapportionment, rural Echols County, the state's least populous with 1,876 residents, cast two votes, while urban Fulton County (Atlanta), its most populous with 556,326 inhabitants, got just six. An Echols County resident's vote had ninety-nine times the weight of one cast in Fulton County. Although the Court had turned aside four previous challenges to the county unit system, it held that this arrangement violated the Equal Protection Clause. Only Harlan dissented, and the now-retired Frankfurter was worried enough about his vote that he invited his clerks over for lunch and some heavy-handed lobbying.[27]

The Court found it easier to invalidate Georgia's county unit system than to suggest a possible remedy that would be constitutional. Bobby Kennedy had to confront that issue, for the attorney general customarily argued one case personally in the Supreme Court, and he chose *Gray v. Sanders*. On Cox's advice, Kennedy avoided taking the position that all votes must be given equal weight. So had the district court, which declared unconstitutional both the statute in effect when the case was filed and a more complex one enacted while it was pending, but held Georgia could still use weighted voting if the resulting disparity between counties was no greater than that between the largest and smallest states in presidential elections. Its Electoral College analogy impressed Harlan. Speaking for the Court, Douglas rejected it as inapposite. "The conception of political equality . . . can mean only one thing," he wrote, "one person, one vote." Only Douglas and Warren originally voted to make that the standard, but six other justices eventually joined them. While agreeing that all votes within a given constituency must count the same, Stewart and Clark emphasized that *Gray* involved statewide elections, not the apportionment of legislative seats. "We do not deal here with the basic ground rules implementing Baker v. Carr," they stressed.[28]

Before confronting that issue, the Court held in *Wesberry v. Sanders* (1964) that Georgia's congressional districts were unconstitutional because they failed to satisfy the one-person, one-vote standard. The Atlanta area had one representative for 823,680 inhabitants, while another district's congressperson represented a population of only 272,154. Everyone but Harlan considered that unconstitutional. As Stewart pointed out in conference, however, they were "hitting Congress where it lives —their jobs are involved." Stewart successfully urged his colleagues to "go slow." Rather than holding that Georgia had violated the Equal Protection Clause, as Clark (prompted by a clerk) argued in a separate opinion that it should, the majority based its decision on Article 1, section 2, which provides that representatives shall be chosen "by the people of the several States." Pointing out that states originally elected all of their congressmen at large, thus giving every citizen equal representation, Black argued for the majority that the Framers could not have intended to allow them to engage in vote-diluting discrimination by dividing themselves into districts. He was mangling history, and neither the plaintiffs, the defendants, nor the solicitor general had relied on Article 1, section 2. But unlike a decision based on the Equal Protection Clause, Black's approach left open the possibility that Congress could authorize congressional districts of unequal size. At the same time, by requiring "that as nearly as is practicable one man's vote in a congressional election is . . . worth as much as another's," Black's opinion provided yet another endorsement of the one-person, one-vote principle.[29]

Three months later, on June 15, 1964, the Court, going further than most would have predicted, held in *Reynolds v. Sims* that this precept also governed the apportionment of both houses of state legislatures. *Reynolds* was one of six challenges to state legislative apportionment, initiated by liberals from both political parties, decided on the same day. Solicitor General Cox coordinated the efforts of all of the plaintiffs and served as their theoretician, yet he was unwilling to sign a brief that endorsed the one-person, one-vote formula. Cox was very much a process liberal, politically committed to reapportionment but convinced the Court should exercise self-restraint and avoid getting too far in front of the country on the issue. In August 1963 he recommended the government argue that while one house of each state legislature must be apportioned on the basis of population, deviations from population equality were permissible in the second. Although the president and the attorney general wanted the government to endorse one person, one vote, Cox would go no further than arguing that apportionments that created irrational inequalities in representation or subordinated the representation of people to that of political subdivisions to such a degree as to create gross inequalities in the weights of different citizens' votes or give control to small minorities violated the Equal Protection Clause. The solicitor general stopped short of saying that the Constitution required allocating all seats in both houses of a legislature in proportion to population. So did most members of the Court. Led by Warren they agreed at a November 22, 1963, conference that only one chamber must comply with the equality of population principle.[30]

Believing that because he had taken an antireapportionment stand as governor of California, he must now squarely face the issue from a judicial viewpoint, the Chief gave himself the job of writing opinions embodying the Court's decision. He found himself unable to do so. Warren started out believing states should be allowed to have an upper chamber that, like California's, represented political subdivisions with differing populations. He soon changed his mind. Bursting into Brennan's chambers to share his revelation, he persuaded him—and later Black, Douglas, and Goldberg —that he was right.[31]

The opinion that Warren wrote in *Reynolds* rejected the idea that legislators spoke for interest groups rather than individuals. They represented "people not trees or acres," he declared. "Legislators are elected by voters, not farms or cities or economic interests." Alabama, whose apportionment was at issue in *Reynolds*, had a constitution that should have provided representation of individuals; it specified that senatorial districts were to be as nearly equal in population as possible and that representatives were to be apportioned among counties on the basis of population, except that each county was guaranteed a minimum of one. The constitution even required the legislature to reapportion itself after every census to ensure that these requirements were met. It had not done so since 1901, however. The result, as Warren pointed out, was like giving citizens living in some parts of the state two, five, or even ten times as many votes as those living in others. Full and effective participation by all citizens in Alabama's government required that each have an equally effective voice in the selection of members of the legislature. "In a society ostensibly grounded on representative government, it would seem reasonable that a majority of the people of a state could elect a majority of that State's legislators," Warren asserted. Like invidious discrimination on the basis of race or economic status, diluting the weight of some people's votes because of where they lived subjected them to impermissible unequal treatment. Thus, it violated their rights under the Fourteenth Amendment. According to Warren, "an individual's right to vote for state legislators is unconstitutionally impaired when its weight is in a substantial fashion diluted when compared with votes of citizens living in other parts of the State." Of course, such dilution occurred in voting for members of the U.S. Senate, where all states, regardless of population, had two seats. Warren dismissed the so-called federal analogy as "inapposite and irrelevant to state legislative districting schemes," arguing that the Framers of the Constitution had not intended its representation scheme to establish a model for the states.[32]

"We hold," he announced, "that, as a basic constitutional standard, the Equal Protection Clause requires that the seats in both houses of a bicameral state legislature must be apportioned on a population basis." Warren acknowledged the "practical impossibility" of arranging legislative districts so that each had an identical number of residents or voters. While "mathematical exactness" was not necessary, however, "the Equal Protection Clause requires that a state make an honest and good faith effort to construct districts, in both houses of its legislature, as nearly of equal population as is practicable." New York, Maryland, Virginia, and Delaware had all failed to do that. Consequently, in companion cases to *Reynolds,* the Court held that the apportionment of their legislatures also violated the Equal Protection Clause.[33]

Stewart did not agree with Warren about all of those states. The reason was that he that simply did not accept the one-person, one-vote standard, which he characterized as unsupported by precedent and "woefully wrong." Stewart accused the Chief of converting a particular political philosophy into a constitutional rule that deprived states of all opportunity for enlightened and progressive innovation in designing their own democratic institutions. In his view, the Equal Protection Clause required only that the apportionment of a legislature be rational in light of the state's own characteristics and needs and that it not permit the systematic frustration of the will of the majority. New York's plan passed that test, so he dissented in its case. Those of Alabama, Virginia and Delaware did not, so Stewart concurred in theirs. He wanted Maryland's case remanded for a finding as to whether its apportionment scheme prevented effective majority rule.[34]

Clark joined his dissent in the New York case and filed a concurring opinion in *Reynolds.* Like Stewart, he objected to the one-person, one-vote rule, the articulation of which he regarded as unnecessary to strike down Alabama's apportionment scheme. All that needed to be said about this "crazy quilt" was that it constituted invidious discrimination, Clark believed. Furthermore, "If one house . . . meets the population standard, representation in the other house might include some departure from it so as to take into account, on a rational basis, other factors in order to afford some representation to the various elements of the state."[35]

Both Stewart and Clark also dissented in *Lucas v. Forty-Fourth General Assembly of the State of Colorado,* the sixth and most difficult of the apportionment cases decided that day. The districts for Colorado's lower house had equal populations. Although its sentorial districts did not, and 36 percent of the voters could elect a majority of the senate, rural areas did not exercise disproportionate control. Indeed, the Denver, Pueblo, and Colorado Springs metropolitan areas actually chose a majority of the senators. The state was divided into four geographic regions, whose topography and economies differed drastically. The distribution of seats in the senate ensured that the interests of all would be represented. Furthermore, Colorado voters overwhelmingly approved it in a 1962 popular referendum, in which a majority in every county voted for this arrangement over an alternative that would have provided population equality in both houses. Cox supported the *Lucas* plaintiffs only because Bobby Kennedy pressured him into doing so, and the Court divided five-to-four in conference. White, who was from Colorado, joined eventual dissenters Clark, Stewart, and Harlan. To him, giving a minority of the people control of the senate seemed like an equal protection problem, but Colorado's apportionment was no Alabama "crazy quilt" and its bicameralism made possible the representation of different interests in the two houses. From Stewart's perspective, that meant the apportionment bore a rational relationship to the attainment of a legitimate objective and, consequently, that it was constitutional. Clark agreed with him about that and argued that courts should not interfere where voters had the opportunity to alter their state's apportionment through initiative or referendum. Warren regarded the availability of those alternatives as without constitutional significance, and he managed to persuade White that determining what the Constitution guaranteed could not be left to the voters "A citizen's constitutional rights can hardly be infringed simply because a majority of the people choose that it be," he wrote in his opinion.[36]

Warren's view contrasted sharply with that of Harlan, who dissented in all six cases. To him, the "'population' principle" was just political ideology; "it is demonstrable that the Fourteenth Amendment does not impose this political tenet on the States or authorize this Court to do so," Harlan contended. The Equal Protection Clause was never intended to inhibit states from using any democratic method they chose to apportion their legislatures. The language of the Fourteenth Amendment, the understanding of its drafters and ratifiers, and the political practices of the states at the time the amendment was adopted all pointed to that conclusion. Announcing his dissent orally from the bench, Harlan accused the majority of amending the Constitution and radically altering the relationship between the states and the national government. Warren was concerned about the harm that not holding malapportionment unconstitutional would do to the individual; "To the extent that a citizen's right to vote is debased, he is that much less a citizen," he wrote. Harlan, in contrast, worried about what judicial intervention would do to the federal system; "These decisions . . . cut deeply into the fabric of our federalism," he wrote. Warren insisted that "the denial of constitutionally protected rights demands judicial protection." Harlan responded that these decisions "support . . . a current mistaken view that every major social ill in this country can find its cure in some constitutional 'principle,' and that this Court should 'take the lead' in promoting reform when other branches of the government fail to act." He insisted the Supreme Court was not "a general haven for reform movements."[37]

Although "a fitting epilogue" to Frankfurter's *Baker v. Carr* dissent, Harlan's opinion also exposed the fundamental flaw in Frankfurter's jurisprudence. As Professor Carl Auerbach pointed out, there was something incongruous about proponents of judicial self-limitation criticizing the Court for "helping to make majority rule effective." The argument for self-restraint, after all, rested on the assumption that judges were reviewing actions of legislators elected and removable by a majority of the people.[38]

Undeterred by Harlan's criticism, on June 22 the Court issued a series of per curiam opinions remanding for resolution consistent with *Reynolds* apportionment cases from Florida, Ohio, Illinois, Michigan, Idaho, Iowa, Connecticut, Oklahoma, and Washington. Within a week it had rendered decisions directly affecting the composition of one-third of the country's state legislatures.[39]

Despite what the *New York Times* characterized as their "unexpected . . . breadth and scope," the reapportionment rulings evoked a generally favorable reaction. Harvard's Paul Freund called their governing principle "simplistic," but the University of Chicago's Philip Kurland (a former Frankfurter clerk and frequent critic of the Warren Court) noted, "Most students of the Court—even the 'nonactivists'—are inclined to approbation." The *Washington Post* praised the Court for going "a long way toward establishing democracy in America." It had, political scientist Robert McCloskey observed, "activated a latent consensus in American opinion." A July Gallup Poll found Americans favoring the reapportionment rulings 47 percent to 30 percent.[40]

Although academics and the general public liked the reapportionment decisions, many politicians did not. The day they were announced, Representative August E. Johnsen (R-Mich.) fired off a letter to House Judiciary Committee chairman Emanuel Celler (D-N.Y.), demanding immediate action on a constitutional amendment authorizing one house of a state legislature to be apportioned on some basis other than population. In early July Judiciary's ranking Republican, William M. McCulloch (R-Ohio), proposed a similar amendment that would allow deviation from equal population in one chamber with the approval of the voters. Celler, who supported the reapportionment decisions, bottled up anti-Court measures in his committee, but William Tuck (D-Va.) managed with the assistance of Howard Smith's Rules Committee to get one to the House floor that would deny the federal courts jurisdiction over apportionment suits. Tuck's bill passed 218–175, but the efforts of Strom Thurmond (R-S.C.) to bring it directly to the Senate floor, without reference to the Judiciary Committee, failed. The Senate took no action on a resolution providing for at least a two-year delay in enforcement of lower court reapportionment rulings, which Minority Leader Everett Dirksen (R-Ill.) introduced as an amendment to a foreign-aid appropriations bill, refusing to invoke cloture to halt a filibuster against it. With input from Cox and Deputy Attorney General Nicholas Katzenbach, however, Dirksen's proposal evolved into a nonbinding "sense of the Senate" resolution, sponsored by Majority Leader Mike Mansfield (D-Mont.), that urged judges to allow legislatures one session plus thirty days in which to obey court orders and to permit the 1964 elections to proceed under existing apportionment systems where no court orders were in effect.

The Senate adopted this compromise forty-four to thirty-eight, but House critics of the Court rejected it.[41]

Meanwhile, the reapportionment rulings had become an issue in the 1964 campaign. On July 12 the Republican National Convention adopted a platform plank pledging support for both legislation and a constitutional amendment that would enable states with bicameral legislatures to apportion one house on a basis of their own choosing. Delegates booed Warren's name, and the GOP set out to mobilize a coalition of those opposed to a number of his Court's recent decisions. Republican presidential candidate Barry Goldwater attacked the Supreme Court vigorously during his campaign, prompting fifty prominent lawyers, including twelve law school deans and five former ABA presidents, to denounce his criticism as inappropriate and irresponsible.[42]

Although Democrat Lyndon Johnson crushed Goldwater in November, the campaign against the apportionment decisions continued. On December 1 the Council of State Governments adopted a resolution that urged amending the Constitution to permit apportioning one house of a state legislature on some basis other than population. Two days later the General Assembly of the States asked Congress to convene a national constitutional convention to adopt such an amendment. By May 20, 1965, twenty-five legislatures had endorsed this proposal. Its supporters hoped to use the threat of a convention—which even opponents of *Reynolds v. Sims* considered potentially dangerous—to force Congress to pass an amendment addressing the reapportionment problem. The Senate Judiciary Committee's Subcommittee on Constitutional Amendments held hearings on several proposals, the most popular of which was sponsored by Senator Dirksen, who insisted the Court's ruling was "an unwarranted intrusion . . . not upon the legislature but upon the people." Senators, representatives, and state legislators testified in favor of amending the Constitution, as did spokesmen for farm and business groups and the ABA. Opposing the Dirksen amendment were the U.S. Conference of Mayors and the American League of Cities, along with labor unions, the NAACP, the ACLU, and other liberal organizations. Since there seemed to be little chance of defeating his proposal, the opposition, spearheaded by the National Committee for Fair Representation, the Leadership Conference on Civil Rights, and Senator Paul Douglas (D-Ill.) stalled for time, waiting for court-ordered reapportionment to transform state legislatures and thereby reduce the pressure they were exerting on Congress. Unable to persuade a majority of the Judiciary Committee to report his amendment, Dirksen attempted to bring it to the Senate floor on August 4 as a substitute for a resolution designating a National American Legion Baseball Week. The vote was fifty-seven to thirty-nine, seven short of the two-thirds needed to pass a constitutional amendment. By threatening to block an administration immigration bill, Dirksen coerced the Judiciary Committee into reporting a modified version of his amendment, but on April 20, 1966, it failed fifty-five to thirty-eight. The number of states adopting calls for a constitutional convention rose to thirty-two by 1968, but Kansas rescinded its resolution in 1970; one house in each of five other legislatures took similar action. The failure of all proposed constitutional

amendments to overturn the reapportionment decisions stamps as astute Cox's observation that it "was unlikely that all this action by professional politicians had much
support among the people."[43]

Even as politicians labored unsuccessfully to overturn them, judges were implementing the reapportionment rulings. Initially, the "substantial equality" standard
that *Reynolds* said would satisfy its one-person, one-vote requirement hampered implementation. A contradiction in terms, it gave lower court judges little guidance concerning how much deviation from arithmetical exactness they might permit. By the
end of 1966, twenty-five states had judicially approved plans under which at least one
house had districts varying from the average by more than 15 percent, but the trend
appeared to be toward demanding increasingly rigid mathematical equality.[44]

Not until *Swann v. Adams* (1967) did lower court judges receive any guidance
from above. In that case the Warren Court held unconstitutional a proposed Florida
apportionment under which the maximum deviations for the Senate and House
respectively were 15.09 percent and 18.3 percent. During oral argument White indicated he found such large departures from equality troubling, apparently unaware
that judicially approved plans in about half the states provided for deviations at least
as great. The opinion he wrote for the Court replaced the substantial equality standard with a new rule: in the absence of special justification, only *de minimis* deviations
were permissible. As Harlan pointed out in dissent, White was reversing the usual
presumption of constitutionality. The Court made clear in a companion case invalidating reapportionment of the Texas legislature, however, that reversing this was
precisely what it intended to do. That plan provided for maximum deviations of
11.64 percent above and 14.84 percent below the average population. Citing *Swann*,
the Court on the same day nullified an Indiana congressional districting scheme
under which the maximum in either direction was 12.8 percent.[45]

Two years later the Court demonstrated that at least where congressional districts
were concerned, even deviations substantially smaller than that might not pass muster.
In *Kirkpatrick v. Preisler* (1969) it invalidated a Missouri plan under which the maximum variances were 3.13 percent above and 2.84 percent below the mathematical
ideal. Speaking for the Court, Brennan took the position that no fixed numerical or
percentage variation was small enough to satisfy automatically the "as nearly as practicable" standard laid out in *Wesberry v. Sanders*. The state must justify every variance.
A desire to create districts with specific interest orientations was not a satisfactory justification. Nor was trying to avoid fragmenting political subdivisions, making districts
geographically compact, nor even attempting to take into account projected population shifts. Although concurring, Fortas accused Brennan of rejecting every type
of justification that could be advanced. George Washington University professor
Robert Dixon charged the Court with pursuing mathematical equality as if it were
the Holy Grail, rendering impossible creative efforts to achieve fair and effective representation.[46]

The public did not share Dixon's dislike for the Court's approach. When asked
in June 1969 whether they preferred the Supreme Court's requirement that upper

houses of state legislatures represent equal numbers of people or a return to earlier methods of apportionment, 52 percent of Gallup Poll interviewees supported the Court. Only 23 percent opposed it. Whether demanding the closest possible approximation of numerical equality in the effect of voters' ballots was just or desirable was debatable. Whether the Warren Court was giving the public what it wanted was not.[47]

In 1967 the Court extended its popular one-person, one-vote rule to representative institutions of local government, holding in *Avery v. Midland County* that the composition of a Texas commissioners court violated the Equal Protection Clause. Speaking through White, the majority held "that the Constitution permits no substantial variation from equal protection in drawing districts for units of local government having general governmental powers over the entire geographic area served by the body." Fortas dissented, arguing that, because the Texas Supreme Court had held Midland County's districting scheme violated the state constitution and ordered redistricting, the writ of certiorari should have been dismissed as improvidently granted. Stewart agreed with him that the Supreme Court should not decide the case. Predictably, Harlan dissented from what he saw as an "unjustified and ill-advised" extension of *Reynolds* to "an estimated 80,000 units of local government." He protested once again what he considered the Court's "insensitivity to the appropriate dividing lines between the judicial and political functions under our constitutional system."[48]

The Court intruded further into local government in *Kramer v. Union Free School District* (1969), holding that states could not limit the right to vote in school board elections to owners and renters of taxable real estate and parents and guardians of school children. According to Warren, such limitations violated the Equal Protection Clause. *Kramer* was not a reapportionment case, but it highlighted how far the Warren Court had traveled since *Baker v. Carr* into what Frankfurter had maintained ought to be forbidden terrain. Experts disagreed about how much the Court actually changed the American political system. On the one hand, Dean Robert McKay of New York University Law School praised its decisions for precipitating "a revolution in the concept and practice of legislative representation." On the other hand, Alexander Bickel argued in 1970, when virtually all state legislatures had been reapportioned, that reapportionment made little or no difference in the results of the political process. Dixon pointed out that, because party and ethnic-group strength was not evenly distributed, merely equalizing the populations of voting districts would not necessarily give a majority of the people control of their government. For example, California Democrats emerged from the postreapportionment 1966 election with majorities of twenty-one to nineteen in the senate and forty-two to thirty-eight in the assembly, despite having polled fewer statewide votes than the Republicans. Kurland thought the reapportionment cases "were concerned more with form than substance" and represented "a sterile concept of equality for the sake of equality." Yale political scientist Douglas Rae took a middle position. "Reapportionment is an important, though not revolutionary, reform," he wrote. "It has made a drastic change within the narrow limits set by existing institutions."[49]

Although the extent to which the reapportionment decisions changed the American political process was debatable, the significance of these rulings for the Supreme Court itself was undeniable. As Frankfurter had predicted, they drew it ever deeper into the "political thicket." There the Court encountered the thorny problem of gerrymandering. If an individual's opportunity to elect a legislator who shared her views was reduced because district boundaries were drawn in such a way as to increase the strength of a particular political party, could she not make a justiciable claim that her rights under the Equal Protection Clause had been violated? In 1986 a much more conservative Supreme Court accepted this argument, holding that political gerrymandering was not nonjusticiable under the political question doctrine. The Court also could not long ignore the consequences of one technique often used to achieve population equality: creating bigger districts with multiple representatives, all of whom were elected at large. This approach could serve to keep members of racial minorities from being elected. The issues posed by gerrymandering and multimember districts were inherently and intensely political, but the Warren Court's reapportionment decisions almost inevitably converted both into legal problems that judges had to solve.[50]

Reapportionment also propelled the Warren Court into a new career as an agent of liberal reform. Frankfurter contended that, because legislatures were chosen by the people and were politically accountable, they were the institutions to which those seeking to change governmental policy should direct their appeals To seek reform through litigation was to invite unelected judges to usurp the power of the people and subject America to rule by an unrepresentative minority. The reapportionment dispute revealed how seriously flawed Frankfurter's premises were. Ultimately, the unelected Supreme Court spoke for the majority, whose interests were injured and will defied by elected legislators. Reforms desired by a majority of the electorate could not be achieved through the electoral process. "As a practical matter," Cox observed, "either the Court must act or nothing would be done." The Court led the attack on school segregation for similar reasons. "If one arm of government cannot or will not solve an insistent problem, the pressure falls upon another," Cox noted. The Court was not being counter-majoritarian; indeed, on many issues it was more responsive to the will of the majority than the elected officials who claimed to speak for the people. "Much of the activism of the Warren Court, not only in reapportionment, but in criminal law and race relations, is the consequence of the neglect of other agencies of the government," Cox wrote in 1968. The Warren Court became the chosen vehicle of liberals unable to persuade unresponsive governmental institutions to implement reforms they sought.[51]

The Supreme Court was, however, an awkward instrument of majoritarianism. Its methods were judicial. The Court could address only those problems litigants brought to it, and only in the form in which they presented them. There was no assurance that briefs and oral arguments that impressed judges reflected what the public desired. Yet, the Court created a means by which those who lost out within the political process could have decisions reversed. Not all of these losers were victims of structural impediments to implementation of the majority will. The victims of malapportionment clearly were, however, and the reapportionment cases accustomed the Warren Court to think of itself as the ultimate defender of majority interests. They started a snowball rolling, encouraging the Court to make itself ever more available to those frustrated by the political process and ever more inclined to provide constitutional solutions for political problems. The reapportionment cases encouraged liberal justices to make constitutional law an instrument of liberal reform.[52]

6

GOD AND THE WARREN COURT

"We ought to impeach these men in robes who put themselves up above God," roared Representative Alvin O'Konski (R-Wis.) in 1962. The target of his outrage was the Warren Court, which had provoked his outburst with its decision declaring that the Constitution forbade praying in public schools. That ruling and one a year later holding that classroom Bible reading also violated the First Amendment's ban on the establishment of religion "probably generated as much discussion, controversy, and criticism of the Court as the school desegregation [and] legislative reapportionment . . . decisions." Yet, like one person, one vote, they survived efforts to overturn them by amending the Constitution. As in the struggle over reapportionment, the opposition was widespread and vocal. The theoretically unrepresentative Supreme Court, however, actually reflected the popular will more accurately than did its critics in the political branches. The Court's decisions outraged those who wanted government to promote religion, but in a nation that was becoming increasingly diverse and divided religiously, there was no consensus concerning what faith government should foster. Ultimately, the only policy that could command the support of a majority of the American people was governmental neutrality toward religion, a concept the Warren Court sought, not always successfully, to embody in its decisions interpreting the First Amendment. Although often accused of hostility toward religion, the Supreme Court was merely accommodating constitutional law to religious pluralism.[1]

The criticism directed at the Court was predictable, for during the years prior to its controversial decisions, the United States was becoming an increasingly religious nation. Bible sales escalated suddenly and dramatically between 1949 and 1953, and during the 1950s church membership rose from 57 percent of the population to 64 percent. By 1958 Americans were spending almost 1 billion dollars per year on new churches, nearly twice as much as on new public hospitals. In 1954, 96 percent of those interviewed by the Gallup Poll said they believed in God. A decade later 63 percent claimed to pray frequently, while only 6 percent admitted never praying at all. Even popular culture reflected the public's religious bent. In 1953 a novel about Jesus, *The Robe,* made the fiction best-seller list, while five nonfiction best sellers also had religious themes. One of television's most popular personalities during the period 1951–58 was Bishop Fulton J. Sheen. In 1952 Congress passed legislation urging the president to proclaim annually a "National Day of Prayer," and two years later, it added the phrase "under God" to the Pledge of Allegiance.[2]

130

Although most Americans were religious, their religious beliefs and affiliations divided rather than united them. Theologian Will Herberg argued that religion was replacing nationality, language, and culture as the chief basis of social differentiation in America. Although ethnic intermarriage increased, religious intermarriage did not. Religion was often the most obvious basis of social cleavage in the burgeoning suburbs, where recent emigrants from ethnic urban neighborhoods, where their faiths had been dominant, clung tightly to the new churches and synagogues they founded in communities in which they were a minority. As children, Catholics often attended their church's parochial schools while Protestants pursued public education. Even socializing with youth of other faiths was limited. As adults, even when Protestants and Catholics joined the same country clubs, they golfed and developed close friendships mainly with others of their own kind. The wall between Gentiles and Jews, although perhaps weakened by reaction to the Holocaust, remained high. They belonged to different country clubs, and their friendships with one another seldom matched in warmth, intimacy, interest, spontaneity, or trust those with others of their own faith. A 1958 study found that Jews and Christians felt distinctly uncomfortable with each other.[3]

The 1960 presidential campaign highlighted the seriousness of the religious divisions in America. John Kennedy was only the second Catholic nominated for president by a major party, and the first since Al Smith, whose Catholicism had contributed significantly to his overwhelming defeat in 1928. Some Methodists attributed the Kennedy candidacy to the political machinations of the Papacy. Fearful that a Catholic president would be controlled by the Church and give government money to Catholic schools, Norman Vincent Peale and other Protestant clergy and laymen organized the National Conference of Citizens for Religious Freedom. The 9.6 million member Southern Baptist Convention also mobilized to defeat Kennedy. The Dallas *Baptist Standard* editorialized that a Catholic president would not be free to exercise his own judgment, an argument JFK soon realized he had to answer if he was to avoid Smith's fate. On September 12 he appeared before the Greater Houston Ministerial Association, proclaiming that he favored a United States that was officially neither Catholic, Protestant, nor Jewish. "I believe in an America where the separation of church and state is absolute," Kennedy declared. His speech was so well received that his Republican opponent, Richard Nixon, agreed that religious issues should be eliminated from the campaign.[4]

Nevertheless, religion significantly influenced the election. Had he been a Protestant Democrat, Kennedy would have gotten about half of the Protestant vote. He actually received 38 percent. On the other hand, a Protestant Democrat would have received 63 percent of the Catholic vote; Kennedy got 80 percent. The Protestant defections occurred mainly in states in the South and agricultural Midwest where one party enjoyed a large advantage, so they did not affect the outcome much. The votes drawn by his Catholicism, which were concentrated in hotly contested northern industrial states, however, did. Thus, religious divisions contributed significantly to Kennedy's narrow victory. Political conflict grounded in religion continued after his election. Most of the battles over issues such as the liberalization of divorce laws and the repeal of laws against birth control devices were fought at the state and local level, but a dispute over whether some of the money should go to parochial schools thwarted Kennedy's own efforts to enact federal aid to education.[5]

The religious cleavages in American society influenced judicial interpretation of the First Amendment. The Warren Court inherited from its predecessors a body of doctrine interpreting that amendment's somewhat discordant clauses proscribing the "establishment of religion" and protecting its "free exercise" that forbade governmental interference with belief and safeguarded the teaching and preaching of religion. As construed prior to 1953, however, the First Amendment did little to prevent any sect or combination of sects that commanded a political majority from exploiting government to foster its values and promote its dogma. Six years before Warren became chief justice, the Supreme Court, speaking through Justice Black, had declared in *Everson v. Board of Education* (1947) that the Establishment Clause erected a "wall of separation between church and state," but had ruled that a New Jersey school district did not breach this wall when it authorized reimbursement of parents for the costs of transporting their children to private schools, including Catholic parochial institutions. Black's opinion outraged Frankfurter, but concerned about the controversy that might arise if a Jew wrote in opposition to state support for Catholic schools, he did not publish the dissent he drafted, instead endorsing ones by Jackson and Rutledge that he urged them to strengthen.[6]

Frankfurter and Black found themselves on the same side a year later in *McCollum v. Board of Education,* in which the Court, by an eight-to-one margin, held that a Champaign, Illinois, "released time" program violated the Establishment Clause. Under that plan teachers employed by private religious groups came to public schools twice weekly during regular school hours (when children were required by compulsory attendance laws to be present) to provide religious instruction to those who wanted it. Although Black refused (then or ever) to renounce *Everson,* his opinion for the Court effectively abandoned its balancing approach to the Establishment Clause in favor of the absolutist position that the "wall between Church and State" must be "high and impregnable." The Court held that the First and Fourteenth Amendments forbade states "to aid any or all religious faiths or sects in the dissemination of their doctrines and ideals." *McCollum* stirred up a nationwide furor among religious groups, most of which operated released-time programs. To quiet their anger, the Court in *Zorach v. Clauson* (1952) upheld a New York City plan under which students were allowed to leave campus during the school day to receive religious instruction or attend devotional exercises. Douglas, who would join Black later in the absolute separation camp, wrote an opinion supporting what Melvin Urofsky characterizes as the Court's first "accommodationist" decision. Observing that "We are a religious people whose institutions presuppose a Supreme being," he emphasized that the Constitution did not require government hostility toward religion or indifference to religious groups. Separation of church and state was a matter of degree, said Douglas. Black and Frankfurter dissented, as did Jackson, who thought the battle for separation of church and state was lost. Black accused the majority of abandoning the neutrality toward religion that the First Amendment required. "It is only by wholly isolating the state from the religious sphere and compelling it to be completely neutral that the freedom of each and every denomination and of all nonbelievers can be maintained," he insisted.[7]

The Warren Court eventually adopted Black's position, but not until after holding constitutional laws that required all businesses to close on the Christian Sabbath. More countries observed Sunday as a day of rest than followed any other custom derived from Christianity, and in America statutes requiring that worldly activities cease on Sunday dated from the colonial period. During the nineteenth century authorities largely stopped enforcing these, but after World War II the development of Sunday merchandising reawakened interest in them. During the 1950s forty-one of the forty-four states having comprehensive restrictions on Sunday activity amended their statutes. While legislatures were adding new prohibitions, groups that observed a different Sabbath, such as Jews (5.51 million in America) and Seventh Day Adventists (330,000 adult members) sought exemptions. By the early 1960s, twenty-one states granted those whose religion required them to rest on Saturday permission to work on Sunday. Exemption provisions often excluded retail merchants, however, and many jurisdictions with large Sabbatarian populations (such as Massachusetts, New York, New Jersey, and Pennsylvania) refused to grant them any relief. In 1958 the New York legislature rejected the Asch-Rosenblatt Fair Sabbath Bill, which would have allowed merchants in New York City to conduct business on Sunday if their religious convictions kept them from working on Saturday. A year later opponents of the "blue laws" decided to take their cause to the Supreme Court.[8]

Although the high tribunal declined to consider the problem throughout the 1950s, repeatedly dismissing cases that raised it as not presenting a substantial federal question, the Court agreed to hear oral argument on the validity of the Maryland, Pennsylvania, and Massachusetts statutes in December 1960. All of these cases arose out of the enforcement of Sunday closing laws against retail merchants. *McGowan v. Maryland* was an appeal by seven employees of a discount department store who were convicted of making sales on Sunday. *Two Guys from Harrison-Allentown v. McGinley* was a suit to enjoin enforcement of the Pennsylvania statute, filed by a discount house whose salespeople were repeatedly prosecuted because of pressure brought to bear on the Lehigh County district attorney by one of the discounter's principal competitors. Similarly, in *Gallagher v. Crown Kosher Super Market*, a store owner sued to enjoin enforcement of the Massachusetts blue law after the Springfield police arrested his partner at the behest of proprietors of small kosher butcher shops. Because those who ran Crown Kosher, as well as the Philadelphia clothing and home-furnishing merchants who attacked the Pennsylvania statute in *Braunfeld v. Brown*, were Orthodox Jews, required by the tenets of their faith to rest on Saturday, they contended that the blue laws interfered with the free exercise of their religion. The *McGowan* appellants also alleged violation of their free exercise rights. All four cases raised Establishment Clause issues. In addition, those attacking the blue laws claimed they violated the Equal Protection Clause by prohibiting some, but not all, Sunday selling.[9]

That argument did not impress any member of the Court. Warren, who spoke for the majority in *McGowan* and *Two Guys* and for a plurality in the other two cases, rejected it, as did Frankfurter, who concurred for himself and Harlan in all four cases, and Brennan and Stewart, who dissented in *Braunfeld* and *Crown Kosher.* Douglas, who dissented in all four cases, simply ignored it.[10]

The argument that Sunday closing statutes violated the Establishment Clause fared little better. Douglas believed they did, for their effect was to put legal sanctions behind the practices of a particular religious group by making its Sabbath a symbol of respect. The question, as he saw it, was "Whether a State can impose criminal sanctions on those who, unlike the Christian majority . . . worship on a different day or do not share the religious scruples of the majority." To him the answer was obviously no.[11]

Douglas lost in conference eight to one. Warren, who assigned the cases to himself, used *McGowan* as his principal vehicle for setting forth the majority's conclusion that Sunday closing laws did not violate the Establishment Clause, including in his discussion of that case an analysis of the history of all such statutes. The Chief conceded that religious motives inspired enactment of the first ones. Even before 1700, however, people began advancing nonreligious arguments for such laws, and they started to lose their totally religious character. More recently, the Chief noted, groups such as labor unions had offered secular justifications for making Sunday a day when everyone could recover from the labors of the past week and prepare for the one ahead. According to Warren, the Establishment Clause did "not ban federal or state regulation of conduct whose reason or effect merely happens to coincide or harmonize with the tenets of some or all religions." The Chief intended to argue that blue laws were constitutional because they did not operate predominantly to support religion, but Black insisted he change his opinion so that "the touchstone [would be] whether legislation does or does not aid religion." Warren quoted at length from Black's *Everson* opinion, then concluded somewhat implausibly that, like repaying the transportation expenses of parochial-school students, requiring Sunday closing did not breach the "wall of separation." In light of the evolution of blue laws throughout the centuries and their recent emphasis on secular considerations, as presently written and administered, most were secular rather than religious in character, he contended; they bore "no relationship to the establishment of religion as those words are used in the Constitution." Had Maryland's purpose in designating Sunday as a universal day of rest been religious, its statute would be unconstitutional, but in selecting the day most people would have chosen on their own, it did no more than take a realistic approach to the problem of enforcement.[12]

Frankfurter agreed with Warren that the blue laws did not violate the Establishment Clause. Nevertheless, he filed a pedantic 101-page concurrence burdened with 143 footnotes. Before oral argument he had circulated a similarly massive memorandum on the four cases, prepared with the assistance of his clerk, Anthony Amsterdam. Frankfurter probably wrote separately because of disappointment that his reasoning had not been made the basis of the Court's opinion, although he claimed that he had to do so because he needed to discuss at length the history of Sunday legislation and objections to Warren's reliance on Black's *Everson* opinion. Acknowledging to the Chief that "some will find little difference between the course of your analysis and that of Felix's separate opinion," Harlan nevertheless joined Frankfurter. He did not, however, dispute Warren's contention that the Establishment Clause permitted blue laws.[13]

Nor did Frankfurter challenge the Chief's assertion that these statutes complied with the Free Exercise Clause. Warren denied that the *McGowan* and *Two Guys* appellants even had standing to raise this issue. He also seemed to have doubts about whether Crown Kosher Super Market could assert the free exercise rights of its Orthodox Jewish customers. He concluded it did not matter, because under the Court's decision in *Braunfeld*, the store would lose on the merits anyhow. In *Braunfeld* he conceded that the Orthodox Jewish merchants challenging Pennsylvania's Sunday closing law were burdened by it, but reiterated the well-established proposition that, while freedom to hold religious beliefs was absolute, freedom to act on them was not. In any event, the state had not regulated the appellants' religious activity, Warren pointed out; it merely made the practice of their religion more expensive by the way it regulated secular conduct. In a nation with almost three hundred denominations, legislators could not be expected to enact only regulations that did not economically disadvantage any sect. A statute whose purpose or effect was to impede religious observances or discriminate among religions would be unconstitutional, even though it burdened faith only indirectly. "But if the State regulates conduct by enacting a general law within its power, the purpose and effect of which is to advance the state's secular goals," Warren asserted, "the statute is valid despite its indirect burden on religious observances unless the State may accomplish its purpose by means which do not impose such a burden." The Jewish Frankfurter agreed with him that the Free Exercise Clause did not require states to exempt Jews from Sunday closing laws. In light of the enforcement problems that having different legal days of rest for various groups would entail, he argued, "a blanket Sunday ban applicable to observers of all faiths cannot be held unreasonable." Predictably, Frankfurter invoked judicial self-restraint. "However preferable, personally, one might deem an exception [for Sabbatarians]," he wrote, "I cannot find that the Constitution compels it."[14]

Brennan and Stewart disagreed with Frankfurter and Warren about that. Dissenting in *Braunfeld*, Brennan argued that the Pennsylvania blue law interfered with the free exercise of religion because it forced an Orthodox Jew to choose between his business and his religion. Only a compelling governmental interest could justify that, and the convenience of having everyone rest on the same day was not compelling. The purpose of the First Amendment was not to facilitate the fulfillment of such collective goals; it was to ensure the preservation of personal liberty. Stewart, who agreed with substantially everything Brennan said, accused Pennsylvania of putting an Orthodox Jew to a "cruel choice" between "his religious faith and his economic survival." Both of them dissented in *Crown Kosher* as well. Douglas insisted there was a Free Exercise Clause violation in all four cases.[15]

Sister Candida Lund observes, "It is possible that [these] Sabbatarian cases might have fared better had they not been linked with the discount house cases." Those highlighted the economic character of the fight over Sunday closing laws and perhaps kept Warren and Black, who normally supported those penalized by government for their convictions, from doing so in these cases. Most justices also did not understand how much sanctioning even mild governmental support for some religions could exacerbate religious tensions in America. Fights over blue-law enforcement and litigation (that went as far as the highest courts of Illinois and Missouri) followed the Sunday closing decisions. Those rulings also precipitated political battles over exemptions in a number of states, including New York, Pennsylvania, New Jersey, Maine, Mississippi, Texas, and Massachusetts.[16]

Although holding that states could require Jews and other Sabbatarians to conform their conduct to Christian principles, Warren did include a caveat in his *McGowan* opinion: Sunday legislation might violate the Establishment Clause if it could be demonstrated that its purpose was to "use the State's coercive power to aid religion." Less than a month later, in *Torcaso v. Watkins,* the Court demonstrated its actual unwillingness to tolerate what its members viewed as governmental coercion with a religious objective. *Torcaso* arose when Maryland denied a justice of the peace commission to a man who would not declare that he believed in God, as the state constitution required. During a discussion of the case in which the possibility that it might be moot received more attention than the question of whether Torcaso's constitutional rights had been violated, no justice expressed any doubt that they had been. Black declared emphatically that "an atheist has a constitutional right to hold state or federal office." Warren proclaimed that despite the reference to the Deity in the Declaration of Independence, a belief in God was not a prerequisite to full citizenship and that nobody lost rights for not being a Christian. There may have been some uncertainty about which of the religion clauses Maryland's belief-in-God requirement violated, for the Chief's opinion never really said, holding that it invaded "the appellants freedom of belief and religion." Warren quoted at length from *Everson,* then "repeat[ed] and reaffirm[ed] . . . that neither a State nor the Federal Government can constitutionally force a person to 'profess belief or disbelief in any religion' . . . or impose requirements which aid all religions as against non-believers." His opinion outraged one man, who wrote to Black that even though *Torcaso* "might appear to be of small importance to some, to a Christian it is a drastic step."[17]

Sherbert v. Verner (1963) kindled less passion, despite representing a more radical departure from the jurisprudence of the past. In that case the Court held that the failure to structure a social welfare program to accommodate religious practices of the Sabbatarian minority was unconstitutional, even if not deliberate discrimination on the basis of religious beliefs. Sherbert, a Seventh Day Adventist, was fired by her South Carolina employer for refusing to work on Saturday and then denied unemployment compensation by the state because of her unwillingness to accept another job that would require labor on her Sabbath. The vote was seven to two in her favor, with only Harlan and White in opposition. The dissenters insisted that because the South Carolina Supreme Court consistently held no one was eligible for benefits whose unemployment was due to personal circumstances, the state might deny them to Sherbert. The Constitution did not entitle her to be treated differently because of her religion. By holding otherwise, Harlan argued in dissent, the Court was in effect overruling *Braunfeld v. Brown*. Apparently realizing this, Brennan tried to write a very narrow opinion, applicable only to those who, like Sherbert, lost their jobs because their employers altered work schedules to conflict with the requirements of their religions. Only Clark would go along with that approach. Hence, Brennan wrote that only a compelling governmental interest could justify forcing someone to choose between the precepts of her faith and unemployment benefits. Since the state failed to demonstrate that paying Sherbert would endanger some "paramount interest," its action violated the Free Exercise Clause. Brennan was trying to utilize a test Warren had announced in *Braunfeld* and to distinguish the two cases on the basis of their facts, but Stewart did not find his efforts persuasive. Furthermore, he argued in a concurring opinion, Brennan's interpretation of the Free Exercise Clause as compelling South Carolina to pay Sherbert benefits because her reasons for refusing to work on Saturdays were religious that it might withhold if they were nonreligious. That was "clearly to require the State to violate the Establishment Clause as construed by this Court." Douglas, who also concurred, would have held simply that depriving someone of something to which she would otherwise have been entitled because of her religion violated the Free Exercise Clause.[18]

Two years later in *Seeger v. United States* (1965), the Court faced the very problem Stewart highlighted in *Sherbert*. Congress exempted from military service religiously motivated conscientious objectors, but not those whose conscientious opposition to any form of war stemmed from nonreligious reasons. In conference most of the justices expressed the view that such discrimination was unconstitutional. Harlan (who eventually concluded the statute was valid) thought they should address this constitutional question. The Court, however, managed to avoid deciding whether the statute violated the Establishment Clause, and also whether failure to accommodate religious pacifists would violate the Free Exercise Clause, by reading the law in a tortured and implausible way. Even Harlan ultimately went along with an interpretation that allowed an agnostic to obtain an exemption that, according to the words used by Congress, seemed to be available only to those who believed in a Supreme Being. In a concurring opinion, Douglas insisted the law had to be read this way; otherwise, under *Sherbert*, it would violate the Free Exercise Clause.[19]

Although the opinion required to justify *Seeger* made little sense, the decision was completely consistent with the stance that the Warren Court was taking by 1965 in all cases involving the relationship between church and state. The Court had by then moved away from the position that government could accommodate the religious practices of the majority to the view that it must be completely neutral, neither discriminating against nor assisting any particular faith or religion in general. The Court first embraced this principle in *Engel v. Vitale* (1962). That decision held unconstitutional the policy of a New York school district that required reading in every class at the beginning of each day, with the teacher present, a prayer composed by the state board of regents: "Almighty God, we acknowledge our dependence upon Thee, and beg Thy blessings upon us, our parents, our teachers and our Country." The storm of controversy provoked by the regents' policy statement recommending the daily recitation of this prayer showed how divisive even such a nonsectarian show of governmental support for religion could be. Major Jewish organizations disputed it. Protestant and Catholic Church leaders supported the regents, but spokesmen for a Peekskill Lutheran congregation accused them of blasphemy for omitting Christ's name to "mollify non-Christian elements." The *Christian Century,* a Protestant publication, considered their prayer an empty formality, without spiritual significance.[20]

That was also the way Warren viewed the prayer. Yet, he was troubled both by the insistence of the school board's lawyer during oral argument that his client was just promoting morality, ethics, and traditional American values and by the lawyer's reluctance to acknowledge that the Hyde Park schools were teaching religion. The board's brief maintained there was no violation of the Constitution because "Recognition of Almighty God in public prayer is an integral part of our national heritage." No child was required to participate in the daily invocation, and any student who wished to be excused was. "The Constitution of the United States is incapable of being so interpreted as to require that the wall of separation of church and State become an iron curtain," the board maintained.[21]

The board's emotional appeal earned just one vote. Frankfurter was ill, and oral argument took place before White's appointment, so only seven justices participated. Six of them thought the board had violated the Establishment Clause. The majority included liberal stalwarts Warren, Black, Douglas, and Brennan, but also Harlan and Clark. Clark, a devout Presbyterian, shared the views of early American members of his denomination about church-state relations and considered the use of prayer for secular purposes, such as promoting civic morality, a threat to the integrity of religion. Harlan feared the political friction that mixing the religious and the secular could create.[22]

Black, worried about how his colleagues would decide this case, was thrilled to learn that almost all shared his view that the "Regents' Prayer" was unconstitutional; he asked Warren to let him write the opinion. A man who had long since drifted away from organized religion, his primary concern was about state compulsion overpowering individual impulses. The fact that students who wished to remain silent or leave the room during the prayer could do so did not impress him, because "When the power, prestige and financial support of government is placed behind a particular religious belief, the indirect coercive pressure upon religious minorities to conform to the prevailing officially approved religion is plain." Nor did the denominational neutrality of the "Regents' Prayer" "free it from the limitations of the Establishment Clause." "The constitutional prohibition against laws respecting an establishment of religion must at least mean," Black wrote, "that in this country it is no part of the business of government to compose official prayers for any group of the American people to recite as a part of a religious program carried on by government."[23]

Douglas agreed, although he conceded their position was inconsistent with the historic meaning of the First Amendment. He did not, however, accept the major premise of Black's argument. "As I see it," Douglas wrote him, "there is no penalty for not praying, no coercion." In a concurring opinion, Douglas contended the real issue in the case was "whether the Government can constitutionally finance a religious exercise." The answer, he insisted, was no. The philosophy of the First Amendment was that government must be neutral in the field of religion. It became a divisive force when it intervened in spiritual matters. The use of public money to pay religious costs was bound to spark squabbling among sects seeking a bigger share; hence, such spending should be considered unconstitutional. Both in private and in his opinion, Douglas acknowledged that many things done by the states and the federal government, including the prayer with which the Supreme Court opened its own sessions, were inconsistent with what he claimed the Establishment Clause demanded.[24]

Stewart viewed these "official expressions of religious faith" as evidence of what the Establishment Clause did not prohibit. His lone dissent argued that they proved the majority "had misapplied a great constitutional principle. I cannot see how an 'official religion' is established by letting those who want to say a prayer say it," Stewart wrote. All the board had done was allow school children to participate in the nation's spiritual heritage.[25]

New York's archbishop, Cardinal Francis Spellman, agreed with him and expressed shock at a decision that, he maintained, struck at the godly tradition in which Americans raised their children. Billy Graham denounced *Engel* as a step toward secularizing the nation, while Dean Griswold faulted the Court for depriving the Christian majority of the opportunity to maintain its religious traditions through public institutions. Their complaints were among the calmer and more rational condemnations of *Engel*. Warren vividly recalled "one bold newspaper headline saying 'Court outlaws God.'" The Supreme Court received more mail denouncing *Engel* than any other decision. Polls showed that this ruling was the Warren Court's most unpopular and that 80 percent of Americans favored prayers in public schools. "They put Negroes into the schools and now they have driven God out of them," ranted Representative George W. Andrews (D-Ala.). Senator Herman Talmadge (D-Ga.) blasted what he called "an outrageous edict." Within days after *Engel*, senators submitted five proposed constitutional amendments to overturn the decision; representatives offered twenty-nine more. Critics in and out of Congress claimed the Court was promoting communistic atheism. Episcopal bishop James A. Pike of San Francisco charged it had "deconsecrated the nation." The National Council of Churches, although endorsing the separation of church and state, insisted that principle should not prevent recognizing the role of religion in the public schools.[26]

Engel also had its defenders. The NAACP joined the ACLU and the American Humanist Association in vigorously supporting the decision, while the National Education Association also reacted positively. Although criticized by the Hearst press and the conservative *Los Angeles Times* and *Chicago Tribune*, the ruling received editorial endorsements from such leading newspapers as the *New York Times, New York Herald Tribune, Washington Post*, and *St. Louis Post-Dispatch*. While the Catholic hierarchy overwhelmingly condemned *Engel*, the official publications of the Kansas City, Missouri, and Portland, Maine, dioceses expressed support. The Protestant clergy was divided. The Baptist Joint Committee on Public Affairs, the country's leading Protestant publication, *The Christian Century*, and the Methodist Church's official organ, the *Christian Advocate*, all backed the Court, however. So did most Jewish rabbis. A Presbyterian minister wrote to Black from Bethesda, Maryland, about a month after the decision, "It is fairly evident by now . . . that the great majority of American church-men heartily endorse the 'prayer' decision." A Vancouver, Washington, woman, who thought "that we must teach our religion to our children and not leave this to some-one else," also supported the Court. President Kennedy expressed similar views, assert-ing that *Engel* should be a welcome reminder to American families to pray more at home, attend church with greater fidelity, and "make the true meaning of prayer much more important in the lives of our children." Kennedy also reminded Ameri-cans that maintaining constitutional principles required supporting even those Supreme Court decisions with which "we may not agree."[27]

Although doubtless comforted by the president's supportive remarks, the justices found disturbing the intensity of public opposition to *Engel.* They did not consider themselves hostile to religion, but agitated by the media, whose interpretation of the decision was incompetent as well as intemperate, many Americans concluded that they were. In August Clark took the unusual step of denouncing the press's misin-formed treatment of the case in a speech to an ABA convention. In 1963 he wrote a majority opinion in *School District of Abington Township v. Schempp* designed to influence positively the public's perception of the Court.[28]

The issue in that case was the constitutionality of reading from the Bible in pub-lic schools, an exercise conducted in 42 percent of continental U.S. districts in 1960. Half of the schools in the country held some sort of homeroom devotional exercises, and when *Engel* was decided, eleven states (mainly in the South) had laws requiring Bible reading. *Schempp* was a challenge by a Unitarian family to a Pennsylvania statute that mandated presentation of at least ten verses without comment at the beginning of each day. In Abbington Township participation in this exercise, which also included recitation of the Lord's Prayer, was voluntary. The school district furnished only the King James version of the Bible, but other versions, as well as the Jewish scriptures, had been used. The plaintiffs in the companion case of *Murray v. Curlett* were a promi-nent atheist, Mrs. Madalyn Murray, and her son, William. They were attacking a Bal-timore School Board rule that required the reading of a chapter from the Bible and/or recitation of the Lord's Prayer each morning. The Murrays lost in the Mary-land state courts, while a federal district court held unconstitutional the practices of the Abington School District and the Pennsylvania statute they implemented.[29]

The Supreme Court affirmed the Pennsylvania decision and reversed the one in *Murray.* When the justices discussed the two cases in conference on March 1, only Stewart opposed deciding them that way. He wanted to remand both "so that states can give every sect a chance to have religious exercises in schools including atheists." Stewart considered establishment an obsolete concept and believed that states had an affirmative duty to create a religious atmosphere in their schools, so that everyone who wished to pray and worship could do so. Although no one else agreed with him, his colleagues were less united than the eight-to-one vote suggests. Clark actually shared Stewart's view that opening the schools to exercises by all religious groups would be constitutional. Harlan, who asked counsel during oral argument to distin-guish *Torcaso* and *Engel,* recognized that the Court could not avoid holding Bible reading unconstitutional unless it reconsidered those rulings, but characterizing his vote in *Murray* as tentative, he told his colleagues he was prepared to look at the whole subject "*de novo.*" "This may in the end come out differently." Warren agreed that unless they were prepared to reverse *Engel,* only one result was possible. The Chief and Goldberg argued, however, that this case presented an even more obvious violation of the Establishment Clause than had *Engel.* Their view prevailed, although what Harlan would do remained in doubt for some time.[30]

Warren assigned the case to Clark, probably because he had a more conservative reputation than Black, whose *Engel* opinion had created such a furor. Also he was devout and active in his church. It was a good choice, for Clark produced on opinion designed to minimize public reaction to the decision. Although *Murray* was docketed first, he made the Unitarian Edward Schempp the captioned plaintiff. Indeed, Clark apparently toyed with the idea of hiding the Murrays' atheism entirely; an early handwritten draft of his opinion contains no discussion of the facts of their case, to which he never did devote as much attention as to those of *Schempp* itself. Clark also took care to avoid writing anything that the public might read broadly as prohibiting all interaction between government and religion. He was careful to emphasize what the Court was not saying and to highlight constitutional ways that those who wished to incorporate the study of religion into public education might do so, such as by teaching religious history or comparative religion.[31]

Clark made it clear, however, that "In light of the history of the First Amendment and of our cases interpreting and applying its requirements, . . . the practices at issue and the laws requiring them are unconstitutional under the Establishment Clause." He acknowledged the close identification of religion with the history and government of the United States, but stressed that religious freedom was also imbedded in American life. The Court's decisions explicating the Establishment and Free Exercise Clauses indicated these required government to manifest a "wholesome 'neutrality'" toward religion. If either the purpose or primary effect of an enactment was to inhibit or advance religion, that law was unconstitutional. History showed powerful sects or groups could bring about a fusion of governmental and religious functions that placed official support "behind the tenets of one or all religions. This the Establishment Clause prohibits." The Free Exercise Clause, by guaranteeing each person's right to choose freely a religious direction without coercion by the state, also supported governmental neutrality toward religion. Excusing those who did not want to participate in public-school religious exercises was insufficient to make those exercises constitutional, Clark argued. He denied that the concept of neutrality, by forbidding government to require religious activities "even with the consent of the majority," deprived that majority of its free exercise rights. To him it was obvious that in America, where the relationship between man and religion was concerned, the government must be "firmly committed to the position of neutrality."[32]

Brennan, seeing "no escape from the conclusion" that the challenged exercises were unconstitutional, "join[ed] fully in the opinion and judgment of the Court." Sensitive to the criticism the Court was receiving, however, he informed his colleagues, even before Warren assigned the case to Clark, that he intended to write separately, in order to distinguish those things the First Amendment permitted from those it prohibited. When Brennan circulated the first printing of his seventy-four-page opinion on May 2, he explained that he wanted it to be an expression of his own views, signed only by himself. "Our holding does not declare that the First Amendment manifests hostility to the practice or teaching of religion," he wrote. "Not every involvement of religion in public life is unconstitutional." According to Brennan, "The First Amendment commands not official hostility toward religion, but only a strict neutrality in matters of religion." As he read the Constitution, it enjoined "those involvements of religion with secular institutions which (a) serve the essentially religious activities of religious institutions; (b) employ the organs of government for essentially religious purposes; or (c) use essentially religious means to serve governmental ends where secular means would suffice." The Establishment Clause reserved to parents, rather than a majority of voters, the choice of whether their children received secular or sectarian educations. "In my judgment," Brennan asserted, "the First Amendment forbids the state to inhibit the freedom of choice by diminishing the attractiveness of either alternative—either by restricting the liberty of the private schools to inculcate whatever values they wish, or by jeopardizing the freedom of the public schools from private sectarian pressures." "Of the four members of the *Schempp* majority who filed opinions," Yale Law School's Louis Pollak thought, "Brennan . . . came much the closest to providing a constitutional framework adequate to the problem."[33]

Douglas and Goldberg also wrote concurrences. Douglas agreed with Clark that public school prayers violated "the 'neutrality' required of the State by . . . the First Amendment," but wanted to reiterate his *Engel* argument that any use of public funds to finance a religious exercise violated the Establishment Clause. Goldberg (speaking also for Harlan) seemed anxious to reassure the public about the limited nature of the Court's decision. The practices being held unconstitutional, he observed, did "not fall within any sensible or acceptable concept of compelled or permitted accommodation and involve the state so significantly and directly in the realm of the sectarian as to give rise to those very divisive influences and inhibitions of freedom which both religion clauses of the First Amendment preclude." Although agreeing "that the attitude of government toward religion must be one of neutrality," Goldberg warned that "untutored devotion to the concept of neutrality" could lead to "a brooding and pervasive devotion to the secular and a passive or even active hostility to the religious."[34]

Stewart, after nearly making the decision unanimous, finally filed a lonely dissent. It charged that banning religious exercises from public schools was not "the realization of state neutrality, but rather . . . the establishment of a religion of secularism." Neutrality meant letting those who wanted to participate in such activities do so. Stewart saw "in these cases a substantial free exercise claim on the part of those who affirmatively desire to have their children's school day open with the reading of passages from the Bible." So long as government designated no particular book or prayer, it was only accommodating religion, he believed. Religious exercises became unconstitutional only when administered in such a way as to place secular authority behind one or more religions or irreligious beliefs. Since the records in these cases were inadequate to determine whether any student who did not wish to participate had been coerced, Stewart wanted them remanded for further hearings.[35]

This time he did not enlist the support of an outraged public. "*Schempp* provoked far less furor than *Engel*," Pollack noted. This did not mean, he warned readers of the *Harvard Law Review,* that "school systems will adhere to *Schempp* with alacrity." In 1964 the Supreme Court had to overturn a decision of the Florida Supreme Court approving prayer and devotional Bible reading, and by 1968 Bible-reading cases were being litigated in eight other states. In the North, when school boards attempted to continue classroom religious practices, state attorneys general ordered them to stop, but in the South public officials promoted resistance. Alabama's governor, George Wallace, prodded his state's board of education to command that Bible reading continue in all public schools. In Tennessee only 51 of 121 districts surveyed made any changes in their policies following *Schempp*, and just one eliminated Bible reading and devotional exercises entirely. A survey by political scientist Frank Way determined that the percentage of classrooms in which prayers were being said dropped from 60 before 1962 to 28 in the 1964–65 school year and the percentage in which Bible reading was taking place went down from 48 to 22, but it also identified a pattern of resistance in the South. Another study found that devotional Bible reading, done in 41.8 percent of schools in 1960, was taking place in only 12.9 percent by 1966, but it too found more noncompliance in the South than elsewhere.[36]

Although southerners resisted the prayer and Bible-reading decisions more vigorously than other Americans, *Schempp* was not really popular anywhere. The Gallup Poll found 70 percent of a national sample opposed to it. Seventy-four percent of those interviewed by the Survey Research Center of the University of Michigan just before the 1964 elections expressed approval of school devotions. Yet, the volume of critical mail received by the Court and by the attorney general was far less than after *Engel*. While average Americans would have preferred that school prayer and Bible reading continue, such individuals normally did not concern themselves much with Supreme Court decisions, which were almost exclusively an object of elite attention, and elite reaction to *Schempp* ranged from muted to positive. In a series of lectures at Northwestern University School of Law, University of Wisconsin professor Wilbur J. Katz expressed a "strong preference" for the principle of state neutrality toward religion, which *Schempp* announced. A study of newspaper editorials published in thirty-five states and the District of Columbia showed 61 percent of them approved of the decision, a marked shift since *Engel*, particularly in the Northeast and Midwest. The reaction of church spokesmen was especially notable. Jewish organizations supported *Schempp*, while the Greek Orthodox Church and the Roman Catholic leadership opposed it. Several Catholic archbishops and bishops, however, issued statements calling for restraint, and Father Robert F. Drinan, S. J., a distinguished legal scholar and dean of the Boston College Law School, echoed Katz. Such major Protestant denominations as the Baptists, Presbyterians, and Lutherans went on record in favor of *Schempp*. Reaction to *Schempp* differed from that to *Engel* in part because that earlier decision made this later one predictable, depriving it of shock effect. Also significant, however, was the strongly southern flavor of resistance to the Bible reading ruling.

Many church leaders felt uncomfortable because some of the harshest critics of *Engel* were also staunch opponents of the Supreme Court's desegregation stand. They were unwilling to help the critics weaken the Court's moral authority.[37]

Southern legislators proposed more than half of the constitutional amendments submitted after *Engel*. Emanuel Celler, the Jewish liberal Democrat from New York who headed the House Judiciary Committee, had no use for any of them, but his Senate counterpart, James Eastland (D-Miss.), scheduled two days of hearings in July and August of 1962, chaired by another southerner, Olin D. Johnston (D-S.C.). Eastland and Johnston were cosponsoring an amendment that would not only protect prayer and Bible reading in schools and other public places, but also give states the right to decide on the basis of their own "public policy" questions of "decency and morality"; it was a measure that seemed designed to wrest control over race relations from the federal courts. Most of the senators and representatives participating in the hearings were southerners, and the tone was ardently anti-*Engel*. The Judiciary Committee received written statements from a few groups (such as the ACLU, the Anti-Defamation League, and the Baptist Joint Committee on Public Affairs) that supported the decision, but the witnesses who testified in person all condemned it. Led by Bishop Pike, they accused the Court of making a concerted attack on God and religion in American life, aiming much of their fire at Douglas's concurring opinion. Senator Willis Robertson (D-Va.) wanted to overcome *Engel*'s effects by recognizing the existence of God with an amendment that would also preserve the separation of church and state. The committee did not report out his paradoxical proposal or any other amendment; it did not even issue a report. "Apart from allowing opponents of the Court and the *Regents Prayer* decision to vent their spleen," William Beaney and Edward Beiser observe, "the hearings accomplished nothing."[38]

Nevertheless, the campaign for a school prayer amendment revived after *Schempp*, led now by Representative Frank J. Becker (R-N.Y.). Becker first introduced his own proposal, then became the tireless champion of one developed by six members of Congress designated to perform that task following a meeting of amendment supporters in August 1963. What became known as the "Becker Amendment" had three substantive sections. The first provided that nothing in the Constitution should be deemed to prohibit "the offering, reading from or listening to prayers or biblical scriptures, if participation therein is on a voluntary basis, in any governmental or public school, institution, or place." The second said that nothing in the Constitution should be taken to forbid referring to a belief in or invoking the aid of God in any governmental document or activity or upon U.S. money. Finally, Becker's proposed amendment declared it did not "constitute an establishment of religion."[39]

Recognizing that Celler would never let this amendment out of committee unless compelled to do so, Becker began collecting signatures on a discharge petition. By April 1964 he had nearly 170 of the 218 required. His success is hardly surprising, for 113 House members introduced their own proposed amendments. Despite the milder public reaction to *Schempp*, nearly twice as many senators and representatives felt impelled to sponsor such measures as had done so after *Engel*. The biggest reason was an orchestrated letter-writing campaign that deluged Capitol Hill with mail. Also important were the efforts of Becker, a zealot who was not running for reelection, and thus had the time to mount a crusade for his prayer amendment. He even threatened to campaign against colleagues who would not support it. Fearful of being branded as opponents of God in an election year, even congressmen with serious reservations about the amendment and/or discharge petitions in general boarded Becker's bandwagon. Facing defeat, in late March Celler announced that his House Judiciary Committee would hold hearings on the amendment, beginning on April 22. He cleverly managed to drag these out into early June, leaving insufficient time for floor action and Senate passage before Congress adjourned for the Republican National Convention.[40]

Ironically, the hearings Becker forced on Celler provided opponents of his amendment with an effective forum. A study published by the Judiciary Committee staff on March 24 gave the critics plenty of ammunition, explicating in detail the problems with the various proposed prayer amendments. Politicians lined up to testify for them anyhow, with two governors and a state attorney general joining ninety-seven House members. But an ad hoc committee of groups opposing amendments, coordinated by Rev. Dean M. Kelley of the National Council of Churches, mobilized a more impressive array of witnesses. These sought to sway wavering congressmen by raising questions such as which version of the Bible would be used and who would decide what prayers would be said. Opposition witnesses included constitutional law scholars Paul Freund of Harvard, Philip Kurland of Chicago, and Paul Kauper of Michigan. Freund, Katz, Drinan, and Leo Pfeffer, general counsel of the American Jewish Congress, submitted a statement signed by 223 of the nation's best-known law school deans and professors. The fact that a number of these were from Catholic institutions helped create the impression that Catholics were joining Protestants and Jews in opposing a school prayer amendment. Even more significant was the testimony of a parade of distinguished theologians that included Dr. Eugene Carson Blake, chief officer of the United Presbyterian Church, and former president of the National Council of Churches; Methodist bishop John Wesley Lord; Dr. Edwin Tuller, general secretary of the American Baptist Convention; Dr. Fredrik Schiotz, president of the American Lutheran Church; and Protestant Episcopal presiding bishop Arthur Lichtenberger. Of 38 clergy and laymen representing religious organizations, 28 opposed amending the Constitution. Some of those who condemned the idea most strongly were deeply religious individuals who feared establishment of a state religion and the harm that rote prayers could do to the personal relationship between believers and their Creator. These spokesmen probably created an exaggerated impression of the extent to which the denominations they represented opposed prayer amendments, but their testimony allowed those seeking to prevent tampering with the First Amendment to capitalize on the prestige of organized religion.[41]

The opposition's tactics worked. Congress received an increasing amount of anti-Becker Amendment mail. When the hearings began, opponents believed a majority of the Judiciary Committee favored the amendment, but by late May, twenty of thirty-five members were probably opposed. Celler still had no intention of letting it reach the floor, and the discharge-petition drive had stalled. Indeed, a number of members who had signed earlier indicated they would remove their names if success appeared likely. By August 5, the Becker Amendment was doomed. Its sponsor had to content himself with getting the Republican National Convention to adopt a platform plank pledging support for amending the Constitution to permit religious exercises in public places.[42]

On March 22, 1966, the GOP's Senate leader, Everett Dirksen (R-Ill.), introduced such a measure. His proposed amendment stated that nothing in the Constitution prohibited those administering schools and other public buildings from providing or permitting voluntary participation by students and others in prayer. Dirksen's amendment purported not to authorize those in charge to prescribe the form or content of any prayer. It received endorsements from over 3,900 members of Protestant Ministers for School Prayers and Bible Reading, the Greek Archdiocese of North and South America, the National Association of Evangelicals, and Dr. Carl McIntre's American Council of Christian Churches. Eventually, forty-seven of Dirksen's colleagues signed on as cosponsors. But spokesmen for the National Council of Churches, the Lutheran Church in America, the Lutheran Church, Missouri Synod, the Seventh-Day Adventists, and the United Presbyterian Church testified against his amendment at hearings of a Senate Judiciary Committee subcommittee. So did Freund, Kauper, and Drinan. Critics focused on the amendment's obscure language and the problems this could create. The nonpartisan Legislative Reference Service of the Library of Congress supported their contention that its use of the word "voluntary" was problematic. Although the Judiciary Committee did not report Dirksen's amendment, the senator managed to get it onto the Senate floor as a substitute for another measure. Garnering forty-nine yeas, with thirty-seven nays and fourteen senators not voting, it fell well short of the two-thirds needed to pass a constitutional amendment. Dirksen tried again in 1967, offering a substantially different amendment, then altering it when his own supporters objected to the language, but his proposal went nowhere.[43]

Meanwhile, support for a prayer amendment was declining in the House. The number of sponsors dropped from 115 in 1964 to 55 in 1966. The movement to overcome *Engel* and *Schempp* via constitutional amendment failed because of religious differences in a nation with some 250 sects. While there was overwhelming popular support for honoring God in schools and other public places, amendment proponents could not formulate language that would accomplish their objective without precipitating endless sectarian wrangling across the country.[44]

The only way to avoid such strife was for government to adhere to a policy of strict neutrality toward religion. That is precisely what the Warren Court held the First Amendment required. The Court continued to interpret the Establishment Clause in this manner until after Warren's retirement. It would not permit the use of the public schools to promote religion, but it also would not mandate the total separation of church and state that Douglas advocated.

In *Epperson v. Arkansas* (1968) the Court unanimously invalidated a statute that made it unlawful for any teacher in a tax-supported school or university to teach the theory of evolution or employ a textbook that did so. The Arkansas Supreme Court declined to express an opinion as to whether this law prohibited explaining the theory or only telling students it was true, so no one could be sure what conduct the law punished. Warren, Black, Douglas, Brennan, and White all wanted to hold it void for vagueness, but Stewart had trouble with that idea. He believed the law violated freedom of speech, and Warren indicated he thought so, too. White had reservations about that approach, and Fortas opposed it. During oral argument he suggested that the statute violated the Due Process Clause because it was arbitrary and unreasonable. While Warren had some sympathy for that approach, the idea of relying on substantive due process outraged Black. Harlan said he thought this was an "Establishment case," Fortas was willing to rely on that ground, and Douglas and Thurgood Marshall went along. Fortas, an advocate of a secular national culture who believed that if public schools did not pursue religious neutrality, the Court should intervene, wrote the opinion. Noting that Arkansas sought to keep its teachers from discussing a theory that contradicted the Book of Genesis, he declared: "There is and can be no doubt that the First Amendment does not permit the State to require that teaching and learning must be tailored to the principles or prohibitions of any religious sect or dogma." Black, Harlan, and Stewart wrote concurring opinions, but only the latter objected to deciding the case under the Establishment Clause, insisting what the statute violated was the First Amendment's "guarantee of free expression."[45]

Everyone else was willing to hold that Arkansas had violated the Establishment Clause, because it had so obviously departed from neutrality toward religion. Much less obvious was that making governmental resources available to church schools would also violate that principle. Assisting only parochial institutions would clearly constitute promoting religion, but *Everson* and *Zorach* suggested that giving them only what public schools and their students received might not violate the Establishment Clause. Catholics, many of whose parochial schools were in financial difficulty, put this theory to the test, seeking many types of aid from Congress and state legislatures. In its *Schempp* opinion the Supreme Court studiously avoided saying anything about the constitutionality of such grants, and only two "parochiaid" cases reached it before Warren retired. The Court resolved them in a manner hardly hostile to religion.[46]

Flast v. Cohen (1968) did give opponents of parochiaid a procedural victory. Seven of them filed suit to enjoin the expenditure of federal funds under Titles I and II of the Elementary and Secondary Education Act of 1965, which provided money for instruction in reading, arithmetic, and other subjects at religious schools and for the purchase of textbooks and instructional materials to be used at such institutions. The plaintiffs claimed that because they paid income taxes, they had standing to ask for a judicial determination of this legislation's validity. Departing from precedent, the Court agreed, creating an exception to a general prohibition on taxpayer suits for ones alleging violation of the Establishment Clause.[47]

On the same day it decided *Flast,* June 10, 1968, the Court rendered another decision favorable to parochiaid. *Board of Education v. Allen* was a challenge to a New York statute that required local public-school authorities to lend textbooks free of charge to all students in grades seven through twelve, including children attending private institutions. Speaking for the majority, White acknowledged that "the line between state neutrality to religion and state support of religion is not easy to locate." It was "a matter of degree." In order to pass constitutional muster, he declared, a statute must have a secular legislative purpose and a primary effect that neither advanced nor inhibited religion. New York's law passed this test because its purpose was furthering educational opportunities for all children, and it gave neither money nor books to parochial schools, only aiding students and their parents.[48]

White's opinion reflected the position Warren had taken in conference. The Chief viewed this, like *Everson*, as "a welfare case for students and not a violation of establishment." Black disagreed, contending that when the government began supplying books to religious schools, it violated the Constitution. Douglas supported him, arguing that while there was nothing ideological about a school lunch or a bus, supplying textbooks smacked of establishment. Fortas joined Black and Douglas in voting against the New York law, finding "offensive" the fact that parochial schools could decide which books were purchased for their students. "That to me is clearly an establishment of religion." All three filed dissenting opinions, Black declaring in his that while some might say this statute made "but a small inroad and does not amount to complete state establishment of religion, that is no excuse for upholding it." He saw a dangerous breach in the wall of separation that could be widened in the future to make constitutional all sorts of government aid to parochial schools.[49]

"My guess," Professor Katz had observed in 1964, "is that the 'no aid' view is held by a large majority . . . of non-Catholic lawyers." Yet, that view did not prevail in *Allen*. Although excoriated for prohibiting prayer and Bible reading in public schools, the Warren Court allowed New York to ease the financial burdens on parochial education. It was committed to the position that government must be neutral toward religion, but as Harlan observed in a concurring opinion, "Neutrality is . . . a coat of many colors." To him the concept meant that government must show no favoritism among sects or between religion and nonreligion. Thus, New York had behaved in a neutral manner. Black viewed what the state had done very differently. Despite having himself upheld in *Everson* a nondiscriminatory program that indirectly benefited church schools, he insisted New York's textbook law violated the Establishment Clause because it compelled unwilling taxpayers to assist religious institutions.[50]

Allen suggested that, at least where parochiaid was concerned, neutrality might not be a viable concept. Even when parochial schools received no more benefits than public ones, the Court itself acknowledged after Warren's 1969 retirement, governmental assistance could lead to excessive and politically divisive entanglements between church and state.[51] Yet, while true neutrality might not be possible, it was the position that Americans supported. A majority of them wanted government to acknowledge religion and promote religious values. As the struggles over the Becker and Dirksen amendments demonstrated, however, in a country as religiously diverse as the United States, beset by serious sectarian divisions, there was no way such acknowledgment could be implemented that would satisfy all believers. Although politicians pandered to proponents of prayer and Bible-reading amendments, Congress could find no language that satisfied even all church leaders, let alone all lawyers. Neutrality was not inherently appealing, but it was the most on which Americans could agree. In interpreting the Establishment and Free Exercise Clauses, the Warren Court at least gave the country what most people could accept, if not what most people wanted.[52] Although accused of putting itself above God, the Court was not guilty even of defying the popular will.

7

CIVIL RIGHTS

On Monday, October 2, 1967, Chief Justice Warren began a new term by announcing that Thurgood Marshall was in the Court to take the judicial oath. There could have been no more appropriate addition to the Warren Court than the famed NAACP litigator. Although it fostered freedom of religion and promoted political democracy, the cause to which it was most strongly committed was racial equality. Warren and his colleagues allied themselves with the NAACP, accepting the organization's arguments and shielding it from attack by southern authorities. While their *Brown* decision may or may not have inspired African Americans to demonstrate against white supremacy, clearly the Warren Court shielded those who did so from legal harassment. It upheld new civil rights laws and expansively interpreted old ones. Furthermore, as former solicitor general Archibald Cox pointed out a year after Marshall's appointment, "The problems of the civil rights revolution . . . affected cases that were apparently unrelated to civil rights." "The constitutional issues precipitated by the civil rights movement . . . became the focal point of the [Warren Court's] work." They inspired it to enlarge the reach and significance of the Equal Protection Clause, "a provision that," as Philip Kurland notes, had not previously been "a strong element in the Supreme Court's arsenal." As Mark Tushnet points out, "The Warren Court accepted and then elaborated the proposition that in our constitutional system all Americans are entitled to the benefits of formal equality."[1]

The NAACP sought to win such equality for African Americans by filing numerous lawsuits in the South. Southern authorities retaliated with stratagems intended to destroy the effectiveness of Marshall's organization, only to be thwarted by the Warren Court. The attorney general of Alabama, for example, sought to enjoin the NAACP from operating in his state because of its alleged failure to comply with a law requiring foreign corporations to register. Although insisting it was not covered by this statute, the civil rights organization eventually agreed to execute the required forms and to produce all of the information the state demanded—except the names of its Alabama "agents" and "members." That refusal earned the group a one-thousand-dollar fine for contempt. Under Alabama law the contempt judgment precluded the NAACP from having its case heard, and the state supreme court twice refused to review it. Black objected strenuously to this "procedure which imposes [a] penalty without giving a chance to defend on the merits." During a January 17, 1958, conference at which the justices voted unanimously for the NAACP, Warren censured the

150

state for cutting into the rights of the organization's members, and Frankfurter condemned Alabama's "unconstitutional assertion of power."[2]

The plan was to announce the result in a brief per curiam opinion, a procedure utilized in most racial litigation since *Brown*. Harlan, to whom Warren assigned the case, soon became convinced, however, that "it would reflect adversely on the Court were we to dispose of [it] without a fully reasoned opinion." The "full-scale" opinion he drafted precipitated conflict. Harlan tried to strike a compromise between Black's insistence that his opinion tie Fourteenth Amendment rights at issue in this case to the First Amendment and Frankfurter's demand that it make no reference to specific provisions in the Bill of Rights. What he wrote upset Douglas, who believed that Alabama could easily satisfy the general Due Process Clause requirement that state actions have a rational basis if that were the only test. "I do not see why a state could not have a rational judgment for believing that an organization like the NAACP was a source of a lot of trouble, friction, and unrest," Douglas told his colleagues. "Once we admit the existence of that kind of test in these racial problems, then I think we are hopelessly lost." He thought the right at issue here should be treated as something "close to the absolute." Black refused to go along with any opinion that did not mention the First Amendment. Apologizing to Frankfurter for his inability to leap directly from the language of the Due Process Clause to condemning Alabama's justification for its treatment of the NAACP, Harlan endeavored to blend the views of Black and Douglas with Frankfurter's insistence that what the state had done was trespass upon the "liberty" that clause guaranteed by fashioning a right of association, related to freedom of expression. In order to firm up the argument that Alabama had violated this right, Harlan subsequently proposed including a sentence that read: "We cannot blink the fact that strong local sentiment exists against the cause which petitioner espouses." Frankfurter pressured him into eliminating what he considered a gratuitous slap at the South. Harlan's balancing of Alabama's interests against those of the NAACP disturbed Clark, who concluded that if the Court were going to do this, the case should be sent back to the state courts so that Alabama could establish why it needed the names it demanded. He prepared a dissenting opinion but withdrew it after both Frankfurter and one of his own clerks, Robert Gorman, urged him not to disrupt "the unanimity of the Court in what is, after all, part of the whole Segregation controversy." Thus Harlan spoke for a unanimous Court.[3]

His opinion declared that the NAACP's claim that its membership lists were immune from state scrutiny was "so related to the right of the members to pursue their lawful private interests privately and to associate freely with others in doing so as to come within the protection of the Fourteenth Amendment." Disclosure of members' names was likely to deter people from joining or remaining in the organization. It was irrelevant, said Harlan, that community pressure, rather than state action, would produce this "repressive effect." Alabama might be able to demand the information it sought if the state had a sufficiently strong need for it, but the identities of rank-and-file members had no substantial bearing on the state's interests, which were determining whether the NAACP was covered by the registration statute and whether its activities justified ouster. Harlan brushed aside the precedent on which the state relied, a decision rejecting the Ku Klux Klan's challenge to a New York law requiring it to turn over membership rosters. The "character of the Klan's activities, involving acts of unlawful intimidation and violence" justified treating it differently, he contended.[4]

Although stripped of his proposed sentence about local hostility toward civil rights, Harlan's opinion in *NAACP v. Alabama* left little doubt about the Warren Court's support for that cause and its unwillingness to tolerate suppression of Marshall's organization. Nevertheless, Alabama judges persisted in trying to enforce their contempt judgment, the state supreme court seeking to justify their defiance by claiming *NAACP* rested on a mistaken assumption that the only reason the association had been held in contempt was its failure to produce membership lists. Pointing out that the case was briefed and argued on precisely that premise, the Supreme Court reversed. The Alabama Supreme Court continued to drag its feet, failing to send the case on to the trial court for a hearing on the NAACP's motion to dissolve the restraining order against it. Marshall's organization sought relief from the federal judiciary, and the case returned again to the Supreme Court. Harlan, who shared Warren's outrage at Alabama's behavior, drafted a per curiam opinion instructing the U.S. District Court for the Middle District of Alabama to determine immediately whether the state courts were delaying in order to prevent a hearing on the underlying constitutional question. Clark objected to having a federal court interfere directly in the state lawsuit, rather than merely requiring Alabama to act promptly, so Harlan revised his opinion into one that ordered Alabama to grant the NAACP a hearing by no later than January 2, 1962, but authorized the district court "to retain jurisdiction over the federal action and take such steps as may appear necessary and appropriate to assure a prompt disposition of all issues involved in, or connected with, the state action." With that gun at his head, a trial judge in Montgomery finally granted the NAACP a hearing on the merits, more than five years after its "temporary" ouster from the state. Predictably, he ruled that the organization was operating in violation of Alabama law and enjoined the NAACP from doing business in the state. The Alabama Supreme Court affirmed, purporting to base its decision on the organization's failure to follow one of the court's rules governing the structure of briefs. Black excoriated this rule as a "trap for the unwary." Fed up with Alabama's obstructionism, the Supreme Court voted unanimously on March 27, 1964, to reverse on the merits. Even Clark was now ready to "formulate a decree." In a signed opinion Harlan brushed aside the contention that the state supreme court's ruling rested on a valid nonfederal ground and ruled that there was no basis for ousting the NAACP from the state. He directed the Alabama Supreme Court to vacate promptly all aspects of the injunction, adding that should he and his colleagues "unhappily be mistaken in our belief" that it would "promptly implement this disposition, leave is given the Association to apply to this Court for further appropriate relief."[5]

While fighting a protracted war against Alabama, the Warren Court also resisted attacks on the NAACP by Arkansas authorities. In 1957 Little Rock and North Little Rock amended their occupational-licensing tax ordinances to require that all organizations operating within those municipalities supply them with information that included the names of their officers, employees, and financial contributors. Since these laws provided that this information was to be public and subject to inspection by all interested persons, a number of people dropped out of the NAACP. Daisy Bates, the custodian of the records for the Little Rock branch, and her North Little Rock counterpart were prosecuted for refusing to supply the names and addresses of their members and contributors. The Supreme Court unanimously reversed these convictions. The only real disagreement concerned whether to base the decision on the rationale of *NAACP v. Alabama* or the First Amendment. Harlan argued strongly for the former approach, which Stewart's opinion for the Court adopted. Compulsory disclosure of membership lists would work a significant interference with the freedom of association of NAACP members, he wrote, and it had no relevant correlation with the municipalities' power to impose occupational-license taxes. Although Stewart deleted a discussion of balancing that had troubled the liberal bloc, Black and Douglas nevertheless filed a concurring opinion arguing that the decision should have been based on the First Amendment.[6]

Ten months after its February 1960 ruling in *Bates v. Little Rock*, the Court thwarted another Arkansas anti-NAACP initiative. *Shelton v. Tucker* involved a statute that required every teacher, as a condition of employment in a state-supported school or college, to file an affidavit listing every organization to which he or she had belonged or regularly contributed during the past five years. It was a tougher case than *NAACP v. Alabama*, for although the statute was "a patent attempt to strike at NAACP members who were teachers," the two public-school instructors and one college professor whom Bates recruited as plaintiffs apparently did not belong to Marshall's organization. Furthermore, precedents from the early 1950s held that public agencies seeking to determine whether their employees were Communists could demand disclosure of organizational memberships that might bear on their job performance, and Arkansas courts ruled that a generalized requirement to disclose all memberships was relevant to job performance. Stewart saw no harassment or discrimination here, and he acknowledged that disclosure of information about teachers was connected to the operation of an efficient school system. He nevertheless voted somewhat hesitantly to reverse a lower court ruling against Shelton. Although offering similar observations about the case, Frankfurter urged affirmance. Clark, Whittaker, and Harlan supported him. On the other side, Warren acknowledged that "this reaches beyond [the] Negro problem," but insisted "Arkansas's statute was too vague." Douglas and Brennan supported him, as did Black, although he added that he "would be willing to go on broader constitutional grounds." Writing for a five-to-four majority, Stewart conceded that this case differed from *Bates* and *NAACP* in that the state's inquiry was relevant to a legitimate governmental interest. The disclosures Arkansas was demanding, however, impaired the right of teachers to free association. Consequently, the question was whether in demanding to know the identity of every single organization to which every one of its teachers belonged, the state was resorting to "means that broadly stifle fundamental personal liberties when the end can be more narrowly achieved." "The statute's comprehensive interference with associational freedom goes far beyond what might be justified in the exercise of the State's legitimate inquiry into the fitness and competency of its teachers," Stewart concluded. By eliminating all implications of balancing and avoiding expressing approval of decisions from which they had dissented during the McCarthy era, he managed to keep Black and Douglas from writing separately. Frankfurter and Harlan dissented, however, and were joined by Clark and Whittaker. Their opinions stressed the need for judicial restraint, with Harlan's also emphasizing the facial neutrality of Arkansas's statute and the absence of "an issue of racial discrimination."[7]

The element of racial discrimination was much more obviously present in *Louisiana ex rel. Gremillion v. NAACP,* a challenge to two Louisiana statutes, one of them an old anti-Klan law that required various types of nonbusiness organizations to file lists of their members and officers with the secretary of state and made it a crime to attend any meeting of a group that had not done so. The other law, a 1958 one aimed at the NAACP, prohibited any "non-trading" association from doing business in Louisiana if it was affiliated with an out-of-state association having any officers or directors who belonged to Communist, Communist-front, or subversive organizations, and required the annual filing of an affidavit attesting that no officers of the out-of-state affiliate were members of such a group. Attorney General John P. F. Gremillion, an official who persistently resisted enforcement of *Brown,* sought to enjoin the NAACP from doing business in the state for failing to comply with this statute. Noting how difficult it would be for Louisiana members to verify the affiliations of the seventy-eight officials of the New York–based NAACP for whom they were required to vouch, the Supreme Court invalidated both this law and the other one. Probably because Douglas's opinion noted that this was "an area where, as Shelton v. Tucker . . . emphasized, any regulation must be highly selective in order to survive challenge under the First Amendment," Frankfurter concurred with the judgment on procedural grounds. Harlan and Stewart did so without opinion. No one, however, dissented.[8]

Cases involving harassment of the NAACP with laws governing the practice of law proved more divisive. In 1956 the Virginia legislature enacted a package of statutes targeting the NAACP's legal activities, one of which authorized disciplinary action against any lawyer who solicited business by using an agent who was not a party to the lawsuit and had no pecuniary interest in the litigation. After hearing arguments on that law's constitutionality in November 1961, the Court voted five to four to uphold it. Warren and Black, who viewed this statute as part of an effort to thwart *Brown,* argued strongly against it, but Clark thought invalidating it would amount to discrimination in favor of African Americans. Frankfurter, who said he could not imagine "a worse disservice than continuing being guardians for Negroes," drafted an elaborate opinion upholding the challenged statute as a constitutionally permissible effort to combat ambulance chasing and related abuses. Before the decision could be announced, however, Frankfurter and Whittaker retired. Following reargument, Goldberg voted with the former minority. Writing for the new majority, in *NAACP v. Button,* Brennan declared that the kind of cooperative organizational activity in which Marshall's organization engaged was protected by the First Amendment, and that a law as vague and overbroad as Virginia's could not be allowed to deter the exercise of constitutionally protected rights. "We cannot close our eyes to the fact that the militant Negro civil rights movement has engendered the intense resentment and opposition of the politically dominant White community of Virginia," Brennan wrote. Only a compelling state interest could justify limiting First Amendment freedoms, and while Virginia's interest in regulating the traditionally illegal practices of barratry, maintenance, and champerty was legitimate, it was not compelling.[9]

Awareness that southern states were harassing Marshall's organization influenced not only the *Button* decision but also the Court's reaction to what legislative committees in Florida, Louisiana, Arkansas, and Mississippi purported to be investigations of subversive activities. The refusal of the president of the NAACP's Miami branch to produce its membership records for the Florida committee, which was allegedly probing Communist infiltration of the civil rights organization, triggered litigation that reached the Court during the 1961–62 term. Although Warren argued that affirming the contempt judgment against Theodore Gibson would effectively overrule *NAACP v. Alabama,* Harlan insisted the two cases were different because this one involved a bona fide investigation of Communism. He drafted an opinion for a five-to-four majority upholding the conviction. As with *Button,* however, the retirements of Frankfurter and Whittaker changed the result. After *Gibson v. Florida Legislative Investigating Committee* was reargued, White voted with Harlan, Clark, and Stewart, but Goldberg joined Warren, Brennan, Black, and Douglas, enabling them to prevail five to four. Speaking for the Court, newcomer Goldberg declared that the legislative power to investigate was limited by the First and Fourteenth Amendments, and that while Florida might have a compelling regulatory concern with Communist activities, the state had failed to demonstrate a nexus between such activities and the Miami branch of the NAACP. Harlan, always reluctant to inquire into the motives underlying ostensibly legitimate governmental actions, dissented. No one dissented when, in 1967, the Court reversed with a per curiam opinion a summary judgment against members of another civil rights organization, the Southern Conference Educational Fund, who were seeking to recover damages from employees of the Senate Internal Security Subcommittee for allegedly conspiring with Louisiana officials to seize their property and records in violation of the Fourth Amendment. While holding legislative immunity shielded members of Congress from liability for such conduct, the Court refused to extend such protection to the subcommittee's counsel.[10]

The Supreme Court also thwarted probable harassment of the NAACP in *Henry v. Mississippi* (1965). The organization's Mississippi president, Aaron Henry, had been convicted of disturbing the peace by making indecent and offensive contact with an eighteen-year-old hitchhiker. The state supreme court initially overturned his conviction because of an unlawful search, but then reversed itself because his lawyer had failed to make a timely objection to the admission of the evidence the search had yielded. Henry claimed to be the victim of a plot by the Clarksdale police chief and a county prosecutor, and the state's brief aroused suspicion about the good faith of Mississippi authorities by implying he had engaged in homosexual acts when nothing in the record substantiated such a claim. During oral argument Warren excoriated a Mississippi assistant attorney general, G. Garland Lyell, for trying to poison the minds of the Court and the public against Henry. In conference, however, he acknowledged that the state really was not guilty of playing fast and loose with its procedural rules and suggested disposing of the case by holding certiorari had been improvidently granted. The others went along, but Brennan, originally willing to treat the admission of the illegally seized evidence as a harmless error, later had second thoughts. He informed his colleagues that he could not accept the planned disposition and intended to circulate a dissent. Brennan's dissent eventually garnered enough support to become an opinion of the Court, vacating the conviction and remanding the case to the Mississippi judiciary to determine whether the defendant had waived his right to object to the admission of the disputed evidence. Black, who wanted to decide the constitutional issues Henry had raised, dissented. So did Harlan, Clark, and Stewart, because they felt the majority was showing disrespect for state procedure and subverting federalism.[11]

The way the Court went about protecting the NAACP had significant doctrinal consequences. *Henry v. Mississippi* confused the established rule that the Supreme Court would not review a state court's determination of a federal question if an adequate and independent state ground for the decision existed, because the ruling treated this principle as not necessarily applicable if the state ground was a procedural default. The Court's determination to protect the NAACP also gave birth to the First Amendment right of freedom of political association, which Harlan created in response to Frankfurter's complaints about his *NAACP v. Alabama* opinion. *Bates v. Little Rock, Shelton v. Tucker,* and *NAACP v. Button* furthered the development of a doctrine whose significance, as Warren acknowledged, "reaches beyond [the] Negro problem." The same was true of the First Amendment overbreadth doctrine, which *Button* revived and developed. The notion that a statute is facially invalid if it is written so broadly that it punishes constitutionally protected speech, along with activity government has a right to proscribe, lay behind such pre–Warren Court decisions as *Cantwell v. Connecticut* (1940) and *Kunz v. New York* (1951). It was in *Button,* however, that Brennan coined the term "overbreadth," pointed out "the danger of tolerating in the area of First Amendment freedoms, the existence of a penal statute susceptible of sweeping and improper application," and laid down the rule that "Because First Amendment freedoms need breathing space to survive, government may regulate in the area only with narrow specificity." To establish that "a vague and overbroad law lends itself to selective enforcement against unpopular causes" he cited the NAACP cases.[12]

Some of Brennan's colleagues objected that altering the law to protect the NAACP from harassment amounted to displaying favoritism toward African American litigants. Harlan lectured his colleagues frequently about the need to avoid creating a body of "Negro law." When he suggested that the Court had agreed to hear one minor contempt case that involved a lawyer only because of its racial overtones, Black expressed regret that Harlan had raised the issue. When Harlan opened a draft of his dissent in *Button* with a sentence "in effect accusing the Court of giving Negroes preferred status as litigants," Brennan protested. Harlan toned down the opinion, but he did not eliminate the implication that the Court was applying different standards in judging whether state actions violated the Fourteenth Amendment when racial problems were involved. Shortly before his retirement Frankfurter too expressed concern that the Court was bending the law to help civil rights activists. "I am sure that you and I are in agreement," he wrote to Black, "that it will not advance the cause of constitutional equality for Negroes for the Court to be taking short cuts, to discriminate as partisans in favor of Negroes."[13]

By then the Warren Court was demonstrating favoritism for African Americans not only in cases arising from southern harassment of the NAACP but also in litigation spawned by civil rights demonstrations. These protests included the 1955–56 Montgomery, Alabama, bus boycott, which catapulted Dr. Martin Luther King Jr. into national prominence, the 1961 Freedom Rides, in which integrated groups of civil rights activists rode buses into the Deep South to challenge the continued segregation of terminal facilities used by interstate carriers, and the student sit-ins at segregated restaurants and other places of public accommodation, which began in Greensboro, North Carolina, in February 1960 and spread quickly through the southern and border states. The Warren Court supported all of these direct-action challenges to white supremacy, beginning with its ruling in *Gayle v. Browder* (1957), which unanimously affirmed a district court decision invalidating the Alabama statutes and municipal ordinances requiring "the segregation of the White and colored races on the motor buses" in Montgomery.[14]

Boynton v. Virginia (1960) laid the groundwork for the Freedom Rides, holding that the Interstate Commerce Act (ICA) gave an African American passenger traveling to Montgomery from Washington, D.C., a federal right to be served without discrimination by a restaurant located in a bus terminal utilized, but not actually operated, by Trailways. The conference vote was five to three; although Stewart withdrew a proposed dissent, Whittaker published one for himself and Clark because certiorari had been granted to decide whether the petitioner's trespassing conviction for refusing to leave the whites-only part of the restaurant violated the Due Process and Equal Protection Clauses. Warren wanted to avoid the Fourteenth Amendment, so he proposed deciding the case under the ICA. Frankfurter liked that idea, and Harlan and Brennan were both inclined to go along with the Chief, although they worried about the broad reach they would be giving the statute if they applied it to a facility the bus company did not control. Black observed realistically that "if it's in a terminal it's part of commerce," but Whittaker insisted there had been no showing of a nexus between the restaurant and the carrier, and Clark, believing Boynton was "trying to get [a] ruling that these private places are terminal facilities" also remained unconvinced. Their dissent argued that the statutory issue had not been properly raised and that if it had been, this trespassing conviction did not violate the ICA. A few months after *Boynton,* the Congress of Racial Equality (CORE) launched the Freedom Rides to test compliance with the decision. In 1965 the Court found itself confronted with a case that had arisen when a group of Freedom Riders, led by Rev. Ralph David Abernathy bought tickets at the Montgomery bus station, then occupied seats at the lunch counter there. A hostile crowd gathered and the sheriff, fearing violence, arrested the demonstrators. Citing *Boynton,* the Court unanimously reversed their convictions with a brief per curiam opinion. In conference, however, Harlan made a point of telling his colleagues that he would not be willing to preclude the police from making arrests like these even when they did not also arrest the crowd, and that if the police had warned the demonstrators to leave before taking them into custody, he would be voting to affirm.[15]

He made these remarks at a time when the justices were engaged in a furious internal debate over related problems generated by the sit-in cases that reached the Court during the early 1960s. At issue were equal protection and free speech. Demonstrators also argued that the laws under which they had been convicted were void for vagueness and that there was no evidence to support their convictions. The Warren Court repeatedly ruled in their favor. In 1966 Loren Miller observed, "In every case in which it granted review . . . [it] upset convictions upheld by state courts." Not until *Adderly v. Florida* (1966) did civil rights demonstrators lose a single case on the merits.[16]

While the Warren Court consistently reversed the convictions of civil rights demonstrators, it did so without ever accepting the constitutional argument that many of them, especially those arrested for trespass and breach of the peace, pressed upon it: that the discriminatory purpose of private individuals should be attributed to the State. Since its decision in the *Civil Rights Cases* (1883), the Supreme Court had adhered to the proposition that only state action could violate the Fourteenth Amendment. During the Vinson years it did attenuate this limitation somewhat, holding that when private persons took on functions normally performed by government, they must comply with the Constitution and, in *Shelley v. Kraemer* (1948), that judicial enforcement of restrictive covenants (by which homeowners bound themselves not to sell their property to nonwhites) sufficiently involved government in their racial discrimination to satisfy the state action requirement. The sit-in demonstrators wanted the Court to go further, imposing on all businesses that served the public the same constitutional norms that applied to governmental actors.[17]

The Court would not do that. It went to great lengths, however, to find some governmental involvement in what was essentially private discrimination. In *Burton v. Wilmington Parking Authority* (1961) it held that the refusal of the Eagle Coffee Shoppe, which leased space in a municipal parking garage from a public agency, to serve an African American because of his race violated the Fourteenth Amendment. Warren viewed the conduct of this private business as "an exercise . . . of state power" and argued that those whose tax monies helped to build a facility such as the parking garage "can't be discriminated against in its use." Harlan, though, could "see no state action whatever." Only Whittaker agreed with him, but both Frankfurter and Stewart wanted to avoid deciding whether the Fourteenth Amendment applied to Eagle. Stewart insisted that a state statute, which permitted restaurant owners to refuse to serve anyone whose presence might offend a majority of their customers (which he thought the Delaware Supreme Court had interpreted as authorizing racial discrimination), supplied the required state action, while Frankfurter wanted the Court to "creep along rather than be general." Stewart concurred, but Frankfurter (although he agreed with the majority on the merits) joined Whittaker and Harlan in dissent, contending the case should be returned to the state courts for clarification of the basis on which they had decided it. Although *Burton* divided the Court, a year later the justices unanimously found state action in the refusal of an airport restaurant, operated under a lease from the City of Memphis, to serve an African American. Its per curiam opinion denied the city a hearing before a three-judge district court on the constitutionality of several allegedly relevant Tennessee statutes and regulations, because "the restaurant was subject to the strictures of the Fourteenth Amendment under *Burton v. Wilmington Parking Authority.*" Even Harlan considered *Burton* determinative.[18]

That decision swept within the ambit of state action a great deal of conduct that had once been considered purely private, and in a heavily regulated economy, where interaction between government and business was pervasive, its rationale could have been extended until it eviscerated the doctrine of the *Civil Rights Cases.* Despite a strong commitment to the elimination of "state-sponsored racial inequality," however, the Warren Court proved unwilling to push it that far. The justices were too attached to what Douglas characterized in *Evans v. Newton* (1966) as "the right of the individual to pick his own associates so as to express his preferences and dislikes." Forced to balance competing values in *Evans,* the Court held that the Equal Protection Clause prohibited the use as a park for whites only of land which a racist citizen had willed to Macon, Georgia, for that purpose—even after the city, realizing it could not legally operate a segregated facility, withdrew as trustee and a state court appointed three private individuals to run it. On one hand, Douglas assumed that Macon was still maintaining the park and emphasized both "the momentum it acquired as a public facility" and the governmental nature of the function it performed. Harlan, on the other hand, saw this as a case of racial discrimination that arose solely out of "individual predilections," and consequently one that the Equal Protection Clause did not touch. Stewart signed his dissent, and although Black and White did not, their separate opinions faulted Douglas for deciding too much. Even Douglas assumed *arguendo* that if someone wanted to "leave a school . . . for the use of one race only and in no way implicated the State in the supervision, control, or management of that facility," there would be no violation of the Constitution. Although urging him not to state flatly that doing so would be permissible, Brennan also believed it was. Despite their very strong commitment to racial equality, even the most liberal members of the Warren Court were "reluctant to impose the obligations of nondiscrimination on private persons engaged in private affairs."[19]

That reluctance complicated the resolution of cases in which sit-in demonstrators were prosecuted on charges such as trespassing and disorderly conduct, rather than for violation of segregation laws. In these the Court searched for some hint that government was promoting racial discrimination, rather than merely using neutral laws to preserve the peace and protect the property of bigoted businessmen. In *Peterson v. City of Greenville* (1963), for example, it pointed to a municipal ordinance that prohibited whites and blacks from dining together, reasoning that, because a trespass law was being used to enforce it, there had been a violation of the Fourteenth Amendment. The Court decided *Gober v. City of Birmingham* (1963) and *Avent v. North Carolina* (1963) on the same basis. *Lombard v. Louisiana* (1963) had arisen in New Orleans, which had no segregation ordinance, so the Court held that the necessary state action was supplied by statements by the mayor and superintendent of police that sit-ins were prohibited. In *Robinson v. Florida* (1964), the Court declared that state health regulations requiring separate toilet and lavatory facilities for white and black customers discouraged serving the races together, and hence constituted state action coercing segregation. The deputizing of the amusement park security guard who made the trespassing arrests in *Griffin v. Maryland* (1964) was enough state action to produce reversal in that case.[20]

The Court resorted to a variety of expedients to overturn convictions without confronting the state action problem. In December 1961, soon after the justices discussed their first sit-in cases, Frankfurter wrote to Warren, saying he agreed with "the view expressed by you . . . that they should be disposed of on the narrowest possible grounds." He endorsed the Chief's proposal that they rely on *Thompson v. Louisville* (1960), a case having nothing to do with African Americans, which had reversed loitering and disorderly conduct convictions because there was no evidentiary support for them, announcing in the process that "it is a violation of due process to convict and punish a man without evidence of his guilt." *Thompson* became a favorite of Warren, who often began discussions of cases involving civil rights demonstrators by asserting that there was "no evidence to justify the judgments of conviction." Harlan objected to this approach, and Douglas also expressed reservations, but the others liked the "no evidence" tactic and the related one of holding the statute under which protesters had been prosecuted void for vagueness. Both yielded reversals without creating broadly applicable precedents.[21]

Yet, in its eagerness to avoid the state action problem, the Court sometimes rendered decisions with considerable precedential significance. One was *Bouie v. City of Columbia* (1964). The protesters in that case were convicted of trespassing for refusing to leave a drugstore restaurant, where they were staging a sit-in, when asked to do so by the manager. The law under which they were prosecuted made entering the premises of another after being prohibited to do so a misdemeanor, but in affirming the convictions, the South Carolina Supreme Court interpreted it as also applying to remaining after being told to leave. Under a well-established doctrine, any criminal statute that failed to give fair warning of what conduct it punished violated the Due Process Clause. In previous cases applying this principle, however, the source of the uncertainty had been the vague and overly broad language of the statute itself. In order to overturn the *Bouie* convictions, the Court declared that a denial of the right of fair warning could also result "from an unforeseeable and retroactive judicial expansion of narrow and precise statutory language." Following this precedent, in 1970 the California Supreme Court dismissed murder charges against a man who had brutally killed his ex-wife's fetus, because previous judicial decisions had construed the state's murder statute as applying only to victims who had been "born alive." In *Cox v. Louisiana* (1965), the Warren Court, in order to reverse convictions of demonstrators who had gathered outside a courthouse to protest the arrest of black students for picketing segregated lunch counters, created another new rule of criminal law, or rather provided a constitutional basis for one proposed by drafters of the American Law Institute's Model Penal Code. It held that the hoary principle that ignorance of the law is no excuse did not apply when the defendant relied on an erroneous explanation of a statute by a public officer charged with interpreting it.[22]

Novel doctrines, "no evidence" rulings, and dubious findings of governmental responsibility enabled the Court to overturn scores of sit-in convictions, but could not prevent a divisive internal debate over how to resolve the conflict of rights and values these cases posed. That controversy began over *Garner v. Louisiana* (1961). The African Americans convicted of disturbing the peace in that case had done nothing more than take seats at a whites-only lunch counter and remain there quietly after being denied service. With Warren writing the opinion, the Court unanimously overturned their convictions using the *Thompson v. Louisville* rationale. That approach appeared to be acceptable to most of the justices when the Chief proposed it in conference. Douglas announced, however, that he had concluded a state could not require segregation of the races in a public place by either legislative or judicial action. "It's nonsense to talk of these [places] as private property—they are as public as jails, streets, or playgrounds," he declared. Frankfurter concluded that Warren and Brennan shared Douglas's "extreme . . . constitutional views regarding sit-ins." He believed all three were starting "from the premise that continuing to remain in what heretofore has been deemed to be 'private' premises after a request to leave is a form of constitutionally protected free speech" and that under this rationale "no 'trespassing' statute, no matter how narrowly drawn," could pass muster with "at least five members of this court." They would eventually "hold such constitutionally protected right overbalances any claim of an exercise of property rights in an irrationally discriminatory way." Harlan assured Frankfurter he did not intend to espouse any "such foolish doctrine as that the 'liberty' protected by the Fourteenth Amendment embraces activities on property which the owner has the right to prevent or object to." He was concerned, however, that once breach-of-the-peace convictions were overturned on *Thompson* grounds, the argument would inevitably be made that trespassing convictions should be also. Harlan glimpsed "the early-flowering seeds of a body of negro law," the creation of which "would be very bad for the Court." Frankfurter too saw this as "only the beginning of a series of cases in which we shall be called upon legally to unwind the tangled skein of sit-in situations," but he deemed it desirable to have a "narrowly written opinion" based on a "narrow ground of decision." He urged Warren to omit "reference to all . . . far-reaching constitutional questions." The Chief produced such an opinion, and Frankfurter concurred on grounds that what the defendants had actually done was not made a crime by the breach-of-the-peace statute under which they had been prosecuted. Harlan, insisting the *Thompson* doctrine did not fit these facts, wrote that the convictions should be overturned because the statute was void for vagueness and, as applied to sitting in with the implied consent of management, interfered with freedom of expression. Douglas also wrote separately, arguing that the state could not use its disturbing-the-peace law against those who engaged in the conduct these defendants had, because restaurants, although "private enterprises . . . are public facilities in which the State may not enforce a policy of racial segregation."[23]

The internal debate ignited by *Garner* continued in connection with six more sit-in cases the following term. By then views had become polarized, and Black emerged as the leading opponent of Douglas's position. The disagreement between these longtime liberal allies over the sit-ins was one consequence of Black's increasing conservatism. During the 1960s his voting pattern on civil rights and civil liberties issues changed, moving him from the Court's left wing to somewhere near the middle. Where sit-ins were concerned, he was on the right. Black found such direct action repugnant. He saw implicit in physical protest threats of violence and disorder, and he believed the civil disobedience employed by Martin Luther King and his followers would lead to anarchy. Black strongly opposed King's August 1963 March on Washington, which he feared would result in rioting. He also saw the sit-ins as a threat to property rights. While acknowledging that Congress or a state legislature could prohibit private firms from practicing racial discrimination, Black insisted that unless they did, the owner of a truly private enterprise, like his father's country store, might exclude anyone he wished; the Constitution did not give African Americans a right to enter any business they chose.[24]

Black forcefully articulated these views when the Court discussed the six cases on November 9, 1962. All involved trespassing, five at restaurants and one at a Maryland amusement park. Warren urged reversing all of them on narrow grounds, taking the position that in Greenville, South Carolina, Durham, North Carolina, Birmingham, and New Orleans, the state compelled restauranteurs to segregate and was thus not merely enforcing private choices when prosecuting for trespass. The amusement park demonstrators had been arrested by an employee with a badge, who had been deputized by the county sheriff, so that case too could be disposed of by attributing the segregation to the state. As for Rev. Fred Shuttlesworth, who had been prosecuted for inciting the Birmingham violations, there was "no evidence he counseled an unlawful act." Black was willing to go along with the Chief because the businesses had not been shown to have freely chosen to exclude blacks. If they had, however, ruling for sit-in demonstrators would require assuming it was unconstitutional for a store owner to choose his own customers. "We have a system of private ownership of property," Black argued, and "if private property is to be protected he has the right to call the police and get help to throw the customer out." Douglas responded forcefully that "retail stores cannot segregate constitutionally." Goldberg thought there was merit in his position, especially in light of *Shelley v. Kraemer,* but Clark agreed with Black that it was "an owner's right to be selective." So did Harlan and Stewart. Brennan did not want to deal with the broad problem Black raised. Nor did Goldberg, who stressed that he "would like to have unity."[25]

That proved difficult to achieve. Warren assigned the writing of the opinions to himself and, at Stewart's suggestion, made *Peterson v. City of Greenville* the leading case. What he wrote did not satisfy his colleagues. White circulated concurring opinions, and Clark informed the Chief that he intended to concur only in the result in two cases, to note his concurrence on different grounds in another, and to write a concurring opinion and two dissents. At a May 16 conference, Stewart and Goldberg, pointing out the great benefit that flowed from the unanimous decisions in the school segregation cases, urged upon their colleagues "the desirability of reaching as nearly a unanimous conclusion as possible." Brennan and White were assigned to prepare revised opinions in *Peterson* and the New Orleans case, *Lombard v. Louisiana.*

Their principal contribution was to eliminate any hint that there could be a violation of the Fourteenth Amendment if the state had not in some way commanded or coerced a restaurant to segregate. This issue was sensitive enough that Goldberg asked Warren to include an explicit disclaimer that "there is nothing in our decision today which holds or suggests that private discrimination itself, regrettable though it be, is outlawed by the Constitution." Bowing to the wishes of his colleagues, Clark decided not to issue his projected opinions.[26]

That enabled Warren to speak for six other justices. He reversed the *Peterson* convictions on the ground that the state had violated the Fourteenth Amendment by leaving restauranteurs with no choice but to segregate. On the authority of that ruling, he vacated the Durham judgments in *Avent v. North Carolina* and reversed the Birmingham judgments in *Gober v. Birmingham*. The latter decision, by overturning the conviction of the individuals the defendants were accused of inciting, begat reversal in *Shuttlesworth*. In *Lombard* the Chief reversed because, due to the statements of executive officials, "The city must be treated exactly as if it had an ordinance prohibiting" integrated service in restaurants. The Court disposed of the amusement park case *Griffin v. Maryland* by setting it down for reargument. Although the now-retired Frankfurter urged Black to "write a separate little piece setting forth the essentials of what you told all of us twice at Conference," he remained silent. Douglas did not. Concurring in *Lombard,* he argued that both by their nature and because they were regulated by government, restaurants were public rather than private, and that in any event judicial imposition of penalties on those seeking service satisfied the state action requirement. Harlan disputed the latter contention. Although faulting the majority for depriving restauranteurs of the right to operate on a segregated basis in any city having a segregation ordinance, he conceded the existence of such a law should force a state to prove that private choice motivated a given exclusion. On the basis of that principle, in a single opinion Harlan concurred or dissented in whole or in part in all of the cases except *Shuttlesworth*.[27]

His opinion and Douglas's were the only public acknowledgments of the sit-in controversy smoldering within the Court. A year later, however, it burst into flame. With *Griffin* already on the docket, the justices also agreed to hear *Bell v. Maryland, Barr v. Columbia, Bouie v. Columbia,* and *Robinson v. Florida.* All were trespassing convictions for sitting down at lunch counters or in restaurants and refusing to leave when denied service. The solicitor general filed a brief urging that, like the previous term's sit-in cases, these be disposed of using narrow rationales, but on October 21 Douglas wrote a memorandum to his colleagues arguing that it "would be unwise to go off on [those] grounds." At a conference two days later, Warren also opposed avoiding the basic issue. He did say, however, that *Barr* and *Bouie* could be reversed on the ground that the police had been enforcing what was actually their policy, something his colleagues agreed to do by votes of eight to one and seven to two (with Black casting two no votes and Harlan one). Warren also argued then and later that the involvement of the deputized park-security guard in *Griffin* supplied the element of state action necessary to overturn those convictions. When they discussed that case again on November 9, only Harlan wanted to affirm.[28]

Although suggesting other grounds on which to decide some cases, Warren insisted the justices had to face the fundamental question. "On the basic issue of [the] right to deny service," Douglas recorded in his notes on the October 23 conference, "the court is 5–4 in favor of the restaurant owner's right to serve only the ones he wants to serve." Insisting that "When a man owns property he owns it," Black claimed that *Shelley v. Kraemer* did not control these cases and said he would overrule *Shelley* rather than invalidate trespass statutes. Clark agreed with everything Black said and Harlan with nearly all. White and Stewart also supported him, at least with respect to *Bell* and *Robinson,* in which Stewart insisted the basic issue should be addressed. Douglas, Warren, Brennan, and Goldberg opposed them. The Chief distinguished homes and warehouses from businesses that served the public, saying that in the field of public accommodations owners abandoned the right of private choice. He joined Douglas and Brennan in arguing that criminal laws could not be employed to enforce an owner's desire to discriminate. When they were used for this purpose, *Shelley v. Kraemer* applied. At a subsequent daylong conference on the sit-in cases, Goldberg argued strongly that in order to sustain these convictions, they would have to overrule *Shelley.* Echoing Douglas, he contended that the majority was legitimizing racial discrimination and, echoing Douglas and Brennan, making the enactment of civil rights legislation impossible. Asking why they were receding from progressive implementation of desegregation, Goldberg characterized the sit-ins as "the most serious problem before the Court in recent years."[29]

He urged deciding these cases on narrow grounds, but the majority resisted. The minority then sought to delay an adverse ruling by requesting the views of the solicitor general on the fundamental issue. Black, Clark, White, and (after changing his mind overnight) Harlan opposed that idea and attached to the Court's November 18 order requesting the filing of a brief a statement saying they did not think the invitation should have been issued. The minority got more than it hoped for; Solicitor General Cox requested double the thirty days the Court had given his office. In addition, while researching the brief, his staff discovered that Florida had a regulation requiring segregated toilets in restaurants. Thus, *Peterson* required reversing the *Robinson* convictions, something the Court did unanimously.[30]

Its spokesman, Black, had been planning to use *Robinson* as the vehicle for rejecting the proposition that the Fourteenth Amendment forbade states from arresting and prosecuting those who refused to leave restaurants when asked to do so for racial reasons. Forced to utilize *Bell v. Maryland* instead, he prepared a fifteen-page draft opinion that Clark, Harlan, Stewart, and White approved. Black circulated this to the full Court on March 12, 1964, and by May 7 Douglas, Goldberg, and Warren had responded with dissents. Although joining these three, Brennan circulated his own dissent on April 18. Ignoring the fundamental issue, Brennan argued for reversal on the basis of state laws enacted after the convictions prohibiting discrimination in places of public accommodation in Baltimore (where *Bell* had arisen). He admitted to Douglas and Goldberg that he would not have taken this tack had the vote gone the other way. He feared, however, that a decision based on Black's constitutional reasoning might adversely affect prospects for passage of the public accommodations title of the civil rights bill Congress was then debating. His concern was not alleviated by the majority's willingness to state explicitly that it was expressing no opinion on the power of Congress to prevent racial discrimination in privately owned businesses.[31]

Brennan managed to delay the handing down of a decision by asking for additional time to alter what he had written in response to new points made by Black. Meanwhile, he and Warren worked to pry a vote away from the majority. Stewart wavered, but when White refused to defect from Black's opinion, he stuck with it too. Then on May 15, Clark informed his colleagues that he had changed his mind and was joining Brennan's dissent. When Black pressured him, arguing that because a majority had voted to decide the case on the merits, they must do so, an angry Clark threatened to join the original minority on the fundamental issue. Brennan also managed to recruit Goldberg, although he persisted in plans to dissent on the merits as well, along with Douglas. Warren joined both of their opinions. Douglas claimed that this "leaves a majority of the Court against the disposition which Brother Brennan has suggested." The two of them debated hotly whether Brennan was proposing "vacating" or "reversing" the judgment of the Maryland courts, and more important, whether there was a majority to do either. This controversy triggered lengthy and complicated negotiations, directed simply at forging some sort of agreement on precisely what a badly fractured Court was doing. The fact that one majority favored in some way setting aside the convictions while an entirely different one wanted to decide the constitutional issue created a seemingly insoluble dilemma.[32]

Clark broke this logjam. On June 7 he informed Douglas that he intended to write for reversal on the merits. Four days later, he circulated a draft, relying on the Fourteenth Amendment and *Shelley*, that was clearly designed to be an opinion of the Court. At a June 11 conference, Clark announced he had five votes, and Warren assigned the case to him. His opinion was apparently only a tactic to prevent a decision on the merits. The maneuver worked, for Stewart, concluding that no resolution of the constitutional issue was better than a bad one, deserted Black for Brennan. Clark then withdrew his opinion, and along with Warren and Goldberg, joined Brennan, making his the opinion of the Court.[33]

Although technically Brennan spoke for a majority, in fact the Court divided into three distinct groups. His opinion resolved *Bell* by holding that "the question of Maryland law raised here by the supervening enactment of the city and state public accommodations laws [requires] us to vacate and reverse the judgment and remand the case to the Maryland Court of Appeals." Only Stewart and Clark fully supported Brennan. Goldberg joined his opinion, but also published a concurrence, which Warren signed, that argued "the Constitution guarantees to all Americans the right to be treated as equal members of the community with respect to public accommodations." A state's use of its criminal trespass laws against African Americans who were seeking service in a restaurant, Goldberg contended, would frustrate their exercise of a "constitutionally guaranteed right," even if the authorities were merely "legitimating a proprietor's attempt at self-help." Douglas also took a position on the merits, joining part of Goldberg's opinion and publishing one of his own, some of which Goldberg (but not Warren) joined. Douglas argued for outright reversal of the convictions and excoriated the Court for defaulting on an issue he believed "the whole nation has to face." He asserted yet again that restaurants were not truly private property and that judicial enforcement of their owners' wishes to exclude blacks was state action. Douglas relied on *Shelley*, but in a dissenting opinion, signed also by Harlan and White, Black insisted this reliance was misplaced. His group contended that the Fourteenth Amendment "does not forbid a State to prosecute for crimes committed against a person or his property, however prejudiced or narrow the victim's views may be" and that the bigotry of the victim could not automatically be attributed to the state. Black protested the Court's refusal to resolve the "crucial issue" of whether the Fourteenth Amendment forbade enforcement of trespass laws against those who refused to leave restaurants after being asked to do so by owners who did not want to serve them because of their race.[34]

He also dissented, along with Harlan and White, in *Bouie, Barr,* and *Griffin.* In all of those cases the Court reversed the convictions without addressing the fundamental issue of whether state enforcement of truly private discrimination violated the Constitution. In *Robinson,* although Douglas claimed the decision should have been based on his *Bell* opinion, Black wrote for an otherwise unanimous Court in reversing the convictions because of the state restroom segregation regulation.[35]

Although reached with great difficulty, the sit-in decisions became largely irrelevant within two weeks after the Court announced them. On July 2 President Johnson signed the Civil Rights Act of 1964. Title II of that law prohibited restaurants, hotels, motels, entertainment facilities, and other places of public accommodation from practicing racial segregation if their discrimination was supported by state action or their operations in some way affected interstate commerce. Since the new statute outlawed most of what the sit-in demonstrators were protesting, and made illegal all of what Douglas and Goldberg had been trying to convince their colleagues was unconstitutional, it freed the Court from having to wrestle any longer with the issue of whether state enforcement of the property rights of bigoted restauranteurs violated the Fourteenth Amendment.[36]

Title II also provided the justices with an easy way to dispose of the many sit-in cases still pending in the courts at the time of its enactment. One provision of the new law, section 203, prohibited punishing or attempting to punish anyone for exercising or attempting to exercise a right or privilege secured by Title II. In *Hamm v. City of Rock Hill,* the Court held that section 203 abated still-pending prosecutions of those who had peacefully attempted to obtain service on an equal basis before its enactment. Black, Harlan, White, and Stewart all filed dissenting opinions, denying that Congress had intended the Civil Rights Act to effect any such abatement. Following *Hamm,* the Court held in *Rachel v. Georgia* (1966) that criminal trespass defendants who had been asked to leave restaurants solely for racial reasons might remove their cases from state to federal court, because the mere pendency of such prosecutions provided sufficient basis for predicting that those charged would be denied or could not enforce in state court the federal right created by Title II.[37]

Passage of Title II did not eliminate all issues generated by the direct action attack on white supremacy, for the Court still had to face the question of how much protection the First Amendment gave participants in demonstrations growing out of the sit-in movement. In *Edwards v. South Carolina* (1963), the Supreme Court overturned breach-of-the-peace convictions imposed on African Americans for peacefully marching on a sidewalk around the grounds of the South Carolina State House to protest racial discrimination. The demonstrators attracted a curious crowd of between two and three hundred, but enough police were on the scene to prevent disorder. The Court overturned the convictions on free speech grounds, taking the position that a state could not make criminal the peaceful expression of unpopular views. Only Clark, who viewed the situation as more dangerous than his colleagues did, dissented, observing that "the power effectively to preserve order cannot be displaced by giving a speaker complete immunity."[38]

Two years after *Edwards,* Harlan, Black, and White joined him in expressing concern about a much larger demonstration. Approximately two thousand protesters from all-black Southern University, led by a CORE field secretary, Rev. B. Elton Cox, had marched on the Baton Rouge, Louisiana, courthouse to protest the arrest of Southern University students for picketing stores with segregated lunch counters. The demonstration (which featured recitation of the Pledge of Allegiance and singing of "God Bless America" and "We Shall Overcome") was peaceful, but when Cox urged the crowd to sit in at twenty stores, the police ordered the group to disperse, then broke it up with tear gas. Cox was subsequently convicted of breach of the peace, obstructing public passages, and (in a separate case) violating a Louisiana statute that made it a misdemeanor to picket "near" a courthouse. The justices realized, as Douglas observed, that "the word 'sit-in' triggered all these convictions." Most of them thought the statutes under which the first two charges were brought were insufficiently specific, giving police too much discretion about whom to arrest. Black, however, seemed to speak for several of his colleagues when he observed, "Congregating outside a courthouse can generate fear and destroy a court." Noting the possibility of "a John Birch crowd [surrounding] this courthouse," he asserted "there is a limit to where they can go." Warren disagreed, but even he expressed concern about the threat of disorder posed by Cox's refusal to end the demonstration when told to do so by the police. Only the Chief and Douglas favored reversing all three convictions. The vote was eight to one on the breach-of-the-peace charge and six to three on the obstruction charge. By a five-to-three margin, with Brennan passing, the justices affirmed the conviction for picketing "near" a courthouse. Goldberg, a member of all three majorities, set out to write opinions that reflected these votes. While working on them, he viewed television coverage of the demonstration, which convinced him the protesters had been where they were (101 feet from the courthouse on the other side of the street) with the acquiescence of the police. Goldberg switched his vote in the picketing case, and because Brennan indicated he would favor reversal if the police had acquiesced, the result was a five-to-four majority to reverse on the third charge. Goldberg produced one opinion that overturned the disturbing-the-peace conviction under *Edwards,* because that statute swept "within its broad scope activities that are constitutionally protected free speech and assembly," and the obstructing-public-passages conviction because that law violated these First Amendment rights by giving unfettered discretion to local officials to control use of the streets for peaceful parades and meetings. His second opinion held that the conviction for picketing "near" the courthouse violated the Due Process Clause, because city officials on the scene had given the demonstrators permission to be where they were. White and Harlan dissented on both the obstruction and picketing charges, joined on the latter by Black and Clark. Black, whose opinion reflected his growing conservatism, asserted: "Minority groups in particular need always to bear in mind that the Constitution, while it requires States to treat all citizens equally and protect them in the exercise of rights granted by the Federal Constitution and laws, does not take away the State's power, indeed its duty, to keep order and to do justice according to law."[39]

His ringing February 23, 1966, dissent in *Brown v. Louisiana,* which he delivered while shaking his finger at the audience, underscored his growing concern for the preservation of order and property rights. Black's dissent in that case reflected a fear of anarchy felt by many Americans in the wake of both a 1964 student uprising at the University of California's Berkeley campus and the 1965 Watts riots. At issue in *Brown* were the breach-of-the-peace convictions of five young African Americans who had refused to leave a segregated Louisiana public library after being told that it did not have the book they wanted. This CORE-sponsored stand-in, which lasted about fifteen minutes, was silent and did not interfere with others' use of the library. The conference vote was five to four to reverse the convictions, but both White, who was on the winning side, and Clark, who went the other way, acknowledged being on the fence. Warren assigned the opinion to Fortas, who soon became concerned about whether the Court had already declared Louisiana's breach-of-the-peace statute unconstitutional in *Cox.* His efforts to resolve that problem with a footnote saying it had been struck down only "as applied" cost him the support of Brennan, who insisted *Cox* was an overbreadth ruling resulting in facial invalidation. White also refused to sign Fortas's opinion, which held the application of the statute to the defendants unconstitutional on somewhat imprecisely articulated First Amendment grounds, arguing in a separate concurrence that the record offered "no evidence" of intent to breach the peace and suggested an equal protection violation. That left Fortas speaking for a plurality of three. Black's dissent (which Clark, Harlan, and Stewart signed) had more support. His opinion "somewhat saddened" Warren, who thought it did "not reflect the better part of his nature." It was actually a toned-down version of a strident draft that, among other things, accused the majority of an antisouthern bias. Black's published dissent denied that the First Amendment guaranteed anyone "the right to use someone else's property, even that owned by government and dedicated to other purposes, as a stage to express dissident ideas." He was concerned that those who wanted to go to the library to learn might be denied that opportunity. "It is high time," Black declared, "to challenge the assumption in which too many people have too long acquiesced, that groups which think they have been mistreated or that have actually been mistreated have a constitutional right to use the public's streets, buildings, and property to protest whatever, wherever, whenever they want, without regard to whom such conduct may disturb." Although his side won, *Brown* convinced Douglas that a majority of the Court was "veering toward the anti-Negro side."[40]

Nine months later, *Adderly v. Florida* (1966) fulfilled his fears. Thirty-one Florida A&M students had appealed their conviction of "trespass with a malicious and mischievous intent" for demonstrating on the grounds of the Tallahassee jail to protest segregation and the arrest of classmates for trying to integrate theaters. Warren argued in conference that *Cox* and *Edwards* controlled *Adderly*, but Black, who viewed this peaceful demonstration as something akin to the storming of the Bastille, prevailed five to four. Noting that the students blocked a driveway, obstructed a jail entrance not normally used by the public, and refused to leave when asked to do so by the sheriff, he rejected the contention that they had been deprived of their rights to freedom of speech, press, and assembly. "The State, no less than a private owner of property, has power to preserve the property under its control for the use to which it is lawfully dedicated," he wrote. "For this reason there is no merit to the . . . argument that [the demonstrators] had a constitutional right to stay on the property, over the jail custodian's objections." Black disputed yet again "the assumption that people who want to propagandize protests or views have a constitutional right to do so whenever and however and wherever they please." Harlan, Stewart, White, and Clark agreed, although the latter signed Black's opinion only after he deleted an assertion that there was no right to demonstrate that was constitutionally paramount to an owner's right to use his own property. Brennan found Black's priorities particularly objectionable when the property owner was the government. "I had thought that our cases drastically limited the application of state statutes when one peacefully goes on *public* property to exercise First Amendment rights," he wrote to Douglas, who was preparing a dissent that Brennan, Fortas, and the Chief signed. "We do violence to the First Amendment when we permit this 'petition for redress of grievances' to be turned into a trespass action," the dissenters maintained.[41]

Adderly was, as Archibald Cox observed, "The first Supreme Court decision which civil rights demonstrators . . . lost on the merits." It was not the last. In *Walker v. Birmingham* (1967), over the objections of the same four dissenters, the Court upheld criminal contempt convictions against organizers of a violence-marred march through Birmingham conducted in defiance of an injunction issued by a state court. This demonstration was part of Dr. King's lengthy 1963 campaign against segregation in the Alabama city that attracted national attention by inducing a violently repressive response from municipal authorities. That crusade already had sent to the Supreme Court *Shuttlesworth v. Birmingham* (1965), which unanimously reversed a demonstration leader's convictions for loitering and refusing to comply with the lawful order of a police officer. Black expressed disagreement with the result in conference but did not dissent. He also lost a March 17, 1967, vote on *Walker*. By a five-to-four margin the justices supported the Chief, who contended that the Birmingham parade ordinance on which the injunction had been based was unconstitutional. Harlan soon had a change of heart and asked for further discussion. After that discussion, the Court split five to four the other way. Writing for the new majority, Stewart conceded that both the generality of the parade ordinance's language and the breadth and vagueness of the injunction raised substantial constitutional issues but held that an injunction must be obeyed until the law it implements is invalidated in appropriate judicial proceedings. "The Court cannot hold that the petitioners were constitutionally free to ignore all the procedures of the law and carry their battle to the streets," he wrote. "Respect for judicial process is a small price to pay for the civilizing hand of law." Two years later in *Shuttlesworth v. Birmingham* (1969) the Court unanimously invalidated the parade ordinance. Because, as written, it gave the city commission unbridled power to prohibit any demonstration on Birmingham streets, Stewart declared, it violated the First Amendment rights of participants in an unauthorized march on Good Friday of 1963. Saying "extraordinary clairvoyance" would have been required for them to anticipate a significant narrowing of the ordinance by the Alabama Supreme Court four years later, he brushed aside its construction of the state law he was holding unconstitutional. Although Harlan, Black, and White all voted to affirm Shuttlesworth's conviction, Harlan concurred, Black noted his concurrence in the result, and White said nothing.[42]

Although disturbed about what they viewed as the anarchic implications of some of the tactics employed by civil rights demonstrators, even the more conservative members of the Warren Court were, after all, strong supporters of the cause these activists championed. They repeatedly joined the liberal bloc in voting to uphold civil rights legislation enacted by Congress. The Court issued one expansive pronouncement after another affirming congressional authority to attack public and private discrimination, using the Thirteenth, Fourteenth, and Fifteenth Amendments, and even the Commerce Clause.[43]

The justices consistently upheld laws designed to enable blacks to vote in the South. Indeed, the Supreme Court had begun attacking the banishment of African Americans from the southern political process even before Congress acted. In 1945 the Stone Court held that the exclusion of black voters from the Texas Democratic primary violated the Fifteenth Amendment, and in 1953 the Vinson Court ruled that keeping them from participating in a pre-primary, run by a "private" political club, did so as well. In *Gomillion v. Lightfoot* (1960) the Warren Court used the Fifteenth Amendment against Tuskegee, Alabama, which had redrawn its municipal boundaries in such a way as to eliminate all but four or five of its four hundred black voters, but not a single white one. The city argued that *Colgrove v. Green* precluded interference by the federal judiciary, but Frankfurter insisted the two cases were distinguishable. Black, Douglas, and Whittaker all maintained this was an equal protection problem. Frankfurter, who desired to have the Court's unanimous decision reflected in a unanimous opinion, "if it is at all possible," worked with the Chief to persuade them not to express their views publicly. He and Warren were only partially successful. Black remained silent and Douglas simply noted that he continued to adhere to his dissent in *Colegrove,* but Whittaker wrote a short concurring opinion, asserting that "the decision should be rested not on the Fifteenth Amendment, but rather on the Equal Protection Clause."[44]

When Congress used the Fifteenth Amendment to legislate against franchise discrimination, no justice objected. In *United States v. Raines* (1960) the Court unanimously reversed a federal district judge who dismissed an action brought by the
Justice Department against officials in Terrell County, Georgia, for refusing to register African Americans to vote because he considered the provisions of the Civil Rights
Act of 1957 on which the government had relied unconstitutional. The only disagreement was over how elaborate the opinion should be. "There are times when one
decides most appropriately without elaborate argument, particularly when there is
such a solid basis for decision as there is in this case," Frankfurter wrote to Brennan
on February 17, 1960. When his colleague refused to recast the "law review discussion"
he had written, Frankfurter concurred separately, joined by Harlan. Their concurrence justified reversal with nothing more than a bare assertion that the presumption
of constitutionality attaching to all congressional legislation had not been overcome.
Although lively, Frankfurter's dispute with Brennan involved only approaches to
opinion writing, particularly whether a "big case" in which "the public has a lively
interest—calls for a big opinion."[45]

On the substantive issue of the constitutionality of the Civil Rights Act of 1957, the
Court was united. In *Hannah v. Larche* (1960) it ruled against Louisiana registrars
who were summoned to testify before the Commission on Civil Rights, a body created by the 1957 law. The Court rejected as without merit their contention that the
statute was inappropriate legislation under the Fifteenth Amendment. It also rebuffed
the registrars' attack on the commission's rules of procedure, which permitted refusing to disclose the identities of persons from whom it had received complaints and
did not allow witnesses against whom complaints had been filed to cross-examine the
sources of evidence against them. The Court held that Congress had authorized the
disputed practices and that they did not violate the Due Process Clause of the Fifth
Amendment. Only Douglas and Black dissented. While emphasizing the importance
of the right to vote, they insisted it would "not do to sacrifice other civil rights in
order to protect [it]."[46]

There was no dissent at all when the Court upheld the sweeping public accommodations provisions of the Civil Rights Act of 1964. Title II was constitutionally
problematic, for in the *Civil Rights Cases* (1883) the Court had struck down a similar
measure on the ground that it proscribed private discrimination rather than state
action. Anxious to avoid a head-on challenge to that decision, Congress, at the urging of the Kennedy and Johnson administrations, based the new law on the Commerce Clause as well as the Fourteenth Amendment. A carefully crafted legislative
history highlighted the adverse effects of racial discrimination on interstate business
activity. Congress was wise to take this approach, for had it relied solely on the Fourteenth Amendment, Harlan would not have supported Title II. As it was, the Court,
after resisting pressure from those challenging the controversial provision to decide
the case before the 1964 presidential election, upheld it unanimously on December
14. Texan Tom Clark, who often arranged for the justices to have afternoon cocktails
with Johnson at the White House, wrote the opinion in *Heart of Atlanta Motel v. United*

States (1964), validating the centerpiece of LBJ's Civil Rights Act. While acknowledging that one of the fundamental objectives of Title II was vindicating the personal dignity of African Americans and that this legislation attacked a moral evil, Clark declared that the Commerce Clause empowered Congress to enact it. He declined to consider whether the Fourteenth Amendment would have done so. Both Goldberg and Douglas wrote concurring opinions asserting that it did. Believing that the right to be free from racial discrimination "occupies a more protected position in our constitutional system than does the movement of cattle, fruit, steel and coal across state lines," Douglas maintained that the Fourteenth Amendment provided a more appropriate basis for the Civil Rights Act than did the Commerce Clause.[47]

The Court had to interpret the commerce power very expansively to hold Title II constitutional as applied in the companion case of *Katzenbach v. McClung.* The involvement of the Heart of Atlanta Motel in interstate commerce was obvious. A 216-room establishment, located near two interstate highways, it advertised nationally, accepted convention trade from other states, and drew 75 percent of its guests from outside Georgia. The defendant in *McClung,* however, seemed disconnected from interstate commerce. Ollie's Barbecue was a family-owned Birmingham restaurant, located eleven blocks from the nearest interstate highway and at an even greater distance from railroad and bus stations. When asked to vote on whether Title II could constitutionally be applied to it, Harlan passed. Even Brennan realized the *McClung* opinion would have to be carefully written to avoid "the danger of expanding federal power without a visible stopping point." The one Clark wrote justified the application of Title II to Ollie's by pointing out that 46 percent of the 150,000 dollars worth of food the restaurant sold in the twelve months prior to passage of the Civil Rights Act consisted of meat purchased from a local supplier, who in turn had procured it outside Alabama. In order to obtain Harlan's support, Clark also had to emphasize that racial discrimination discouraged people from traveling and moving from one state to another, thereby decreasing business in general. Thus, *McClung* became a striking application of the *Wickard v. Filburn* (1942) doctrine that Congress may regulate localized activities having a minimal impact on interstate commerce if the cumulative effect of the actor's contribution and those of others similarly situated is substantial.[48]

South Carolina v. Katzenbach (1966) upheld an equally striking federal intrusion into local affairs, the Voting Rights Act of 1965. That law contained what Warren, writing for the Court, characterized as "a complex scheme of stringent remedies aimed at areas where voting discrimination has been most flagrant." The sections at issue applied automatically to any state, or political subdivision thereof, that as of November 1, 1964, utilized a literacy, educational, knowledge, good character, or similar "test or device" to determine who could vote and where less than half of the voting-age population was registered or had participated in the 1964 presidential election. The act suspended all tests and devices and required the prior approval of the Justice Department or the U.S. District Court for the District of Columbia before any new voting qualification or regulation could be implemented. It also authorized the attorney general to appoint federal voting examiners who were empowered to ensure compliance with the Fifteenth Amendment by adding would-be voters to the rolls. South Carolina challenged these provisions "on the fundamental ground that they exceed the powers of Congress and encroach on an area reserved to the States by the Constitution." It also raised a variety of constitutional objections to particular sections. Notable was its attack on the law's coverage formula, which South Carolina contended violated the principle of the equality of the states, denied due process by employing an invalid presumption, and served as a bill of attainder. The Court rejected all of the state's arguments. "We here hold," Warren declared, "that the portions of the Voting Rights Act properly before us are a valid means of carrying out the commands of the Fifteenth Amendment." "As against the reserved powers of the States," he said, "Congress may use any rational means to effectuate the constitutional prohibition of racial discrimination in voting." Although endorsing those portions of the Chief's opinion sustaining the power of Congress under section 2 of the Fifteenth Amendment, Black dissented from those approving the preclearance procedures, which he maintained would undercut the self-respect of white southerners, breed resentment and resistance, and "distort our constitutional structure of government."[49]

It was Harlan and Stewart who sounded the discordant note in *Katzenbach v. Morgan* (1966), as the rest of the Court endorsed section 4(e) of the Voting Rights Act. Designed to enfranchise Puerto Ricans living in New York by overriding a state law requiring voters to be literate in English, that provision forbade denying anyone the right to vote because of inability to read or write English if they had completed the sixth grade in a school flying an American flag that taught its students in some other language. Section 4(e) presented a difficult problem for the Court. In enacting it, Congress had purported to utilize the authority granted it by section 5 of the Fourteenth Amendment to enforce the rest of the amendment by appropriate legislation. In *Lassiter v. Northampton County Board of Elections* (1959), however, the Court had held that literacy tests for would-be voters did not violate the Equal Protection Clause. Thus, arguably, under the guise of enforcing the amendment, Congress had altered its meaning. In conference Harlan objected that only the Court could say what the Equal Protection Clause meant. Led by Warren and Black, the others supported section 4(e), although an indecisive Stewart leaned toward Harlan. Warren asked Black to write the opinion, but he declined because he thought his views were too extreme to command the support of a majority. Brennan tried, but his draft elicited a dissent from Douglas. White considered joining Harlan, and Stewart did so. In the end Brennan managed to produce something seven justices could accept. It was not for the Court to determine whether New York's English literacy requirement violated the Equal Protection Clause, he wrote. "Accordingly, our decision in *Lassiter* is inapposite." By including section 5, Brennan argued, the framers of the Fourteenth Amendment sought "to grant Congress, by a specific provision applicable to the Fourteenth Amendment, the same broad powers expressed in the Necessary and Proper Clause" as interpreted by *McCulloch v. Maryland* (1819). Section 4(e) was constitutional because it met the requirements *McCulloch* established; it was a means to the legitimate end of enforcing the Equal Protection Clause, "plainly adapted" to furthering that end, and consistent with the letter and spirit of the Constitution. Insisting that the majority "confused the issue of how much enforcement power Congress possesses under section 5 with the distinct issue of what questions are appropriate for congressional determination and what questions are essentially judicial in nature," Harlan dissented. The majority's reasoning, he contended, would permit Congress to change the Court's constitutional decisions, and thus "the substantive scope of the [Fourteenth] Amendment." By passing laws they claimed enforced the guarantees of the Equal Protection and Due Process Clauses, legislators could dilute them. Brennan denied this could happen, and the majority was obviously unwilling to let the possibility that it might happen interfere with upholding section 4(e). Even Harlan took pains to say that he did not mean "to disparage Congress' exertion of authority in the field of civil rights."[50]

So supportive was the Warren Court of legislation in this field that it expansively interpreted the power of Congress, even when the statutes at issue had been enacted during Reconstruction. Sections 241 and 242 of the federal criminal code derived respectively from the Ku Klux Act of 1871 and the Civil Rights Act of 1866. Section 241 made it a felony to conspire to injure, threaten, or intimidate someone to keep him from enjoying a right or privilege secured by the Constitution or federal law. Section 242 made it a misdemeanor willfully to deprive another of the same rights or privileges while acting "under color of law" (i.e., under governmental authority). The Supreme Court had interpreted these laws very restrictively, holding they were violated only if the defendant acted with the specific intent to deprive the victim of a particular right, and (by splitting four to four on the question) making it doubtful that they protected Fourteenth Amendment rights at all. In addition, although section 241 did not include its companion's "under color of law" language, the Court had taken the position that it could be employed constitutionally only if the violation involved state action. That interpretation rendered section 241 useless against lynching; thus a crime that southern states would not punish became one the federal government could not. The Justice Department sometimes employed section 242 to prosecute police brutality, but the Court's decisions severely limited its utility as well. Then, prodded by public outrage over the murders during the summer of 1964 of three civil rights workers in Mississippi and of a black U.S. Army Reserve officer in Georgia, federal prosecutors initiated two cases that could not be sustained under the existing interpretations of those laws.[51]

When district judges dismissed the indictments, the prosecutors appealed. In *United States v. Price* (1966) the Supreme Court held unanimously that where private individuals cooperated with law enforcement officers in carrying out a lynching, all of those involved could be prosecuted under section 242, and that among the privileges protected by section 241 was the right not to be deprived of life without due process of law. In *United States v. Guest* (1966) the Court held that section 241 also encompassed rights guaranteed by the Equal Protection Clause and a right of interstate travel. *Guest* posed a more difficult problem than *Price*, for none of the defendants was a public employee. Writing for the Court, Stewart strained to find a smidgen of state action in the case, implausibly interpreting one count of the indictment as alleging cooperation between Ku Klux Klansmen and police. Anxious to assure Congress that their colleague's opinion did not mean the Court might invalidate legislation against anti–civil rights violence it was then considering, both Brennan (speaking also for Warren and Douglas) and Clark (for himself, Black, and Fortas) wrote concurring opinions, asserting that section 5 of the Fourteenth Amendment authorized enactment of laws punishing all conspiracies to interfere with the exercise of Fourteenth Amendment rights, whether or not state officers were involved; they disagreed only about whether section 241 represented an exercise of that authority. Harlan, in contrast, insisted that federal prosecution of even a conspiracy targeting the right to travel was constitutional only if there was state action.[52]

He dissented also when the majority fashioned an open-housing law out of another old statute in *Jones v. Alfred H. Mayer Co.* (1968). Jones, an African American, sued a Missouri developer for refusing to sell him a home in its Paddock Woods community because of his race. Warren wanted to rule for him on the basis of *Marsh v. Alabama* (1946), which had held that a company town that looked and acted like a municipality had a comparable obligation to comply with the Fourteenth Amendment. White and Marshall also favored extending *Marsh*'s logic to housing developments, but prompted by his clerk, Laurence Tribe, Stewart argued for a "much broader" decision, based on 42 U.S.C. section 1982. Part of the Civil Rights Act of 1866, that law gave all other citizens the same rights as whites to inherit, purchase, lease, sell, hold and convey real property. What appealed to Stewart about section 1982, as his questions during oral argument revealed, was that it predated the Fourteenth Amendment, making its constitutional basis the Thirteenth Amendment, which contained no state action limitation. Black, the author of *Marsh*, also favored reliance on section 1982, contending it had been passed to cover situations like this one. Harlan, however, objected strenuously to Stewart's approach, insisting the 1866 law could not be valid in the absence of state action. He wanted to leave the housing discrimination problem to Congress, which, as the Chief pointed out, was then considering legislation on the subject. The conference vote went unanimously for Jones, but when Stewart produced an opinion based on his theory, Harlan and White deserted him. The Court held "that § 1982 bars all racial discrimination, private as well as public, in the sale or rental of property, and that the statute, thus construed, is a valid exercise of the power of Congress to enforce the Thirteenth Amendment." Stewart's opinion potentially relieved Congress of the need to rely on the Fourteenth Amendment for authority to attack racial discrimination, thus freeing it from the shackles of the state action doctrine. "Surely Congress has the power under the Thirteenth Amendment rationally to determine what are the badges and incidents of slavery, and the authority to translate that determination into effective legislation," he wrote. Stewart took pains to point out differences between section 1982 and the open-housing provisions of the just-enacted Civil Rights Act of 1968. Dissenting for himself and White, Harlan disputed his contention that the 1866 statute was intended to prohibit purely private as well as state-authorized discrimination and also argued force-fully that passage of the new law so diminished the "public importance" of *Jones* that "by far the wisest course would be for this Court to refrain from decision."[53]

That his colleagues would hand down a decision having such potentially momen-tous implications without any pressing need to do so is indicative of what an assertive champion of racial equality the Warren Court had become by 1968. Marshall's appointment a year earlier only heightened its already strong identification with the cause of civil rights. The Court's first African American justice was the son of a rail-road dining-car waiter and a kindergarten teacher. Born in Baltimore in 1908, he attended segregated public schools, all-black Lincoln University (from which he received a bachelor's degree in 1930), and all-black Howard University Law School, (from which he received an LL.B. in 1933.). At Howard, Marshall studied under the legendary Charles Hamilton Houston, who as dean built a once-marginal institution into a high-powered seminary for civil rights lawyers. Barely six months after launch-ing a solo practice in Baltimore, Marshall filed suit on behalf of a black man seeking admission to the segregated University of Maryland Law School, and soon he was heavily involved in litigating civil rights cases for the NAACP. In 1936 Houston, who had left Howard to head up that organization's courtroom campaign against segre-gation, invited Marshall to join his staff in New York. When his mentor returned to Washington in 1938, Marshall replaced him as special counsel of the NAACP's Legal Defense and Educational Fund (LDF). For the next two decades, he was America's best-known and most successful civil rights litigator.[54]

Marshall's high visibility commended him to John Kennedy. Early in his adminis-tration Kennedy sought to demonstrate a commitment to African Americans, while avoiding the political risks inherent in decisive initiatives against segregation, by mak-ing high-profile black appointments. Bobby Kennedy tried to interest Marshall in a district court judgeship, but he held out for the U.S. Court of Appeals for the Sec-ond Circuit. On September 23, 1961, the president nominated Thurgood Marshall to be only the second black circuit judge ever. The *New York Times* enthusiastically endorsed the nomination, and both the ABA and the New York State Bar Associa-tion, overcoming earlier reservations, rated him highly qualified. Nevertheless, Mar-shall did not win confirmation until September 12, 1962. The Judiciary subcommittee charged with evaluating him was chaired by southerner Olin Johnston (D-S.C.). Prac-ticing what Senator Kenneth Keating (R-N.Y.) called inexcusable delay, he held no hearings until May 1, 1962. When the subcommittee finally took up the nomination, no adverse witnesses appeared, but a member of its staff prolonged the proceedings with a lengthy interrogation of the nominee that featured Red baiting and extensive questioning about the alleged professional misconduct of another LDF attorney. Only after Jacob Javits (R-N.Y.) threatened to have the full Senate rip the nomina-tion away from the Judiciary Committee did Senator Eastland finally bring it to a vote. His committee approved Marshall eleven to four, and on September 11, 1962, after a brief floor debate, the full Senate confirmed him by a margin of fifty-four to sixteen. Southern Democrats cast all of the negative votes.[55]

Marshall retained his hard-won judgeship only until 1965. His service on the bench ended when Lyndon Johnson, consciously grooming him to become the first African American on the Supreme Court, made Marshall solicitor general. Archibald Cox wanted to remain in that job, but he felt that after winning election to a term of his own in 1964, LBJ should have the opportunity to pick his own man. He submitted his resignation, hoping the president would refuse it, but Johnson pounced on this opportunity to appoint Marshall. During two years as solicitor general, the former NAACP lawyer argued eighteen cases before the Supreme Court, far fewer than Cox and somewhat less than average. Ironically, only six involved civil rights or broad issues of constitutional law. Most were business cases.[56]

Johnson told Marshall that his willingness to become solicitor general had "nothing to do with any Supreme Court appointment," but even if there was no quid pro quo, it clearly did. Before he was ever confirmed, black congressman Adam Clayton Powell (D-N.Y.) was pressuring the White House to make him a justice. Not content to wait for a vacancy, LBJ created one for Marshall, as he had for Fortas. In September 1966 the president made Attorney General Nicholas Katzenbach undersecretary of state and gave Justice Clark's son, Deputy Attorney General Ramsey Clark, his old job on an acting basis. After testing young Clark's loyalty for six months, LBJ somewhat reluctantly nominated him to be attorney general, a move bound to create a vacancy on the Supreme Court. Tom could not continue to sit while Ramsey headed the Justice Department without creating serious conflicts of interest in cases in which the government was a party. Realizing this, Justice Clark informed the Chief on October 3 that if his son became attorney general, he intended to retire. On the afternoon that the appointment was disclosed, Warren released a statement in which Tom, expressing "pride and joy over Ramsey's nomination," announced his retirement. Johnson's wife, Lady Bird, urged him to fill the resulting vacancy with a woman, and Fortas advised him that Marshall was less intellectually capable than other possible black nominees, particularly Judge William Hastie of the Third Circuit. Katzenbach, however, vouched for his intellect and told LBJ that if he appointed any African American, it had to be Marshall, who was a hero to both blacks and liberal lawyers. The solicitor general appealed to the populist president, because as LBJ told Clarence Mitchell, "he knows the law and he's never lost touch with the ordinary people." On June 13 the president had Ramsey Clark instruct Marshall to report to the White House without telling him why. LBJ then disclosed his intention to announce his nomination immediately. Marshall recalled later asking to call his wife, only to have the president preempt him by picking up the phone and giving her the news himself. "I've just put your husband on the Supreme Court," he told Cissy Marshall.[57]

Oddly, placing him there proved easier than getting him onto the Second Circuit. Most southern senators accepted the nomination silently; only Strom Thurmond (D-S.C.) vocally opposed it. Joseph Kraft of the *Washington Post* regarded Marshall's intellect as ordinary, and both the *Washington Evening Star* and right-wing journalist James J. Kilpatrick grumbled about his liberalism, but otherwise, there was little adverse comment. The confirmation hearings were not as difficult as those in 1962 had been, although southerners Thurmond, John McClellan (D-Ark.), and Sam Ervin Jr. (D-N.C.) did play to their constituencies. McClellan probed Marshall's views on criminal justice, and Ervin drew him into an extended discussion of proper methods of interpreting the Constitution, faulting the Supreme Court for making law rather than discovering it. Marshall responded that the Constitution was a living document that could not be interpreted simply by looking to the original intent of its framers. Throughout his lengthy exchange with Ervin, a former judge widely regarded as a constitutional expert, he defended his position ably. Content to let the southerners play their political game, Marshall's supporters remained largely silent. With no substantial opposition to him, the Judiciary Committee approved the nomination eleven to five. The full Senate debated it for six hours on August 30, 1967, with Ervin again bemoaning the Court's activism. Marshall's supporters declined to attribute racist motives to the opposition. Philip Hart (D-Mich.) did insist, however, that "we cannot ignore the fact of his race. I think it is a symbol of progress, of hope, and of opportunity." Apparently agreeing with him, the Senate voted sixty-nine to eleven to confirm the first black justice. Again, all of the opposition was southern.[58]

The Court's newest member was a Great Society liberal who supported the expansive use of national power, both legislative and judicial, especially on behalf of minorities and civil liberties. A renowned story teller, Marshall also had an irascible streak, and he could be brutally blunt in questioning counsel from the bench. Caring far more about facts than academic theories and legal technicalities, he gave his clerks more freedom in drafting opinions than did his colleagues. Marshall defined the central focus and rationale, then let them organize arguments consistent with his prior opinions. Although resenting being singled out because he was African American, he regularly focused his colleagues' attention on racial issues. They were receptive, of course. Fortas had helped then–vice president Johnson draft the executive order creating the President's Equal Employment Opportunity Commission, and the same year Marshall joined the Court, Warren hired a black clerk, Tyrone Brown from Cornell.[59]

Marshall's appointment offered dramatic evidence of the progress African Americans had made since he argued *Brown*. By 1967 the Court's strong commitment to civil rights was transforming not only their legal position but the Equal Protection Clause itself. Equality had become a far more important constitutional principle than ever before. The Warren Court's "revitalization of the constitutional prohibition against racial discrimination" had, Cox observed in 1968, "given impetus to review of other inequalities in American life."[60]

It had not, however, significantly affected the virtual immunity from challenges based on equal protection that regulatory legislation had enjoyed since the late 1930s. "In the area of economic regulation and taxation," Philip Kurland observes, "the [Warren] Court almost invariably sustained the state classifications." The only major win for a taxpayer was the invalidation of a measure that taxed domesticated foreign corporations at a different rate than local ones. In *Williamson v. Lee Optical* (1955) the early Warren Court upheld (even while conceding it was needless and wasteful) an Oklahoma statute that regulated the sale of spectacles by opticians but did not apply to over-the-counter sales of ready-to-wear eyeglasses. In 1963 the justices rejected challenges to a Kansas statute that prohibited anyone but lawyers from engaging in debt adjustment and to a California law that discriminated against Florida avocados. Their only significant equal protection ruling against a regulatory law was *Morey v. Doud* (1957), which struck down an Illinois statute that exempted the American Express Company from a requirement that firms that issued or sold money orders secure licenses and submit to regulation. Had the statute simply excused concerns having certain characteristics that only American Express possessed, the Court would have upheld this law unanimously, but many justices found offensive what looked like the granting of a monopoly. Burton wrote an opinion for a six-to-three majority condemning the Community Currency Exchange Act for its invidious discrimination and holding that it violated the Equal Protection Clause. Frankfurter, who had "no difficulty in saying this is OK," dissented for himself and Harlan, faulting the majority for acting like a super legislature. Black dissented, too. He was "disturbed by the case," but thought that "unless state legislatures have power to make distinctions that are not plainly unreasonable, then the ability of the States to protect their citizens by regulating business within their boundaries can be seriously impaired." Such a view usually prevailed on the Warren Court.[61]

When it discerned racial discrimination, however, the Court's willingness to accept the decisions of state authorities evaporated, and it fashioned novel doctrines to justify overturning them. Reacting to years of resistance to *Brown*, the Court recast what seemed to be just a prohibition of segregation into a requirement that southerners integrate their schools. At the time of *Cooper v. Aaron* it had carefully avoided even the word "integrated," using "desegregated" instead to avoid giving offense. The justices eventually discovered, however, that they had seriously underestimated white southerners' determination to avoid race mixing in schools and seriously overestimated the value of understanding and compassion. Their approach had placed primary responsibility for dismantling the old system on local public school officials, who were prone to resent and resist judicial efforts to change it. Anxious to get the desegregation process moving, the Court condoned (by refusing to review challenges to them) grade-a-year plans, procedural requirements, and pupil-placement laws, all designed to delay or evade substantial compliance with *Brown*. As time passed without appreciable progress toward the elimination of school segregation, however, the justices grew impatient.[69]

Despite the Court's increased firmness, southern public education remained largely segregated. In the 1964–65 school year only 1.17 percent of black students in the eleven states of the old Confederacy attended school with whites. Title VI of the 1964 Civil Rights Act increased the pressure for integration by forbidding recipients of federal funds to discriminate on the basis of race. In order to continue receiving money from Washington, most southern districts adopted freedom-of-choice plans that purported to allow children to attend whatever school they wished. The right to exercise choice was significantly restricted, however, and black parents who elected to send their children to white schools risked economic reprisal. No white students enrolled in black schools. Dissatisfied with the lack of results produced by freedom of choice, the Department of Health, Education, and Welfare established goals and timetables to speed desegregation. In *United States v. Jefferson County Board of Education* (1967) the Fifth Circuit adopted HEW's guidelines as the standard for determining whether desegregation plans complied with *Brown*, which the court interpreted as requiring demonstrated progress toward the mixing of white and black students.[63]

In *Green v. County School Board of New Kent County, Virginia* (1968), the Warren Court followed the Fifth Circuit's lead. At issue in *Green* was the freedom-of-choice plan adopted by a rural county with only two schools and no housing segregation. Under it no white student had enrolled in the negro school, and while 115 African Americans attended the formerly all-white school, 85 percent of black children continued to receive a segregated education. The easiest way to change that would have been to divide New Kent County into two attendance zones, and the failure of the board to take this obvious step seems to have convinced most justices that it was acting in bad faith. Only Black defended freedom of choice and voted to uphold the board's plan. Nevertheless, Brennan had to temper his opinion to retain the support of Harlan and Stewart and keep Black from disrupting the Court's traditional public unanimity in school desegregation cases by writing a concurrence. Even the modified version made obvious the Court's impatience with southern stalling. Noting that the board had not adopted its program until eleven years after *Brown*, Brennan insisted the sort of "dual systems" that decision had condemned "must be abolished." A freedom-of-choice plan was not necessarily unconstitutional, "but if it fails to undo segregation, other methods must be used to achieve this end." School boards were "charged with the affirmative duty to take whatever steps might be necessary to convert to a unitary system in which racial discrimination [was] eliminated root and branch." His opinion, Warren assured Brennan, would change "the traffic light . . . from *Brown* to *Green*."[64]

For those bent on discriminating against African Americans, the light was red. In *Whitus v. Georgia* (1967), for example, the Court held that procedures permitting officials to use juror-pool lists that indentified the race of those on them were unconstitutional if statistics showed they produced racially disproportionate results. The realism and lack of sympathy for white supremacy the Court displayed in *Whitus* was also evident in its rejection of facially nondiscriminatory miscegenation laws. Racial intermarriage violated the white South's most fervently held taboo, and as late as 1956, anxious to avoid exacerbating tensions in the region, Warren and his colleagues refused on specious grounds (the Chief privately characterized the decision as "total bullshit") to consider a challenge to Virginia's miscegenation statute. By 1964, however, the Court had grown much bolder and more assertive in its support of African American rights. In *McLaughlin v. Florida* it unanimously invalidated a Florida law that made it a misdemeanor for a white person of one sex and a black one of the other to occupy habitually the same room at night. White denied that this statute was constitutional because it imposed the same penalties on members of both races. Taking the position that because the law classified on the basis of race, it could pass muster under the Equal Protection Clause only if it served an overriding state purpose, he declared that preventing elicit premarital and extramarital promiscuity was not sufficiently important to justify trenching upon the constitutionally protected right to be free from invidious discrimination. White also observed that, since the central purpose of the Fourteenth Amendment was to eliminate official racial discrimination, any classifying by race was constitutionally suspect. Although deciding *McLaughlin* did not require passing on Florida's miscegenation law, Harlan, who was reluctant to attack such statutes, and Black both considered their eventual invalidation inescapable.[65]

The inevitable happened in *Loving v. Virginia* (1967). There a state argued that its miscegenation laws did not amount to invidious racial discrimination because they punished equally both participants in an interracial marriage. No justice supported Virginia, even in conference. Speaking for a unanimous Court, Warren rejected "the notion that the mere 'equal application' of a statute containing racial classifications is enough to remove the classifications from the Fourteenth Amendment's proscription of all invidious racial discriminations." "At the very least," he declared, "the Equal Protection Clause demands that racial classifications . . . be subjected to the most rigid scrutiny." They could be constitutional only if "shown to be necessary to the accomplishment of some permissible state objective, independent of the racial discrimination which it was the object of the Fourteenth Amendment to eliminate." Although avoiding holding that all racial classifications were unconstitutional, the Warren Court forced their supporters to overcome a presumption of invalidity that few, if any, could surmount.[66]

The Supreme Court also fashioned an abstruse doctrine that made extremely difficult the elimination of any laws civil rights advocates managed to enact. In *Reitman v. Mulkey* (1967) the Court invalidated California's Proposition 14, which prohibited the state and its agencies and political subdivisions from limiting the absolute discretion of real estate owners to sell, lease, or rent to anyone they chose. Although the purpose of this voter-approved initiative was to get rid of two fair-housing laws passed by the legislature, the California Supreme Court interpreted it as going beyond repealing them to authorize and encourage private discrimination in the housing market. That, it held, was state action violating the Fourteenth Amendment. "We accept this holding of the California Court," wrote White for the majority. Dissenting for himself, Black, Clark, and Stewart, Harlan maintained all California had done was repeal its laws forbidding private discrimination, and that this no more violated the Fourteenth Amendment than would not passing such laws in the first place. The state simply "decided to remain 'neutral' in the realm of private discrimination affecting the sale or rental of private residential property." Harlan considered this decision a short-sighted one that would provide opponents of antidiscrimination legislation with an argument for not enacting it in the first place.[67]

White managed to invalidate Proposition 14 without really addressing the difficult question of when private racial discrimination becomes unconstitutional state action, because the California Supreme Court had already answered it for him. He could not avoid that problem in *Hunter v. Erickson* (1969), a challenge to the constitutionality of a voter-enacted amendment to the Akron, Ohio, city charter under which an ordinance regulating the sale, rental, or financing of real property on the basis of race, color, religion, national origin, or ancestry could become effective only if approved by a majority of the electorate. This measure rendered ineffective a fair-housing measure the city council had adopted in 1964 and required a referendum to replace it. The Ohio Supreme Court held that the amendment did not violate the Equal Protection Clause. Warren disagreed because, as he told his colleagues in conference, "This particular discriminatory legislation makes it harder to promote open housing than other things." White, and even Harlan, agreed. White's efforts to explain why that made the amendment a violation of the Equal Protection Clause were less than satisfactory, however. If it treated people differently on the basis of race, the legislation was inherently suspect and only the weightiest justification could make it constitutional. Although White wrote an opinion that treated the amendment as that type of law, all the Akron measure actually did was single out for special treatment certain kinds of governmental decisions involving race. On its face, the amendment did not discriminate against anyone. White argued that although it "treats Negro and White, Jew and gentile [sic] in an identical manner, the reality is that the law's impact falls on the minority. The majority needs no protection against discrimination." Concurring, Harlan somewhat more successfully articulated the Court's rationale: Akron had "not attempted to allocate governmental power on the basis of any general principle," but instead had adopted a provision having "the clear purpose of making it more difficult for certain racial and religious minorities to achieve legislation that is in their interest." If its charter amendment amounted to state action violating the Fourteenth Amendment, however, would not any measure rescinding a past action beneficial to minorities do so as well? Dissenting, Black protested vigorously against what he viewed as the "use of the Equal Protection Clause to bar States from repealing laws that the Court wants the States to retain."[68]

While employing the Equal Protection Clause in novel ways to assist African Americans, the Warren Court also extended the clause's benefits to other disfavored minorities. Even before *Brown,* the Chief, in *Hernandez v. Texas* (1954), rejected the contention that "there are only two classes—White and Negro—within the contemplation of the Fourteenth Amendment." Despite objections from Clark, who reminded his colleagues that Mexicans were segregated in West Texas schools, the Court held systematically excluding persons of Mexican descent from juries violated the Equal Protection Clause. Community prejudices were "not static," Warren observed, and "from time to time other differences from the community norm [might] define other groups which need the same protection."[69]

One group long victimized by community prejudices was illegitimates. In *Levy v. Louisiana* (1968) the Court held that a state had violated the Fourteenth Amendment when it denied children born out of wedlock the opportunity to recover damages for the wrongful death of their mother. Louisiana was also violating the Equal Protection Clause by refusing to allow a mother to recover for the wrongful death of her illegitimate son, it ruled in the companion case of *Glona v. American Guarantee & Liability Insurance Company* (1968).[70]

Harlan dismissed *Levy* and *Glona* as "constitutional curiosities," but they were in fact evidence that the Warren Court was willing to subject long-tolerated forms of discrimination to heightened judicial scrutiny. The real boom in the use of that approach to enhance the Equal Protection rights of groups other than African Americans did not begin until after Warren's retirement, however. Not until 1971, for example, did the Court hold that classifications based on alienage were inherently suspect and subject to close judicial scrutiny.[71]

Particularly striking is the failure of the Warren Court to contribute anything to the emerging Women's Liberation movement. As Linda Kerber has observed, the justices "generally were certain that discrimination on the basis of race was not equal treatment under the law . . . [but] they were not at all certain that discrimination on the basis of sex was equally questionable." Indeed, the Warren Court did not invalidate a single law that treated women differently from men, nor subject any such measure to more than a rational relationship review. It did, in *United States v. Dege* (1960), reject the common-law doctrine that a woman could not be guilty of conspiring with her husband; Frankfurter emphasized in his opinion that vast changes in the status of women had wiped out the traditional submission of wives to their husbands. The following year, however, in *Hoyt v. Florida* (1961), the Court held that a woman convicted of second-degree murder for killing her husband, who was abusive and about to leave her, was not denied equal protection by a state statute that excluded women from jury service unless they explicitly asked to serve. The Court declined to reconsider *dicta* in *Strauder v. West Virginia* (1879) that a state might constitutionally restrict jury duty to males. It was somewhat less insensitive to women's rights than Harlan's opinion suggested, however. At the urging of clerk Timothy Dyk, Warren argued in conference for reversal of Gwendolyn Hoyt's conviction, contending that her case demonstrated why female defendants sometimes needed the help of female jurors. Douglas and Black supported the Chief, and Brennan apparently wavered for a time before voting with Frankfurter, Harlan, Clark, Stewart, and Whittaker to affirm. Reluctant to waste the limited political capital of a Court already under fire for its handling of African American rights and other controversial issues by highlighting its division over a type of discrimination he believed was dying anyhow, Warren did not dissent. Rather, he opted for a brief concurrence in which the minority disassociated itself from Harlan's assertion that treating men and women differently with respect to jury service was reasonable; as justification for supporting the decision they offered instead the narrow ground that the record failed to show Florida was not making a good-faith effort to avoid discrimination. Warren's obscure one-paragraph opinion offered little solace to those challenging the constraints that traditional gender roles imposed on women, especially when compared with the majority's assertion that "Despite the enlightened emancipation of women from the restrictions and protections of bygone years, and their entry into many parts of community life formerly considered to be reserved to men, woman is still . . . the center of home and family life."[72]

Although unable to see anything especially suspicious about laws that treated the sexes differently, the Warren Court did increase dramatically the use of the Equal Protection Clause to protect implied fundamental rights. Only once before Warren became chief justice had the Court used that clause to invalidate a law that treated people differently with respect to a liberty not explicitly mentioned in the Constitution. *Skinner v. Oklahoma* (1942) struck down a statute that subjected most habitual criminals to involuntary sterilization, but exempted those convicted of certain white-collar offenses. Douglas condemned this law for impinging upon a fundamental right of procreation, the existence of which was first announced in his opinion. *Skinner* presaged the Warren Court's development of a body of "substantive equal protection" law, that as Stanford's Gerald Gunther observed, "bore the closest resemblance to freewheeling substantive due process, [because] it circumscribed legislative choices in the name of newly articulated values that lacked clear support in constitutional text and history."[73]

The progenitor of this new doctrine was Douglas, and the ruling that best epitomized it was *Harper v. Virginia State Board of Elections* (1966), "one of the most activist decisions of the later Warren Court." At issue in *Harper* was the constitutionality of a $1.50 annual levy that residents had to pay to vote in state elections. By 1966 such poll taxes (once widely used to disfranchise African Americans) were on the verge of being legislatively extinguished. The Twenty-Fourth Amendment (ratified in 1964) outlawed these taxes in federal elections, and all but four states had eliminated them. Although dying, the poll tax appeared invulnerable to constitutional attack, for the Supreme Court had held in *Breedlove v. Suttles* (1937) that it did not violate the Equal Protection Clause. Nevertheless, Warren, Douglas, and Goldberg wanted to invalidate Virginia's poll tax. The others considered the arguments against its validity so insubstantial that they agreed to dispose of *Harper* with a one-sentence per curiam. That provoked a draft dissent from Goldberg, discussing the equal protection cases the Court had decided since *Breedlove*, emphasizing those (such as *Reynolds v. Sims*) that involved voting and also stressing the need to ensure that the poor had the same right to vote as the rich. His circulation persuaded Black, forcing the Court to junk the per curiam and schedule oral argument for January 1966. At the conference that followed it, Warren argued passionately that the poll tax discriminated against blacks and the poor and that *Breedlove* could be distinguished. The waffling Black led the opposition. Contending that the poll tax was not necessarily discriminatory, he acknowledged Congress could ban it, but objected to the Court usurping the legislature's role in order to make social policy. Black lost six to three.[74]

Nevertheless, Douglas felt compelled to add to his opinion for the Court a sentence denying the outcome was founded "on what we think governmental policy should be," rather than "on what the Equal Protection Clause requires." He had more than a little trouble explaining why poll taxes denied the equal protection of the laws. Initially, relying on *Skinner,* Douglas simply condemned as invidious discrimination the use of the "irrelevant" factor of wealth to determine who could vote. Wealth, however, had not been held to be a suspect basis of classification, and although Douglas appears to have wanted the Court to treat it like race, all he could get his colleagues to accept was an assertion that both were "traditionally disfavored." *Skinner* had invalidated a measure that reeked of class discrimination, but that law treated white-collar criminals and other felons differently with respect to the exercise of a fundamental right, and there was no explicit constitutional right to vote in state elections.

Douglas acknowledged this, but asserted that if a state chose to grant the franchise to anyone, any line-drawing in which it then engaged was governed by the Equal Protection Clause. He quoted *Reynolds v. Sims* to establish that "'the right of suffrage is a fundamental matter'" and "'any alleged infringement on the right of citizens to vote must be carefully and meticulously scrutinized.'" The right to vote "being too precious, too fundamental" to be burdened by a wealth distinction, the poll tax was unconstitutional. Harlan agreed with Douglas that this holding was a logical result of *Reynolds*, but having dissented from that decision, he protested this one too. Conceding that the poll tax was "not in accord with current egalitarian notions of how a modern democracy should be organized," Harlan nevertheless insisted it was rational and that implementing "political doctrines popularly accepted at a particular moment of our history" was a legislative function. Black considered writing a concurring opinion, but ultimately he dissented too. Like Harlan, he saw no justification for subjecting the poll tax to anything more than a rational basis test, for all voting laws discriminated, denying the franchise to some groups, such as the young and convicted felons, while giving it to others. If measured by the proper standard, the poll tax was clearly constitutional; raising revenue and asking those who wished to participate in a state's elections to demonstrate their commitment to furthering its welfare were rational practices. Professing to share the majority's dislike for the disputed levy, Black insisted their policy preferences did not justify holding it unconstitutional. The Court, he contended was "using the old 'natural-law-due-process formula' to justify striking down state laws as violations of the Equal Protection Clause." Douglas acknowledged as much. "In determining what laws are unconstitutionally discriminatory," he wrote, "we have never been confined to historic notions of equality, any more than we have restricted due process to a fixed catalogue of what was at a given time deemed to be the limits of fundamental rights."[75]

His approach licensed the Court to identify other values as "fundamental" and subject laws that frustrated their realization to strict scrutiny and likely invalidation under the Fourteenth Amendment. In *Shapiro v. Thompson* (1969) Brennan declared interstate movement to be a fundamental right for equal protection purposes. *Thompson*, which invalidated residency requirements for the receipt of welfare, had far more to do with justices' concern for the poor than with the right to interstate travel itself. The Warren Court, however, was never willing to declare wealth a suspect basis of classification and thus give the impoverished the same entitlement to special judicial protection that African Americans enjoyed. Expanding the list of fundamental rights guaranteed by the Equal Protection Clause enabled the Supreme Court to join its ally, Lyndon Johnson, and his Great Society administration in their "War on Poverty" without giving the Constitution a reading that had socialistic implications. Substantive equal protection was an alternative means of affording constitutional validation to the claims of a group that, like blacks, was disadvantaged within the political process. Significantly, the second time the Warren Court used the Equal Protection Clause to invalidate a law because of its impact on the fundamental right to vote, the beneficiaries were the propertyless; the casualty was a measure that excluded some people from participating in school elections because they did not own or lease taxable real estate. Like numerous other decisions, it stamped this both as a Court committed to assisting those disadvantaged by lack of economic resources or by the color of their skin and as a tribunal willing to fashion novel constitutional doctrines in order to promote the interests of such citizenry.[76]

It was, in short, a Court committed to the promotion of equality in a variety of forms and for a variety of groups. That commitment was an outgrowth of a deep involvement in the struggle of African Americans for civil rights, thrust upon the Court by *Brown*, by the intransigence and creativity of white southerners determined to preserve segregation, and by the militancy of black activists equally committed to destroying it. The litigation and legislation inspired by the civil rights movement repeatedly challenged the Warren Court to expand the constitutional envelope. Sometimes, as in the sit-in cases, it resisted doing so. More often, in order to advance the cause of civil rights, it creatively reinterpreted the Constitution, boldly fashioning novel doctrines grounded more in the egalitarian political ideology of the 1960s than in constitutional text or history. By 1967, when Thurgood Marshall took his seat, making civil rights law had become almost as central to the Supreme Court's jurisprudence as it had been to his career as a lawyer. Speaking in support of Marshall's nomination, Senator Jacob Javits (R-N.Y.) pronounced it "inevitable." Given what he had always been and what the Warren Court had become, perhaps it was.[77]

Chief Justice Earl Warren's first day at the Court, October 1953. Photograph by Harris & Ewing. Collection of the Supreme Court of the United States.

Group photograph of the October 1959–term Court. (Front row, left to right) Justice William O. Douglas, Justice Hugo Black, Chief Justice Earl Warren, Justice Felix Frankfurter, and Justice Tom Clark; (rear row, left to right) Justice Potter Stewart, Justice John Marshall Harlan, Justice William Brennan, and Justice Charles Whittaker. Photograph by Abdon Daoud Ackad. Collection of the Supreme Court of the United States.

Justice Hugo L. Black, February 1, 1956. Photograph by Harris & Ewing. Collection of the Supreme Court of the United States.

*Justice Felix Frankfurter.
Photograph by Pach Brothers
Studio. Collection of the
Supreme Court of the United
States.*

*Justice William Brennan.
Collection of the Supreme
Court of the United States.*

Chief Justice Earl Warren at President Kennedy's inaugural luncheon, 1961. Collection of the Supreme Court of the United States.

Group photo of the October 1962–term Court. (Front row, left to right) Justice Tom Clark, Justice Hugo Black, Chief Justice Earl Warren, Justice William O. Douglas, and Justice John Marshall Harlan; (rear row, left to right) Justice Byron White, Justice William Brennan, Justice Potter Stewart, and Justice Arthur Goldberg. Photograph by Harris & Ewing. Collection of the Supreme Court of the United States.

Abe Fortas with President Lyndon Johnson at the White House. Photograph by Yoichi Okamoto. Collection of the Supreme Court of the United States.

Justice Thurgood Marshall. Photograph by Abdon Daoud Ackad. Collection of the Supreme Court of the United States.

Chief Justice Earl Warren at a White House dinner held in honor of Vice President Hubert Humphrey. Collection of the Supreme Court of the United States.

Billboard with the slogan "Impeach Earl Warren." Collection of the Supreme Court of the United States.

8

INDIVIDUALISM, PRIVACY, AND SELF-EXPRESSION

Equality was not the Warren Court's only priority. More consistently than earlier and later Courts, it gave freedom of expression a preferred status. This Court also prized individualism, and that commitment helped recast the First Amendment. If all citizens were to have equal voices in their government, as the reapportionment decisions dictated, then the focal point of constitutional analysis had to be the individual and the crucial inquiry whether government had done something that left one person with fewer or more limited rights than others. For the post–Frankfurter Court the individual became the "privileged unit of social action." Disillusioned by southern resistance to desegregation, the Court grew cynical about federalism, devaluing it in favor of national protection of individual rights. That meant also devaluing the local cultures that federalism preserved and valorizing individual differences. Those who sought to promote community values by curtailing personal liberty faced strong opposition from the Warren Court.[1]

Warren's Court extended constitutional protection to individual expression that was unconventional and even shocking. Its primary motivation was a determination to open up the national political debate The free speech doctrines that Nadine Strossen credits Warren and his colleagues with pioneering all served mainly to protect communication about political matters. Yet, many of the Warren Court's most controversial decisions, involved expression that dealt with sex. In an era when sexual mores were changing rapidly, individuals often flouted the traditional community norms embodied in laws restricting sexual activity and the depiction and discussion of sex. To judges who valued individualism, these nonconformists were dissidents, whose activities, although offensive to the majority, merited constitutional protection. That perception inspired decisions enhancing individual rights, not just in the marketplace of ideas but also in the adult bookstore and the bedroom. These rulings increased personal freedom, but they also created doctrinal confusion and inspired outraged attacks on the Supreme Court.[2]

Although less controversial, the Court's rulings enhancing the First Amendment rights of political dissenters were even more numerous. Frankfurter's retirement tilted the Court toward the liberal side in such cases. Since he usually got Stewart's vote, the liberal bloc had been losing by a five-to-four margin. Now, the frequency with which civil liberties claimants won rose from 57.8 percent in the 1958–61 terms to 79.1 percent in the 1962–64 terms. Frankfurter's departure eliminated a voice that in 1960 had argued against striking down a Los Angeles ordinance forbidding the distribution of anonymous handbills because forty states had legislation restricting political advertising that cut even more deeply into freedom of expression. "We're trying too hard to make the states justify what they have done," he insisted. Frankfurter's retirement strengthened the hand of his old rival, Black, who had emphasized in his opinion in *Talley v. California* (1960) the Court's decisions recognizing that "identification and fear of reprisal might deter perfectly peaceful discussion of public matters of importance."[3]

Goldberg's views on the First Amendment were closer to Black's than to Frankfurter's. A Jew and a former lawyer for a radical industrial union, he was (like Black, Douglas, Warren, and Brennan), an outsider, and his appointment created a majority in civil liberties cases sympathetic to the claims of underdogs. The result, notes S. Sidney Ulmer, was a pattern of "dramatically lower levels of support for the claims of government." Although Fortas was also a Jewish liberal outsider, whose law practice had included the defense of high-profile victims of McCarthyism, the Court became somewhat less protective of civil liberties after he replaced Goldberg. It remained, however, much more likely to rule in favor of civil liberties claimants than it had been during the four terms prior to Frankfurter's retirement and slightly more likely to do so than it had been during the 1956 and 1957 terms. It was especially protective of freedom of expression. From 1964 onward, the Warren Court adopted Dr. Alexander Meiklejohn's theory that the constitutional guarantees of freedom of speech and press define reserved powers, totally withheld from the government by the people.[4]

Reflecting Meiklejohn's priorities, the Court became especially protective of political expression, sweeping away numerous legal leftovers from the McCarthy era. In *Yellin v. United States* (1963), for example, it held that HUAC had violated the First Amendment by denying a witness's request for a closed hearing. *DeGregory v. Attorney General of New Hampshire* (1966) reversed a state contempt conviction for refusing to answer questions about Communist activities in the rather distant past, taking the position that the First Amendment forbade investigative probing not justified by present needs. The Court also clamped down hard on state loyalty programs. In *Baggett v. Bullitt* (1964) it invalidated a complex of statutes from the state of Washington that mandated two separate loyalty oaths, holding these laws void for vagueness. While basing its decision on the Due Process Clause, the Court noted that the impact of these statutes on First Amendment liberties aggravated the problem created by their abstruseness. Two years later in *Elfbrandt v. Russell* (1966) it again employed the void-for-vagueness rationale, this time to invalidate an Arizona law requiring state employees to take an oath to uphold the constitution and laws of Arizona and the U.S. Constitution and to defend them against all enemies, which, as interpreted by the legislature, made knowing membership in the Communist Party a crime. *Keyishian v. Board of Regents* (1967) reexamined New York's Feinberg Law, which had survived a First Amendment challenge in the Vinson era, condemning it and related statutes for unconstitutional vagueness. A few months later in *Whitebill v. Elkins* (1967) the

Court employed the same rationale to strike down a teachers' oath imposed by the regents of the University of Maryland. While relying on the Due Process Clause, Douglas stressed that "we are in the First Amendment field." The Warren Court killed loyalty oaths with what amounted to "a kind of fusion between due process of law and First Amendment rights," thus admitting long-stifled radical voices to the political debate.[5]

Although the context was very different, *Red Lion Broadcasting v. Federal Communications Commission* (1969) exhibited a similar commitment to preserving "an uninhibited marketplace of ideas in which truth will ultimately prevail." At issue was the FCC's "fairness doctrine," which required broadcasters to give targets of personal attacks and those who disagreed with their political editorializing free airtime to respond. Red Lion argued that these rules inhibited the exercise of its First Amendment rights, but the Court unanimously disagreed. Upholding the fairness doctrine, White declared, "There is no sanctuary in the First Amendment for unlimited private censorship operating in a medium not open to all." The constitutional guarantee of free speech did not preclude "the Government from requiring a licensee to share his frequency with others and . . . to present those views and voices which are representative of his community and which would otherwise . . . be barred from the airwaves." The people retained "their interest in free speech by radio and their collective right to have the medium function consistently with the ends and purposes of the First Amendment."[6]

Those ends and purposes included the promotion of an open political debate from which even the most extreme voices might not be excluded. On the same day that it decided *Red Lion,* June 9, 1969, the Court, in *Brandenburg v. Ohio,* overturned the conviction of a KKK leader who had spoken in vague terms during a Klan rally about marching on Washington and about taking "revengence" if the government did not stop suppressing the white race. The Court held unconstitutional the 1919 criminal syndicalism law under which he had been prosecuted, declaring that it failed to meet a stringent new test articulated for the first time in this case. A state might forbid or proscribe advocacy of the use of force or of violation of the law, *Brandenburg* announced, only "where such advocacy is directed to inciting or producing imminent lawless action and is likely to incite or produce such action." Although this rule sheltered far more seditious expression than had the old "clear and present danger" test before the Vinson Court watered it down in *Dennis,* there were no dissents. Only Black and Douglas protested, and their complaint was that the Court had not gone far enough because it had failed forthrightly to repudiate the "clear and present danger" rule. Not only did this major change in First Amendment doctrine elicit no dissents, it was announced in an unsigned per curiam opinion, started by Fortas and, after he unexpectedly resigned, completed by Brennan.[7]

That the Court so casually promulgated such a rule—essentially making impossible the prosecution of anything less than express incitement of immediate lawless action—indicates how protective of political speech it had become by 1969. Fueling this enhancement of protection for political expression was the Court's strong commitment to safeguarding the rights of African Americans. *Talley v. California,* for example, facilitated a boycott by an organization protesting employment discrimination against blacks, as well as Mexicans and Asians. University of Chicago professor Harry Kalven and the ACLU's legal director, Mel Wulf, both spotlighted the Court's tendency to interpret the First Amendment more generously in cases involving the civil rights movement. Strossen agrees there was a connection. The development of the First Amendment right of freedom of association proves the point.[8]

This right really originated in *NAACP v. Alabama* (1957), where Harlan created it in order to hold unconstitutional a southern state's demand that the NAACP turn over the names of its members. The initial circulation of his opinion held for the civil rights organization on the ground that Alabama had violated its free speech rights, but Frankfurter, who found what Harlan had written objectionable for seeming to endorse Black's position on the incorporation of the First Amendment, suggested there was a right of association that was part of the liberty protected against state interference by the Due Process Clause. Harlan managed to satisfy him by blending his approach with the free speech one demanded by Black and Douglas, formulating a right of association related to freedom of expression. The result, notes Bernard Schwartz, was "the first decision holding that there is a constitutional right to organize and join an association for advancement of beliefs and ideas." Subsequent NAACP cases *Bates v. Little Rock* (1959), *Shelton v. Tucker* (1960), and *NAACP v. Button* (1963) elaborated this right, which the Court forthrightly acknowledged in *Button*, "rested on the First Amendment as absorbed in the Fourteenth." Civil rights had spawned a new free speech principle, whose significance, Warren realized, reached beyond race cases.[9]

The same thing could be said of the overbreadth doctrine. The notion that a statute is facially invalid if it is so broad that it proscribes constitutionally protected speech, along with activity that government has a right to punish, was not completely new, but it was in *Button* that Brennan coined the term "overbreadth" and pointed out "the danger of tolerating in the area of First Amendment freedoms, the existence of a penal statute susceptible to sweeping and improper application." It was also in this NAACP case that he laid down the rule that "Because First Amendment freedoms need breathing space to survive, government may regulate in the area only with narrow specificity." To establish that "a vague and overbroad statute lends itself to selective enforcement against unpopular causes," Brennan cited earlier NAACP-NAACP cases. At the urging of crusaders for racial justice, he soon enhanced the importance of the doctrine he had articulated in *Button* by expanding the jurisdiction of the federal courts in cases where it might apply. Civil rights demonstrators, who often risked prosecution under overly broad state criminal statutes, demanded access to federal trial courts to seek injunctions restraining enforcement of such laws before they were actually used against them. In *Dombrowski v. Pfister* (1965), the Warren Court gave them what they wanted, holding that someone threatened with prosecution under an overly broad state law was entitled to an injunction forbidding the authorities to prosecute or continue to harass him.[10]

The Warren Court's commitment to thwarting interference with the civil rights movement also enhanced First Amendment protection for speakers who outraged hostile audiences. In *Feiner v. New York* (1951) the Vinson Court had upheld the disorderly conduct conviction of a street-corner agitator, arrested after he ignored requests from police to cease vitriolic denunciations of public officials and the American Legion and intemperate calls for armed struggle by blacks. Feiner provoked many onlookers, and one threatened him with violence, but *Edwards v. South Carolina* (1963) seemed to present a stronger case for governmental restriction of expression. The 187 student civil rights protestors who were appealing breach-of-the-peace convictions in *Edwards* had outraged 200 to 300 white onlookers by invading the grounds of the South Carolina State House to sing songs, hear speeches, and display signs denouncing segregation, and then had ignored police orders to disperse. Yet, the Warren Court reversed their convictions. This was, Stewart insisted, "a far cry from the situation in Feiner." As John Nowak and Ronald Rotunda point out, "The situation in Edwards might have been potentially more dangerous." The Warren Court reversed because it "appreciated the ability of an expansive *Feiner* doctrine to suppress civil rights demonstrations." In *Edwards* it announced that one function of free speech was to invite dispute, and that the prejudices of others could not be permitted to silence speakers with unpopular messages. The Court went on to overturn convictions of other civil rights protesters on similar grounds in *Gregory v. Chicago* and *Cox v. Louisiana* (1965). In *Cox*, Douglas argued for reversal because, "The word 'sit-in' triggered all these convictions." Along with *Edwards* and *Gregory* that decision established, according to Laurence Tribe, a constitutional principle that even imminent spectator violence will not justify suppression of protected speech if reasonable crowd-control tactics could have prevented the violence.[11]

Like that doctrine, the limitations the Warren Court imposed on defamation were byproducts of its campaign to prevent southerners from suppressing expression that promoted civil rights. In injecting the First Amendment into what had been merely a branch of state tort law, the Court was reacting to a legal assault on an advertisement, headlined "Heed Their Rising Voices," that the *New York Times* ran on March 29, 1960. The ad trumpeted the fact that thousands of "Southern Negro students" were engaging in nonviolent demonstrations to affirm constitutional rights and denounced the "unprecedented wave of terror" mounted against them by those who would "negate or deny" the Constitution. The ad had been placed by the Committee to Defend Martin Luther King and the Struggle for Freedom in the South, a group of union officials, ministers and entertainers, cochaired by veteran civil rights leader A. Philip Randolph, that was raising money to support the civil rights movement. "Heed Their Rising Voices" bore the names of sixty-four prominent individuals sponsoring the 4,800-dollar advertisement and those of four Alabama ministers (including King's top aide, Rev. Ralph David Abernathy) that the committee had included without consulting them. It also contained some inaccuracies, most of them relatively minor. The ad erroneously stated that police had "ringed" the campus of Alabama State College, that its dining hall had been padlocked in an attempt to starve student demonstrators, that student leaders had been expelled from Alabama State for singing "My Country 'Tis of Thee" on the steps of the state capital (rather than for participating in lunch counter sit-ins), that the entire student body had protested these expulsions by not re-registering for classes (actually, registration was down only slightly), and that Dr. King had been arrested seven times (the real number was four). An alert reporter at the *Montgomery Advertiser* spotted some of these inaccuracies, and after his paper editorially accused the *Times* of lying, L. B. Sullivan, the city commissioner responsible for overseeing the police, wrote to both it and the four Alabama ministers whose names appeared in the ad, demanding a retraction. After the *Times* responded with a letter asking Sullivan how the statements in the advertisement reflected on him, he filed a libel action. He also named the four ministers as defendants, apparently in order to eliminate the diversity of citizenship between opposing parties that would otherwise have enabled the newspaper to remove the case to federal court. A few weeks later Governor John Patterson also demanded a retraction. The *Times* responded by publishing a story apologizing to Patterson and retracting the paragraphs containing factual errors. Nevertheless, the governor sued too, adding King to the list of defendants. The mayor of Montgomery and present and former city commissioners joined Sullivan and Patterson as plaintiffs, seeking a total of 3 million dollars in damages. This strong reaction to relatively minor mistakes was due in part to resentment over the slant the northern media was giving news coverage of the civil rights struggle; Montgomery whites considered reporting on their city's bus boycott unfair. Also driving these libel actions was hostility toward the civil rights struggle. Sullivan had facilitated a Ku Klux Klan attack on Freedom Riders, and both he and Patterson had endeavored to crush the sit-in movement with violence and intimidation. As Kermit Hall observes, "Southern whites were committed to [the] destruction" of the civil rights movement.[12]

Awareness of their motives influenced the way the Warren Court reacted to *New York Times v. Sullivan* (1964), a case in which a Montgomery County jury had awarded the commissioner five hundred thousand dollars, without specifying what portion of the damages was compensatory and what part was punitive. Alabaman Hugo Black thought its action reflected "the feeling that the Times belongs to a foreigner who is an enemy of Ala[bama]." The state supreme court nevertheless affirmed the verdict. The *Times* Alabama circulation was less than four hundred copies per day, and the advertising revenues it had received from that state in the past six months totaled only about eighteen thousand dollars, far less than the five-hundred-thousand-dollar judgment. The *Montgomery Advertiser* correctly viewed libel suits as a means of checkmating this unpopular New York paper and other like-minded publications. So did the Supreme Court. "Whether or not a newspaper can survive a succession of such judgments," it declared, "the pall of fear and timidity imposed upon those who would give voice to public criticism is an atmosphere in which the First Amendment freedoms cannot survive."[13]

Historically, as Sullivan's attorney, Ronald Nachman, reminded the Court, libel had been treated as outside the First Amendment. But Columbia Law School professor Herbert Wechsler, representing the *Times*, countered that damage awards like the one against his client would suppress criticism of the government just as surely as had the notorious Sedition Act of 1798. Although identifying narrower alternatives available to the Court, Wechsler argued that the First Amendment created an absolute privilege to criticize the way public officials did their jobs, a privilege so broad that it protected even statements that were false.[14]

The Court would not accept his absolutist position, but stopped only a little short of it. At their January 10, 1964, conference, the justices voted unanimously to reverse the judgment against the *Times*. Douglas stated he was doing so "on the First Amendment." The vote to reverse Sullivan's verdict against the Montgomery ministers in *Abernathy v. Sullivan* was also unanimous, most of Warren's colleagues agreeing with him that there was no evidence to support it. Black acknowledged that setting aside the verdict against the *Times* would be difficult if libel laws applicable to press criticism of official conduct were valid, but that as far as he was concerned," the purpose of [the] First Amendment is to keep public affairs open to discussion," and "*at least in the field of public affairs* a state can't keep a person from talking." Harlan disagreed, arguing that the First Amendment did not prohibit libel laws that applied to statements about public affairs and insisting upon the need to accommodate private rights. Even he acknowledged, however, "We must lay down new rules for state libel laws." Brennan agreed with him that the "First Amendment does not outlaw all libel laws even in this field," but argued that the press was entitled to considerable freedom in criticizing public officials. He endorsed Harlan's contention that federal standards were needed. The difficult issue was what those should be. Warren and Douglas believed publishers ought to enjoy the protection of the First Amendment so long as their inaccuracies were part of "fair comment" on public affairs. Harlan, Brennan, and Clark favored imposing on plaintiffs in cases like this a higher burden of proof for all the elements of libel (Brennan suggested the "clear and convincing evidence" standard). The justices also disagreed about damages. Clark thought the Constitution gave the Court no authority to control those; Harlan, backed by Brennan, argued for prohibiting punitive damages, except where there was proof of actual malice. Stewart and White suggested that the Court's obscenity decisions might provide an analogy that would be useful in resolving the difficulties that confronted them.[15]

Finding a resolution acceptable to Supreme Court colleagues fell to Brennan. The first draft of his opinion rejected the contention that the First Amendment prohibited any sanctions against defamatory criticism of public officials that reflected upon the performance of their duties and employed the "clear and convincing evidence" principle he had proposed in conference. It also relied heavily on the rule, followed in a minority of states, that in a libel action by a public official against a critic of his official conduct, the plaintiff must prove not only that the disputed statement was false and defamatory, but also that it was made with "actual malice." By the time Brennan circulated his opinion, everything about the standard of proof had been eliminated, and this rule, presented as one mandated by the First Amendment, had become the rationale for the decision. According to Brennan, the failure of the Alabama courts to require proof of actual malice dictated reversal of the judgments against the *Times* and the ministers. Because there was no evidence of actual malice, Sullivan was not entitled to a new trial.[16]

Black, Douglas, and Goldberg did not think Brennan had gone far enough. They wanted the Court to accept Wechsler's argument. Black circulated, and ultimately published, a concurring opinion that argued that allowing a public official to sue for libel on the basis of criticism of the way he did his job violated the Constitution—even in the absence of actual malice. "I base my vote to reverse on the belief that the First and Fourteenth Amendments not merely 'delimit' a State's power to award damages to 'public officials against critics of their official conduct' but completely prohibit a State from exercising such power," he wrote. Goldberg, after initially concurring "in the Court's opinion and judgment," ultimately endorsed only "the result." "In my view," he declared in a concurring opinion, "the First and Fourteenth Amendments . . . afford to the citizen and to the press an absolute unconditional privilege to criticize official conduct despite the harm which may flow from excesses and abuses." Douglas signed both Goldberg's concurrence and Black's.[17]

That left six justices supporting Brennan's opinion, if no one else defected. For a time it appeared that Harlan and Clark might do so over the question of whether the Court should foreclose the possibility of a new trial. Initially, Harlan wanted the Supreme Court to enter judgment for the defendants. He persuaded Brennan, but after Black attacked Harlan's argument and accused him of being inconsistent with his own views on federalism, Brennan had second thoughts. After he expressed his concerns to Harlan, his conservative colleague reversed direction, taking the position that not only should the Court not foreclose the possibility of a new trial, it should say nothing at all about the sufficiency of the evidence, "since the judgment must in any event be reversed for failure of the trial judge to differentiate between general and punitive damages making it impossible [because Alabama required proof of malice for the former but not the latter] to say that the verdict did not include an award of general damages resting on a constitutionally invalid rule of state law." Brennan believed, however, that an analysis of "the constitutional insufficiency of the proofs of actual malice" was essential for the guidance of both the parties and the legal profession. Unwilling to endorse such a discussion, Harlan wrote a separate opinion. Clark then drafted one supporting him. Confronting the possibility of being left without a majority, Brennan accepted offers by Douglas and Goldberg to note, while continuing to assert that the actual malice standard was inadequate, their belief that even under that standard, the evidence was constitutionally insufficient. The result would be different majorities for different parts of the opinion of the Court. Black objected to this strategy. Fortunately, Clark eliminated the need for it by agreeing to withdraw his opinion and join Brennan's if it were modified to present the analysis of the evidence as required for effective judicial administration. At the last minute Harlan, too, had second thoughts about writing separately, telephoning Brennan the night before the decision was handed down to tell him he was withdrawing his opinion and joining the Court's.[18]

Brennan's opinion declared that "the Constitution delimits a State's power to award damages for libel actions brought by public officials against critics of their official conduct." It made exceedingly clear the Court's rationale for imposing First Amendment limitations on this branch of tort law. "We consider this case against the background of a profound national commitment to the principle that debate on public issues should be uninhibited, robust, and wide-open," Brennan wrote. Criticism of official conduct was shielded by the Constitution, and "neither factual error nor defamatory content suffices to remove [that] constitutional shield." According to Brennan, the Constitution required "a federal rule that prohibits a public official from recovering damages for a defamatory falsehood relating to his official conduct unless he proves that the statement was made with 'actual malice,'—that is, with knowledge that it was false or with reckless disregard of whether it was false or not." After discussing at length why the Court considered the evidence in *Sullivan* constitutionally defective and insufficient, he remanded the case to the Alabama Supreme Court.[19]

Although Brennan's opinion revolutionized defamation law by creating a constitutional privilege that immunized from liability most false statements about public officials, many important questions remained unanswered. At Harlan's request, he included a footnote stating, "We have no occasion here to determine how far down into the lower ranks of government employees the 'public official' designation would extend for purposes of this rule, or otherwise to specify categories of persons who would or would not be included." The Warren Court and its successors would wrestle for years with questions *Sullivan* left unanswered.[20]

The rule the Court announced did enable it finally to resolve *Garrison v. Louisiana* (1964). Jim Garrison, the district attorney of Orleans Parish, had been convicted under a Louisiana criminal-defamation statute for making slanderous statements at a press conference attributing a large backlog of pending cases to the inefficiency, laziness, and excessive vacations of some judges and accusing them of hampering enforcement of the vice laws in New Orleans. The Louisiana Supreme Court rejected Garrison's contention that the statute unconstitutionally abridged freedom of expression. When the U.S. Supreme Court first considered the matter on April 24, 1964, five justices voted to reverse, and two (Harlan and Clark) to affirm. Stewart wanted to remand the case, and White passed. Assigned to write the opinion, Brennan produced a draft that seemed to hold that all criminal prosecutions for criticizing public officials or the government were unconstitutional. His draft elicited dissents from Clark (joined by Harlan) and White. Because Black and Douglas were concurring on the absolutist ground that the First Amendment prohibited any kind of libel action for statements about public officials, Brennan lacked a majority. The case was set down for reargument, and by the time the justices discussed it again on October 23, they had decided *Sullivan*. Warren now urged his colleagues to reverse Garrison's conviction because there was no showing of actual malice. Stewart, Clark, Harlan, and Brennan agreed. Again assigned the opinion, Brennan wrote that the reasons that had led the Court to hold in *Sullivan* that a public official might be allowed to recover civil damages for libel "only if he establishes that the utterance was false and that it was made with knowledge of its falsity or in reckless disregard of whether it was false or true . . . apply with no less force merely because the remedy is criminal." Reaffirming their absolutist position, Black and Douglas concurred, as did Goldberg, who insisted that "the Constitution accords citizens and press an unconditional freedom to criticize official conduct." For a while it appeared that Brennan's opinion would be unable to secure a majority because Clark, Harlan, Stewart, and White objected to ruling that Louisiana might not retry Garrison, but Brennan won their support by concluding the opinion with a simple "reversed." Even as modified it was likely to encourage the boldness "in probing and exposing unsavory acts of wayward public officials" that the New Orleans television and radio station WDSU had predicted *Sullivan* would inspire.[21]

The extent to which such activity would take place depended on who was a "public official" for purposes of the *New York Times* rule. In *Rosenblatt v. Baer* (1966) the Court finally addressed the issue Harlan had insisted be left open in *Sullivan*. *Rosenblatt* was a libel suit based on a column in the *Laconia* (New Hampshire) *Evening Citizen* that allegedly contained defamatory falsehoods about Frank Baer's performance as supervisor of a publicly owned and operated recreation area. When the case reached the Supreme Court during the 1964–65 term, Brennan recognized that the crucial question was whether Baer was a "public official." He thought the supervisor was definitely in that category, because the social interest in free discussion required that it be defined broadly enough to include everyone whose conduct was a matter of public interest in a political context. Brennan suggested that the Court could avoid defining "public official" in a way that might be unacceptable to some justices by summarily disposing of *Rosenblatt* with a brief per curiam opinion merely asserting he was one because he was directly responsible to the governing body of the county and his conduct was a matter of the highest public concern. Harlan objected to that approach, so the Court heard oral argument on October 20, 1965. A solid majority then emerged for reversing the judgment Baer had obtained below. During two conferences, the justices could not agree upon a rationale, however. Brennan drafted an opinion taking the position that anyone in the hierarchy of government employees who had, or appeared to have, substantial responsibility for or control over the conduct of governmental affairs was a public official. Douglas, countering that the record did not contain the necessary "factual building blocks" for resolving the question of who was a public official, proposed dismissing the writ of certiorari as improvidently granted, a suggestion Clark, Stewart, and Fortas endorsed. Conceding that "the facts are not sufficient to decide the 'public official' issue," Brennan still wanted to frame "some principles for decision." He insisted that "the interests protected in *Times* included *both* free discussion of public issues *and* free discussion of persons in positions of responsibility for and influence on such issues" and that both factors should influence the "public official" determination. Warren, White, Harlan, and Stewart supported him, although Harlan rejected part of his opinion, and Stewart converted a dissent into a concurrence only after he inserted a paragraph alluding to the "important social values" underlying the law of defamation and to society's strong interest in redressing attacks upon reputation. Fortas dissented, while Clark concurred in the result, refraining from publishing a separate opinion only after Brennan protested that the Texan had written it so late that he did not have time to respond to its arguments. Douglas and Black, while supporting reversal, objected to protecting discussion of public issues only when it involved persons deemed to hold public office.[22]

Their opinions highlighted a problem with Brennan's approach that accounts for Warren's agitated reaction when the justices discussed the petition for certiorari in *Curtis Publishing Co. v. Butts* (1967) three days before announcing *Rosenblatt.* Wally Butts, who had successfully sued the *Saturday Evening Post* for libel after it accused him of conspiring to fix a college football game by passing information about his school's team to the head coach of an archrival, was the former athletic director and head coach at the University of Georgia. What upset Warren (enough for him to threaten to change his vote in *Rosenblatt*) was the suggestion that Butts might be a "public official." The justices postponed voting on certiorari until the beginning of the 1966–67 term, when they agreed to hear Butts's case, along with an appeal from a libel judgment that General Edwin Walker had obtained against the Associated Press for distributing a dispatch that depicted him as taking command of a violent crowd during 1962 rioting against the admission of an African American student to the University of Mississippi. Walker had received five hundred thousand dollars in compensatory damages, but the trial judge had thrown out a jury award of punitive damages because there was no evidence of the actual malice that Texas law required for those. That meant, of course, that if the *Times* rule applied to Walker—a retired U.S. Army general who had commanded the troops at Little Rock—he was not entitled to compensatory damages either. In *Butts* the trial judge determined that there was ample evidence of reckless disregard concerning the article's truthfulness but held that this did not matter because the plaintiff was not a public official. Thus, both cases raised the issue of the reach of the *New York Times* rule.[23]

The justices voted unanimously to reverse in *Walker*, in which the evidence showed that the defendant had been at worst slightly negligent, but because the *Saturday Evening Post* had done virtually nothing to substantiate a report from a source of obviously dubious reliability, they found *Butts* more difficult to decide. The Court divided four to four at one conference, with Harlan passing, and five to four at the next one, with his vote tipping the balance in favor of affirming the judgment for the coach. As Warren, who was part of the majority, explained in a concurring opinion, all members of the Court agreed "that the basic considerations underlying the First Amendment require that some limitations be placed on the application of state libel laws to 'public figures' [such as Butts and Walker] as well as 'public officials.'" What they could not agree on was what those limitations should be. Harlan, to whom the Chief assigned the case, took the position that libel suits brought by public figures were not, like those brought by public officials, analogous to seditious libel prosecutions, and consequently that the *New York Times* rule should not apply to them. Only Clark, Stewart, and Fortas supported him. Warren agreed with Harlan that the judgment in favor of Butts should be affirmed (a position the Chief's clerks jokingly accused him of taking because he was a sports fan), but he insisted the *Times* rule should apply to public figures as well as public officials. Brennan (speaking also for White) agreed with Warren about the standard to be applied, but took the position that there should be a reversal in *Butts,* so that a properly instructed jury could determine whether there had been actual malice. Pursuant to an agreement with Brennan, both Black and Douglas, while reiterating their view that the *Times* rule was "wholly inadequate," concurred in that part of an opinion by Warren reversing *Walker* "in order for the Court to be able at this time to agree on (a disposition of) this important case based on the prevailing constitutional doctrine."[24]

The following year in *St. Amant v. Thompson* (1968), although still insisting *Sullivan* had not gone far enough, Black and Douglas again supported a decision based on its rule. In *St. Amant* the Court defined "reckless disregard" so restrictively as to render those making false and defamatory statements about public officials and public figures immune from liability under all but the most extreme circumstances. The decision reversed a judgment against a candidate for public office who quoted someone else's assertion that the plaintiff, a deputy sheriff, had taken money from a crooked labor leader. While conceding the defendant had not knowingly broadcast a falsehood, the Louisiana Supreme Court concluded, for purposes of the *Times* rule, that he had been "reckless." The U.S. Supreme Court disagreed. Speaking for an eight-to-one majority, White declared that "reckless conduct is not measured by whether a reasonably prudent man would have published, or would have investigated before publishing. "There must be," he said, "sufficient evidence to permit the conclusion that the defendant in fact entertained serious doubts as to the truth of his publication." A Pennsylvania congressman wrote to Warren, protesting the decision "in the strongest terms possible" and predicting that "rulings such as this one . . . will have the effect of discouraging good men from running for public office." The Warren Court seemed prepared to risk that possibility, because it was convinced that, in White's words, "to insure the ascertainment of the truth about public affairs, it is essential that the First Amendment protect some erroneous publications."[25]

That belief led the Court down a libertarian path that Kalven had foreseen immediately after *Sullivan*. "The invitation to follow a dialectic progression from public official to government policy to public policy to matters in the public domain . . . seems to me to be overwhelming," he observed. Kalven predicted *Sullivan* would lead to the acceptance of something close to the complete constitutional protection for expression on public matters that Meiklejohn advocated. Meiklejohn himself saw *Sullivan* as "an occasion for dancing in the streets." After *St. Amant* the Supreme Court reporter for the *Washington Post* observed how far the logic of the *Times* case had carried the Court. "*New York Times v. Sullivan* and its progeny have carved out a press freedom to print news without fear of libel judgments under standards more generous and permissive to the fourth estate than the standards set by responsible newspapers for themselves," he wrote. Not surprisingly, the press applauded the Court's sensitivity to its economic and professional needs.[26]

Warren and his colleagues had fashioned a constitutional shield that protected the media—not only from libel suits but also from actions for invasion of privacy. The Court injected the *New York Times* rule into the latter field in *Time v. Hill* (1967), a suit against the publishers of *Life Magazine,* brought under a New York statute that authorized any person whose portrait or picture was used for advertising or trade purposes without his consent to sue for damages. In 1953 James Hayes published a novel, *Desperate Hours,* that depicted the adventures of a family held hostage in their home by three escaped convicts. His book was based in part on the experiences of the Hills. In 1955 *Life* ran a picture story about *Desperate Hours* being made into a play, showing the cast recreating scenes from the drama in the house where the Hills had lived during their ordeal. Following the invasion of their home, the family had discouraged all efforts to keep them in the public spotlight, even moving to another state, and the appearance of the *Life* article caused Mrs. Hill to become severely ill. Her husband sued. He denounced the magazine for creating the false impression that the play mirrored his family's experience and for sensationalizing the incident by adding violence that had not occurred. Hill also objected to the brief text that accompanied the pictures, which characterized the play as a "re-enactment" of what had happened to his family and from which an editor had deleted the qualifying phrase "somewhat fictionalized." After two trials and extensive appellate review, he emerged from the New York courts with a thirty-thousand-dollar award for a "false light" invasion of privacy. Time Inc. appealed to the Supreme Court, where the oral argument attracted considerable press attention because former vice president Richard Nixon appeared as counsel for Hill. Nixon emphasized that "*Life* magazine lied and . . . knew that it lied," noting that the story had a three-month lead time, giving the editors ample opportunity to verify its accuracy. Although he contended that the New York privacy statute made actionable only "intentionally false statements," the lawyer for Time Inc. insisted it did not require proof of either malice or falsity. He argued that nondefamatory language deserved at least as much constitutional protection as the Court had given defamation in *Sullivan*.[27]

When the justices voted on April 29, 1966, Hill prevailed six to three. Warren, who had not even wanted to hear the case, sided with his old enemy, Nixon, saying he saw no threat to freedom of the press and no First Amendment problem. The Chief assigned the opinion to Fortas, who also had voted to deny review. He considered privacy crucial and was skeptical of the press (indeed, according to one of his clerks, he feared and loathed the fourth estate). The efforts of Black and Douglas to shield the news media with the First Amendment bemused Fortas, whose ambition was to narrow the scope of *Sullivan*. In *Hill* he produced a draft opinion that condemned *Life* for inflicting "needless, heedless, wanton and deliberate injury." "Magazine writers and editors are not, by reason of their high office, relieved of the common obligation to avoid deliberately inflicting wanton and unnecessary injury," he asserted. Fortas startled his colleagues by insisting that the New York statute under which Hill had sued was based upon a constitutional right to privacy. This law did not violate the First Amendment, he insisted, because it allowed recovery only for fictionalized accounts that were commercially exploited. White disagreed, contending that the New York Court of Appeals had suggested the statute might impose liability for publishing a truthful account of a newsworthy event solely for purposes of trade. If it made such material actionable, he insisted, it was overbroad, and therefore unconstitutional. Fortas responded by revising his opinion to say that the New York statute required intentional fictionalization, but, recognizing that he had failed to allay the doubts White had aroused, he called for reargument to clarify the statute's meaning. Just before reargument began, on October 18, 1966, Black circulated a memorandum that mocked the Fortas draft and faulted it for employing the sort of balancing Harlan advocated in freedom of expression cases. Black disputed Fortas's contention that the Constitution enshrined a right to privacy and argued for reversal "on the ground that the New York statute as applied is a gross, flagrant refusal to give Time the benefit of the First Amendment." Black's arguments proved persuasive. When the justices voted again on October 21, Time Inc. prevailed seven to two. Only Warren supported Fortas.[28]

This time Brennan wrote for the Court. His opinion argued that the guarantees of freedom of speech and press were not limited to "political expression or comment upon public affairs" and that "exposure of the self to others in varying degrees is a concomitant of life in a civilized community." According to Brennan, "The risk of exposure is an essential incident to life in a society which places a primary value on freedom of speech and of press." There was no doubt that the *Life* article dealt with a matter of public interest, and erroneous statements about such subjects were as inevitable as ones about public affairs. With both "if innocent or merely negligent '. . . [they] must be protected if the freedoms of expression are to have the breathing space they need . . .' to survive." "We hold," Brennan declared, "that the constitutional protections for speech and press preclude the application of the New York statute to redress false reports of matters of public interest in the absence of proof that the defendant published the report with knowledge of its falsity or in reckless disregard of the truth." As they did in *Walker* during the same term, Black and Douglas, while insisting that the *Times* rule was insufficiently protective of First Amendment rights, concurred "in order for the Court to be able at this time to agree on an opinion . . . based on the prevailing constitutional doctrine expressed in New York Times Co. v. Sullivan." They had to do so, or there would have been no majority for Brennan's opinion. Fortas dissented, arguing that other values were as entitled to protection as those reflected in the First Amendment, and that "among these is the right to privacy." Warren and Clark joined him. Harlan concurred in the reversal of the judgment, but maintained that on remand a jury could constitutionally hold Time Inc. liable if it found the defendant had been merely negligent. Brennan would not even have had Stewart's essential fifth vote had he not added a paragraph expressly leaving open the question of the rules that would apply in libel actions brought by private individuals.[29]

Hill badly divided the justices because it pitted freedom of expression against another value the Warren Court had elevated to the status of a constitutional right two years earlier. In *Griswold v. Connecticut* (1965) the Supreme Court had constitutionalized the right to privacy in order to protect personal autonomy with respect to sex, thereby enlisting in a "sexual revolution" that transformed American attitudes and practices during the 1960s. During that era, the social stigma attached to unwed pregnancy of white females declined dramatically. Ceasing to be viewed as psychologically disordered, sexually active young women came to be viewed instead as rebellious champions of social change. Helen Gurley Brown celebrated female sexual liberation in her 1962 bestseller *Sex and the Single Girl*, and the number of women having intercourse while "going steady" or involved in other dating relationships increased significantly. By 1973 three-fourths of all college students were sexually active, and one survey found that the females were actually more active than their male counterparts. Hugh Hefner, who had launched *Playboy* magazine in 1953, saw the circulation of his "men's magazine" skyrocket to 800,000 by 1959; in the 1960s he presided "over a commercial empire of sex."[30]

Facilitating the sexual revolution that Hefner exploited were oral contraceptives, which became available during the 1960s. While birth control swept the country and a sexual revolution transformed popular attitudes, the Warren Court wrestled with the question of what limits the Constitution placed on governmental interference with the conduct that changing mores seemed to sanction. The justices first confronted this issue in *Poe v. Ulman* (1961), a challenge to Connecticut statutes that prohibited using contraceptive devices and giving medical advice related to their use. The plaintiffs were a married couple who had lost three babies born with multiple birth defects, a married woman who had recently undergone a pregnancy that caused illness and unconsciousness and left her partially paralyzed, and a physician legally unable to counsel them concerning methods of preventing conception. Connecticut had prohibited the use of "any drug, medicine, article or instrument" to prevent conception since 1879. Beginning in 1923, repeated efforts were made to repeal this law, or at least to exempt doctors from its penalties, but vigorous opposition from the Catholic Church defeated all of these initiatives. Finally, in 1957 the Planned Parenthood League of Connecticut organized a judicial challenge to the birth-control law, securing as plaintiffs Dr. Charles Lee Buxton, chairman of the Obstetrics and Gynecology Department at Yale Medical School, and two of his patients.[31]

The three plaintiffs alleged that the state's attorney intended to prosecute them. He had, however, not yet done so, nor even threatened them with prosecution. Only five justices wanted to hear the case, and during oral argument Frankfurter, Harlan, and Stewart all asked questions that called attention to the fact that Connecticut never prosecuted anyone under the birth-control law. Stewart suggested this declaratory judgment action was just an abstract attack on the statute, and when they took up the case in conference, Warren echoed his concern. Although the Chief thought the law could be declared invalid as applied, he did not believe it was unconstitutional on its face, and he disliked deciding what he considered "contrived litigation." Frankfurter (who warned his colleagues against issuing what would amount to an advisory opinion) voted with Warren to dismiss the case, as did Clark, Whittaker, and Brennan. Opposing them were Harlan, Stewart (who contended the lack of birth-control clinics in Connecticut showed the statute was not a dead letter), Douglas (who wanted to hold the law "unconstitutional on its face"), and Black (who thought the Constitution permitted prohibiting the use of contraceptives but also believed the First Amendment forbade punishing as aiders and abettors of a crime doctors who advised their patients to use them). The normally reserved Harlan argued passionately that the statute was "egregiously unconstitutional" because it infringed a "right to be let alone" that was protected by the Due Process Clause. Frankfurter, to whom Warren assigned the case, avoided the constitutional issue by dismissing the suits as nonjusticiable. Highlighting their "unreality," he noted that although contraceptives were sold openly in Connecticut drugstores, the only prosecution ever brought under the challenged law had been dismissed on motion of the state. The Court ruled that no real controversy existed between the parties.[32]

Black, Douglas, Harlan, and Stewart dissented, verifying a clerk's observation that no other case during the term "depend[ed] so much upon the whole philosophy which a Justice brings to the case." Ever the activist, Black published a one-sentence assertion that "the constitutional questions should be reached and decided." Douglas insisted that, by prohibiting a doctor from advising his patients, the Connecticut statute violated the First Amendment and, as applied to married couples, offended the Due Process Clause. Stewart joined his dissent and Harlan's. Although refraining "from a discussion of the constitutional issues" because the appeals had been dismissed, he left little doubt about how he would have decided them.[33]

The Harlan dissent that Stewart endorsed was "an activist, value-oriented, free-wheeling piece of judicial lawmaking" that contrasted starkly with the judicial restraint its author generally espoused. Unlike Frankfurter, Harlan did not regard the cannons of process liberalism as ends in themselves; he would abandon them when they stood in the way of affirming values about which he cared more deeply. To him, the birth-control law represented an outrageous interference with personal privacy, not "far removed from one that sought to punish a marital relationship not resulting in procreation. "I can hardly believe that such a statute would be deemed constitutional," he wrote to a law school dean. Harlan's problem was that no constitutional language explicitly forbade such legislation. Invalidating the Connecticut statute would require holding that it violated some substantive right implicit in the vast vagueness of the Due Process Clause. Black had long argued that the only rights found there were those enumerated in the Bill of Rights. Harlan rejected his incorporation theory. Encouraged by one of his clerks, Charles Fried, he argued that due process had a substantive content apart from the first eight amendments and that this limited the states' broad power to regulate matters such as public health. No mere procedural safeguard, the Due Process Clause had a substantive content, defined not by the Bill of Rights, but by history and tradition. Although the meaning of "due process" could not be reduced to a formula, the Court's decisions showed it "represented the balance which our nation, built upon postulates of respect for the liberty of the individual, has struck between that liberty and the demands of organized society," Harlan asserted. From his perspective, the liberty the Due Process Clause protected fell along "a rational continuum which, broadly speaking includes a freedom from all substantial arbitrary impositions and purposeless restraints." Connecticut's birth-control statute involved "what, by common understanding throughout the English-speaking world must be granted to be a most fundamental aspect of 'liberty,' the privacy of the home in the most basic sense." Hence, the statute should receive strict judicial scrutiny. A law that abridged an important fundamental liberty protected by the Fourteenth Amendment required more justification than "simply that the statute is rationally related to the effectuation of a proper state purpose." Such "obnoxiously intrusive means" were not needed to enforce Connecticut's moral judgments, as both the novelty of the state's law and the infrequency with which it was enforced demonstrated. "There are limits to the extent to which a legislatively represented majority may conduct experiments at the expense of the 'dignity and personality' of the individual," Harlan concluded.[34]

Four years later, a majority of his colleagues decided he was right, striking down the birth-control law in *Griswold*. Unlike *Poe*, this case arose out of a criminal prosecution. Outraged that the Planned Parenthood League of Connecticut had opened a birth-control clinic in New Haven, a Catholic layman filed a complaint with local authorities, and Dr. Buxton and the league's executive director, Estelle Griswold, seized upon this opportunity for another judicial challenge. They enlisted the assistance of two patients who agreed to testify against them, thus ensuring their conviction for violation of a companion statute that made an accessory of anyone who counseled or assisted the prevention of conception. Fined one hundred dollars each, Buxton and Griswold appealed to the Connecticut Supreme Court of Errors, and, after losing there, to the U.S. Supreme Court. By now more than half of married Catholic women were using methods of contraception condemned by the Church hierarchy, and many priests, and even Boston's archbishop, Richard Cardinal Cushing, had acknowledged that they did not oppose repeal of anticontraception statutes. With polls showing 78 percent of Catholics (up from 52 percent two years earlier) and 82 percent of Protestants in favor of making birth-control information available to anyone who wanted it, the Court unanimously agreed to hear *Griswold*.[35]

The decision on the merits was seven to two, with only Black and Stewart wishing to affirm the convictions. Agreeing on a rationale proved more difficult. Although no one disputed Warren's contention that, because Griswold and Buxton had been prosecuted for aiding and abetting violations of the birth-control law, they had standing to challenge its constitutionality, the members of the majority could not agree on why the 1879 measure was invalid. Yale Law School professor Thomas Emerson, representing Griswold and Buxton, had suggested two possibilities. One was that application of the Connecticut statutes to his clients violated their First Amendment right to freedom of speech. The other was that these laws denied due process because they invaded in an unwarranted way a right of privacy derived from a composite of the Third, Fourth, Fifth, and Ninth Amendments. Harlan, restating his position in *Poe v. Ulman*, endorsed the latter rationale, which also appealed to Brennan (who had told English barristers soon after *Poe* that he considered governmental intrusion into the marriage chamber an indefensible invasion of privacy) and to Clark (who considered this an area where a person "has the right to be left alone"). Warren and Douglas found the First Amendment more attractive, although they thought Connecticut had violated it by infringing on freedom of association rather than freedom of speech. Black mocked that rationale, declaring: "The right of association is for me a right of assembly and the right of the husband and wife to assemble in bed is a new right of assembly to me." Goldberg thought both First Amendment and substantive due process justified reversal. Had Harlan written the opinion, it would have rested on the latter rationale, but Warren, whose clerk, John Hart Ely, had argued against reading a right to privacy into the Constitution, assigned the case to Douglas. He also opposed reliance on substantive due process.[36]

Douglas drafted a six-page opinion, based on the First Amendment, that failed even to make clear whether the Connecticut legislation violated freedom of expression or freedom of association. Brennan, to whom he showed a draft before circulating it, found his opinion troubling. "I hesitate to bring the husband-wife relationship within the right to association we have constructed in the First Amendment," he informed Douglas. What the First Amendment protected was grouping together for purposes of advocacy. Brennan would "prefer a theory based on privacy," for that was the interest Douglas was really vindicating, and grounding this in the First Amendment would afford groups such as the Communist Party an opportunity to resist regulation as a violation of their privacy rights. He suggested that, rather than expanding the right of association the Court had spun off from the First Amendment, Douglas should make similar use of provisions in other amendments. In Brennan's view, "where fundamentals are concerned, the Bill of Rights guarantees are but expressions or examples of . . . rights, and do not preclude applications or extensions of those rights to situations unanticipated by the framers." The Connecticut statute would on this reasoning run afoul of a right to privacy created out of the Fourth Amendment and the self-incrimination clause of the Fifth, together with the Third. Douglas quickly adopted Brennan's suggestion, employing it in another draft, which also reflected his own broad conception of privacy.[37]

His opinion invalidated the Connecticut birth-control law for violating a right found in "penumbras, formed by emanations from" various guarantees in the Bill of Rights. To those suggested by Brennan, Douglas added the Ninth Amendment and the First Amendment right to freedom of association. His opinion was so poorly reasoned that it elicited scorn from clerks in other chambers. The only justice who really liked it was Clark. Douglas would not have spoken for a majority had not Warren (who had been warned by Ely not to endorse his opinion), signed Goldberg's concurrence that relied on a different line of reasoning but joined the opinion of the Court, rather than White's, which concurred only in the judgment. Even Brennan, deterred from writing separately by Douglas's adoption of his approach, signed the Goldberg opinion.[38]

Like Douglas, Goldberg maintained that Connecticut's birth-control law violated a right of marital privacy. To establish the existence of such a right, however, he relied primarily on the Ninth Amendment's declaration that "The enumeration in the Constitution of certain rights shall not be construed to deny or disparage others retained by the people." In an opinion drafted by his clerk, Stephen Breyer, Goldberg cited that amendment to establish that merely because "no particular provision of the Constitution explicitly forbids the State from disrupting the traditional relation of the family—a relation as old and as fundamental as our entire civilization . . . does not show that the Government was meant to have the power to do so." The Ninth Amendment expressly recognized that there were "fundamental personal rights . . . protected from abridgment by the Government though not specifically mentioned in the Constitution"; the Fourteenth Amendment protected these from infringement by the states, which could abridge them only if doing so were necessary to achieve some compelling governmental interest. Connecticut claimed its prohibition of contraceptives served to discourage infidelity, but that interest could have been promoted by a much more narrowly tailored law that did not intrude upon the privacy of married couples.[39]

White also "fail[ed] to see how the ban on the use of contraceptives by married couples in any way reinforces the State's ban on illicit sexual relationships." Consequently, as applied to married couples, he wrote in a concurring opinion, the statute was a deprivation of "'liberty' without due process of law." Although White did not acknowledge doing so, he was relying on substantive due process. Harlan much more forthrightly condemned the Connecticut statute on that basis. Again rejecting Black's version of incorporation, which he purported to find implicit in the Douglas opinion, Harlan declared that as far as he was concerned, "the proper constitutional inquiry in this case is whether this Connecticut statute infringes the Due Process Clause of the Fourteenth Amendment because the enactment violates basic values 'implicit in the concept of ordered liberty.'" For the reasons set out in his *Poe* dissent, he believed it did.[40]

Both Black and Stewart, who signed each other's dissenting opinions, vigorously disputed the approach of White and Harlan, as well as what they viewed as the majority's creation of a new constitutional right. They declined to defend the policy embodied in what Stewart characterized as "an uncommonly silly law," but insisted the Supreme Court had no business invalidating statutes merely because it considered them unwise or unreasonable. "I do not believe that we are granted power by the Due Process Clause or any other constitutional provision or provisions to measure constitutionality by our belief that legislation is arbitrary, capricious or unreasonable, or accomplishes no justifiable purpose, or is offensive to our own notions of 'civilized standards of conduct,'" wrote Black. "Such an appraisal of the wisdom of legislation is an attribute of the power to make laws, not of the power to interpret them." He insisted that Harlan and White had found the Connecticut statute unconstitutional on the basis of nothing more than their own appraisal of its wisdom and necessity. Responding to the contention that the law was invalid because it violated the right to privacy, Black declared, "I like my privacy as well as the next one, but I am nevertheless compelled to admit that government has a right to invade it unless prohibited by some specific constitutional provision." Like him, Stewart could "find no . . . general right of privacy in . . . the Constitution."[41]

Although some criticized *Griswold*, press reaction was generally positive. The *New York Times* praised the decision as "a milestone in the judiciary's march toward enlarged guardianship of the nation's freedoms." The Protestant *Christian Century* commended the Court for, among other things, protecting and honoring marriage. The reaction of the Roman Catholic hierarchy was relatively subdued and that of Catholic editorial writers, although somewhat muffled, was generally positive. *Commonweal* called the invalidation of the Connecticut birth-control law "long overdue." That journal did observe, however, that "from a legal point of view, the decision was a muddy one." Numerous legal commentators agreed. Some faulted Douglas for weak reasoning and for his use of the term "penumbras," while others criticized the way he, and especially Goldberg, had employed the Ninth Amendment.[42]

Griswold and its establishment of what the *Times* recognized immediately as a new right of privacy excited far less criticism than did the Court's floundering efforts to define the extent of constitutional protection enjoyed by books and movies that probed the outer limits of the nation's increasingly permissive attitudes toward sex. As William O'Neill notes, "The most conspicuous development in literature after 1960 was the triumph of sexual freedom." America experienced a "surfacing of erotic literature." After federal courts ruled that D. H. Lawrence's *Lady Chatterley's Lover* was not obscene, the United States Post Office abandoned its long campaign to keep people from reading the book. The increasingly aggressive efforts of publishers to distribute long-suppressed erotic literature forced the Warren Court to grapple with the First Amendment implications of governmental efforts to stop such distribution. The justices, most of whom were products of a rather puritanical middle class, were surprised by and not well prepared to deal with the emergence of sexuality into the mainstream of popular culture. Recognizing the close connections between democratic political institutions and democratic culture, however, they expanded constitutionally protected expression to include many of the latter's increasingly sexual manifestations. Unfortunately, the Court was "conspicuously unsuccessful in pleasing commentators" or in reaching internal consensus on how to handle obscenity.[43]

Although widely criticized, the Warren Court's rulings were pioneering "simply because there were no constitutional decisions whatsoever on the . . . issue prior to 1957." Indeed, a respectable body of opinion, for which Meiklejohn was the most prominent spokesman, maintained that the First Amendment protected only political speech. That a Court headed by Earl Warren should have blazed trails into the constitutional wilderness of obscenity is ironic, for the chief justice was personally hostile to pornography. Something of a prude, he refused to watch the films at issue in obscenity cases and blanched at the thought of his daughters being exposed to pornographic material. Warren considered decency basic to a civilized existence and believed in protecting potentially susceptible individuals from indecency. The deterioration of resistance to it distressed him. Adding further irony, where obscenity was concerned, the attitudes of the conservative Harlan were more liberal than Warren's. When he missed the screening of an allegedly obscene film, Harlan delighted in probing his embarrassed clerks about the details. He considered most controls on obscenity silly. However, neither Harlan nor Warren became the Court's spokesman in this controversial area. Brennan did. Obscenity offended Justice Brennan's Catholic sensibilities, but no one else wanted anything to do with these cases, and the Chief had confidence in Brennan's ability to strike a proper balance between First Amendment values and society's need to protect itself from smut.[44]

Brennan made his first attempt to do that in *Roth v. United States* and *Alberts v. California,* which the Court decided together on June 24, 1957. Four months earlier, in disposing of *Butler v. Michigan,* Frankfurter had evaded the issues those two cases raised. Butler had been convicted of violating a law that criminalized making available to the general public any publication whose lewd, lascivious, obscene, or immoral nature might tend to incite minors to violent, depraved, or immoral acts. The vote to reverse his conviction was six to two, but Frankfurter passed, Black and Reed were reluctant to invalidate the statute, and the members of the majority differed in their reasoning. Apparently trying to secure Frankfurter's support for reversal, Warren assigned him the opinion. Having wanted to wait to decide the case until he heard the arguments in *Roth*, Frankfurter eventually proposed that they resolve *Butler* "on a narrow ground on which the whole Court . . . can agree." Even Brennan, who originally wanted a "full dress treatment," acceded to his suggestion. With a brief opinion, devoid of explanatory reasoning, a unanimous Court overturned the conviction on the ground that a law that reduced "the adult population of Michigan to reading only what is fit for children" arbitrarily curtailed "one of those liberties now enshrined in the Due Process Clause of the Fourteenth Amendment."[45]

Frankfurter's opinion was not "worth much in clarifying the field of obscene literature," but as Clark noted, "there are more cases coming which will provide that opportunity." In one, Samuel Roth had been found guilty of violating a federal obscenity statute by sending obscene circulars and advertising through the mails. Another was an appeal of David Alberts's conviction on state charges of "lewdly" keeping for sale obscene and indecent books and writing and publishing an obscene advertisement for them. Four members of the Court did not even want to hear these cases, but Warren, Harlan, and Brennan joined Black and Douglas in voting to grant certiorari. Only the two First Amendment absolutists favored reversing Alberts's conviction. Although part of the majority in that case, Harlan voted with Black and Douglas in *Roth*. He opposed Supreme Court interference with state efforts to protect morality, but considering obscenity a local problem, believed the federal government had no business censoring anything but hardcore pornography. Warren, in contrast, insisted that both the states and the national government might guard against filth. All of the others supported him, but Brennan disputed his contention that formulating a definition of obscenity was unnecessary, contending instead that the justices should develop a legal test, so as to make the question of a publication's obscenity one for the judiciary, rather than for a jury. Although disagreeing with Brennan about that, Warren assigned him the case. The result was an opinion establishing as the test for obscenity "whether to the average person, applying contemporary community standards, the dominant theme of the material taken as a whole appeals to prurient interest." According to Brennan, anything meeting that definition was outside the protection of the First Amendment because it was "utterly without redeeming social importance." Arguing that this litigation was really about conduct, that the Court's focus should be on the defendants' commercial exploitation of shameful cravings, and that it should not be reaching beyond their cases, the chief justice concurred only in the judgment; he was concerned that Brennan's broad language might eventually be used to restrict freedom of communication in the arts, sciences, and other areas. Harlan also criticized Brennan's "sweeping formula," which he thought rested on the faulty assumption that obscenity was "a peculiar genus of 'speech and press' which is as distinct, recognizable, and classifiable as poison ivy is among other plants." He believed that the value of each communication was unique, and that each suppression raised its own constitutional problem, which appellate courts could not avoid because a trier of fact, applying some generalized definition, had labeled something "obscene." Douglas and Black protested making the justification for censorship offensiveness to community standards and denied that any form of expression could be placed "beyond the pale of the absolute prohibition of the First Amendment." While they emphasized the repressive implications of Brennan's opinion, it was, as Samuel Krislov has pointed out, "perversely promising. By stating that obscenity was suppressible because worthless, it suggested that that which was not worthless was neither obscene nor suppressible."[46]

That principle was easier to articulate than to apply. On the same day *Roth* was decided, in *Kingsley Books v. Brown* a majority of the Court upheld a New York statute authorizing municipal officials to secure injunctions preventing the sale or distribution of obscene material. Brennan, who objected to that law's failure to provide for a jury trial, found himself dissenting, along with Warren (who insisted it imposed an invalid prior restraint), Douglas, and Black. Two years later in *Smith v. California* he spoke for the Court when it invalidated a Los Angeles ordinance that made unlawful the possession of any obscene or indecent writing in a place where books were sold, holding that because of the law's failure to require that the defendant know the contents of the offending publication, it necessarily had "a tendency to inhibit constitutionally protected expression." The decision was unanimous, but Harlan objected to Brennan's reasoning, and Frankfurter wrote separately to interpret the Court's decision as "not intended to nullify the conceded power of the State to prohibit booksellers from trafficking in obscene literature." Douglas and Black also concurred, condemning "fluid tests of obscenity . . . which require judges to read condemned literature and pass judgment on it." They predicted: "We are on the way to national censorship."[47]

The Court did eventually sanction censorship of motion pictures, but only if such action was accompanied by specified procedural safeguards. Its first movie case, *Kingsley International Pictures v. Regents* (1959), was more divisive than the unanimous decision suggested. The Motion Picture Division of the New York Education Department had refused to issue Kingsley a license to display *Lady Chatterley's Lover* because it depicted adultery in a favorable light. Although the statute that purportedly authorized the department's action made obscenity grounds for denying a license, the New York Court of Appeals had held this film was not obscene. Hence, the state was preventing the exhibition of the picture merely for "advocat[ing] an idea that adultery under certain circumstances may be proper behavior." Only Frankfurter indicated any willingness to uphold that notion. Nevertheless, Stewart's opinion, which declared the statute unconstitutional because "the First Amendment's basic guarantee is freedom to advocate ideas," won the total support only of Brennan and the Chief. Harlan, Frankfurter, Whittaker, and Clark all concurred solely in the result. Stewart spoke for a majority only because Douglas and Black, who considered *all* censorship of movies "a form of 'previous restraint' . . . at war with the First Amendment," signed his opinion.[48]

Two years later, in *Times Film Corp. v. Chicago,* a five-to-four majority directly repudiated their position. Times Film's permit application to exhibit *Don Juan* had been turned down solely because the company refused to submit the film for examination, as required by a Chicago ordinance. Times then filed suit, claiming the ordinance was an unconstitutional prior restraint. Taking the position that the case presented only an abstract question of law, a federal district court dismissed it as not justiciable. Warren wanted to hold that ruling erroneous and remand the case for trial, but Brennan thought the justices should decide the constitutional issue. If they were going to do so, Clark maintained, they should reject the contention that all prior restraints are unconstitutional and hold that in some circumstances government might review a film before it was exhibited. Harlan supported him, as did Stewart, Frankfurter, and Whittaker. Trying to hold a narrow five-to-four majority together, Clark drafted an opinion that both incorporated Stewart's view that "freedom from previous restraint . . . is not absolute" and accommodated Harlan's unwillingness to endorse anything that "might convey the impression that we are saying that this sort of prior restraint is good in all circumstances." "At this time," he wrote, "we say no more than this—that we are dealing only with motion pictures and, even as to them, only in the context of the broadside attack presented on this record." Warren thought *Times Film Corp.* had much wider implications. In a dissent joined by Black, Douglas, and Brennan, he maintained that the issue that had been posed was "our approval of unlimited censorship of motion pictures before exhibition through a system of administrative licensing." The Court's ruling, the Chief contended, "presents a real danger of eventual censorship of every form of communication." He joined a Douglas dissent attacking movie censorship as unconstitutional prior restraint.[49]

Having approved prior restraint of films, the Court then had to deal with administrative restraints on the distribution of printed material. Rhode Island had created the Commission to Encourage Morality in Youth, which was empowered to educate the public concerning anything that contained obscene, indecent, or impure language or manifestly tended to the corruption of young people and to investigate and recommend the prosecution of violators. When a majority of its members found a book or magazine objectionable for sale to persons under eighteen, it notified the publisher, which would often withdraw the condemned item from the market in order to avoid legal action. Confronted in *Bantam Books v. Sullivan* (1963) with a challenge to both the statute and the commission's practices, the Court ignored the law and held the methods used to implement it unconstitutional. Brennan's opinion declared that, despite their informal nature, the commission's activities amounted to censorship. Prior administrative restraints carried a heavy presumption of invalidity. The Court had upheld such schemes only when they operated under judicial supervision that assured almost immediate review. Rhode Island's did not operate in such a manner. Furthermore, although supposedly created to protect youthful readers, the commission also deprived adults of access to the suppressed publications. Only Harlan supported Rhode Island in conference and, while Clark wrote a concurring opinion faulting Brennan for failing to provide adequate guidance concerning what would be permissible, he alone dissented.[50]

Freedman v. Maryland (1965) produced no dissents. Brennan managed to satisfy Clark and even Harlan by eschewing a broad attack on movie censorship in favor of procedural restrictions on its implementation that would prevent the suppression of what was not obscene. A Baltimore theater owner appealed a conviction for showing the film *Revenge at Daybreak* without first submitting it to the Maryland State Board of Censors, as state law required. Maryland conceded the film was not obscene, that it did not violate the statute on any other basis, and that he could have gotten permission to show it had he asked. The defendant contended, however, that because the law allowed a censorship board to prevent exhibition of a movie while the exhibitor undertook a time-consuming appeal to the courts, it imposed unconstitutional prior restraint and threatened to suppress protected expression. Everyone but Clark, Harlan, and Stewart supported his position. Brennan, to whom the case was assigned, showed his opinion to Clark before circulating it. Clark found the draft inconsistent with *Times Film*. At his suggestion, Brennan changed the opinion to incorporate a passage providing that the prior submission of a film to a censor was constitutional "only if it takes place under procedural safeguards designed to obviate the dangers of the censorship system." The burden of proving a film was not protected had to be on the censor. The final decision to restrain exhibition must be made by a court, and the burden of going to court had to be placed on the censors. Any restraint imposed in advance of final adjudication must be limited to "the shortest fixed period compatible with sound judicial administration." Furthermore, Brennan declared (citing *Bantam Books*), "The procedure must . . . assure a prompt final judicial decision to minimize the deterrent effect of an interim and possibly erroneous denial of a license." "Although I voted the other way at the Conference," Harlan wrote to him, "I am satisfied with the way you have handled the matter and so join your opinion." Warren was reluctant to endorse something so clearly inconsistent with his ringing attack on censorship in *Times Film*, but on the night before the decision was announced, he abandoned plans to concur only in the judgment. The sole concurrence was by Douglas and Black, who wanted to "put an end to all forms and types of censorship."[51]

While the other justices managed to find common ground on the procedural aspects of movie censorship, the Warren Court never managed to reach anything approaching consensus on the substantive issue of what constituted obscenity. In *Manual Enterprises v. Day* (1962), Harlan could get only one other justice to sign what was supposed to be the opinion of the Court. *Day* was a challenge to a U.S. Post Office Department ruling prohibiting shipment of magazines filled mainly with photographs of nude or near-nude men and advertisements offering such pictures for sale. Warren, who thought Congress had a right to ensure that the mails were used only for "decent" purposes, had no doubt that this homosexual material was obscene. Only Frankfurter and Whittaker supported him. Five justices favored reversal, and although wanting to rule that the writ of certiorari had been improvidently granted, Stewart thought that "this literature for homosexuals is no worse than strip tease calendars are for others." Trying to write for the majority, Harlan utilized *Roth*'s prurient interest standard, but added that something was obscene if it was "so offensive on [its] face as to affront current community standards of decency—a quality that we shall hereafter refer to as 'patent offensiveness' or 'indecency.'" That addition to the definition of obscenity pleased Stewart, but not Brennan, who admitted the *Roth* test would have to be refined some day, but considered this a bad case in which to do so. Brennan also had "some difficulty with the element of 'patent offensiveness,'" which, he thought, would serve to limit obscenity to "'hard core' pornography." "And I have trouble defining 'hard core,' although no trouble at all recognizing it when I see it," he informed Harlan. Brennan wrote a concurrence arguing that reversal was required because the statute that the government claimed gave the postmaster general the power to censor obscenity actually authorized only criminal prosecution, not administrative proceedings. Warren and Douglas signed his opinion, while Clark dissented on the ground that the magazines were nonmailable because they contained advertisements for obscene material. Whittaker's retirement and Frankfurter's incapacitation at the time the decision was announced on June 25, 1962, left Harlan speaking only for himself and Stewart.[52]

Brennan did no better in *Jacobellis v. Ohio* (1964), where he wound up speaking only for himself and Goldberg. Nico Jacobellis had been convicted of possessing and exhibiting an obscene film, and the issue was whether the Ohio courts had properly found that *Les Amants* was obscene. Before discussing the case with his colleagues, Brennan believed "that the Court should embrace this opportunity to attempt a clarification of the applicable constitutional principles." At the conference, however, he confessed that while he had once thought *Roth* could be rewritten, he no longer did. Warren stood by the 1957 decision, saying "we don't know how to do any better by any test." Harlan agreed that "if a test has to be verbalized Roth is as good as any." He added, however, that "it is impossible to verbalize it"; the only real test was offense to one's taste or mind. Stewart, White, and Goldberg thought only hardcore pornography was not protected by the First and Fourteenth Amendments. Warren wanted a national community standard for obscenity; Harlan believed the states should have flexibility, but acknowledged the Court could not allow a book to be condemned in one jurisdiction and cleared in another. Perhaps the most revealing remark during a lengthy discussion was Brennan's admission that he went on a "Constitutional hunch" in these cases. The vote was six to three to reverse (with Harlan, Clark, and Warren in the minority), and Brennan was assigned to dispose of *Jacobellis* with a per curiam opinion. He quickly produced one that stated simply, "We have viewed the motion picture and conclude it is not obscene within the test of obscenity announced in [*Roth* and *Alberts*]."[53]

Brennan eventually abandoned this per curiam in favor of a full-blown opinion, which acknowledged the *Roth* test's inherent difficulties, but maintained that any substitute would raise equally thorny problems. Hence, "We . . . adhere to that standard." He seemed, however, to modify the test along the lines he had been considering before the conference, adding that to forfeit constitutional protection, something must be "'utterly without redeeming social importance." The mere fact that a work of art, literature, or science portrayed sex did not make it obscene. Black and Douglas, of course, insisted all censorship was unconstitutional. Goldberg thought suppression was sometimes permissible, but wrote briefly to explain why it was not justified here. White concurred in the judgment only, giving no reason. Stewart was the most candid. Contending that criminal laws could punish only "hard-core pornography," he added "I shall not today attempt to further define the kinds of material I understand to be embraced within that shorthand description. But I know it when I see it, and the motion picture involved in this case is not that." Warren, dissenting for himself and Clark, insisted Ohio could condemn *Les Amants*. Adding that for "all the sound and fury that the Roth test has generated, it has not proved unsound," he urged trying to live with *Roth* until a better definition of obscenity evolved.[54]

Four years later Brennan offered one he considered an improvement, but only one other justice joined the Chief in endorsing it. In fact, the three obscenity cases the Court decided in 1966 elicited fourteen opinions. The most important was Brennan's in *A Book Named "John Cleland's Memoirs of a Woman of Pleasure" v. Attorney General of Massachusetts*. That case involved a book, popularly known as *Fanny Hill*, that had been adjudged obscene in a civil equity proceeding authorized by state statute. It was decided along with *Ginzburg v. United States*, an appeal from federal criminal convictions for sending through the mails *Eros* (an expensive hardcover magazine, containing articles and photo-essays on love, sex, and sexual relations), *Liason* (a newsletter on sexual topics that included articles that had appeared earlier in professional journals and a report of an interview with a psychotherapist), and *The Housewife's Handbook on Selective Promiscuity* (a purportedly autobiographical account of the author's sexual experiences). *Eros* had unsuccessfully sought mailing privileges from the postmasters of Intercourse and Blue Ball, Pennsylvania, before obtaining them in Middlesex, New Jersey, from which it and several million circulars soliciting subscriptions were mailed out. The third case, *Mishkin v. New York*, was an appeal of a state criminal conviction for publishing, possessing, and hiring others to prepare obscene books. Some of the fifty works involved "depict[ed] relatively normal heterosexual relations, but more depict[ed] such deviations as sadomasochism, fetishism, and homosexuality." Many had covers with drawings of scantily clad women being whipped, tortured, and otherwise abused. Black, Harlan, and Stewart voted to hear all three cases, joined in *Ginzburg* and *Mishkin* by Goldberg and in *Memoirs* by Douglas and Fortas (who in the meantime had replaced Goldberg). On the merits the justices split five to four in all three cases, but the alignments were not the same. Warren, Brennan, Clark, and White voted three times to affirm, and Black, Douglas, and Stewart supported reversal with equal consistency. Harlan voted to affirm in the two state cases and to reverse in the federal one. *Ginsburg* yielded a qualified five-to-four majority to affirm, with Fortas, in what seems to have been an unsuccessful vote-trading gambit to keep *Fanny Hill* from being held obscene, supporting affirmance of the *Liason* and *Eros* convictions but reversal of the *Handbook* one.[55]

After the conference he apparently continued to work on Brennan, who had drawn the thankless job of trying to speak for a badly fractured Court. In order to retain Fortas's crucial fifth vote in *Ginzburg* and *Mishkin*, Brennan decided to write an opinion supporting reversal in *Fanny Hill*, a result he justified by applying a new threefold definition of obscenity that had made its first appearance in his draft *Ginzburg* opinion. For something to be obscene, he wrote: "Three elements must coalesce: it must be established that (a) the dominant theme of the material taken as a whole appeals to a prurient interest in sex; (b) the material is patently offensive because it affronts contemporary community standards relating to the description or representation of sexual matters; and (c) the material is utterly without redeeming social value." Under this test *Fanny Hill* was not obscene, for a Massachusetts court had found it possessed "a modicum of literary and historical value." That "redeeming social importance" was sufficient to save the work. Brennan managed to win Warren's support by telling him of Fortas's position and reminding him of his own dissenting opinion in *Kingsley Books*. White, however, objected to the three-pronged definition of obscenity on which the *Fanny Hill* decision now rested, and his objections forced Brennan to remove the new test from his opinion in *Ginzburg* (where White was part of a five-to-four majority) and move it to *Fanny Hill*. Stewart was willing to endorse the part of the *Fanny Hill* opinion that now articulated the test, so that some definition of obscenity would have the support of a majority of the Court, but when Clark drafted a dissent in that case (leaving Brennan with only three other votes), he withdrew his partial concurrence. That left a five-man majority that included Black and Douglas, both of whom supported reversal on their usual absolutist grounds, and only two of Brennan's colleagues endorsing his new test for obscenity.[56]

Brennan's method of disposing of the other two cases heightened the confusion in an already muddled area of the law. He upheld Ginzburg's convictions on the ground that the defendant had sought to market his publications by representing them as erotically arousing. "Where the purveyor's sole emphasis is on the sexually provocative aspects of his publications," Brennan declared, "that fact may be decisive in the determination of obscenity." Since Warren had argued in his *Kingsley Books* dissent that the Court should judge the conduct of the individual rather than the content of his publications, Brennan's adoption of this pandering strategy no doubt helped him secure the Chief's support. Such an approach had not previously been discussed even in conference, however, and the solicitor general's office found as surprising as did Ginzburg a decision holding to be obscene material he had marketed after carefully studying existing obscenity law. Fortas signed Brennan's opinion only after getting him to add the word "sole" to its key sentence, and White and Clark did so only after he moved his three-part test to *Fanny Hill*. He used neither the new test nor his *Ginzburg* gambit in *Mishkin*, although the defendant in that case almost certainly had been pandering, too. Considering the books Mishkin had been marketing beyond the protection of the First Amendment no matter how they were sold, Brennan held them obscene using the *Roth* test. The New York courts had interpreted that state's obscenity statute as applying only to hardcore pornography, he observed, so they had used a standard even more stringent than the old rule. Mishkin had contended that some of his publications were not obscene under *Roth* because they depicted "deviant" sexual practices, and thus did not meet its requirement of appeal to a prurient interest of the average person. Brennan dismissed that argument by declaring: "Where the material is designed for and primarily disseminated to a clearly defined deviant sexual group, rather than to the public at large, the prurient-appeal requirement of the *Roth* test is satisfied if the dominant theme of the material taken as a whole appeals to the prurient interest in sex of the members of that group."[57]

As if his use of a different approach in each of the three cases and his announcement of a new test for obscenity in a plurality opinion did not confuse matters enough, Brennan's colleagues added eleven more opinions to his three. Douglas concurred in *Fanny Hill* and wrote one dissenting opinion for both *Ginsburg* and *Mishkin*. Black dissented in both *Ginzburg* and *Mishkin*. Harlan also wrote a dissenting opinion in *Ginzburg*, because he thought the federal statute used to prosecute the defendant reached only "hardcore pornography" and because he objected to what he viewed as Brennan's use of pandering to convert something that was not obscene into obscenity. But unlike Douglas and Black, Harlan also dissented in *Fanny Hill*, complaining about Brennan's addition of a without-redeeming-social-value prong to the test for obscenity and reiterating his view that states should be able to do essentially whatever they wanted in this area. Stewart dissented in both *Ginzburg*, where he contended that the defendant's due process rights had been violated because no federal statute made "'commercial exploitation' or 'pandering' or 'titillation' a criminal offense," and in *Mishkin*, where he declared simply that since the books in question were "not hard-core pornography," they were "protected by the First and Fourteenth Amendments." In addition, he and Black concurred in the reversal of *Fanny Hill* "for the reasons stated in their respective dissenting opinions in Ginzburg v. United States." Conversely, both White and Clark dissented in *Fanny Hill*. White merely protested briefly the addition of the lack-of-social-importance stipulation to the *Roth* rule, but Clark weighed in with a lengthy jeremiad, moaning that "the public should know of the continuous flow of pornographic material reaching this Court and the increasing problem States have in controlling it." He had stomached the decisions of the past ten years, Clark declared, but this book was too much even for him. He then plunged into a discussion of its contents. "With fourteen opinions filed in three cases, propounding at least five separate tests, coherence was hard to come by," a perceptive political scientist observed.[58]

The following year the justices threw up their hands and conceded they were incapable of bringing order out of the chaos they had wrought. Although most of his colleagues did not want to review any more obscenity cases, Fortas pressed them to resolve important questions raised by petitions that were pending when the 1966 trilogy was decided. The Court agreed to hear three cases that concerned him. At the conference that followed oral argument, although at least five votes to reverse were cast in each case, the grounds suggested were even more diverse than in 1966. None of the three opinions Fortas drafted could command a majority. Nor could the three that Harlan wrote or the two Brennan composed. Soon there were six different opinions in each case. With the likelihood of even more to come, the Court confronted the danger of yet another embarrassing display of disunity. To prevent this, Stewart drafted a brief per curiam that avoided the issues on the basis of which review had been granted and held simply that "the distribution of the publications in each of these cases is protected by the First and Fourteenth Amendments from governmental suppression." Outlining the approaches taken by the various justices in determining whether or not something was obscene, Stewart concluded, "Whichever of these constitutional views is brought to bear upon the cases before us, it is clear the judgments cannot stand." After Stewart removed a footnote stating that four members of the Court rejected the "'pandering concept of the First Amendment" (which Brennan found objectionable), all but Harlan and Clark joined the per curiam, which was published as *Redrup v. New York*. *Redrup* initiated a new policy under which per curiams were used to reverse obscenity convictions whenever at least five justices, applying their separate tests, concluded the material was not obscene. This tactic would be employed by the Court in at least thirty-one cases over the next six years.[59]

In his *Redrup* per curiam Stewart noted that none of the cases the Court was resolving involved "a claim that the statute in question reflected a specific and limited state concern with juveniles." The law challenged in *Ginsberg v. New York* (1968) did. The defendant in that case had been prosecuted for selling two "girlie magazines" to a sixteen-year-old boy in violation of a statute making it a crime knowingly to sell to someone under seventeen any picture depicting nudity that was harmful to minors or any magazine containing such pictures that, taken as a whole, would be harmful to them. The conference vote was five to four to affirm the conviction, but the majority initially divided over whether the case was moot because the defendant had received only a suspended sentence. Brennan eventually managed to resolve that issue to the satisfaction of Harlan and Stewart with a lengthy footnote. He also managed to write an opinion on the merits that proved acceptable to a majority of the Court. His first draft took the position that "state infringement of First Amendment rights is justified by the overriding state interest in the welfare of children." This seemed to White a less-desirable approach than "pursu[ing] further the idea that obscenity is outside the area of First Amendment protection." He favored taking the position that the magazines, although protected with respect to adults, were not when sold to children because as to them "they have no social value." Brennan revised his opinion to satisfy White, declaring that "the concept of obscenity or of unprotected matter may vary according to the group to whom the questionable material is directed or from whom it is quarantined." Sustaining the New York law, then, required "only that we be able to say that it was not irrational for the legislature to find that exposure to material condemned by the statute is harmful to minors." Brennan also rejected Ginsberg's contention that the law under which he had been prosecuted was void for vagueness. Douglas dissented for himself and Black, and Fortas also wrote a dissenting opinion, in which he protested "the Court's failure to circumscribe state power by defining its limits in terms of the meaning of 'obscenity' in this field." Harlan, concurring in *Ginsberg* but dissenting in two companion cases, outlined the differences among the justices over whether the Court itself should be determining whether particular items were obscene. Complaining that "the current approach has required us to spend an inordinate amount of time in the absurd business of pursuing and viewing the miserable stuff that pours into the Court," he insisted the only way to alleviate this "chaotic state of affairs" was to give the states wide discretion to control the dissemination of obscene material.[60]

A majority of his colleagues was unwilling to provide the states with such sweeping power. Indeed, in its last obscenity decision, the Warren Court overturned a conviction under a Georgia law that made the private possession of obscene material a crime. State officers had discovered the offending films while executing a warrant that authorized them to search Robert Stanley's home for evidence of bookmaking activity. The outraged justices voted unanimously to reverse Stanley's conviction. They divided, however, over the appropriate rationale. Some favored basing the decision on the Fourth Amendment, while others wanted to hold that, as Black put it, "possession cannot be made a crime." Marshall, to whom the case was assigned, took the latter approach. Although acknowledging that *Roth* and its progeny had declared obscenity enjoyed no constitutional protection, he concluded that "the First and Fourteenth Amendments prohibit making mere private possession of obscene material a crime." "If the First Amendment means anything," Marshall wrote, "it is that a State has no business telling a man, sitting alone in his own house, what books he may read or what films he may watch." Stewart, White, and Brennan concurred only in the result, taking the position that the films had been seized in violation of the Fourth Amendment. To Professor Al Katz, *Stanley* revealed "the difficulty the Court has in shaping a conceptually defensible rationale for its judgments in the obscenity area."[61]

The Supreme Court had "meandered about in a series of rulings that gave little guidance to the lower courts." Furthermore, its obscenity decisions pleased almost no one. Academic critics lambasted them. Political scientist C. Peter McGrath, for example, condemned the Court's "continuing inability to provide an intelligible definition of obscenity" and faulted the justices for "needlessly confound[ing] a confusing set of questions and . . . display[ing] a penchant for individual dogmatism and murky opinions." A minister and his wife attacked *Roth*, which they viewed as having "much to do with the low morals . . . [that are] bringing this nation to destruction." The anti-obscenity *Ginsburg* decision faired no better, eliciting harsh criticism from *Newsweek*, the *Saturday Evening Post, Library Journal*, the *Wall Street Journal*, the *New York Herald Tribune*, the *Wilmington Journal*, the *Greensboro* (North Carolina) *News*, the *San Francisco Examiner*, and a host of other newspapers, most with moderate-Republican editorial orientations. These publications condemned *Ginsburg* as "bewildering" and "outrageous." Meanwhile, Citizens for Decent Literature mobilized those who wanted even more publications declared obscene for a "religious crusade." That organization spearheaded a correspondence campaign that flooded the Court with letters and postcards, and its members also pressed for the enactment of more repressive legislation. A friend of Warren's reported to him from San Francisco that hundreds of incidents of censorship had occurred in Northern California and that groups such as the John Birch Society were targeting not only hardcore pornography but also a *Harper*'s magazine article on homosexuality and J. D. Salinger's novel, *Catcher in the Rye*. He feared that the Court's decisions were giving "encouragement to the censors." Yet, the Chief also received complaints from members of Congress that they had unleashed a flood of "filth" upon the country.[62]

Although almost everyone disliked the Warren Court's obscenity rulings, the reaction they elicited was evidence of how much the Court had achieved in just a few years. While fighting over how to define a category that a majority of its members continued to insist lay outside the realm of constitutionally protected expression, the

Court had managed to shield with the First Amendment most books and movies that dealt with sex in the more open and explicit manner sanctioned by changes in popular attitudes. Furthermore, it had invented a right to privacy that protected sexual intimacy. *Griswold* and the obscenity decisions were both part of a broader trend. They exemplified the Warren Court's determination to facilitate individual expression and autonomy, even when that meant limiting the capacity of communities to prohibit words and even conduct that outraged what the youth of the 1960s derided as "the Establishment." Although rooted in concerns about political repression, this judicial world view had wider implications. By the time Earl Warren retired in 1969, constitutional protections for individual freedom extended far beyond the political realm.

His Court followed more than led changes in society. By 1965 the sexual revolution had progressed so far that Hollywood was showing bare breasts. Two years later *Newsweek* ran a signpost story announcing "Anything Goes," and *Time* put Hugh Hefner on its cover. The Warren Court was really just riding a tidal wave that was transforming American society. The justices did not cause that wave, but they also did not try to hold it back. The Court facilitated and assisted the sexual revolution, just as it facilitated and assisted the civil rights movement and the triumph of liberalism over McCarthyism. Although perhaps not as much of a pioneer as either its champions or its critics claimed, the Warren Court significantly expanded the rights of individuals against the community. This was a substantial achievement. It was also a cause of constitutional confusion. Furthermore, it added fuel to the fires of hostility kindled by the Warren Court's revolutionary transformation of criminal procedure.[63]

9

THE CONSTITUTIONALIZATION
OF CRIMINAL PROCEDURE

As a district attorney, Earl Warren did not have to worry much about the Constitution. When he was an Alameda County prosecutor, the Bill of Rights had little bearing on state criminal justice and affected hardly at all the way local police and prosecuting attorneys did their jobs. By the time Warren retired from the Supreme Court in 1969, a district attorney had to be an expert on constitutional law. During its last eight years, his Court revolutionized criminal procedure, taking the lead in one of the most dramatic developments in twentieth-century American law. As Lawrence Friedman observes, "Constitutional law and criminal procedure came together with a bang, like the *Titanic* and its iceberg." Under Warren's leadership, the Supreme Court rejected Frankfurter's federalism-based view that the Constitution did not impose the same limits on state and local law enforcers as it did on their federal counterparts. Concerned that American criminal justice favored the well-to-do and knowledgeable over the poor and uneducated, egalitarian justices also expanded the content of constitutionally guaranteed defendants' rights.[1]

They did so at a time when demographic trends and social unrest were fueling a rapid rise in the crime rate. Much of the blame for what many perceived as a breakdown of law and order was placed on the Warren Court, which became a favorite whipping boy for conservative politicians. Yet, at the very time that conservative politicians were accusing it of coddling criminals, the Court was handing down numerous decisions highly beneficial to law enforcement.

Before Warren became chief justice, few politicians would have thought to blame the Supreme Court for the crime rate. Even though the Supreme Court supervised federal criminal trials and federal law enforcement, it played a small and relatively unimportant role in American criminal justice. More than 99 percent of all prosecutions were brought in the state systems. In those cases, both the Court's pronouncements and the Constitution were largely irrelevant.[2]

The states did, of course, have to comply with the Fourteenth Amendment, which forbade them from depriving any person of life or liberty without due process of law. As interpreted by the Supreme Court, however, the Due Process Clause required only that the states afford defendants fair and decent trials and left them free within very broad limits to determine what satisfied that requirement. During the 1930s and

1940s, while holding that the First Amendment freedoms were part of the liberty protected by the Due Process Clause, the Court seemed reluctant to nationalize the criminal-procedure rights contained in the Fourth, Fifth, Sixth, and Eighth Amendments. It did hold in *Powell v. Alabama* (1932) that the Fourteenth Amendment required states to appoint lawyers for indigent defendants in capital cases. This was, however, not because the Sixth Amendment applied to such cases, but only because some actions that would violate the Bill of Rights if undertaken by the federal government also happened to be denials of due process if done by the states. From the 1930s through the 1950s the Supreme Court grappled with the question of what rights those were. In *Palko v. Connecticut* (1937), Justice Benjamin Cardozo explained that they were those which were "of the very essence of a scheme of ordered liberty," which lay "at the base of all our civil and political institutions," and the denial of which would be shocking. The prohibition against double jeopardy at issue in *Palko* did not meet those criteria. Indeed, beyond the right to counsel in capital cases and the right to have a coerced confession excluded from evidence, it was unclear what did.[3]

The *Palko* approach required case-by-case application. While that pleased Frankfurter, Black eventually became convinced that what he condemned as a "natural law" method of determining whether the Due Process Clause had been violated permitted too much judicial discretion. Dissenting in *Adamson v. California* (1947), he argued that those who drafted the Fourteenth Amendment had intended to make all of the Bill of Rights guarantees applicable to the states. Three of his colleagues supported his "total incorporation" position, but Stanford Law School professor Charles Fairman savaged it in a famous law review article. After 1949 only Black and Douglas endorsed a theory that Frankfurter endeavored to convince other justices would produce "monstrous results." The triumphant fair-trial interpretation of the Due Process Clause produced among other things his opinion in *Wolf v. Colorado* (1949), which held that the Fourteenth Amendment required states to afford the security against arbitrary intrusions by the police that lay at the core of the Fourth Amendment, but not to comply with the federal exclusionary rule, which prohibited the use at trial of evidence obtained through unreasonable searches and seizures. Frankfurter also spoke for the Court in *Rochin v. California* (1952), where it ruled that pumping a defendant's stomach in order to seize drugs he had swallowed violated the Due Process Clause because it shocked the conscience.[4]

The fair trial approach persisted through the first half of Warren's chief justiceship. During those years the Supreme Court played a small, traditional, and generally supportive role in law enforcement. The Chief's long experience in city, county, and state government had led him "to the conclusion that, within reason, government should be kept as close as possible to the people," and his background also inclined him toward supporting the police. He was, after all, the son of a murder victim. District Attorney Warren was "a favorite in law enforcement circles." In the infamous *Point Lobos* case his office employed evidence obtained through surreptitious electronic eavesdropping and a confession secured in the absence of counsel. It also exploited both an extensive delay between arrest and arraignment and pretrial publicity unfavorable to the accused. When Warren ran for attorney general in 1938, most of California's district attorneys, police chiefs, and sheriffs supported him. His pre-Court career did, to be sure, offer hints that he would not be a hardline law-and-order judge. As district attorney Warren urged Alameda County to hire a public defender to represent indigents charged with crimes, and as governor he exhibited an interest in prison reform. A believer in rehabilitation, he promoted legislation making it possible for ex-convicts who lived lawfully after their releases to secure pardons and have their civil rights restored. Warren maintained that in criminal cases what mattered was not which side won but whether "justice has been done." Once he saw the American justice system from the vantage point of the Supreme Court, he was struck by the gap between the enlightened law enforcement that he favored and the inequality and coercion so common in many places. Although he eventually became protective of defendants' rights, however, his initial tendency was to favor the prosecution.[5]

Other members of the early Warren Court leaned the same way. Frankfurter did so because of his commitments to judicial restraint and federalism. Thus, in 1957 he informed a colleague that despite "my deep feelings against capital punishment," he favored affirming a death sentence imposed following a retrial occasioned by the reversal of a conviction for second degree murder, because the case raised "an issue even more important . . . than the appropriate application of the double jeopardy clause to [these] circumstances. That issue is the proper exercise of the judicial function." Although quarreling often with Frankfurter on that subject, Black could be even more conservative than his colleague in some criminal cases. The Alabaman was extremely uncomfortable with the flexible language of the Fourth Amendment's prohibition of "unreasonable" searches and seizures and the Eighth Amendment's ban on "cruel and unusual" punishments, which, he realized, authorized the sort of judicial discretion he disliked. While acknowledging that such provisions required him to balance competing interests, he read the Fourth Amendment more restrictively than any other justice in modern times and was quite deferential to the government in cases involving the Eighth Amendment as well. Although Black sympathized enough with those convicted of crimes to lead the fight to abolish the convict lease system in Alabama, he disdained arguments that the death penalty violated the Cruel and Unusual Punishment Clause. His reservations about flexible standards of reasonableness and fairness made him a less-rigorous enforcer of the Fourth Amendment than Frankfurter or Harlan. Although firmer than Black in that area, Harlan generally showed great deference to governmental authority, resisting the imposition of detailed rules limiting the discretion of those charged with enforcing the criminal law. As a state judge, the otherwise liberal Brennan had interpreted defendants' rights restrictively, exhibiting an orthodoxy that favorably impressed New Jersey's Republican chief justice, Arthur Vanderbilt.[6]

A tribunal composed of men such as these was unlikely to impose many constitutional constraints on state criminal justice systems, and the early Warren Court did not. It continued to adhere to the fair-trial interpretation of the Due Process Clause, despite the bizarre and confusing results the approach produced in cases such as

Irvine v. California (1954). The evidence used to convict Irvine of bookmaking included recordings of conversations in his house, which the police had obtained by breaking into it three times to install and move a concealed microphone. The Court voted five to three to affirm the conviction, with Black passing. He and Douglas eventually dissented on the ground that the use of other evidence against the defendant violated his Fifth Amendment right against compulsory self-incrimination. Frankfurter also dissented (for himself and Burton), but his reason was that what the police did was "revolting," and hence the recordings should have been excluded under the *Rochin* rule. Warren and Jackson agreed that their behavior was distasteful, but in conference Jackson responded to Frankfurter's arguments by saying, "If you take each case by itself you cannot give the rule necessary for law enforcement." He wrote an opinion for a four-man plurality, which asserted that the recordings had been unlawfully obtained (indeed it urged the Justice Department to prosecute those involved in the surreptitious entries), but held that under *Wolf* they were admissible. Clark provided the crucial fifth vote. In a concurring opinion he stated bluntly that had he been on the Court in 1949, he would have voted to apply the exclusionary rule to the states. Yet, he declined to "sterilize the rule announced in *Wolf* by adopting a case-by-case approach." That would make for intolerable "uncertainty and unpredictability." Instead, Clark opted to follow *Wolf,* in the hope that "strict adherence . . . may produce needed converts for its extinction."[7]

Clark continued to chart an ambiguous course in *Breithaupt v. Abram* (1957), an involuntary manslaughter case arising out of a fatal traffic accident. The evidence against Paul Breithaupt included testimony that he had been driving while intoxicated, which was based on a blood sample a physician, at the urging of a state patrolman, had taken while he was unconscious in the hospital. Breithaupt argued that the admission of this evidence violated his rights under both the Fourth and Fifth Amendments, but citing *Wolf,* Clark disagreed. Speaking for the Court, he also denied that reversal was required, because "the taking of a sample of blood . . . under the protective eye of a physician" was either "brutal" or "offensive." Warren joined Black and Douglas in dissent. *Irvine* had affected his thinking, and he was no longer willing to practice judicial restraint when that would leave constitutional rights unenforced. Declaring his intellectual independence from Frankfurter, the Chief thereafter "voted with Black and Douglas in virtually all cases involving individual rights."[8]

One of those was *Bartkus v. Illinois* (1959). After Bartkus was acquitted in federal court on charges of robbing a federally insured savings and loan association, Illinois prosecuted him for the same crime under a state robbery statute, using evidence supplied by the FBI. This time he was convicted. Bartkus claimed the state prosecution was unconstitutional double jeopardy. His argument was difficult to make, for in *United States v. Lanza* (1922) the Court had promulgated the "dual sovereignty doctrine," under which the national and state governments could punish the same act if both had criminalized it. *Lanza* involved a state prosecution followed by a federal one, and in *Abate v. United States* (1959), a companion to *Bartkus,* the Court reiterated its holding that this scenario did not violate the Fifth Amendment's Double Jeopardy Clause. Deciding whether reversing the order of the trials posed a constitutional

problem proved more difficult, for it triggered yet another debate over incorporation. When the justices first discussed the case in November 1957, Frankfurter, Burton,
Clark and Harlan supported the state, while Black, Douglas, Warren, and Whittaker
backed Bartkus. Brennan's failure to participate produced an evenly divided Court,
thus affirming the decision below. On May 26, 1958, the justices granted a rehearing.
After reargument, Black advocated applying the Double Jeopardy Clause to the states.
He maintained, however, that even under the "shocks the conscience" approach, reversal was required. Frankfurter responded that "to reverse would be to cut deep into
our federalism." Brennan and Warren staked out a middle ground, advocating reversal because a federal officer had participated in the state prosecution. That argument appealed to the indecisive Whittaker, but Frankfurter's intense preconference
lobbying won his vote. Stewart said the matter "was not crystal clear to him," precipitating a sometimes nasty struggle for his crucial fifth vote that continued during the
writing of opinions. The testiness that Frankfurter displayed during this tug of war
may have been due to a heart attack that he suffered while the *Bartkus* opinions were
being written; his illness seems to have exacerbated his tendency to browbeat colleagues. Black considered him "an obviously sick man." His physical condition may
explain why he insisted on using his *Bartkus* opinion to "make the case against the
'incorporation' theory as devastingly [*sic*] conclusive as possible," despite Clark's
efforts to dissuade him. The *Lanza* precedent made mounting a persuasive argument
for reversal based on incorporation nearly impossible, Clark argued, and all he was
doing was opening up "a Pandora's box of abstractions." In order to retain Clark's
support, Frankfurter agreed to delete some passages, but he resisted abandoning his
attack on incorporation. Clark "reluctantly" went along, enabling Frankfurter to
retain the majority he achieved when Stewart joined him. Brennan dissented from
Frankfurter's opinion of the Court on the ground that the domination of the state
trial by federal officers made Bartkus's conviction a violation of the Double Jeopardy
Clause. Warren and Douglas joined his opinion, as well as one by Black, which contended that the Due Process Clause made the Fifth Amendment's double jeopardy
prohibition applicable to the states.[9]

Although Frankfurter saw himself as defending the interests of the states, their
conception of what those were differed from his. Less than five months after *Bartkus*,
the Illinois legislature passed a law negating the effects of the decision. It made a
prior federal conviction or acquittal a defense when the state prosecuted someone
for the same conduct. Approximately sixteen other states already had such laws. By
1992 a majority would.[10]

Although of dubious utility to the states, Frankfurter and Harlan's restricted conception of the Due Process Clause was more than just a rationalization for pro-prosecution
positions, as the case of Caryl Chessman demonstrated. A career criminal who had
allegedly terrorized lovers' lanes while impersonating a police officer, Chessman was
convicted of kidnaping three women for purposes of robbery and sentenced to
death under California's "Little Lindbergh Law." During a dozen years on death row,
he carried his case to the Supreme Court seventeen times. Only twice did the Court
render decisions in his favor, once in 1955 and again in 1957. Those opinions, written

by Frankfurter and Harlan respectively, addressed alleged improprieties in the preparation of the record utilized in Chessman's state appeal, holding that the handling of this matter had denied him due process. They neither overturned his convictions nor invalidated his death sentence. Yet, Harlan insisted "that the fair administration of justice" required granting a Chessman petition for certiorari, even though the Court had already turned down four others that raised the same issue, and Frankfurter used his case to push for reform of the way the Court handled in forma pauperis petitions from prisoners. Meanwhile, the more liberal but less process-oriented Douglas complained about "a needless detour in a case already long drawn-out by many appeals." By late 1959 even Frankfurter had become exasperated with the amount of time that had elapsed since Chessman's conviction, writing to his colleagues, "There is a serious defect somewhere in the scheme of the law when this happens." On April 25, 1960, the Court turned down eight to zero (with former California governor Warren abstaining) a final plea for a stay of execution. One week later America's most famous death-row inmate died in the San Quentin gas chamber. His case had by then become a focal point for the anti–capital punishment sentiment that had been gaining strength in the United States during the 1950s, but rather than using judicial power to promote that cause, the Warren Court did little for Caryl Chessman beyond delaying the inevitable with demands that the state afford him procedural due process.[11]

Its failure to affect significantly the outcome of such a celebrated case highlights how unimportant the early Warren Court was to state criminal justice. The Court played a more significant role in federal cases; in those arising out of the domestic cold war, it was quite protective of defendants. For example, in *Mesarosh v. United States* (1957) the Court overturned a Smith Act conviction because of the false testimony that a paid informer, who appeared as a prosecution witness, had given before a Senate committee. The following year, the Supreme Court thwarted one of the favorite tactics of prosecutors in such cases: repeatedly asking defense witnesses a question they knew no Communist would ever answer—whether someone else was a member of the CPUSA—and thus subjecting them to punishment for multiple counts of contempt. In *Yates v. United States* (1957) the Court held that when a witness made clear the first time she was asked that she would never identify anyone else as a Communist, she was guilty of only one act of contempt, no matter how many times she refused to respond. In *Kremen v. United States* (1957) the Court overturned on Fourth Amendment grounds the convictions of three people who had hidden two *Dennis* defendants while they were fugitives from justice.[12]

The principal exception to this pattern of protecting the rights of defendants in internal security cases was *Abel v. United States* (1960). Col. Rudolph Abel was a notorious Soviet spy who had been convicted of conspiracy to commit espionage. Some of the evidence against him, including a forged New York birth certificate, had been seized during a warrantless search of the hotel room where he was arrested. The arrest was problematic, for while knowing that Abel was a spy, the FBI had failed to seek a warrant to arrest him for espionage. Instead, the Bureau notified the Immigration and Naturalization Service, and the head of the New York INS office issued an administrative warrant that authorized seizing him for purposes of deportation. Agents from both agencies went to Abel's hotel room, but only after FBI efforts to interrogate him failed, did the INS men enter and arrest the spy. They then searched his room. The Bureau appeared to have involved INS in the case in order to circumvent the rigorous requirements governing the issuance of warrants in criminal cases, and Warren and Black considered the administrative warrant unconstitutional. The other justices disagreed, and the Chief eventually proposed that they hold this issue had been waived below. After two conferences the Court did so, upholding Abel's conviction five to four. The opinion, written by Frankfurter, ruled the disputed evidence had been obtained through a proper search incident to a lawful arrest. The Court emphasized repeatedly, however, that "the matter would be totally different had the evidence established . . . that the administrative warrant was . . . employed as an instrument of criminal law enforcement to circumvent the latter's legal restrictions." Douglas, Black, Warren and Brennan dissented. They viewed *Abel* as proof of the old adage that hard cases make bad law. "We must take care to enforce the Constitution without regard to the nature of the crime or the nature of the criminal," Brennan warned.[13]

The early Warren Court failed to follow Brennan's warning when deciding cases involving notorious organized crime figures, such as the 1956 appeal of Frank Costello's tax evasion conviction. A mobster who had branched out into a number of legitimate businesses and established both a corrupt grip on New York City politics and a reputation as the ruler of a vast criminal empire, Costello gave televised testimony in March of 1951 that was one of the highlights of the highly publicized investigation of racketeering and organized crime led by Senator Estes Kefauver (D-Tenn.). He claimed his constitutional rights had been violated in the tax case because the only witnesses who testified against him before the grand jury were investigating officers, and thus all of the evidence on which his indictment rested was hearsay. The Court unanimously rejected this argument. Even in private no justice supported Costello. The fact that Frankfurter tailored the opinion in an unrelated tax case so Costello could not exploit the government's inconsistent interpretation of the relationship between two provisions of the tax code strongly suggests that who he was affected his fate. A desire to avoid giving aid and comfort to organized crime also appears to have influenced the Court's handling of Anthony "Blinky" Palermo's 1959 tax evasion case. Until Robert Kennedy became attorney general, the rest of the federal government did little to combat mobsters, but the Warren Court took a hard line against them.[14]

Organized crime cases were not the only ones in which the justices' rulings favored prosecutors. For example, in 1957 the Court held that the National Motor Vehicle Theft Act, which made it a crime to transport a "stolen" car across a state line, could be used to punish someone who had lawfully obtained possession of another person's automobile in South Carolina and then unlawfully sold it in Maryland. In 1959, over the objections of Black, Douglas, Brennan, and Warren, the Court decided that Rule 42(b) of the Federal Rules of Criminal Procedure, which authorized summary punishment of contempt committed in the presence of the court, could be used against someone who, after refusing to answer a question in a grand jury hearing, was taken before a judge and again refused to answer. In *Green v. United States* (1961), with the same four justices dissenting, the Court rejected the contention that a trial judge had violated another provision of the Federal Rules, which mandated that before sentence could be imposed, the defendant must be given an opportunity to make a statement in his own behalf. When the trial judge asked Green if he wished to say something, his lawyer responded, but the defendant himself said nothing. The defendant contended the rule had not been complied with, and Warren agreed. With Frankfurter writing the opinion, however, the Court held that the judge had complied with the rule, because he had directed to Green the question that elicited the attorney's statement.[15]

Although the early Warren Court leaned in a pro-prosecution direction, it also provided hints of the egalitarianism that would eventually propel it along a different course. One was *Griffin v. Illinois* (1956), in which the Court for the first time "sought to eliminate the invidious effects of poverty on individuals' constitutional rights when facing the administration of justice." After being convicted of armed robbery, Judson Griffin and James Crenshaw asked the trial judge for a certified copy of the record, which, they contended, they needed to prosecute an appeal and could not afford because they were poor. He denied their request because the state provided free transcripts only in capital cases. *Griffin* suggested the criminal justice system discriminated on the basis of wealth and class, which bothered Douglas. Led by Warren, six of his colleagues joined him in voting to reverse. All but Burton and Minton followed the lead of Warren. Moving away from his early pro-prosecution position, the Chief argued that Illinois "can't have one rule for rich and one for poor." Burton thought the Court was interfering in a matter that should be left to the discretion of the states, but even Frankfurter and Harlan supported Warren. After the conference Harlan had second thoughts. One of his clerk's research into Illinois law persuaded him that Griffin and Crenshaw could have appealed without obtaining a copy of the trial record. Black, to whom the case had been assigned, was not impressed, pointing out that during oral argument the state's lawyer had agreed this was not possible. His opinion held that Griffin and Crenshaw had been victims of unequal treatment, which violated the Equal Protection and Due Process Clauses. Frankfurter concurred, declaring, "The State is not free to produce such a squalid discrimination." He wrote separately to address an issue that would bedevil the Court throughout the coming criminal-procedure revolution: whether the principle it was announcing should have only prospective application. Frankfurter argued that it should, advising against indulging in the fiction that the new rule had always been the law and then refusing relief to those who had been denied its benefits on the specious ground that they had waived their rights by failing to assert them. Despite Black's objections, he urged the Court to "recognize candidly the considerations that give prospective content to a new pronouncement of the law." Burton dissented, insisting Illinois's appellate procedures did not deny due process and adding that, because the only discrimination they involved—between capital and noncapital cases—was rational, there was no violation of the Equal Protection Clause. The Constitution did "not require the States to provide equal financial means for all defendants." Minton signed Burton's dissent, as did Reed and Harlan, whom Clark had unsuccessfully sought to dissuade from doing so.[16]

The decision Harlan opposed proved to be "a watershed in the Warren Court's jurisprudence." *Griffin v. Illinois* was its first broad pronouncement in favor of economic equality in the criminal process. *Mallory v. United States* (1957) evinced a similar sympathy for the disadvantaged. The defendant was a nineteen-year-old African American of limited intelligence who had been convicted in the District of Columbia of raping a white woman. He confessed after being interrogated for nine or ten hours by numerous police officers, confronted by the complaining witness, and given a lie detector test—all before he was brought before a magistrate for arraignment, as Rule 5(a) of the Federal Rules of Criminal Procedure required, although there was one in the same building where the police headquarters was located. Speaking through Frankfurter, the Court declared, "We cannot sanction this extended delay, resulting in confession, without subordinating the general rule of prompt arraignment to the discretion of arresting officers." Even Burton and Harlan went along. Because *Mallory* freed a rapist, the decision evoked a bitter reaction from the District of Columbia press and criticism from Washington's police chief that was tinged with racism. In Congress, southern Democrats and internal-security-conscious Republicans added it to their bill of particulars against the Warren Court.[17]

The controversy ignited by *Mallory* foreshadowed larger storms that would swirl around the Court after 1961 as it labored to bring criminal procedure into line with changes in American legal culture. By then the exercise of largely unchecked discretion by police, wardens, and others charged with preventing, detecting, and punishing crime had become much less acceptable than it once had been. Increasingly, rules constrained those who administered criminal justice and protected defendants and prisoners from unfair treatment and abuse. The pace of change was uneven, however. Some communities, states, and regions lagged behind national trends. These deviations seemed unacceptable to many citizens of a country where, since World War II, nationally circulated magazines, mass marketing, chain stores, franchises, and television networks had homogenized popular culture. "Undoubtedly, the democratization of the marketplace with its emphasis on uniformity prompted expectations of equal treatment, just as it dimmed the belief in the values of diversity and difference," David Bodenhamer observes. The mechanism that implemented national standards and enforced equality was the Warren Court's incorporation of the Bill of Rights into the Fourteenth Amendment.[18]

That revolution began with the Fourth Amendment. Although continuing to follow the fair-trial approach in search and seizure cases, some justices were becoming increasingly sensitive about intrusions into the home, as *Frank v. Maryland* (1959) demonstrated. The question in *Frank* was whether a city health inspector's warrantless search of a house for rats, which resulted in the arrest of the homeowner and imposition of a twenty dollar fine, violated the Fourteenth Amendment. Since the Fourth Amendment had been held to apply only in criminal contexts, this seemed like an easy issue. Warren announced that because of the small size of the fine, he would consider this search reasonable even in a criminal case, and the Court voted eight to one to affirm. Only Douglas objected. Shutting himself up in his office for three days, he ground out a dissent so persuasive that Black, Brennan, and even the Chief changed sides. Whittaker wavered, threatening Frankfurter, to whom the case had been assigned, with loss of his majority. In the end it held, but Stewart insisted that the opinion not suggest the protection of the Fourth Amendment was "available exclusively or even primarily against searches for evidence to be used in criminal proceedings." What Frankfurter published was an erudite essay, but one whose holding was so fact-specific that its significance for other cases was unclear. "In light of the long history of this kind of inspection and of modern needs," he wrote, "we cannot say that the carefully circumscribed demand which Maryland here makes on appellant's freedom has deprived him of due process of law." Douglas's dissent had a much clearer thesis: the Due Process Clause imposed upon the states "the guarantee of privacy embodied in the Fourth Amendment." He accused the Court of diluting "the right to privacy which every homeowner has the right to believe was part of our American heritage."[19]

Douglas's opinion resonated with the public. Harvard Law School professor Albert Sacks saw dangerous implications in what Frankfurter had written, believing his rationale could not be confined to noncriminal cases. Newspapers as diverse as the *Christian Science Monitor,* the *Wall Street Journal,* and the *Richmond Times-Dispatch* joined the Illinois legislature in condemning *Frank.* The New Orleans radio and television station WDSU charged that the decision had "left the American home less sacred." "Does the enforcement of public health inspection laws require the violation of a citizen's right to privacy?" asked an outraged *Winston-Salem Journal.*[20]

Besides outraging the public, *Frank* triggered a nasty squabble within the Court over *Eaton v. Price* (1960). Decided a few months later, that case involved a criminal prosecution of a homeowner for refusing to admit housing inspectors. Frankfurter, Harlan, Clark, and Whittaker insisted the case was controlled by *Frank* and should be summarily affirmed. Warren argued strongly that they were dissimilar because in *Frank* the officer had reason to believe there was a violation on the premises and the fine was only twenty dollars. Frankfurter insisted these differences were not constitutionally significant, which infuriated Warren, who accused him of emphasizing the smallness of the fine during the *Frank* conference. Douglas charged that Frankfurter's rationale for not hearing oral argument was contradicted by a memorandum he himself had written in another case. Ultimately, the Court affirmed the Ohio Supreme Court four to four, with Stewart recusing himself because of his father's involvement in the case. Although the uniform practice in cases affirmed because of an even division had been to withhold any expression of views on the merits, Brennan published an opinion for himself, Warren, Black, and Douglas. It emphasized that "the judgment is without force as precedent," attacked *Frank,* and condemned the view that the judiciary was free "to administer a watered-down, subjective version of the individual guarantees of the Bill of Rights when state cases come before us." Brennan had no use for Frankfurter's view that "it would be a wrong way of getting at our problem in the *Frank* case to determine whether it would or wouldn't constitute a violation of the Fourth Amendment and from that conclude that, therefore, it does or doesn't violate the Fourteenth Amendment." The tide was beginning to run in Brennan's direction.[21]

"The fair-trial approach to search-and-seizure issues was substantially undermined by the Court's decision in *Elkins v. United States* in 1960," Richard Cortner notes. The defendants in *Elkins* had been convicted of wiretapping and conspiracy. The evidence against them included recordings of telephone calls and a recording machine that Oregon law enforcement officers had procured through a search and seizure that two state courts considered unlawful. Although assuming the search was unreasonable, a federal district judge refused to suppress the disputed items. Under the so-called silver platter doctrine, evidence turned over to federal prosecutors after being illegally obtained by state officers was admissible in federal court. This rule rested on the proposition, which *Wolf* had repudiated, that the Fourth Amendment did not apply to the states. Warren argued that they should abolish the rule, and five justices favored doing so, including Stewart, who believed that because this was a federal case, the federal exclusionary rule should apply, and Black, who considered the silver platter doctrine just a judge-made rule of evidence, not a command of the Fourth Amendment. The Chief assigned the case to Stewart. He produced an opinion pointing out that the foundation that supported the doctrine—the proposition that unreasonable state searches did not violate the Constitution—had been destroyed by *Wolf* and invoked "the Court's supervisory power over the administration of criminal justice in the federal courts" to "hold that evidence obtained by state officers during a search which, if conducted by federal officers, would have violated the defendant's immunity from unreasonable searches and seizures under the Fourth Amendment is inadmissible . . . in a federal criminal trial." Frankfurter, Clark, Harlan, and Whittaker sought to dissuade the majority from "reversing out of hand a course of adjudications in this Court that began . . . more than forty-six years ago." When that effort failed, all four dissented. Harlan (writing for himself, Clark, and Whittaker), urged retention of the silver platter doctrine, while Frankfurter (joined in part by the other three) advocated excluding evidence gathered by officers from states whose own courts would not have admitted it. While rejecting the dissenters' view that at least some illegally obtained evidence should be admissible in federal courts, Stewart's opinion avoided the issue of whether the Fourth Amendment required its exclusion. His initial draft explicitly stated that the exclusionary rule was not a constitutional command, but at Brennan's urging, he revised it.[22]

A year later in *Mapp v. Ohio* (1961) the Court endorsed the proposition Stewart had nearly disavowed. *Mapp* was an odd vehicle for constitutionalizing the exclusionary rule, for it was really a First Amendment case. Dollree Mapp had been convicted of knowingly possessing lewd and lascivious books, pictures, and photographs. Cleveland police officers found these after smashing their way into and rummaging through her house, in what they claimed was a search for a bombing suspect and gambling paraphernalia. Although having plenty of time to obtain a search warrant, they did not bother to get one. The issue of primary concern to the Ohio Supreme Court, however, was whether the state's possession-of-obscenity statute violated the

First Amendment. The briefing and oral argument in the U.S. Supreme Court focused on the same issue, although an amicus brief filed by the ACLU did contain a short paragraph urging the Court to reexamine *Wolf* and hold that the Fourteenth Amendment required the exclusion of unconstitutionally seized evidence from state criminal proceedings. When interrogated by Frankfurter about whether he was asking the Court to do that, Mapp's lawyer dodged his questions. The ACLU's Bernard Berkman used some rebuttal time to say his organization did want that decision overruled, but when the justices took up the case, they too spent most of their time discussing the Ohio obscenity statute, which everyone seemed to agree was an overly broad restriction on freedom of expression. Only Douglas and Brennan, who viewed it as an alternative basis for a decision in Mapp's favor, had much to say about the search-and-seizure aspect of the case. Warren and Clark also indicated they would be willing to overrule *Wolf,* but the whole subject received so little attention that Stewart did not remember it being "even discussed at the Conference." The vote was unanimous, and "We all agreed, as I recollect it," he wrote to Clark a month later, "that the judgment should be reversed on First Amendment grounds."[23]

Stewart was reacting to a Clark opinion written for the Court that "came as quite a surprise." Although the Texan had not said much in the conference, Mapp's case apparently reminded him of one he had handled early in his law practice. Dallas police, searching without a warrant, had torn up his client's house in order to find a half-pint of whiskey, which they handed over to federal prosecutors. Despite Clark's objections, the alcohol was admitted into evidence in a Prohibition Act prosecution under the silver platter doctrine. While riding back downstairs on the elevator with Black and Brennan, Clark asked them, "Wouldn't this be a good case to apply the exclusionary rule and do what *Wolf* didn't do?" Probably encouraged by Brennan (who had expressed the same thought in conference and later praised what he wrote as "magnificent and wonderful"), he set to work drafting an opinion based on that rationale. Unaware of Clark's change of direction, Douglas wrote what was intended to be a concurring opinion, advocating that they "apply the Fourth Amendment with full force" to the states and make the exclusionary rule "part and parcel of the constitutional guarantee." He never circulated it, because Clark adopted his position. Clark's would not be the opinion of the Court, however, unless he got one more vote. While Black wanted to overrule *Wolf*'s partial application of the Fourth Amendment to the states and fully incorporate it, he was averse to compelling the states to comply with the exclusionary rule, which he did not regard as constitutionally required. Warren, Douglas, and Brennan went together to see him, and after intense lobbying by these close allies, Black caved in. He did, however, publish a concurring opinion, putting his own spin on the decision: "I agree with what appears to be a plain implication of the Court's opinion, that the federal exclusionary rule is not a command of the Fourth Amendment, but is a judicially created rule of evidence which Congress might negate."[24]

Although Black went along with Clark somewhat grudgingly, Stewart, Harlan, Whittaker, and Frankfurter would not do so. Harlan professed to be "unable to understand why a ground for deciding this case should have been chosen which is not only highly debatable and divisive, but also requires the overruling of a decision to which the Court has many times adhered over the past dozen years." If *Wolf* were going to be overruled, Stewart protested, that should happen only after argument by counsel and full discussion in conference. He remained part of the majority, but published a short "Memorandum" that endorsed the judgment on the ground that the Ohio obscenity statute violated freedom of thought and expression, and he declined to take a position on the constitutional question the Court was deciding. Harlan dissented. In a part of his opinion with which Stewart expressed agreement, he faulted the majority for reaching out to decide an issue it did not need to resolve. *Mapp*, he maintained, furnished "a singularly inappropriate occasion" for reconsidering *Wolf.* Harlan went on to dispute Clark's contention that the exclusionary rule was a constitutional requirement, rather than a dictate of the Court in its capacity as supervisor of the federal judiciary. Defending his position, Clark wrote to his colleague, "If the right to privacy is really so basic as to be constitutional in rank and if it is really to be enforceable against the states (*Wolf*), then we cannot carve out of the bowels of that right the vital part, the stuff that gives it substance, the exclusion of evidence." He added, "I have a court and therefore my theory at least has support." Unable to change Clark's mind, Harlan denounced the majority for forgetting "the sense of judicial restraint which . . . should enter into deciding whether a past decision of this Court should be overruled." Whittaker signed his dissent, as did Frankfurter, who considered the Court's decision premature and ill-advised, because a majority of the states had already adopted the exclusionary rule on their own, and others would probably soon do so. "Why substitute platonic guardianship for the deeper education possible on democracy's long march?" he asked. Frankfurter, objecting to "concentration of governmental powers in one central government," opposed *Mapp* and explained to his colleagues, "I care deeply about our federalism."[25]

Although the California Supreme Court was among those courts that had adopted the exclusionary rule, that state's attorney general, Stanley Mosk, welcomed the decision Frankfurter condemned, because it would "take the pressure off the local judges." Douglas was perfectly happy to do that, for he believed *Wolf* had "reduced the guarantee against unreasonable searches and seizures to 'a dead letter.'" His concurring opinion endorsed Clark's position. Black's, in contrast, denied that the Fourth Amendment mandated the exclusionary rule and objected to the way Clark handled incorporation. His justification for supporting the decision was that "the Fourth Amendment's ban against unreasonable searches and seizures . . . considered together with the Fifth Amendment's ban against compelled self-incrimination" provided a constitutional basis for the exclusionary rule. Although Clark persuaded him not to say they were impliedly overruling a decision holding the latter did not apply to the states, Black did insist his colleague accept his interpretation of the most important sentence in Clark's opinion: "Since the Fourth Amendment's right of privacy has been declared enforceable against the States through the Due Process Clause of the Fourteenth, it is enforceable against them by the same sanction of exclusion as is used against the Federal Government." Black insisted they were "holding . . . that the Fourth Amendment *as a whole* is applicable to the States and not some imaginary and unknown fragment designated as the 'right to privacy.'" If not, he would be unwilling to decide in this state case that the Fourth Amendment required the exclusionary rule. Clark tried to persuade Harlan that his opinion was no "windfall to 'incorporation' enthusiasts," but because of the terms on which Black provided him with his crucial fifth vote, it was a major victory for supporters of incorporation. "The margin was slim," Bodenhamer notes, "but the abandonment of the fair trial interpretation of constitutional guarantees was unmistakable." *Mapp* was an "incorporation breakthrough."[26]

That breakthrough occurred because Clark considered the exclusionary rule essential to deterring police misconduct. Two years later in *Ker v. California* (1963), eight justices agreed that the constitutionality of state searches and seizures was to be determined using the same standards that applied to federal searches and seizures. Harlan refused to sign Clark's opinion, "which I read to embrace 'incorporation' in full-blown form." Concurring only in the judgment, he protested "this further extension of federal power." Yet, while Brennan thought it "especially important that we emphasize the same federal standards of reasonableness apply in federal and state cases," Clark took care to point out that not all of the principles governing the admission of evidence in federal trials came from the Constitution. "Mapp sounded no death knell for our federalism," he claimed. The four justices for whom Clark spoke disagreed with dissenters Brennan, Warren, Douglas, and Goldberg, however, not about what constitutional standard applied but only over whether it had been satisfied in this case.[27]

While reading *Mapp* broadly, the Court limited its immediate impact by refusing to make the decision retroactive. Harlan, who believed his colleagues were setting the stage for "a jail delivery of uncertain but obviously serious proportions," objected to disposing summarily of cases that raised the question of whether the new rules it had announced required "the reopening of cases long since finally adjudicated"; he also objected to hiding behind the fiction that the Court's recent decisions had only proclaimed what was already the law. In *Linkletter v. Walker* (1965) his colleagues finally addressed what had by then "become a most troublesome question in the administration of justice." During a conference discussion Black argued strongly that "if we hold something unconstitutional then it should apply wherever adherence to [the] old view would do an injustice." Only Douglas supported him. The colloquy revealed that the "fair trial" approach retained more vitality than the Court was publicly acknowledging. Because *Mapp* was designed to deter police misconduct rather than to ensure a fair trial, said Clark, he was inclined to make its rule entirely prospective. Harlan took a similar position, as did Warren, Brennan, Stewart, and Goldberg. Several justices maintained that *Mapp*'s holding should be treated differently from the right to counsel, which went "to the essence of a fair trial." With Clark writing the opinion, the Court held that the exclusionary rule did not apply retrospectively, and hence did not require reversal of convictions that had become final before *Mapp*. Only Black and Douglas dissented.[28]

Although unwilling to extend *Mapp*'s benefits to all who had been convicted using evidence the decision made inadmissible, the Warren Court did, on the basis that "the fundamental protections of the Fourth Amendment are guaranteed by the Fourteenth Amendment against invasion by the States," impose federal standards that state judges must follow in issuing search warrants. In *Stanford v. Texas* (1965), the Court unanimously annulled a warrant that authorized rummaging through a man's home to look for written material concerning the Communist Party of Texas. The lawyers from the state attorney general's office who executed this warrant seized over three hundred books and pamphlets, as well as private documents and papers. What they had employed looked to the justices like the very sort of "general warrant" the Fourth Amendment had been intended to prohibit. Black and Warren disagreed, however, over whether reversal could be justified on the basis of *Aguilar v. Texas* (1964).[29]

In *Aguilar* the Court had held that a search warrant might be based on hearsay information supplied by a policeman who, though claiming to have obtained the tip from an anonymous informant, lacked direct personal knowledge of the facts alleged in the affidavit he filed with the issuing magistrate. The magistrate had to be informed, however, of the underlying circumstances on which the officer based his conclusions and which led him to consider the informant credible and his report reliable. These principles already applied in federal courts, Goldberg declared, and although *Ker* had concerned a search without a warrant, it dictated "that the standard for obtaining a search warrant [be] 'the same under the Fourth and Fourteenth Amendments.'" Harlan agreed. "If *Ker* means anything an affidavit not good for a federal search would not be good for a state search" either, he told his colleagues. Harlan somewhat reluctantly concurred, convinced that a contrary ruling "would tend to 'relax Fourth Amendment standards . . . in the federal system.'" Clark, who believed the Court should not be claiming supervisory authority over state searches, dissented for himself, Stewart, and Black. Yet, the following year, he, Harlan, Stewart, Black, and White acknowledged that the two-pronged test established by *Aguilar* applied also to police claims of probable cause to arrest or search without a warrant. In *Spinelli v. United States* (1969) the Court, as it often did in the era of incorporation, applied a rule developed to limit the discretion of state judges in a federal case. Interpreting and enlarging upon *Aguilar*, it held that not only must an informant's report be measured against the standards laid down in *Aguilar*, but if his tip failed to satisfy those, the standards must be applied to other allegations in the affidavit that might tend to corroborate the tip. Black protested that "all probable cause cases are now potentially reviewable in this Court."[30]

Even while developing and enforcing rigorous national standards for the issuance of warrants, the Court was also extending the reach of the Fourth Amendment in order to protect privacy against electronic intrusion. *Olmstead v. United States* (1928) had held, over dissents by Brandeis and Holmes, that wiretapping did not violate the Fourth Amendment because it involved no physical entry onto premises belonging to the defendant. Arguably, *Silverman v. United States* (1961) did not involve a trespass either, for the District of Columbia police officers who overheard conversations in the row house they alleged was a gambling establishment merely drove a "spike mike" through the common wall separating it from the adjacent dwelling. Warren, Frankfurter, Douglas, and Brennan saw this case as an opportunity to overrule *Olmstead*. but Black, Clark, and Harlan were unwilling to do that. In order to get a majority to reverse the convictions, the Chief and his allies had to base the decision on a narrower, alternative rationale he suggested: that the penetration of the mike through the wall of the row house really was a trespass, and hence a warrantless search violating the Fourth Amendment.[31]

The antipathy for electronic surveillance that produced the *Silverman* decision manifested itself again in *Berger v. New York* (1967). There the Court held unconstitutional a state law that authorized issuance of an "ex parte order for eavesdropping" upon oath or affirmation of a prosecutor or police officer attesting that there was "reasonable ground to believe" that evidence of a crime might be obtained and describing the person or persons whose communications were to be overheard or recorded. With Clark writing the opinion, the Court held "that the language of New York's statute is too broad in its sweep, resulting in a trespassory intrusion into a constitutionally protected area and is, therefore, violative of the Fourth and Fourteenth Amendments." Stewart objected that the challenged law contained provisions more stringent than the Fourth Amendment required, and Black, who dissented along with Harlan and White, censured the Court for making "completely impossible" any state or federal eavesdropping statute.[32]

The hostility toward what it considered the "dirty business" of high-tech snooping that Black thought animated the majority led the Court to hold a few months later in *Katz v. United States* (1967) that the FBI had violated the Fourth Amendment when it obtained evidence of illegal interstate transmission of wagering information by attaching a listening and recording device to the outside of a public telephone booth without first obtaining a warrant. The government argued strenuously that the booth was not a constitutionally protected area, and that the Fourth Amendment did not apply to this kind of surveillance because there was no physical intrusion. Warren insisted, however, that Katz had "[paid] a fee to use the box," had sought privacy there, and had "a right to it the same as in any other registered place." The Court split four to four, with the newly-appointed Marshall not participating. A couple of weeks after the conference, Stewart, who had voted to affirm, circulated a memorandum calling for reversal of Katz's conviction. *Olmstead* had been so eroded by subsequent decisions, he now believed, "that the 'trespass' doctrine there enunciated can no longer be regarded as controlling. The Government's activities in electronically listening to and recording [Katz's] words violated the privacy upon which he justifiably relied while using the telephone booth and thus constitute a 'search and seizure' within the meaning of the Fourth Amendment." The fact that the listening device the agents had employed did not penetrate the wall of the phone booth "can have no constitutional significance," Stewart maintained. He drafted an opinion for the majority his switch created, and White and Harlan also changed sides. That left Black as the lone dissenter. White, supported by Fortas, did insist on the inclusion of a declaration that the Court was not deciding whether this type of electronic surveillance would be permissible in national security investigations. He added a concurring opinion high-lighting that disclaimer and setting forth his view that search warrants were not required in such cases. Harlan also contributed a concurring opinion in which he interpreted the opinion of the Court as holding that a telephone booth was, like a home, protected against both physical and electronic intrusion, because in both places "a person has a constitutionally protected reasonable expectation of privacy." His words summarized in a particularly compelling way the thinking behind the Court's assertion that "the Fourth Amendment protects people—and not simply 'areas'—against unreasonable searches and seizures." The Supreme Court was moving toward a redefinition of the scope of this constitutional guarantee. Harlan's phrase "reason-able expectation of privacy" came to define what it was that the Fourth Amendment protected.[33]

The Court declined to apply *Katz* retroactively, or to hold information obtained through judicially sanctioned wiretaps inadmissible because it represented neither the fruits nor the instrumentality of a crime. Nevertheless, the chief justice of Geor-gia accused it of sanctioning "a criminal invasion of the general public's right to pro-tection against criminals." His was a type of complaint heard with increasing frequency during the middle and late 1960s as the Warren Court imposed more and more con-stitutional constraints on law enforcement. Most of these regulated criminal proce-dure, but the Court's incorporation of the Bill of Rights also imposed some federal standards on state substantive criminal law. The first decision to do so was the enig-matic *Lambert v. California* (1958), which overturned a conviction for failure to com-ply with a Los Angeles ordinance making it a crime for any person who had been convicted anywhere of an offense punishable in California as a felony to remain in the city for more than five days without registering with the chief of police. This law struck Warren as vague and arbitrary, and the other justices followed his lead in vot-ing to reverse Lambert's conviction. Douglas wrote an opinion that held the ordi-nance unconstitutional because the phrase "punishable as a felony" was too vague to satisfy due process. That approach proved acceptable only to Black. Among those who objected to it was Clark, who contended Douglas's draft would "wreck a host of state statutes." After consulting with him, as well as Black and Brennan, Douglas rewrote his opinion. The final version reversed Lambert's conviction because she had not received actual notice of the registration requirement. "Where a person did not know of the duty to register and where there was no proof of the probability of such knowl-edge, he may not be convicted consistently with due process," Douglas declared. Frank-furter, who thought this rationale "would cut too deeply into the criminal law," dissented (joined by Harlan and Whittaker). He faulted the Court for trying to draw a constitutional line between acts and omissions. Frankfurter ignited a testy exchange by castigating Douglas from the bench for placing under a cloud countless federal and state statutes that subjected people to punishment for failure to comply with requirements of which they had no notice. He accurately predicted that *Lambert* would "turn out to be . . . a derelict on the waters of the law." Uncertainty about what exactly the ruling prohibited kept it from doing much but creating confusion.[34]

Though also somewhat ambiguous, *Robinson v. California* (1962) did clearly establish that the Eighth Amendment's Cruel and Unusual Punishment Clause applied to the states. Lawrence Robinson had been convicted of violating a statute that made it a crime for a person to "be addicted to the use of narcotics." To Harlan punishing in this manner "the status of being a drug addict" raised "serious constitutional questions, which are at least, if not more, substantial than those which we decided in *Lambert v. California*." Douglas considered addiction an illness; consequently, being an addict was something that could not be made a crime. Brennan and Stewart supported him, and so did Warren, albeit somewhat reluctantly. The vote was four to three. The Chief assigned the case to Stewart, hoping for a moderate opinion that could command a majority. His strategy worked, for Stewart won over Black. His opinion characterized the California statute as one "which makes the 'status' of narcotic addiction a criminal offense" and held that "a state law which imprisons a person thus afflicted as a criminal, even though he has never touched any narcotic drug within the State or been guilty of any irregular behavior there, inflicts cruel and unusual punishment in violation of the Fourteenth Amendment." Stewart's opinion assumed, without establishing, that the Eighth Amendment applied to the states, an issue that had received only passing mention in the briefs and oral argument. Stewart could get away with appealing to Black in this way because the ailing Frankfurter took no part in the case. Douglas added a concurring opinion setting forth his view that addiction was an illness, and, consequently, that it was "'cruel and unusual' punishment . . . to treat as a criminal a person who is a drug addict." Harlan distanced himself from that view, but faulted California for punishing "a bare desire to commit a criminal act." Only White and Clark dissented, with the latter insisting California's law was really part of a drug-treatment program. Neither objected to the majority's incorporation of the Eighth Amendment.[35]

The complete incorporation of the Sixth Amendment right to counsel sparked even fewer fireworks. The Court had been searching for an opportunity to overrule *Betts v. Brady* (1942), which had held that a state defendant enjoyed a constitutional right to an appointed lawyer only if his case involved special circumstances. By the late 1950s *Betts* had become a hollow shell, for the Court had not turned down a single claim that a case met that requirement. Black campaigned against *Betts,* and even Frankfurter became convinced that, because of changed circumstances, it should be abandoned. The Court nearly overruled the decision in *Carnley v. Cochran* (1962), a habeas corpus case in which the petitioner had been convicted for having incestuous sexual intercourse with his thirteen-year-old daughter. Confusion had arisen over which of two sets of Florida statutes applied to what the illiterate Carnley was alleged to have done, and the state supreme court had imputed a waiver of assistance of counsel from the mere fact that the record showed he did not have a lawyer. Even under *Betts,* Carnley was clearly entitled to have his conviction reversed, and the justices voted unanimously to do so. Although Black wanted to seize this opportunity to discard *Betts,* Frankfurter objected that because of *Carnley*'s unsavory facts, he could not "imagine a worse case . . . to overrule a long standing decision." The Court did not do what Black desired, but in a concurring opinion, which Warren and Douglas joined, he reaffirmed his belief that the Supreme Court should hold that the Fourteenth Amendment made the Sixth Amendment's guarantee of the right to counsel in all criminal cases applicable to the states.[36]

The Court did so a year later in *Gideon v. Wainwright* (1963). Warren had instructed his clerks to be on the lookout for a case that could be used to overrule *Betts,* and Clarence Earl Gideon presented them with what they were seeking. Gideon had been charged with breaking and entering a poolroom with the intent to commit a misdemeanor, which was a felony in Florida. He asked the trial judge to appoint a lawyer to represent him, but was informed that state law authorized this only when the defendant was charged with a capital offense. Gideon sought a writ of habeas corpus from the Florida Supreme Court, claiming the state's refusal to give him a lawyer violated the Bill of Rights. Denied relief, he filed with the U.S. Supreme Court an in forma pauperis petition, laboriously scrawled out by hand in pencil. The Court voted six to one to hear his case, with only Clark opposed. It appointed Abe Fortas, then practicing with Arnold, Fortas, and Porter, to represent Gideon and asked both sides to address the question of whether *Betts v. Brady* should be overruled.[37]

Fortas did not argue that the Fourteenth Amendment had made the Sixth Amendment's Assistance of Counsel Clause applicable to the states. Instead, he contended that no indigent defendant could get a fair trial in a state criminal case unless he had a lawyer, and therefore that even under the fair trial approach, *Betts* should be overruled. Worried that some justices might think he was advocating an intolerable intrusion on states' rights, Fortas stressed that the existing special-circumstances rule was worse for federalism, because the case-by-case review of state decisions by federal courts that it necessitated inevitably created conflict between the two judicial systems. He received support from an unexpected source. Seeking backing in *Betts,* Florida's assistant attorney general, Bruce Jacob, invited the attorneys general of other states to intervene in *Gideon* as amicus curiae. Only those from Alabama and North Carolina supported him. Organized by Walter Mondale of Minnesota and Edward McCormack Jr. of Massachusetts, attorneys general from twenty-three other states filed a brief urging the Court to reverse *Betts* and hold counsel must be appointed in all serious state criminal cases. As Cortner points out, "The intervention of twenty-three states urging reversal of *Betts v. Brady* dramatically underlined Fortas's argument that the special-circumstances rule could not be supported on the basis of considerations of federalism."[38]

The outcome was inevitable. Gideon won nine to zero. With Black writing the opinion, the Court explicitly overruled *Betts v. Brady*. "Reason and reflection require us to recognize," it declared, "that in our adversary system of criminal justice, any person hailed into court, who is too poor to hire a lawyer, cannot be assured a fair trial unless counsel is provided for him." Fortas had made this point during oral argument, seeking thereby to avoid having to claim explicitly that the Fourteenth Amendment had made the Assistance of Counsel Clause applicable to the states. He sought to skirt the incorporation minefield by saying he did not care how the Court explained overruling *Betts* and applying the right to counsel to the states. The ACLU, however, filed an amicus brief, signed by former solicitor general Rankin and New York University professor Norman Dorsen, that urged directly that the Fourteenth Amendment be held to incorporate the right recognized in federal courts under the Sixth Amendment. Although bowing in the direction of the fair-trial approach, Black gave the ACLU what the organization wanted. "We accept Betts v. Brady's assumption . . . that a provision of the Bill of Rights which is 'fundamental and essential to a fair trial' is made obligatory upon the States by the Fourteenth Amendment," he wrote. "We think the Court in Betts was wrong, however, in concluding that the Sixth Amendment's guarantee of counsel is not one of those fundamental rights." Harlan offered only a mild protest. While agreeing that *Betts* should be overruled and that the right to counsel should be "recognized as a fundamental right embraced in the Fourteenth Amendment," he declined "to embrace the concept that the Fourteenth Amendment 'incorporates' the Sixth Amendment as such." Nevertheless, *Gideon* was "a major victory for incorporationists.[39]

The decision's effect on American criminal justice was modest, however, at least outside Florida. Within three years of *Gideon,* that state granted new trials to 2500 inmates who had been convicted in proceedings in which they were not represented by counsel, and 1300 prisoners were released. In addition, the state legislature created a public-defender system. The Court's action merely added Florida to the thirty-seven states that already provided lawyers to indigent defendants. Similar moves were soon under way in the remaining minority of jurisdictions that had not guaranteed counsel to everyone. The federal government was already providing lawyers to indigents, but required them to serve pro bono. In 1964 Congress agreed to pay for attorneys to represent poor defendants.[40]

Although *Gideon* did little more than further the implementation of a principle that was already widely accepted when the Supreme Court ruled, the decision did directly affect *Douglas v. California* (1963), which the Court decided three months later. William Douglas and his codefendant, both indigent, had requested the appointment of counsel when they appealed their convictions on thirteen felony charges. The California Court of Appeal, acting pursuant to a statute that authorized denial of such a request if its own examination of the record convinced it that the services of a lawyer would not be helpful to the court or to the defendant, turned them down. That ruling was one of several bases on which they appealed. The Court came close to using *Douglas* to overrule *Betts,* but after Fortas agreed to argue *Gideon,* it elected to set the California case down for reargument. When the justices considered it again on January 18, 1963, the vote was six to three to reverse. Douglas's opinion for the Court did not even mention *Gideon.* Instead, employing a rationale actually developed the year before, it relied on *Griffin v. Illinois* and the Equal Protection Clause. As Harlan, who joined Clark and Stewart in dissent, pointed out, this line of reasoning made *Gideon*'s analysis "wholly unnecessary." That case could have been decided by simply holding that a state deprived an indigent of equal protection whenever it failed to furnish him legal services. Although rhetorically inconsistent with *Gideon, Douglas* announced a principle that was completely compatible with it: indigents had a constitutional right to counsel during the first stage of a state's appellate process.[41]

The Warren Court went on to hold that the right to counsel existed in other contexts as well. On the same day that the *Douglas* decision was announced, the Court made clear that an indigent defendant must be provided with a lawyer at his arraignment. Its 1961 *Hamilton v. Alabama* ruling required the provision of a lawyer in capital cases in states where the law treated defenses not raised at this point as abandoned. Now, in *White v. Maryland,* the Court generalized *Hamilton*'s holding. The state had used against White at his trial a guilty plea he had entered at a preliminary proceeding (which the state insisted was not the real arraignment), where he had no lawyer. Reversing his conviction, the Court took the position that any hearing at which a defendant was asked to enter a plea was a "critical stage" in his prosecution; hence, he had a right to counsel there. Three years later in *Mempa v. Rhay* (1967), it ruled that a lawyer had to be provided at a proceeding that could result in the revocation of probation.[42]

In another 1967 case, *United States v. Wade,* the Court held that the accused was entitled to counsel at a lineup, which was conducted after indictment but before trial, because that was a critical stage in a criminal prosecution. The presence of a lawyer could avert prejudice and assure meaningful confrontation with witnesses later. This holding had the support of six members of the Court, including Brennan, who wrote the opinion, and Clark, both of whom had originally voted to affirm Wade's conviction. Brennan became convinced after the conference that the lineup was a critical stage at which a lawyer played an essential role, and Clark went along with him in return for getting the conviction in the companion case of *Stovall v. Denno* affirmed. A very different majority (which included the three dissenters on the right-to-counsel issue) held that requiring a defendant to participate in a lineup did not violate his privilege against compulsory self-incrimination. *Wade,* along with *Stovall* and a third lineup case, *Gilbert v. California,* badly fragmented the Court. In both *Gilbert* and *Wade,* six justices dissented from at least one of the multiple holdings. Brennan's opinion in *Wade* declared unconstitutional the admission of in-court identifications of witnesses who had viewed the defendant earlier at a postindictment lineup conducted without notice to his appointed counsel, unless a prior determination had been made that the witnesses were of independent origin and had not been tainted by the illegal lineup. The group of justices who endorsed that holding was different from the one that supported *Gilbert*'s ruling, also written by Brennan, that requiring a defendant to provide handwriting exemplars did not violate his Fifth Amendment privilege against compulsory self-incrimination or any other constitutional right. In *Stovall* the Court (again with Brennan as its spokesman) limited the impact of *Wade* and *Gilbert* by holding that the exclusionary rule they had created did not operate retroactively, because being without a lawyer at a lineup, unlike being without one at trial, did not always result in unfairness to the accused. The same six-to-three majority also held that Stovall had not been deprived of due process because he was brought to a hospital room so he could be identified by a woman (whom he had allegedly stabbed while murdering her husband) who was physically unable to visit the jail. Only Clark endorsed every part of all three Brennan opinions. Harlan, Stewart, and White opposed all defendants on all issues in all three cases. Warren, Black, Douglas, and Fortas joined Brennan and Clark in holding the right to counsel existed at a lineup because it was a critical stage. Although Stewart would have been willing to rule on the basis of the Supreme Court's supervisory authority over the lower federal courts that Wade had been entitled to a lawyer, he would not accede to Brennan's view that "the right to counsel [at a lineup] should be declared a constitutional right." Despite joining Brennan in making that right a constitutional guarantee, Black, Douglas, and Fortas disputed his refusal to make it retroactive.[43]

Although hopelessly fragmenting the Court, the 1967 lineup cases did extend the right to counsel, now secured by both the Sixth and Fourteenth Amendments, to an important noncourtroom setting. They represented a significant addition to a growing body of constitutional rules regulating the treatment of suspects during the investigative phase of criminal cases, which had to be followed if confessions were to be admissible at trial. In creating these rules Warren and his colleagues departed from the position the Supreme Court had taken since 1936, which was that, where confessions were concerned, all the Fourteenth Amendment required of the states was fundamental fairness. For three decades the Court employed a due process "voluntariness" test, under which the admissibility of a defendant's statement depended upon a judicial assessment of the totality of the circumstances. At first interested only in whether the methods used to obtain a confession would produce one that was reliable, the Court became increasingly attentive to whether the defendant had been allowed to decide freely if he would talk to the police. As Laurence Benner observes, "The Court progressively civilized the meaning of due process until the clause forbade not only physical force, but also psychological coercion." On the rare occasions when it reviewed the admission of a confession in a federal case, the Court used essentially the same approach, except that it based these rulings mainly on the Fifth Amendment's Self-Incrimination Clause.[44]

Employing the voluntariness doctrine, the Supreme Court overturned a murder conviction in *Spano v. New York* (1959), ruling inadmissible a confession made after the police repeatedly denied the defendant's requests to see his attorney, who had advised him before he turned himself in not to answer any questions. The police had worn Spano down with prolonged questioning and appeals from an officer who was a childhood friend; the officer, following instructions, had lied to Spano, saying the defendant had gotten him into trouble. Warren thought, "In the totality of this picture, due process [was] denied," and the Court unanimously reversed the conviction. The Chief's opinion relied on traditional grounds, emphasizing that "The abhorrence of society to the use of involuntary confessions does not turn alone on their inherent untrustworthiness. It also turns on the deep-rooted feeling that the police must obey the law." Douglas, Brennan, Black, and Stewart argued in concurring opinions that the rationale should have been the absence of counsel when the confession was elicited. This, they thought, rendered it inadmissible under the Fourteenth Amendment, a contention the Chief found it "unnecessary to reach."[45]

Five years later the absence of counsel when a defendant made damaging admissions became the focus of the Court. It rendered three major confession decisions in 1964, and only *Jackson v. Denno* employed the traditional fundamental-fairness approach. The issue in *Denno* was the constitutionality of a New York procedure under which the trial judge submitted to the jury, along with the other issues in a case, the question of whether a defendant's confession was voluntary, telling jurors to disregard his statement if they believed it was involuntary, but to determine its reliability and how much weight to give it if they concluded he had freely confessed. The Court voted six to three to hold this practice unconstitutional, with Clark, Harlan, and Stewart in the minority. In his opinion for the Court, White noted that a finding of deprivation of due process was "now axiomatic" if a defendant's conviction rested on a confession that was involuntary. "In our view," he declared, "the New York procedure employed in this case did not afford a reliable determination of the voluntariness of the confession offered in evidence at the trial." In determining whether a confession was voluntary, jurors might well be influenced by whether they believed it was true; even a confession that they found involuntary might still influence their verdict. Thus, White held unconstitutional a procedure the Court had approved earlier in *Stein v. New York* (1953). Dissenting for himself, Clark, and Stewart, Harlan faulted the majority for disregarding precedent and the dictates of federalism. In conference he had indicated he would be willing to overrule *Stein* if *Denno* were a federal case. "Even under the broadest view of the restrictive effect of the Fourteenth Amendment," however, Harlan did not consider "it open to doubt that the States were free to allocate the trial of issues . . . between judge and jury as they deemed best." Black, who also objected to the majority's failure to follow *Stein,* expressed concern that its opinion might be read as "relying on the loose definition of 'due process' as anything that is offensive to this Court's sense of decency or the basic principles of fundamental fairness." White assuaged these concerns by reformulating his statement of the issue, focusing on the "constitutionality," rather than the "fairness," of New York's procedure. Black disagreed with more than just his choice of words, however. "My idea of the question presented in this case is whether a man can be compelled to be a witness against himself contrary to the command of the Fifth Amendment, which is made applicable to the States by the Fourteenth Amendment," he informed White.[46]

A week earlier in *Malloy v. Hogan* (1964) the Court had incorporated the right on which Black wanted to base the *Denno* decision. Malloy had been adjudged in contempt for refusing to answer the questions of a judicial officer who, in the course of investigating gambling and related criminal activities, had asked him about events surrounding his earlier arrest and conviction for pool selling. He contended he did not have to respond, because answering might tend to incriminate him. Malloy's attorney, Harold Strauch, endeavored to convince the Connecticut Supreme Court of Errors that the Fifth Amendment privilege against self-incrimination applied to the states, but following numerous U.S. Supreme Court precedents, it ruled against him. Later, before the Supreme Court, Strauch argued that the Fourth Amendment and the Self-Incrimination Clause complimented one another, and that if the former applied to the states, the latter must also, but he denied advocating total incorporation. When Harlan asked him whether he was suggesting abandoning two precedents rejecting that concept—*Adamson* and *Twining v. New Jersey* (1908)—Brennan jumped in to assure Strauch: "You start with four members of the Court who have already indicated that those cases should be overruled." Malloy got one additional vote, and incorporation prevailed five to four. "We hold today," Brennan declared for the majority, "that the Fifth Amendment's exception from compulsory self-incrimination is also protected by the Fourteenth Amendment against abridgment by the States." He added that the same standards applied in both state and federal cases. "Decisions of the Court since Twining and Adamson have departed from the contrary view expressed in those cases," Brennan maintained, brushing aside (without bothering to overrule) precedents the attorney general of California had urged the Court to reaffirm. His evasiveness was probably calculated to win over Clark, Harlan, or Stewart, all of whom had announced during the conference that they opposed overturning *Twining*, but it angered Douglas. On June 1 he withdrew his endorsement of Brennan's opinion, leaving it without a majority. Brennan responded that he had modeled his opinion on Black's *Gideon* one, which Douglas had joined, while noting his continued commitment to total incorporation. Brennan asked Douglas to suggest changes, but received instead a lengthy letter faulting him for avoiding basic constitutional questions and drawing fine but unpersuasive distinctions. Douglas "had been reading your opinions with my heart as well as my mind," but now "realized the spirit of Felix still [is] the dominant force here." Bowing to pressure, Brennan eliminated assertions that the only rights the Fourteenth Amendment had been held to secure against state abridgement were those comprehended by the concept "due process of law" and that the Fifth Amendment privilege against self-incrimination was protected by the Fourteenth Amendment because of its "fundamental nature." Douglas then concurred with a brief statement expressing continued adherence to the position he had taken in *Gideon*. Brennan could not satisfy Harlan at all. In a dissenting opinion, he faulted the Court for accepting in fact what it purported to reject in theory: "the application to the States via the Fourteenth Amendment, of the forms of federal criminal procedure embodied within the first eight amendments to the Constitution." The logical gap between the majority's premises and its "novel constitutional conclusion" could be bridged "only by the additional premise that the Due Process Clause of the Fourteenth Amendment is a shorthand directive to this Court to pick and choose among the provisions of the first eight Amendments and apply those chosen, freighted with their entire accompanying body of federal doctrine, to law enforcement in the states," he charged. Cortner agrees. "With an incorporationist majority clearly in control . . . , the nationalization process took on an inexorable quality after . . . *Malloy v. Hogan*," he writes.[47]

So did Supreme Court supervision of state criminal procedure. A year later, in *Griffin v. California* (1965), the Court invalidated a law that allowed prosecutors to comment on the failure of defendants to testify, holding that such an action violated the right against self-incrimination. *Malloy* also laid part of the constitutional foundation for national rules regulating police interrogation of suspects. The rest was supplied by two 1964 right-to-counsel decisions.[48]

The first of these, handed down on May 18, dealt "not with a state court conviction, but with a federal case, where the specific guarantee of the Sixth Amendment directly applies." The defendant in *Massiah v. United States* (1964) had been indicted for possession of narcotics. He retained a lawyer, entered a not-guilty plea, and was released on bail. While free on bond, Massiah made a number of incriminating statements during a conversation with his codefendant in the front seat of the latter's car. Unbeknownst to Massiah, the codefendant was now cooperating with the authorities. His car was wired, and a federal agent recorded the entire conversation, which was later used as evidence against Massiah. The justices voted six to two to reverse, with Clark expressing uncertainty, but leaning toward reversal. Stewart wanted to base the decision on *Spano,* but the other members of the majority endorsed the analysis of the concurring justices in that case and argued that Massiah's right to counsel had been violated. Assigned the opinion, Stewart failed to satisfy Black, who accused him of relying on Frankfurter's "view that the Due Process Clause permits the court to hold a court practice unconstitutional that offends 'the rudimentary requirements of a civilized order.'" Stewart deleted a Frankfurter quotation that offended Black and rested the decision unambiguously on what he acknowledged was the position of a majority of those voting to reverse. His published opinion declared that Massiah's Sixth Amendment rights had been violated by the admission of incriminating statements that were deliberately elicited after his indictment and in the absence of his lawyer. In dissent, White, Harlan, and Clark protested the creation of a constitutional rule "barring the use of evidence which is relevant, reliable and highly probative." While they thought the Court had gone too far, Black wanted a broader rationale. "My reason for reversing," he had written to Stewart "is that the confession used against petitioner was obtained in a way that I believe violated his Fifth Amendment right not to be compelled to be a witness against himself, and his Sixth Amendment right to have the assistance of counsel, both of which Amendments are made applicable to the States by the Fourteenth."[49]

In linking the rights recognized by *Gideon* and *Malloy,* Black envisioned the foundation for national rules governing the interrogation of suspects. *Escobedo v. Illinois* (1964), decided one week after *Massiah,* showed why these rules were needed. The evidence used to convict Danny Escobedo of murder included an incriminating statement he had made after lengthy and perhaps deceptive questioning by the Chicago police. Escobedo, a Mexican American who lacked previous experience with law enforcement, was never advised of his constitutional rights, and although he repeatedly asked to consult with his attorney, who was at the station and demanding to see him, he was never allowed to do so. The Court voted six to three to reverse his conviction, but the majority had some difficulty settling upon a rationale. Two possibilities suggested themselves to Warren, Black, and Goldberg: totality of the circumstances and denial of the right to counsel. Stewart objected vigorously to holding that a suspect was entitled to have a lawyer present during questioning, a rule he feared would have "staggering" consequences, while White thought *Massiah* had adequately delineated the right to counsel. Brennan, however, insisted they had taken *Escobedo* to decide about that and refused to go along with the totality-of-the-circumstances approach. Douglas and other members of the majority came around to his position. A draft of Goldberg's opinion of the Court, circulated on May 19, stated that this case presented "questions concerning the admissibility, under the Due Process Clause of the Fourteenth Amendment, of an incriminating statement made by petitioner while in police custody after his request to consult with his retained attorney had been denied." By June 2 the "critical question" had become whether refusing to let Escobedo talk to his lawyer was a denial of assistance of counsel that violated the Sixth Amendment. The Court held that it was. Unlike Massiah, Escobedo had not yet been indicted, but the majority felt "that fact should make no difference." "We hold," Goldberg wrote:

> that where . . . the investigation is no longer a general inquiry into an unsolved crime but has begun to focus on a particular suspect, the suspect has been taken into police custody, the police carry out a process of interrogations that lends itself to eliciting incriminating statements, the suspect has requested and been denied an opportunity to consult with his lawyer, and the police have not effectively warned him of his absolute constitutional right to remain silent, the accused is denied "the Assistance of Counsel" in violation of the Sixth Amendment to the Constitution as made obligatory upon the States by the Fourteenth Amendment.

This ruling would "seriously and unjustifiably [fetter] perfectly legitimate methods of criminal law enforcement," Harlan protested. He dissented, along with Stewart and White, who considered it "naive to think that the new constitutional right announced will depend upon whether the accused has retained his own counsel." White saw *Escobedo* as another major step toward barring "from evidence all admissions obtained from an individual suspected of crime whether involuntarily made or not."[50]

Policemen and politicians liked the decision even less. Los Angeles police chief William Parker accused the Court of "handcuffing the police," and during a symposium on the decision, attended by Warren and Brennan, former New York police commissioner Michael Murphy charged the Court with "unduly hampering the administration of criminal justice" while "vicious beasts" roamed the streets. Although University of Michigan Law professor Yale Kamisar attacked Murphy's position as "simplistic, narrow-minded, and politically expedient," and accused police of trying to make the Supreme Court a scapegoat for society's inability to cope with crime, Republican presidential candidate Barry Goldwater echoed the former commissioner. Blaming the justices for a breakdown of law and order, he made their rulings an issue in the 1964 campaign. Hostility toward the Court's criminal-procedure decisions also fueled the right-wing drive to "Impeach Earl Warren."[51]

Escobedo raised not only tempers but also questions about precisely what standards law enforcement must meet. As *Time* magazine pointed out, legislation could accomplish far better than constitutional interpretation the sort of detailed rule-making the situation required. Although it maintained the "burden is now on Congress and

state legislatures," politicians found criticizing the Court more appealing than enacting laws to regulate police practices. An American Law Institute committee, chaired
by Harvard professors Paul Bator and James Vorenberg, proposed that the police be
given four hours to question a suspect without his lawyer present, provided the questioning was taped, but its Model Code of Pre-Arraignment Procedures sparked disagreement and was not adopted until 1975. Legislative action was "only sporadically
forthcoming." Nor did state supreme courts step forward; only those in California,
Oregon, and Rhode Island accepted what amounted to an invitation from the U.S.
Supreme Court to devise their own rules. Meanwhile, "*Escobedo* cases" inundated the
high tribunal. On November 3, 1965, Warren informed his colleagues that none
would appear on the lists for Friday's conference "because there are so many of them
we might not have time to go over them and also the regular cases." On December
9 the justices declined to hear 66 *Escobedo* cases, but by June 16, 1966, 155 more
awaited their attention. During the summer of 1965 Warren had told his new clerks
that he expected to decide one during the forthcoming term and instructed them to
look for suitable cases. They identified twenty "good ones" and, after reading their
memos, the justices selected four.[52]

The defendants in *Miranda v. Arizona, Vignera v. New York, Westover v. United States*,
and *California v. Stewart* had all confessed to crimes following station-house interrogations by local police or prosecutors who had not given them full and effective
warnings of their constitutional rights to remain silent and to have a lawyer present
during questioning. The Justice Department feared the Court would use these cases
to prohibit police from interrogating suspects at all, or at least to do so without a
lawyer present. Attorney General Katzenbach and the head of the Criminal Division
hoped to persuade the justices to rule instead that interrogation was permissible if
preceded by warnings of the type already given by the FBI, and Solicitor General
Thurgood Marshall, although suspected by some of his subordinates of harboring
views less protective of defendants, urged the Court to adopt the Justice Department's position. His audience was receptive. Questioning from the bench betrayed
little sympathy for prohibiting interrogation or for allowing it only with a lawyer present, focusing instead on whether warnings should be required. Warren made clear
that he thought they should be, asking counsel at one point: "Wouldn't the best test
be simply that the authorities must warn him?"[53]

The Chief took the same position in conference. He began the justices' March
18, 1966, discussion by reading a prepared statement. What confronted them, he said,
was basically a Self-Incrimination Clause issue. Warren believed, however, that "*Gideon*
controls," for the right to counsel commenced at the moment a suspect was taken
into custody. He must be given an opportunity to get a lawyer before being interrogated, unless he knowingly and intelligently waived that right, and the burden of proving there had been a waiver must be on the prosecution. Interrogation might take
place only if a suspect were advised of his right to remain silent, that what he said
might be used against him, and that "in time [the] court will appoint a lawyer." With
respect to what rights an accused had, "no distinction should be made between one
who has a lawyer and one who does not." Black also viewed these as self-incrimination

cases and believed that the right not to be a witness against oneself attached the moment someone was taken into custody. He agreed with most of what Warren said, as did Brennan and Fortas. Clark, emphasizing that the Fifth Amendment applied to interrogation and that anyone grilled by the police who could not afford a lawyer should be entitled to a court-appointed one, declared himself "pretty close" to the Chief. Douglas also "largely" agreed with Warren. Although he considered interrogation a critical stage for right-to-counsel purposes, he would have preferred to treat this as "a legislative problem only." Harlan led the opposition. He accused Warren and his supporters of repudiating "all our precedents and history," as well as ABA proposals. Harlan insisted they should "leave law reform to others." Seeing no need for "radical" innovation, he advocated unhurried change, to take place only after "more empirical data being assembled." Noting there had been no coercion in these cases, Stewart too expressed disagreement with Warren. So did White. The vote was six to three in all four cases—to reverse in *Miranda, Vignera,* and *Westover* and to affirm the California Supreme Court's decision overturning the conviction in *Stewart*.[54]

Warren assigned these cases to himself. By May 9 he had an opinion written but did not immediately circulate it to the entire Court. Instead, the Chief sought Brennan's advice. The resulting lengthy critique of his draft questioned Warren's approach. Brennan agreed that procedural safeguards were needed to make effective the constitutional right against compulsory self-incrimination. He objected, however, to holding, as Warren's draft did, that there was "only a single constitutionally required solution to the problems of testimonial compulsion inherent in custodial interrogation." Although Brennan could not think of any procedure other than the warning given by the FBI that would serve the purpose, he recognized that mandating it, as Warren's opinion did, would make the Court vulnerable to criticism for going beyond "the scope of judicial responsibility and authority." "Should we not leave Congress and the States latitude to devise other means (if they can) which might also create an interrogation climate which has the similar effect of preventing the fettering of a person's own will?" he asked. Brennan also questioned a passage in Warren's draft that discussed police violence against racial minorities. What united those they were trying to protect, he believed, was poverty, not race. Brennan also recommended that Warren's first sentence be rewritten to say that these cases were not about the role society must assume in prosecuting crime, but about "the *restraints* society must *observe*" in doing so.[55]

The Chief made that change and also deleted the passage about the relationship between race and police brutality, but his published opinion mandated the sort of precise rules Brennan had opposed. It held that the prosecution might "not use statements . . . stemming from custodial interrogation of the defendant unless it demonstrates the use of procedural safeguards effective to secure the privilege against self-incrimination." Warren conceded that the use of physical violence to extract confessions was now exceptional, but he emphasized that in-custody interrogation was still done secretly and in private and that it was designed to be psychologically coercive and to compel the suspect "to speak where he would not otherwise do so freely." Hence, "Prior to any questioning, the person must be warned that he has a right to remain silent, that any statement he does make may be used as evidence against him, and that he has a right to the presence of an attorney, either retained or appointed." If indigent, he must be told that the public would pay for his lawyer. A suspect might waive these rights, but any waiver had to be made "voluntarily, knowingly and intelligently." If at any point he indicated in any manner that he wished to consult with an attorney before speaking, "there can be no questioning."[56]

In deference to Brennan's views, Warren acknowledged that the Constitution did not require adherence "to any particular solution for the inherent compulsions of the interrogation process" and encouraged Congress and the states to continue "their laudable search" for effective ways to protect suspects. His opinion made clear, however, that any alternative procedures they might adopt must be at least as effective in safeguarding the right to silence as those mandated by the Supreme Court. Brennan was satisfied until Harlan circulated a dissent. He reacted to it by drafting a concurring opinion, which emphasized that the Court was doing nothing that would prevent states from devising and applying their own prophylactic means to safeguard against the inherent dangers of interrogation, provided those could not be circumvented by police prevarication. When he showed a draft of his concurrence to Warren, the Chief objected strenuously. Although Brennan insisted he was only correcting the minority's misreading of his opinion, which already said essentially the same thing, Warren worried that by writing separately, he would dilute the power and effectiveness of *Miranda*. Bowing to the Chief's objections, Brennan did not issue, or even circulate, his concurrence.[57]

The Harlan dissent to which he was responding insisted *Miranda* would inevitably handicap sound efforts at reform by eliminating options that had to be part of any just compromise reconciling the competing interests at stake. Harlan criticized Warren's position on both constitutional and policy grounds. The Court's rules, he contended, would "impair, if they will not eventually serve wholly to frustrate, an instrument of law enforcement that has long and quite reasonably been thought worth the price paid for it." Stewart and White joined Harlan's opinion, and all three of them signed a dissent by White attacking Warren's premise that "in-custody interrogation, without more [is] a violation of the Fifth Amendment." Although furnished copies of both of these opinions before they were circulated, Clark joined neither. Contending that the Court's "opinion goes too far on too little, while my dissenting brethren do not go quite far enough," he wrote separately. Defending custodial interrogation and accusing the majority of going beyond *Escobedo*, Clark advocated a totality-of-the-circumstances approach for determining whether confessions were voluntary.[58]

He and the other dissenters all signed Warren's opinion in the companion case of *Johnson v. New Jersey* (1966), which held that neither *Miranda* nor *Escobedo* applied retroactively. The principles those decisions promulgated governed only cases commenced after the decisions were handed down. Brennan, however, used *Davis v. North Carolina* (1966) to emphasize that "prisoners whose trials have already been completed may still seek new trials on the ground that the confessions relied on to convict them were the product of unconstitutional coercion and therefore involuntary."

Although *Johnson* did not immunize all pre-*Miranda* confessions from Supreme Court review, it ensured that few convicts would get out of prison because they had not received the warnings *Miranda* mandated. The Court further reduced the potential impact of its landmark ruling when it held in *Jenkins v. Delaware* (1969) that a defendant whose conviction was reversed on appeal after *Miranda* was decided could not have a confession obtained in violation of its rules excluded from his retrial.[59]

Despite the Court's efforts to curry favor with the public by applying its rules only prospectively, *Miranda* evoked outrage. Indeed, the decision proved to be, in the short run at least, the most controversial of all those handed down by the Warren Court. Newspaper editorials deplored it, while cartoonists lampooned its logic. Congress responded to *Miranda* by attempting to invalidate its holding with a provision of the Omnibus Crime Control and Safe Streets Act of 1968. As Warren himself pointed out, the ensuing hostility to the decision arose in large part because "police and indignant citizens were overwhelmed with a wave of violence that flooded the land, [and] they found in the Court a stationary target and made us responsible for the increasing crime rate." What really bothered those who accused the justices of "handcuffing the police" was America's failure, as Louis Michael Seidman puts it, "to control the new and frightening social disintegration that urban crime seemed to presage." Furthermore, while *Miranda* reflected the same egalitarianism that produced the Court's civil rights and reapportionment rulings, it did not fill the same sort of moral void. By the time the Court ruled, the ALI committee had produced its draft Model Code, the President's Commission on Law Enforcement and the Administration of Justice had been established at least in part to reform criminal procedure, and some state legislatures had mandated reforms in custodial interrogation. As G. Edward White points out, "The *Miranda* decision brushed aside these developments and established a uniform code of police procedure." The ruling was paternalistic in approach and legislative in both form and substance.[60]

Although *Miranda* represented a questionable exercise of judicial power and was perhaps unnecessary, its holdings were realistic. Informal pressure to speak could constitute compulsion within the meaning of the Self-Incrimination Clause, and warnings were needed to dispel this sort of compulsion, which accompanied any custodial interrogation. Furthermore, the controversial decision hardly proved to be the disaster for law enforcement that its critics predicted. Having received the warnings that *Miranda* required, suspects generally waived their rights and talked to the police anyhow. Interrogation tactics and techniques did not change, and while two studies found declines of ten and twenty percent, respectively, in confession rates, in most places the flow of self-incriminating statements continued unabated. Fewer interrogations took place, but within a year or two conviction and clearance rates had returned to pre-*Miranda* levels.[61]

Harlan's prediction that *Miranda*'s rules would "ultimately render inadmissible in evidence any confession taken by the police without the presence of counsel" also proved unwarranted. On the other hand, those rules did not remain confined to the police station interrogation room, whose isolation and inherently coercive atmosphere Warren had emphasized in his opinion. In 1968 the Court held inadmissible, because he had not received *Miranda* warnings, oral statements the defendant in a tax-fraud case had made to a federal agent while he was in prison serving a state sentence. During conference discussion of *Mathis v. United States,* Warren argued successfully that one could not "distinguish between [a] police station and [a] prison cell." In *Orozco v. Texas* (1969), the Court overturned a murder conviction because of the use against the defendant of admissions he had made to the Dallas police, who questioned him without informing him of his rights. This interrogation took place at 4:00 A.M., and the accused was under arrest at the time, but the location was his own bedroom. Black declared that *Miranda* warnings had to be given whenever officers questioned anyone who was "'in custody.'" Harlan went along with *Orozco* "purely out of respect for stare decisis," but White and Stewart dissented, protesting that this decision carried *Miranda* "to a new and unwarranted extreme."[62]

Orozco was decided just three months before Warren retired. By then his Court had not only subjected interrogation to sweeping constitutional supervision but had also imposed upon the states almost all of the criminal justice provisions of the Bill of Rights. Its 1965 ruling in *Pointer v. Texas* required them to comply with the Sixth Amendment's Confrontation Clause. Bob Pointer had been convicted of robbery largely on the basis of testimony given at a preliminary hearing by a witness who subsequently moved out of the state, did not appear at his trial, and was never cross-examined by the defendant. Prior rulings of the Supreme Court left no doubt that Pointer had been denied the sort of confrontation and cross-examination guaranteed by the Sixth Amendment. The Court now held, with Black writing the opinion, that "the Sixth Amendment's right of an accused to confront the witnesses against him is . . . a fundamental right . . . made obligatory on the states by the Fourteenth Amendment." The Supreme Court was unanimous in reversing Pointer's conviction, but neither Harlan nor Stewart would join Black in holding that the Confrontation Clause applied to the states.[63]

Harlan also objected to incorporating the Sixth Amendment's guarantee of a speedy trial. Peter Klopfer had been prosecuted for criminal trespass following a melee during a sit-in demonstration. His trial ended with a hung jury. The prosecutor then sought to enter a nolle prosequi in the case, which would have kept Klopfer from being retried immediately, but left him subject to retrial at another time, and thus on a sort of de facto probation. Knowing the state could not retry him successfully because of the Supreme Court's decisions in *Hamm v. Rock Hill* and *Luper v. Arkansas,* his lawyer objected. He contended Klopfer was being denied a speedy trial, a right that was protected by the Fourteenth Amendment, whether viewed from a fundamental fairness perspective or an incorporationist one. The Court agreed. Without making clear which approach he was employing, Warren held that the right to a speedy trial was fundamental and consequently applied to the states through the Fourteenth Amendment. The decision was unanimous, but in a concurring opinion Harlan objected to what he considered its incorporationist basis.[64]

Washington v. Texas (1967), an appeal that was argued only a few days after the *Klopfer* decision, had a clearer doctrinal foundation. A convicted murderer had been prevented from calling the other alleged participant in his crime by a Texas procedural rule that prohibited persons charged as principals, accomplices, or accessories in the same crime from testifying for each other. The Court granted certiorari for the expressed purpose of determining whether the Sixth Amendment right to compulsory process to obtain witnesses was "applicable to the States through the Fourteenth Amendment." Even the attorney for Texas agreed that it was, disagreeing with Washington's lawyer only about whether the state's procedural rule violated the Compulsory Process Clause. The Court held that it did. Harlan concurred, but declared that he still could not "accept the view that the Due Process Clause . . . 'incorporates' in its terms the specific provisions of the Bill of Rights."[65]

Harlan continued to fight a rearguard action against incorporation in *Duncan v. Louisiana* (1968). The African American defendant in that case had been prosecuted for misdemeanor battery after he intervened in a confrontation between his cousins and four white boys. Convinced this prosecution was part of a pattern of anti–civil rights violence and intimidation in Plaquimines Parish, Louisiana, Richard Sobel of the Lawyers Constitutional Defense Committee took the case. He requested a jury trial, but because the state constitution authorized one only when capital punishment or imprisonment at hard labor might result, the trial judge refused. Duncan was convicted, sentenced to sixty days in jail, and fined 150 dollars. On appeal Sobel argued that Louisiana had denied him a federal constitutional right. The Supreme Court agreed, holding that because a "trial by jury in criminal cases is fundamental to the American scheme of justice," the Fourteenth Amendment required states to afford one in any case which, if it were "tried in a federal court—would come within the Sixth Amendment's guarantee." That did not mean jury trials were required for petty crimes, but they had to be offered to defendants charged with "serious offenses" (a term the Court avoided defining). White's opinion was also evasive concerning the test that determined that the jury-trial right was protected by the Fourteenth Amendment, but in a concurrence, Black reiterated his long-standing contention "that the Fourteenth Amendment made all of the provisions of the Bill of Rights applicable to the states." Harlan and Stewart responded that its framers had intended no such thing. Taking another slap at selective incorporation, Harlan proclaimed, "I have raised my voice many times before against the continuing undiscriminating insistence upon fastening on the States federal notions of criminal justice, and I must do so again." He did not want states burdened with "the sometimes trivial accompanying baggage of judicial interpretation in federal contexts." Fortas, who had voted with the dissenters in conference, shared his concern. In a concurring opinion he endorsed *Duncan's* holding, but opposed automatically importing "all of the ancillary rules which have been or may hereafter be developed incidental to the right to jury trial in the federal courts."[66]

Harlan and Stewart received no support at all in *Benton v. Maryland*, a June 23, 1969, decision that marked the culmination of the Warren Court's nationalization of criminal procedure. Benton had been convicted of burglary and acquitted of larceny. After the Maryland Court of Appeals overturned his conviction, he was reindicted and convicted of both offenses. The Supreme Court granted certiorari to consider whether the Fourteenth Amendment had made the Fifth Amendment's

Double Jeopardy Clause applicable to the states, and if it had, whether Maryland had violated this constitutional guarantee. *Palko v. Connecticut* had held that the Due Process Clause did not require the states to comply with it, but demonstrating how far the incorporation revolution had progressed, the Court overruled *Palko*, with Marshall (who had refused to follow it in a Second Circuit case) writing the opinion. Observing "that the double jeopardy prohibition of the Fifth Amendment represents a fundamental ideal in our constitutional heritage," he held "that it should apply to the States through the Fourteenth Amendment." Predictably, Harlan and Stewart dissented. They complained about "the complete overruling of one of the Court's truly great decisions." Harlan lamented that his colleagues had become "impervious to the pervasive wisdom of the constitutional philosophy embodied in Palko." They had, as he understood, rejected its conception of federalism in favor of the nationalization of the criminal-procedure provisions of the Bill of Rights. The Court did hold in *North Carolina v. Pearce,* which it decided on the same day, that neither the Double Jeopardy Clause nor the Equal Protection Clause imposed an absolute bar to the imposition of a more severe sentence upon a reconvicted defendant who had gotten his original conviction reversed on appeal. In the process, however, as Stewart, who wrote the opinion, later acknowledged, it implicitly made *Benton* retroactive. Thus culminated a remarkably effective campaign by a selective incorporationist majority that often set its own agenda and employed cases the litigants saw as raising other issues to promote the sort of liberal nationalism that Harlan deplored.[67]

He liked no better the habeas corpus decisions rendered by his colleagues that granted greater federal court access to state prisoners alleging violations of their constitutional rights. Prior to Frankfurter's retirement, the Court had exhibited a rather negative attitude toward this sort of federal intervention in state proceedings. After 1962, it became more sympathetic toward those seeking habeas corpus relief. In *Sanders v. United States* (1963) (a case brought by a federal prisoner) the Supreme Court held that a court to which a petition was directed might give controlling weight to the denial of a prior application for habeas corpus only if the same ground were presented in both, the prior determination was on the merits, and "the ends of justice would not be served by reaching the merits of the subsequent application."[68]

Sanders was one of three major habeas corpus decisions rendered within two months in the spring of 1963. The winners in the other two cases were state prisoners. *Fay v. Noia* favored an inmate whose confession was later determined by New York's highest court—in a case involving his codefendants—to have been obtained under coercive circumstances; the Court ruled that his failure to appeal his conviction earlier did not preclude him from obtaining a federal writ, although under a state procedural rule, that default meant his case could not be reopened. The Supreme Court had long held that on direct review it would not reach the merits of constitutional claims if the judges below had relied upon adequate state grounds, even if those grounds were procedural rather than substantive. Whether the same principle should apply in habeas corpus cases was a question Brennan had addressed in a lecture at the University of Utah in October 1961, and by the time *Fay* reached the Court, he and Harlan had already subjected their colleagues to an exchange of memos on the subject. Harlan's position was that, under the habeas corpus statute, the writ was available only if a prisoner's custody violated federal law: the existence of an adequate state ground, even if it was only procedural, indicated no violation of federal law. Brennan, in contrast, insisted "procedural defaults are not crimes for which people are sent to prison." One might preclude challenging a conviction on appeal, "But the effect of the default is only to cut off certain remedies and not at all to make the detention lawful." Brennan's views prevailed in the January 11, 1963, conference, and he wrote an opinion for the Court holding that a federal judge could grant habeas relief, despite the applicant's failure to pursue state remedies no longer available to him when he applied for it. Harlan, joined by Clark and Stewart, dissented, contending that the majority had "struck a heavy blow at the foundations of our federal system." Drawing on the work of his former clerk Paul Bator, he criticized what he saw as a departure from precedent that would encourage premature and excessive intervention by federal district courts in state criminal cases.[69]

White joined Harlan, Clark, and Stewart as dissenters in *Townsend v. Sain*, which was decided on the same day as *Fay*. The facts of *Townsend* outraged Warren; the evidence used to convict the petitioner of murder included a confession made after he was injected with phenobarbital and scopolamine. At the February 23, 1962, conference, however, only Black and Douglas voted with the Chief to reverse the federal district judge who had denied Townsend a writ of habeas corpus on the basis of written pleadings and the opinion the Illinois Supreme Court produced in rejecting his appeal. Four justices wanted to affirm, while Brennan and Stewart favored returning the case to the district court for an evidentiary hearing. The retirements of Frankfurter and Whittaker necessitated reargument and also changed the alignment. White took the same position Whittaker had, but unlike Frankfurter, Goldberg voted to reverse. Now in the majority, Warren assigned the opinion to himself. Brennan managed to persuaded the Chief to modify his first draft, shifting the focus from the substantive issue of whether the confession had been coerced to the procedural one of when a hearing was required. The result was a holding that a hearing must be granted whenever the applicant alleged facts that, if proved, would entitle him to relief, and when he had not been given a full and fair hearing on these allegations by a state court. *Townsend* thus became a companion to *Fay*.[70]

Together they posed what many perceived as a threat to state sovereignty. Chief Justice J. Ed Livingston of Alabama denounced them. So did Chairman James Eastland of the Senate Judiciary Committee, who introduced a bill to strip the Supreme Court of the power to review cases involving state criminal laws. The Council of State Governments sponsored a constitutional amendment that would set up a Court of the Union, composed of state chief justices, to review the Court's decisions. Warren seized the opportunity afforded by a September 23 dinner, given in his honor by the California Bar, to answer the critics. If state courts vigilantly protected individual rights, he said, the Supreme Court would seldom have to challenge states' rights. The Court proved his point in *Henry v. Mississippi* (1965). In that case the supreme court of a segregationist state had sought to protect an NAACP leader from the consequences of a procedural default by his own attorneys, all of whom, it erroneously believed, were from out of state and unfamiliar with local procedure. The Warren Court defended Mississippi's interests, ruling that a defendant who deliberately failed to make a timely objection should be deemed to have forfeited his state court remedies.[71]

Although not as hostile to the legitimate interests of the states as its critics often claimed, the later Warren Court was determined to facilitate access to the federal courts by those claiming violation of their constitutional rights. *Johnson v. Avery* (1969) held that states could not prohibit inmates from assisting each other in preparing habeas petitions unless they provided them with assistance in preparing them. "Since the basic purpose of the writ is to enable those unlawfully incarcerated to obtain their freedom, it is fundamental that access of prisoners to the courts for purpose of presenting their complaints not be denied or obstructed," the Court declared.[72]

Besides making the assertion of constitutional rights easier for prisoners and others, the later Warren Court increased the number and scope of those rights. For example, *Brady v. Maryland* (1963) held that the Fourteenth Amendment forbade prosecutors to withhold from defense attorneys potentially exculpatory evidence.[73]

In addition to protecting defendants from deceitful prosecutors, the Warren Court also shielded them from the news media, beginning before Frankfurter's retirement and with his full support. *Irvin v. Dowd* (1961) was a contentious habeas corpus case that had been dismissed by the district judge because the petitioner had failed to exhaust his state remedies. In 1959 the Court remanded the case for a decision on the merits. At that point Frankfurter's concern was "the limits of our jurisdiction in reviewing state convictions." When the case returned in 1961, however, the Court focused on the impartiality of the jury that had convicted the petitioner of murder and sentenced him to death. A unanimous Court held that it had not been impartial. A "barrage of newspaper headlines, articles, cartoons and pictures was unleashed against him during the six or seven months preceeding the trial," Clark declared. This "continued adverse publicity caused a sustained excitement and fostered a strong prejudice" against him, depriving him of due process of law. Warren doubtless spoke for all of his colleagues when he told the conference that he "would have hated to be tried by this jury." Frankfurter felt just as strongly about the prejudicial pretrial publicity, lamenting that not a term passed without the Court "being importuned to review convictions, . . . in which substantial claims are made that a jury trial has been distorted because of inflammatory newspaper accounts—too often, as in this case, with the prosecutor's collaboration." Harlan too believed "a parade of publicity . . . violates Due Process." Two years later in *Rideau v. Louisiana* the Court overturned the murder conviction of a defendant who had been denied a change of venue after a local television station broadcast on three occasions a twenty-minute film of him admitting to committing crimes with which he was charged.[74]

The Supreme Court's thinking was in line with that of the ABA, which had adopted in 1937 a judicial canon prohibiting courtroom photography and radio coverage of trials and amended it in 1952 to include television. Douglas agreed completely with the ABA's position. On May 10, 1960, he told a University of Colorado audience that the end of protecting defendants' rights was "best served by banning all photography, broadcasting, and televising. The camel should be kept out of the tent, lest he take it over completely." The Court prohibited the photographing or broadcasting of its own proceedings, and Warren told Fred Friendly of CBS News in 1964 that it was unlikely ever to change that rule.[75]

Douglas and Warren were both part of the majority in *Estes v. Texas* (1965), which overturned the conviction of a notorious swindler because live telecasting of pretrial proceedings and parts of his trial had deprived him of his Fourteenth Amendment right to due process of law. *Estes* badly divided the Court. Warren, Douglas, Harlan, and Goldberg all believed Billie Sol Estes had been denied a fair trial. The Chief insisted banning television from the courtroom would not violate freedom of speech or press, and Harlan denied that such a prohibition would infringe the Sixth Amendment's guarantee of a public trial, which "doesn't mean for me that [the] public has [a] right to a public performance." Douglas also maintained, "A trial is not a spectacle." Black too opposed cameras in the courtroom, but he could find nothing in the Constitution that prohibited them, and Brennan reminded his colleagues that America's legal heritage included trials that had become public spectacles. The two of them voted with Clark, White, and Stewart to affirm Estes's conviction, and Stewart drafted an opinion for the Court. It evoked dissents from Harlan, Goldberg, and Warren. The Chief, who insisted that the courtroom must not be allowed to become a public spectacle, may also have lobbied Clark on their morning walks, for the Texan experienced a change of heart. He informed his colleagues in a May 25, 1965, memorandum that he had "become disturbed at what could result from our approval of this emasculation by TV of the trial of a case." Clark listed ten undesirable elements he felt television could inject into criminal proceedings. Among his concerns was that only "horrendous" trials, involving "the most sordid crimes" or appealing "to the prurient interest," would be broadcast. Within two days Clark's memorandum had become an opinion for the new majority his switch created. He significantly modified it before publication, however, eliminating both an express denial that either the press or the people had a right to a public trial and a per se rule that televising a trial violated due process. Clark made the latter change in response to a revised draft of Stewart's opinion (now a dissent, joined by Black, White, and Brennan), which characterized the introduction of television into the courtroom as unwise policy, but opposed "escalat[ing] this personal view into a per se constitutional rule." White and Brennan also published dissents, the latter insisting "today's decision is not a blanket constitutional prohibition against the televising of state criminal trials." Warren (joined by Douglas and Goldberg) published his former dissent as a concurrence, and Harlan also concurred.[76]

In sharp contrast to *Estes*, *Sheppard v. Maxwell* (1966) produced only one opinion. This habeas corpus case challenged the constitutionality of an infamous Ohio trial of a prominent doctor, charged with murdering his wife. Before that proceeding a barrage of newspaper stories and editorials proclaimed the defendant's guilt, and during the trial the courtroom was crowded with news media representatives, who caused such a commotion that it was often impossible for witnesses and counsel to be heard or for the defendant and his lawyer to converse confidentially. Jurors were exposed to this saturation media coverage, both before and during the proceedings, and were also photographed by the press. Although the Supreme Court declined to review the case on direct appeal in 1956, Frankfurter found the "Roman holiday" atmosphere surrounding the trial so disturbing that he published a memorandum emphasizing that denial of certiorari did not mean approval of the Ohio Supreme Court decision affirming Sheppard's conviction. In 1966 the justices voted seven to two to overturn the verdict. Only White and Warren, who said he did "not think the pre-trial publicity was anything we could complain about," wanted to affirm. Both of them eventually joined an opinion of the Court, written by Clark, who also had said there was "nothing to the publicity issue." He developed a broader rationale, holding that the trial judge had not fulfilled "his duty to protect Sheppard from the inherently prejudicial publicity which saturated the community and to control disruptive influences in the courtroom." Only Black, who had wanted a different rationale, dissented, and he did so without opinion. The majority spoke with one voice in *Sheppard* because, however divided they may have been over television, all were determined to ensure that the media would not deprive defendants of fair trials.[77]

While shielding adult defendants from journalistic excess, the Warren Court also gave rights to minors charged with crimes. Juvenile delinquency proceedings had always been viewed as beyond the scope of constitutional regulation. Then in *In re Gault* (1967), with Fortas writing the opinion, the Court held that the Due Process Clause required states to give juveniles threatened with commitment to a reformatory notice of the charges against them, of their right to confront and cross-examine witnesses, of the privilege against self-incrimination, and of their rights to be represented by counsel and to have a lawyer appointed for them if their parents could not afford one. Why youth enjoyed only these rights, rather than all of those adults possessed, Fortas did not explain, but the reason may have been that in conference not only Harlan—who cast the one vote to affirm a juvenile court's commitment of Gerald Gault to the Arizona State Industrial School for making an obscene phone call— but also Warren and Brennan indicated they did not favor giving young people even the privilege against self-incrimination. While Fortas's opinion went further than they wanted, it did not go far enough for Black, who reiterated his commitment to total incorporation. On the other hand, in a partial dissent Harlan said he did not think due process demanded everything the Court was requiring of the states. The only true dissenter was Stewart, who objected to using "an obscure Arizona case as a vehicle to impose upon thousands of juvenile courts throughout the Nation restrictions that the Constitution made applicable to adversary criminal trials." He considered *Gault* "wholly unsound as a matter of constitutional law and sadly unwise as a matter of judicial policy." Most of those who wrote to Fortas about the ruling disagreed with Stewart. Influential newspapers also supported Fortas.[78]

"Once again," Ed Cray observes, "the Warren Court had boldly extended the Constitution to the unprotected." *Gault* was typical, for during what the authors of a leading treatise call "the Warren Court's criminal procedure 'revolution,'" "guarantees were extended into new areas previously viewed as beyond the scope of constitutional regulation, and constitutional standards in areas subject to regulation were made more rigorous." So rapid and wide ranging was this expansion of rights that in less than a decade decisions of the Warren Court "outstripped all of the expansionist rulings over the Court's entire prior history in the degree of additional regulation imposed upon the combined state and federal criminal justice processes."[79]

This enhanced regulation resulted in some decisions favoring unpopular defendants. By the mid-1960s the Court was even ruling in favor of organized crime figure Frank Costello. It held that a statute authorizing deportation of an alien who was convicted of two crimes of moral turpitude could not be used against Costello because he was a naturalized citizen when he committed his offenses, even though he had procured his citizenship through willful misrepresentation. *Marchetti v. United States* (1968) and *Grosso v. United States* (1968) aided gamblers. In those cases the Court held that the privilege against self-incrimination barred prosecutions for conspiracy to evade payment of a federal occupational tax on wagering, not paying that levy or an excise tax on gambling, and failing to register as a gambler. The reason was that anyone who did register and supply the information that the tax legislation required would thereby identify himself to federal and state prosecutors and provide evidence they could use to convict him. Similarly, in 1969 the Court overturned the conviction of the guru of the drug culture, Dr. Timothy Leary, for violation of two federal laws against marijuana trafficking, holding that his rights under the Due Process and Self-Incrimination Clauses had been violated.[80]

With drug use, teenage violence, racial tensions, and urban street crime on the rise, such rulings outraged many people. Americans increasingly blamed the anxieties of urban life on judicial decisions. Even Philip Kurland, one of the Warren Court's most persistent critics, conceded in 1970, however, that all the Court had done was "demand that the state criminal process come up to the same standards being imposed on federal criminal process." But that looked to much of the public like coddling criminals. Because the crime rate was rising at the same time that the Court was developing higher standards for criminal procedure, people inferred a casual relationship. They complained that the Supreme Court was undermining federalism not so much because they cared about which government made what rules as because they were worried about crime, disorder, and social disintegration. By 1968, these concerns had made the Court "the object of sustained political attack."[81]

The assault included enactment of Title II of the Omnibus Crime Control and Safe Streets Act of 1968, which contained provisions designed by Senator Sam Ervin (D-N.C.) to overturn *Mallory*, *Miranda*, and *Wade*. This law made voluntary confessions admissible, even if those making them had not been warned of their constitutional rights. It authorized police to hold suspects for up to six hours (more under some circumstances) before presenting them for arraignment, without rendering inadmissible any statements they might obtain in the interim. If the trial judge determined, based on his assessment of all of the circumstances, that a confession had been made voluntarily, he was to admit it. These rules applied only to federal trials. Law professors universally condemned Title II, but Senator McClellan promoted the measure with wild rhetoric blaming the Court for the spiraling crime rate; the assassination of Senator Robert Kennedy while the bill was before the Senate fueled the drive for its enactment. Liberals beat back an effort to forbid any federal court, including the Supreme Court, from reviewing a state trial judge's decision that a confession was voluntary if the decision had been affirmed by the highest court of his state. Nevertheless, passage of Title II represented a victory for those bent on unshackling the police. Fearful of the political consequences of a veto, President Johnson reluctantly signed it into law.[82]

The June enactment of the Omnibus Crime Control and Safe Streets Act did not end the political attacks on the Warren Court's criminal-procedure decisions. The assaults continued throughout the 1968 campaign. Both the Republican presidential candidate, Richard Nixon, and the nominee of the American Independent Party, George Wallace, made "law and order" a central theme. They blamed the Supreme Court for the crime problem and accused it of coddling criminals and handcuffing the police. All across the land, Nixon claimed, the guilty were going free. "Something has gone terribly wrong in America," he asserted. "Some of our courts and their decisions . . . have gone too far in weakening the peace forces against the criminal forces in this country."[83]

Although such charges helped Nixon win the presidency, they were inaccurate. The Warren Court was neither friendly to the criminal forces nor hostile to the interests of law enforcement. Indeed, during its last years it rendered a number of decisions decidedly beneficial to prosecutors and police. One of these was *Schmerber v. California,* handed down on June 20, 1966, just one week after *Miranda. Schmerber* revisited the question of whether a drunk-driving suspect could be required to furnish a blood sample. Warren, Black, and Douglas, all of whom had dissented in *Breithaupt v. Abraham* (1957), announced that they remained committed to the position they had taken in that case, but only Fortas joined them. Brennan was at first undecided, but seeing an opportunity to soften the impact of *Miranda,* he voted to affirm Schmerber's conviction. Since his was the swing vote, Clark assigned the case to him. Even while writing, Brennan continued to waver concerning the proper result, but in the end he produced an opinion that reaffirmed *Breithaupt* on due process grounds and rejected two arguments based on rights that had been incorporated since that decision. There had been no violation of the privilege against self-incrimination, which protected "an accused only from being compelled to testify against himself, or otherwise provide the State with evidence of a testimonial or communicative nature," Brennan wrote. Nor had the Fourth Amendment been violated, because it prohibited only those intrusions into the body that were not justified under the circumstances. Ample justification exited for testing Schmerber's blood, and this had been done in a reasonable manner. In response to a dissent by Black, Brennan removed language from his opinion suggesting that he was balancing the need for effective means of law enforcement against the guarantees of the Bill of Rights.[84]

In fact, however, during the Warren Court's final years, it repeatedly balanced law enforcement against the Bill of Rights. As early as the 1966–67 term, it began to move in a more conservative direction in criminal-procedure cases. In *McCray v. Illinois* (1967), the Court upheld a warrantless arrest based on information from an informer in a narcotics case, and in *Warden v. Hayden* (1967) it held that the police had not violated the Fourth Amendment when, without a warrant, they entered a house in hot pursuit of a suspect and then searched it not only for him but also for his weapons and the fruits of his crime.[85]

Particularly notable was the December 12, 1966, decision upholding the conviction of corrupt labor leader Jimmy Hoffa and others for attempting to bribe members of the jury in Hoffa's trial for violation of the Taft-Hartley Act. The evidence against Hoffa included incriminating statements he and another defendant had made in a hotel room during private conversations that included Edward Partin, a government informant. They contended that the deceptive means the government had used to obtain these admissions violated their rights under the Fourth, Fifth, and Sixth Amendments, but the Court rejected those claims. It also held in *Osborn v. United States,* a prosecution of one of Hoffa's lawyers for attempting to bribe a juror, that a tape-recording of a conversation in the attorney's office, secretly made by a defense investigator, who, unbeknownst to the attorney, was also a government informant, could be used as evidence against the lawyer.[86]

As these decisions indicate, during its last years, the Warren Court became more willing to accept what were arguably violations of the Fourth Amendment. In *Camara v. Municipal Court* (1967), the Court held that, because administrative searches by municipal health and safety inspectors constituted significant intrusions upon interests protected by the Fourth Amendment, they were subject to its warrant requirement. The Court went on, however, to reject the contention that a warrant might be issued only if there were probable cause to believe that a particular building contained violations, holding instead that inspections of all structures in a given area were reasonable in light of the goals of code enforcement, and hence that the requisite probable cause existed if reasonable legislative or administrative standards for conducting an area inspection were met. In the companion case of *See v. City of Seattle,* involving a defendant convicted for refusing to permit the warrantless fire inspection of a locked warehouse, the Court declared that the principles announced in *Camara* applied to commercial as well as residential property, but it indicated that inspections of businesses would be considered reasonable in far more situations than searches of homes. Clark, Harlan, and Stewart dissented in both cases, protesting that "inspections of this type have been made for over a century and a half without warrants" and that the majority was "prostitut[ing] the command of the Fourth Amendment that 'no warrant shall issue, but upon probable cause.'"[87]

In *Terry v. Ohio* (1968), Warren applied *Camara*'s balancing approach to street encounters between citizens and police, producing an interpretation of the Fourth Amendment decidedly beneficial to law enforcement. A Cleveland detective, Martin McFadden, had observed three men behaving in a suspicious manner, which suggested to him that they were "casing" a store for a robbery. He questioned them and, dissatisfied with their responses, patted them down. McFadden found a gun in Terry's pocket, and he was subsequently convicted of carrying a concealed weapon. The Court voted unanimously to affirm his conviction. Warren and Black argued that in such a situation an officer who feared for his life had a right to protect himself, and no one disagreed. However, reconciling the result everyone favored with the language of the Fourth Amendment was not easy. Warren, Black, and Brennan all believed the appropriate standard was "probable cause." Indeed, Black explicitly rejected the idea that "reasonable suspicion" could be enough. But with respect to what was probable cause required? Warren thought it was the search. Although Brennan tried to persuade him that "the threshold issue was whether the 'stop' was consistent with the Fourth Amendment," the Chief told his clerks to concentrate on the frisk. The printed opinion he circulated conceded that McFadden had lacked probable cause to arrest Terry, but argued that he did have probable cause to believe his life was in danger, and that because of the minimal intrusion that a frisk entailed, this was enough to satisfy the Fourth Amendment. Black objected to what he recognized as a balancing approach, while Douglas questioned the Chief's failure to deal with the stop. White and Harlan also emphasized the stop in concurring opinions that they drafted. Harlan's insisted "that *new* constitutional rules are necessary to sanction this sort of police work" and argued that the Court should adopt the "reasonable suspicion" formulation approved by the ALI. Responding to his colleagues' concerns, Warren massively revised his opinion. The published version dismissed "probable cause" as a standard applicable only to the Fourth Amendment's Warrant Clause and held that where a policeman observed unusual conduct that led him reasonably to conclude that criminal activity might be afoot and that the person he was confronting might be armed and dangerous, and where he first identified himself and made reasonable inquiries that failed to dispel his fear for his own safety or that of others, he was entitled "to conduct a carefully limited search of the outer clothing" of that individual "in an attempt to discover weapons which might be used to assault him. Such a search," Warren concluded, "is a reasonable search under the Fourth Amendment, and any weapons seized may properly be introduced in evidence against the person from whom they were taken."[88]

Only Douglas dissented, somewhat surprisingly, insisting that the Fourth Amendment permitted neither search nor seizure without probable cause. "There have been powerful hydraulic pressures throughout our history that bear heavily on the Court to water down constitutional guarantees and give the police the upper hand," he wrote. "That hydraulic pressure has probably never been greater than it is today." Douglas was almost certainly correct. Yet, only a year later, the Court actually increased Fourth Amendment limitations on law enforcement. Overruling two old cases, which appeared to allow officers making an arrest to conduct a warrantless search of the entire home in which they found the suspect, *Chimel v. California* (1969) held that such a search incident to arrest might not extend beyond "the area into which an arrestee might reach in order to grab a weapon or evidentiary items."[89]

Although having swum against the law-and-order tide in *Chimel,* during its last years the Warren Court upheld the so-called informer's privilege (allowing the government to withhold the identity of its informant at a suppression hearing) and rejected the general assumption that errors of constitutional magnitude were not subject to the harmless-error rule. In addition, the Court eschewed opportunities to expand constitutional rights. In *Powell v. Texas* (1969), for example, it rejected the argument that punishing an alcoholic for public drunkenness violated the cruel and unusual punishment prohibition. The Court actually voted five to four to overturn Leroy Powell's conviction, but Fortas, who was passionate about the case, managed to lose his majority. He drafted an opinion that built upon and extended the logic of *Robinson v. California*, taking the position that punishing Powell was unconstitutional because his public intoxication was not a voluntary act, but rather the symptom of a disease. Black disputed the applicability of *Robinson*. The contention that criminal liability could not be imposed on conduct that was part of the pattern of a disease infuriated him, for he viewed it as inconsistent with most states' version of the insanity defense. He and Warren both circulated proposed dissents. In order to hold onto Stewart, Fortas modified his opinion, deleting numerous references to behavior and acts and emphasizing that the defendant was being punished for a condition. Nevertheless, White deserted him too, drafting a separate opinion that argued a chronic alcoholic could be punished for being drunk in public, unless he established that drinking in private was impossible for him. Warren reassigned the case to Marshall, who wrote an opinion based on the Chief's draft dissent. While sympathetic to the problems of alcoholics, both realized that facilities for treating them were woefully inadequate and considered the opportunity to sober up in jail better than nothing. Marshall's opinion represented an example of the sort of social engineering he had engaged in as an NAACP litigator, but this time the results were not in accord with the liberal agenda.[90]

Nor did the Warren Court implement liberal desires for the elimination of capital punishment, despite sympathy for that cause within the Court. In October of 1963 Goldberg circulated to his colleagues a memorandum questioning the value of the death penalty as a deterrent and expressing concern about the mistaken execution of innocent defendants. It noted that "most civilized nations of the western world" had done away with capital punishment and that "the world-wide trend is unmistakenly [*sic*] in the direction of abolition." Goldberg argued that the death penalty constituted cruel and unusual punishment, and thus violated the Eight and Fourteenth Amendments. His memorandum crystalized thinking at the NAACP Legal Defense and Education Fund, which, at the urging of Anthony Amsterdam, a brilliant young law professor, mounted a large-scale attack on the death penalty. NAACP attorneys managed to obtain a moratorium on executions by raising constitutional challenges to every aspect of capital punishment. By 1967 the justices were ready to work through the challenges to reach a final decision on the constitutionality of capital punishment. Yet, by the time Warren retired, they still had not decided the issue.[91]

By June 1969 the Court's sole accomplishment regarding the matter was its holding that "death-qualified" juries were unconstitutional. An Illinois statute allowed prosecutors to challenge for cause any juror who stated that he had conscientious scruples against capital punishment. William Witherspoon was convicted of murder and sentenced to death by a jury from which forty-seven veniremen were excluded because of their views on the death penalty, although only five said they would never vote to impose it. When he sought review by the Supreme Court, it voted not to hear his case. Stewart, however, drafted a dissent from the denial of certiorari that changed his colleagues' minds, in part because he had defined the issue narrowly. With Stewart writing the opinion, the Court held merely that capital punishment could not be imposed or recommended by a jury "chosen by excluding veniremen for cause simply because they voiced general objections to the death penalty or expressed conscientious or religious scruples against its infliction." In a nation where less than half of the people believed in capital punishment, a jury composed entirely of its supporters could not speak for the community, he reasoned. Imposition of the death penalty by such a "hanging jury" violated due process. Black, Harlan, and White dissented, the latter concluding that the Court should "restrain its dislike for the death penalty and leave the decision about appropriate penalties to [elected] branches of government."[92]

The Warren Court never rendered the decision abolishing the death penalty that White seemed to fear, but not because of judicial restraint. After *Witherspoon,* Amsterdam sought a ruling prohibiting capital punishment for rape. There was reason for optimism. In October 1963 Douglas and Brennan had joined Goldberg in dissenting from the denial of certiorari in a case which they believed raised this issue. That opinion was the first in which any justice openly questioned the constitutionality of the death penalty. In early 1969 Amsterdam and his NAACP associates offered the Court the case of Willie Maxwell, an African American sentenced to death in Arkansas for raping a white woman. The justices voted eight to one to reverse, but those favoring reversal were divided. Warren wanted the Court to impose standards for the imposition of the death penalty. Harlan opposed that idea, because it would preclude a compassionate jury from sparing the life of someone who met those standards. He and Fortas found unacceptable the use of a single proceeding to determine guilt and impose a death sentence. Although the Court had approved unitary trials in *Spencer v. Texas* (1967), this format tended to discourage testimony by defendants, leaving jurors unaware of facts that might be relevant in determining what penalty to impose. That seemed especially unfair in a capital case. Warren assigned *Maxwell v. Bishop* to Douglas, who drafted an opinion that addressed both issues and pleased almost no one. The majority unraveled, as Harlan and Fortas, along with White and Stewart, deserted Douglas. He eliminated a discussion of standards to win over Fortas, but that prompted Brennan to draft a concurrence for himself and Warren. When Fortas resigned from the Court, Harlan's vote became crucial; without it Douglas lacked a majority. Unable to make up his mind, Harlan proposed reargument. Having no real choice, Douglas agreed. By the time *Maxwell* came up again, the Warren Court had become the Burger Court.[93]

Its failure to rule on the constitutionality of the death penalty was part of a broader pattern. As Yale Kamisar has observed, "In its final years, the Warren Court was not the same Court that handed down *Mapp* or *Miranda.*" Although the Court became more timid and less innovative as the political reaction to its rulings escalated, during the Warren years its record of achievement was nevertheless extraordinary. By nationalizing almost all the provisions of the Fourth, Fifth, Sixth, and Eighth Amendments, the Warren Court affected a truly revolutionary transformation of American criminal procedure. Besides requiring the states to comply with those guarantees, it expanded their scope considerably. Justice Goldberg later claimed "that the advancement of the criminal defendant's constitutional rights during the Warren years was not as great a departure from the past as the Court's critics would have us believe." In a sense he was right, for often the Supreme Court's rulings during Warren's tenure merely extended to the poor, minorities, and residents of the country's most backward states protections many Americans already enjoyed. Yet, as Goldberg acknowledged, "To say this is not to downgrade the fundamental nature of the Warren Court's criminal law decisions." Those rulings fundamentally altered the American system of criminal justice. Although the most controversial part of the Warren Court's legacy, they are also its most substantial achievements.[94]

10

THE TRUE WARREN COURT

"The later Warren Court," writes Mark Tushnet, "is the Warren Court that has entered our culture." Unlike the Supreme Court of the years 1953–62, this true Warren Court was consistently liberal. Although innovative and provocative decisions made it more conspicuous than the tribunal that Frankfurter so often controlled, this Court was no more active than the pre-1962 one. While the number of cases decided remained about the same, their nature changed. Fewer involved the variety of non-constitutional matters that had traditionally composed much of the Supreme Court's workload. The true Warren Court was, much more than the one of Warren's first nine terms, a constitutional court. While continuing to render important decisions on matters of taxation, immigration, civil procedure, and federal jurisdiction, the Court paid less attention to admiralty and administrative procedure. It also displayed less interest in constitutional questions unrelated to civil rights, civil liberties, and criminal procedure, while litigation inspired by its activism in those areas occupied an increasing amount of the justices' attention. The later Warren Court shared with the early one a keen interest in antitrust and labor law, but mainly because those areas afforded excellent opportunities for promoting the agenda of substantive liberalism. The years 1962–69 were above all, as Russell Galloway notes, "a period in which liberal activists exercised almost complete control over the Court's decisions."[1]

During this era of constant liberal dominance, the Court continued to devote time and effort to overseeing the rest of the federal judiciary. In both 1963 and 1966 the justices squabbled over amendments to the Federal Rules of Civil Procedure. Black and Douglas continued, as they had in 1961, to oppose a procedure that permitted such amendments to take effect upon their submission to Congress by the Supreme Court, without the legislative branch or the president taking affirmative action or expressing approval. The two justices insisted this practice was unconstitutional because, while some of the new rules were simply housekeeping details, "many contain matters so substantially affecting the rights of litigants in law suits that in practical effect they are the equivalent of new legislation." When the Court forwarded amendments to the Federal Rules of Criminal Procedure to Congress in 1969, Douglas protested that responsibility for promulgating these should rest with the Judicial Conference, which had appointed the advisory committee that proposed the changes, rather than with the Supreme Court. Congress also charged the Court with adopting rules of practice and procedure for the federal magistrates whose positions it created in 1968, necessitating the devotion of conference time to that subject.[2]

Besides supervising the lower federal courts, the justices continued to perform a variety of nonjudicial duties, both great and small. For example, a committee composed of Douglas, Clark, and Fortas met with the archivist of the United States, one of his assistants, and the marshal to discuss how tapes of the Court's oral arguments might be transferred to the National Archives. Of vastly greater significance was Warren's service as chair of the commission that investigated the assassination of President Kennedy, a duty he did not want. Warren refused to reduce his work as Chief Justice during the assassination inquiry, devoted only a small portion of his time to the work of the "Warren Commission," and wrote only selected portions of its 1964 report. Lyndon Johnson insisted he head the panel, however, because he considered him an important symbol whose participation would give the commission's findings credibility.[3]

The Chief's service on the assassination commission temporarily heightened his personal workload, but the workload of the Court as a whole did not increase substantially between the 1962 and 1969. Nor was it much greater than it had been during the less activist era before Frankfurter's retirement. The Court did dispose of substantially more cases. The average for each term between 1953 and 1958 had been 1,542. In Frankfurter's last term (1961–62) the Court disposed of 2,142 cases. The number rose to 2,401 in the 1963–64 term, fell back to 2,180 in 1964–65, then climbed steadily to 3,117 in 1968–69. Most of these cases, however, were disposed of summarily; they were neither fully briefed nor argued orally. Nor did they elicit published opinions. Clark presented a more accurate picture of the Court's workload when he told a Cornell Law School audience on March 18, 1965, "Last term there were 2,294 cases filed with our Clerk, of which 175 were appeals and 1,939 petitions for certiorari. Out of this total number we heard arguments only in 144 and handed down full dress opinions in 111." When summary dispositions of appeal cases and denials of cert are eliminated, and only cases that produced full written opinions are considered, what emerges is a picture of a relatively constant workload. The average number of cases disposed of by full opinion between 1953 and 1958 was 116 per term. During Frankfurter's last term it was 121. The number rose to 147 in the 1962–63 term. Subsequently, the Court issued 143 full opinions in 1963–64, 132 in 1964–65, 130 in 1965–66, 170 in 1966–67, 184 in 1967–68, and 167 in 1968–69. These numbers suggest the Court was working much harder during Warren's last three terms, but that is an inaccurate impression created by the Court's habit of disposing of more than one case with the same opinion. The numbers of full-blown opinions of the Court and per curiam opinions of comparable length written in each term from 1963–64 (the first for which the *Harvard Law Review* compiled this statistic) through 1968–69 were 131, 119, 115, 134, 146, and 134, respectively.[4]

Although the total number of real decisions did not increase dramatically, the percentage in which the principal issue was constitutional did. During Warren's first term as chief justice, only 27 percent of cases decided with full opinions (21 out of

78) were primarily constitutional. In the 1957–58 term, 32 percent (38 out of 119) were. During Frankfurter's final term the figure was 30 percent (29 out of 96). In the years after his departure the Court devoted more and more of its attention to cases of this kind:

Term	Constitutional cases	Total cases	Percentage of total
1962–63	36	117	31%
1963–64	50	127	39%
1964–65	53	114	46%
1965–66	41	107	38%
1966–67	56	119	47%
1967–68	59	127	46%

During Warren's final term as chief justice in 1968–69, a majority of the cases the Court decided with full opinions (65 out of 120, or 54 percent) were constitutional in nature. His Court had become primarily a constitutional tribunal, whose principal function was explicating and enforcing the nation's fundamental charter.[5]

Warren's Court devoted less attention to other matters that had once been important components of the Supreme Court's business. Ironically, one of these was federal criminal cases. While constitutionalizing, and thereby revolutionizing, the criminal procedure of the states, the Warren Court substantially reduced the number of federal criminal appeals it decided. During the Chief's first nine terms, such cases accounted for 17.1 percent of its decisions. During the last seven, that figure dropped to 11.5 percent. The average number of federal criminal cases decided in each term between 1953 and 1961 was 17.4. During Frankfurter's last term the Court decided 13; the average for the seven terms after his retirement was 13.6.

Some of these rulings were nonconstitutional. For example, the 1964 decision in *Hardy v. United States* (which held that an indigent defendant who sought to appeal and was represented by a different attorney from the one who defended him at trial must be given a complete transcript at government expense) rested on Rule 52(b) of the Federal Rules of Criminal Procedure. Other cases, such as *United States v. Blue* (1966), while not technically constitutional rulings, involved constitutional issues. In *Blue* the Court held that the possible use in a criminal tax prosecution of evidence obtained by the government in a civil deficiency suit did not justify dismissal of the indictments against the defendant. Blue claimed that he was being forced to choose between becoming a witness against himself and defaulting in the deficiency action, but the Court took the position that even if his Fifth Amendment rights were violated, that would entitle him only to suppression of the incriminating evidence, not dismissal of his indictments. Other decisions in federal criminal cases were clearly constitutional. *Singer v. United States* (1965), for example, upheld the constitutionality of Rule 23(a) of the Federal Rules of Criminal Procedure, which effectively gave the government and the judge, as well as the accused, the right to demand a jury trial by requiring that the accused obtain their consent to waive one.[6]

Thus, the later Warren Court often functioned as an interpreter of the Constitution even in the reduced number of federal criminal appeals it decided. As it became more of a constitutional court, the importance of some of its traditional functions declined. Original jurisdiction cases had not been numerically significant even during Warren's first nine terms, but the five cases the Court decided then included momentous disputes over submerged oil lands and Colorado River water with vast economic and political significance. The five it resolved during his last seven terms were so unimportant that they aroused little interest, let alone controversy.[7]

Even in a purely quantitative sense, the interpretation of federal statutes became less important. Between the terms that began in 1953 and ended in 1962, 4.5 percent of the Court's decisions were in federal criminal cases that turned on issues of statutory construction. For the 1962–63 through 1968–69 terms, only 1.1 percent were. The Court decided no cases at all of this type during the 1964–65, 1966–67, and 1967–68 terms.

Of course, the Supreme Court had to interpret federal statutes in order to resolve civil suits as well. Unfortunately, the *Harvard Law Review* compiled no statistics on cases of this type, as it did on ones interpreting criminal statutes. Its editors do seem to have believed, however, that the Court was not deciding as many of these that were truly important, for it included fewer (other than the antitrust and National Labor Relations Act cases) in the yearly issue that highlighted the past term. There were, to be sure, some significant statutory construction decisions during Warren's last seven terms. In 1963, for example, the Court held that the Natural Gas Act, which gave the Federal Power Commission exclusive jurisdiction over wholesale natural gas prices, preempted state efforts to achieve a fair division of production among wells in a given area by telling buyers how much they must purchase from each. The *Harvard Law Review* thought that ruling might lead to "a substantial expansion of federal regulation in this area." During the same term the Court held that federal prisoners might recover damages for injuries they sustained due to the negligence of corrections officials, although the Tort Claims Act made governmental liability dependent upon whether a private individual would have been liable in the same circumstances under state law, and in a number of states jailers enjoyed immunity from suits by convicts. Warren and his colleagues not only read the Tort Claims Act in a manner favorable to criminals but did so in a case in which one of the plaintiffs was Henry Winston, a Communist Party leader and *Dennis* defendant.[8]

Although not as notorious as Winston, the beneficiaries of the Court's 1968 decision in *King v. Smith* were also politically unpopular. That decision held that the "man in-the-house" rule used by many states to deny welfare benefits to women and children otherwise eligible to receive them under Aid to Families with Dependent Children violated subchapter IV of the Social Security Act. Douglas wanted to hold that the Alabama regulation at issue in the case was consistent with the statute, then rule that it denied needy children whose mothers cohabited with men the equal protection of the laws. Warren's opinion, however, treated this as merely a statutory interpretation case, not a constitutional one. The same was true of Black's opinion in *First*

Agricultural National Bank v. State Tax Commission (1968). Speaking for a five-to-three majority (with Fortas not participating), he read the National Bank Act as conferring immunity from most state taxation on banks chartered by the federal government. Marshall, Harlan, and Stewart protested that the legislative history did not support his interpretation. They wanted the Court to decide whether the Constitution itself exempted national banks from state taxation.[9]

Although in *King* and *First Agricultural Bank* the Court seems to have resorted to statutory interpretation to avoid deciding controversial cases on constitutional grounds, *SEC v. National Securities, Inc.* (1969) was a ruling inspired by nothing more than the need to provide guidance concerning the relationship between two important federal statutes. Section 10(b) of the Securities Exchange Act of 1934, along with SEC Rule 10b-5, which applied it, had become by 1969 the most litigated portions of the federal securities laws. In *National Securities* the Court held eight to one that the SEC could undo a merger of two Arizona insurance companies that occurred after one bought a controlling interest in the other and then, using a solicitation that allegedly omitted some material facts and misrepresented others, sought the remaining shareholders' approval for combining the companies. Acting pursuant to a state statute, the Arizona director of insurance had approved the merger. This led both the district court and the Ninth Circuit to conclude that section 10(b) did not empower the SEC to undo the deal, for section 2(b) of the McCarran-Ferguson Act of 1945 provided that no federal statute should be construed as superseding any state law regulating insurance. The Supreme Court disagreed, holding that the relationship between an insurance company and its stockholders was outside the business of insurance, and hence remained subject to the securities laws.[10]

Statutes governing intellectual property rights gave rise to similarly complicated issues. The Warren Court addressed one of these in 1965, when it held unlawful a company's practice of charging royalties calculated on the extent to which a machine was used after the patents incorporated into that machine had expired. The following year in *Brenner v. Manson* the Court construed a statute providing that patents were to be granted for the invention of "useful" products and processes. The process at issue in *Brenner* yielded a chemical compound that was being tested on mice to determine if it had tumor-inhibiting effects, but at the time of the litigation had no known use. The Court held the compound was not patentable, concluding that unless something had a specific use, there was insufficient benefit to society to justify the granting of the monopoly rights that a patent conferred. After it ruled in 1968 that a cable company that carried motion pictures to its customers without obtaining a license from United Artists authorizing it to do so was not guilty of copyright infringement because its activities did not constitute public performances, the *Harvard Law Review* reported, "Mr. Justice Stewart, for the majority, viewed the issue of infringement as one of narrow statutory construction hinging on the meaning of the term 'perform.'"[11]

That was the type of issue in which the Warren Court seemed less and less interested, perhaps in part because of the demise of the domestic cold war and the consequent waning of the sorts of individual-rights issues it had spawned. The early

Warren Court often used statutory construction as a way to give some life to civil liberties "while avoiding direct clashes with Congress." By 1962 the need to do that was largely gone. Besides, the Court's focus was squarely on the Constitution.[12]

The Warren Court did continue to render important decisions in some of the nonconstitutional fields in which it had been active prior to Frankfurter's retirement. One of these, where the Supreme Court's rulings often had constitutional implications, was federal jurisdiction and procedure. During the 1953–54 through 1961–62 terms, 9.6 percent of the cases the Court decided involved civil procedure. Subsequently, through the 1968–69 term, the figure fell to 8.9 percent.

The most criticized of these rulings involved the problem of when in deciding cases within their diversity jurisdiction, federal courts must follow state substantive law and also state procedural rules that might effectively determine the outcome of litigation. Philip Kurland accused the Warren Court of undermining this entire body of law with decisions such as *Hannah v. Plumer* (1965), which held that process could be served on the executor of an estate by leaving it with his wife, as authorized by Rule 4(d)(1) of the Federal Rules of Civil Procedure, even though in Massachusetts, where the executor resided, the law required that such service be "by delivery in hand." The Court rejected contentions that Rule 4(d)(1) was unauthorized by statute and unconstitutional. Kurland accused it of ruthlessly expanding federal jurisdiction and of ignoring the core principle of the so-called *Erie* doctrine by declaring the existence of a federal common law that was as broad as the Court wished to make it. Some of the rhetoric that annoyed him, however, garnished an opinion supporting an eight-to-one decision holding that a U.S. district court should follow state law in deciding a contract dispute involving an oil and gas lease that had been issued under a federal statute. In *Wheeldin v. Wheeler* (1963) the Court rejected an opportunity to create a whole new branch of federal common law by refusing to hold that the Fourth Amendment gave rise to a cause of action for civil damages. The justices ruled instead that someone injured by a federal officer's violation of this part of the U.S. Constitution must seek redress in a state court. Warren and his colleagues were more assertive where diversity jurisdiction was concerned, but as Circuit Judge J. Skelly Wright pointed out, diversity jurisdiction was under severe attack. In May 1965 the ALI proposed slashing it nearly in half. The post-Frankfurter Warren Court probably did have a bias toward expanding the dominion of the federal courts, but it fell far short of waging the sort of aggressive war on the *Erie* doctrine and state judicial authority that Kurland claimed.[13]

The Court did not, to be sure, have much affection for abstention. Under the "abstention doctrine," when the outcome of a constitutional issue depended upon the interpretation of a state statute, a federal court was supposed to decline to exercise its jurisdiction until state judges could construe their own law. Abstention was a Frankfurter creation and was employed extensively during his years on the bench. The practice became something of a judicial orphan after 1962. In the first seven cases following Frankfurter's retirement in which the abstention doctrine might have been applied, the Court found its use improper. Four of these decisions overruled lower federal courts that had abstained. Probably the most important was *Dombrowski v. Pfister* (1965), in which Brennan, for a five-to-four majority, held that the abstention doctrine was inapplicable where a state statute regulating speech was the target of a justifiable facial attack on its vagueness, brought by persons whose conduct was neither within the reach of any acceptable limiting construction that might be readily anticipated to result from a single criminal prosecution nor the sort of "hard core" conduct obviously prohibited by the statute. Brennan also spoke for the Court in 1964 when it reversed a federal district judge who, after staying an action so a state court could interpret a Louisiana law involving chiropractors, allowed that court also to decide the constitutional issue in the case.[14]

He also wrote the opinion in *United Mine Workers v. Gibbs* (1966), which construed liberally the "pendant jurisdiction" of the federal judiciary. Lower courts had concluded that the question of when they might properly decide cases posing both federal and state law issues depended on the extent to which the two claims relied on the same facts. Whether complete factual identity was required, however, or whether something less would do was uncertain. In *Gibbs* Brennan declared that the constitutional requirement that both claims be part of a case arising under federal law was satisfied whenever they arose from a "common nucleus of operative facts."[15]

Unlike its decisions regarding *Erie*, abstention, and pendant jurisdiction, most of the later Warren Court's civil procedure rulings had little effect on the division of authority between the federal and state judicial systems. In 1964, for example, the Supreme Court specified when a case might properly be transferred from one federal district court to another pursuant to section 1404(a) of the Judicial Code and established a permissive concept of agency for purposes of service of process under Rule 4(d)(1) of the Federal Rules of Civil Procedure. In 1967 the Court handed down decisions clarifying the procedure that federal courts of appeal were to use when trial judges improperly denied motions for judgment notwithstanding the verdict and interpreting provisions of Rule 24(a) that governed the right of nonparties to intervene in a case. The *Snyder v. Harris* (1969) decision refused to permit the aggregation of separate and distinct claims to reach the minimum amount in controversy of ten thousand dollars then required for a federal court to exercise diversity jurisdiction.[16]

Like resolving technical issues of federal civil procedure, reviewing the actions of federal administrative agencies remained an important part of the Court's workload. Fifteen percent of decisions during Warren's first nine terms had involved such cases, as did 14.5 percent in his last seven. Well over half of the administrative agency cases the Court decided in both periods involved labor relations and trade and commerce, and while the former declined slightly (from 4.5 percent of total decisions to 3.4 percent), the latter remained essentially constant (falling only from 5.2 percent to 4.9 percent). Although numerically significant, cases involving review of administrative agency proceedings seldom received much attention In this respect 1962–63 was exceptional. Commenting on that term, political scientist Benjamin Schoenfeld declared, "The Supreme Court handed down important decisions in several aspects of the administrative process." Among its thirty rulings were major ones involving the scope of the Federal Power Commission's jurisdiction over natural gas production and its discretion with respect to natural gas pricing. The Court increased both the authority of the FPC vis a vis the states and the degree of judicial deference to the commission's determinations. During the same term the Court also decided two important cases involving the Interstate Commerce Commission. One set aside an injunction that a railroad had obtained, thwarting the ICC's efforts to prevent it from reducing its rates to levels that would undercut those of water carriers. The other held that a provision of the Interstate Commerce Act, which gave the commission authority to suspend carrier-initiated rate changes for a maximum of seven months pending a decision on their reasonableness, precluded courts from enjoining the proposed rates even after seven months. In 1967 the Court sustained the ICC's claim that, although lacking explicit authorization from Congress, it nevertheless possessed the power to coordinate the "piggyback" service that railroads were offering to other forms of transportation, particularly freight-laden trucks and trailers.[17]

During that same term the Court also handed down three decisions allowing pre-enforcement review of regulations promulgated under the Federal Food, Drug, and Cosmetic Act that observers viewed as "a triumph for proponents of judicial review of administrative action." These rulings, which resolved a conflict between the Second and Third Circuit Courts of Appeal, were somewhat unusual, however; the later Warren Court did not often exhibit much interest in administrative procedure. When the *Duke Law Journal* initiated an annual commentary on major developments in federal administrative law by analyzing what it considered to be the forty-five most important procedural decisions of 1969, only three of them were Supreme Court decisions. Just one had been handed down before Warren's retirement. *NLRB v. Wyman-Gordon Company* held the National Labor Relations Board could not use its adjudicatory powers to promulgate requirements that were purely prospective in effect, thereby avoiding the formal rule-making process spelled out in the Administrative Procedure Act.[18]

Besides avoiding the complexities of administrative procedure, the Warren Court also spent less time wrestling with highly technical tax issues. For the 1953–54 through 1961–62 terms, federal tax cases composed 6.8 percent of its workload. During the 1962–63 through 1968–69 period, they composed only 4.2 percent. One 1967 tax decision had significant implications for federalism. The Supreme Court held that a state trial court's ruling on property law issues did not preclude a federal judge from making an independent determination of tax law questions, even when doing so might involve deciding the property issues differently. Most tax cases, however, involved nothing more than interpreting the Internal Revenue Code and regulations implementing it, usually to resolve disagreements among courts of appeal or between one or more of those and the U.S. Tax Court. In 1966, for example, the justices had to devote some of their limited time to reconciling the application of three long-established rules benefitting livestock raisers. The Court also addressed such complicated issues as the deductibility of the depreciation of an asset in a year when that asset was sold (in this case for an amount greatly in excess of its depreciated value) and the legitimacy of a "bootstrap" transfer of a business to a charitable organization as a means of converting what would otherwise have been ordinary income to the shareholders into capital gains taxable at a lower rate. Although these cases might suggest otherwise, political scientist Martin Shapiro concluded, "The two most striking features of the Warren Court's record on substantive tax issues are its desire to avoid over-involvement in complex economic matters and its general, but not complete submission to the guidance of the Internal Revenue Service."[19]

Immigration and naturalization matters were less complex, and the Court's declining involvement with those was probably due mainly to the waning of the Cold War. During the 1953–54 through 1961–62 terms, 2.89 percent of the cases that it decided were in this field, compared to only 1.92 percent of those in the next seven terms. One 1967 case did address a Cold War–related issue. In *United States v. Laub* the Court held that visiting Communist Cuba in defiance of a State Department policy against traveling there without a passport specifically validated for that purpose did not constitute violation of a provision of the Immigration and Nationality Act of 1952 that made it a crime to depart from or enter the United States without a valid passport. Most of the high-profile cases the later Warren Court decided in the immigration and naturalization field, however, were constitutional attacks on congressional legislation revoking the citizenship of persons who had engaged in disfavored conduct having little or nothing to do with the Cold War. In *Kennedy v. Mendoza-Martinez* (1963) the Court invalidated statutes permitting the expatriation, without criminal proceedings, of citizens who had departed from or remained outside the United States in time of war or national emergency in order to evade military service. *Schneider v. Rusk* (1964) struck down a section of the Immigration and Nationality Act of 1952 that revoked the citizenship of a naturalized citizen who resided continuously for three years in the country of her birth. Three years later the *Harvard Law Review* reported: "The Court in *Afroyim v. Rusk* continued a decade-long trend of holding unconstitutional yet another of the statutory provisions which declared specified conduct to result in the loss of American citizenship." *Afroyim* invalidated a 1940 law that expatriated persons who voted in foreign elections.[20]

While the number of tax and immigration cases that were decided declined slightly after 1962, the Warren Court's level of activity in those fields remained somewhere near where it had been before Frankfurter's retirement. Other subjects, however, received vastly less attention. Admiralty cases comprised 4.5 percent of the Supreme Court's workload from the 1953–54 through 1961–62 terms, but for the 1962–63 through 1968–69 terms they represented only .6 percent of it. The Court rendered two important admiralty decisions in 1963. *Guterrez v. Waterman S.S. Corp.* extended the benefits of the warranty of seaworthiness to a longshoreman injured on a pier by defective packaging, holding that the warranty rendered a nonnegligent shipowner liable to the wounded man. This significant expansion of the near-absolute liability that the seaworthiness doctrine imposed elicited protests from Harlan and the *Harvard Law Review*. Both considered *Gutierrez* inconsistent with precedent and faulted the Court for summarily changing the law with a holding that was at best only an alternative basis for its decision. In *Reed v. The Yaka* (1963) "the Court added still another weapon to the already formidable legal arsenal at the disposal of injured longshoremen and

harbor workers." This decision held that a stevedore injured due to an unseaworthy condition on a vessel his employer had chartered could bring an "in rem" proceeding against the ship itself, even though the availability of such an action depended
on someone being personally liable to him, and the combined effect of the charter
and the Harbor Workers' Compensation Act seemed to be a situation in which no
one was liable. The following term the Court interpreted that statute in a manner
more favorable to shipowners, ruling that an owner held liable to a longshoreman
for injuries suffered when a rope supplied by his employer snapped might seek
indemnification from the stevedoring company for which the injured man worked.
After 1964 significant admiralty rulings became rarities. Indeed, during Warren's
final term, the Court decided no admiralty cases at all.[21]

Like admiralty, the vast expanse of constitutional law lying outside the realm of
civil rights and civil liberties failed to elicit many decisions from the later Warren
Court. The justices decided only a few cases involving alleged state interference with
interstate and foreign commerce. Two 1964 decisions restrictively interpreted the
scope of the authority that the Twenty-First Amendment gave the states over alcoholic beverages. During the same term the Court upheld a Washington tax on the
privilege of engaging in wholesaling that was measured by a company's gross receipts
in the state, declaring it could constitutionally be applied even to revenue derived
from sales of auto parts and accessories shipped from a warehouse in Oregon upon
receipt of orders from local retailers, although these were not the direct result of any
marketing activity within Washington. Three years later, however, the justices took a
much harder line with Illinois, which had required an out-of-state mail-order firm to
collect a use tax for the state, even though the company had no property or personnel there and solicited customers only by sending them catalogues and direct mail
advertising. The Court held that the Illinois statute violated both the Commerce
Clause and the Due Process Clause of the Fourteenth Amendment.[22]

While occasionally ruling on such issues, the later Warren Court hardly ever
addressed separation-of-powers questions. Its only important ruling in this area was
Powell v. McCormack (1969), in which it held that the House of Representatives had
acted unconstitutionally in refusing to seat a controversial member because of his
alleged misconduct. In order to reach the merits, the Court had to rule that the
political question doctrine did not preclude judicial resolution of the case. Although
Powell was the Supreme Court's most important explication of that doctrine between
Baker v. Carr (1962) and *United States v. Nixon* (1974), *Powell* was the later Warren
Court's only contribution to separation-of-powers law.[23]

During Warren's last seven terms his Court took far more interest in civil rights,
criminal procedure, reapportionment, and the First Amendment. The ways in which
its workload changed reflected these priorities. For example, appeals of state criminal convictions, which produced only 7.3 percent of the cases the Court decided during the 1953–54 through 1961–62 terms, accounted for 17.6 percent of those it
resolved in the terms from 1962–63 through 1968–69. The criminal-procedure revolution was not the sole cause of the increase: state criminal cases implicating freedom

of expression more than doubled, rising from 1 percent during Warren's first nine terms to 2.2 percent in his last seven. Appeals combining equal protection and due process issues also fueled the increase, accounting for 3.7 percent of the Court's workload after 1962. In addition, the number of habeas corpus cases brought by state prisoners rose. Fortas, who lauded *Fay v. Noia* as "another Brennan milestone," outranked in importance only by *Baker v. Carr*, exaggerated only a little, for as the *Brooklyn Law Review* noted, by changing the exhaustion of state-remedies doctrine, that decision "permitted the filing of a greater number of habeas petitions by state prisoners." During Warren's first nine terms, such petitions generated only 1.5 percent of the cases the Supreme Court heard. During his last seven they accounted for 2.7 percent. Of the twenty-two habeas decisions rendered after Frankfurter's retirement, thirteen came down during Warren's last two terms, making them the busiest of his entire chief justiceship.[24]

Like habeas corpus actions and appeals challenging state criminal convictions, state and local government litigation originating in the lower federal courts increased dramatically after 1962. During the terms beginning in 1953 and ending in 1962 such cases represented only 3.8 percent of the Court's workload; from the 1961–62 term through the 1968–69 term, they rose to 8.1 percent. The biggest generators of this type of litigation were reapportionment and voting, which accounted for 2.2 percent of the Court's workload during the years after Frankfurter retired. Next in importance were racially based equal-protection disputes, which generated 15 percent of the state and local government cases and accounted for 1.2 percent of the Court's total workload. Other equal protection and due process cases accounted for an additional 1.1 percent.

One indication of how substantially the Warren Court's transformation of criminal procedure and its growing commitment to the promotion of civil rights, reapportionment, and freedom of expression changed its workload is the dramatic drop in the number of labor relations cases that the Court decided. During Warren's first nine terms such cases accounted for 13.7 percent of its decisions. In his last seven only 6.2 percent of the Court's rulings involved labor relations.

Yet, the true Warren Court was at least as committed to promoting the interests of organized labor as was the Frankfurter-dominated tribunal of 1953–62. Beginning in 1964 the Supreme Court revitalized the concept of picketing as a form of free speech protected by the First Amendment, which had been in eclipse for about a decade. One decision utilized rather strained statutory interpretation to reach the conclusion that 1959 amendments to the Taft-Hartley Act did not forbid consumer picketing directed at a nonunion product being distributed by a retailer who was neutral in the labor dispute. In *Food Employees Local 590 v. Logan Valley Plaza, Inc.* (1968) the Court ruled that a state judge had violated the First Amendment when he enjoined peaceful picketing of a business located in a privately owned shopping center.[25]

While making greater use of the First Amendment to promote union interests, the later Warren Court exhibited the same tendency as the earlier one to construe national labor legislation in a way that preempted state authority. In *Railroad Trainmen v. Terminal Company* (1969), for example, it held that even though no federal statute governed secondary picketing at a railroad terminal, paramount federal policies of nationwide import limited the application of state law to this activity. According to Theodore St. Antoine, when Warren became chief justice, "the pre-emption doctrine in its application to labor relations was still in its adolescence." His Court brought it to maturity. Over one-third of the important labor cases it decided by December 1968 dealt "either directly with the metes and bounds of the pre-emption doctrine, or with issues which would not have arisen but for the displacement of state law by federal." Pre-1962 rulings, such as *Garner v. Teamsters Union* (1953) and *San Diego Building Trades Council v. Garmon* (1959) ushered in the elements of the strong preemption doctrine that the Warren Court developed, but numerous decisions during that Court's last seven terms made it more expansive and restricted further the autonomy of the states in labor matters. One decision declared that while a state might use its police power to maintain order, it could not take over a public utility to halt a strike. Another announced that the permissible scope of state remedies for claims involving force and violence was "strictly confined to the direct consequences of [illegal conduct] and does not include any consequences resulting from associated peaceful picketing or other union activity." A 1966 decision imposed restrictions on state libel law when the alleged defamation occurred in connection with a labor dispute. According to Warren biographer G. Edward White, the Chief's "stance in preemption cases was . . . consistently one of support for federal regulation of labor disputes." So was his Court's. Congress had failed in the National Labor Relations Act to make any general allocation of power between the states and the federal government, and "the Warren Court filled this void with a strong preemption doctrine."[26]

Warren's Court also defended the interests of organized labor. That is not to say the true Warren Court never ruled in favor of employers. In 1966 a majority held that a railroad had not violated the Railway Labor Act when it responded to a strike by unilaterally changing the working conditions of its employees without notice or mediation. In two 1965 cases arising under the National Labor Relations Act, the Court reversed decisions of the NLRB holding lockouts illegal. After a bargaining impasse was reached, the American Shipbuilding Company had shut down its plant and laid off employees in an effort to pressure the union into accepting the company's position. The Court held unanimously (with Goldberg writing a concurring opinion) that the company's actions did not violate sections 8(a)(1) and 8(a)(3) of the act. It also ruled that these provisions had not been violated when, during a "whipsaw" strike against one member of a multi-employer bargaining unit, the other employers locked out their workers and joined the struck one in hiring temporary replacements. During the same term the Court also ruled in *Textile Workers v. Darlington Manufacturing Company* (1965) that, while an employer would be guilty of an unfair labor practice for shutting down part of its enterprise in order to avoid dealing with a union, it would not be for going out of business entirely. Because a majority of the stock in the manufacturing company that had closed down was owned by a textile-selling house that also operated other mills and was controlled by the president of the firm that was closing and his family, the category in which this case belonged was highly debatable, and in conference Warren, Black, and Clark all expressed dislike for what the company had done.[27]

Most of the later Warren Court's labor decisions manifested the pro-union leanings suggested by the three justices' comments about Darlington's practices. In 1964 the Court held that the secondary boycott provisions of the Labor Management Relations Act did not bar picketing directed at encouraging consumers not to buy an employer's product, a reading of the statute the *Harvard Law Review* found "unexpected." The same term produced two pro-union decisions that reflected "the Warren Court's ideological commitment to grievance arbitration as the road to industrial peace." One held that a union could compel an employer to arbitrate, under the grievance procedures of their contract, even work assignments or representational disputes within the jurisdiction of the NLRB, and the other decided that whether a collective bargaining agreement survived a merger between the employer and another firm was an issue that the new employer must submit to arbitration under the grievance provisions of the contract. Later in 1964, continuing its policy of expanding the range of matters subject to mandatory collective bargaining, the Court ruled that a company had violated the National Labor Relations Act when it contracted out all of the maintenance work at one of its plants for economic reasons without bothering to consult the union that represented the company's maintenance employees. The true Warren Court also gave a broad reading to labor's exemption from the antitrust laws, taking the position that the procompetition approach those laws embodied must yield to policies promoting collective bargaining. While holding that an agreement between a union and large coal operators to force smaller companies out of business by demanding wages the big companies could afford but the small ones could not was subject to the antitrust laws, the Court ruled that a multi-employer contract with a butchers' union that prohibited selling meat at night was lawful, despite its negative effects on competition among grocery stores. Likewise, regulations of the American Federation of Musicians prohibiting members from booking their own "club dates" and fixing the prices charged for various types of services associated with such performances were not actionable under the Sherman Act. In Warren's final term he spoke for a unanimous Court in *NLRB v. Gissel Packing Co.* (1969), upholding the power of the NLRB to order collective bargaining when a union had gathered cards authorizing it to represent a majority of the employees and, in addition, the employer's unfair labor practices made it unlikely that an election on the question of representation would be fair. "*Gissel* was a decision wholly favorable to the interests of organized labor."[28]

Among other things it appeared to restrict employer speech concerning a union. The Warren Court supported labor even when doing so required limiting freedom of expression. The Chief believed that the economic dependence of employees gave employer speech a potential for coercion that distinguished it from political speech, and his Court treated less favorably the right of bosses to comment on matters particularly affecting the operation of their businesses than it did the right of newsmen and politicians to speak on matters of public concern. However, it responded positively to pleas from then-solicitor general Thurgood Marshall to shield the heated rhetoric of labor leaders. When a federal district judge dismissed a libel suit filed by a company official against an employee, a union, and two of its officers, based on allegedly false and defamatory statements made during an organizing campaign, the Court reversed his ruling, but did so on the ground that the National Labor Relations Act precluded *either* party to a labor dispute from recovering for defamation without proving that the offending statements had been made with malice and resulted in actual harm.[29]

Besides being decidedly pro-union, the true Warren Court was strongly committed to the antitrust laws. In that respect, it reflected the views of Warren himself, who voted against liability in only 3 of 101 cases between 1953 and 1968. The later Warren Court appears to have taken an even greater interest in antitrust enforcement than the earlier one. Richard Arnold found that of the 1,381 cases decided by full opinion during the Warren Court's first thirteen terms, 84 (or 6.1 percent) dealt with antitrust. During the 1965–66 term 11 out of 107 (or 10.3 percent) did, making this the busiest term for antitrust down to 1967. The quietest had been Warren's first, when only 2 of 94 cases dealt with this area of the law.[30]

In some cases the commitment of the true Warren Court to antitrust enforcement collided with its devotion to the interests of organized labor. When this happened, the latter generally prevailed. "Unions did not obtain from the Warren Court total exemption from the antitrust laws," Lee Modjeska reports, but "extremely wide latitude . . . was accorded legitimate union activity." While Black insisted that "antitrust law [is] not repealed by labor law," Harlan was equally insistent that because of congressional policy embodied in statutes such as the Norris-La Guardia Act and section 6 of the Clayton Act, the legality of provisions of collective bargaining agreements that ran afoul of antitrust law should not be assessed using antitrust principles. Goldberg maintained that no antitrust penalties should attach to any accord involving a subject of mandatory collective bargaining. In his opinion for the Court in *United Mine Workers v. Pennington* (1965) (a case that Harlan thought presented "a head on conflict between antitrust and labor laws"), White rejected the notion of such a sweeping exemption, taking the position that a union was not automatically immune from the Sherman Act because the conspiracy in which it was alleged to have engaged was an agreement reached through mandatory collective bargaining. A violation would have been committed if a union agreed with one set of employers to impose a certain wage scale on other employers, the Court held. In the companion case of *Local 189, Amalgamated Meat Cutters v. Jewel Tea Company* (1965), however, White declared that, unless there was a conspiracy, a labor-management agreement would not violate the antitrust laws if the value of the benefit it provided to the union outweighed its negative effects on competition in a product market. The fact that keeping meat counters open at night hurt employees was sufficient to exempt a contract prohibiting that practice from the antitrust laws, Clark argued in conference. Likewise, the Court held in *American Federation of Musicians v. Carroll* (1968) that the need to protect the salaries of member musicians justified union regulations dictating the cost of booking orchestras. In that case, noted the *Harvard Law Review,* it "gave a broad reading to the labor exemption from the antitrust laws."[31]

When labor was not involved, the Court generally supported those alleging antitrust violations. As of 1967, the Justice Department had lost only three out of forty cases. Two of the defeats came during the post-1962 period, but both were qualified losses. In *United States v. Pan American World Airways, Inc.* (1963) the Court held that, with respect to the defendant's conduct, another regulatory regime had superseded the antitrust laws. *White Motor Company v. United States* (1963) merely reversed the granting of a Justice Department motion for summary judgment, holding that a trial was needed to determine the "economic and business stuff" out of which a territorial limitation imposed by the defendant on dealers in its product had emerged. Four years later in *United States v. Arnold Schwinn and Company* (1967), Fortas, despite a probusiness reputation, produced one of the Warren Court's most radical antitrust opinions, holding that, whatever the reasons for them, customer and resale restrictions imposed by a manufacturer on distributors were per se illegal.[32]

With the exceptions of *White* and *Pan American,* Justice Department antitrust enforcers won consistently during Warren's last seven terms. In 1963 the Court supported their efforts to enjoin a merger between the second- and third-largest banks in Philadelphia, and a year later it agreed with them that combining the first- and third-largest ones in the Lexington, Kentucky, area violated section 1 of the Sherman Act. In *United States v. Aluminum Company of America* (1964) the justices narrowly interpreted a Clayton Act prohibition on one company acquiring another in the same "line of commerce," and in *United States v. Continental Can Company* (1964) they relied upon a broad interpretation to achieve the same objective of invalidating mergers of large companies with their smaller alleged competitors. Also in 1964, the Court ruled unlawful the acquisition by the only interstate pipeline company then supplying natural gas to the California market of a firm in the Pacific Northwest that could serve the same market in the future and the formation by two chemical companies of a joint-venture corporation established to produce and market sodium chlorate. A 1966 decision upheld an action brought by the Justice Department against the Grinnell Corporation, which owned controlling interests in three burglar alarm companies that together supplied nearly 90 percent of the "accredited central station protective services" in the country, reasoning that such services, rather than property protection generally, constituted the relevant market. The Court also for the first time invalidated a merger without finding that it would substantially lessen competition, holding that one between the third- and sixth-largest supermarket chains in Los Angeles violated section 7 of the Sherman Act because chains were forcing small groceries out of business. During Warren's final term his Court ruled that competing firms chilled competition when they exchanged prices quoted to identified customers, and therefore violated section 1 of that law.[33]

The Warren Court supported the Federal Trade Commission nearly as consistently as it did the Justice Department, ruling for the FTC in eighteen of twenty cases decided during its first thirteen terms. The commission's two losses came in 1958; it was undefeated in the true Warren Court, which produced rulings such as *FTC v. Sun Oil Company* (1963). This case held that a gasoline refiner that lowered its whole-sale price to a single dealer was guilty of discriminatory pricing in violation of the Robinson-Patman Act, even though it did so to enable the dealer to respond to a price cut by a competing retailer. The *Harvard Law Review* criticized this application of the statute as "unwise," but in *FTC v. Borden Co.* (1966) the Court again read the Robinson-Patman Act in a way that favored the commission, validating its efforts to sanction Borden for illegal price discrimination, based on the company's selling of the same evaporated milk for different prices under its own label and certain "pri-vate brands." Warren, who viewed the FTC as a protector of small business, wrote an opinion in *FTC v. Fred Myer, Inc.* (1968) upholding the commission's contention that a supermarket chain had violated the Robinson-Patman Act by soliciting and obtain-ing promotional allowances and price reductions from suppliers with whom it dealt directly when the same incentives and discounts were unavailable to the wholesalers who served the supermarket's retail competitors. The Court also supported FTC efforts to prevent conglomerate mergers. In 1965 it held that the reduction in com-petition resulting from the acquisition by Consolidated Foods of a producer of dehy-drated garlic and onion used by food processors, who in turn sold to distributors such as Consolidated, was substantial enough to constitute a violation of section 7 of the Clayton Act and merited the divestiture the commission had mandated. Two years later the Court upheld an FTC ruling that the acquisition of bleach maker Clorox by Procter & Gamble violated the same section, rejecting the contention that economic efficiency could justify a merger that adversely affected competition. The Court also ruled that the commission could obtain a preliminary injunction restrain-ing consummation of a merger pending adjudication of whether it was legal. Fortas, who contended that Congress had deliberately determined not to authorize the FTC to obtain preliminary relief, dissented, proclaiming publicly that "not all mergers are bad." The true Warren Court, however, seemed to think they were. It also exhibited distaste for deceptive advertising, upholding FTC actions against a paint company's two-cans-for-the-price-of-one promotion and Colgate-Palmolive's use of a mock-up to create the false impression that applying "Rapid Shave" to sandpaper would enable one to shave the sand off the paper immediately.[34]

The Court did not support private antitrust plaintiffs as consistently as it did the FTC and the Justice Department. Indeed, during Warren's first thirteen terms, such plaintiffs won only fourteen out of twenty-four cases decided on full opinion. They did better after 1962, however. *Silver v. New York Stock Exchange* (1963) exemplifies the true Warren Court's solicitude for private antitrust plaintiffs. There it ruled in favor of a nonmember over-the-counter dealer in a suit alleging that a NYSE order to member firms to terminate their private wire connections with him violated section 1 of the Sherman Act. The Court took the position that the self-regulation of the exchange authorized by the Securities Exchange Act did not immunize it from the award of an injunction and treble damages. The following year it ruled in favor of a service-station operator who had violated a consignment agreement that Union Oil forced on those wishing to lease stations from the company, under which Union retained title to all gasoline until it was sold and determined what the retailer might charge. Writing for a majority of five, Douglas declared this method of retail price maintenance a violation of the Sherman Act. During Warren's last term the Court ruled, in a treble-damages suit filed by a builder who was complaining that United States Steel had made its extension of credit to him contingent upon his using most but not all of the funds to buy its prefabricated houses, that such an arrangement would under certain circumstances constitute a "tie-in" prohibited by the antitrust laws. Although the opinion was written by Black, this decision was just one of many that reflected Warren's commitment to employing the antitrust laws to protect small producers and consumers from the effects of corporate size and power.[35]

Like so many of his Court's antitrust decisions, it was designed to implement liberal values. The true Warren Court relentlessly used judicial power to promote substantive liberalism. The tribunal Frankfurter so often controlled had a liberal image, but its reputation corresponded only imperfectly with reality. The same was not true of the post-1962 Court. The liberals who controlled it were more than willing to support Congress when the national legislature joined in the legal revolution they were promoting, and in an era when liberal Democrats controlled both Capitol Hill and the White House, the justices often found themselves marching in step with the political branches. But the true Warren Court was more than willing to invalidate acts of Congress in order to advance its agenda. It struck down 50 percent more national legislation than any previous Supreme Court, in addition to invalidating more state constitutional provisions and statutes and more local ordinances than any previous Court. Only the conservative Taft Court of the 1920s invalidated legislation at a faster rate. Warren and his colleagues threw out judge-made law as readily as they did legislation. His Court reversed more of its predecessors' decisions than any previous Supreme Court; it did so, however, in a creative, rather than a destructive, manner. The Warren Court exploited constitutional litigation to make law, operating, Kurland lamented, in a manner more legislative than judicial. Especially between the years 1962 and 1969, Galloway observes, "The liberals exercised their dominance with a great deal of judicial activism."[36]

They did not exercise their power entirely without opposition, but a five-vote liberal majority existed throughout the period 1962–69 (with the possible exception of the 1966–67 term). At its core were Warren and Brennan, as well as Goldberg and his replacement, Fortas. Marshall joined them after his appointment in 1967, and Douglas occupied the Court's left wing. He agreed most frequently with Warren, Brennan, Fortas, and Marshall, and during the early 1960s with Black. By 1966 Black had moved to the right and was voting with Harlan and Stewart as much as with Douglas, but his position was still slightly to the left of the Court's center. Not surprisingly, Douglas disagreed most frequently with Harlan and Stewart. The true Warren Court's truest conservative, Harlan, drew support from Stewart more often than from any other justice. Stewart also disagreed less with Harlan than he did with Douglas or even Warren. White compiled a moderate voting record. Aligning himself most often with Brennan and Clark, he was near the center of a continuum that ran from Douglas on the left to Harlan on the right.[37]

Voting alignments were not consistent throughout the 1962–69 period. During the 1964–65 and 1965–66 terms, the liberals broke ranks, and a two–five–two division emerged. Brennan and Warren lined up more or less in the middle (between Douglas and Black on the left and Harlan and Stewart on the right), where they were joined by Clark, White, and Goldberg/Fortas. During the 1966–67 term Black, White, and Clark moved to the right, producing a four–one–four split (with Black now in the middle and Warren, Brennan, and Fortas joining Douglas on the left) that briefly challenged liberal dominance. During Warren's last two terms, with Marshall now occupying Clark's seat, "the liberals resumed almost complete control over the Court's decisions, thus completing the most liberal period in the history of the United States Supreme Court."[38]

It was an era during which an activist majority sought to promote social justice by equalizing rights and facilitating a more equitable distribution of society's benefits. The Warren Court ruled in favor of America's underdogs (such as African Americans, criminal defendants, and the poor) with great regularity. States and local governments prevailed against the traditionally disadvantaged barely over 20 percent of the time. In the Warren Court even the federal government had less than a 40 percent chance of success against society's underdogs. "For the first time in American history," Morton Horwitz contends, "the Supreme Court demonstrated its concern and support for the weak and the powerless, the marginal and the socially scorned." The Warren Court became "the first Supreme Court in American history to champion the legal position of the underdog and the outsider."[39]

The Court did so most fully and consistently during Warren's last seven terms, a period in which the Supreme Court shifted the focus of its attention significantly, becoming much more of a constitutional court. Exhibiting reduced concern for traditionally important aspects of the Court's business that ranged from admiralty through statutory interpretation to the Commerce Clause, it involved itself deeply in civil rights and civil liberties and in the types of litigation spawned by its initiatives in those areas. Antitrust enforcement and advancing the interests of organized labor remained high priorities, but they were now just small components of a larger liberal agenda. Like no other Court before or since, the true Warren Court committed itself to promoting "an expansive conception of the democratic way of life." That ideal shaped not just its interpretation of the Constitution but its entire jurisprudence.[40]

11

THE END OF AN ERA

On April 4, 1968, an assassin's bullet felled the country's best-known civil rights leader, Dr. Martin Luther King Jr. On June 5, Senator Robert Kennedy, campaigning for president as an opponent of the increasingly unpopular Vietnam War, was gunned down after a celebration of his victory in the California Democratic primary. America seemed to be coming apart. The national epidemic of divisiveness and violence devastated Earl Warren. Four days after Kennedy's death, during his regular weekly luncheon with his clerks, a shaken chief justice told them that he had decided to retire at the end of the term. "I felt I was bearing witness to the end of an era, not only in the life of the Supreme Court, but in the life of the country," Clerk Tyrone Brown recalled later. Although Warren believed "that his era had come to an end," the epoch was not yet over. The failure of President Johnson to make Abe Fortas his successor would force the Chief to serve one more term. That curtain call would not be a happy one. Vietnam and the escalating protests against the war presented the Court with difficult and divisive issues. Still firmly under liberal control, the Warren Court went out in a blaze of liberal activism, even though "the mood of the nation was swinging away from liberalism." A Court that had long reflected popular sentiment and implemented popular aspirations for reform found itself out of step with public opinion. A president who had campaigned against its decisions chose the new chief justice, and the Warren Court staggered to an end amid scandal and controversy.[1]

Warren had envisioned a far different finale on June 11 when he asked Fortas to arrange a meeting with the president. The Chief wanted to retire immediately, for reasons that were both personal and political. During a fifteen-minute meeting on the morning of June 13, he handed Johnson a one-sentence retirement letter, accompanied by a second letter explaining that he was stepping down "not because of reasons of health or on account of any personal or associational problems, but solely because of age." Warren was seventy-eight. Many of his contemporaries were dying off. Clark had retired at sixty-seven, and Warren did not want to cling to his own seat too long, as he believed the eighty-two-year-old Black (whose opinions had become increasingly erratic) and the seventy-year-old Douglas (who seemed to have lost interest in the job) had done. The Chief considered his work finished, for the Court had laid down legal guidelines in all the major areas of social concern. He wanted to enjoy himself more, travel with his wife, Nina, and work on behalf of a new organization,

World Peace through Law. His forty-thousand-dollar salary would continue as retirement income, giving him no financial incentive to remain on the Court, but he did have political reasons for choosing this moment to leave. The election of conservative Republican Ronald Reagan to the California governorship in 1966 suggested to the Chief that the tide had turned against liberal governmental activism, and Bobby Kennedy's death made it highly likely that his old political enemy, Richard Nixon, would be elected president in November. If Warren waited, Nixon would probably appoint his successor.[2]

The shorter of the two letters he gave to Johnson advised the president of "my intention to retire as Chief Justice of the United States, effective at your pleasure." On June 26, after nearly two weeks of rumors and press speculation about Warren's impending retirement, LBJ announced that the chief justice was stepping down and publicly accepted his "decision to retire effective at such time as a successor is qualified." The two men apparently agreed on this arrangement because they believed that, even during its summer recess, the Court needed a chief justice. Should some emergency arise that might necessitate the calling of a special session, Black, as the senior associate justice, would have to function temporarily as the head of the Court, and Warren did not think his health would permit him to do so. By remaining available if needed, he could protect his friend from public embarrassment. Furthermore, as Attorney General Ramsey Clark, who stressed the "need for continuity in the office of Chief Justice," reminded the president, a "hiatus of leadership and supervision" would hurt not only the Supreme Court but the entire federal judiciary, over which the Chief had administrative responsibility. Johnson told Clark he wanted the reply to Warren's letter of resignation carefully drafted, so that Warren's retirement would become effective upon the qualification of a successor and could be withdrawn if none qualified. This arrangement was unusual. Indeed, when Brennan succeeded Minton, one of the Chief's clerks had advised him that "the case of a Justice being appointed to this Court so that he is in a position to take office right on the heels of his predecessor's retirement or resignation is without precedent." He was not quite correct; Deputy Attorney General Warren Christopher discovered that in 1902 Justice Horace Gray had submitted a resignation "to take effect on the appointment and qualifying of my successor." What had sent Christopher mining for precedents was the negative reaction of many senators to Warren's contingent resignation. One powerful member of the Judiciary Committee, Sam Ervin (D-N.C.), maintained that the office of chief justice was not vacant. Even the *Washington Post* called on Warren to submit a less equivocal letter of resignation.[3]

Johnson insisted there was a vacancy because he was determined to fill it with his old friend Fortas. During their meeting, LBJ asked Warren if he had a successor in mind. Although the Chief apparently believed Brennan should succeed him, he replied, "No Mr. President, that's your problem." Johnson then asked him what he thought about Fortas. Warren answered, "I think Abe would be a good Chief Justice." So did Douglas, who wrote to Johnson when he learned about the vacancy, urging him to elevate his former protégé. Doing that would, of course, leave Fortas's seat vacant. The man Johnson had in mind to fill it was Judge Homer Thornberry of the

Fifth Circuit. A graduate of the University of Texas School of Law, Thornberry had practiced in Austin, where he also served as district attorney. From 1937 to 1939 he was a member of the Texas legislature, and from 1946 to 1948 he served on the Austin City Council, acting as mayor pro tem for the last year of his term. In 1948 Thornberry succeeded Johnson as the representative from Texas's Tenth Congressional District. He became a federal district judge in 1963, and in 1965 LBJ elevated him to the Fifth Circuit. Fellow Texan Ramsey Clark recommended him, and Warren congratulated the president on the selection of "Mr. Justice Fortas as my successor and of Judge Homer Thornberry to succeed him."[4]

The Chief touted both as "men of whom you can well be proud." Others were less enthusiastic about Johnson's choices. Secretary of Defense Clark Clifford, a lawyer and longtime adviser, was alarmed. LBJ was a lame duck, and with the Republicans convinced they would win the White House in November, he did not think it would be possible to get Fortas confirmed. Coupling his nomination with that of Thornberry would just make a bad situation worse. Although the Texan had earned the respect and support of colleagues on the Fifth Circuit and other federal judges who wrote letters endorsing his candidacy, he was bound to be viewed as just an LBJ crony. Clifford suggested that the President nominate a nonpolitical Republican lawyer, such as Albert Jenner of Chicago, chair of the ABA's Committee on the Federal Judiciary. On June 22 Johnson discussed Jenner—as well as Senator Edmund Muskie (D-Me.), Secretary of the Treasury Henry Fowler, and former secretary of the army Cyrus Vance—with Attorney General Clark. Three days later though, he told Clark he had decided to nominate Fortas and Thornberry.[5]

That evening the attorney general telephoned Jenner, asking him to seek confidentially his committee's reaction. The following morning Jenner called back to report that during a just-concluded conference call, the committee had unanimously found both men "highly acceptable from the viewpoint of their professional qualifications." Later in the day Jenner sent Johnson a letter declaring that the committee had reached this conclusion about Fortas "as a result of our investigation." Of course, no one had investigated anything. The Senate was not about to endorse Fortas so quickly and easily.[6]

For one thing, the associate justice was even more vulnerable than Thornberry to charges of cronyism. Even after joining the Court, Fortas continued to respond to pleas from LBJ for assistance and advice. He had a private, direct telephone line installed in his Supreme Court office and gave the number to the White House operators and the president, who used it to consult him regularly. Fortas advised LBJ on everything from the establishment of the Kennedy Center to the war in Vietnam. He made recommendations on appointments, served as a back channel for communications between the White House and the Israeli embassy, and assisted in writing LBJ's 1966 State of the Union Address. In October 1967, with the Vietnam War becoming increasingly unpopular, Fortas drafted a memorandum urging the administration to seek an early opportunity to state emphatically that it was going to see the conflict through to a successful conclusion. He also advised the White House on how to manage the antiwar demonstrators who poured into Washington. Fortas found his role as a presidential adviser more absorbing than his work on the Court, and his colleagues worried about the amount of time he spent at the White House. According to Douglas,"there were no instances in which his consultations with LBJ in any way implicated cases coming to the Court." Still, they did not look good.[7]

Johnson, who had a well-deserved reputation as a master politician, was nevertheless sure he could get his friend confirmed. When questions about their relationship had arisen during his 1965 confirmation hearings, Fortas successfully deflected them, along with inquiries about his views on legal issues, and even conservative segregationist James Eastland, the chair of the Senate Judiciary Committee, had supported him. This time, however, Eastland informed the White House that Fortas could not be confirmed and that there would be a filibuster against him. Southerners, such as Ervin, Robert Byrd (D-W.Va.) (who considered the nominee a "leftist"), and John McClellan (D-Ark.)(who called him an "SOB") were hostile, but Eastland reported that even one nonsouthern Democrat had declared he would oppose confirmation because "liberalism is dead." The northern and western senators with whom the White House checked favored Fortas, but they were unenthusiastic about Thornberry. Johnson believed, though, that the powerful Richard Russell (D-Ga.), who controlled the votes of at least a dozen other southerners, would swallow Fortas in order to get Thornberry. He thought he could count on Minority Leader Everett Dirksen to blunt Republican opposition. Before the nomination was announced, Johnson summoned Dirksen to the White House, where they discussed a number of possible nominees. The president then asked the minority leader what he thought of Fortas. Dirksen said he knew nothing negative about him. Johnson enlisted the senator's support by prolonging the life of the Subversive Activities Control Board, a moribund relic of the McCarthy era valued by conservatives. Unfortunately for LBJ's strategy, Russell angrily deserted him after erroneously concluding that the president was holding up a Georgia judicial appointment in order to ensure his support for Fortas. Dirksen's backing proved far less valuable than LBJ had expected, for the minority leader's power within the GOP was eroding. He could not even get his son-in-law, Howard Baker, who represented Fortas's home state of Tennessee, to support him. Freshman Robert Griffin (R-Mich.) surprised Dirksen by mounting an organized campaign against the nomination, rallying opposition with the argument that the appointment should be made by the winner of the November election. The day Johnson announced Warren's resignation and the nominations of Fortas and Thornberry, the Chief's secretary informed him that "some of the Republicans are making loud noises . . . about a Lame Duck President appointing a Chief Justice." Eighteen GOP senators joined Griffin in signing a statement declaring that the Senate should not confirm anyone Johnson nominated. By the July 4th weekend, Griffin and Russell had struck a deal, and, although the president and Fortas did not know it yet, the nomination was dead.[8]

The nominee's opponents sought to turn the fight over his confirmation into a referendum on the Warren Court. Although one of its newer members, Fortas made a splendid target for those upset about the course the Court had charted. He was, as Clifford noted, committed to "the liberal cause." Fortas, who evaded and lied when questioned about his relationship with Johnson, had advised the president to sponsor a domestic program focusing on education, unemployment, urban development, health, and culture. As a justice he championed the cause of outsiders, taking positions that placed him on the left wing of the Court. He believed in positive government action to protect the powerless and, while cooperating behind the scenes with the FBI to protect its wiretapping and keep Brennan from appointing a former Berkeley student radical, Michael Tigar, as his clerk, publicly championed the rights of dissident minorities against the state As his biographer, Laura Kalman, writes, "Few symbolized liberalism's promise and paradoxes as well as Abe Fortas." Nor did anyone better epitomize the Warren Court's activism. Fortas considered law indeterminate and did not really care much about it. He sought consistently to legalize his personal prejudices, instructing clerks to "decorate" unsupported opinions with precedents that would rationalize the results. Strangely, the only member of the Court who disliked him was Black; the venerable activist considered Fortas an unprincipled opportunist. His other colleagues liked and respected him, and because he had been the managing partner of his law firm, he was well qualified to serve as their chief.[9]

The record they had compiled, however, made his nomination a lightning rod. In a Gallup Poll conducted during the last week of June, a mere 8 percent of respondents rated the Supreme Court's performance as excellent and only 28 percent considered it even good. In contrast, 21 percent thought it was poor and 32 percent viewed it as only fair. Confirmation hearings before the Senate Judiciary Committee, which began on July 11, suggested why the Court's popularity was so low. After some squabbling over whether there really was a vacancy and after an appearance by Griffin, who lambasted the administration for making partisan, lame-duck appointments and conjured up the specter of cronyism, Fortas himself testified. Declining to follow the examples of Edward White and Harlan Stone, who, when elevated from associate justice to chief justice, had announced it would be inappropriate for them to appear before the committee, the nominee subjected himself to four days of interrogation. Senators grilled him not only about his relationship with Johnson but also about rulings with which they disagreed. Under questioning by Eastland, Fortas dishonestly denied believing that the Supreme Court should spearhead social, economic, and political change. Apparently unconvinced, Ervin repeatedly condemned the Warren Court for legislating.[10]

He also criticized its criminal-procedure decisions, but it was Strom Thurmond (R-S.C.) who mounted the most aggressive attack on those. Thurmond fumed about *Mallory*, ripping a ruling he charged had freed an admitted rapist on a technicality and shackled law enforcement. He demanded to know whether such decisions would not encourage the commission of more rapes and other serious crimes. Stunned by a vicious assault that was based on a case decided eight years before he joined the Court, Fortas elected not to answer Thurmond. Although he had debated decisions with Ervin, the nominee now insisted that discussing them would be inconsistent with constitutional limitations on members of the Court. "I cannot respond to questions of this sort, because I cannot and I will not be an instrument by which the separation of powers specified in our Constitution is called into question," Fortas responded when asked about the reapportionment rulings. Thurmond, more concerned about crime than constitutional boundaries, asked the nominee whether Supreme Court decisions had not made it "terribly difficult to protect society from crime and criminals" and whether they were not "among the principal reasons for the turmoil and near-revolutionary conditions which prevail in our country, and especially in Washington?" After pausing for several moments to compose himself, an angry Fortas answered, "No." A junior-high principal who had charged the Court the previous month with sharing the "responsibility to a great extent for the terrible violence that we have in this country because of their decisions which have greatly handicapped law enforcement" would not have agreed with his answer.[11]

The Warren Court's obscenity decisions also drew heavy fire. When Thornberry testified on July 20, only four senators showed up, and he left Washington convinced he would not be confirmed. The attention the nominee should have received went instead to James Clancy of the Citizens for Decent Literature, whose appearance Thurmond had arranged. After examining fifty-two of the Court's recent obscenity decisions, Clancy told the committee, he had concluded that in forty-nine of them Fortas had cast the deciding vote to hold something was not obscene. He brought with him a thirty-eight-minute slide show, containing highlights of some pornographic movies the Court's rulings had allowed to be shown, as well as numerous pictures from pornographic magazines, and one pornographic film he found particularly offensive. Clancy and Thurmond volunteered to arrange a private screening for lawmakers and the press, an offer many senators accepted. Clancy charged that Fortas's actions were responsible for the "release of the greatest deluge of hard-core pornography ever witnessed by any nation," a flood of filth that had caused "a pronounced breakdown in public morals and general movement toward sexual degeneracy throughout our nation." He badly misrepresented the nominee's position on obscenity, but Fortas's earlier refusal to discuss cases prevented him from mounting an effective defense. He declined Eastland's offer to let him testify again. Both Dirksen and Majority Leader Mike Mansfield (D-Mont.) felt the "dirty movies" issue had hurt Fortas badly.[12]

Also "hurtful," they agreed, were revelations concerning the fifteen thousand dollars Fortas had received for conducting a summer seminar for seventeen students at American University's Washington College of Law. By the time Congress adjourned for the party conventions, the nomination was clearly in trouble, despite the fact that, as Fortas reported to Warren, "Newspapers covering the entire political spectrum have carried editorials favorable to our cause." A filibuster appeared likely, and Johnson had only fifty-seven votes, not enough to impose cloture. In early August Eastland visited LBJ in Texas, informing him bluntly that Fortas could not be confirmed. Although the president refused to give up the fight, the testimony that Dean B. J. Tennery gave when the confirmation hearings resumed on September 13 rendered it hopeless. Tennery revealed that the money to pay for the seminar had come from several wealthy businessmen. He was less than completely successful in

disguising the fact that it had been solicited from them by Fortas's former law partner, Paul Porter, who had actually conceived the idea of having the justice teach this
class (on which he did very little work) as a way of supplementing his income. Kentucky
Republicans Thruston Morton and John Sherman Cooper immediately deserted the
nominee. On September 20 GOP whip Hugh Scott of Pennsylvania informed the
White House that the revelations about the fifty-thousand-dollar fee "had struck a
damaging blow to the Fortas case;" his mail was now running very heavily against the
nomination.[13]

That bad news arrived on the same day that the Judiciary Committee endorsed
Fortas by an eleven-to-six margin. Scott and one other Republican joined nine Democrats in the majority, while three GOP senators backed Eastland, Ervin, and McClellan. The administration's victory in the committee would be meaningless unless it
could round up enough votes for cloture. When the nomination reached the Senate
floor on September 25, the opposition launched a filibuster, ignoring the Lawyers
Committee on Supreme Court Nominations—consisting of 151 attorneys from forty-
nine states, including seven former ABA presidents, numerous present and past state
bar association officers, and twenty law school deans—which had condemned this
tactic in a September 11 press release. The *Washington Post* editorialized that "only
the crassest political partisanship could explain a failure to confirm the President's
nomination," and a survey of 476 newspapers across the country, conducted in late
August, found 47.5 percent supported Fortas, while only 24 percent opposed him,
and 28.5 percent were neutral. Even after the American University revelations, polls
still showed the public favored confirmation by a margin of two to one. The mail of
many senators was running heavily against Fortas, however, and on September 26 the
filibuster received a major boost when Dirksen announced he would not support cloture. When Mansfield called for a vote on October 1, only forty-five of eighty-eight
senators voted to cut off debate.[14]

That night Fortas asked Johnson to "withdraw my nomination as Chief Justice.
Continued efforts to secure confirmation . . . , even if ultimately successful, would
result in a continuation of the attacks upon the Court which have characterized the
filibuster." The following day, Johnson announced with "deep regret" that he was withdrawing the Fortas nomination. On October 3 Thornberry also gave up the fight.[15]

He and Fortas were not the only losers in the confirmation battle. The Warren
Court had suffered defeat as well. Explaining to constituents why he intended to vote
against the two men, Senator Norris Cotton (R-N.H.) declared it was "because confirmation of these two nominations . . . will perpetuate the policies of the Warren
Court for many years to come, and that, in my opinion, would be a catastrophe."
Thurmond condemned Fortas as a "protégé of Earl Warren," citing as a reason why
he should not be confirmed the fact that he had voted with the chief justice in 97
out of 112 cases during the 1966–67 term. Political scientists stress that issues alone
do not explain Fortas's defeat, and it is no doubt true, as Kalman has argued, that
some other individual closely identified with the jurisprudence of the Warren Court,
such as Brennan or Goldberg, could have been confirmed. Fortas carried the added

burden of a close association with an increasingly unpopular president. "By the summer of 1968," as Kalman notes, "liberals on the Supreme Court and in the White House were on the defensive." At least in part because of persistent attacks by hostile politicians, the left-leaning justices had become estranged from a substantial segment of the public, which included "a large, vocal minority eager to discredit the Court in every conceivable way." Such critics welcomed any excuse to retaliate for the creation of what a Californian man had characterized more than a year earlier in a letter to Douglas as "a system of jurisprudence . . . that has made us the most lawless country in the world." He insisted that if Americans had a chance to vote on whether or not to retain the members of the Supreme Court, "seven or eight of the present incumbents would be out of their sinecure by a 3 to 1 majority." Life tenure precluded such a referendum, but the Fortas nomination afforded foes of the Warren Court an opportunity to reiterate grievances, vent animosities, and inflict a stinging political defeat on the liberal-activist tribunal they hated.[16]

The irony, of course, was that Fortas's withdrawal prolonged the life of the Court its enemies despised. When the new term opened on Monday, October 7, Earl Warren was still in the center seat. Presidential aide DeVier Pierson had recommended "sending up another nomination," reasoning that Nixon's views made it "highly unlikely that he would pick a successor in the Warren tradition" and that consequently the White House had everything to gain and nothing to lose by trying again. Senator Ernest Gruening (D-Alaska) urged Johnson to appoint Goldberg, predicting he would be quickly confirmed. On October 10, however, the president announced both that he would not send another name to the Senate and that Warren had agreed to remain in office. The Chief did not withdraw his conditional letter of resignation. Doing that would look terrible, he believed, because it would create the impression that he had decided to retire only to keep Nixon from appointing his successor. Unwilling to tarnish his reputation for rectitude and personal morality, Warren now presided as the lamest of lame ducks, subject to instant removal by the president who took office in January.[17]

That, the chief justice realized, put the Court in a bad position. It might well have heard arguments in half of the cases on the docket before his successor was nominated and confirmed, but the decisions in most of them would not yet have been announced. These cases would have to be resolved by an eight-man Court, creating the possibility of four-to-four splits that would necessitate reargument in the following term or dispositions that failed to resolve the legal issues they raised. Consequently, in late November, after Nixon scored his anticipated victory, the chief justice extended a feeler to the president-elect through his son-in-law, John Daly, a vice president of ABC News, who discussed the situation with the incoming secretary of state, William Rogers, during a round of golf. Warren's wishes corresponded with Nixon's needs, for the president-elect was busy filling cabinet and sub-cabinet posts and was not anxious to rush into the appointment of a chief justice. On December 4, he telephoned Warren to ask him formally to serve until the end of the term, so as to avoid serious disruption in the work of the Supreme Court. Observing "the polite rituals of official Washington," Nixon also asked the retiring chief justice to swear him in. On a cold, raw January 20, 1969, Earl Warren administered the oath of office to his bitter political enemy.[18]

Then the Chief returned to the work of the Supreme Court. Like the new administration, it was wrestling with issues generated by the Vietnam War. For example, in *O'Callahan v. Parker* (1969) the Court addressed the reach of court-martial jurisdiction over hundreds of thousands of young draftees. The justices threw out convictions of an army sergeant for attempted rape, housebreaking, and assault with intent to commit rape in an incident that had occurred in a Honolulu hotel room when the defendant was out of uniform and on an evening pass. With Douglas writing the opinion and Harlan dissenting for himself, Stewart, and White, the Court held that court-martial jurisdiction extended only to crimes committed by members of the armed forces that were "service connected." The justices originally voted six to three to decide the case the other way. Harlan wrote what was supposed to be the opinion of the Court, only to lose his majority after he refused to modify a draft declaring that any court-martial of a member of the armed forces on any charge was constitutional. One of those who deserted him, eventually supporting what had started out as a Douglas dissent, was Fortas. He could not, he said, "agree that every person on active duty in the Armed forces can be tried by military courts for every offense whatever, wherever committed, merely because he is in the military."[19]

The Warren Court had already acted to excuse some young men from even serving in the military. In 1965 it extended conscientious-objector status to potential conscripts to whom Congress rather clearly had not intended to grant it. Section 6(j) of the Universal Military Training and Service Act excused from combatant training and service in the armed forces all persons who by virtue of their religious training and belief were conscientiously opposed to participation in war in any form. The act went on to define "religious training and belief" as "an individual's belief in a relation to a Supreme Being involving duties superior to those arising from any human relation, but . . . not . . . essentially political, sociological, or philosophical views or a merely personal moral code." In *United States v. Seeger* (1965) the Court interpreted this language as entitling two men to be treated as conscientious objectors, even though they did not belong to any organized religion and one of them rather clearly was an agnostic. Clark's opinion took the position that when Congress used the expression "Supreme Being" rather than the word "God," it had merely been clarifying the meaning of religious training and belief so as to embrace all religions. "We believe," he wrote, "that under this construction the test of belief 'in relation to a Supreme Being' is whether a given belief that is sincere and meaningful occupies a place in the life of its possessor parallel to that filled by the orthodox belief in God of one who clearly qualifies for the exemption." The Court gave section 6(j) this implausible reading in order to avoid holding it unconstitutional. Black, Harlan, and Stewart considered the statute's discrimination in favor of those who believed in God an equal protection violation, while Warren and Stewart thought it offended the Establishment Clause. Nobody, however, wanted to invalidate section 6(j) and leave the nation without any draft exemption for those conscientiously opposed to military service. Harlan thought the Court would have to face the constitutional issue, but Clark suggested this could be avoided by interpreting the statute as simply requiring religious belief and treating the reference to a Supreme Being as adding nothing to that requirement. Warren assigned him the case, and their colleagues persuaded Harlan and Goldberg not to publish opinions that raised the constitutional issue. In a concurrence, Douglas stated publicly what all had acknowledged in private: unless section 6(j) were given the implausible interpretation Clark had imposed upon it, a decision holding the statute unconstitutional would be difficult to avoid.[20]

Three years later, with Douglas as its spokesman, the Court gave a restrictive interpretation to another provision of the Selective Service laws, thereby foiling vindictive draft boards that were bent on punishing registrants who protested conscription and the war. James Ostereich had received the exemption that section 6(g) of the Military Selective Service Act of 1967 authorized for "students preparing for the ministry." When he turned in his registration certificate to express his opposition to the war, however, his board declared him delinquent and changed his classification to the induction-eligible 1-A. After losing an administrative appeal of this reclassification, Ostereich filed suit in a Wyoming federal court. Its dismissal of his complaint was affirmed by the Tenth Circuit. Both decisions relied on section 10(b)(3) of the Selective Service Act, which said that there should be no pre-induction judicial review of a registrant's classification or processing. That law required a draftee seeking judicial review of some action of his draft board either to raise its alleged illegality as a defense to a criminal prosecution or to accept induction and then seek release from the armed forces by petitioning for a writ of habeas corpus. The Supreme Court reversed, ruling that pre-induction judicial review was not precluded in Ostereich's case because Congress had not authorized Selective Service to deny a registrant an unequivocal statutory exemption to which he was entitled because of conduct unrelated to that exemption. Douglas added that delinquency proceedings might not be used for punitive purposes. Draft boards could not be permitted to become "freewheeling agencies meeting out their brand of justice in a vindictive manner." The decision was unanimous, but the original vote had been only five to four in Ostereich's favor. A concurring opinion by Harlan indicated some justices had gone along with Douglas only because they believed section 10(b)(3) posed potentially serious constitutional problems if it were interpreted as precluding registrants from raising a constitutional issue in some competent forum. The Court was more concerned with ensuring that Congress would not deprive the judiciary of jurisdiction conferred on it by Article 3 than with the abuse of antiwar protesters by freewheeling draft boards.[21]

Indeed, despite its otherwise strong commitment to safeguarding freedom of expression, the later Warren Court was not particularly protective of protest against the Vietnam War. The Supreme Court shared the public's antipathy for the tactics of many protesters. Antiwar demonstrations were often chaotic, and many Americans, viewing them as antithetical to social peace, reacted strongly against these disruptive protests. A 1967 poll disclosed that those with unfavorable opinions of antiwar demonstrations outnumbered those who approved of them by a three-to-one margin. Indeed, 70 percent of Americans considered them to be acts of disloyalty. In a 1969 book, *Points of Rebellion,* Douglas defended the youthful activists who carried their fight against the Vietnam War into the streets, insisting that even violent dissent was protected by the First Amendment. Fortas strongly disagreed, writing in his own 1968 book, *Concerning Dissent and Civil Disobedience,* that violence could not be tolerated and that to survive, liberty must be restrained. Black also found the tactics of antiwar activists unacceptable, fearing they might trigger a public reaction that would destroy free speech and lead to repressive rule. As far as he was concerned, while the First Amendment afforded absolute protection to pure speech, it did not protect conduct at all, even when engaged in for communicative purposes. Warren, who believed demonstrations might shake the "Establishment" out of its complacency, was less hostile toward them than some of his colleagues, but he too deplored violent protest.[22]

The type of antiwar activist who appealed to the Chief and his colleagues was Julian Bond. Orderly and law abiding, Bond was also black. In 1965 he became one of the first two African Americans since 1907 to win election to the Georgia legislature. The state House of Representatives voted 184 to 12 not to seat him, giving as its reason his endorsement of a statement issued by SNCC, an organization of which he was the communications director, which had denounced the Vietnam War and expressed support for men who refused to submit to the draft. Warren viewed Bond as a victim of racial discrimination, and his colleagues probably did also. Rejecting Georgia's contention that the federal judiciary lacked jurisdiction to review a decision by its legislature not to seat someone, the Chief declared that by disqualifying Bond "because of his statements," the House had "violated [his] right of free expression under the First Amendment," the "central commitment" of which was that "debate on public issues should be uninhibited, robust and wide-open." Although Stewart and Clark had voted against Bond in conference, neither dissented.[23]

Among the factors that made the young legislator appealing to the justices was his insistence that he had never counseled nor advocated that anyone burn a draft card. In *United States v. O'Brien* (1968), the Warren Court rejected the constitutional argument of an antiwar activist who had resorted to this common but very unpopular form of protest against conscription and the war. Draft-card burning violated a 1965 statute that criminalized the knowing destruction or mutilation of a Selective Service certificate. Senator Thurmond and Representative L. Mendel Rivers (D-S.C.) had introduced this measure because of their outrage at public draft-card burning. It passed overwhelmingly, winning adoption in the House by a 392 to 1 margin and in the Senate on a voice vote. A few months later, David Paul O'Brien and three companions were convicted of violating the new law by igniting their registration certificates on the steps of the South Boston courthouse. The First Circuit overturned their convictions, holding that the statute unconstitutionally abridged freedom of expression. Seeking to persuade the Supreme Court to affirm its decision, O'Brien's lawyers argued that the conduct the law sought to punish was "a peaceful act of symbolic speech." Warren, who thought there were plenty of other ways to protest the war, was rcluctant to accept their contention, asking during oral argument whether a soldier in Vietnam who broke his rifle in front of others would be engaging in constitutionally protected expression. Two days later at the Court's conference, the Chief argued strongly against O'Brien's position. His colleagues all supported him, although Douglas did urge disposing of the case with a short per curiam opinion.[24]

Instead, Warren assigned *O'Brien* to himself and set out to produce a full-blown defense of the statute's constitutionality. He faced behind-the-scenes resistance from the Court's clerks, who belonged to the same generation as the defendant, shared his views about Vietnam, and "engaged in virtual guerilla warfare against the decision." They sought to make the opinion as weak as possible. The Chief added to his problems by telling the one to whom he assigned the case, Larry Simon, that he wanted to hold draft-card burning was not speech at all for First Amendment purposes. Since the Court had treated other types of conduct as protected expression, Simon found it necessary to create a very narrow exception for those kinds that had an immediately harmful impact not arising from their communicative effect. Only Black found his draft opinion persuasive. Harlan considered it "illogical, unsound, and in conflict with prior decisions of this Court." "I am unable," he wrote, "to endorse a doctrine which dictates that all . . . nonverbal modes of expression are entirely without the ambit of the First Amendment." The proper approach, Harlan believed, was balancing. Although Warren had told Simon he wanted none of that in his opinion, Harlan's views eventually prevailed. After weeks passed without anyone but Black joining him, the Chief asked Simon what they could do to attract support. The clerk recommended saying draft-card burning could be punished because "even though speech, it is not protected speech." Warren adopted his suggestion, along with Brennan's that they treat such conduct as within the scope of the First Amendment but then hold that a compelling governmental interest justified regulating it.[25]

The final version of his opinion conceded for the sake of argument that the "alleged communicative element in O'Brien's conduct" might be sufficient to bring the First Amendment into play, but added: "This Court has held that when speech and 'nonspeech' elements are combined in the same course of conduct, a sufficiently important governmental interest in regulating the nonspeech element can justify incidental limitations on First Amendment freedoms." The regulation in question had to be within the constitutional power of the government, Warren said, and must further an "important or substantial [but not necessarily 'compelling'] governmental interest" unrelated to the suppression of expression. If it met those criteria and the "incidental restriction on alleged First Amendment freedoms" was no greater than necessary, the regulation was constitutional. The 1965 law "meets all of these requirements," he maintained, "and consequently . . . O'Brien can be constitutionally convicted of violating it." Warren insisted that the draft-card mutilation statute was designed to assist Congress in raising and supporting armies, brushing aside evidence that with respect to the accomplishment of that objective, it added little to regulations already on the books. He refused to consider legislative history, which revealed that the real purpose of those responsible for the law's enactment was to suppress an unpopular form of expression. Only Douglas dissented, and he devoted his opinion to arguing that the draft was unconstitutional because Congress had not declared war in Vietnam.[26]

Although not even Douglas was willing to treat draft-card burning as constitutionally protected expression, a few months later the Court held that the wearing of black armbands at public secondary schools was. Fortas, White, Black, and Harlan opposed granting certiorari in *Tinker v. Des Moines School District* (1969), but the vote following oral argument was seven to two in favor of the three students who had been suspended for engaging in this form of symbolic protest against the war. All but Black and Harlan thought school officials had violated their First Amendment rights. Two factors appear to have influenced the majority. One is that while prohibiting the wearing of black armbands to express opposition to U.S. involvement in Vietnam, school officials had permitted students to display a variety of mainstream political and religious symbols and even to wear Iron Crosses. Such blatant discrimination outraged Warren and troubled Brennan, Douglas, and Stewart. Even more significant was the complete lack of any evidence supporting the district's contention that the wearing of black armbands would disrupt Des Moines's schools. White emphasized this during conference discussions of the case, and other justices rallied around his suggestion that they make it the basis of their decision. Fortas's opinion for the Court stressed that the record failed to "demonstrate any facts which might reasonably have led school authorities to forecast substantial disruption of or material interference with school activities" and that "no disturbances or disorders on the school premises in fact occurred." Any student conduct, in or out of class, that "materially disrupts classwork or involves substantial disorder or invasion of the rights of others is, of course, not immunized by the constitutional guarantee of freedom of speech," he added. Although signing Fortas's opinion, both Stewart and White wrote separately, the former to fault him for his "uncritical assumption" that children generally enjoyed the same First Amendment rights as adults, and the latter to emphasize that the Court continued to recognize a distinction between communicating by words and communicating by conduct. Since Fortas had disregarded that distinction, Black was bound to dissent, but what he published was an emotional jeremiad that railed against "uncontrolled and uncontrollable liberty," which he saw as the "enemy of domestic peace." Black, whose grandson had recently been suspended from a New Mexico high school for helping to write and distribute an underground newspaper, lamented that "groups of students all over the land are already running loose, conducting break-ins, sit-ins, lie-ins, and smash-ins." Apparently wanting no part of this intemperate tirade, the courtly Harlan filed his own short dissent. While Black's rhetoric was extreme, most of his colleagues shared both his concerns about the anarchic bent of student antiwar protest and his reluctance to give it much First Amendment protection.[27]

They reacted very differently to protest against racial discrimination. *Street v. New York* (1969) involved flag burning, a tactic often associated with antiwar demonstrations, but the defendant was a black man who had ignited Old Glory in angry reaction to the shooting of James Meredith during a 1966 civil rights march. While burning the flag, Sidney Street declared, "We don't need no damn flag" and "If they let that happen to Meredith we don't need an American flag." He was convicted of violating a New York statute that made it a misdemeanor to "mutilate, deface, defile, or defy, trample upon, or cast contempt upon either by words or act" any flag of the United States in public. Although reaching the Court in December 1967, it was held over until after *O'Brien* was decided, apparently because this case too involved symbolic expression. Following the belated oral argument, Warren told his colleagues that as far as he was concerned, public flag burning was conduct, not speech or symbolic speech, and states could punish it to prevent riots. Explaining his position to his clerks, the Chief declared, "I'm just not going to vote in favor of burning the American flag." Only Black supported him. The majority backed Harlan, who pointed out that in light of the wording of the New York statute, and because Street had both burned the flag and expressed contempt for it orally, one could not be certain whether he had been punished for his conduct or his speech. Fortas, who had held in *Brown v. Mississippi* that library sit-ins were a form of protected expression but later insisted draft-card burning was not because it violated a valid law, initially supported the majority, probably because this case involved civil rights, rather than the war. After circulating a concurrence, which framed the issue as whether Street might constitutionally be convicted for his speech, independent of the flag burning, however, he abandoned that opinion in March 1969. Now taking the position "that the conviction was for the conduct of publicly burning the flag and not for the words used," Fortas asserted that "the First Amendment does not preclude a State from enacting a statute making it a criminal offense publicly to mutilate, deface, or defile the flag." "Protest does not exonerate lawlessness," he wrote in a dissenting opinion. Warren, Black, and White (another defecter from the original majority) also dissented.[28]

When the cause was civil rights and the powerful symbolism of the flag was not involved, even the *Street* dissenters were willing to give First Amendment protection to protest activity, as *Gregory v. Chicago* (1969) demonstrated. Comedian Dick Gregory had led a march through Chicago to express dissatisfaction with the slow pace of school desegregation there. When a hostile crowd menaced the marchers, the police asked them to leave. The protesters refused and were then arrested for violation of the city's disorderly conduct ordinance—despite the fact that, "Gregory and his group [had done] all in their power to maintain order." The conference vote was nine to zero to reverse the convictions. Warren proposed basing the decision on the *Thompson v. Louisville* "no evidence" rationale the Court had used so often in southern civil rights cases. Although the others agreed, Black, to whom the Chief assigned the case, produced an expansive opinion that focused on what he viewed as the vagueness and overbreadth of the disorderly conduct ordinance. While acknowledging the important role that street marches had played in promoting desegregation, Black asserted that the power of government to regulate expressive conduct was broader than its power to regulate pure speech and stressed that if this were not so, "anyone with a complaint" could "do anything he pleased, wherever he pleased and whenever he pleased," with horrific consequences for others. Only Douglas signed his opinion. Fortas, Harlan, and Stewart all prepared concurrences that criticized its breadth. Warren circulated one based on the "no evidence" rationale that attracted so much support that it became the opinion of the Court, leaving Black to publish his lengthy essay as a concurrence.[29]

The commitment of the dying Warren Court to black civil rights proved strong enough to protect even the angry rhetoric of an African American whose intemperate outburst damned not only racism but also conscription and the war. *Watts v. United States* (1969) was a prosecution for the offense of threatening the life of the president. During a public rally on the Washington Monument grounds, Robert Watts declared, "I have already received my draft classification as 1-A and I have got to report for my physical this Monday morning. I am not going. If they ever make me carry a rifle, the first man I want to get in my sights is LBJ." But Watts, an eighteen-year-old African American, also proclaimed, "They are not going to make me kill my black brothers," and he spoke all of these words during a discussion of police brutality. The Court reversed his conviction with a per curiam opinion, written by Marshall, that declared the government had failed to prove his utterance was a true threat. Marshall characterized it as mere "political hyperbole" and suggested that interpreting the threatening-the-life-of-the-president statute as being applicable to such speech would pose First Amendment problems. He concluded that Watts was guilty only of "a kind of crude offensive method of stating political opposition to the President." Fortas, who called this a "trivial case" (Watts had received only a suspended sentence), objected to deciding at all the issues Marshall discussed. So did Stewart and Black, but no one supported punishing Watts for his outburst.[30]

Pure antiwar protest having no racial dimension was another matter, as illustrated by *Gunn v. University Committee to End the War in Vietnam*. The plaintiffs in that case were several demonstrators who, after being attacked by a hostile crowd when they arrived to protest a 1967 speech by the president near Ft. Hood, Texas, were arrested for disturbing the peace. The county attorney requested dismissal of the charges when it was discovered that the alleged offense had taken place on a federal military reservation, but the protesters filed suit, seeking an injunction against future enforcement of the statute they had been accused of violating. A three-judge district court held the statute was unconstitutionally overbroad, and Warren managed to get a majority to affirm its ruling. He assigned the case to Fortas, who left the Court before his opinion could be published, but not before Stewart and White had drafted dissents. "Surely if recent history has taught us anything," Stewart wrote, "it [is] that noise is not necessarily speech—that sound and fury can as often stifle free expression as promote it." The sentiments he voiced explained the contrasting fates of *Gunn* and the landmark free speech case *Brandenburg v. Ohio*, on which Fortas was also working when he resigned. Brennan finished up that opinion, which the Court issued as a per curiam. *Gunn* had to be set down for reargument.[31]

The Warren Court had difficultly deciding cases arising out of demonstrations against the Vietnam War and often resolved them in ways inconsistent with its libertarian image. It would not even consider cases challenging the legality of the war. Ten times between the spring of 1967 and the end of the 1968–69 term, litigants seeking a ruling that the Vietnam conflict was unlawful asked the Supreme Court to hear their cases. In every single instance it refused to grant review. "I thought the Court did a great disservice to the nation in not resolving this, the most important issue of the sixties to reach [it]," Douglas wrote later.[32]

The Court's "strange silence" on this issue did not reflect support for the war, which a solid majority of its members opposed. The only one who was clearly a "hawk" was Fortas. Although he opposed the initial decision to commit American ground troops to Vietnam and often suggested alternatives to approaches that Johnson adopted, he worked faithfully to execute LBJ's Vietnam policies. "In his unofficial capacity as friend, counselor and strategist," Larry Berman writes, "Fortas supported an unrestrained policy of stepping up the war." In an October 14, 1967, memorandum, he pointed out that backing for the military effort in Southeast Asia was eroding and urged the administration to "take or make an early opportunity to state emphatically, that we're going to see this through to a successful conclusion." White may have shared Fortas's hawkish views, although there is not much evidence to indicate where he stood on Vietnam.[33]

There is a great deal of evidence showing that most of their colleagues were, or at least became, "doves." For example, in 1964, although he was an old friend of LBJ, Douglas "gave the President hell" about his Vietnam policy. In private Black characterized the war as "insanity" and "the worst thing that has ever happened to this country." When Fortas wrote an opinion that referred to what was going on in Southeast Asia as a "war," Stewart protested so vociferously that his hawkish colleague was forced to substitute euphemisms, such as "hostilities" and "conflict."[34]

Like a majority of his Court, Earl Warren became an opponent of the Vietnam War. The Chief Justice liked and admired Johnson, and initially he supported his Southeast Asia policy, convinced the White House would not have gone to war unless it was necessary and in the national interest to do so. By the fall of 1966, however, Warren had become concerned about the escalating hostilities and the effect they were having on America's standing in other countries, especially those with nonwhite populations. During 1967, as both the war and domestic opposition to it heated up, he began to entertain serious doubts about Johnson's policies. In August, when the president asked him to visit Vietnam on a fact-finding mission, the chief justice declined, saying the judiciary should not entangled itself in a political issue.[35]

David Currie applauds Warren and his colleagues for staying out of the dispute over Vietnam, commending the Court for its "realistic awareness of the practical limits of judicial power." Rodric Schoen disagrees. "No valid or legitimate reasons explain or justify" judicial silence on this subject, he contends. Furthermore, "The practical legal effect of the Court's silence was to validate the Government's prosecution of the war." The Warren Court's caution on Vietnam doubtless reflected the ambivalence of a public that wanted out of the war but was unwilling to accept the Communist takeover that would have followed immediate withdrawal. Not even the Court's liberal allies could agree on how to cure this national cancer. Furthermore, as Schoen concedes, by refusing even to hear cases attacking the legality of the war, the justices avoided placing a stamp of approval on it. "Silence produces no precedents," he notes. The government had won all of these cases below, generally because trial judges dismissed them under the political question doctrine. By repeatedly denying certiorari, the Supreme Court let the government win individual disputes and avoided criticism for tying up military operations, without legitimizing what was going on in Vietnam. The Court kept its options open, forcing the administration to reckon constantly with the possibility that someday its war might be declared unconstitutional. Ironically, however, by failing to render a decision implementing the policy preferences of its members, the Supreme Court missed an opportunity to require affirmative congressional authorization of future military operations in Vietnam, and thus a chance not only to facilitate early termination of the war but to ensure that the decision about when and how the United States would extricate itself from the quagmire in Southeast Asia was actually made by the people's elected representatives.[36]

Adding to the irony was the stark contrast between this questionable exercise of judicial restraint and the Court's advanced liberal activism in other areas. During Warren's final term "the liberal bloc . . . exercised almost complete control over [the Supreme Court's] decisions." Free speech rulings reflected this dominance. In *Brandenburg v. Ohio* (1969) the Court announced almost casually that advocacy of violence or violation of the law could be punished only if it were both directed at inciting or producing imminent lawless action and actually likely to do so. Because *Brandenburg*'s incitement requirement precluded censorship of all but the most extreme forms of radical political expression, it was "of great significance." As Samuel Walker reports, "After a fifty-year struggle, the ACLU had finally persuaded the Court to accept its view of the First Amendment." *Stanley v. Georgia* (1969) looked revolutionary. Although under fierce attack for its obscenity decisions, the Court held that the First Amendment prohibited making the private possession of obscene material a crime. *Stanley* seemed "to sabotage the *Roth* premise that obscenity is *per se* outside the protection of the First Amendment"; hence, Harry Kalven notes, it generated expectations that its logic would "inevitably extend beyond the possession to the distribution of obscene materials."[37]

The Court staked out advanced positions on equal protection as well as free speech. *Wells v. Rockefeller* (1969) and *Kirkpatrick v. Preisler* (1969) addressed the meaning of equality in the context of congressional redistricting. The New York legislature had divided that state into seven regions and subdivided each of those into districts with equal populations. The populations of the resulting districts varied from 6.5 percent above to 6.6 percent below the statewide mean. Missouri had come even closer to absolute equality, adopting a redistricting plan with variances ranging only from 3.13 percent above the mean to 2.84 percent below it. The Court held that neither plan satisfied *Wesberry v. Sanders*'s requirement that a state's congressional districts come as close as practicable to population equality. It rejected Missouri's argument that some fixed numerical or percentage variance could be considered *de minimis*, and hence in compliance with *Wesberry*. Adopting the position Warren had advocated in conference, Brennan wrote that the burden was on the state to present acceptable reasons for any variations from absolute equality. His opinions had the support of only five justices, for Harlan, Stewart, and White dissented, and Fortas concurred separately in order to reject the rule Brennan articulated. Marshall, who provided the crucial fifth vote, held back from joining Brennan because of lobbying by one of his clerks (who felt New York's recognition of regional interests was proper) and because he did not want to reverse a former Second Circuit colleague in *Wells*. Warren persuaded him to endorse Brennan's opinions by emphasizing the importance of defining the scope of the 1964 reapportionment rulings before new appointments changed the balance of power within the Court on reapportionment issues.[38]

Like *Kirkpatrick* and *Wells*, *Kramer v. Union Free School District* (1969) exhibited a commitment to the promotion of equality. There the Court struck down a New York law that restricted the right to vote in certain school districts to residents who owned or leased taxable real estate or had children enrolled in the public schools. Warren, who contended in conference that this statute embodied "a classification not supported by proper reasons," spoke for a six-to-three majority in holding that it violated the Equal Protection Clause. Laws that distributed the franchise were not entitled to the presumption of constitutionality generally afforded to state statutes, he declared, but must be given "close and exacting examination." Black thought only racial classifications, which the Constitution explicitly prohibited, should receive such special treatment, but Warren argued that measures restricting the franchise also had to be more than merely rational. Whenever a statutory provision "grants the right to vote to some bona fide residents of requisite age and citizenship and denies [it] to others, the Court must determine whether the exclusions are necessary to promote a compelling state interest," he insisted. New York claimed it was trying to limit participation in school elections to those primarily interested in or affected by them, but Warren thought its law failed to accomplish this purpose with sufficient precision to pass strict scrutiny. Dissenting for himself, Harlan, and Black, Stewart responded that no justification existed for using the exacting equal protection test the chief justice had employed.[39]

In its last term the Warren Court used the Due Process Clause as well as the Equal Protection Clause to promote its reform agenda. *Sniadach v. Family Finance Corporation* (1969) held that when a state allowed a creditor with no special need to do so to garnish an alleged debtor's wages prior to a hearing, it denied the debtor procedural due process in violation of the Fourteenth Amendment. In *Sniadach*, the Warren Court demonstrated yet again what Morton Horwitz characterizes as "its concern and support for the weak and the powerless." The decision rested on a realistic understanding of the hardship that garnishment works on poor defendants, who are often denied any realistic opportunity for a judicial hearing by the pressing need to settle with plaintiffs in order to mollify their bosses.[40]

Determined to ensure fundamental fairness for the weak and the powerless, during its final term the Warren Court went to the brink of making welfare a constitutional right. In the mid-1960s the Johnson administration launched a highly publicized "War on Poverty," and the Warren Court appeared poised to develop a doctrinal framework that would enable it to utilize aggressive judicial review to support this drive to eradicate economic inequality. Legal academics offered suggestions. In 1964–65 Yale's Charles Reich published two seminal articles arguing that was an entitlement to welfare. Poverty was an inevitable product of the existing economic structure, he maintained, and thus public assistance was in effect a government subsidy to the poor to compensate them for low wages and frequent unemployment, both of which were systemically necessary. A few years later Harvard's Frank Michelman suggested that the state had a duty to protect against certain hazards endemic in a society characterized by inequalities of wealth. Michelman advocated "minimum protection," which as applied to "economic hazards . . . would mean that persons are entitled to have certain wants satisfied—certain existing needs filled—by government." "The equal protection clause is the constitutional text which most naturally suggests itself to one who would claim a legal right to have certain wants satisfied out of the public treasury," he observed. Michelman seemed ambivalent about this equality approach, but its avoidance of the outright substitution of judicial for legislative policy-making (demanding only that legislatures distribute benefits evenhandedly) made it the most politically viable way for activist judges to assist the poor. The Warren Court, apparently recognizing this, carefully avoided holding that there was a fundamental right to welfare.[41]

Instead, in *Shapiro v. Thompson* the Supreme Court relied on equal protection analysis and the right to travel in striking down state and District of Columbia statutory restrictions that prohibited new residents from receiving welfare benefits until a year after their arrival. The Court did not reach this decision easily. Despite the fact that a former solicitor general, Archibald Cox, appropriately working without pay, represented the would-be welfare recipients, the Court voted five to four on May 3, 1968, to reverse the three-judge district courts in Connecticut, Pennsylvania, and Washington, D.C., that had held these durational residency requirements unconstitutional. All three programs had been approved by the secretary of Health, Education, and Welfare, acting pursuant to a provision of the Social Security Act that said he might not approve any plans requiring more than one year's residence. Warren viewed this provision as congressional authorization for what the three jurisdictions had done and told his colleagues he did not see how he could say their residency requirements were unconstitutional. The Chief prepared an opinion that expressed sympathy for the poor, but declared that "the relevant provisions of the Social Security Act . . . require a reversal of the judgments below." He denied that the requirements violated equal protection or impermissibly burdened a constitutional right to travel. Fortas drafted a dissent challenging the Chief on both grounds. It elicited a short note from Brennan, who had expressed reservations during the conference about his vote supporting the Chief, and he now announced that while he had difficulty with Fortas's equal protection argument, he could join his conclusion, and about everything he said, "that relates to burden on the right to travel." His defection left the Chief without a majority, and when the justices considered the case again at the June 13 conference, Stewart (part of the original minority) refused to vote, creating a four-to-four tie. The justices scheduled reargument for the following term.[42]

After reargument, the vote was five to three to affirm. Douglas, Fortas, Brennan, Marshall, and Stewart now comprised the majority, White passed, and only Harlan and Black supported Warren. With the Chief in the minority, Douglas assigned the case to Brennan. Despite previously rejecting the equal protection rationale, Brennan now made it the basis of his opinion. His approach differed from that Fortas had taken the year before, however. Fortas had argued that durational residency requirements violated the equal protection requirement because they discriminated invidiously between poor people and rich people who might wish to travel from one state to another. Brennan took the position that the requirements were unconstitutional because they treated differently two classes of needy families, those who had resided in a jurisdiction for more than one year and those who had not. This classification imposed a burden on the right to travel from one state to another, and thus mere rationality was not enough to make it constitutional. The "traditional criteria" did not apply because the right of interstate movement was fundamental. The constitutionality of this classification "must be judged by the stricter standard of whether it promotes a compelling state interest," Brennan wrote. "Under this standard, the waiting-period requirement clearly violates the Equal Protection Clause." His line of analysis troubled Stewart, who thought the compelling-interest approach should be reserved for cases involving racial discrimination and the First Amendment. Brennan was unwilling to abandon his reasoning in favor of invalidating the waiting-period requirements under the rationality test; the Court had never found any law that failed to pass that test, and its use in this case "might invite a flood of challenges to ordinary economic or social legislation having no relation to the right to travel or any other underlying constitutional right." Fortunately for Brennan, Stewart changed his mind, agreeing to join his opinion if he made certain minor modifications.[43]

He almost won the Chief over too. As a former governor, Warren felt strongly that waiting periods were essential to protect states that gave liberal benefits from being swamped with destitute migrants, but he also wanted to avoid the spectacle of a dissent by the chief justice in such an important case. He and Brennan worked out a compromise under which a paragraph stating categorically that Congress could not authorize the states to impose residency requirements would be deleted from the opinion of the Court, in return for which Warren would go along with an interpretation of the Social Security Act as not authorizing the imposition of one-year waiting periods. The other members of the majority rejected this deal, however, and Warren wound up dissenting. His opinion declared that, as far as he was concerned, the issue was simply whether Congress, acting under one of its enumerated powers, could impose minimal nationwide residency requirements or authorize the states to do so; he asserted his conviction that it could. Black, who at one point had agreed to Brennan's opinion, signed the Chief's instead. Harlan also dissented. While conceding that citizens had a constitutional right of interstate travel, he felt that a balancing approach should be used to determine if the right had been violated, and that if this test were applied, durational residency requirements for welfare would pass muster. Furthermore, Harlan disagreed strongly with Brennan's approach, faulting him for applying "an equal protection doctrine of relatively recent vintage: the rule that statutory classifications which either are based upon certain 'suspect' criteria or affect 'fundamental rights' will be held to deny equal protection unless justified by a 'compelling' interest." Harlan found the second branch of this doctrine particularly troublesome, because, "I know of nothing which entitles this Court to pick out particular human activities, characterize them as 'fundamental,' and give them added protection under an unusually stringent equal protection test," he wrote. Extending the compelling-interest test in such a manner would go a long way toward making the Supreme Court a superlegislature.[44]

Harlan directed that complaint to colleagues who were no longer inclined to show deference to legislators. In his final opinion, which he announced on June 16, 1969, Warren ordered the United States House of Representatives to seat a controversial member whom fellow congressmen wanted to exclude. The House had refused to seat African American representative Adam Clayton Powell after he would not supply information to a committee investigating his alleged misuse of House funds; additionally, he allegedly abused congressional immunity in order to avoid having to defend a lawsuit in his home state of New York. Powell and thirteen voters from his Harlem district, which had reelected him despite a subcommittee report alleging financial misconduct, sued Speaker John McCormack and four other representatives, contending that the House could properly exclude someone only for failure to meet the age, citizenship, and residency requirements for membership spelled out in Article 1, section 2, of the Constitution. A district court dismissed their suit, and the U.S. Court of Appeals for the District of Columbia Circuit affirmed its decision, but the Supreme Court reversed. It held in *Powell v. McCormack* (1969) that the House "was without power to exclude [Representative Powell] from membership," because in judging the eligibility of its members, Congress was "limited to the standing qualifications prescribed in the Constitution." Having concluded that the Court must speak through its chief because of the case's inherent potential for creating conflict with the legislative branch, Warren wrote the opinion himself. Although he was personally appalled by Powell's behavior and considered the flamboyant Harlem legislator a disgrace to his office and his race, the Chief insisted that Congress did not enjoy unreviewable power to deny a duly elected member his seat. Even Harlan considered the respondents' argument untenable, and no one disputed Warren's rejection of their contention that *Powell v. McCormack* posed a nonjusticiable "political question." Although conceding that deciding the matter could involve the judiciary in a potentially embarrassing confrontation with Congress, Warren insisted the American system of government required "that federal courts on occasion interpret the Constitution in a manner at variance with the construction given the document by another branch." This was such an occasion, for a fundamental principle of representative government was at stake, one Douglas characterized in a concurring opinion as "the basic integrity of the electoral process." When voters chose a person who was "repulsive to the Establishment in Congress," he asked, "by what constitutional authority can that group of electors be disfranchised?"[45]

"*Powell v. McCormack* makes the point that Congress, like all others, is bound by the Constitution," NYU professor Robert McKay declared. Hans Linde of the University of Oregon considered the Court's ruling a victory for constitutional democracy. Along with *Bond v. Floyd*, the *Powell* decision had established "the inapplicability of the political question doctrine in cases . . . involving infringements of constitutional rights," Donald Weckstein of the University of Connecticut believed. Yet, as Lewis Donald Asper and Sanford Jay Rosen of the University of Maryland reminded fans of the ruling, one could easily read too much into this challenge to congressional authority. *Powell* did not represent "abandonment by the Supreme Court of the position that there are some issues which can be dealt with only by political processes. Its reaction to challenges to the constitutionality of the Vietnam War testifies to that."[46]

One week after deciding *Powell,* and without ever having addressed that most momentous of constitutional issues, the Warren Court came to an official end. Two events had already been held to celebrate the Chief's retirement. On April 23 President Nixon honored Warren and his family at a White House dinner, attended by the entire Court, most of the cabinet, and practically everybody who was anybody in official Washington. Nixon toasted the chief justice warmly for his years of distinguished public service, and Warren responded to his old enemy's "decorous insincerity" with an expression of appreciation. "I approach retirement with no malice in my heart toward anyone," he proclaimed.[47]

That is highly unlikely, for the Warren Court had plenty of reason to be upset with the Nixon administration over *Alderman v. United States.* The Court's March 10 decision in that wiretapping case had agitated the Justice Department, because *Ivanov v. United States* and *Butenko v. United States,* which the Court had decided along with *Alderman,* both involved Soviet espionage. The Justice Department tried to persuade the Supreme Court to accept its own ex parte determination that none of the overheard conversations in these cases was arguably relevant to the prosecutions, but the Court remanded the cases to the district courts in which they originated for hearings on that issue. The Supreme Court also rejected the government's request that it be allowed to submit the transcripts to the trial judges for examination in camera. Attorney General John Mitchell, the solicitor general, and other Justice Department lawyers read the opinions in *Alderman* as requiring that the text of any conversation obtained by illegal electronic surveillance be turned over to the defense. That interpretation inspired concern, for Justice knew that illegal electronic surveillance had occurred not only in the two espionage cases but also in those of Jimmy Hoffa and heavyweight boxing champion Cassius Clay, who was being prosecuted for draft resistance. The Justice Department's reading of *Alderman* alarmed the FBI, the CIA, and the State Department, which knew that forty-six foreign embassies were under constant electronic surveillance and that others were bugged occasionally.[48]

On March 12 Jack Landau, the director of public relations for the Justice Department, contacted Brennan's office, asking to talk with him. During a conversation in his chambers, Landau revealed that Justice was concerned about a story the *New York Times* was going to run on the results that would flow from the *Butenko* and *Ivanov* decisions. He also informed Brennan about the electronic surveillance of the embassies (something Justice had mistakenly assumed the Court already knew because White, Fortas, and Marshall had all held positions in which they should have become aware of the practice). "He said that it would be most embarrassing to our foreign relations officially to admit the practice and therefore it could not be made the subject of a formal petition for rehearing or other document to be filed with the Court," Brennan recalled later. Concluding that it would be inappropriate for either the attorney general or the solicitor general to see the chief justice about the matter, Landau reported, Justice had decided to employ him to communicate its concerns. Justice considered itself at fault in the situation and was willing to help the Court avoid any congressional reaction that might lead to a constitutional amendment or legislation to curtail its jurisdiction, he volunteered. Brennan took Landau in to see Warren, who was surprised to learn the extent of federal electronic surveillance. Both he and Brennan expressed doubts about the propriety of the way Justice had disclosed this fact. Warren told Landau "there was nothing for the Court to consider unless and until an appropriate petition for rehearing or other document was filed and that if and when it was filed, it would be disposed of in the usual course under applicable principle." The Chief found the Justice Department's attempt to influence the Court's disposition of a case with a clandestine communication sufficiently disturbing that he called a special conference on March 17 to discuss the matter. At that meeting an outraged Douglas asked him whether he had questioned Landau concerning the bug Douglas believed was hidden in the conference room. On March 24 the Court, with only one dissent, announced that all wiretap cases posing the same issue as *Alderman*, including the two espionage ones, would be handled in the same manner as that case. "It is pretty clear that the Department of Justice has picked on a group that will not be panicked or frightened or pushed around," Douglas asserted in a memorandum for the files. He also thought it "pretty apparent that [Deputy Attorney General] Richard Kleindienst, and perhaps Mitchell himself, has a cause and the cause is to give the Court as much trouble as possible."[49]

By the time of Warren's second retirement dinner on June 6, it was obvious how prescient Douglas had been. That night a dozen active and retired justices and their spouses dined aboard the presidential yacht *Sequoia*. With Black serving as master of ceremonies, they feted the Warrens, presenting the Chief with a custom-made Winchester shotgun and his wife with a bracelet engraved "To Nina Warren, First Lady of the Judiciary 1953–1969." Only seven sitting associate justices were present. Fortas was not there because he had resigned on May 14, following exposure of his financial relationship with New York financier Louis Wolfson. In late 1965, feeling bored and isolated in his new job at the Supreme Court, Fortas had agreed to serve Wolfson's family foundation as a consultant on race relations in Florida. For doing so he would be paid $20,000 per year (more than half his $39,500 judicial salary) for life, and after his death his wife would continue to receive that amount for the rest of her life. Wolfson, who had serious legal problems with the SEC, discussed these troubles with Fortas, who apparently also reviewed documents prepared by his attorneys. On June 21, 1966, after the SEC referred two cases against Wolfson to the Justice Department for criminal prosecution, Fortas sent the foundation a letter saying that, because of the burden of his Supreme Court work, he was canceling their arrangement, but not until December 15 did he return the $20,000 he had been paid. In 1967 and 1968 Wolfson was convicted of conspiracy to violate securities laws, selling unregistered stock, and perjury. A prosecution witness, who was a Wolfson financial adviser, disclosed his client's arrangement with Fortas to lawyers from the U.S. Attorney's Office in Manhattan, and in September 1968 the Senate Judiciary Committee received an anonymous tip about the deal. Senator Griffin's office tried to get the FBI to investigate, but when told the Bureau could do this only with the approval of Attorney General Clark, it dropped the matter. The story was eventually broken by a *Life* reporter, William Lambert, whose account of the Fortas-Wolfson relationship hit the newsstands on May 5, 1969.[50]

Fortas had learned about Lambert's investigation from Clark, who had been alerted by U.S. Attorney Robert Morgenthau in New York. He tried unsuccessfully to satisfy Lambert by having his former law partner, Paul Porter, grant him an interview, in which Porter explained that the money had been returned. Also, on March 26 Fortas wrote to Warren, disqualifying himself from a case involving Wolfson. Unfortunately for him, an interview Lambert conducted with Will Wilson, head of the Justice Department's Criminal Division, alerted Wilson to the existence of the scandal. With the collaboration of the new attorney general, John Mitchell, FBI director Hoover, and the president, Wilson launched his own inquiry, the objective of which was to force Fortas off the Court. Wolfson, apparently seeking leniency, offered to provide prosecutors with a statement concerning his relationship with Fortas. He was unable to provide evidence of any illegal conduct, but in the meantime the Justice Department launched a grand jury investigation into allegations that Arnold and Porter had withheld subpoenaed documents in a price-fixing case, an inquiry that targeted Fortas's wife, Carol Agger. Nixon dissuaded Republican congressional leaders from initiating an impeachment inquiry, but after the Criminal Division obtained from the Internal Revenue Service, which had subpoenaed correspondence between Fortas and Wolfson, a copy of the justice's contract with the foundation, Mitchell arranged to see Warren. Slipping secretly into the U.S. Supreme Court Building through a garage entrance shortly before noon on May 7, he met for about half an hour with the chief justice. Mitchell showed Warren the contract and gave him excerpts from minutes of the Wolfson Family Foundation board of trustees and four letters that confirmed the relationship. The Chief was very upset. "He has to go," he told his secretary. Numerous administration leaks and a *Newsweek* article implying the existence of even more damaging evidence on Fortas kept the pot boiling. Fortas tried to cool the mounting furor by announcing publicly that he was either taking no fee for speaking engagements or turning anything he was paid over to charity. On May 12 Justice sent Warren additional correspondence and foundation minutes, along with the contract and Wolfson's statement to the FBI.[51]

By then Fortas was considering resignation and discussing that option with friends and associates, among them Black, Douglas, and Clark Clifford. Black, with whom he talked on May 10, urged him to quit in order to protect the Court, only to reverse his field after Fortas predicted that if he did so, his enemies would put him through hearings that would kill his wife. Douglas entreated his protégé not to resign, but Agger was urging him to quit because of what the controversy had done to their lives, and Clifford, sensing Fortas's unhappiness on the Court, apparently offered similar counsel. Many federal judges believed the public interest would be best served if he stepped down. On May 13 Warren convened all of the justices, including Fortas, to discuss the situation. The Chief quietly laid out all the material Mitchell had given him. Fortas responded that he had done nothing improper. In view of the outcry in the press, however, he had concluded it would be best for the Supreme Court if he stepped down. The following day Fortas submitted to the chief justice "a memorandum with respect to my association with the Wolfson Family Foundation, and a statement of the reasons which in my judgment indicate that I should resign in order that the Court may not continue to be subjected to extraneous stress which may adversely affect the performance of its important functions."[52]

Although gone, Fortas was far from forgotten. His downfall inspired conservative Republicans in Congress, such as Strom Thurmond, to target another liberal justice. Since 1960 Douglas had, for $12,000 per year, directed the work of the Parvin Foundation, a charitable trust interested in various "phases of the international situation." In 1966 he assured Warren, "Nothing coming before the Court has involved matters in which the Foundation has had even an indirect, remote, interest." That was good enough then. In the wake of the Fortas scandal, however, with talk of impeachment emanating from the Capitol Building, Douglas tendered his resignation to the Parvin Foundation on May 21, 1969. A few days later, at a special session, the Judicial Conference adopted a resolution providing that no federal judge should accept "compensation of any kind" for outside activities of its members, unless authorized to do so by the judicial council of his circuit, following a determination that the services in question were in the public interest or justified by exceptional circumstances and that performing them would not interfere with his judicial duties. A majority of the justices decided that dealing with the outside activities of members of the Supreme Court would be "inappropriate" at the moment, but Brennan, Stewart, White, and Marshall (who had received as much as $10,000 for a single lecture) requested that it be reported they agreed in principle with the standards of conduct the Judicial Conference had adopted and intended to comply with them.[53]

Besides inspiring some soul-searching by his fellow judges concerning their extrajudicial activities, Fortas's resignation created an immediate vacancy. On May 19, Nixon announced his choice to succeed Warren: Warren Earl Burger. Burger had headed the Justice Department's Civil Division during the Eisenhower administration and was now a judge on the U.S. Court of Appeals for the District of Columbia Circuit. Eighteen days later the Senate confirmed him seventy-four to three, and he took his seat on June 10. The incoming chief justice was a conservative, a strict constructionist, and a critic of the Warren Court's criminal-procedure decisions. Not surprisingly, no one consulted the man he would replace about the appointment. Indeed, Warren was informed of Nixon's choice "as a courtesy" only a few hours before the public announcement. Yet, he had predicted to both his clerks and to Tom Clark that Burger would be the nominee. Warren had anticipated that Nixon would select a lower court judge, and he obviously expected him to choose someone very different from himself.[54]

Both his old adversary from the White House and the man who was to take his seat were on hand when the Warren Court assembled for its final session on June 23, 1969. The president, clad in a cutaway coat and striped trousers, sat quietly while the Court announced the last three decisions of the term. Then, he rose and moved to the lawyer's lectern. After remarking on the nervousness he had felt when he stood there as an advocate, arguing *Time Inc. v. Hill*, Nixon launched into a laudatory seven-minute review of Warren's career that even the man he was describing considered warm and generous. "To the Chief Justice of the United States, all of us are grateful today that his example, the example of dignity, the example of integrity, the example of fairness, as the chief law official of this country, has helped to keep America on the path of continuity and change, which is essential for our progress," the president declared. The retiring chief justice responded with a short speech, in which he reminded Nixon "because you might not have looked into the matter, that [the Supreme Court] is a continuing body." He seemed bent on persuading the new president that he could not undo what the Warren Court had accomplished, pointing out to him "that the Court develops consistently the eternal principles of our Constitution in solving the problems of the day." The Chief's colleagues had sent him a retirement letter, in which they praised his "unswerving devotion to liberty and justice" and expressed pride over having "had the opportunity to be members of the Court over which you have presided during one of the most important and eventful eras of our Nation." In return, he expressed confidence that a tribunal "manned by men . . . like those who sit today" would remain a vital force in the affairs of the nation. After wishing his replacement happiness and success, Warren proceeded to administer the oath of office to a judge who was not at all like most of those who had manned his Court at the peak of its power. His last official task completed, Earl Warren turned to the audience and announced, "I present the new Chief Justice of the United States." Then it was finished.[55]

12

The Legacy of the Warren Court

Like an old soldier, Earl Warren faded away into a quiet retirement. The Warren Court did not. Idealized by some and demonized by others, it remained controversial long after the departure of the man Brennan came to refer to as the "Super Chief." Decisions handed down during Warren's tenure had revolutionized constitutional law, and the Court's foes hoped and its friends feared that his successor would lead a conservative counterrevolution that would sweep away much of what his Court had wrought. The Burger years brought as much continuity as change, however, and the Warren Court lived on in the corpus of the law. It survived also as a symbol, loathed by conservatives, who hated it for the causes it had championed, and romanticized by liberals, who longed for a return to what they recalled fondly as a sort of judicial Camelot.[1]

Soon after the retirement of the man who had given this controversial Court its name, Thurgood Marshall lauded him as "the greatest chief justice who ever lived." On the evening of Sunday, June 29, 1969, nearly a thousand people who shared Marshall's enthusiasm for Warren, including former justice Arthur Goldberg and CBS news commentator Eric Sevareid, celebrated the Chief's accomplishments during an unpublicized "national tribute" at the Lincoln Memorial. Doubleday considered his achievements important enough to offer him $75,000 for his memoirs, and despite having once vowed never to write such a book, Warren now agreed to do so in order to ensure that Nina would have financial security in her old age. He kept putting off work on his autobiography to do other things, though. The Warrens traveled widely, visiting Europe, Asia, and Africa. The retired chief justice met the pope and attended conferences of the World Peace through Law movement, which honored him in 1971 for his "landmark decisions upholding human rights." Warren's special joy was speaking on college campuses, where he generally received a hero's welcome from students with whom he seemed to have an amazing empathy. The retired chief justice retained an office at the Supreme Court, but most of what he performed there was make-work. For awhile he had a cordial relationship with his successor, who invited him and Nina to dinner at the Court, but eventually it cooled as Burger, intimidated by his predecessor's reputation, began to worry that Warren might steal his thunder. The old chief justice reacted very negatively when a blue-ribbon committee, which Burger had appointed because of his concern about the Supreme Court's growing caseload, recommended creation of a "National Court of Appeals"

306

to screen all of the petitions for review then being filed with the high tribunal. Viewing the report of the so-called Freund Committee as an attack on his Court, Warren condemned its proposal in a Law Day address and sought to mobilize his former clerks to defeat it. This was the only controversial issue on which the retired chief justice took a public stance.[2]

He watched the developing Watergate crisis from the sidelines, appalled by the number of lawyers who were being indicted and convicted. Warren viewed the whole affair as proof that Nixon's character was as badly flawed as he had always believed. He did not live to see his old enemy resign from the presidency. Warren had been experiencing chest pains since the spring of 1972, and in January 1974 he suffered a heart attack. He recovered quickly, but his health was failing, and in May he was hospitalized again for about a week. Although he went home on June 2, his condition continued to deteriorate. On July 9 Brennan and Douglas visited their former chief at his apartment. They informed him that the Court had just voted eight to zero to require Nixon to turn over tapes of his White House conversations with aides indicted in the Watergate case. "Thank God!" Warren exclaimed. Contented, he died in his sleep at 8:00 P.M.[3]

By the time its chief expired, the Warren Court had passed away too. Like him it departed gradually. Except for the addition of Burger, the Court Warren had led remained intact through the 1969–70 term, as Senate rejection of Nixon nominees Clement Haynesworth and G. Harold Carswell kept Fortas's seat vacant. The man who eventually claimed it, Judge Harry Blackmun, proved to be a moderate, as did Lewis Powell, whom Nixon nominated to replace Black in 1971, and Judge John Paul Stevens, to whom Gerald Ford gave what had been Douglas's seat in 1975. William Rehnquist, named by Nixon in 1971 as a successor to Harlan, was an aggressive conservative, but although having a similar orientation, his Stanford Law School classmate Sandra Day O'Connor, nominated by Ronald Reagan in 1981 to replace Stewart, eventually moved toward the middle of the Court on many issues. The only members of the Warren Court who remained when Burger retired in 1986 were Brennan, Marshall, and White, but the transformation of Warren's Court into Burger's had been gradual and the results far less dramatic than many had anticipated. As David Currie notes, "If there was to be a counterrevolution, . . . it was slow in coming." For a time, Brennan, who had been Warren's loyal lieutenant and chief tactician, was the real leader of, and frequent spokesman for, what was only nominally Burger's Court. Changes in membership eventually reduced his power and made him a frequent dissenter, while Stewart, who had opposed many of the most important decisions of the Warren era, and White, who had sided with him periodically, especially in criminal-procedure cases, gained influence. Stewart had always coveted the role of the cautious, prudent "swing man," and White favored a narrow, fact-specific approach to cases. Their jurisprudence, which had often put them at odds with the liberal majority on the later Warren Court, was well suited to the less ideological and more moderate Burger Court.[4]

That Court was the product of a political culture vastly more conservative than the one that had prevailed while the Warren Court was rendering its most libertarian and controversial decisions. Not surprisingly, since all of the justices appointed between 1969 and 1981 were nominees of conservative Republican presidents, not one was as supportive of civil liberties claims as the Warren Court judge he or she replaced. Stevens took the liberal side in more than half of such cases, however, and Blackmun and Stewart did so about 40 percent of the time. Although White shifted somewhat to the right during the Burger years, he still opted for the liberal position in about one-third of civil liberties cases, and Powell was close behind him. Rehnquist compiled a solidly conservative voting record, opposing such claims more than 80 percent of the time, but even the Chief Justice sometimes deserted him. As Charles Lamb and Stephen Halpern observe, "Without at least five solid votes consistently in the conservative column, no new era of constitutional jurisprudence could be expected." None materialized. An ambivalence that often seemed to mirror "America's post-Vietnam, post-Watergate sense of drift" characterized the jurisprudence of the Burger Court, which Earl Maltz insists was, on balance, even more liberal than that of its predecessor.[5]

The Court that Burger's followed had profoundly changed constitutional law, overruling forty-five prior decisions, compared to eighty-eight by all previous Supreme Courts combined. Longtime critic Philip Kurland questioned the Warren Court's creativity, insisting the major doctrines it sought to effectuate had all originated earlier. Even he conceded, however, that "the Warren Court accepted with a vengeance the task of protector of the individual against government and of minorities against the tyranny of majorities." To William Nelson, who views the work of the Warren Court more positively, its acceptance of this responsibility is evidence of moral virtue and proof of a willingness to take "responsibility for transforming America's ideology into reality." Morton Horwitz, also a fan of the Warren Court's efforts to empower the oppressed, declares, "Like no other Court before or since, it stood for an expansive conception of the democratic way of life as the foundational ideal of constitutional interpretation." The Warren Court stood also for the nationalization of the Bill of Rights, for increased federal judicial supervision of the states and their political subdivisions, and for the imposition of constitutional constraints on aspects of the law, such as defamation, that had long been considered purely private. As Bernard Schwartz points out, "During Warren's tenure, the Supreme Court virtually rewrote the corpus of our constitutional law." In 1974 the *American Bar Association Journal* invited readers to vote for the most significant milestones in American judicial history. They ranked *Miranda* fourth, *Brown* fifth, *In re Gault* ninth, *Gideon* thirteenth, and *Mapp* sixteenth. So significant were the decisions of Warren's Court that Schwartz considers his chief justiceship one of the "two great creative periods in American public law" (the other being the one overseen by John Marshall). Although obviously biased, Fortas was essentially correct when he characterized the work of the Court on which he served as a "profound and pervasive revolution."[6]

That revolution was largely a legal one. The rulings of the Warren Court do not seem to have changed life in America all that much. Although Horwitz contends "that the decision in *Brown v. Board of Education* served both as a catalyst for and as a legitimation of social change," it rather clearly did not desegregate southern public schools, something that was accomplished (to the extent it ever was) by the Civil Rights Act of 1964 and the threat of losing out on federal financial aid to education. Michael Klarman has argued persuasively that what *Brown* actually did was crystalize southern resistance to racial change. Although disputing him, Tushnet concedes, "He is surely correct that lawyers have overestimated the importance of *Brown v. Board of Education* in the transformation of race relations that occurred in the latter part of the twentieth century." Gerald Rosenberg supports Klarman but goes further, rejecting even his contention that *Brown's* long-term effects were positive because the reaction to the violent southern defense of white supremacy the decision triggered pressured Congress into enacting effective civil rights legislation. "By stiffening resistance and raising fears before the activist phase of the civil rights movement was in place," he contends, "*Brown* may actually have delayed the achievement of civil rights." Rosenberg adds that public-opinion data, press coverage, congressional and presidential responses to civil rights legislation, and the timing of sit-ins and other forms of civil rights demonstrations all fail to confirm that judicial decisions either energized African Americans or legitimized their objectives in the eyes of whites. "The evidence suggests that *Brown's* major positive impact was limited to reinforcing the belief in a legal strategy for change of those already committed to it," he contends.[7]

Rosenberg also insists that the Warren Court's criminal-procedure decisions produced little real change. He points to studies showing that failure to comply with *In re Gault* was widespread, that *Mapp's* exclusionary rule did not deter illegal searches and seizures to any significant extent, and that despite *Miranda*, suspects continued to confess. Rosenberg concedes that *Gideon* led to a tremendous increase in the number of public-defender organizations and private lawyers providing representation to the indigent, but because these have been badly underfunded and overworked, he questions whether the result has been effective assistance of counsel for the poor.[8]

The reapportionment rulings may actually have harmed those whose interests the Warren Court sought to promote. The Court's one-person, one-vote rule enjoyed overwhelming public support, being viewed as preferable to the arrangements it replaced by a two-to-one margin among members of all political parties and in all parts of the country. Yet, while it produced dramatic change in some states, such as California, studies of the extent to which the Court's rule increased legislative turnover have arrived at conflicting results. Whatever reform occurred was almost entirely procedural, rather than substantive, Rosenberg contends. Although studies of the sorts of policies adopted by reapportioned legislatures have yielded mixed results, "an overall reading seems to be that any effects that can be traced to reapportionment are small." What *Baker, Reynolds,* and their progeny clearly did do was enhance the political power of those who opposed the Great Society. The principal beneficiaries of reapportionment were not the large cities, where liberalism was strong, but the burgeoning suburbs that voted overwhelmingly Republican. The school-prayer and Bible-reading decisions further damaged the liberal cause, for the GOP exploited them to document how far out of touch with Middle American values the Great Society coalition had become. Although even Kurland conceded in 1970 that "our society has been substantially modified during the existence of the Warren Court," it seems doubtful that the Court's decisions caused much of that change. Furthermore, some of what they did bring about was neither intended nor desired by the justices themselves.[9]

Although failing to transform American society, the Warren Court did transform American legal culture by helping elevate equality to a central position in the law. "The Warren Court's inclusive idea of democracy was built on the revival of the Equal Protection Clause in *Brown*," Horwitz notes. Not content with attacking discrimination against African Americans, the Court moved on to condemn handicaps and disadvantages imposed on all people because of their race, ethnicity, poverty, place of residence, illegitimacy, or affiliation with radical political organizations or minority religions. Because interest-group politics could not ensure such outsiders full participation in American democracy, they needed judicial protection. The Warren Court's activism was designed to promote what Lawrence Friedman calls "plural equality," and as he points out, "A theory of plural equality underlies modern legal culture." The Court itself did not carry implementation of this concept beyond eliminating inequalities of access to governmental institutions and enforcing formal equality in the enjoyment of rights of citizenship. It never really grappled with the problems posed by informal discrimination and the unequal distribution of private power. Equality came to have a broader and deeper meaning, however, and the Warren Court helped to bring about this redefinition. It legitimated pluralism, promoting acceptance both of the idea that America is "a kind of confederation of groups, all of equal worth and with equally valid cultures," and of the principle that minorities have rights that must be respected.[10]

The Warren Court also contributed to the development of modern American legal culture by stimulating rights consciousness. "[A] momentum toward an increasingly broad definition of the rights attaching to American citizenship" characterized its jurisprudence. The concept of natural rights had fallen into disfavor among progressive legal thinkers, who considered it a conservative creation designed to shield property from governmental regulation. The Warren Court encouraged "the resurrection of rights discourse." This Supreme Court's objective, however, was to safeguard people, not property. While Warren served as chief justice, "personal rights and liberties became the very focus of the Court's enforcement of the . . . Constitution." The highly publicized rulings that recognized and enforced rights for the benefit of some outsiders encouraged others to demand them too. As ACLU historian Daniel Walker reports, "The rights revolution reached across the country." Millions of women, homosexuals, poor people, students, and persons with physical and mental disabilities discovered their own voices and began demanding fair treatment and personal dignity. "The empowerment of these previously silent groups was a political development of enormous significance." Like these groups of victims, ordinary Americans developed new expectations about personal freedom. The ACLU cast these aspirations into constitutional arguments that it pressed on the Supreme Court, both before and after Warren's retirement. In 1964, for example, the ACLU committed itself to eliminating laws criminalizing abortion, and in 1970, reversing past policy, it endorsed an equal rights amendment to eliminate discrimination on the basis of gender. This "rights revolution was the longest-lasting legacy of the 1960s," and the Warren Court both reflected and contributed to that revolution, as well as to the heightened rights consciousness that pervaded America.[11]

The Warren Court also legitimated resort to the judiciary to accomplish reform. As biographer Bernard Schwartz acknowledges, Warren was "the paradigm of the 'result-oriented' judge, who used his power to secure the result he deemed right in the cases that came before his Court." He employed judicial power to advance his vision of a just society. Frankfurter fans at the Harvard Law School mocked his habit of asking counsel during oral argument whether a particular legal position was "just," but as far as Warren was concerned, the basic ingredient of a proper decision was principle not doctrine. His emphasis on fairness and justice "led him to join hands with Justices Black and Douglas and their activist approach to constitutional law." After Frankfurter's retirement they had a secure majority, and Warren's became "the quintessentially 'activist' Court."[12]

The Warren Court moved, in the words of critic Kurland, "toward the legislative mode and away from the judicial mode of carrying on its business." "It preferred to write codes of conduct rather than resolve particular controversies." The Warren Court also imitated a legislature by providing that some of its most important criminal-procedure decisions should operate only prospectively and by readily accepting briefs from nonlitigants interested in issues it had under review. In addition, the justices often took to the hustings to defend their decisions. "The Warren Court has moved closer to the legislative form than most of its predecessors . . . not because it has made new law but because in making new law it has come closer to emulating the legislative process than did any of its predecessors," Kurland contends. Warren viewed the Court as having the last word in governmental affairs and as speaking for the whole American people. His Progressivism led him to believe that legislatures were neither democratic nor representative of public opinion and that the Court could do a better job of speaking for the people than their elected representatives. Although this was a somewhat elitist outlook, as G. Edward White points out, "The Warren Court's activism was . . . distinguishable from that of other activist courts in the past in the nonelitist character of its beneficiaries." It used elite power to assist outsiders, often in contexts where the consequence of judicial restraint would have been the perpetuation of restrictions on their rights. "In some of its decisions," White acknowledges, "the Warren Court seemed to be distinguishing between the corrosive elitism of legislatures and its own benevolent elitism, and arguing that the Constitution encouraged only the latter."[13]

Despite an approach reminiscent of the activist Court of the 1930s, Warren's Court escaped a similar fate because the results of its activism accorded so well with the core values of the liberal political culture of the 1960s. "Greatness in a judge who adopts Warren's approach seems inextricably linked to public acceptance of the rightness of that judge's ethical stance," White notes. Yet the Warren Court's approach survived the collapse of liberalism in the late 1960s. In the foreword to a 1983 collection of essays on the Burger Court, Anthony Lewis commented that "the great conflict between judicial 'restraint' and activism is history. We are all activists now." Wrote Victor Blasi in the same book, "By almost any measure, the Burger Court has been an activist Court." So has the Rehnquist Court. The Burger years witnessed the disappearance of the controversy that dominated Warren Court decision making. During the 1960s justices had debated whether decisions that embodied principles most of them regarded as morally and socially "right" were properly crafted and sufficiently sensitive to institutional considerations, such as federalism. Later, their arguments had a different focus. "The Burger Court's debates . . . were debates about substance, not debates pitting substance against process."[14]

Although the Warren Court died, Warren Court activism lived on, applauded by academic admirers who labored to provide theoretical justifications for the methodology that had produced decisions they revered. During the 1960s constitutional commentators, such as Kurland and Bickel, had preached Frankfurter's gospel of judicial self-restraint, but during the Burger era the commentators were as activist as the Court. A new generation of legal academics had gone to law school and entered the teaching of law while Warren was chief justice, often after clerking at his Court. As Laura Kalman observes, this group of brilliant young scholars (which included Jesse Choper, Bruce Ackerman, Ronald Dworkin, John Hart Ely, Owen Fiss, Frank Michelman, and Laurence Tribe) "saw Earl Warren as the emperor, and . . . wanted to give him and his Court clothes." Dworkin, for example, argued that attacking the Warren Court for failing to treat the Constitution as binding text was wrong because "if we wish to treat fidelity to the text as an overriding requirement of constitutional interpretation, then it is the conservative critics of the Warren Court who are at fault, because their philosophy ignores the direction to face issues of moral principle that the logic of the text demands." Pining for their judicial Camelot, such scholars continued to formulate justifications for its activist jurisprudence. In the mid-1970s many law professors became estranged from the Burger Court, but that was because they disliked the substance of its rulings. Much of their scholarship was directed toward reawakening the spirit of the Warren Court. "Many constitutional scholars continued 'living off the remains of the Warren Court,'" notes Kalman, "writing articles that justified it and glorified courts as the great engine of social and political change." For them it remained a powerful symbol.[15]

The Warren Court was a beacon for many judges as well. Because Nixon and Reagan appointments made the U.S. Supreme Court more conservative and because the Court ceased expanding upon some of the libertarian doctrines forged during the Warren era, liberal supreme courts in a number of states stopped deferring to Washington. Rediscovering their own constitutions, they began exploiting doctrines of federalism and states' autonomy to increase the rights of their citizens. Between 1969 and 1986 state supreme courts handed down more than 450 rulings that either interpreted recognized rights more broadly than had the Burger Court or secured ones it had left entirely unprotected.[16]

While continuing to serve as a legal lighthouse for liberal law professors and judges, the Warren Court became a target for those disaffected with legal liberalism. Skeptical about social engineering by judges, conservative constitutional theorists mounted telling attacks on the proposals of those who wanted to carry on the work of the

Warren Court, branding some as too utopian while condemning others as too pragmatic. In 1977 legal historian Raoul Berger accused the Warren Court of converting the Constitution into a scrap of paper by rendering decisions purportedly based on the Fourteenth Amendment that conflicted with the intent of its framers. Attacks came from the left as well as from the right. In the 1980s, scholars identified with the new Critical Legal Studies movement condemned the "hocus-pocus" of the sort of rights-centered liberalism the Warren Court had championed, assailing conservatives as well as liberals for practicing "liberal legalism." "Republicanism" became a fad among legal academics in the late 1980s and early 1990s because it seemed to offer to those haunted by the ghost of Earl Warren a way "to go beyond his Court's liberalism" to help those it had sought to benefit in a "communitarian" way that did not rely on individual rights against the majority.[17]

Whether they loathed or loved it, no one forgot Warren's Court. As Tushnet points out, its "definition of the Supreme Court's role in government remains prominent in contemporary political discussion." Today, "liberals . . . yearn for a return to the Warren Court's true course, just as conservatives take the Warren Court to represent everything a Supreme Court should not be." For those at both ends of the political spectrum, Earl Warren's Court possesses immense symbolic significance.[18]

It always has. In October of 1970, at a time when alienation, radicalism, and disaffection with American institutions had infected colleges across the country, the recently retired chief justice spoke at the University of California's San Diego campus. As he began his talk, several students unfurled a large banner. Many in the audience cringed, expecting to see an expletive-laced condemnation of such a prominent representative of what many young people condemned as "the Establishment." Instead, the sign read "RIGHT ON, BIG EARL!" This unexpected outpouring of admiration and affection for Warren impressed a young history professor who was in the audience that day. "I . . . learned that this great bear of a man, who looked every inch the Chief Justice and who had presided over the nation's most August judicial forum, had become a symbol for many young people of their own rebellion against the social, political, and economic deformities of American life," Michael Parrish recalled years later.[19]

The man Thurgood Marshall considered "the greatest chief justice who ever lived" remained a symbol for many of those who believed that America could do better, even after he had passed away and they had passed into middle age. So did his Court. "The Warren Court was," as Horwitz reminds us, "an expression of both the spirit and the contradictions of liberal American jurisprudence." By the mid-1980s liberalism had changed so much that the specific political agenda with which Warren's Court was associated had become largely irrelevant. But the idea that lawyers and judges could make a difference, the feeling that innovations in constitutional law could change society, and the belief that courts could serve as effective instruments of reform retained their appeal. They were survivors from an era before Vietnam and Watergate, a time when cynicism had not yet become pervasive and liberalism was an advancing political tide that seemed to be sweeping away much that was outmoded and unfair and making America a better place. John Kennedy symbolized that age as well, but assassination ended his presidency before he had really accomplished much. His successors aroused more animosity than admiration, and after passing the Voting Rights Act in 1965, Congress likewise did little to commend itself to the public. The Warren Court lasted longer than Kennedy and left behind a far more meaningful record of achievement. For better or worse, its decisions became the most significant and enduring embodiments of the liberalism of the 1960s. Even more than the martyred president, the Warren Court was, and seems likely to remain, the symbol for that age.[20]

Notes

ABBREVIATIONS

AF   Abe Fortas Papers, Sterling Library, Yale University

AS   Administration Series, Papers of Dwight D. Eisenhower as President, Dwight D. Eisenhower Presidential Library

BD   Harold Burton Diary, Harold Burton Papers, Manuscript Division, Library of Congress

CF   Chornological Files Pertaining to Abe Fortas and Homer Thornberry, Lyndon Baines Johnson Presidential Library

DDEL   Dwight D. Eisenhower Presidential Library

EW   Earl Warren Papers, Manuscript Division, Library of Congress

FF-H   Felix Frankfurter Manuscripts, Harvard Law School

FF-LC   Felix Frankfurter Papers, Manuscript Division, Library of Congress

HB   Harold Burton Papers, Manuscript Division, Library of Congress

HLB   Hugo L. Black Papers, Manuscript Division, Library of Congress

JFK   John F. Kennedy Presidential Library

JMH   John Marshall Harlan Papers, Seeley G. Mudd Manuscript Library, Princeton University

LBJ   Lyndon Baines Johnson Presidential Library, Austin, Texas

OF   Official Files

PS   Potter Stewart

RHJ   Robert H. Jackson Papers, Manuscript Division, Library of Congress

TCC   Tom C. Clark Papers, Tarlton Law Library, University of Texas, Austin, Texas

TM   Thurgood Marshall Papers, Manuscript Division, Library of Congress

WHCF   White House Central Files

WJB   William J. Brennan Papers, Manuscript Division, Library of Congress

WOD   William O. Douglas Papers, Manuscript Division, Library of Congress

INTRODUCTION

1. Robert H. Bork, *The Tempting of America: The Political Seduction of the Law* (New York: Free Press, 1990), 69; Bernard Schwartz, ed., *The Warren Court: A Retrospective* (New York: Oxford University Press, 1996), ix; Morton J. Horwitz, *The Warren Court and the Pursuit of Justice* (New York: Hill and Wang, 1998), 3.

2. Mark V. Tushnet, "The Warren Court as History: An Interpretation," in *The Warren Court in Historical and Political Perspective,* ed. Mark V. Tushnet (Charlottesville: University of Virginia Press, 1993), 1.

3. Lucas A. Powe Jr., *The Warren Court and American Politics* (Cambridge, Mass.: Harvard University Press, 2000), 501.

4. Ibid., 1, 501.

1. ARRIVAL OF THE SUPER CHIEF

1. Earl Warren, *The Memoirs of Earl Warren* (Garden City, N.Y.: Doubleday, 1977), 275–76, 278–79.

2. G. Edward White, *Earl Warren: A Public Life* (New York: Oxford University Press, 1982), 161; Bernard Schwartz, *A History of the Supreme Court* (New York: Oxford University Press, 1993), 263.

3. Morton J. Horwitz, "The Warren Court and the Pursuit of Justice," 50 *Washington and Lee Law Review* 5–13 (1993).

4. G. Edward White, "Warren Court," in *American Constitutional History,* ed. Leonard W. Levy, Kenneth L. Karst, and Dennis J. Mahoney (New York: Macmillan, 1989), 279.

5. Paul L. Murphy, *The Constitution in Crisis Times, 1918–1969* (New York: Harper & Row, 1972), 293–94.

6. Except as otherwise noted, materials in this section are from Warren, *Memoirs,* 10–15, 47–52, 60, 67–69, 71–72, 117, 119–20, 155–56, 239–40, 252–56, 268–69; White, *Warren,* 9–13, 16, 19–34, 45, 47, 49–51, 55–57, 131–40, 143; and Bernard Schwartz, *Super Chief: Earl Warren and His Supreme Court—A Judicial Biography* (New York: New York University Press, 1983), 1–2, 7–9, 12–13, 18.

7. Schwartz, *History,* 265.

8. Ed Cray, *Chief Justice: A Biography of Earl Warren* (New York: Simon & Schuster, 1997), 246–47; Herbert Brownell *Advising Ike: The Memoirs of Attorney General Herbert Brownell,* with John Burke (Lawrence: University Press of Kansas, 1993), 164–65; Warren, *Memoirs,* 252–56; White, *Warren,* 138–40, 143; Dwight D. Eisenhower, *The White House Years: Mandate for Change, 1953–1956* (Garden City, N.Y.: Doubleday, 1963), 228; Warren to Dwight D. Eisenhower, November 5, 1952, and Ike Eisenhower to Earl Warren, November 9, 1952, box 38, AS.

9. Brownell, *Advising,* 164–65; Eisenhower, *Mandate,* 228.

10. Brownell, *Advising,* 165–66; Eisenhower, *Mandate,* 228; Warren to the president, June 30, 1953, and July 31, 1953, box 38, AS.

11. Brownell, *Advising,* 166; Eisenhower, *Mandate,* 226–28; Warren, *Memoirs,* 260–61; Schwartz, *Super Chief,* 4–5; Mary Frances Berry, *Stability Security, and Continuity: Mr. Justice Burton and Decision-Making in the Supreme Court 1945–1958* (Westport, Conn.: Greenwood Press, 1978), 153; Young B. Smith to President Eisenhower, September 11, 1953, and Dwight D. Eisenhower to Young B. Smith, September 14, 1953, box 36, AS; Dwight D. Eisenhower, *Ike's Letters to a Friend, 1941–1958,* ed. Robert Griffith (Lawrence: University Press of Kansas, 1984), 135; James C. Hagerty, *The Diary of James C. Hagerty: Eisenhower in Mid-Course 1954–1955,* ed. Robert H. Ferrell (Bloomington: Indiana University Press, 1983), 67.

12. Eisenhower, *Mandate,* 226–28; Brownell, *Advising,* 166–67; Eisenhower to Smith, September 14, 1953; White, *Warren,* 149.

13. Brownell, *Advising,* 167–68; Warren, *Memoirs,* 270–71; Schwartz, *Super Chief,* 5–7; White, *Warren,* 150; telegram, Earl Warren to the president, September 30, 1953, OF 100-A, WHCF, DDEL.

14. Senate Concurrent Resolution No. 5, April 20, 1954, William F. Knowland to the president, September 25, 1953, and Dwight D. Eisenhower to William F. Knowland, October 6, 1953, and memorandum for the president, October 13, 1953, all in OF 100-A, WHCF, DDEL; Chester J. Pach Jr. and Elmo Richardson, *The Presidency of Dwight D. Eisenhower,* rev. ed. (Lawrence: University Press of Kansas, 1991), 142.

15. Brownell, *Advising*, 169–71; *Cong. Record*, 83rd Cong., 2nd sess. (March 1, 1954): 2381.

16. Schwartz, *Super Chief*, 169–71; Dwight D. Eisenhower to the Chief Justice, March 23, 1954, box 38, AS.

17. On Black's pre-Court career, see Howard Ball, *Hugo L. Black: Cold Steel Warrior* (New York: Oxford University Press, 1996), 29–106; Tony Allen Freyer, *Hugo L. Black and the Dilemma of American Liberalism* (Glenview, Ill.: Scott Foresman / Little Brown, 1990), 1–71; Gerald T. Dunne, *Hugo Black and the Judicial Revolution* (New York: Simon & Schuster, 1977), 1–173; Roger K. Newman, *Hugo Black: A Biography* (New York: Pantheon, 1994), 1–263; and James F. Simon, *The Antagonists: Hugo Black, Felix Frankfurter and Civil Liberties in Modern America* (New York: Simon & Schuster, 1989), 68–98. For the vote on his confirmation, see *Cong. Record*, 75th Cong., 1st sess. (August 17, 1937): 9103.

18. On Frankfurter's pre-judicial career, see Michael E. Parrish, *Felix Frankfurter and His Times: The Reform Years* (New York: Free Press, 1982); Melvin I. Urofsky, *Felix Frankfurter: Judicial Restraint and Individual Liberties* (Boston: Twayne, 1991), 1–44; Simon, *Antagonists*, 24–64.

19. Urofsky, *Frankfurter*, 44–47, 62; Melvin I. Urofsky, *Division and Discord: The Supreme Court under Stone and Vinson, 1941–1953* (Columbia: University of South Carolina Press), 35–36.

20. On Douglas's pre-Court life and career, see James F. Simon, *Independent Journey: The Life of William O. Douglas* (New York: Harper & Row, 1980), 1–194; Bruce Allen Murphy, *Wild Bill: The Legend and Life of William O. Douglas* (New York: Random House, 2003), 1–175; Simon, *Antagonists*, 184–87, 190; G. Edward White, *The American Judicial Tradition: Profiles of Leading American Judges*, 2nd ed. (New York: Oxford University Press, 1988), 370–78. On his nomination, see Urofsky, *Division*, 23. Powe, a Douglas clerk, reports his constitutional law grade in *Warren Court*, 6.

21. On Jackson's pre-Court life and career, see Eugene C. Gerhart, *America's Advocate: Robert H. Jackson* (Indianapolis and New York: Bobbs-Merrill, 1958), 25–234; Jeffrey D. Hocket, *New Deal Justice: The Constitutional Jurisprudence of Hugo L. Black, Felix Frankfurter, and Robert H. Jackson* (Lanham, Md.: Rowman & Littlefield, 1996), 215–40.

22. Daniel I. Breen, "Stanley Forman Reed," in *The Supreme Court Justices: A Biographical Dictionary*, ed. Melvin I. Urofsky (New York: Garland, 1994), 367. The only full-scale biography of Reed is an uncritical account by a former clerk, John D. Fassett, *New Deal Justice: The Life of Stanley Reed of Kentucky* (New York: Vantage, 1994).

23. On Burton's appointment and pre-Court career, see Berry, *Stability*, 3–25; Urofsky, *Division*, 151–52.

24. The most extensive discussion of Minton's pre-Court career is Linda C. Gugin and James E. St. Clair, *Sherman Minton: New Deal Senator, Cold War Justice* (Indianapolis: Indiana Historical Society, 1997), 1–177. See also Richard Kirkendall, "Sherman Minton," in *The Justices of the United States Supreme Court: Their Lives and Major Opinions*, ed. Leon Friedman and Fred L. Israel, 3rd. ed. (New York and Philadelphia: Chelsea House, 1991), 4:1362–65; Urofsky, *Division*, 155–56, David N. Atkinson, "From New Deal Liberal to Supreme Court Conservative," 1975 *Washington University Law Quarterly* 361, at 372–82 (1975).

25. Michal R. Belknap, "Tom C. Clark," in *American National Biography*, ed. John A. Garraty and Mark L. Carnes (New York: Oxford University Press, 1998), 4:948–51; Urofsky, *Division*, 154–55.

26. Berry, *Stability*, 87, 146; White, *Judicial Tradition*, 319–20, 324.

27. White, *Judicial Tradition*, 324–25; Parrish, *Frankfurter*, 20–21, 167–69; James Bradley Thayer, "The Origin and Scope of the American Doctrine of Constitutional Law," 7 *Harvard Law Review* 129, at 144 (1893); Urofsky, *Frankfurter*, 49; *Lochner v. New York*, 198 U.S. 45, 74 (1905) (Holmes, J., dissenting); Michael Parrish, "Felix Frankfurter, the Progressive Tradition and the Warren Court," in Tushnet, *Warren Court*, 59; Felix Frankfurter to John M. Harlan, May 9, 1957, box 97, FF-H.

28. Frankfurter to John M. Harlan, October 29, 1957, box 42, JMH; Herbert Wechsler, "Toward Neutral Principles of Constitutional Law," 73 *Harvard Law Review* 1, at 15–20 (1959); White,

Judicial Tradition, 230–31, 322–23; Kermit L. Hall, *The Magic Mirror: Law in American History* (New York: Oxford University Press, 1989), 310–12. Morton J. Horwitz, *The Transformation of American Law, 1870–1960: The Crisis of Legal Orthodoxy* (New York: Oxford University Press, 1992), 253–54; Urofsky, *Frankfurter,* 98–99, 126.

29. Hockett, *New Deal Justice,* 241–45; White, *Judicial Tradition,* 231, 241–46.

30. White, *Judicial Tradition,* 389–90, 403–5, 415, 417; Melvin I. Urofsky, "William O. Douglas as Common-Law Judge," in Tushnet, *Warren Court,* 64–65, 76, 78, 83; Schwartz, *Super Chief,* 52.

31. Ball, *Black,* 135; Freyer, *Black,* 1–2; Tony Freyer, "Hugo L. Black and the Warren Court in Retrospect," in Tushnet, *Warren Court,* 87; Howard Ball and Philip J. Cooper, *Of Power and Right: Hugo Black, William O. Douglas, and America's Constitutional Revolution* (New York: Oxford University Press, 1992), 10–11; Tinsley Yarbrough, *Mr. Justice Black and His Critics* (Durham, N.C.: Duke University Press, 1988), 20–21, 27, 66–67, 80; White, *Judicial Tradition,* 335.

32. Michael E. Parrish, "Earl Warren and the American Judicial Tradition," 1982 *American Bar Foundation Research Journal* 1179, at 1184–86 (1982); Paul Murphy, *Crisis Times,* 265–66; Urofsky, *Frankfurter,* 108; Simon, *Antagonists,* 108.

33. Quoted in Newman, *Black,* 413.

34. Yarbrough, *Black,* 127, 130–33; Freyer, "Black," 97–98.

35. Yarbrough, *Black,* 79; Newman, *Black,* 350–52; Simon, *Antagonists,* 178–79; Freyer, *Black,* 101–2, 118; Urofsky, *Frankfurter,* 63, 93–98, 149, 152, 163; *Adamson v. California,* 332 U.S. 46, 68 (1948) (Black, J., dissenting); *Palko v. Connecticut,* 302 U.S. 319 (1937); Parrish, "Frankfurter," 62.

36. David Currie, *The Constitution in the Supreme Court: The Second Century 1888–1986* (Chicago: University of Chicago Press, 1990), 370–71; Schwartz, *History,* 255–56; White, *Judicial Tradition,* 245–46.

37. White, *Judicial Tradition,* 330; Berry, *Stability,* 147; Urofsky, *Frankfurter,* 47–48, 57; White, *Warren,* 175–77; Schwartz, *Super Chief,* 38–40.

38. Quoted in Parrish, "Frankfurter," 52.

39. Simon, *Antagonists,* 192–93; Melvin I. Urofsky, "Conflict among the Brethren: Felix Frankfurter, William O. Douglas and the Clash of Personalities and Philosophies on the United States Supreme Court," 1988 *Duke Law Journal* 71, at 100–103, 106, 110 (1988); Schwartz, *Super Chief,* 54–55; Urofsky, *Division* 35–36; William J. Brennan Jr., "A Personal Remembrance," in Schwartz, *Retrospective,* 9.

40. Simon, *Antagonists,* 189–91; White, *Judicial Tradition,* 386–87; William O. Douglas to William Brennan, June 3, 1964, box 1299, WOD; G. Edward White, "The Anti-Judge: William O. Douglas and the Ambiguities of Individuality," 74 *Virginia Law Review* 17, at 36, 42 (1988); Simon, *Independent Journey,* 430–33; Schwartz, *Super Chief,* 51.

41. Urofsky, *Division,* 137–45; Ball and Cooper, *Power,* 93–98.

42. Schwartz, *History,* 248, 243–54.

43. Jan Palmer and Saul Brenner, "Determinants of the Amount of Time Taken by the Vinson Court to Process Its Full-Opinion Cases," 1990, *Journal of Supreme Court History,* 141, 145.

44. Except as otherwise indicated, the discussion from this point until the end of the chapter is based upon Warren, *Memoirs,* 117, 148–49, 169–71, 218–20, 232, 275–77, 282–83, 322–33, 334–35, 345–48; White, *Warren,* 42–44, 67–76, 101–5, 126–27, 154–55, 161, 172–74, 178–80, 218, 228–30, 248, 332, 335, 337.

45. Michal R. Belknap, *Cold War Political Justice: The Smith Act, the Communist Party, and American Civil Liberties* (Westport, Conn.: Greenwood, 1977), 236–37.

46. Brownell, *Advising,* 172.

47. White, *Judicial Tradition,* 337, 339.

48. Schwartz, *Super Chief,* 146–52, 206; Berry, *Stability,* 30; Frankfurter to Warren, October 12, 1953, Frankfurter to Warren, October 8, 1953, and Frankfurter to Warren, December 8, 1954, all in box 353, EW; Newman, *Black,* 470–71.

49. Schwartz, *Super Chief,* 134, 140, 199; G. Edward White, "Earl Warren as Jurist," 67 *Virginia Law Review* 461, at 462, 471–72, 476 (1981).

50. G. Edward White, "Earl Warren's Influence on the Warren Court," in Tushnet, *Warren Court,* 39–40; Schwartz, *History,* 267.

51. Schwartz, *History,* 266–67; Schwartz, *Super Chief,* 131–32, 286; "Andy" Stewart to Chief Justice, box 358, EW; diary entry of December 1, 1956, reel 4, BD.

52. Thurgood Marshall, interview by T. H. Baker, July 10, 1969, transcript, 18, LBJ Oral History Project, LBJ; Newman, *Black,* 427.

53. Schwartz, *Super Chief,* 143–46, 266–69; White, *Judicial Tradition,* 429.

54. Quoted in Schwartz, *Super Chief,* 31.

2. THE SCHOOL DESEGREGATION CASES

1. Morton Horwitz, "The Jurisprudence of Brown and the Dilemmas of Liberalism," 14 *Harvard Civil Rights-Civil Liberties Law Review* 599, at 599–600, 612 (1979); Horwitz, "Pursuit," 5.

2. Mark V. Tushnet, *Making Civil Rights Law: Thurgood Marshall and the Supreme Court, 1936–1961* (New York: Oxford University Press, 1994), 12–15, 116, 70; Tushnet, *The NAACP Legal Strategy against Segregated Education, 1925–1950* (Chapel Hill: University of North Carolina Press, 1987), 72–75; Michael J. Klarman, *From Jim Crow to Civil Rights: The Supreme Court and the Struggle for Racial Equality* (New York: Oxford University Press, 2004), 146–52; *Missouri ex rel. Gaines v. Canada,* 305 U.S. 339 (1939).

3. Tushnet, *Civil Rights Law,* 127–28; Klarman, *Jim Crow,* 174–75, 204–12.

4. Tushnet, *Civil Rights Law,* 187–88, 68, 70; *Sweatt v. Painter,* 339 U.S. 629 (1950); *McLaurin v. Oklahoma State Regents,* 339 U.S. 637 (1950); Simon, *Antagonists,* 209–12; Berry, *Stability,* 20–21.

5. Tushnet, *Civil Rights Law,* 91–92, 129–49 (quote at 147); Loren Miller, *The Petitioners: The Story of the Supreme Court of the United States and the Negro* (Cleveland and New York: Meridian Books, 1966), 324; *Shelly v. Kraemer,* 334 U.S. 1 (1948).

6. *Briggs v. Elliott,* 98 F. Supp. 529 (D. S.C. 1951), *vacated and remanded,* 342 U.S. 350 (1952); *Brown v. Board of Education,* 98 F. Supp. 797 (D. Kan. 1951); *Davis v. County School Board,* 103 F. Supp. 337 (E.D. Va. 1952); *Gebhardt v. Belton,* 32 Del. Ch. 343, 87 A.2d 862 (1952), *aff'd* 33 Del. Ch. 144, 91 A.2d 137 (1952); *Brown v. Board of Education,* 344 U.S. 1 (1952) (noting pendency of the unreported *Bolling v. Sharpe* in the court of appeals and inviting petition for certiorari). For the pre-Supreme Court history of these cases, see Richard Kluger, *Simple Justice: The History of Brown v. Board of Education and Black America's Struggle for Equality* (New York: Knopf, 1976), 287–540; Tushnet, *Civil Rights Law,* 150–67; Dennis Hutchinson, "Unanimity and Desegregation: Decisionmaking in the Supreme Court, 1948–1958," 68 *Georgetown Law Journal* 1, at 30–32 (1979); James T. Patterson, *Brown v. Board of Education: A Civil Rights Milestone and Its Troubled Legacy* (New York: Oxford University Press, 2001), 21–45; Robert J. Cattral, Raymond T. Diamond, and Leland B. Ware, *Brown v. Board of Education: Caste, Culture, and the Constitution* (Lawrence: University Press of Kansas, 2003), 119–39; Peter Irons, *Jim Crow's Children: The Broken Promise of the Brown Decision* (New York: Penguin, 2002), 43–132.

7. Document written by FF during summer of 1952 and revised September 26, 1952, box 571, EW.

8. Freyer, *Black,* 123; Simon, *Antagonists,* 217–18; Kluger, *Simple Justice,* 590–91, 595–99; Tushnet, *Civil Rights Law,* 188–91; Vincent [L. McKusick] to Alexander Bickel, September 2, 1952, reel 4, frame 00239, FF-H. Bernard Schwartz disputes the contention that Jackson shared Rehnquist's views. See his "Chief Justice Rehnquist, Justice Jackson, and the *Brown* Case," 1988 *Supreme Court Review* 245, at 245–47, 267.

9. Tushnet, *Civil Rights Law,* 161–63, 172–73; *Brown v. Board of Education,* 98 F. Supp. at 797–98; Philip Elman, "The Solicitor General's Office, Justice Frankfurter, and Civil Rights Litigation, 1946–1960: An Oral History," 100 *Harvard Law Review* 817, at 825–27 (1987).

10. Kluger, *Simple Justice*, 543–48; FF, memorandum for the Conference, November 28, 1952, reel 4, frame 23, FF-H.

11. Entries of December 9–11, 1952, reel 2, Harold Burton Diaries, BD; Tushnet, *Civil Rights Law*, 173–86; Kluger, *Simple Justice*, 564–81. The oral arguments in *Brown* are published in full in Leon Friedman, ed., *Argument: The Oral Argument before the Supreme Court in Brown v. Board of Education of Topeka, 1952–1955* (New York: Chelsea House, 1969), and Philip Kurland and Gerhard Casper, eds., *Landmark Briefs and Arguments of the Supreme Court of the United States*, vol. 49A (Arlington, Va.: University Publications of America, 1975). Robert Carter's statement appears in the latter source at 280.

12. Elman, "Solicitor General," 827–29; Robert L. Stern to Harold Wiley, Nov. 12, 1952, box 184, RHJ; Kluger, *Simple Justice*, 561.

13. This account of the December 13, 1952, conference is based on the following sources: BD, December 13, 1952; Douglas, memorandum for the file, May 17, 1954, box 1148, WOD; retyped conference notes, box 1149, WOD; Frankfurter to Reed, undated, reel 4, frame 403, FF-H; conference notes, box A-27, TCC; conference notes [misdated December 23, 1952], box 184, RHJ; Tushnet, *Civil Rights Law*, 187–94; Klarman, *Jim Crow*, 293–300.

14. Schwartz, *Super Chief*, 78–82; Tushnet, *Civil Rights Law*, 195; Felix Frankfurter, memorandum for the Conference, May 27, 1953, and Hugo L. Black, memorandum for the Conference, June 13, 1953, both in box A-27, TCC; Newman, *Black*, 433; Felix Frankfurter to Tom Clark, June 4, 1953 (frame 211), Felix Frankfurter, memorandum for the Conference (frames 222–23), and Frankfurter to Warren, June 8, 1953 (frames 237–38), all on reel 4, FF-H; *Brown v. Board of Education*, 345 U.S. 972 (1953).

15. Kluger, *Simple Justice*, 656; Frankfurter to C. C. Burlingham, reel 3, frame 699, FF-H; Schwartz, *Super Chief*, 97, 219, 138; Cray, *Chief Justice*, 160–61, 185, 166, 278; *Hernandez v. Texas*, 347 U.S. 475 (1954); White, *Warren*, 163.

16. Tushnet, *Civil Rights Law*, 197–203; Alfred H. Kelly, "The School Desegregation Case," in *Quarrels That Have Shaped the Constitution*, ed. John Garraty, 2nd ed. (New York: Harper & Row, 1987), 325–27.

17. Alexander Bickel to Frankfurter, August 2, 1953, reel 4, frames 212–14, FF-H; FF, memorandum to the Conference, December 3, 1953, box 263, HB. Frankfurter circulated another version of the memorandum, revised by both him and Bickel, on May 18, 1954. Reel 4, frames 723–83, FF-H. It was later published as Bickel, "The Original Understanding of the Fourteenth Amendment," 69 *Harvard Law Review* 1–65 (1955) .

18. Elman, "Solicitor General," 852; Tushnet, *Civil Rights Law*, 205–7; Kluger, *Simple Justice*, 667–74.

19. Brownell, *Advising*, 189–94; Elman, "Solicitor General," 832–36; Supplemental Brief for the United States on Reargument, at 187, *Brown v. Board of Education of Topeka*, 347 U.S. 483 (1954). Although collapsing two conversations into one and erroneously stating that Brownell argued the case, Eisenhower supports the essence of his attorney general's account. See Dwight D. Eisenhower, *The White House Years: Waging Peace 1956–1961* (Garden City, N.Y.: Doubleday, 1965), 150.

20. Warren, *Memoirs*, 285; conference notes, 12–12–53, on *Briggs v. Elliott* and *Davis v. County School Board of Prince Edward County*, box 1149, WOD; Mark Tushnet, with Katya Lezin, "What Really Happened in *Brown v. Board of Education*," 91 *Columbia Law Review* 1867, at 1912–14 (1991).

21. FF, to "Dear Brethren," January 15, 1954, box 263, HLB; BD, December 17, 1953; Schwartz, *Super Chief*, 90–93; Cattral et al., *Brown v. Board*, 174–75.

22. Warren, *Memoirs*, 2, 285; Kluger, *Simple Justice*, 687–94; Schwartz, *Super Chief*, 93–94.

23. Kluger, *Simple Justice*, 698; R [Stanley Reed] to Frankfurter, May 21, 1954, reel 4, frame 408, FF-H.

24. Cray, *Chief Justice*, 284; Newman, *Black*, 434; Warren, *Memoirs*, 285–86; Douglas, memorandum for the file; Warren, "Memorandum to Members of Court," May 7, 1954, box 184, RHJ;

Schwartz, *Super Chief,* 96–97; drafts of memorandum [apparently prepared May 5, 1954] and Burton to Warren, May 8, 1954, all in box 571, EW; EW to Frankfurter, May 4, 1954, reel 4, frame 196, FF-H; BD, May 8, 1954.

25. Draft memoranda and undated cover note by E. D. [Elsie Douglas] on one of them, box 184, RHJ; Kluger, *Simple Justice,* 695, 697–98; Jeffrey D. Hockett, "Justice Robert H. Jackson and Segregation: A Study of the Limitations and Proper Basis of Judicial Action," 1989 *Yearbook of the Supreme Court Historical Society,* 52, 52–57; Schwartz, "Rehnquist," 264–67; Tushnet, "What Happened," 1915–17.

26. Schwartz, *Super Chief,* 101; BD, May 15, 1954; Douglas, memorandum for the files.

27. Brownell, *Advising,* 172; Kluger, *Simple Justice,* 701–2.

28. Schwartz, *Super Chief,* 109; *Brown v. Board of Education of Topeka,* 347 U.S. 483 (1954); ibid. at 493.

29. 347 U.S. at 494, 495; Kluger, *Simple Justice,* 705–6.

30. Edmund Cahn, "Jurisprudence," 30 *New York University Law Review* 150, at 159–61 (1955); Ernest Van den Haag, "Social Science Testimony in the Desegregation Cases—A Reply to Professor Kenneth Clark," 6 *Villanova Law Review* 69, 74–79 (1960); Learned Hand, *The Bill of Rights* (New York: Atheneum, 1968), 54–55; Wechsler, "Neutral Principles," 32–34; Louis H. Pollak, "Racial Discrimination and Judicial Integrity: A Reply to Professor Wechsler," 108 *University of Pennsylvania Law Review* 1–34 (1959); Charles L. Black Jr., "The Lawfulness of the Segregation Decisions," 69 *Yale Law Journal* 419, 421–23 (1960).

31. EP [Earl Pollock] to Chief Justice, undated, box 571, EW; Hutchinson, "Unanimity," 44– 50; *Meyer v. Nebraska,* 262 U.S. 390 (1923); *Pierce v. Society of Sisters,* 268 U.S. 510 (1925); *Farrington v. Tokushige,* 273 U.S. 284 (1927); *Bolling v. Sharpe,* 347 U.S. 497, 499–500 (1954).

32. *New York Times,* May 18, 1954, 28, 19, May 19, 1954, 19–20. On May 19, the *Times* published extracts from the editorials of other newspapers on the *Brown* decision.

33. Tushnet, *Civil Rights Law,* 217–18.

34. Warren, *Memoirs,* 302–3; William T. Coleman Jr. to Frankfurter, May 20, 1954, reel 3, frame 939, FF-H; Harry H. Lun Jr. to Burton, October 27, 1954, box 337, HB; Richard T. McSorley to Frankfurter, May 23, 1954, reel 3, frame 945, FF-H; Newman, *Black,* 440; Mrs. William Dickinson to Hugo L. Black, August 19, 1954, box 322, HB; "A Joint Resolution Stating the Policy of the State of North Carolina with Reference to the Mixing of Children of Different Races in the Public Schools of the State, and Creating an Advisory Committee on Education," box 337, HB; Schwartz, *Super Chief,* 110–11; Frankfurter to Warren, July 8, 1954, box 184, RHJ; untitled report on public education, box A-27, TCC; Powe, *American Politics,* 39; Frankfurter to Warren, July 21, 1954, box 353, EW.

35. Tinsley E. Yarbrough, *John Marshall Harlan: Great Dissenter of the Warren Court* (New York: Oxford University Press, 1992), 1–88; Eisenhower, *Mandate,* 230; Lloyd Wright to president, November 16, 1954, OF 100-A, WHCF, DDEL; Learned Hand to the president, October 22, 1954, box 182, JMH.

36. Yarbrough, *Harlan,* 90–109; *Cong. Record,* 84th Cong., 1st sess (March 16, 1955): 3036.

37. Dwight D. Eisenhower to Harlan, April 6, 1955, OF 100-A(1), DDE; Charles Fried, "The Conservatism of Justice Harlan," 36 *New York Law School Law Review* 33, at 36–37 (1991); Yarbrough, *Harlan,* viii.

38. Yarbrough, *Harlan,* 89–92; Burton to Harlan, November 22, 1954, box 490, JMH; Warren to Harlan, December 14, 1954, box 605, JMH; Hutchinson, "Unanimity," 51; Kluger, *Simple Justice,* 741.

39. Schwartz, *Super Chief,* 115–16; Tushnet, *Civil Rights Law,* 220–21; Draft 1, undated, reel 4, frames 429–33, FF-H; "Law Clerks Recommendations for Segregation Decree," undated, box 337, EW.

40. "Brief for U.S. on the Further Argument of Questions of Relief," at 23, 349 U.S. 294 (1955); Brownell, *Advising*, 196–97; Pach and Richardson, *Presidency*, 143.

41. Tushnet, *Civil Rights Law*, 324–27; Schwartz, *Super Chief*, 114; Kurland and Casper, *Landmark Briefs and Oral Arguments*, 49A:1188–95.

42. Hutchinson, "Unanimity," 53–55; conference notes, 4–16–54 [*sic*], box 1148, WOD; Tushnet, *Civil Rights Law*, 229; Kluger, *Simple Justice*, 737–39.

43. Schwartz, *Super Chief*, 119–20; EW, memorandum for the Conference, May 26, 1955, box 337, EW; *Brown v. Board of Education of Topeka*, 349 U.S. 294, 298–99 (1955).

44. Patterson, *Brown v. Board*, 84–85; Brownell, *Advising*, 174, 198; Cray, *Chief Justice*, 296. Michael Klarman calls *Brown II* "a solid victory for white southerners," *Jim Crow*, 318.

45. Powe, *American Politics*, 52; Michael J. Klarman, "How *Brown* Changed Race Relations: The Backlash Thesis," 81 *Journal of American History* 81, at 82 (1994); Judith A. Hagley, "Massive Resistance: The Rhetoric and the Reality," 27 *New Mexico Law Review* 167, at 190 (1997). The "Southern Manifesto" is reprinted in its entirety in Brownell, *Advising*, 359–63.

46. Hagerty, *Diary*, 54; Eisenhower, *Mandate*, 230; Brownell, *Advising*, 197–98, 204–5; Dwight D. Eisenhower to James F. Byrnes, July 23, 1957, box 25, DDE Diaries Series (Ann Whitman File), DDEL; Schwartz, *Super Chief*, 174–75; Warren, *Memoirs*, 289–90.

47. Melvin I. Urofsky, *A March of Liberty: A Constitutional History of the United States*, 2nd ed. (New York: Knopf, 1988), 777; Patterson, *Brown v. Board*, 99–100; Michal R. Belknap, *Federal Law and Southern Order: Racial Violence and Constitutional Conflict in the Post-Brown South* (Athens: University of Georgia Press, 1987), 27–30; Brownell, *Advising*, 205.

48. Tushnet, *Civil Rights Law*, 235–38, 244–45; *Hawkins v. Board of Control*, 350 U.S. 413 (1956); *Shuttlesworth v. Birmingham Board of Education*, 358 U.S. 101 (1958).

49. Herbert Brownell Jr. to the president, November 7, 1957, box 8, AS, DDEL; Tony Freyer, *The Little Rock Crisis: A Constitutional Interpretation* (Westport, Conn.: Greenwood Press, 1984), 15–114; Brownell, *Advising*, 210–11.

50. Tushnet, *Civil Rights Law*, 258–59; *Cooper v. Aaron*, 163 F. Supp. 13 (E.D. Ark. 1958), *rev'd*. 257 F.2d 33 (8th Cir. 1958), *cert granted*, 358 U.S. 27 (1958); *Aaron v. Cooper*, 358 U.S. 27 (1958); *Cooper v. Aaron*, 358 U.S. 5 (1958).

51. BD, May 3, 1956; Gugin and St. Clair, *Minton*, 274, 276. Minton to the president, September 7, 1956, and Herbert Brownell Jr. to the president, October 11, 1956, OF 100-A, WHCF, DDEL; Eisenhower, *Mandate*, 230; Brownell, *Advising*, 179–80; Horwitz, *Warren Court*, 9, 103; Cong. Record, 86th Cong., 1st Sess. 1957, 3936–46.

52. On Brennan's pre-Court career, see Kim Isaac Eisler, *A Justice for All: William J. Brennan Jr. and the Decisions That Transformed America* (New York: Simon & Schuster, 1993), 17–85.

53. Reed to president, undated, and Dwight D. Eisenhower to Reed, January 28, 1957, both in OF 100-A, WHCF, DDEL; Brownell, *Advising*, 180–81; Herbert Brownell Jr. to president, March 3, 1957 [?], OF 100-A(2), WHCF, DDEL; Michael A. Kahn, "Shattering the Myth about President Eisenhower's Supreme Court Appointments," 22 *Presidential Studies Quarterly* 47, at 53 (1992); Henry J. Abraham, *Justices, Presidents, and Senators: A History of the U.S. Supreme Court Appointments from Washington to Clinton* (Lanham, Md.: Rowman & Littlefield, 1999), 203–4.

54. Berry, *Stability*, 212, 225–26.

55. Ibid., 226; Burton to president, July 17, 1958, OF 100-A(2), WHCF, DDE; Abraham, *Justices*, 205.

56. Berry, *Stability*, 226; BD, September 26, 1958; Kahn, "Shattering," 53–54; Abraham, *Justices*, 205; *Cong. Record*, 86th Cong., 1st sess. (May 5, 1959): 7472.

57. *Aaron v. Cooper*, 358 U.S. 27 (1958); Tushnet, *Civil Rights Law*, 260; William Rogers to Wayne Upton, September 7, 1958, and William Rogers to Dean Dauley, September 7, 1958, both in box 14, WJB.

58. Tushnet, *Civil Rights Law*, 259–61; Schwartz, *Super Chief*, 292.

59. Schwartz, *Super Chief*, 293; FF and JMH, memorandum for the Conference, September 11, 1958, box A-73, TCC; *Cooper v. Aaron*, 358 U.S. 5 (1958).

60. Tushnet, *Civil Rights Law*, 263–64; Yarbrough, *Harlan*, 168–71; notes for Conference, undated, and untitled, undated response to Harlan's suggestions, both in "Aaron v. Cooper" folder, box i4, WJB; WOD to Bill, September 22, [1958], box 14, WJB; Warren, *Memoirs*, 298.

61. "Memorandum by Mr Justice Frankfurter on Little Rock," August 27, 1958, reel 36, frames 501–4, FF-H; Hutchinson, "Unanimity," 76–77; Schwartz, *Super Chief*, 292, 303; Freyer, *Black*, 132; BD, September 29, 1958; Yarbrough, *Harlan*, 171–72; "Mr Justice Harlan concurring in part, expressing a dubitante in part and dissenting in part," undated, box 325, HB; *Cooper v. Aaron*, 358 U.S. 20 (1958) (Frankfurter, J., concurring).

62. 358 U.S. 1, 14, 16, 17, 18 (1958).

63. Memorandum for record, August 22, 1958–telephone call, box 31, AS, DDEL; Dwight D. Eisenhower to E. E. Hazlett, July 22, 1957, box 25, DDE Diaries, DDEL; undated statement, box 17, William Rogers Papers, DDEL.

64. Powe, *American Politics*, 164; *Watson v. Memphis*, 373 U.S. 526, 530 (1963).

65. *Goss v. Board of Education*, 373 U.S. 683 (1963); *Griffin v. Prince Edward County Board of Education*, 377 U.S. 218 (1964); conference notes, April 3, 1964, box 1304, WOD; 377 U.S. at 234.

66. Gerald N. Rosenberg, *The Hollow Hope: Can Courts Bring About Social Change?* (Chicago: University of Chicago Press, 1991), 50–52; Herbert O. Reid Sr., "State of the Art: The Law and Education since 1954," 52 *Journal of Negro Education* 234, at 237 (1963); Robert L. Crain and Rita E. Mahard, "Desegregation and Black Achievement: A Review of the Research," 42 *Law and Contemporary Problems* 17, at 31–33 (1978).

67. Lawrence Friedman, *American Law in the 20th Century* (New Haven, Conn.: Yale University Press, 2000), 294; *Mayor & City Council of Baltimore v. Dawson*, 350 U.S. 877 (1955); *Holmes v. City of Atlanta*, 350 U.S. 879 (1955); *Gayle v. Browder*, 352 U.S. 903 (1956); Schwartz, *Super Chief*, 125–27; Kurland, *Politics*, 71, 124.

68. William E. Nelson, "The Changing Meaning of Equality in Twentieth-Century Constitutional Law," 52 *Washington and Lee Law Review* 3, at 4, 76, 100 (1995).

69. For examples of scholarship questioning Brown's significance and effectiveness, see Klarman, "Backlash Thesis"; Klarman, "Brown, Racial Change, and the Civil Rights Movement," 80 *Virginia Law Review* 7 (1994); Klarman, *Jim Crow*, 342–442; Rosenberg, *Hollow Hope*, 42–71; and Raymond Wolters, *The Burden of Brown: Thirty Years of School Desegregation* (Knoxville: University of Tennessee Press, 1984). For defenses of its significance, see David J. Garrow, "Hopelessly Hollow History: Revisionist Devaluing of *Brown v. Board of Education*," 80 *Virginia Law Review* 151 (1994); and Mark Tushnet, "The Significance of *Brown v. Board of Education*," 80 *Virginia Law Review* 179 (1994). The arguments of the critics are ably summarized by James T. Patterson, who nevertheless concludes that *Brown* made positive contributions to American law and race relations. See *Brown v. Board*, 206–23.

70. *Warren*, 170.

3. COLD WAR, COMMUNISM, AND CONFRONTATION

1. David Caute, *The Great Fear: The Anti-Communist Purge under Truman and Eisenhower* (New York: Simon & Schuster, 1978), 146.

2. *American Communications Association v. Douds*, 339 U.S. 94 (1950); *Dennis v. United States*, 341 U.S. 494 (1951); Ellen Schrecker, *Many Are the Crimes: McCarthyism in America* (Boston: Little, Brown, 1998), 190; *Joint Anti-Fascist Refugee Committee v. McGrath*, 341 U.S. 123 (1951); *Bailey v. Richardson*, 341 U.S. 918 (1951); *Gerende v. Election Board*, 341 U.S. 56 (1951); *Garner v. Board of*

Public Works of Los Angeles, 341 U.S. 716 (1951); *Adler v. Board of Education,* 342 U.S. 485 (1952); *Wieman v. Updegraff,* 344 U.S. 183 (1952).

3. Richard M. Fried, *Nightmare in Red: The McCarthy Era in Perspective* (New York: Oxford University Press, 1990), 178–83, 136–43; Belknap, *Cold War,* 214–31.

4. Fried, *Nightmare,* 184.

5. *Wilson v. Girard,* 354 U.S. 525 (1957); EW, memorandum for the Conference, June 19, 1957, box 1182, WOD; Felix Frankfurter to Earl Warren, June 12, 1957, box 353, EW; EW, memorandum for the Conference, June 20, 1957, box 328, HLB; appendix B, 354 U.S. at 544; Schwartz, *Super Chief,* 247–49; Boris Bittker to Jerome A. Cohen, reel 27, frame 666, FF-H.

6. "Notes for Conference Re No.'s 701 and 710," undated, box A-48, TCC; conference notes, May 4, 1956, box 1163, WOD; docket book entries for *Kinsella v. Krueger* and *Reid v. Covert,* box 369, EW; Reed, memorandum to the Conference, May 14, 1956, and TCC to "Our Five," May 23, 1956, box A-48, TCC; *Kinsella v. Krueger,* 351 U.S. 470 (1956); *Reid v. Covert,* 351 U.S. 487 (1956).

7. 351 U.S. at 481–85; Harlan to Frankfurter, June 6, 1956, reel 24, frame 339, FF-H; memoranda from Frankfurter to Warren, Black and Douglas, September 19, 1956, reel 24, frame 344, FF-H; memorandum from Frankfurter to Warren, Black and Douglas, September 20, 1956, reel 24, frame 346, FF-H; circulated dissent by Frankfurter, September 20, 1956, memorandum by Black, September 21, 1956, and memorandum from Harlan for Reed, Burton, Clark and Minton, September 26, 1956, all in box A-48, TCC; conference list for week of October 1, 1956, box A-49, TCC; Schwartz, *Super Chief,* 243; Harlan, memorandum for the Conference, October 10, 1956, box 1, WJB; Clark to Reed and Burton, October 29, 1956, box A-48, TCC. In *United States ex rel. Toth v. Quarles,* 350 U.S. 11 (1956), the Court had held that an honorably discharged former serviceman could not constitutionally be subjected to trial by court-martial for a crime committed while he was on active duty.

8. Conference notes, March 1, 1957, box 1163, WOD; docket book entries for *Kinsella v. Krueger* and *Reid v. Covert,* box 403, WJB; Frankfurter to Warren, March 6, 1957, box 1, WJB; *Reid v. Covert,* 354 U.S. 4 (1957).

9. Schwartz, *Super Chief,* 245–46; 354 U.S. at 16–19; Frankfurter to "Dear Brethren," May 20, 1957, reel 18, frames 383–85, FF-H.

10. *Kinsella v. United States ex rel. Singleton,* 361 U.S. 234 (1960); *Grisham v. Hagan,* 361 U.S. 278 (1960); *McElroy v. United States ex rel. Guagliardo,* 361 U.S. 281 (1960); conference notes, October 23, 1959, box 1213, WOD; Clark, memorandum to the Conference, October 24, 1959, box A-93, TCC; 361 U.S. at 249 (Harlan, J., concurring in part and dissenting in part); 361 U.S. at 259 (Whittaker, J., concurring in part and dissenting in part).

11. White, *Warren,* 38–42, 58–60, 114, 120–22 (quote at 114); Edward R. Long, "Earl Warren and the Politics of Anti-Communism," 51 *Pacific Historical Review* 51, at 54 (1982); Belknap, *Cold War,* 236–37.

12. White, *Warren,* 199; "The Blessings of Liberty: Address of Earl Warren, Chief Justice of the United States at the Second Century Convocation of Washington University, St. Louis, Missouri," February 19, 1955, OF 100-A, WHCF, DDEL; Belknap, *Cold War,* 237; Schwartz, *Super Chief,* 151. The ABA speech is quoted in Belknap, *Cold War,* at 237. The *Fortune* article is reprinted in *The Public Papers of Chief Justice Earl Warren,* ed. Henry M. Christman (New York: Simon & Schuster, 1955), 236–37.

13. Urofsky, *Frankfurter,* 143, 147.

14. Simon, *Antagonists,* 235–39; Belknap, *Cold War,* 239.

15. Yarbrough, *Harlan,* 119–29; Simon, *Antagonists,* 239–40.

16. Yarbrough, *Harlan,* 128; Schwartz, *Super Chief,* 216–17.

17. Robert S. Marsel, "The Constitutional Jurisprudence of Justice Potter Stewart: Reflections on a Life of Public Service," 55 *Tennessee Law Review* 1, at 11–12 (1987); Gail Binion, "Justice

Potter Stewart: The Unpredictable Vote," 1992 *Journal of Supreme Court History* 99, at 119 (1992); Simon, *Antagonists*, 249.

18. Belknap, *Cold War*, 237–39; *United States v. Flynn*, 216 F.2d 354 (2d Cir. 1954); Yarbrough, *Harlan*, 86; memorandum of Harlan, *Noto v. United States*, November 21, 1955, box A-40, TCC.

19. *Emspak v. United States*, 349 U.S. 190 (1955); docket book entries for *Emspak v. United States*, box 367, EW; Schwartz, *Super Chief*, 177–79; Frankfurter to Black, May 15, 1954, box 320, HLB; conference notes on *Quinn v. United States* and *Emspak v. United States*, April 9, 1955, box 1155, WOD; *Quinn v. United States*, 349 U.S. 155 (1955).

20. *Ullman v. United States*, 350 U.S. 425 (1956); 68 Stat. 745 (1954); *Peters v. Hobby*, 349 U.S. 331 (1955); *Cole v. Young*, 351 U.S. 557 (1956).

21. *Slochower v. Board of Higher Education of the City of New York*, 350 U.S. 551 (1956); conference notes, October 21, 1955, and March 8, 1956, box 1163, WOD; Frankfurter to Chief Justice, March 13, 1956, reel 15, frame 391, FF-H; *Slochower*, 350 U.S. at 559, 565.

22. Conference notes, November 18, 1955, and March 8, 1956, box 1163, WOD; "Communist Party case discussion," box 494, JMH; TCC, memorandum for the Conference, February 24, 1956, and JMH, memorandum for the Conference, March 7, 1956, both in box A-43, TCC.

23. Schwartz, *Super Chief*, 186; FF to "Dear Brethren," April 2, 1956, TCC, memorandum for the Conference, April 4, 1956, and FF, memorandum for the Conference, April 4, 1956, all in box 494, JMH; Clark, draft memorandum to the Conference (not used), April 17, 1956, box A-43, TCC; Burton to Frankfurter, April 4, 1956, HB; *Communist Party v. Subversive Activities Control Board*, 351 U.S. 116, 125 (1956); ibid. at 125, 128.

24. *Pennsylvania v. Nelson*, 350 U.S. 497 (1956); *Commonwealth v. Nelson*, 377 Pa. 58, 104 A.2d 133 (1954); conference notes, November 18, 1955, box 1164, WOD; docket book entry, box 367, EW; conference list, conference of Friday, November 18, 1955, reel 20, frame 673, FF-H. Douglas, Frankfurter, and Warren disagree about how Harlan and Reed voted.

25. *Mesarosh v. United States*, 352 U.S. 1 (1956); docket book entry, box 370, EW; *Mesarosh v. United States*, 352 U.S. 862 (1956); 352 U.S. at 9, 4.

26. *Schware v. Board of Bar Examiners of the State of New Mexico*, 353 U.S. 232 (1957); docket book entry in no. 92, Schware vs. Board of Bar Examiners of the State of New Mexico, box 370, EW; Clark to Black, May 2 [1957], box 330, HLB; *Konigsberg v. State Bar of California*, 353 U.S. 252 (1957); conference notes on Konigsberg, January 18, 1957, box 1123, WOD; *Konigsberg*, 353 U.S. at 274 (Frankfurter, J., dissenting) and at 276 (Harlan, J., dissenting).

27. *Kremen v. United States*, 353 U.S. 346 (1957); *Jencks v. United States*, 353 U.S. 657 (1957); conference notes on *Jencks*, October 19, 1956, November 2, 1956, and March 22, 1957, box 1173, WOD; *Jencks*, 353 U.S. at 672; ibid. at 681 (Clark, J., dissenting); Schwartz, *Super Chief*, 226–28; Arthur J. Sabin, *In Calmer Times: The Supreme Court and Red Monday* (Philadelphia: University of Pennsylvania Press, 1999), 147.

28. *Service v. Dulles*, 354 U.S. 363 (1957). For a complete history of the *Amerasia* case, see Harvey Klehr and Ronald Radosh, *The Amerasia Spy Case: Prelude to McCarthyism* (Chapel Hill: University of North Carolina Press, 1996).

29. *Yates v. United States*, 354 U.S. 301 (1957); Schneiderman conference notes, October 12, 1956, reel 20, frames 376–81, FF-H; 354 U.S. at 339; Schwartz, *Super Chief*, 232–34; docket book entry, box 370, EW; Belknap, *Cold War*, 245; JMH., "Confidential Memorandum for Messrs. Bator and Schlei," July 8, 1956, box 483, JMH; 354 U.S. at 344.

30. Belknap, *Cold War*, 246, 258–61; *Yates*, 354 U.S. at 324–25.

31. *Watkins v. United States*, 354 U.S. 215 (1957); ibid. at 217; Sabin, *Calmer*, 154; conference notes, March 8, 1957, box 1173, WOD; White, *Warren*, 242–44; 354 U.S. at 197; Parrish, "Frankfurter," 60; Frankfurter to Chief Justice, May 27, 1957, reel 27, frames 606–8, FF-H; pages from Warren's draft opinion with suggested changes, reel 27, frames 587–90, FF-H; Schwartz, *Super Chief*, 238–39; 354 U.S. at 216 (Frankfurter, J., dissenting); Yarbrough, *Harlan*, 201.

32. *Sweezy v. New Hampshire,* 354 U.S. 269 (1957); conference notes, March 8, 1957, box 1173, WOD; docket book page for *Sweezy v. New Hampshire,* box 270, EW; Warren to Frankfurter, June 5, 1957, box 580, EW; Harlan to the Chief Justice, May 31, 1957, box 29, JMH; 354 U.S. at 255; ibid. at 267.

33. Schwartz, *Super Chief,* 250, 280–81; Fried, *Nightmare,* 186; Sabin, *Calmer,* 193; Powe, *American Politics,* 98–99; *The Gallup Poll,* 3 vols. (New York: Random House, 1972), 3:1502–3; *New York Times,* June 25, 1957, 15, and July 8, 1957, 15. McCarthy is quoted by Schwartz.

34. Warren, *Memoirs,* 5; Dwight D. Eisenhower to Chief Justice, June 21, 1957, box 104, EW; Eisenhower to William Rogers, May 12, 1958, box 33, DDE Diaries Series, DDEL.

35. Warren to president, July 15, 1957, box 104, EW; Warren, *Memoirs,* 321–27, 330–31; Frankfurter to Warren, November 8, 1956, box 353, EW.

36. Walter F. Murphy, *Congress and the Court: A Case Study in the American Political Process* (Chicago: University of Chicago Press, 1962), 164, 127–53; 71 Stat. 595 (1957).

37. Belknap, *Cold War,* 254–58; Sabin, *Calmer,* 195; Walter Murphy, *Congress,* 160–71, 196–208; Powe, *American Politics,* 130–33; Act to Define the Term "Organize," Pub. L. No. 87–486, 76 Stat. 103 (1962).

38. Powe, *American Politics,* 141–42; Walter Murphy, *Congress,* 246; Sabin, *Calmer,* 202.

39. *Wellman v. United States,* 354 U.S. 931 (1957); *Scales v. United States,* 355 U.S. 1 (1957); *Lightfoot v. United States,* 355 U.S. 2 (1957); Belknap, *Cold War,* 160, 247, 169; Frankfurter to "Dear Brethren," October 26, 1956, box 320, HB; Schwartz, *Super Chief,* 312; *Yates v. United States,* 355 U.S. 66 (1957), 356 U.S. 365 (1958).

40. *In re Sawyer,* 360 U.S. 622 (1959); conference notes, May 22, 1959, box 1200, WOD; 360 U.S. at 646 (Stewart, J., concurring); ibid. at 647, 649 (Frankfurter, J., dissenting).

41. *Kent v. Dulles,* 357 U.S. 117 (1958); *Dayton v. Dulles,* 357 U.S. 144 (1958); conference notes, undated, box A-71, TCC; Schwartz, *Super Chief,* 309–11; preliminary circulation of concurring opinion by Frankfurter, May 13, 1958, reel 29, frame 249, FF-H; Whittaker to Douglas, June 13, 1958, box A-71, TCC; *Kent,* 357 U.S. at 130; 357 U.S. at 154. For an extended discussion of *Kent v. Dulles,* see Stanley I. Kutler, *The American Inquisition: Justice and Injustice in the Cold War* (New York: Hill and Wang, 1982),101–14.

42. *Greene v. McElroy,* 360 U.S. 474 (1959); ibid. at 493; conference notes, *Greene v. McElroy* docket book entry, box 405, WJB; 360 U.S. at 509; ibid. at 510; *Taylor v. McElroy,* 360 U.S. 709 (1959); preliminary circulation of per curiam opinion in *Taylor v. McElroy,* box A-88, TCC; conference notes, April 3, 1959, box 1200, WOD; *Vitrarelli v. Seaton,* 359 U.S. 545 (1959); "Memorandum of Justice Frankfurter on No. 101—October Term, 1958," undated, box 21, WJB.

43. *Shelton v. Tucker,* 364 U.S. 479 (1960); Schwartz, *Super Chief,* 367; 364 U.S. at 490 (Frankfurter, J., dissenting); ibid. at 496, 497 (Harlan, J., dissenting).

44. Walter Murphy, *Congress,* 123, 184, 190, 231; Ball and Cooper, *Power,* 157.

45. *Sacher v. United States,* 356 U.S. 576 (1958); Douglas to Frankfurter, April 23, [1958], Frankfurter to Douglas, April 23, 1958, and Harlan to Frankfurter, April 23, 1958, reel 23, frames 618–20, 624–25, FF-H.

46. *Barenblatt v. United States,* 360 U.S. 109 (1959); conference notes, March 24, 1961, box 1234, WOD; Yarbrough, *Harlan,* 201–4; Warren to Frankfurter, June 5, 1957, box 580, EW; 360 U.S. at 128; Frankfurter, "Memorandum to Harlan re. No. 35 . . . ," June 3, 1959, box 533, JMH; 360 U.S. at 166 (Brennan, J., dissenting); ibid. at 134, 141, 143 (Black, J., dissenting).

47. Thurman Arnold to Black, June 10, 1959, box 337, HLB; *Braden v. United States,* 365 U.S. 431 (1961); *Wilkinson v. United States,* 365 U.S. 399 (1961); conference notes, *Braden v. United States* docket book pages, box 407, WJB; *Deutch v. United States,* 367 U.S. 456 (1961).

48. *Uphaus v. Wyman,* 360 U.S. 72 (1959), *previously vacated and remanded,* 355 U.S. 16 (1957); conference notes, *Uphaus v. Wyman* docket book entry, box 405, WJB; conference notes, box

A-74, TCC; Harlan to Clark, December 4, 1958, box A-78, TCC; 360 U.S. at 82 (Brennan, J., dissenting); ibid. at 108 (Black, J., dissenting); memorandum from Douglas, undated, and memorandum by Frankfurter on motion for bail, July 7, 1960, both in box A-90, TCC; *Uphaus v. Wyman*, 364 U.S. 388 (1960).

49. *Beilan v. Board of Education, School District of Philadelphia*, 357 U.S. 405 (1958); *Lerner v. Casey*, 357 U.S. 468, 475 (1958); *Nelson v. County of Los Angeles*, 362 U.S. 1 (1960).

50. *Konigsberg v. State Bar of California*, 366 U.S. 36 (1961); *In re Anastaplo*, 366 U.S. 82 (1961); conference notes, December 16, 1960, box 1233, WOD; *Anastaplo*, 366 U.S. at 89; ibid. at 97 (Black, J., dissenting); *Konigsberg*, 366 U.S. at 56 (Black, J., dissenting).

51. *Communist Party of the United States v. Subversive Activities Control Board*, 367 U.S. 1 (1960); conference notes, docket book entry for *CPUSA v. SACB*, box 407, WJB; conference notes, undated, box A-105, TCC; JMH, memorandum for the Conference, January 24, 1961, and separate memorandum on *Communist Party of the United States v. Subversive Activities Control Board*, January 10, 1961, box 47, TCC; 367 U.S. at 115 (Warren, C.J, dissenting); ibid. at 169 (Douglas, J., dissenting); ibid. at 191 (Brennan, J., dissenting); ibid. at 137, 164 (Black, J., dissenting); Charles Hughes to Justice Frankfurter, June 7, 1961, reel 59, frame 559, FF-H.

52. *Scales v. United States*, 353 U.S. 657 (1957); Belknap, *Cold War*, 265–67; Mark A. Sheft, "The End of the Smith Act Era: A Legal and Historical Analysis of *Scales v. United States*," 36 *American Journal of Legal History* 164, at 186 (1992); FF to "Dear Brethren, Re: Nos. 29 and 32 . . . ," October 23, 1956, reel 33, frames 749–50, FF-H; Clark, circulated memoranda on *Communist Party v. SACB, Scales v. United States*, June 26, 1959, box 72, JMH, and on *CP* and *Noto v. United States*, February 3, 1960, box 347, HLB; Frankfurter to Clark, February 5, 1960, box 493, JMH.

53. *Scales v. United States*, 367 U.S. 203 (1961); Sheft, "End," 192–97; Yarbrough, *Harlan*, 195; 367 U.S. at 262 (Douglas, J., dissenting); ibid. at 259 (Black, J., dissenting); ibid. at 278 (Brennan, J., dissenting).

54. Sheft, "End," 193; *Noto v. United States*, 367 U.S. 299 (1961); docket bok entry, *Noto v. United States*, box 407, WJB; Clark to Harlan, February 21, 1966, box A-104, TCC; 367 U.S. at 298; Sabin, *Calmer*, 203; Belknap, *Cold War*, 271–72. Brennan, Black, and Douglas concurred in *Noto*.

55. Sheft, "End," 198; Belknap, *Cold War*, 270–71; *Green v. United States*, 356 U.S. 165 (1958); *Fleming v. Nestor*, 363 U.S. 603 (1960).

56. *Abel v. United States*, 362 U.S. 217 (1960); Schwartz, *Super Chief*, 339–41, 366–67; *Cafeteria and Restaurant Workers Union Local 473 v. McElroy*, 367 U.S. 886 (1961); Schwartz, *Super Chief*, 366–67.

57. Leon Friedman, "Byron R. White," in Friedman and Israel, *Justices*, 4:1581–82; David L. Stebenne, *Arthur J. Goldberg: New Deal Liberal* (New York: Oxford University Press, 1996), 80, 107–9, 317–18. According to Russell J. Galloway Jr., during the 1957–61 terms (October 1957–June 1961), the Court exhibited conservative voting patterns in a wide variety of cases, not just those involving internal security. "The Second Period of the Warren Court: The Liberal Trend Abates (1957–1961)," 19 *Santa Clara Law Review* 947 (1979).

58. Nationality Act of 1940, ch. 876, Pub. L. No. 76–853, 54 Stat. 1137; Leonard B. Boudin, "Involuntary Loss of American Nationality," 73 *Harvard Law Review* 1510, at 1513 (1960); *Perez v. Brownell*, 356 U.S. 44 (1958); *Trop v. Dulles*, 356 U.S. 88 (1958); Schwartz, *Super Chief*, 313, 315; White, *Judicial Tradition*, 349–56; Urofsky, *Frankfurter*, 80–81; FF, memorandum for the Conference, June 7, 1957, reel 32, frame 501, FF-H; White, *Warren*, 232; *Trop*, 356 U.S. at 91–104; Brennan to Warren, March 12, 1958, box 10, WJB; *Trop*, 356 U.S. at 105–14 (Brennan, J., concurring); ibid. at 114, 119–28 (Frankfurter, J., dissenting); *Perez*, 356 U.S. at 57–62; Frankfurter to Whittaker, March 5, 1958, reel 32, frames 599–604, FF-H; *Trop*, 356 U.S. at 129 (Frankfurter, J., dissenting).

59. *Kennedy v. Mendoza-Martinez* and *Rusk v. Cort*, 372 U.S. 144 (1963); Schwartz, *Super Chief*, 357–58, 404–7; *Mackey v. Mendoza-Martinez*, 362 U.S. 384 (1960); *Kennedy v. Mendoza-Martinez*,

369 U.S. 832 (1962); *Rusk v. Cort*, 369 U.S. 367 (1962); 372 U.S. at 187 (Brennan, J., concurring); "Mr. Justice Stewart's Second Circulation in Mendoza-Martinez," box 73, WJB; 372 U.S. at 201 (Stewart, J., dissenting); ibid. at 197.

60. Charles Gordon, "The Citizen and the State: The Power of Congress to Expatriate American Citizens," 53 *Georgetown Law Journal* 315, at 331–33 (1965); *Schneider v. Rusk*, 377 U.S. 163 (1964); *Marks v. Esperdy*, 377 U.S. 214 (1964); *Afroyim v. Rusk*, 387 U.S. 255 (1967); ibid. at 270 (Harlan, J., dissenting).

61. *Russell v. United States*, 369 U.S. 749 (1962); *Yellin v. United States*, 374 U.S. 485 (1963); note from Bill [Brennan] to Chief, undated, box 348, EW; *Gojack v. United States*, 384 U.S. 702 (1966).

62. Fried, *Nightmare*, 195–96.

63. *Gibson v. Florida Legislative Investigating Committee*, 372 U.S. 539 (1963); ibid. at 583 (White, J., dissenting); *DeGregory v. Attorney General of New Hampshire*, 383 U.S. 825, 829 (1966); ibid. at 830 (Harlan, J., dissenting).

64. *Baggett v. Bullitt*, 377 U.S. 360 (1964); ibid. at 372; *Elfbrandt v. Russell*, 384 U.S. 11 (1966); ibid. at 19 (White, J., dissenting).

65. *United States v. Brown*, 381 U.S. 465 (1965); ibid. at 462; *Aptheker v. Secretary of State*, 376 U.S. 500 (1964); *Lamont v. Postmaster General of the United States*, 381 U.S. 301 (1963).

66. *American Committee for the Protection of Foreign Born v. Subversive Activities Control Board*, 380 U.S. 503 (1965); ibid. at 506 (Douglas, J., dissenting); *Veterans of the Abraham Lincoln Brigade v. Subversive Activities Control Board*, 380 U.S. 514 (1965); 380 U.S. 503 at 511 (Black, J., dissenting in both cases); docket book entry and conference notes, box 11, WJB; Brennan, memorandum to chief justice, Black, Warren, Douglas and Goldberg, January, 1965, box 82, HLB; *Albertson v. Subversive Activities Control Board*, 382 U.S. 70 (1965).

67. *United States v. Robel*, 389 U.S. 258 (1967); docket book entry and conference notes, box 415, WJB; Schwartz, *Super Chief*, 709–11; WJB Jr., "Memorandum to the Chief," May 22, 1967; 389 U.S. at 389 (White, J., dissenting).

68. *Dallas Morning News*, December 13, 1967.

4. Turning Point

1. Russell W. Galloway Jr., "The Third Period of the Warren Court: Liberal Dominance (1962–1969)," 20 *Santa Clara Law Review* 773, at 775 (1980); Schwartz, *History*, 273; White, *Judicial Tradition*, 346; Tushnet, "History," 4, 7, 12–13.

2. E. P. Cullinan, Deputy Clerk, "Memorandum for Chief Justice," January 4, 1961, box A-102, TCC; "The Supreme Court, 1961 Term," 76 *Harvard Law Review* 78, at 78–79 (1962). The statistics presented here and later in this chapter are based on data contained in the *Harvard Law Review*'s annual reviews of the Supreme Court term for the terms 1953 through 1961. These appear in the November issues of volumes 68–76. For the pages on which this data appears, see chapter 10, notes 5 and 7, below.

3. Schwartz, *Super Chief*, 399; Erwin N. Griswold, "Forward: Of Time and Attitudes—Professor Hart and Judge Arnold," 74 *Harvard Law Review* 81, at 82–84 (1960); Yarbrough, *Harlan*, 130–31; Henry M. Hart, "Forward: The Time Chart of the Justices," 73 *Harvard Law Review* 84, at 100, 124 (1959).

4. Thurman Arnold, "Professor Hart's Theology," 75 *Harvard Law Review* 1298, at 1314 (1960); William O. Douglas, "The Supreme Court and Its Case Load," April 8, 1960, box 59, HLB. Douglas's speech was published with minor editorial changes in 45 *Cornell Law Quarterly* 401 (1960).

5. White, *Judicial Tradition*, 369; Warren, *Memoirs*, 356–58; Clark, Harlan, and Brennan, memorandum to the Conference, March 18, 1959, and EW, "Memorandum for Brethren," September 29, 1958, box 1199, WOD; Statement by Justice Douglas, April 15, 1961, box A-102, TCC;

EW, "Memorandum for Brethren," December 10, 1962, box 84, WJB; "Statement by Mr. Justice Black and Mr. Justice Douglas on the Rules of Civil Procedure and the Proposed Amendments," January 16, 1963, box 484, JMH.

6. Schwartz, *Super Chief,* 63–64; Yarbrough, *Harlan,* 131; Griswold, "Of Time," 85; Douglas, memorandum to the Conference, December 22, 1961, box A-118, TCC.

7. Schwartz, *Super Chief,* 60–71; [Frankfurter], untitled, undated memo to chief justice, box 353, EW; Tushnet, "History," 26.

8. Tushnet, "History," 27–28; Schwartz, *Super Chief,* 129; TCC, memorandum for the Conference, October 7, 1957, box A-60, TCC; Frankfurter, memorandum for the Conference, September 5, 1956, box 353, EW; FF to Brethren, February 26, 1962, box A-118, TCC.

9. *Perez v. Brownell,* 356 U.S. 44 (1958); *Trop v. Dulles,* 356 U.S. 86 (1958); *Rusk v. Cort,* 369 U.S. 367 (1962); *Galvan v. Press,* 347 U.S. 522 (1954); *Jay v. Boyd,* 350 U.S. 892 (1955).

10. *Marcello v. Bonds,* 349 U.S. 302 (1955); *Shaughnessy v. Pedreiro,* 349 U.S. 48 (1955); *Shaughnessy v. United States ex rel. Accardi,* 349 U.S. 280 (1955); *United States v. Zucca,* 351 U.S. 91 (1956); *United States v. Minker,* 350 U.S. 179 (1956).

11. "The Supreme Court, 1953 Term," 68 *Harvard Law Review* 96, at 157 (1954); *Madruga v. Superior Court,* 346 U.S. 556 (1954); *Maryland Casualty Co. v. Cushing,* 347 U.S. 409 (1954); *Pope & Talbot, Inc. v. Hawn,* 346 U.S. 406 (1953); *Alaska Steamship Co. v. Petterson,* 347 U.S. 396 (1954); *British Transport Commission v. United States,* 354 U.S. 129 (1957); *Lake Tankers Corp. v. Henn,* 354 U.S. 147 (1957); *Romero v. International Terminal Operating Co.,* 358 U.S. 354 (1959); *Kermarec v. Compagnie Generale Transatlantique,* 358 U.S. 625 (1959); *The Tungus v. Skovgaard,* 358 U.S. 588 (1959); *United N.Y. & N.J. Sandy Hook Pilots Association v. Halecki,* 358 U.S. 613 (1959); *United States v. Isthmian S.S. Co.,* 359 U.S. 314 (1959); *Kossick v. United Fruit Co.,* 365 U.S. 731 (1961); *Vaughn v. Atkinson,* 369 U.S. 527 (1962); *Calbeck v. Travelers Insurance Co.,* 370 U.S. 114 (1961); *Morales v. City of Galveston,* 370 U.S. 165 (1962).

12. Frankfurter to Burton, November 2, 1955, box 490, JMH; *Tank Truck Rentals, Inc. v. Commissioner,* 356 U.S. 30 (1958); *Hoover Motor Express Co. v. United States,* 356 U.S. 38 (1958); *Commissioner v. Sullivan,* 356 U.S. 27 (1958); *Camarano v. United States,* 358 U.S. 498 (1959); *Commissioner v. Bilder,* 369 U.S. 499 (1962); *Peurifoy v. Commissioner,* 358 U.S. 58 (1958); *Libson Shops, Inc. v. Koehler,* 353 U.S. 382 (1957); *Putnam v. Commissioner,* 352 U.S. 82 (1956).

13. *General American Investors Co. v. Commissioner,* 348 U.S. 434 (1955); *Commissioner v. Glenshaw Glass Co.,* 348 U.S. 426 (1955); *Commissioner v. LoBue,* 351 U.S. 243 (1956); *James v. United States,* 366 U.S. 213 (1961); *Corn Products Refining Co. v. Commissioner,* 350 U.S. 46 (1955); *Commissioner v. G. Lake, Inc.,* 356 U.S. 260 (1958).

14. *Automobile Club v. Commissioner,* 353 U.S. 180 (1957); *United States v. Leslie Salt Co.,* 350 U.S. 383 (1956); *Commissioner v. Estate of Sternberger,* 348 U.S. 187 (1955); *Meyer v. United States,* 364 U.S. 410 (1960); *Fidelity-Philadelphia Trust Co. v. Smith,* 356 U.S. 274 (1958).

15. *Baltimore Contractors, Inc. v. Bolinger,* 348 U.S. 176 (1955); *Sears Roebuck & Co. v. Mackey,* 351 U.S. 427 (1950); *Cold Metal Process Co. v. United Engineering & Foundry Co.,* 351 U.S. 445 (1956); *La Buy v. Howes Leather Co.,* 352 U.S. 249 (1957); *Byrd v. Blue Ridge Rural Electrical Cooperative,* 356 U.S. 525 (1958); *Beacon Theaters, Inc. v. Westover,* 359 U.S. 500 (1959); *Horton v. Liberty Mutual Insurance Co.,* 367 U.S. 348 (1961); *Norwood v. Kirkpatrick,* 349 U.S. 29 (1955); *Schnell v. Peter Eckrich & Sons, Inc.,* 365 U.S. 260 (1961); *Kesler v. Department of Public Safety,* 369 U.S. 153, 156–77 (1962); *Smith v. Sperling,* 354 U.S. 91 (1957); *Swanson v. Traer,* 354 U.S. 114 (1957); *Leiter Minerals, Inc. v. United States,* 352 U.S. 220 (1957); *Sam Fox Publishing Co. v. United States,* 366 U.S. 683 (1961).

16. *Greene v. McElroy,* 360 U.S. 474 (1959); *Dickinson v. United States,* 346 U.S. 389 (1953); *Public Utilities Commission v. United Air Lines,* 346 U.S. 402 (1953); *FCC v. ABC,* 347 U.S. 284 (1954); *Pan-Atlantic Steamship Corp. v. Atlantic Coast Line Railroad,* 353 U.S. 436 (1957); *St. Regis Paper Co.*

v. United States, 368 U.S. 208 (1961); *California v. FPC*, 369 U.S. 482 (1962); *Frozen Food Express v. United States*, 351 U.S. 40 (1956); *United States v. Storer Broadcasting Co.*, 351 U.S. 192 (1956).

17. *Boynton v. Virginia*, 361 U.S. 958 (1960).

18. *Monroe v. Pape*, 365 U.S. 167 (1961); Frankfurter, "Memorandum for the Conference Re: No 59, Monroe v. Pape," November 9, 1960, box 51, WJB; memorandum from Frankfurter, November 9, 1960, box A-107, TCC; Frankfurter, "Memorandum of Views Expressed in Conference of Friday," November 11, 1960, undated, and handwritten notes, reel 67, frames 929–33, FF-H; conference notes, box 407, WJB; *Screws v. United States*, 325 U.S. 91 (1945); 365 U.S. at 192 (Harlan, J., concurring).

19. *Monroe v. Pape*, 365 U.S. at 202 (Frankfurter, J., dissenting); Charles Alan Wright, *Law of Federal Courts*, 5th ed. (St. Paul, Minn.: West Publishing Co., 1994), 132–33.

20. *Louisiana v. United States*, 363 U.S. 1 (1960); *United States v. California*, 332 U.S. 19 (1947); *United States v. Louisiana*, 339 U.S. 699 (1950), 340 U.S. 899 (1950); *United States v. Texas*, 339 U.S. 707 (1950), 340 U.S. 900 (1950); Eisenhower, *Mandate*, 204–7; Submerged Lands Act of 1953, 67 Stat. 29; *Alabama v. Texas*, 347 U.S. 272 (1954); *United States v. Louisiana*, 354 U.S. 515 (1957); JMH, memorandum for the Conference, September 22, 1958, box A-91, TCC; *United States v. Florida*, 363 U.S. 121 (1960); ibid. at 132 (Harlan, J., dissenting).

21. *Arizona v. California*, 373 U.S. 546 (1962); Archibald Cox to Black, April 27, 1964, box 370, HLB; Douglas, memorandum for the Conference, January 30, 1962, Black to Harlan, February 1, 1962, Douglas, memorandum to the Conference, February 1, 1962, Black, memorandum for the Conference, February 1, 1962, and JMH to Black, February 1, 1962, all in box A-134, TCC.

22. *Kern-Limerick, Inc. v. Scurlock*, 347 U.S. 110 (1954); *Michigan-Wisconsin Pipe Line Co. v. Calvert*, 347 U.S. 157 (1954); *Miller Bros. Co. v. Maryland*, 347 U.S. 340 (1954); *Braniff Airways, Inc. v. Nebraska State Board of Equalization*, 347 U.S. 590 (1954); *Railway Express Agency, Inc. v. Virginia*, 358 U.S. 434 (1959).

23. *Bibb v. Navajo Freight Lines, Inc.*, 359 U.S. 520 (1959); conference notes on *Bibb v. Navajo Freights [sic] Lines, Inc., Et al.*, undated, box 205, WJB; Schwartz, *Super Chief*, 334–35; *Eli Lilly & Co. v. Save-On Drugs Inc.*, 366 U.S. 276 (1961); *Central Railroad v. Pennsylvania*, 370 U.S. 607 (1962).

24. *Youngstown Sheet & Tube Co. v. Bowers* and *United States v. Plywood Corp.*, 358 U.S. 534 (1959); *Kern-Limerick, Inc. v. Scurlock*, 347 U.S. 110 (1954); *United States v. City of Detroit*, 355 U.S. 466 (1958); *United States v. Township of Muskeegeon*, 355 U.S. 484 (1958); *Carroll v. Lanza*, 349 U.S. 408 (1955); *Watson v. Employers Liability Assurance Corp.*, 348 U.S. 66 (1954); *McGee v. International Life Insurance Co.*, 355 U.S. 220 (1957).

25. *Western Union Telegraph Company v. Pennsylvania*, 368 US. 71 (1961); *Morey v. Doud*, 354 U.S. 457 (1957); conference notes, April 26, 1956, WOD.

26. *Goldblatt v. Town of Hempstead*, 369 U.S. 590 (1962); *Griggs v. Allegheny County*, 369 U.S. 84 (1962); *United States v. Twin Cities Power Co.*, 350 U.S. 222 (1956); *United States v. Virginia Electric & Power Co.*, 365 U.S. 624 (1961).

27. *Wiener v. United States*, 357 U.S. 349 (1958); Lee Modjeska, "Labor and the Warren Court," 8 *Industrial Relations Law Journal* 479, at 545 (1986); *Brooks v. NLRB*, 348 U.S. 96 (1954); White, *Warren*, 293, 301.

28. White, *Warren*, 282–85; Modjeska, "Labor," 533–35; *San Diego Building Trades Council v. Garmon*, 359 U.S. 236, 244–46 (1959); *Guss v. Utah Labor Relations Board*, 353 U.S. 1 (1957); *International Association of Machinists v. Gonzales*, 356 U.S. 634 (1958); *Automobile Workers v. Russell*, 356 U.S. 634 (1958); Kurland, *Politics*, 60.

29. Modjeska, "Labor," 485–86, 503–6, 496–503, 518–22, 506–10; *NLRB v. Babcock & Wilcox Co.*, 351 U.S. 105 (1956); *NLRB v. Erie Resistor Corp.*, 373 U.S. 221 (1963); *NLRB v. Wooster Division of Borg-Warner*, 356 U.S. 342 (1958); *NLRB v. Katz*, 369 U.S. 736 (1962); *Railway Employees'*

Department v. Hanson, 351 U.S. 225 (1956); *Local 1976, United Brotherhood of Carpenters v. NLRB*, 357 U.S. 93 (1958); *Local 761, IUE v. NLRB*, 366 U.S. 667 (1961).

30. Modjeska, "Labor," 512–15; *Textile Workers Union v. Lincoln Mills*, 353 U.S. 448 (1957); Katherine Van Wezel Stone, "The Post-War Paradigm in American Labor Law," 90 *Yale Law Journal* 1509, at 1515, 1525–29 (1981); *United Steelworkers v. American Manufacturing Co.*, 363 U.S. 564 (1960); *Steelworkers v. Warrior & Gulf Navigation Co.*, 363 U.S. 574 (1960); *Steelworkers v. Enterprise Corp.*, 363 U.S. 593 (1960); Stebenne, *Goldberg*, 219–21.

31. *Railway Employees' Department v. Hanson*, 351 U.S. 225 (1956); *International Association of Machinists v. Street*, 367 U.S. 740 (1961); *Lathrop v. Donohue*, 367 U.S. 820 (1961); Schwartz, *Super Chief*, 371–76; Black to Brennan, June 15, 1961, box 61, WJB; conference notes, box 407, WJB; Brennan, memorandum to the Conference, June 13, 1961, and WJB, "Re: No. 4–International Association of Machinists v. Street," June 13, 1961, both in box 45, WJB; *Street*, 367 U.S. at 775 (Douglas, J., concurring); ibid. at 780 (Black, J., dissenting); ibid. at 797 (Frankfurter, J., dissenting); *Lathrop*, 367 U.S. at 848 (Harlan, J., concurring); ibid. at 865 (Black, J., dissenting); ibid. at 877 (Douglas, J., dissenting).

32. Thomas E. Kauper, "The 'Warren Court' and the Antitrust Laws: Of Economics, Populism, and Cynicism," 67 *Michigan Law Review* 325, at 325–31 (1968); Richard Arnold, "The Supreme Court and the Antitrust Laws 1953–1967," 34 *Antitrust Law Journal* 2, at 2–5 (1967); *Brown Shoe Co. v. United States*, 370 U.S. 294 (1962).

33. White, *Warren*, 295; Warren, *Memoirs*, 315; Arnold, "Antitrust Laws," 6–8; Black, draft dissent in *Willard Dairy Corp. v. National Dairy Products Corp.*, May 27, 1963, box 84, WJB.

34. *Federal Baseball Club of Baltimore v. National League of Professional Baseball Clubs*, 259 U.S. 200 (1922); *Toolson v. New York Yankees*, 346 U.S. 356, 357 (1953); ibid. (Burton, J., dissenting); Schwartz, *Super Chief*, 162–64, 213–14; *United States v. International Boxing Club of New York*, 348 U.S. 236 (1955); conference notes on *United States v. International Boxing Club*, November 13, 1954, box 1155, WOD; *International Boxing Club*, 348 U.S. at 249 (Frankfurter, J., dissenting); first circulation of Frankfurter's dissent, January 11, 1955, box A-36, TCC; *United States v. Shubert*, 348 U.S. 222 (1955); JMH, "Memorandum to Brennan Re: Radowich [*sic*]," February 1, 1957, box 486, JMH; *Radovich v. National Football League*, 352 U.S. 445, 452 (1957); ibid. at 455 (Frankfurter, J., dissenting); ibid. at 456 (Harlan, J., dissenting).

35. *United States v. E. I. du Pont de Nemours & Co.*, 351 U.S. 377 (1956); ibid. at 413 (Frankfurter, J., concurring); ibid. at 415, 426 (Warren, C.J., dissenting).

36. Schwartz, *Super Chief*, 222–24; docket book entries, box 292, HB; conference notes, November 11, 1956, box 1173, WOD; Yarbrough, *Harlan*, 134–35; *United States v. E. I. du Pont de Nemours & Co.*, 353 U.S. 586 (1957); Powe, *American Politics*, 121; 353 U.S. at 608 (Burton, J., dissenting); conference notes, February 24, 1961, box 1233, WOD; conference notes, box 407, WJB; *United States v. E. I. du Pont de Nemours & Company*, 366 U.S. 316 (1961); ibid. at 335 (Frankfurter, J., dissenting).

37. Schwartz, *Super Chief*, 253–58, 261–63, 352, 400; *New York Times*, April 25, 1961, 1; Cray, *Chief Justice*, 370–71. All of the quotations are from Schwartz, *Super Chief*, except for the one beginning "degrading this court," which is from Cray, *Chief Justice*.

38. Frankfurter, memorandum to the Conference, October 1, 1956, box A-40, TCC; Douglas, memorandum for the files, May 28, 1960, and memorandum to the Conference, November 21, 1960, both in box 1213, WOD; Newman, *Black*, 509; Schwartz, *Super Chief*, 258, 306; Yarbrough, *Harlan*, 134–37; Douglas to Harlan, April 18, 1957, box 514, JMH.

39. White, *Judicial Tradition*, 322–25, 344–45; Gerald Gunther, *Learned Hand: The Man and the Judge* (New York: Knopf, 1994), 652–60, 665; Schwartz, *Super Chief*, 267; Yarbrough, *Harlan*, xi; FF to "Dear Boys," May 18, 1960, reel 55, frame 673, FF-H; Frankfurter to Warren, April 13, 1960, box 354, EW.

40. Schwartz, *Super Chief,* 267–72; memorandum by Frankfurter, May 17, 1961, box A-114, TCC; Black, memorandum for the Conference, April 9, [1957], box A-60, TCC.

41. October Term, 1959–Greetings, September 29, 1959, reel 55, frame 674, FF-H; Frankfurter, memorandum for the Conference, September 5, 1956, and memorandum for the Conference, September 27, 1955, both in box 353, EW; October Term 1958 Greetings, box 499, JMH.

42. Frankfurter, October Term 1957, Greetings, September 30, 1967, and Warren, memorandum for the Conference, October 7, 1957, both in box 353, EW; Douglas, memorandum to the Conference, October 23, 1961, and handwritten annotations on October Term, 1961–Greetings, both in box 499, JMH.

43. Parrish, "Frankfurter," 54.

44. Newman, *Black,* 482, 518; Statement of Charles E. Whittaker, Associate Justice of the United States Supreme Court, March 29, 1962, Ex. FG 535/A, WHCF, JFK; Warren to John F. Kennedy, March 16, 1962, box 358, EW; Whittaker to Warren, January 29, 1963, Whittaker to Colonel Robert C. Hunter, March 7, 1963, and Medical Board Proceedings, March 16, 1962, all in box 358, EW; Kennedy to Whittaker, March 28, 1962, Ex FG 535/A, WHCF, JFK.

45. Urofsky, *Frankfurter,* 173; Warren, memorandum to Black, Douglas, Clark, Harlan, Brennan, Stewart, and White, April 25, 1962, and attachment dated April 30, 1962, box 534, JMH; Yarbrough, *Harlan,* 278; John F. Kennedy to Frankfurter, August 28, 1962, Ex. FG 535/A, WHCF, JFK; Simon, *Antagonists,* 252–54; Margaret McHugh to Chief Justice, August 16, 1962, box 359, EW; Felix Frankfurter to president, August 28, 1962, Ex. FG 535/A, WHCF, JFK.

46. Frankfurter to Chief Justice and Associate Justices, September 28, 1962, box 35, EW; Newman, *Black,* 518–19; Simon, *Antagonists,* 255; Urofsky, *Frankfurter,* 174.

47. James Edwin Livingston to President Kennedy, January 2, 1963, Ex. FB 535/A, WHCF, JFK; Gallup, *Poll,* 3:1767.

48. Dennis J. Hutchinson, *The Man Who Once Was Whizzer White: A Portrait of Justice Byron R. White* (New York: Free Press, 1998), 14–286.

49. Ibid., 313–31; Arthur M. Schlesinger Jr., *Robert Kennedy and His Times* (Boston: Houghton Mifflin, 1978), 377–78; Schlesinger, *A Thousand Days: John F. Kennedy in the White House* (Boston: Houghton Mifflin, 1965), 698; Joseph F. Dolan, interview by Charles Morrissey, December 1, 1964, transcript, 98–102, John F. Kennedy Library Oral History Project, JFK; Harrison Loesch to James O. Eastland, April 6, 1962, Byron R. White Name File, WHCF, JFK.

50. Schlesinger, *Robert Kennedy,* 378; Stebenne, *Goldberg,* 3–9.

51. Stebenne, *Goldberg,* 11–130.

52. Ibid., 167, 160–61, 174, 195–96, 216–17.

53. Ibid., 233, 238–53, 290–98, 309–10; Ken Gormley, *Archibald Cox: Conscience of a Nation* (Reading, Mass.: Addison-Wesley, 1997), 171; Schlesinger, *Robert Kennedy,* 378–79; Schlesinger, *Thousand Days,* 698; Ralph Y. Yarborough, telegram to president, August 30, 1962, and Barry Goldwater, telegram to president, August 30, 1964, both in Ex. FG 535/A, WHCF, JFK; Paul Douglas, telegram to president, August 30, 1962, General FG 535/A, WHCF, JFK; Emanuel Celler to president, Arthur J. Goldberg Name File, WHCF, JFK.

54. William E. Nelson, "Byron R. White: A Liberal of 1960," in Tushnet, *Warren Court,* 139–54; Jonathan D. Varat, "Justice White and the Breadth and Allocation of Federal Authority," 58 *University of Colorado Law Review* 371, at 371 (1987); Allan Ides, "The Jurisprudence of Byron White," 103 *Yale Law Journal* 419, at 457, 447 (1993); Hutchinson, *Whizzer,* 346 (quoting college classmate).

55. Hutchinson, *Whizzer,* 341; Dennis L. Thompson, "The Kennedy Court: Left and Right of Center," 26 *Western Political Quarterly* 263, at 269, 271 (1973); Stebbene, *Goldberg,* 8–9, 85, 108–9.

56. Parrish, "Frankfurter," 54; Thompson, "Kennedy Court," 271, 275–79.

57. Except as otherwise indicated, the following discussion is based on Laura Kalman, *Abe Fortas: A Biography* (New Haven, Conn.: Yale University Press, 1990), 3, 7–19, 43–160, 217, 200–203, 209–12, 230, 240–48.

58. Stebenne, *Goldberg,* 346–48.

59. Kalman, *Fortas,* 241–48; Abe to president, July 19, 1965, FG 535, WHCF, LBJ; Nicholas deB. Katzenbach to president, July 22, 1965, FG 535/A, WHCF, LBJ; William O. Douglas, *The Court Years 1939–1975: The Autobiography of William O. Douglas* (New York: Random House, 1980), 318–19; Schwartz, *Super Chief,* 584; Bruce Allen Murphy, *Fortas: The Rise and Fall of a Supreme Court Justice* (New York: Morrow, 1988), 172–83; *Cong. Record,* 89th Cong, 1st sess. (Aug. 11, 1965): 20,079.

5. THE MOST IMPORTANT ISSUE

1. *Baker v. Carr,* 369 U.S. 186 (1962); Warren, *Memoirs,* 306, 308; Morton Horwitz, "The Warren Court: Rediscovering the Link Between Law and Culture," 55 *University of Chicago Law Review* 452, at 455–56 (1988); White, *Judicial Tradition,* 359; Laura Kalman, *The Strange Case of Legal Liberalism* (New Haven, Conn.: Yale University Press, 1996), 43.

2. Kalman, *Liberalism,* 43; Galloway, "Third Period," 773–74.

3. Allen J. Matusow, *The Unraveling of America: A History of Liberalism in the 1960s* (New York: Harper & Row, 1984), 60–62, 47–48; Richard Polenberg, *One Nation Divisible: Class, Race and Ethnicity in the United States since 1938* (New York: Penguin, 1980), 128, 173; James Gilbert, *Another Chance: Postwar America, 1945–1968* (New York: Knopf, 1981), 189–90.

4. Matusow, *Unraveling,* 181; Gordon E. Baker, *The Reapportionment Revolution: Representation, Political Power, and the Supreme Court* (New York: Random House, 1967), 89–94.

5. Gordon Baker, *Revolution,* 70–80.

6. Ibid., 23–32.

7. Robert B. McKay, *Reapportionment: The Law and Politics of Equal Representation* (New York: Twentieth Century Fund, 1965), 36–40, 55–58.

8. McKay, *Reapportionment,* 50–51; Richard C. Cortner, *The Apportionment Cases* (Knoxville: University of Tennessee Press, 1970), 4–5.

9. Cortner, *Cases,* 5–8.

10. *Keogh v. Neeley,* 50 F.2d 685 (7th Cir. 1931); *dismissed,* 285 U.S. 526, *cert denied* 286 U.S. 529; *petition for writ of mandamus dismissed,* 286 U.S. 534 (1932); *Wood v. Broom,* 287 U.S. 1, 8 (1932).

11. *Luther v. Borden,* 7 How. 1 (1849).

12. *Colgrove v. Green,* 328 U.S. 549, at 552–54, 556 (1946); ibid. at 568, 571–73 (Black, J., dissenting); ibid. at 564 (Rutledge, J., concurring); Cortner, *Cases,* 23–25; *Truman v. Cook and Duckworth v. Fortson,* 329 U.S. 675 (1946); *South v. Peters,* 339 U.S. 276 (1950), *Cox v. Peters,* 342 U.S. 936 (1952); *Colgrove v. Barrett,* 342 U.S. 936 (1952); *Remmy v. Smith,* 342 U.S. 916 (1952); *Anderson v. Jordan,* 343 U.S. 913 (1952). For a thorough discussion of the Court's handling of *Colgrove,* see Urofsky, *Division,* 145–48.

13. *Gomillion v. Lightfoot,* 364 U.S. 339 (1960); FF to Whittaker, November 4, 1960, box 50, WJB; 364 U.S. at 349 (Whittaker, J., concurring).

14. *Baker v. Carr,* 369 U.S. 186 (1962); Cortner, *Cases,* 29–30, 33–34, 27–41, 56–57; *Kidd v. McCanless,* 200 Tenn. 273, 292 S.W.2d 40, *appeal dismissed,* 352 U.S. 920 (1956); *Baker v. Carr,* 179 F. Supp. 824 (M.D. Tenn. 1959).

15. Cortner, *Cases,* 76–78, 83–84, 89–91; Schlesinger, *Robert Kennedy,* 397.

16. Gormley, *Cox,* 165; Warren, *Memoirs,* 310; White, *Warren,* 237; Schwartz, *Super Chief,* 411–12; Newman, *Black,* 517; conference notes, April 20, 1961, and April 28, 1961, and vote count with

handwritten annotation, dated October 9, 1961, all in box 1267, WOD; docket book entry for no. 103, box 407, WJB. Douglas claimed later that Stewart voted tentatively with Warren, but neither Brennan's contemporary notes nor Douglas's own support this contention. See Douglas, *Court Years,* 135–36.

17. Schwartz, *Super Chief,* 413; Frankfurter to Whittaker, October 6, 1961, reel 80, frames 514–15, FF-H; FF, memorandum for the Conference, October 10, 1961, and memorandum of Frankfurter on no. 6, *Baker v. Carr,* undated, both in box A-119, TCC; Frankfurter to Stewart, October 13, 1961, Reel 80, frame 518, FF-H.

18. JMH to Whittaker and Stewart, October 11, 1961, box 65, FF-LC.

19. Conference notes and docket book entry, box 408, WJB; conference notes, reel 82, frames 546–49, FF-H; conference notes, October 13, 1961, box 1267, WOD; Brennan, memorandum to the Conference, October 12, 1961, box 9, WJB; Schwartz, *Super Chief,* 415–18.

20. Schwartz, *Super Chief,* 418–24; Douglas, *Court Years,* 136; White, *Judicial Tradition,* 185; Brennan to Stewart, January 22, 1962, box 69, WJB; memorandum to chief justice, Black, and Douglas, January 27, 1962, and Brennan to Black, January 31, 1962, all in box 69, WJB; JMH to Stewart, February 8, 1962, reel 80, frame 391, FF-H; TCC to Frankfurter, February 3, 1962, reel 80, frame 250, FF-H; TCC to Frankfurter, March 7, 1962 (with handwritten addendum to Harlan), box 493, JMH; WJB, memorandum to chief justice, Black, and Douglas, March 10, 1962, box 69, WJB.

21. *Baker v. Carr,* 369 U.S. 186, at 237.

22. Brennan, notes for oral announcement of decision, undated, box 70, WJB; *Baker,* 369 U.S. at 241 (Douglas, J., concurring); ibid. at 251, 258 (Clark, J., concurring); ibid. at 265–66 (Stewart, J., concurring).

23. *Baker,* 369 U.S. at 330 (Harlan, J., dissenting); Robert C. Post, "Justice William J. Brennan and the Warren Court," 8 *Constitutional Commentary* 11, at 12–13 (1991); 369 U.S. at 339–40.

24. *Baker,* 369 U.S. at 266, 299 (Frankfurter, J., dissenting).

25. *Washington Post,* March 28, 1962; William S. White, "Apportionment Ruling Assailed," *Washington Evening Star,* March 28, 1962; Alexander M. Bickel, "The Great Apportionment Case," *New Republic,* April 9, 1962, at 13, 14; Powe, *American Politics,* 203–4; Cortner, *Cases,* 146–48.

26. Cortner, *Cases,* 222–26;Warren, *Memoirs,* 312; Gallup, *Poll,* 3:1830 [this poll was taken May 23–28, 1963]; Information Service, American Bar Association, "Proposals for Amending the Constitution Approved by the General Assembly of the States: A Summary of State Legislative Action (May 1964)," box 660, EW.

27. Robert G. McCloskey, "Forward: The Reapportionment Case," 76 *Harvard Law Review* 54, at 70, 72 (1962); *Gray v. Sanders,* 372 U.S. 368 (1963); Yarbrough, *Harlan,* 279. The earlier county unit cases, none of which received full-Bench consideration were *Cook v. Fortson,* 329 U.S. 675 (1946); *South v. Peters,* 339 U.S. 276 (1950); *Cox v. Peters,* 342 U.S. 936 (1952); and *Hartsfield v. Sloan,* 357 U.S. 916 (1958). See McKay, *Reapportionment,* 84.

28. Schlesinger, *Robert Kennedy,* 396–98; *Sanders v. Gray,* 203 F. Supp. 158 (N.D. Ga. 1962); *Gray,* 372 U.S. at 384–85 (Harlan, J., dissenting); ibid. at 378, 381; MJF [Martin J. Flynn], note to Justice Clark, February 6, [1963], box A-143, TCC; 372 U.S. at 382 (Stewart, J., concurring).

29. *Wesberry v. Sanders,* 376 U.S. 1 (1964); conference notes, box 1300, WOD; 376 U.S. at 20 (Harlan, J., dissenting); JLMcH to Clark, undated, box A-152, TCC; 376 U.S. at 18 (Clark, J., concurring in part and dissenting in part); Robert G. Dixon Jr., *Democratic Representation: Reapportionment in Law and Politics* (New York: Oxford University Press, 1968), 183, 185, 187–89; 376 U.S. at 7–8; Powe, *American Politics,* 244.

30. *Reynolds v. Sims,* 377 U.S. 533 (1964); Dixon, *Representation,* 199–200, 252, 255–56; Gormley, *Cox,* 171–74; Schlesinger, *Robert Kennedy,* 399–400; Brief for the United States as Amicus Curiae, at 29–49, *Maryland Committee for Fair Representation v. Tawes,* 377 U.S. 656 (1964); Brief

for the United States as Amicus Curiae, at 32, *Lucas v. Colorado General Assembly*, 377 U.S. 713 (1964); Schwartz, *Super Chief*, 503.

31. Warren, *Memoirs*, 310; Schwartz, *Super Chief*, 503.

32. *Reynolds*, 377 U.S. at 562, 538–40, 562–63, 565–67, 572–73.

33. Ibid. at 568, 577; *WMCA, Inc. v. Lorenzo*, 377 U.S. 633 (1964); *Maryland Committee for Fair Representation v. Tawes*, 377 U.S. 656 (1964); *Davis v. Mann*, 377 U.S. 678 (1964); *Roman v. Sincock*, 377 U.S. 695 (1964).

34. *Lucas v. Forty-Fourth General Assembly of the State of Colorado*, 377 U.S. 713, 744–54, 758–65 (Stewart, J., dissenting); *Reynolds*, 377 U.S. at 588 (Stewart, J., concurring); *Davis*, 377 U.S. at 693–94 (Stewart, J., concurring); *Roman*, 377 U.S. at 712 (Stewart, J., concurring); *Tawes*, 377 U.S. at 677 (Stewart, J., concurring).

35. *Lucas*, 377 U.S. at 741; *Reynolds*, 377 U.S. at 588–89 (Clark, J., concurring).

36. *Lucas*, 377 U.S. at 717–18; Schlesinger, *Robert Kennedy*, 400; Gormley, *Cox*, 175–76; docket book entry for *Lucas v. Forty-Fourth General Assembly of the State of Colorado*, box 410, WJB; conference notes, April 3, 1964, box 1304, WOD; *Lucas*, 377 U.S. at 754–59 (Stewar, J., dissenting); ibid. at 741–42 (Clark, J., dissenting); Schwartz, *Super Chief*, 506; *Lucas*, 377 U.S. at 736–37.

37. *Reynolds*, 377 U.S. at 589–91 (Harlan, J., dissenting); Cortner, *Cases*, 234; *Reynolds*, 377 U.S. at 566; ibid. at 624 (Harlan, J., dissenting); ibid. at 566; ibid. at 624–25 (Harlan, J., dissenting).

38. Dixon, *Representation*, 265; Carl Auerbach, "The Reapportionment Cases: One Person, One Vote—One Vote, One Value," 1964 *Supreme Court Review* 1, at 2.

39. *Swann v. Adams*, 378 U.S. 533 (1964) (Florida); *Nolan v. Rhodes* and *Sive v. Ellis*, 378 U.S. 556 (1964) (Ohio); *Germano v. Kerner*, 378 U.S. 560 (1964) (Illinois); *Marshall v. Hare*, 378 U.S. 561 (1964) (Michigan); *Hearne v. Smylie*, 378 U.S. 563 (1964) (Idaho); *Pinney v. Butterworth*, 378 U.S. 564 (1964) (Connecticut); *Hill v. Davis*, 378 U.S. 565 (1964) (Iowa); *Baldwin v. Moss*, 378 U.S. 558 (1964) (Oklahoma); *Meyers v. Thigpen*, 378 U.S. 554 (1964) (Washington). See Cortner, *Cases*, 237.

40. *New York Times*, June 18, 1964, 34; Philip Kurland, "The Supreme Court, 1963 Term: Forward," 78 *Harvard Law Review* 143, at 156, 143 (1964); *Washington Post*, June 17, 1964, A-18; McCloskey, "Forward," 74 (1962); Gallup, *Poll*, 3:1897.

41. *New York Times*, June 16, 1964, 1, 28, 31, 32; Cortner, *Cases*, 237–40; Dixon, *Representation*, 385–86; *Cong. Record*, 88th Cong., 2d sess. (Aug. 19, 1964): 20,300.

42. Cortner, *Cases*, 236, 240–42.

43. Cortner, *Cases*, 246; Everett Dirksen, interview by Joe B. Frantz, March 21, 1969, tape 1, transcript, 7–9, LBJ Oral History Project, LBJ; Dixon, *Representation*, 404–15; *Cong. Record*, 89th Cong., 1st sess. (August 4, 1965): 19,373; ibid., 2nd sess. (April 20, 1966): 8,583; Arthur Freund to Wally Sandack, box 660, EW; Archibald Cox, *The Warren Court: Constitutional Decision as an Instrument of Reform* (Cambridge, Mass.: Harvard University Press, 1968), 120.

44. Dixon, *Representation*, 439–44.

45. Ibid., 440–42, 444–48; *Swann v. Adams*, 385 U.S. 440, 444 (1967); ibid. at 447 (Harlan, J., dissenting); *Kilgalin v. Hill*, 386 U.S. 120, 122 (1967); *Kirkpatrick v. Preisler*, 385 U.S. 459 (1967).

46. *Kirkpatrick v. Preisler*, 394 U.S. 526 (1969); ibid. at 537 (Fortas, J., concurring); Robert G. Dixon Jr., "The Warren Court Crusade for the Holy Grail of 'One Man–One Vote,'" 1969 *Supreme Court Review* 219, at 219–20. See also *Wells v. Rockefeller*, 394 U.S. 542, 546 (1969).

47. Gallup, *Poll*, 3:2205–6.

48. *Avery v. Midland County*, 390 U.S. 474, 484–85 (1968); ibid. at 495 (Fortas, J., dissenting); ibid. at 509 (Stewart, J., dissenting); ibid. at 486–87 (Harlan, J., dissenting).

49. *Kramer v. Union Free School District*, 395 U.S. 621 (1969); Robert B. McKay, "Reapportionment: Success Story of the Warren Court," 67 *Michigan Law Review* 223, at 225 (1968); Alexander

M. Bickel, "The Supreme Court and Reapportionment," in *Reapportionment in the 1970s*, ed. Nelson W. Polsby (Berkeley and Los Angeles: University of California Press, 1971), 57; Robert G. Dixon, "The Court, the People, and 'One Man, One Vote,'" in Polsby, *1970s*, 185. Kurland, *Politics*, 161; Douglas W. Rae, "Reapportionment and Political Democracy," in Polsby, *1970s*, 105.

50. Dixon, "Court," 31–34; *Davis v. Bandamer*, 478 U.S. 109 (1986); *Whitcomb v. Chavis*, 403 U.S. 124 (1971).

51. Cox, *Warren Court*, 118.

52. See Bickel, *Progress*, 113.

6. GOD AND THE WARREN COURT

1. J. Herbert Laubach, *School Prayers: Congress, the Courts and the Public* (Washington, D.C.: Public Affairs Press, 1969), 2 (O'Konski quote); Paul G. Kauper, "The Warren Court: Religious Liberty and Church-State Relations," 67 *Michigan Law Review* 269, at 269 (1968). For a fuller development of the argument made in this chapter, see Michal R. Belknap, "God and the Warren Court. The Quest for a Wholesome Neutrality," 9 *Seton Hall Constitutional Law Journal* 401 (1999).

2. Gilbert, *Another Chance*, 238–39; Gallup, *Poll*, 2:1293, 3:1863; Powe, *America Politics*, 182.

3. Polenberg, *One Nation*, 146–48.

4. Ibid., 164–67; Matusow, *Unraveling*, 22–23. Kennedy is quoted by Matusow.

5. Polenberg, *One Nation*, 167–68; Matusow, *Unraveling*, 27–28, 169–72.

6. Belknap, "God," 408–11; *Everson v. Board of Education*, 330 U.S. 1, 15, 17–18 (1947); Urofsky, *Division*, 234.

7. *McCollum v. Board of Education*, 333 U.S. 203 (1948); Urofsky, *Division*, 233, 235–37; 333 U.S. at 211–12; *Zorach v. Clauson*, 343 U.S. 306 (1952); ibid. at 319 (Black, J., dissenting).

8. Robert F. Drinan, *Religion, Courts, and Public Policy* (New York: McGraw-Hill, 1963), 203–5; Sister Candida Lund, "The Sunday Closing Cases," in *The Third Branch of Government: 8 Cases in Constitutional Politics*, ed. C. Herman Pritchett and Alan F. Westin (New York: Harcourt, 1963), 276–77.

9. Philip B. Kurland, "Of Church and State and the Supreme Court," 29 *University of Chicago Law Review* 1, at 83 (1961); *McGowan v. Maryland*, 366 U.S. 420 (1961); *Two Guys from Harrison-Allentown v. McGinley*, 366 U.S. 582 (1961); Lund, "Sunday Closing," 278–79, 283–85; *Gallagher v. Crown Kosher Super Market*, 366 U.S. 617 (1961); *Braunfeld v. Brown*, 366 U.S. 599 (1961).

10. *McGowan*, 366 U.S. at 425–28; *Crown Kosher*, 366 U.S. at 622–24; *Two Guys*, 366 U.S. at 589–92; *Braunfeld*, 366 U.S. at 600–601; *McGowan*, 366 U.S. at 535 (separate opinion by Frankfurter, J.); *Braunfeld*, 366 U.S. at 610 (Brennan, J., dissenting); ibid. at 616 (Stewart, J., dissenting). For the dissenting opinion of Justice Douglas in all four cases, see 366 U.S. at 561.

11. *McGowan*, 366 U.S. at 576–77, 573, 561 (Douglas, J., dissenting).

12. Docket book entry, *McGowan v. Maryland*, box 407, WJB; *McGowan*, 366 U.S. at 442–44, 451–53; Frankfurter, "Memorandum on Changes in Chief Justice's Sunday Law Opinions," circulations of 3/9 and 5/24, reel 63, frames 604–6, FF-H.

13. Frankfurter, memorandum on *McGowan v. Maryland, Gallagher v. Crown Kosher Super Market, Two Guys from Harrison-Allentown, Inc. v. McGinley*, and *Braunfeld v. Gibbons*, December 8, 1960, reel 63, frames 607–715, and Frankfurter to "Dear Brethren," December 7, 1960, reel 64, frames 175–76, FF-H; *McGowan*, 366 U.S. at 459–60 (Frankfurter, J., dissenting); Harlan to Warren, May 26, 1961, reel 65, frame 5, FF-H.

14. *McGowan*, 366 U.S. at 429–30; *Two Guys*, 366 U.S. at 592; *Crown Kosher*, 366 U.S. at 630–31; *Braunfeld*, 366 U.S. at 603, 605–6, 607; *McGowan*, 366 U.S. at 520 (Frankfurter, J., dissenting).

15. *Braunfeld*, 366 U.S. at 611, 613–14, 610 (Brennan, J., dissenting); ibid. at 616 (Stewart, J., dissenting); *Crown Kosher*, 366 U.S. at 642 (Brennan and Stewart dissenting); *McGowan*, 366 U.S. at 420 (Douglas, J., dissenting).

16. Lund, "Sunday Closing," 307, 302–4; Drinan, *Religion,* 216.

17. *McGowan,* 366 U.S. at 453; conference notes on *Torcaso v. Watkins,* April 28, 1961, box 1234, WOD; conference list for conference of Friday, April 28, 1961, box A-102, TCC; *Torcaso v. Watkins,* 367 U.S. 488, 496, 495 (1961); W. B. Baughan to Black, June 27, 1961, box 351, HLB.

18. *Sherbert v. Verner,* 374 U.S. 398 (1963); docket book entry, box 409, WJB; 374 U.S. at 419–23 (Harlan, J., dissenting); Schwartz, *Super Chief,* 468–70; 374 U.S. at 403–9; ibid. at 414–17 (Stewart, J., concurring); ibid. at 412–23 (Douglas, J., concurring).

19. *United States v. Seeger,* 380 U.S. 163 (1965); conference notes, box 411, WJB; Yarbrough, *Harlan,* 230–31; 380 U.S. at 188 (Douglas, J., concurring). For a fuller discussion of all the issues raised by *Seeger,* see Michal R. Belknap, "The Warren Court and the Vietnam War: The Limits of Legal Liberalism," 33 *Georgia Law Review* 65, at 122–25 (1998).

20. *Engel v. Vitale,* 370 U.S. 421 (1962); Leo Pfeffer, "The New York Regents Prayer Case," 4 *Journal of Church and State* 150, at 150–51 (1962).

21. Schwartz, *Super Chief,* 440; Brief for Respondents, at 124, 137–38, 126, *Engel v. Vitale,* 370 U.S. 421 (1960).

22. Ellis M. West, "Justice Tom Clark and American Church-State Law," 54 *Journal of Presbyterian History* 387, at 400, 394 (1976); Yarbrough, *Harlan,* 227; Newman, *Black,* 521.

23. Newman, *Black;* 521; *Engel,* 370 U.S. at 430–31, 425.

24. Douglas to Black, May 28, 1962, box 354, HLB; *Engel,* 370 U.S. at 437, 439–44 (Douglas, J., concurring); Douglas to Black, June 11, 1962, box 354, HLB.

25. *Engel,* 370 U.S. at 446–50, 445 (Stewart, J., dissenting).

26. Wilber G. Katz, *Religion and American Constitutions* (Evanston, Ill.: Northwestern University Press, 1964), 35–36, 41; Warren, *Memoirs,* 316; Laubach, *Prayers,* 1; Thomas M. Mengler, "Public Relations in the Supreme Court: Justice Tom Clark's Opinion in the School Prayer Case," 6 *Constitutional Commentary* 331, at 336 (1989); Joseph A. Fisher, "The Becker Amendment: A Constitutional Trojan Horse," 11 *Journal of Church and State* 427, at 428 (1969); "Editorial: Religion Sponsored by the State," 4 *Journal of Church and State* 141, at 142 (1962); Powe, *American Politics,* 187. With respect to the poll results, it should be noted that a study by Kenneth M. Dolbeare and Phillip E. Hammond found that half of those favoring prayer at the start of the school day nevertheless liked the *Engel* decision. *The School Prayer Decision: From Court Policy to Local Practice* (Chicago: University of Chicago Press, 1971), 15.

27. "Religion Sponsored," 142–43; Mrs. C. G. Hickman to Brennan, August 31, 1963, box 95, WJB; Mengler, "Public Relations," 337; Philip Kurland, "The Regents' Prayer Case: Full of Sound and Fury, Signifying . . . ," 1962 *Supreme Court Review* 1, at 2; James G. MacDonnel to Black, July 22, 1962, and Mrs. Delores E. Rayfield to Black, July 3, 1962, both in box 354, HLB; Paul Murphy, *Crisis Times,* 394.

28. Mengler," Public Relations," 338–46; Warren, *Memoirs,* 316; Yarbrough, *Harlan,* 227–28. On the religious views of the justices, see Belknap, "God," 403–5.

29. Dolbeare and Hammond, *School Prayer,* 29; *School District of Abington Township v. Schempp* and *Murray v. Curlett,* 374 U.S. 203 (1963); *Schempp v. School District of Abington Township,* 201 F. Supp. 815 (E.D. Pa. 1962); *Murray v. Curlett,* 228 Md. 239, 179 A.2d. 698 (1962).

30. Docket book entries for *Murray v. Curlett and School District of Abington Township, Pennsylvania v. Schempp,* both in box 409, WJB; conference notes on *Murray v. Curlett,* March 1, 1963, box 1280, WOD; Schwartz, *Super Chief,* 466; MJF [Martin J. Flynn] to Mr. Justice [Clark], undated, box A-143, TCC.

31. Schwartz, *Super Chief,* 467–68; Henry J. Abraham and Barbara J. Perry, *Freedom and the Court: Civil Rights and Civil Liberties in the United States,* 6th ed. (New York: Oxford University Press, 1994), 272–73; Mengler, "Public Relations," 339–41, 344–45; West, "Clark," 395; *Schempp,* 374 U.S. at 224–25.

32. *Schempp,* 374 U.S. at 205, 222, 225–26.

33. Ibid. at 231–32 (Brennan, J., concurring); Edward V. Heck, "Justice Brennan and the Heyday of Warren Court Liberalism," 20 *Santa Clara Law Review* 841, at 851 (1980); Schwartz, *Super Chief,* 467; *Schempp,* 374 U.S. at 232, 295, 231, 242 (Brennan, J., concurring); Louis H. Pollak, "Forward: Public Prayers in Public Schools," 77 *Harvard Law Review* 62, at 69 (1963).

34. *Schempp,* 374 U.S. at 228–29 (Douglas, J., concurring); ibid. at 307, 306 (Goldberg, J., concurring).

35. Schwartz, *Super Chief,* 467; *Schempp,* 374 U.S. at 313, 312, 315, 317–18 (Stewart, J., dissenting).

36. Pollak, "Public Prayers," 63; *Chamberlain v. Dade County,* 377 U.S. 402 (1964); Laubach, *Prayers,* 98; Fisher, "Becker Amendment," 441–42; Robert H. Birkby, "The Supreme Court and the Bible Belt: Tennessee Reaction to the 'Schempp' Decision," in *Prayer in the Public Schools,* ed. Robert Sikorkie (New York: Garland, 1993), 1:444; H. Frank Way, Jr., "Survey Research on Judicial Decisions: The Prayer and Bible Reading Cases," 21 *Western Political Quarterly* 189, at 191, 199, 203–4 (1968); Frank J. Sorauf, *The Wall of Separation: The Constitutional Politics of Church and State* (Princeton, N. J.: Princeton University Press, 1966), 296–98.

37. Laubach, *Prayers,* 138; Dolbeare and Hammond, *School Prayer,* 21; William M. Beaney and Edward N. Beiser, "Prayer and Politics: The Impact of *Engel* and *Schempp* on the Political Process," 13 *Journal of Public Law* 476, at 483–85 (1964); Katz, *Religion,* 39; Fisher, "Becker Amendment," 436.

38. Beaney and Beiser, "Prayers," 478–80; Fisher, "Becker Amendment," 428–30; Robert S. Alley, *School Prayer: The Court, the Congress, and the First Amendment* (Buffalo, N.Y.: Prometheus Books, 1994), 111–17; Senate Committee on the Judiciary, *Offerings on Prayer in Public Schools and Other Matters before the Senate Committee on the Judiciary,* 87th Cong., 2nd sess., 1962.

39. Beaney and Beiser, "Prayer," 494–95; Alley, *School Prayer,* 123–24; House Committee on the Judiciary, *Hearings on School Prayers before the House Committee on the Judiciary,* 88th Cong., 2nd sess., 1964, 2008.

40. Beaney and Beiser, "Prayer," 492–99.

41. Fisher, "Becker Amendment," 438–39, 453–54; Beaney and Beiser, "Prayer," 498–500.

42. Beaney and Beiser, "Prayer," 500–503; Alley, *School Prayer,* 150–51; Laubach, *Prayers,* 94–95.

43. Laubach, *Prayers,* 141–49; *Cong. Record,* 89th Cong., 2nd sess. (Sept. 21, 1966): 23,556.

44. Laubach, *Prayers,* 150–51; Fisher, "Becker Amendment," 433.

45. *Epperson v. Arkansas,* 393 U.S. 97 (1968); conference notes, box 1429, WOD; conference notes, box 416, WJB; Schwartz, *Super Chief,* 753–55; Kalman, *Fortas,* 273–75; 393 U.S. at 106–7; ibid. at 116 (Stewart, J., concurring).

46. Leo Pfeffer, "The Schempp-Murray Decision on School Prayers and Bible Reading," 5 *Journal of Church and State* 165, at 173 (1963); Pfeffer, *Church, State and Freedom,* rev. ed. (Boston: Beacon Press, 1967), 520–21.

47. *Flast v. Cohen,* 392 U.S. 83 (1968); John E. Nowak and Ronald D. Rotunda, *Constitutional Law,* 7th ed. (St. Paul, Minn.: West Publishing, 2004), 88.

48. *Board of Education of Central School District No. 1 v. Allen,* 392 U.S. 236 (1968); ibid. at 243–44.

49. Docket book entry and conference notes, box 415, WJB; *Allen,* 392 U.S. at 253 (Black, J., dissenting).

50. Katz, *Constitutions,* 73; *Allen,* 392 U.S. at 249 (Harlan, J., concurring); ibid. at 250 (Black, J., dissenting).

51. See *Lemon v. Kurtzman,* 403 U.S. 602 (1971).

52. John Sexton, a law professor, disputes the doctrinal significance of the Warren Court's decisions. He writes, "Quite simply, the Warren Court cases on church and state that were noteworthy political and social events added little to the jurisprudence of the First Amendment's Religion Clauses." "The Warren Court and the Religious Clauses of the First Amendment," in Schwartz, *Retrospective,* 104, at 104.

7. CIVIL RIGHTS

1. Announcement by the Chief Justice, October 2, 1967, box 356, EW; Cox, *Warren Court*, 6; Kurland, *Politics*, 89, 98, 110; Tushnet, "History," 3. For contrasting views on the subject of whether *Brown* inspired the civil rights movement, see Donald G. Nieman, *Promises to Keep: African-Americans and the Constitutional Order, 1776 to the Present* (New York: Oxford University Press, 1991), 162 (contending that it did), and Klarman, "Backlash Thesis," (arguing that it did not).

2. Klarman, *Jim Crow*, 335; *National Association for the Advancement of Colored People v. Alabama, ex rel. Patterson*, 357 U.S. 449 (1958); conference notes, January 17, 1958, box 1185, WOD.

3. JMH, memorandum for the Conference, April 22, 1958, box 46, JMH; Tushnet, *Civil Rights Law*, 285–87; Douglas to Harlan, April 22, 1958, box 1184, WOD; Frankfurter markup of preliminary circulation of Harlan's opinion, reel 32, frame 61, FF-H; Harlan to Frankfurter, undated, reel 32, frame 70, FF-H; JMH, memorandum for the Conference, May 23, 1958, box 10, WJB; Yarbrough, *Harlan*, 161–63; draft dissenting opinion by Clark, June 25, 1958, and Frankfurter to Clark, June 25, 1958, both in box A-66, TCC; TCC, memorandum to the Conference, June 30, 1958, box 10, WJB.

4. *NAACP v. Alabama*, 357 U.S. at 466, 462–65. The Ku Klux Klan case on which Alabama relied is *New York ex rel. Bryant v. Zimmerman*, 278 U.S. 63 (1928).

5. *National Association for the Advancement of Colored People v. Alabama, ex rel. Patterson*, 268 Ala. 531, 109 So.2d 138 (1959), *rev'd*, 360 U.S. 240 (1959); JMH, memorandum for the Conference, April 26. 1959, box 27, WJB; Tushnet, *Civil Rights Law*, 289; draft opinion by Harlan in *NAACP v. Gallion*, October 17, 1961, box A-128, TCC; *National Association for the Advancement of Colored People v. Gallion*, 190 F. Supp. 583 (M.D. Ala. 1960), *aff'd* 290 F.2d 337 (5th Cir. 1961), *cert granted*, 368 U.S. 16 (1961); 368 U.S. at 16–17; JMH, memorandum for the Conference, October 17, 1961, box A-128, TCC; *Natl. Ass'n for Adv. of Colored People v. State of Alabama*, 274 Ala. 544, 150 So.2d 677 (1963); conference notes on *NAACP v. Alabama Ex Rel. Flowers*, March 27, 1964, box 1303, WOD; *National Association for the Advancement of Colored People v. Alabama ex rel. Flowers*, 377 U.S. 288 (1964); ibid. at 310.

6. *Bates v. City of Little Rock*, 361 U.S. 516 (1960); docket book entry and attached conference notes, box 406, WJB; Brennan to Black, January 5, 1960, and Stewart to Chief Justice, Black, Douglas, and Brennan, January 19, 1960, both in box 340, HLB; 361 U.S. at 419 (Black, J., concurring).

7. *Shelton v. Tucker*, 364 U.S. 479 (1960); Miller, *Petitioners*, 382; Tushnet, *Civil Rights Law*, 294–95; conference notes, November 11, 1960, box 1233, WOD; docket book entry and attached conference notes, box 407, WJB; 364 U.S. at 488, 490; PS to Black and Douglas, December 2, 1960, box 344, HLB; 364 U.S. at 490–96 (Frankfurter, J., dissenting); ibid. at 496–99 (Harlan, J., dissenting).

8. *Louisiana ex. rel. Gremillion v. National Association for the Advancement of Colored People*, 366 U.S. 293 (1961); Miller, *Petitioners*, 382–83; 366 U.S. at 296; ibid. at 297 (Harlan, J. and Stewart, J., concurring in the judgment); ibid. at 297–98 (Frankfurter, J., concurring in the judgment).

9. Tushnet, *Civil Rights Law*, 274–80; *National Association for the Advancement of Colored People v. Button*, 371 U.S. 415, 430, 434, 435, 432–35, 438–39 (1963).

10. Tushnet, *Civil Rights Law*, 296–300; Yarbrough, *Harlan*, 210–12; docket book entry and attached conference notes, box 409, WJB; JMH, memorandum for the Conference, October 4, 1962, box A-133, TCC; *Gibson v. Florida Legislative Investigating Committee*, 372 U.S. 539 (1963); *Dombrowski v. Eastland*, 387 U.S. 82 (1967). The facts of *Dombrowski* are discussed more fully in *Dombrowski v. Pfister*, 380 U.S. 479, 481–82 (1965).

11. *Henry v. Mississippi*, 379 U.S. 443 (1965); Schwartz, *Super Chief*, 572–73; *Washington Post*, October 14, 1964; conference notes and WJB, memorandum for the Conference, October 20,

1964, both in box A-166, TCC; 379 U.S. at 453 (Black, J., dissenting); ibid. at 457–65 (Harlan, J., dissenting).

12. Michal R. Belknap, "The Warren Court and Equality," in *Constitutionalism and American Culture*, ed. Sandra F. Van Burkleo, et al. (Lawrence: University Press of Kansas, 2002), 211, at 222–24; Wright, *Law*, 402–3; *NAACP v. Alabama*, 357 U.S. at 460–61; Schwartz, *Super Chief*, 304–5; conference notes on *Shelton v. Tucker*, November 11, 1960, box 1233, WOD; Owen M. Fiss, "Dombrowski," 86 *Yale Law Journal* 1102, at 1103 (1977); Robert C. Post, "William J. Brennan and the Warren Court," in Tushnet, *Warren Court*, 123, at 132–33; *Button*, 371 U.S. at 433, 435–36; Tushnet, "History," 9.

13. Yarbrough, *Harlan*, 236–37; draft dissent in *Holt v. Virginia*, May 7, 1965, box 129, WJB; HLB to Harlan, May 10, 1965, box 484, JMH; Brennan to Douglas, January 9, 1963, box 85, WJB; *Button*, 371 U.S. at 448 (Harlan, J., dissenting); Frankfurter to Black, February 19, 1962, box 366, HLB.

14. *Gayle v. Browder*, 352 U.S. 903 (1956); *Browder v. Gayle*, 142 F. Supp. 707, 710 (M.D. Ala. 1956).

15. *Boynton v. Virginia*, 364 U.S. 454 (1960); docket book entry and attached conference notes on Boynton, box 407, WJB; PS, memorandum to the Conference, December 2, 1960, box A-103, TCC; conference notes on *Boynton*, box 1233, WOD; 364 U.S. at 464 (Whittaker, J., dissenting); *Abernathy v. Alabama*, 380 U.S. 447 (1965); conference notes on *Abernathy*, box 1330, WOD.

16. "Memorandum from Chief Justice Re: The Sit-In Cases," undated, box 83, WJB; Miller, *Petitioners*, 402–03; *Adderly v. Florida*, 385 U.S. 39 (1966).

17. "Memorandum from Chief Justice Re: Sit-In Cases"; *Civil Rights Cases*, 109 U.S. 3 (1883); *Marsh v. Alabama*, 326 U.S. 501 (1946); *Shelley v. Kraemer*, 334 U.S. 1 (1948).

18. *Burton v. Wilmington Parking Authority*, 365 U.S. 715 (1961); conference notes on *Burton*, February 24, 1961, box 1234, WOD; docket book entry no. 164 and attached conference notes, box 407, WJB; 365 U.S. at 726–27 (Stewart, J., concurring); 365 U.S. at 727–28 (Frankfurter, J., dissenting); FF to Clark, April 12, 1961, box A-113, TCC; 365 U.S. at 728–29 (Harlan, J., dissenting); *Turner v. City of Memphis*, 369 U.S. 350, 353 (1962); conference notes on *Turner*, box 1259, WOD.

19. *Evans v. Newton*, 382 U.S. 296, 298 (1966); ibid. at 316 (Harlan, J., dissenting); ibid. at 312 (Black, J., dissenting); ibid. at 303–5 (separate opinion by White, J.); ibid. at 300; Brennan to Douglas, December 6, 1965, box 139, WJB; Kurland, *Politics*, 171.

20. *Peterson v. City of Greenville*, 373 U.S. 244 (1963); *Gober v. City of Birmingham*, 373 U.S. 374 (1963); *Avent v. North Carolina*, 373 U.S. 375 (1963); *Robinson v. Florida*, 378 U.S. 153 (1964); *Griffin v. Maryland*, 378 U.S. 130 (1964).

21. FF to Chief Justice, December 4, 1961, box 534, JMH; *Thompson v. Louisville*, 362 U.S. 199, 206 (1960); conference notes on *Garner v. Louisiana*, box 408, WJB; conference notes on *Shuttlesworth v. Birmingham*, box 416, WJB; conference notes on *Shuttlesworth v. City of Birmingham*, November 9, 1962, box 1280, WOD; conference notes on *Abernathy v. Alabama*, October 16, 1964, box 1328, WOD; conference notes on *Brown v. Louisiana*, December 10, 1965, box 1352, WOD; *Garner v. Louisiana*, 368 U.S. 157, 185–86 (Harlan, J., concurring); Yarbrough, *Harlan*, 242–45; Cox, *Warren Court*, 41; "Memorandum from Chief Justice Re: Sit-In Cases"; *Barr v. City of Columbia*, 378 U.S. 146 (1964).

22. *Bouie v. City of Columbia*, 378 U.S. 347, 351–52 (1964); *Keeler v. Superior Court of Amador County*, 2 Cal. 3d 619, 87 Cal. Rptr. 481, 470 P.2d 617 (1970); *Cox v. Louisiana*, 379 U.S. 559, 571 (1965); Belknap, "Equality," 227.

23. *Garner v. Louisiana*, 368 U.S. 157 (1961); conference notes on *Garner v. Louisiana*, box 408, WJB; Yarbrough, *Harlan*, 242–45; Frankfurter to Harlan, December 1, 1961, reel 83, frames 867–68, FF-H; Harlan to Frankfurter, December 4, 1961, and Frankfurter to Chief Justice, December

4, 1961, both in box 534, JMH; 368 U.S. at 174 (Frankfurter, J., concurring); ibid. at 185, 198, 202, 205 (Harlan, J., concurring); ibid. at 157 (Douglas, J., concurring).

24. Burton M. Atkins and Terry Sloope, "The 'New' Hugo Black and the Warren Court," 18 *Polity* 621, at 622–26 (1986); Newman, *Black,* 541–43; Freyer, *Black,* 148.

25. *Peterson v. City of Greenville,* 373 U.S. 244 (1963); *Avent v. North Carolina,* 373 U.S. 375 (1963); *Gober v. City of Birmingham,* 373 U.S. 374 (1963); *Shuttlesworth v. Birmingham,* 373 U.S. 262 (1963); *Lombard v. Louisiana,* 373 U.S. 267 (1963); *Griffin v. Maryland,* 378 U.S. 130 (1964); Schwartz, *Super Chief,* 479–82; conference notes for *Peterson v. City of Greenville* and *Shuttlesworth v. City of Birmingham,* both dated November 9, 1962, box 1080, WOD; conference notes on Sit-ins, O.T. 62, box A-135, TCC.

26. Schwartz, *Super Chief,* 482–86; TCC to Chief Justice, May 3, 1963, box A-135, TCC; Warren to Douglas, May 18, 1963, box 1280, WOD; Goldberg to Chief Justice, February 12, 1963, box 370, HLB.

27. *Peterson v. City of Greenville,* 373 U.S. 244 (1963); *Avent v. North Carolina,* 373 U.S. 375 (1963); *Gober v. City of Birmingham,* 373 U.S. 374 (1963); *Lombard v. Louisiana,* 373 U.S. 267, 273 (1963); *Griffin v. Maryland,* 373 U.S. 920 (1963); [Frankfurter] to Black, May 6, 1963, box 484, JMH; *Lombard,* 373 U.S. at 274–83 (Douglas, J., concurring); *Peterson,* at 248–61 (Harlan, J., concurring).

28. *Bell v. Maryland,* 378 U.S. 226 (1964); *Barr v. City of Columbia,* 378 U.S. 146 (1964); *Bouie v. City of Columbia,* 378 U.S. 347 (1964); *Robinson v. Florida,* 378 U.S. 153 (1964); Schwartz, *Super Chief,* 508–9; Douglas, memorandum to the Conference, October 14, 1963, box 1299, WOD; conference notes on *Griffin v. Maryland,* October 23, 1963, box 1300, WOD; docket book entries for no. 9 (*Barr*) and no. 10 (*Bouie*), box 410, WBJ; "The Deliberations of the Justices in Deciding the Sit-In Cases of June 22, 1964," 2, 6–7, box 376, HLB (this is a collection of transcribed conference notes, judges notes, memoranda and other documents, compiled by Black clerks A. E. Dick Howard and John G. Kester).

29. Docket book entry for *Bell v. Maryland* and attached conference notes, box 410, WJB; October 23 conference notes; conference notes on no. 6–O.T. 1963, October 25, 1963, box 1300, WOD; "Deliberations," 3–6; Schwartz, *Super Chief,* 509–12.

30. Schwartz, *Super Chief,* 512–13; JMH to Chief Justice, October 26, 1963, box 102, WJB; *Griffin v. Maryland,* 375 U.S. 918 (1964); Archibald Cox to Chief Justice, November 21, 1963, box 102, WJB; *Robinson,* 378 U.S. at 155–57.

31. Schwartz, *Super Chief,* 513–17; draft opinion of the Court by Black in *Bell v. Maryland* and draft dissent by Warren in *Barr v. City of Columbia,* reprinted in Bernard Schwartz, ed., *The Unpublished Opinions of the Warren Court* (New York: Oxford University Press, 1985), 149–72; Douglas to Goldberg, May 8, 1964, box 1314, WOD; JMH to Black, May 6, 1964, box 484, JMH.

32. Schwartz, *Super Chief,* 517–22; Douglas, memorandum for files, June 20, 1964, box 1314, WOD; Douglas, memorandum to the Conference, May 27, 1964, WJB, memorandum to the Conference, May 28, 1964, and WOD, memorandum to the Conference, May 28, 1964, all in box 103, WJB.

33. Schwartz, *Super Chief,* 522–24; WOD to Clark, June 8, 1964, box A-151, TCC; draft opinion of Clark in *Bell v. Maryland,* in Schwartz, *Unpublished,* 173–86; EW to conference, June 11, 1964; "Deliberations," 34; WJB, memorandum to the Conference, June 16, 1964, box 103, WJB.

34. *Bell,* 378 U.S. at 239; ibid. at 286, 311 (Goldberg, J., concurring); ibid. at 243–45, 254–55 (separate opinion by Douglas, J.); ibid. at 327–28, 318 (Black, J., dissenting). For a good analysis of all of the opinions in *Bell* and the other 1964 cases, see Monrad G. Paulsen, "The Sit-In Cases of 1964: 'But Answer Came There None,'" 1964 *Supreme Court Review* 137.

35. *Bouie v. City of Columbia,* 378 U.S. 347 (1964); *Barr v. City of Columbia,* 378 U.S. 146 (1964); *Griffin v. Maryland,* 378 U.S. 130 (1964); *Robinson v. Florida,* 378 U.S. 153 (1964).

36. Pub. L. 88–352, § 201, 78 Stat. 243.

37. *Hamm v. City of Rock Hill,* 379 U.S. 306 (1964); *Georgia v. Rachel,* 384 U.S. 780 (1966); ibid. at 804; docket book entry, box 512, WJB; *City of Greenwood v. Peacock,* 384 U.S. 808 (1966); ibid. at 826; ibid. at 836 (Douglas, J., dissenting).

38. *Edwards v. South Carolina,* 372 U.S. 229 (1963); ibid. at 245 (Clark, J., dissenting).

39. *Cox v. Louisiana,* 379 U.S. 536 (1965); ibid. at 559; docket book entry for no. 24 and attached conference notes, box 411, WJB; conference notes on no. 24, October 23, 1964, box 1329, WOD; Schwartz, *Super Chief,* 557–59; Goldberg, memorandum to the Conference, November 18, 1964, A-168, TCC; 379 U.S. at 552 (Goldberg quote); ibid. at 584 (Black, J., dissenting).

40. Powe, *American Politics,* 274; Newman, *Black,* 548–49; *Brown v. Louisiana,* 383 U.S. 131 (1966); docket book entry and attached conference notes, box 412, WJB; conference notes, December 10, 1965, box 1352, WOD; AF, "Memorandum for Brethren Re: No. 41, *Brown v. Louisiana,*" circulated December 30, 1965, box 2, AF; Schwartz, *Super Chief,* 607–9; 383 U.S. at 151 (White, J., concurring); Warren, memorandum to Fortas, box 2, AF; 383 U.S. at 166–67, 162 (Black, J., dissenting); undated note from Douglas to Fortas, box 2, AF.

41. *Adderly v. Florida,* 385 U.S. 39 (1966); conference notes, October 21, 1966, box 1385, WOD; conference list, October 21, 1966, box 147, WJB; 385 U.S. at 47–48; Schwartz, *Super Chief,* 631; Brennan to Douglas, November 8, 1966, box 149, WJB; 385 U.S. at 52 (Douglas, J., dissenting).

42. Cox, *Warren Court,* 110; *Walker v. Birmingham,* 388 U.S. 307 (1967); *Shuttlesworth v. Birmingham,* 382 U.S. 87 (1965); docket book entry and attached conference notes on no. 5 [*Shuttlesworth*], box 412, WJB; conference notes attached to docket book entry for no. 249 [*Walker*], box 414, WJB; conference notes on *Walker v. City of Birmingham,* March 17, 1967, box 1389, WOD; conference list, March 17, 1967, box 147, WJB; Schwartz, *Super Chief,* 632–33; conference list, March 24, 1967, box 147, WJB; 388 U.S. 316–17, 321; *Shuttlesworth v. Birmingham,* 394 U.S. 147 (1969); conference notes on no. 42 [*Shuttlesworth*], November 22, 1968, box 1430, WOD; docket book entry on no. 42, box 416, WJB.

43. Cox, *Warren Court,* 70; Kurland, *Politics,* 155.

44. *Smith v. Allwright,* 321 U.S. 649 (1944); *Terry v. Adams,* 345 U.S. 461 (1953); *Gomillion v. Lightfoot,* 364 U.S. 339 (1960); conference notes, October 21, 1960, box 1293, WOD; docket book entry and attached conference notes, box 407, WJB; Schwartz, *Super Chief,* 379; Frankfurter to Black, November 1, 1960, reel 62, frame 934, FF-H; Note from WOD to Felix [Frankfurter], undated, reel 62, frame 942, FF-H; 364 U.S. at 349 (Whittaker, J., concurring).

45. *United States v. Raines,* 362 U.S. 17 (1960); FF, memorandum for the Conference, February 11, 1960, box 36, WJB; Frankfurter to Brennan, February 17, 1960, reel 51, frame 750, FF-H; 362 U.S. at 28 (Frankfurter, J., concurring); Harlan to Brennan, February 18, 1960, box 36, WJB; Frankfurter to Harlan, February 23, 1960, reel 51, frame 754, FF-H.

46. *Hannah v. Larche,* 363 U.S. 420 (1960); ibid. at 494 (Douglas, J., dissenting).

47. *Civil Rights Cases,* 109 U.S. 3 (1883); *Heart of Atlanta Motel v. United States,* 379 U.S. 241 (1964); Yarbrough, *Harlan,* 253; HLB, "Memorandum to Chief Justice Re Motion in *Heart of Atlanta Motel* Case," box 382, HLB; Newman, *Black,* 578; 379 U.S. at 293 (Goldberg, J., concurring); ibid. at 279 (Douglas, J., concurring). For a good short history of *Heart of Atlanta* and its companion case, *Katzenbach v. McClung,* see Richard C. Cortner, *Civil Rights and Public Accommodations: The Heart of Atlanta and McClung Cases* (Lawrence: University Press of Kansas, 2001).

48. *Katzenbach v. McClung,* 379 U.S. 294 (1964); *Heart of Atlanta,* 379 U.S. at 243; docket book entry, box 412, WJB; Brennan to Clark, November 25, 1964, and Harlan to Clark, November 30, 1964, both in box A-179, TCC.; *Wickard v. Filburn,* 317 U.S. 111 (1942).

49. *South Carolina v. Katzenbach,* 383 U.S. 301, 315, 323, 336, 324 (1966); Freyer, *Black,* 146; 383 U.S. at 358 (Black, J., dissenting).

50. *Katzenbach v. Morgan,* 384 U.S. 641 (1966); *Lassiter v. Northampton County Board of Elections,* 360 U.S. 45 (1959); Schwartz, *Super Chief,* 599–602; docket book entry, box 413, WJB; 384 U.S. at 671; ibid. at 666–67 (Harlan, J., dissenting); ibid. at 671 (Harlan, J., dissenting). Douglas

joined all of the Court's opinion except its discussion of whether the congressional remedies adopted in section 4(e) constituted means not prohibited by, but consistent with, the letter and spirit of the Constitution; on that he reserved judgment. 384 U.S. at 658.

51. Belknap, *Federal*, 4–19, 159–71.

52. *United States v. Price*, 383 U.S. 787 (1966); *United States v. Guest*, 383 U.S. 745 (1966); ibid. at 774–84 (Brennan, J., concurring in part and dissenting in part); ibid. at 762 (Clark, J., concurring); ibid. at 762–63 (Harlan, J., concurring in part and dissenting in part); Belknap, *Federal*, 172–82.

53. *Jones v. Alfred H. Mayer Co.*, 392 U.S. 409 (1968); *Marsh v. Alabama*, 326 U.S. 501 (1946); docket book entry and attached conference notes, box 415, WJB; Yarbrough, *Harlan*, 260; Schwartz, *Super Chief*, 701–3; 392 U.S. at 413, 440; ibid. at 450 (Harlan, J., dissenting).

54. On Marshall's early life, education, and career with the NAACP, as well as Houston's work and influence on his protege, see Tushnet, *Civil Rights Law*, and Kluger, *Simple Justice*, 105–238.

55. Mark V. Tushnet, *Making Constitutional Law: Thurgood Marshall and the Supreme Court* (New York: Oxford University Press, 1997), 9–12; Richard L. Revesz, "Thurgood Marshall's Struggle," 68 *New York University Law Review* 237, at 237–48 (1993); *Cong. Record*, 87th Cong., 2nd sess. (September 11, 1962): 19,007–55.

56. Tushnet, *Constitutional Law*, 18–21.

57. Thurgood Marshall, interview, 10–16; Marvin [Watson], memorandum for the president, July 20, 1965, Ex. FG-535, WHCF, LBJ; Tushnet, *Constitutional Law*, 3–4, 25; Edwin Weisel Jr., interview by Joe B. Frantz, May 23, 1969,transcript, 21, LBJ Oral History Project, LBJ; press release given out the afternoon Ramsey Clark's appointment as attorney general was announced by the president, February 28, 1967, box 349, EW; Clarence Mitchell, interview by Thomas H. Baker, April 30, 1969, tape 2,transcript, 31, LBJ Oral History Project, LBJ.

58. Tushnet, *Constitutional Law*, 25–27; Senate Committee on the Judiciary, *Hearings on the Nomination of Thurgood Marshall . . .* , 90th Cong., 1st sess., 1967, 67–100; Dirksen interview, 14–15; *Cong. Record*, 90th Cong., 1st sess. (August 30, 1967): 24,583–657. For the Hart quote, see ibid., 24,639. For the vote, see ibid. 24,565.

59. Tushnet, *Constitutional Law*, 4, 7; Glen Darbyshire, "Clerking for Justice Marshall," 77 *ABA Journal* 48, at 50–51 (1991); Kalman, *Fortas*, 210; Cray, *Chief Justice*, 488.

60. Cox, *Warren Court*, 6.

61. Kurland, *Politics*, 163; *WHYY, Inc. v. Borough of Glassboro*, 393 U.S. 117 (1968); *Williamson v. Lee Optical*, 348 U.S. 483, 488–89 (1955); *Ferguson v. Skrupa*, 372 U.S. 726 (1963); *Florida Lime & Avocado Growers v. Paul*, 373 U.S. 132 (1963); *Morey v. Doud*, 354 U.S. 457 (1957); "Conference Notes on No. 475–Morey v. Doud, April 26, 1956 [*sic*]," box 1173, WOD; 354 U.S. at 475 (Frankfurter, J., dissenting); ibid. at 471 (Black, J., dissenting).

62. Powe, *American Politics*, 294–95; Brennan to Clark, May 23, 1963, box 97, WJB; Robert L. Carter, "The Warren Court and Desegregation," 67 *Michigan Law Review* 238, at 244–45 (1968).

63. Carter, "Desegregation," 245; Nieman, *Promises*, 176–79; *United States v. Jefferson County Board of Education*, 372 F.2d 836 (5th Cir. 1966); Frank T. Read, "Judicial Evolution of the Law of School Integration since *Brown v. Board of Education*," 39 *Law and Contemporary Problems* 7, at 20–28 (1975).

64. *Green v. County School Board of New Kent County, Virginia*, 391 U.S. 430 (1968); Schwartz, *Super Chief*, 703–6; 391 U.S. at 438, 435, 438–40; Warren, memorandum to Brennan, May 22, 1968, box 177, WJB.

65. *Whitus v. Georgia*, 385 U.S. 545 (1967); Tushnet, "History," 5; *Naim v. Naim*, 350 U.S. 891 (1955); Powe, *American Politics*, 286; *McLaughlin v. Florida*, 379 U.S. 184 (1964); *Pace v. Alabama*, 106 U.S. 583 (1883); conference notes on *McLaughlin v. Florida*, October 16, 1964, box 1329, WOD; conference notes, undated, box A-167, TCC; Yarbrough, *Harlan*, 267–68; 379 U.S. at 184, 197 (Harlan, J., concurring).

66. *Loving v. Virginia,* 388 U.S. 1 (1967); docket book entry, box 414, WJB; 388 U.S. at 8; ibid. at 11; Kurland, *Politics,* 156–57.

67. *Reitman v. Mulkey,* 387 U.S. 369 (1967); *Lincoln v. Mulkey,* 64 Cal. 2d 529, 50 Cal. Rptr. 881, 413 P.2d 825, 834 (1966); 387 U.S. at 378; ibid. at 389, 395 (Harlan, J., dissenting).

68. William E. Nelson, "Deference and the Limits to Deference in the Constitutional Jurisprudence of Justice Byron R. White," 58 *University of Colorado Law Review* 347, at 353–54 (1987); *Hunter v. Erickson,* 393 U.S. 385 (1969); *State ex rel. Hunter v. Erickson, Mayor et al.,* 12 Ohio St. 2d 116, 233 N.E. 2d 129, 131 (1967); conference notes attached to docket book entry, box 416, WJB; 393 U.S. at 391–92; ibid. at 395 (Harlan, J, concurring); ibid. at 396 (Black, J., dissenting).

69. *Hernandez v. Texas,* 347 U.S. 475, 477–78 (1954); conference notes, January 16, 1954, box 1147, WOD; 347 U.S. at 478.

70. *Levy v. Louisiana,* 391 U.S. 68 (1968); ibid. at 71; *Glona v. American Guarantee & Liability Insurance Company,* 391 U.S. 73 (1968).

71. *Glona,* 391 U.S. at 76; *Graham v. Richardson,* 403 U.S. 365 (1971).

72. Linda K. Kerber, *No Constitutional Right to Be Ladies: Women and the Obligations of Citizenship* (New York: Hill and Wang, 1998), 172, 124–27, 177–82; Ruth Bader Ginsburg, "Sexual Equality under the Fourteenth and Equal Rights Amendments," 1979 *Washington University Law Quarterly* 161, at 163–64 (1979); *United States v. Dege,* 364 U.S. 51, 54 (1960); *Hoyt v. Florida,* 368 U.S. 57 (1960); conference notes on *Hoyt v. Florida,* box 408, WJB; Schwartz, *Super Chief,* 400–401; 368 U.S. at 69 (Warren, C. J., concurring); ibid. at 62.

73. *Skinner v. Oklahoma,* 316 U.S. 535 (1942); Kurland, *Politics,* 167; Gerald Gunther, "Forward, In Search of Evolving Doctrine on a Changing Court: A Model for a Newer Equal Protection," 86 *Harvard Law Review* 1, at 8 (1977).

74. White, "Anti-Judge," 72; *Harper v. Virginia State Board of Elections,* 383 U.S. 663 (1966); *Breedlove v. Suttles,* 302 U.S. 277 (1937); Schwartz, *Super Chief,* 596–97; preliminary circulations of dissenting opinions by Goldberg, February 27, 1965, March 3, 1965, and March 4, 1965, box 249, JMH; Black, memorandum for the Conference, March 4, 1965, box 249, JMH; conference notes, January 28, 1966, box 1363, WOD; conference notes attached to docket book entry for *Harper v. Virginia Board of Elections,* box 412, WJB.

75. WOD, memorandum to the Conference on nos. 48 and 655, March 22, 1966, box 249, JMH; Douglas, preliminary circulation of opinion of the Court in *Harper v. Virginia State Board of Elections,* February 4, 1966, box 249, JMH; White, "Anti-Judge," 72–73; 383 U.S. at 665, 667, 670; ibid. at 682–83, 686 (Harlan, J., dissenting); Newman, *Black,* 569; 383 U.S. at 673–74, 675 (Black, J., dissenting); ibid. at 669.

76. *Loving v. Virginia,* 388 U.S. 1, 12 (1968); *Shapiro v. Thompson,* 394 U.S. 618, 630 (1969); Tushnet, *Constitutional Law,* 96–97; Ronald Kahn, *The Supreme Court and Constitutional Theory, 1953–1993* (Lawrence: University Press of Kansas, 1994), 43; *Kramer v. Union Free School District,* 395 U.S. 621 (1969).

77. *Cong. Record,* 90th Cong., 1st sess. (August 30, 1967): 24,640.

8. INDIVIDUALISM, PRIVACY, AND SELF-EXPRESSION

1. Nadine Strossen, "Freedom of Speech in the Warren Court," in Schwartz, *Retrospective,* 71; Robert C. Post, "William J. Brennan and the Warren Court," in Tushnet, *Warren Court,* 124–27.

2. Strossen, "Speech," 68–69. The seven First Amendment doctrines Strossen credits the Warren Court with formulating or meaningfully developing are the following: (1) freedom of association; (2) academic freedom; (3) the right to receive information and ideas; (4) public forum; (5) chilling effect; (6) vagueness and overbreadth; and (7) less-restrictive alternatives.

3. Newman, *Black,* 501–2; Lawrence Baum, "Measuring Policy Change in the U.S. Supreme Court," 82 *American Political Science Review* 905, at 909 (1988); conference notes on *Talley v. California,* box 406, WJB; *Talley v. California,* 362 U.S. 60, 65 (1960).

4. Horwitz, "Pursuit," 10–12; S. Sidney Ulmer, "Governmental Litigants, Underdogs, and Civil Liberties in the Supreme Court: 1903–1968 Terms," 47 *Journal of Politics* 899, at 906 (1985); Kalman, *Fortas,* 131; Baum, "Measuring," 909; Cox, *Warren Court,* 10.

5. *Yellin v. United States,* 374 U.S. 109 (1963); *DeGregory v. Attorney General of New Hampshire,* 383 U.S. 825 (1966); *Baggett v. Bullitt,* 377 U.S. 360 (1964); *Elfbrandt v. Russell,* 384 U.S. 11 (1966); *Keyishian v. Board of Regents of the University of the State of New York,* 385 U.S. 589 (1967); *Whitehill v. Elkins,* 389 U.S. 54 (1967); ibid. at 59; Alfred H. Kelly and Winfred A. Harbison, *The American Constitution: Its Origins and Development,* 3rd ed. (New York: Norton, 1976), 928–29.

6. *Red Lion Broadcasting Co. v. Federal Communications Commission,* 395 U.S. 367, 390 (1969); ibid. at 392, 389, 390.

7. *Brandenburg v. Ohio,* 395 U.S. 444 (1969); ibid. at 447; ibid. at 440–50 (Black, J., concurring); ibid. at 454 (Douglas, J., concurring); Black, memorandum to Fortas, April 15, 1969, box FL 11, AF; Warren to Brennan, May 22, 1969, box 54, TM. File 492 in box FL of the Fortas Papers contains three circulations of his *Brandenburg* opinion, dated April 11, April 18, and April 22, 1969.

8. Strossen, "Speech," 76–79.

9. Tushnet, *Civil Rights,* 285–86; Yarbrough, *Harlan,* 161; JMH, "Memorandum for the Conference Re: No. 91–NAACP v. Alabama," April 22, 1958, box 46, JMH; *NAACP v. Alabama, ex rel. Patterson,* 357 U.S. 459, 460–61 (1958); Schwartz, *Super Chief,* 304–5; *Bates v. Little Rock,* 361 U.S. 516, 523 (1960); *Shelton v. Tucker,* 364 U.S. 479, 487–88 (1960); *NAACP v. Button,* 371 U.S. 415, 428–30; ibid. at 444; conference notes on *Shelton v. Tucker,* November 11, 1960, box 1233, WOD.

10. Fiss, "Dombrowski," 1103, 1112–16; Post, "Brennan," 132–33; *NAACP v. Button,* 371 U.S. at 435–36; *Dombrowski v. Pfister,* 380 U.S. 479, 433 (1965).

11. *Feiner v. New York,* 340 U.S. 315 (1951); *Edwards v. South Carolina,* 372 U.S. 229, 236–38 (1963); Nowak and Rotunda, *Constitutional Law,* 1113; *Gregory v. Chicago,* 394 U.S. 111, 112; *Cox v. Louisiana,* 379 U.S. 551 (1965); conference notes attached to docket book entry on no. 24, B. Elton Cox vs. Louisiana, box 411, WJB; Laurence H. Tribe, *American Constitutional Law,* 2nd ed. (Mincola, N.Y.: Foundation Press, 1988), 854.

12. Anthony Lewis, *Make No Law: The Sullivan Case and the First Amendment* (New York: Random House, 1991), 9–14; Kermit L. Hall, "Justice Brennan and Cultural History: *New York Times v. Sullivan* and Its Times," 27 *California Western Law Review* 339, at 343–44, 346–50 (1991) (quote at 344).

13. *New York Times v. Sullivan,* 376 U.S. 254, 262 (1964); conference notes, box 1301, WOD; *Sullivan v. New York Times,* 273 Ala. 656, 144 So. 2d 25 (1962); Hall, "Cultural History," 351; 376 U.S. at 278.

14. Lewis, *No Law,* 130–32, 136–37; Schwartz, *Super Chief,* 531.

15. Docket book entry and attached conference notes, box 410, WJB; "Conference Notes No. 39–New York Times v. Sullivan, January 10, 1964," and "Conference Notes, No. 40—Abernathy v. Sullivan, January 10, 1964," both in box 1301, WOD.

16. Lewis, *No Law,* 166–70; Schwartz, *Super Chief,* 533.

17. Note from HLB to Douglas, February 26, 1964, box 1301, WOD; Schwartz, *Super Chief,* 534; *Sullivan,* 376 U.S. at 293 (Black, J., concurring); ibid. at 297–98 (Goldberg, J., concurring).

18. Schwartz, *Super Chief,* 534–41; Lewis, *No Law,* 172–82; WJB, memorandum to the Conference, March 3, 1964, box 497, JMH (quotation on Harlan's misgivings about discussing sufficiency of the evidence from this memo); Brennan to Harlan, March 2, 1964, box 194, JMH; note from Brennan to Douglas, March 4, 1964, box 1301, WOD; 376 U.S. at 284–85.

19. 376 U.S. at 283, 270, 273, 279, 292.

20. Harlan to Brennan, February 26, 1964, box 194, JMH; Yarbrough, *Harlan,* 223; 376 U.S. at 284 n. 23.

21. *Garrison v. Louisiana,* 379 U.S. 64 (1964); *State v. Garrison,* 244 La. 787, 154 So. 2d 400 (1963); conference list, April 24, 1964, box 101, WJB; Schwartz, *Super Chief,* 566–68; Yarbrough, *Harlan,* 225; Harlan to Clark, June 12, 1964, box A-166, TCC; docket book entry, box 410, WJB; 379 U.S. at 74; ibid. at 79 (Black, J., concurring); ibid. at 81–82 (Douglas, J., concurring); ibid. at 88 (Goldberg, J., concurring); WJB, memorandum to Clark, Harlan, Stewart, and White, November 19, 1964, box A-166, TCC; WDSU-TV and WDSU-Radio, "The Supreme Court and Freedom of the Press," March 19, 1964, box 380, HLB.

22. *Rosenblatt v. Baer,* 383 U.S. 75 (1966); Schwartz, *Super Chief,* 612–17; WJB, memorandum to the Conference, March 2, 1965, box 136, WJB; 383 U.S. at 81, 85; Brennan to Douglas, November 20, 1965, box 135, WJB; 383 U.S. at 96–97 (Harlan, J., concurring); ibid. at 86; ibid. at 100 (Fortas, J., dissenting); ibid. at 88 (Clark, J., concurring in the result); ibid. at 90 (Douglas, J., concurring); ibid. at 94 (Black, J., concurring and dissenting).

23. Schwartz, *Super Chief,* 617, 648–49; *Curtis Publishing Co. v. Butts* and *Associated Press v. Walker,* 388 U.S. 130 (1967); *Associated Press v. Walker,* 393 S.W.2d 671 (Tex. Civ. App. 1965).

24. 388 U.S. at 156–59; Schwartz, *Super Chief,* 648–52; conference lists, February 24, 1967, and March 10, 1967, box 147, WJB; docket book entries for no. 37, *Curtis Publishing Company v. Wallace Butts,* and no. 150, *The Associated Press v. Edwin A. Walker,* both in box 414, WJB; 388 U.S. at 162 (Warren, C.J., concurring); 388 U.S. at 154–55; JMII, memorandum for the Conference, June 8, 1967, box 545, JMH; 388 U.S. at 163 (Warren, C.J., concurring); ibid. at 172–73 (Brennan, J., concurring in *Walker* and dissenting in *Butts*); Brennan to Warren, June 7, 1967, box 156, WJB; 388 U.S. at 170–71 (Black, J., concurring in the result in *Walker* and dissenting in *Butts*).

25. *St. Amant v. Thompson,* 390 U.S. 727 (1968); *Thompson v. St. Amant,* 250 La. 405, 424, 196 So. 2d 255, 262 (1967); 390 U.S. at 731; Lawrence G. Williams to Warren, May 9, 1968, box 176, WJB; 390 U.S. at 732; Powe, *American Politics,* 321.

26. Harry Kalven Jr., "The New York Times Case: A Note on 'The Central Meaning of the First Amendment,'" 1964 *Supreme Court Review* 191, at 221; John P. MacKenzie, "The Warren Court and the Press," 67 *Michigan Law Review* 303, at 303 (1968).

27. *Time, Inc. v. Hill,* 385 U.S. 374, 376–80, 392–93 (1967); Harry Kalven Jr., "The Reasonable Man and the First Amendment: Hill, Butts, and Walker," 1967 *Supreme Court Review* 267, at 272–73; Kalman, *Fortas,* 262–63; Schwartz, *Super Chief,* 642–43; typescript of oral argument in *Time, Inc. v. Hill,* box 7, AF.

28. Conference list, April 29, 1966, box 132, WJB; Schwartz, *Super Chief,* 643–47; Kalman, *Fortas,* 263–66; Schwartz, *Unpublished,* 240, 243, 251, 242–57, 275; draft dissent by White, June 9, 1966, box 7, AF; Newman, *Black,* 590; conference list, October 21, 1966, box 147, WJB.

29. 385 U.S. at 387–88; ibid. at 398 (Black, J., concurring); ibid. at 401–2 (Douglas, J., concurring); ibid. at 411–12 (Fortas, J., dissenting); ibid. at 402 (Harlan, J., concurring in part and dissenting in part); Schwartz, *Super Chief,* 648.

30. Rickie Solinger, *Wake Up Little Susie: Single Pregnancy and Race before Roe v. Wade* (New York and London: Routledge, 1992), 217–18; William O'Neill, *Coming Apart: An Informal History of America in the 1960s* (New York: Quadrangle Books, 1971), 268; Powe, *American Politics,* 336; Gilbert, *Another Chance,* 71.

31. *Poe v. Ulman,* 367 U.S. 497 (1961); David J. Garrow, *Liberty and Sexuality: The Right to Privacy and the Making of Roe v. Wade* (New York: Macmillan, 1994), 15–17, 21–23, 27–28, 32–37, 77, 100, 92–93, 95–97, 106–7, 110–11, 113–16, 119–23, 125–28, 137–38, 141–42, 159–60, 143–47; FF, Re: *Poe v. Ulman,* March 6, 1961, reel 70, frame 603, FF-H.

32. Docket book entry and attached conference notes, box 407, WJB; Garrow, *Sexuality,* 169, 178–86; Schwartz, *Super Chief,* 351–52; 367 U.S. at 501–2.

33. "Dan" to Frankfurter, undated, reel 70, frame 511, FF-H; 367 U.S. at 509 (Black, J., dissenting); ibid. at 513, 515 (Douglas, J., dissenting); ibid. at 555 (Stewart, J., dissenting).

34. White, *Judicial Tradition,* 356; Yarbrough, *Harlan,* 313, 311–12; Harlan to Dean Joseph Omera, September 19, 1962, box 583, JMH; 367 U.S. at 541–43, 548, 553–55 (Harlan, J., dissenting).

35. *Griswold v. Connecticut,* 381 U.S. 479 (1965); Garrow, *Sexuality,* 202–13, 228–29; *State v. Griswold,* 151 Conn. 544, 200 A.2d 479 (1964); docket book entry, box 411, WJB.

36. Conference list, April 2, 1965, box 118, WJB; conference Notes, box 411, WJB; conference notes, box 1346, WOD; Garrow, *Sexuality,* 233, 238, 199, 242–43; Schwartz, *Super Chief,* 577–78.

37. Schwartz, *Unpublished,* 231–36; Garrow, *Sexuality,* 245–48; Brennan to Douglas, April 24, 1965, box 130, WJB; James F. Simon, "William O. Douglas," in Schwartz, *Retrospective,* 218.

38. 381 U.S. at 484–85; Garrow, *Sexuality,* 248–52; Schwartz, *Super Chief,* 580.

39. 381 U.S. at 488, 495–99 (Goldberg, J., concurring); Garrow, *Sexuality,* 250.

40. 381 U.S. at 505, 502 (White, J., concurring); ibid. at 500 (Harlan, J., concurring).

41. Ibid. at 527 (Stewart, J., dissenting); ibid. at 507, 512, 511, 510 (Black, J., dissenting); ibid. at 530 (Black, J., dissenting).

42. Garrow, *Sexuality,* 256–57, 263–64; *New York Times,* June 9, 1965, 46; "Supreme Court Reverses Birth Control Law," *Christian Century,* June 13, 1965, 797; "The Connecticut Decision," *Commonweal,* June 23, 1965, 427.

43. *New York Times,* June 9, 1965; O'Neill, *Coming Apart,* 204–5; Horwitz, *Warren Court,* 102, 99; Harry Kalven Jr., "'Uninhibited, Robust, and Wide-Open'—A Note on Free Speech and the Warren Court," 67 *Michigan Law Review* 289, at 301 (1968).

44. Kalven, "Uninhibited," 300; Horwitz, *Pursuit,* 100; White, *Warren,* 250–54; Schwartz, *Super Chief,* 221–22; Hunter R. Clark, *Justice Brennan: The Great Conciliator* (Secaucus, N.J.: Carol Publishing, 1995), 183, 185. For an extensive discussion of obscenity law, including cases decided by the Warren Court, see Edward de Garza, *Girls Lean Back Everywhere: The Law of Obscenity and the Attack on Genius* (New York: Random House, 1992).

45. *Roth v. United States* and *Alberts v. State of California,* 354 U.S. 476 (1957); *Butler v. Michigan,* 352 U.S. 380 (1957); conference notes on *Butler v. Michigan,* October 19, 1956, WOD; docket book entry for *Butler v. Michigan,* box 370, EW; "Memorandum for Brethren," February 18, 1957, box A-50, TCC; WJB Jr. to Frankfurter, February 19, 1957, reel 21, frame 642, FF-H; 352 U.S. at 383–84.

46. Clark to Frankfurter, February 18, 1957, box A-50, TCC; *Roth* and *Alberts,* 354 U.S. at 476 (1957); docket book entries for *Alberts v. California* and *Roth v. United States,* box 403, WJB; docket book page, *Alberts v. California,* box 370, EW; Schwartz, *Super Chief,* 219–20; Yarbrough, *Harlan,* 215–16; 354 U.S. at 489, 483–84; ibid. at 494–96 (Warren, C.J., concurring); ibid. at 497 (Harlan, J., concurring in the result in *Alberts* and dissenting in *Roth*); ibid. at 512–14 (Douglas, J., dissenting); Samuel Krislov, "From Ginzburg to Ginsberg: The Unhurried Children's Hour in Obscenity Litigation," 1968 *Supreme Court Review* 153, at 160.

47. *Kingsley Books, Inc. v. Brown,* 354 U.S. 436 (1957); ibid. at 448 (Brennan, J., dissenting); ibid. at 446, (Warren, C.J., dissenting); ibid. at 446–47 (Douglas, J., dissenting); *Smith v. California,* 361 U.S. 147, 148, 152, 153 (1960); ibid. at 162 (Frankfurter, J., concurring); ibid. at 170–72 (Harlan, J., concurring in part and dissenting in part); ibid. at 169 (Douglas, J., concurring); ibid. at 159 (Black, J., concurring).

48. *Kingsley International Pictures Corp. v. Regents of the University of the State of New York,* 360 U.S. 684 (1959); ibid. at 688; docket book entry and attached conference notes, box 505, WJB; 360 U.S. at 697 (Douglas, J., concurring); ibid. at 690 (Black, J., concurring).

49. *Times Film Corp. v. City of Chicago,* 365 U.S. 43 (1961); docket book entry and attached conference notes, box 407, WJB; Schwartz, *Super Chief,* 368; Stewart to Clark, November 22, 1960, and Harlan to Clark, November 3, 1960, both in box A-107, TCC; 365 U.S. at 50; ibid. at 50–51 (Warren, C.J., dissenting); ibid. at 78 (Douglas, J., dissenting).

50. *Bantam Books, Inc. v. Sullivan,* 372 U.S. 58 (1963); Note from MJF [Martin J. Flynn] to Clark, December 29, 1962, box A-143, TCC; 372 U.S. at 75 (Clark, J., concurring); ibid. at 76 (Harlan, J., dissenting).

51. *Freedman v. Maryland,* 380 U.S. 51 (1965); docket book entry, box 411, WJB; Schwartz, *Super Chief,* 368–70; Clark to Brennan, December 21, 1964, and JMH to Brennan, February 4, 1965, box 125, WJB; 380 U.S. at 58–59; JMH to Brennan and EW to Brennan, February 25, 1965, both in box 125, WJB; 380 U.S. at 61–62 (Douglas, J., concurring).

52. *Manual Enterprises v. Day,* 370 U.S. 478 (1962); conference notes, March 2, 1962, box 1259, WOD; Yarbrough, *Harlan,* 217–18; Brennan to Harlan, June 9, 1962, box 543, JMH; 370 U.S. at 500, 518–19, 495 (Brennan, J., concurring); ibid. at 520 (Clark, J., dissenting).

53. *Jacobellis v. Ohio,* 378 U.S. 184 (1964); "Memorandum of Mr. Justice Brennan in Re: The Obscenity Cases," undated, box 101, WJB; conference notes, April 3, 1964, WOD; docket book entry, box 410, WJB; conference list, April 3, 1964, box 101, WJB.

54. 378 U.S. at 191; "Memorandum in Re: The Obscenity Cases"; 378 U.S. at 196 (Black, J., concurring); ibid. at 198 (Goldberg, J., concurring); ibid. at 197 (Stewart, J., concurring); ibid. at 196 (White, J., concurring in the judgment); ibid. at 200, 204 (Warren, C.J., dissenting).

55. Schwartz, *Super Chief,* 616–19; *A Book Named "John Cleland's Memoirs of a Woman of Pleasure" v. Attorney General of Massachusetts,* 383 U.S. 413 (1966); *Ginzburg v. United States,* 383 U.S. 463 (1966); *Mishkin v. New York,* 383 U.S. 502, 505 (1966); docket book entry for "A Book Named 'John Cleland's Memoirs of a Woman of Pleasure' v. Attorney General of Massachusetts," box 413, WJB; docket book entries for *Mishkin v. New York* and *Ginzburg v. United States,* both in box 412, WJB; Kalman, *Fortas,* 343.

56. Schwartz, *Super Chief,* 619–20; *Memoirs,* 383 U.S. 418, 421; ibid. at 428, 433 (Douglas, J., concurring); ibid. at 421 (Black, J., concurring in the reversal for reasons set forth in his dissent in *Ginzburg*); *Ginzburg,* 383 U.S. at 516 (Black, J., dissenting).

57. *Ginzburg,* 388 U.S. at 470; Schwartz, *Super Chief,* 621–22; Krislov, "Ginzburg to Ginsberg," 162; *Mishkin,* 383 U.S. at 511, 507–8.

58. *Memoirs,* 383 U.S. at 424 (Douglas, J., concurring); *Ginzburg* and *Mishkin* at 482 (Douglas, J., dissenting); *Ginzburg,* 383 U.S. at 515 (Black, J., dissenting); *Mishkin,* 383 U.S. at 515 (Black, J., dissenting); *Ginzburg,* 383 U.S. at 493–95 (Harlan, J., dissenting); *Memoirs,* 383 U.S. at 456, 459–60 (Harlan, J., dissenting); *Ginzburg,* 383 U.S. at 500 (Stewart, J., dissenting); *Mishkin,* 383 U.S. at 518 (Stewart, J., dissenting); *Memoirs,* 383 U.S. at 421 (Black, J., and Stewart, J., concurring); ibid. at 460–62 (White, J., dissenting); ibid. at 441 (Clark, J., dissenting); Krislov, "Ginzburg to Ginsberg," 163.

59. Fortas, memorandum to the Conference, April 13, 1966, box 133, JMH; Schwartz, *Super Chief,* 652–56; *Redrup v. New York,* 386 U.S. 767, 769–71 (1967); Nowak and Rotunda, *Constitutional Law,* 1389–90.

60. 386 U.S. at 769; *Ginsberg v. New York,* 390 U.S. 629 (1968); Schwartz, *Super Chief,* 706–9; 390 U.S. at 633 n. 2; White to Brennan, March 4, 1968, box 169, WJB; 386 U.S. at 636, 641, 643–45; ibid. at 629 (Douglas, J., dissenting); ibid. at 674 (Fortas, J., dissenting); *Ginsberg v. New York,* 390 U.S. 676, 706–9 (1968) (Harlan, J., concurring in no. 47 and dissenting in nos. 56 and 64).

61. *Stanley v. Georgia,* 394 U.S. 557 (1969); docket book entry and attached conference notes, box 416, WJB; 394 U.S. at 560, 568, 565; ibid. at 572 (Stewart, J., concurring in the result); Al Katz, "Privacy and Pornography: Stanley v. Georgia," 1969 *Supreme Court Review* 203, at 203.

62. C. Peter McGrath, "The Obscenity Cases: Grapes of Roth," 1966 *Supreme Court Review* 7, at 8; Rev. and Mrs. Ira R. Dubal to Black, December 9, 1965, box 388, HLB; Kenneth Rexroth, "Obscenity Case Backlash," *San Francisco Examiner,* June 14, 1966; Morris Lowenthal to Warren, April 15, 1966, and Rep. Maston O'Neal to Warren, March 7, 1969, both in box 366, EW.

63. Powe, *American Politics,* 355–56.

9. THE CONSTITUTIONALIZATION OF CRIMINAL PROCEDURE

1. Yale Kamisar, "The Warren Court and Criminal Justice," in Schwartz, *Retrospective,* 116; Lawrence M. Friedman, *Crime and Punishment in American History* (New York: Basic Books, 1993), 295; White, *Judicial Tradition,* 359; David J. Bodenhamer, *Fair Trial: Rights of the Accused in American History* (New York: Oxvford University Press, 1992), 113; Tushnet, "History," 22; Schwartz, *History,* 283.

2. Wayne LaFave and Jerold H. Israel, *Criminal Procedure,* 2nd ed. (St. Paul, Minn.: West Publishing Co., 1992), 46.

3. Friedman, *Crime,* 299–300; Richard C. Cortner, *The Supreme Court and the Second Bill of Rights: The Fourteenth Amendment and the Nationalization of Civil Liberties* (Madison: University of Wisconsin Press, 1981), 46, 49, 124, 126, 133, 135–36; Bodenhamer, *Fair Trial,* 93–99; *Powell v. Alabama,* 287 U.S. 45, 71 (1932); *Palko v. Connecticut,* 302 U.S. 319, 325, 322 (1937).

4. Cortner, *Second,* 137–38, 144–49, 150, 152, 165–71; Bodenhamer, *Trial,* 100–105, 108; *Adamson v. California,* 332 U.S. 46, 85 (1947); Frankfurter to Warren, November 19, 1954, box 353, EW; *Wolf v. Colorado,* 338 U.S. 25, 28 (1949); *Rochin v. California,* 342 U.S. 165 (1982).

5. Warren, *Memoirs,* 169, 126, 117, 121; White, *Warren,* 43, 277–78, 195; Warren to Douglas, October 23, 1958, box 350, EW; Warren to John L. Kane Jr., March 20, 1967, box 366, EW; Schwartz, *Super Chief,* 192–93.

6. FF to Black, November 6, 1957, box A-64, TCC; Newman, *Black,* 554–55; Yarbrough, *Black,* 209, 214, 225; Freyer, *Black,* 38; Yarbrough, *Harlan,* 178–79, 296–97; Eisler, *Justice for All,* 70–71.

7. *Irvine v. California,* 347 U.S. 128 (1954); docket book entry, box 367, EW; 347 U.S. at 139–42 (Black, J., dissenting); ibid. at 150, 145–46 (Frankfurter, J., dissenting); conference notes, December 5, 1953, box 1146, WOD; 347 U.S. 132–34, 137; undated memorandum by Clark, annotated "This draft was never circulated or released; only Jackson, J. has seen a copy of it," box A-28, TCC; 347 U.S. at 138–39 (Clark, J., concurring).

8. *Breithaupt v. Abram,* 352 U.S. 432 (1957); Schwartz, *Super Chief,* 207.

9. *Bartkus v. Illinois,* 359 U.S. 121 (1959); *United States v. Lanza,* 260 U.S. 377 (1922); *Abbate v. United States,* 359 U.S. 187 (1959); annotated conference list, November 21, 1957, box A-60, TCC; Schwartz, *Super Chief,* 322–24; *Bartkus v. Illinois,* 355 U.S. 281 (1958); conference notes, box 1200, WOD; docket book entry and conference notes, box 405, WJB; FF, "Memorandum for the Conference, Re: No. 1—Bartkus v. Illinois," January 30, 1959, reel 36, frame 847, FF-H; WJB, "Memorandum to the Conference Re: No. 1—Bartkus v. Illinois," February 6, 1959, reel 36, frames 850–52, FF-H; Newman, *Black,* 482; Frankfurter to Clark, February 24, 1959, and Clark to Frankfurter, February 4, 1959, both in box A-75, TCC; handwritten note from Clark to Frankfurter, February 24, [1959], reel 36, frame 682, FF-H; 359 U.S. at 168 (Brennan, J., dissenting); ibid. at 168 (Black, J., dissenting).

10. Walter T. Fisher to Frankfurter, August 13, 1955, reel 36, frame 511, FF-H; LaFave and Israel, *Procedure,* 1192–93.

11. Susan E. Gunter, "Caryl Whittier Chessman," in Garraty and Carnes, eds., *Biography,* 4:790–91; Friedman, *Crime,* 320; *Chessman v. Teets,* 350 U.S. 3 (1955); *Chessman v. Teets,* 354 U.S. 156 (1957); Harlan, memorandum for the Conference, April 2, 1957, box A-58, TCC; memorandum of Frankfurter on in Forma Pauperis Petitions, November 1, 1954, box 6, WJB; 354 U.S. at 166 (Douglas, J., dissenting); *Chessman v. Dickson,* 362 U.S. 965 (1960); memorandum of Frankfurter, October 21, 1959, box A-89, TCC; Samuel Walker, *Popular Justice: A History of American Criminal Justice* (New York: Oxford University Press, 1980), 250.

12. *Mesarosh v. United States,* 352 U.S. 1 (1956); Belknap, *Cold War,* 169; *Yates v. United States,* 355 U.S. 66 (1957); *Kremen v. United States,* 353 U.S. 346 (1957).

13. *Abel v. United States,* 362 U.S. 217 (1960); Schwartz, *Super Chief,* 339–41; 362 U.S. at 230, 226; ibid. at 241 (Douglas, J., dissenting); ibid. at 248 (Brennan, J., dissenting).

14. David R. Bewley-Taylor, "Frank Costello," in Garrity and Carnes, eds., *Biography*, 5:58–59; Friedman, *Crime*, 272; *Costello v. United States*, 350 U.S. 359 (1956); conference notes, January 20, 1956, WOD; FF, memorandum for the Conference, May 21, 1957; Schwarz, *Super Chief*, 215; *Palermo v. United States*, 360 U.S. 343 (1959); conference notes, May 1, 1959, box 1200, WOD; Brennan to Chief Justice, Black, and Douglas, May 8, 1959, and WJB to Chief Justice, Black, and Douglas, June 11, 1959, both in box 26, WJB; 360 U.S. at 360–66; Walker, *Popular*, 207–8. The unrelated tax case was *Achilli v. United States*, 353 U.S. 373 (1957).

15. *United States v. Turley*, 352 U.S. 417 (1957); *Brown v. United States*, 359 U.S. 41 (1959); *Green v. United States*, 365 U.S. 43 (1961); conference notes attached to docket book entry for *Green v. United States*, box 407, WJB.

16. *Griffin v. Illinois*, 351 U.S. 12 (1956); Arthur J. Goldberg, "The Warren Court and Its Critics," 20 *Santa Clara Law Review* 831, at 833 (1980); William O. Douglas, "Vagrancy and Arrest on Suspicion" (speech given at University of New Mexico Law School, March 15, 1960), box 59, HLB; docket book entry, box 368, EW; Schwartz, *Super Chief*, 193; conference notes, December 9, 1955, box 1163, WOD; Berry, *Stability*, 186; Yarbrough, *Harlan*, 183–87; JMH, memorandum for the Conference, February 27, 1956, box 429, EW; memorandum by Black *In re* Harlan's Memorandum in No. 95, *Griffin and Crenshaw v. Illinois*, undated, box A-44, TCC; 351 U.S. at 26–29 (Burton, J., dissenting); ibid. at 629 (Harlan, J., dissenting).

17. *Mallory v. United States*, 354 U.S. 449, 451–52, 455 (1957); Paul Murphy, *Crisis Times*, 330; Powe, *American Politics*, 108.

18. Friedman, *Crime*, 297, 300; Bodenhamer, *Trial*, 112.

19. Cortner, *Second*, 173–74; *Frank v. Maryland*, 360 U.S. 914 (1959); docket book entry and attached conference notes, box 405, WJB; Urofsky, "Douglas," in Tushnet, *Warren Court*, 79; Whittaker to Frankfurter, April 25, 1959, reel 37, frame 817, FF-H; Stewart to Frankfurter, April 10, 1959, reel 37, frame 809, FF-H; 360 U.S. at 373; ibid. at 374 (Douglas, J., dissenting).

20. To "Dear Al," June 29, 1959, reel 37, frames 763–66, FF-H; "A Priceless Right Is Weakened," reel 37, frames 747–48, FF-H; Senate Resolution No. 38, May 28, 1959, and WDSU editorial, May 8, 1959, both in box 25, WJB.

21. *Ohio ex rel. Eaton v. Price*, 364 U.S. 263 (1960); Schwartz, *Super Chief*, 342–44; Douglas, memorandum for the Conference, May 16, 1959, box 25, WJB; Frankfurter to Brennan, June 22, 1960, box 32, WJB; 364 U.S. at 264, 275–76 (opinion of Brennan, J.); Frankfurter to Brennan, April 23, 1959, box 25, WJB.

22. Cortner, *Second*, 177; Schwartz, *Super Chief*, 345–46; *Elkins v. United States*, 364 U.S. 206, 213, 216, 223 (1960); Frankfurter, Clark, Harlan, and Whittaker, memorandum to Majority in Silver-Platter Cases, April 13, 1960, box A-95, TCC; 364 U.S. at 251 (Harlan, J., dissenting); ibid. at 237 (Frankfurter, J., dissenting); letter to Mr. Justice [Clark], undated, box A-95, TCC.

23. *Mapp v. Ohio*, 367 U.S. 643 (1961); Cortner, *Second*, 181–84; docket book entry and attached conference notes, box 407, WJB; conference notes, March 31, 1961, box 1254, WOD; Ball and Cooper, *Power*, 212; Stewart to Clark, May 1, 1961, box A-115, TCC. Secondary accounts of what occurred at the *Mapp* conference differ significantly, reflecting discrepancies between Brennan's and Douglas's notes on that meeting. While Douglas's show that Warren, Clark, and Brennan said they would overrule *Wolf*, Brennan's do not indicate that anyone other than Douglas had anything to say on that subject. Most probably, Douglas, looking for endorsements of his position, interpreted as such brief comments or even gestures that Brennan did not consider important enough to record. A letter from Clark to Harlan partially supports Douglas's version, saying of the search-and-seizure issue: "At Conference three gave the latter as an alternative ground for reversal." Clark to Harlan, May 4, 1961, box A-115, TCC.

24. Stewart to Clark, May 1, 1961; Paul R. Bair, "Justice Clark, the Voice of the Past, and the Exclusionary Rule," 64 *Texas Law Review* 415, at 416–17 (1985); Schwartz, *Super Chief*, 393;

Douglas, conference notes; Brennan to Clark, May 1, 1961, box 62, WJB; Newman, *Black*, 555; 367 U.S. at 661 (Black, J., concurring).

25. Harlan to Clark Re: No. 236–Mapp v. Ohio, May 1, 1961, box 125, JMH; Stewart to Clark, May 1, 1961, box A-115, TCC; 367 U.S. at 672 (memorandum of Stewart, J.); ibid. at 678 (Harlan, J., dissenting); Clark to Harlan, May 4, 1961, box A-115, TCC; 367 U.S. at 672 (Harlan, J., dissenting); Parrish, "Frankfurter," 62; Frankfurter to "Dear Brethren," January 30, 1962, box 62, WJB.

26. Douglas to Clark, January 25, 1962, box 62, WJB; 367 U.S. at 670 (Douglas, J., concurring); ibid. at 662 (Black, J., concurring); Yarbrough, *Harlan*, 273; 367 U.S. at 655; Clark to Black, June 6, 1961, and Black to Clark, June 15, 1961, both in box 349, HLB; Schwartz, *Super Chief*, 273; Bodenhamer, *Trial*, 115; Cortner, *Second*, 187.

27. Powe, *American Politics*, 197; *Ker v. California*, 374 U.S. 23, 30–31 (1963); Harlan to Clark, May 8, 1963, box A-139, TCC; 374 U.S. at 45 (Harlan, J., concurring in the result); Brennan to Clark, undated, box A-139, TCC; 374 U.S. at 46 (Brennan, J., concurring).

28. Yarbrough, *Harlan*, 297; *Pickelsimer v. Wainwright*, 375 U.S. 2, 2 (1962) (Harlan, J., dissenting); *Linkletter v. Walker*, 381 U.S. 618, 619 (1965); conference notes, *Linkletter v. Walker*, March 12, 1965, box 1331, WOD; 381 U.S. at 639–40.

29. *Stanford v. Texas*, 379 U.S. 476, 481 (1965); docket book entry and attached conference notes, box 411, WJB; 379 U.S. at 485–86.

30. *Aguilar v. Texas*, 378 U.S. 108, 114 (1964); ibid. at 110; conference notes, box 1304, WOD; 378 U.S. at 116 (Harlan, J., concurring); ibid. at 116–22 (Clark, J., dissenting); *Spinelli v. United States*, 393 U.S. 410, 415–16 (1969); ibid. at 429, 433–34 (Black, J., dissenting).

31. *Olmstead v. United States*, 277 U.S. 438 (1929); *Silverman v. United States*, 365 U.S. 505 (1961); docket book entry and attached conference notes, box 407, WJB; Schwartz, *Super Chief*, 386–87.

32. *Berger v. New York*, 388 U.S. 41, 54, 44 (1967); ibid. at 68 (Stewart, J., concurring); ibid. at 71 (Black, J., dissenting).

33. 388 U.S. at 71 (Black, J., dissenting); *Katz v. United States*, 389 U.S. 347, 351, 352 (1967); conference notes, box 319, docket book entry, box 415, WJB; memorandum from Justice Stewart, November 7, 1967, and draft opinion by Stewart, November 17, 1967, both in box 301, JMH; 389 U.S. 364 (Black, J., dissenting); AF to Stewart, November 30, 1967, box 552, EW; 389 U.S. at 363 (White, J., concurring); ibid. at 360 (Harlan, J., concurring); ibid. at 353; Edmund W. Kitch, "Katz v. United States: The Limits of the Fourth Amendment," 1968 *Supreme Court Review* 133, at 133; LaFave and Israel, *Procedure*, 134; *Desist v. United States*, 394 U.S. 244 (1969); *Warden v. Hayden*, 387 U.S. 294 (1967); Powe, *American Politics*, 405.

34. *Desist v. United States*, 394 U.S. 244 (1969); *Warden v. Hayden*, 387 U.S. 294 (1967); Powe, *American Politics*, 406; W. H. Duckworth to Harlan, December 28, 1967, box 545, JMH; *Lambert v. California*, 355 U.S. 225 (1958); Schwartz, *Super Chief*, 307; Douglas to Frankfurter, December 16, 1957, reel 31, frame 692, FF-H; TCC to Douglas, November 14, 1957, box A-64, TCC; Douglas, memorandum to the Conference, November 21, 1957, box 9, WJB; 355 U.S. at 230; Frankfurter to Douglas, December 16, 1957, reel 31, frame 691, FF-H; 355 U.S. at 230–31 (Frankfurter, J., dissenting); Douglas to Frankfurter, December 16, 1957, reel 31, frame 693, FF-H; 395 U.S. at 232 (Frankfurter, J., dissenting).

35. *Robinson v. California*, 370 U.S. 660 (1962); JMH, memorandum for the Conference, November 15, 1961, box 496, JMH; Schwartz, *Super Chief*, 438–39; 370 U.S. at 666, 667; Cortner, *Second*, 191; 370 U.S. at 676, 668 (Douglas, J., concurring); ibid. at 683–85 (Clark, J., dissenting).

36. Newman, *Black*, 525–26; HLB note to Bill [Douglas], April 29, 1964, box 1299, WOD; *Carnley v. Cochran*, 369 U.S. 506, 507–13 (1962); docket book entry and attached conference notes, box 408, WJB; Schwartz, *Super Chief*, 407–9; 369 U.S. at 512; ibid. at 517–20 (Black, J., concurring).

37. Schwartz, *Super Chief*, 458–59; *Gideon v. Wainwright*, 372 U.S. 335, 336–38; Cortner, *Second*, 194–95; docket book entry, box 409, WJB. For an interesting and well-written contemporary history of *Gideon v. Wainwright*, see Anthony Lewis, *Gideon's Trumpet* (New York: Vintage Books, 1964).

38. Cortner, *Second*, 195–96; Kalman, *Fortas*, 181–82.

39. 372 U.S. at 345, 344; Cortner, *Second*, 198–202; 372 U.S. at 342; ibid. at 349, 352 (Harlan, J., concurring); Bodenhamer, *Trial*, 118.

40. John Morton Blum, *Years of Discord: American Politics and Society, 1961–1974* (New York: Norton, 1991), 208–9; Cortner, *Second*, 202; Criminal Justice Act of 1964, Pub. L. No. 88–445, 78 Stat. 552 (1964).

41. *Douglas v. California*, 372 U.S. 353, 353–54 (1963); Powe, *American Politics*, 382–84; docket book entry for no. 476, *Douglas and Meyes v. California*, box 375, EW; conference list, January 18, 1963, box 83, WJB; 372 U.S. at 355–56; ibid. at 363 (Harlan, J., dissenting); ibid. at 356.

42. *Hamilton v. Alabama*, 368 U.S. 52 (1961); *White v. Maryland*, 373 U.S. 59 (1963); *Mempa v. Rhay*, 389 U.S. 128 (1967); Paul Murphy, *Crisis Times*, 435.

43. *United States v. Wade*, 388 U.S. 218, 236–37 (1967); WJB Jr., memorandum to the Conference, June 6, 1967, box 159, WJB; docket book entry, *United States v. Wade*, box 414, WJB; Schwartz, *Super Chief*, 656–63; *Wade*, 388 U.S. at 221–23; *Gilbert v. California*, 388 U.S. 263, 272, 266 (1967); *Stovall v. Denno*, 388 U.S. 293, 299–300, 302 (1967); "Memorandum to Chief Justice, Mr. Justice Black, Mr. Justice Douglas, and Mr. Justice Fortas," April 24, 1967, box 159, WJB.

44. LaFave and Israel, *Procedure*, 309–10; Laurence A. Benner, "Requiem for *Miranda:* The Rehnquist Court's Voluntariness Doctrine in Historical Perspective," 67 *Washington University Law Quarterly* 59, at 114 (1989).

45. *Spano v. New York*, 360 U.S. 315 (1959); conference notes attached to docket book entry, box 405, WJB; 360 U.S. at 321–24, 320; ibid. at 325–26 (Douglas, J., concurring); ibid. at 326 (Stewart, J., concurring); 360 U.S. at 320.

46. *Jackson v. Denno*, 378 U.S. 368 (1964); docket book entry and attached conference notes, box 410, WJB; 378 U.S. at 376–77, 383, 386, 381; ibid. at 427–28 (Harlan, J., dissenting); Black to White, February 21, 1964, box 506, EW.

47. *Malloy v. Hogan*, 378 U.S. 1 (1964); *Malloy v. Hogan*, 150 Conn. 220, 187 A.2d 744 (1963); Cortner, *Second*, 208, 210, 217; docket book entry, box 410, WJB; 378 U.S. at 6, 10; conference notes, March 6, 1964, box 1299, WOD; Douglas to Brennan, June 1, 1964, Brennan to Douglas, June 2, 1964, Douglas to Brennan, June 3, 1964, and preliminary circulations of Opinion of the Court in Malloy v. Hogan, dated April 28, 1964, and June 5, 1964, all in box 113, WJB; 378 U.S. at 15 (Harlan, J., dissenting).

48. *Griffin v. California*, 380 U.S. 609 (1965); Cortner, *Second*, 216.

49. *Massiah v. United States*, 377 U.S. 201, 205, 202–3 (1965); docket book entry, box 410, WJB; handwritten notes on Massiah conference, undated, box A-159, TCC; conference notes, March 6, 1964, box 1303, WOD; Black, memorandum to Stewart, April 11, 1964, and Stewart to Black, April 13, 1964, both in box 484, JMH; 377 U.S. at 206; ibid. at 208 (White, J., dissenting).

50. Black, memorandum to Stewart, April 11, 1964; *Escobedo v. Illinois*, 378 U.S. 478 (1964); docket book entry, box 410, WJB; conference notes, box 1304, WOD; Goldberg, preliminary circulations of opinion of Court in *Escobedo v. Illinois*, May 29, 1964, and June 2, 1964, box 505, EW; 378 U.S. 485, 490; ibid. at 493 (Harlan, J., dissenting); ibid. at 495 (White, J., dissenting).

51. Powe, *American Politics*, 391; Paul Murphy, *Crisis Times*, 381.

52. Paul Murphy, *Crisis Times*, 383; Powe, *American Politics*, 392–94; "The Revolution in Criminal Justice," *Time*, July 16, 1965, 23; Cray, *Chief Justice*, 455, 457; EW, memorandum to the Conference, November 3, 1965, EW, memorandum for the Conference, December 9, 1965, and

Warren, "Escobedo Cases for Conference," Thursday, June 16, 1966, all in box 133, EW; EW, memorandum to the Conference, undated, box A-180, TCC.

53. *Miranda v. Arizona*, 384 U.S. 436, 445, 491–99 (1964); Tushnet, *Constitutional Law*, 24; Liva Baker, *Miranda: Crime, Law and Politics* (New York: Atheneum, 1985), 140–46; Schwartz, *Super Chief*, 389.

54. Conference notes, *Miranda v. Arizona*, March 18, 1966, box 1354; handwritten notes on Miranda, folder 1, box 616, EW; docket book entries and attached conference notes for *Miranda v. Arizona*, *Vignera v. New York*, and *Westover v. United States*, all in box 413, WJB; conference list, March 18, 1966, box 132, WJB; Schwartz (*Super Chief*, 589–90) errs in stating both that this conference took place on March 4, 1966, and that the vote was five to four, as Brennan's conference list and docket book entries and Douglas's conference notes demonstrate. Harlan did inform a friend in Australia that "the cases went by a five-to-four vote," but he seems to have been referring to the alignment at the time the decisions were announced, rather than to that during the conference. See Harlan to Sir Howard Beale, June 29, 1966, box 483, JMH.

55. Draft opinion dated May 9, 1966, and attached note from EW to Bill [Brennan], box 145, WJB; Brennan to Warren, box 616, EW; Schwartz, *Super Chief*, 590–92; Cray, *Chief Justice*, 459.

56. 384 U.S. 444, 445–56, memorandum from Kenneth Ziffren to the chief justice, May 2, 1966, Charles Hallam to Charles C. Thomas, May 2, 1966, and Charels Hallam to C. O. Reville, Jr., May 9, 1966, all in box 616, EW; 384 U.S. at 465, 473.

57. 384 U.S. at 467; Schwartz, *Super Chief*, 592–93; memorandum from Jim Hale, Mike Smith and Ken Ziffren to Chief Justice, undated, box 616, EW.

58. 384 U.S. at 524, 505, 513, 516 (Harlan, J., dissenting); ibid. at 530 (White, J., dissenting); TCC to White, June 6, 1966, and Harlan to White, June 7, 1966, both in box A-194, TCC; 384 U.S. at 499–503 (Clark, J., dissenting in *Miranda*, *Vignera*, and *Westover*, and concurring in *Stewart*).

59. *Johnson v. New Jersey*, 384 U.S. 755 (1966); *Davis v. North Carolina*, 384 U.S. 737 (1966); statement announcing decision in *Davis v. North Carolina*, undated, box 146, WJB; *Jenkins v. Delaware*, 395 U.S. 213 (1969).

60. White, *Warren*, 364, 271, 365; Richard J. Leo, "The Impact of *Miranda* Revisited," 86 *Journal of Criminal Law and Criminology* 621, at 622 (1996); Omnibus Crime Control and Safe Streets Act of 1968, Pub. L. No. 90–351, tit. III, § 701 (a), 82 Stat. 197, 210; Warren, *Memoirs*, 316; Cox, *Warren Court*, 86; Louis Michael Seidman, "*Brown* and *Miranda*," 80 *Harvard Law Review* 673, at 678–79 (1992).

61. Stephen J. Schulhofer, "Reconsidering Miranda," 54 *University of Chicago Law Review* 435, at 436, 456 (1987); Leo, "Impact," 645. For a study disputing the conventional academic wisdom that *Miranda* has not harmed law enforcement, see Paul G. Cassell, "*Miranda*'s Social Costs: An Empirical Reassessment," 90 *Northwestern University Law Review* 387 (1996). Cassell's analysis of the data on the ruling's impact is in turn disputed by Schulhofer in "*Miranda*'s Practical Effect: Substantial Benefits and Vanishingly Small Social Costs," 90 *Northwestern University Law Review* 500, at 502–3 (1996). Cassell and Richard Fowles argue that crime clearance statistics demonstrate the decision's adverse impact in "Handcuffing the Cops? A Thirty-Year Perspective on *Miranda*'s Harmful Effects on Law Enforcement," 50 *Stanford Law Review* 1055 (1998).

62. Harlan to Sir Howard Beale; *Mathis v. United States*, 391 U.S. 1 (1968); conference notes attached to docket book entry for *Mathis v. United States*, undated, box 415, WJB; *Orozco v. Texas*, 394 U.S. 324, 325–26 (1969); ibid. at 328 (Harlan, J., concurring); ibid. (White, J., dissenting).

63. *Pointer v. Texas*, 380 U.S. 400, 401 (1965); Cortner, *Second*, 219–25.

64. *Klopfer v. North Carolina*, 386 U.S. 213, 222–26 (1967); Cortner, *Second*, 234–42; 386 U.S. at 226 (Harlan, J., concurring).

65. *Washington v. Texas,* 388 U.S. 14 (1967); Cortner, *Second,* 230–31; 388 U.S. at 24 (Harlan, J., concurring).

66. *Duncan v. Louisiana,* 391 U.S. 145, 146–47 (1968); Cortner, *Second,* 246–53, 260; 391 U.S. at 149, 157–61, 148–49; ibid. at 174–76, 173 (Harlan, J., dissenting); docket book entry, box 415, WJB; 391 U.S. at 171 (Fortas, J., concurring).

67. *Benton v. Maryland,* 395 U.S. 784, 785–89 (1969); Cortner, *Second,* 265–67, 274, 290; Tushnet, *Constitutional Law,* 15, 33; 395 U.S. at 794; conference notes attached to docket book entry for *Benton v. Maryland,* box 416, WJB; 395 U.S. at 808, 809 (Harlan, J., dissenting); *North Carolina v. Pearce,* 395 U.S. 711, 722, 717 (1969); Stewart, memorandum to the Conference, December 29, 1969, box 349, JMH; Bodenhamer, *Trial,* 128.

68. Schwartz, *Super Chief,* 342; *Sanders v. United States,* 373 U.S. 1, 15 (1963).

69. *Fay v. Noia,* 372 U.S. 391 (1963); LaFave and Israel, *Procedure,* 1315; Schwartz, *Super Chief,* 470–72; memorandum of Brennan, December --, 1962, box 93, WJB; 372 U.S. at 398–99; ibid. at 449 (Harlan, J., dissenting); Yarbrough, *Harlan,* 236.

70. *Townsend v. Sain,* 372 U.S. 293 (1963); Schwartz, *Super Chief,* 472–73; conference notes, February 23, 1962, and October 12, 1962, box 1280, WOD.

71. Schwartz, *Super Chief,* 470, 473–74; *Henry v. Mississippi,* 379 U.S. 443 (1965).

72. *Johnson v. Avery,* 393 U.S. 483 (1969); ibid. at 485.

73. *Brady v. Maryland,* 373 U.S. 83 (1963).

74. *Irvin v. Dowd,* 366 U.S. 717 (1961); *Irvin v. Dowd,* 153 F. Supp. 531 (N.D. Ind. 1957), *aff'd,* 251 F.2d 548 (7th Cir. 1958), *remanded,* 359 U.S. 394 (1959); 366 U.S. at 723–26; conference notes, November 11, 1960, box 1233, WOD; 366 U.S. at 730 (Frankfurter, J., concurring); conference notes from *Baldanado v. California,* May 10, 1961, box 1234, WOD; *Rideau v. Louisiana,* 373 U.S. 723 (1963).

75. Friedman, *Crime,* 400; William O. Douglas, "The Public Trial and the Free Press," speech given at the University of Colorado, May 10, 1960, box 59, HLB; Schwartz, *Super Chief,* 543.

76. *Estes v. Texas,* 381 U.S. 532, 534–35, 550–51 (1965); docket book entry and attached conference notes, box 411, WJB; Schwartz, *Super Chief,* 543–52; Clark, memorandum to the Conference, May 25, 1965, box A-175, TCC; Schwartz, *Unpublished,* 191–94, 209–10, 220–21; 381 U.S. at 601–2 (Stewart, J., dissenting); ibid. at 615 (White, J., dissenting); ibid. at 617 (opinion of Brennan, J.); ibid. at 552 (Warren, C.J., concurring); ibid. at 587–95 (Harlan, J., concurring).

77. *Sheppard v. Maxwell,* 384 U.S. 333, 335–39 (1965); *Sheppard v. Ohio,* 352 U.S. 910, 911 (1956) (memorandum of Frankfurter, J.); conference notes, box 1368, WOD; docket book entry, box 413, WJB; 384 U.S. at 363; ibid. (Black, J., dissenting).

78. Wayne LaFave and Jerold H. Israel, *Criminal Procedure,* 2nd ed. (St. Paul, Minn.: West Publishing Co., 1992), 75; *In re Gault,* 387 U.S. 1 (1967); Kalman, *Fortas,* 252–54; docket book entry and attached conference notes, box 414, WJB; 387 U.S. at 61–62 (Black, J., concurring); ibid. at 72 (Harlan, J., concurring in part and dissenting in part); ibid. at 78 (Stewart, J., dissenting). The letters to Fortas concerning *Gault* are in box FL 2 of AF.

79. Cray, *Chief Justice,* 490; LaFave and Israel, *Procedure,* 74–75.

80. *Costello v. Immigration and Naturalization Service,* 376 U.S. 120 (1964); *Marchetti v. United States,* 390 U.S. 39 (1968); *Grosso v. United States,* 390 U.S. 62 (1966); *Leary v. United States,* 395 U.S. 6 (1969).

81. Blum, *Discord,* 215, 207; Kurland, *Politics,* 82; Cortner, *Second,* 82.

82. Omnibus Crime Control and Safe Streets Act, Title II, Pub. L. No. 90–351, Title III, § 701, 82 Stat. 197, 210–11 (1968); Yale Kamisar, "Can (Did) Congress Overrule *Miranda,*" 85 *Cornell Law Review,* 883, at 887–91, 899–901 (2000); Paul Murphy, *Crisis Times,* 438–39; Blum, *Discord,* 215.

83. Liva Baker, *Miranda,* 211–12; The Nixon quotes are from Bodenhamer, *Trial,* 127, and Cortner, *Second,* 263, respectively.

84. *Schmerber v. California,* 384 U.S. 757 (1966); docket book entry and attached conference notes, box 413, WJB; Schwartz, *Super Chief,* 594–95; 384 U.S. at 760, 761.

85. Paul Murphy, *Crisis Times,* 429–31; *McCray v. Illinois,* 386 U.S. 300 (1967); *Warden v. Hayden,* 387 U.S. 294 (1967).

86. *Hoffa v. United States,* 385 U.S. 293, 309 (1966); *Osborn v. United States,* 385 U.S. 323 (1967).

87. *Camara v. Municipal Court of the City and County of San Francisco,* 387 U.S. 523, 534–39 (1967); *See v. City of Seattle,* 387 U.S. 541, 545–46 (1967); ibid. at 550, 547 (Clark, J, dissenting).

88. Schwartz, *Super Chief,* 388–92; *Terry v. Ohio,* 392 U.S. 1, 4–7 (1968); docket book entry and attached conference notes, box 415, WJB; Brennan to Warren, January 30, 1968, box 171, WJB; Douglas to Warren, February 26, 1968, box 1415, WOD; B. R. W. to Warren, February 21, 1968, box 402, HLB; preliminary circulation of concurring opinion by Harlan, February 27, 1968, box 305, JMH; 392 U.S. at 20, 30.

89. 392 U.S. at 35, 39 (Douglas, J., dissenting); *Chimel v. California,* 395 U.S. 752, 768, 763 (1969).

90. Kamisar, "Criminal Justice," 116; *McCray v. Illinois,* 386 U.S. 300 (1967); *Chapman v. California,* 386 U.S. 18 (1967); *Powell v. Texas,* 392 U.S. 514 (1968); docket book entry, box 415, WJB; Kalman, *Fortas,* 257–59; Tushnet, *Constitutional Law,* 181–83; handwritten annotation on preliminary circulation of opinion of the Court, May 17, 1968, box 46, AF; 392 U.S. at 549–51 (White, J., concurring); 392 U.S. at 528.

91. Memorandum to the Conference from Justice Goldberg, undated, box 102, WJB; Tushnet, *Constitutional Law,* 147. Goldberg's memorandum is published in Schwartz, *Unpublished,* 401–11, and is analyzed in Robert S. Marsel, "Mr. Justice Arthur J. Goldberg and the Death Penalty: A Memorandum to the Conference," 27 *South Texas Law Review* 467 (1986).

92. *Witherspoon v. Illinois,* 391 U.S. 510, 512 (1968); Tushnet, *Constitutional Law,* 147–48; Stewart, preliminary circulation of dissent from denial of petition for writ of certiorari, *Witherspoon v. Illinois,* January 10, 1968, and Warren to Stewart, January 11, 1968, both in box 358, EW; 391 U.S. at 513–14, 521, 519–20; ibid. at 542 (White, J., dissenting).

93. *Rudolph v. Alabama,* 375 U.S. 889, 889 (1963) (Goldberg, J., dissenting); Marsel, "Death Penalty," 485; Tushnet, *Constitutional Law,* 148–49; Schwartz, *Unpublished,* 396–400; Schwartz, *Super Chief,* 738–42; *Spencer v. Texas,* 385 U.S. 554 (1967). The opinions that Douglas, Stewart, Black, Brennan, and Harlan wrote in *Maxwell v. Bishop* during the spring of 1969 are published in Schwartz, *Unpublished,* 412–40.

94. Kamisar, "Criminal Justice," 116; Goldberg, "Critics," 837.

10. THE TRUE WARREN COURT

1. Tushnet, "History," 12; Galloway, "Third Period," 773 (1980).

2. Preliminary circulation of statement of Black and Douglas on rules of civil procedure and proposed amendments, January 16, 1963, box 484, JMH; 368 U.S. 1012 (1961) (statement of Black, J.); ibid. at 1014 (statement of Douglas, J.); preliminary circulation of dissenting opinion by Douglas to amendments to Federal Rules of Criminal Procedure, February 15, 1969, both in box 386, HLB; Warren, memorandum for the Conference, April 22, 1969, box 403, HLB.

3. WOD, TCC, and AF, memorandum for the Conference, January 17, 1967, box 148, WJB; White, *Warren,* 193, 210–11.

4. Tom C. Clark, "The Decisional Process of the Supreme Court," 50 *Cornell Law Quarterly* 385, at 389 (1965). The statistics for the terms from October 1961 through October 1968 that appear in this paragraph and throughout chapter 10 are, unless otherwise indicated, based on data presented in the *Harvard Law Review*'s summaries of the past term for those years. These data may be found at the following locations: "The Supreme Court, 1961 Term," 76 *Harvard Law Review* 54, at 81–82 (1962); "The Supreme Court, 1962 Term," 77 *Harvard Law Review* 62,

at 83–92 (1963); "The Supreme Court, 1963 Term," 78 *Harvard Law Review* 143, at 180–85 (1964); "The Supreme Court, 1964 Term," 79 *Harvard Law Review* 56, at 106 (1965); "The Supreme Court, 1965 Term," 80 *Harvard Law Review* 91, at 143–47 (1966); "The Supreme Court, 1966 Term," 81 *Harvard Law Review* 69, at 127–33 (1967); "The Supreme Court, 1967 Term," 82 *Harvard Law Review* 63, at 303–12 (1968); "The Supreme Court, 1968 Term," 83 *Harvard Law Review,* at 278–82 (1969). The statistics for the terms between October 1953 and October 1957 presented here are based on the table that appears in "The Supreme Court, 1957 Term," 72 *Harvard Law Review* 77, at 106 (1958). Until its summary of the October 1963 term, the data published by the *Harvard Law Review* disclosed only the number of cases in various categories disposed of by full opinion, not the number of opinions expressing the position of the Court that resulted from those dispositions. Consequently, only for the terms from 1963 on is it possible to determine the extent to which the apparent number of opinions of the Court or lengthy per curiams is exaggerated, due to the double counting of opinions that disposed of more than one case.

5. Statistics on the October 1953 term come from "The Supreme Court, 1953 Term," 68 *Harvard Law Review* 96, at 191 (1954). Those on the October 1957 term are taken from "The Supreme Court, 1957 Term," 72 *Harvard Law Review* 77, at 100 (1958).

6. *Hardy v. United States,* 375 U.S. 277 (1964); *United States v. Blue,* 384 U.S. 251 (1966); *Singer v. United States,* 380 U.S. 24 (1965).

7. The statistics for the October 1953–October 1961 terms presented in this paragraph and the rest of chapter 10 are based on data presented in "1953 Term," 188–92; "The Supreme Court, 1954 Term," 69 *Harvard Law Review* 119, at 200–207 (1955); "The Supreme Court, 1955 Term," 70 *Harvard Law Review* 83, at 99–103 (1956); "The Supreme Court, 1956 Term," 71 *Harvard Law Review* 91, at 97–105 (1957); "1957 Term," 99–100; "The Supreme Court, 1958 Term," 73 *Harvard Law Review* 128, at 132–35 (1959); "The Supreme Court, 1959 Term," 74 *Harvard Law Review* 97, at 103 (1960); "The Supreme Court, 1960 Term," 74 *Harvard Law Review* 40, at 103 (1961); "1961 Term," 81–82.

8. *Northern Natural Gas Co. v. State Corporation Commission,* 372 U.S. 84 (1963); "1962 Term," 187, 135; *United States v. Muniz,* 374 U.S. 150 (1963). *Muniz* affirmed two different Second Circuit decisions, *Muniz v. United States,* 305 F.2d 285 (2d Cir. 1962), and *Winston v. United States,* 305 F.2d 253 (2d Cir. 1962).

9. *King v. Smith,* 392 U.S. 309 (1968); ibid. at 333–36 (Douglas, J., concurring); *First Agricultural Bank v. State Tax Commission,* 392 U.S. 339 (1968); ibid. at 348 (Marshall, J., dissenting).

10. *SEC v. National Securities, Inc.,* 393 U.S. 453 (1969); "1968 Term," 252–53; Securities Exchange Act of 1934, § 10(b), 15 U.S.C. § 78j(b) (1997); McCarran-Ferguson Act, § 2(b), 15 U.S.C. § 1012(b) (1997).

11. *Brulotte v. Thys Co.,* 379 U.S. 29 (1964); *Brenner v. Manson,* 383 U.S. 519 (1966); 35 U.S.C. § 101 (1964); *Fortnightly Corp. v. United Artists Television, Inc.,* 392 U.S. 390 (1968); "1968 Term," 272.

12. William M. Beaney, "Civil Liberties and Statutory Construction," 8 *Journal of Public Law* 66, at 78 (1959).

13. Kurland, *Politics,* 62–64; *Hannah v. Plumer,* 380 U.S. 460 (1965); *Wallis v. Pan American Petroleum Corp.,* 384 U.S. 63, 72, 68 (1966); *Wheedlin v. Wheeler,* 373 U.S. 647, 652 (1963); J. Skelly Wright, "The Federal Courts and the Nature and Quality of State Law," 13 *Wayne Law Review* 317, at 317, 320 (1967).

14. Nowak and Rotunda, *Constitutional Law,* 119–121; *Dombrowski v. Pfister,* 380 U.S. 479, 489–91 (1965); *England v. Louisiana State Board of Medical Examiners,* 375 U.S. 411 (1964).

15. *United Mine Workers v. Gibbs,* 383 U.S. 715, 725 (1966); "1966 Term," 221–22.

16. *Van Dusen v. Barrack,* 376 U.S. 612 (1964); *National Equipment Rental, Ltd. v. Szukhent,* 375 U.S. 311 (1964); *Neely v. Martin K. Eby Construction Co.,* 386 U.S. 317 (1967); *Cascade Natural Gas Corp. v. El Paso Natural Gas Co.,* 386 U.S. 129 (1967); *Snyder v. Harris,* 394 U.S. 332 (1969).

17. Benjamin J. Schoenfeld, "Significant Administrative Law Decisions of the United States Supreme Court during the October 1962–1963 Term," 2 *Duquesne University Law Review* 47, at 47 (1963); *Northern Natural Gas Co. v. State Corporation Commission*, 372 U.S. 84 (1963); *Wisconsin v. FPC*, 373 U.S. 294 (1963); "1962 Term," 186, 190; *ICC v. New York, N.H. & H.R.R.*, 372 U.S. 744 (1963); *Arrow Transportation Company v. Southern Railway*, 372 U.S. 658 (1963); *American Trucking Associations v. Atchison, Topeka & Santa Fe Railway*, 387 U.S. 397 (1967).

18. *Abbot Laboratories v. Gardner*, 387 U.S. 136 (1967); *Toilet Goods Association v. Gardner*, 387 U.S. 158 (1967); *Gardner v. Toilet Goods Association*, 387 U.S. 167 (1967); "1966 Term," 225–26; "Project: Federal Administrative Law Developments–1969," 1970 *Duke Law Journal* 67 (1970); *NLRB v. Wyman-Gordon Co.*, 394 U.S. 759 (1969); ibid. at 779 (Douglas, J., dissenting); ibid. at 281 (Harlan, J., dissenting). The *Duke Law Journal* included cases from both the 1968–69 and 1969–70 terms of the Supreme Court in its survey, which reviewed decisions rendered in calendar 1969. One of the lower court decisions that it discussed was affirmed by the Court during the 1970 part of the 1969–1970 term, and another was vacated. It did not analyze those rulings. Ibid. at 69–72.

19. John B. Jones Jr., "Recent Developments in Federal Taxation," 16 *Tulane Tax Institute* 9, at 11 (1967); *Commissioner v. Estate of Bosch*, 387 U.S. 456 (1967); *United States v. Cato*, 384 U.S. 102 (1966); *Fribourg Navigation Co. v. Commissioner*, 383 U.S. 272 (1966); *Commissioner v. Brown*, 380 U.S. 563 (1965); Martin Shapiro, "The Warren Court and Federal Tax Policy," 36 *Southern California Law Review* 208, at 209 (1963).

20. *United States v. Laub*, 385 U.S. 475 (1967); *Kennedy v. Mendoza-Martinez*, 372 U.S. 144 (1963); "1967 Term," 126; *Afroyim v. Rusk*, 387 U.S. 253 (1967).

21. *Gutierrez v. Waterman, S.S. Corp.*, 373 U.S. 206 (1963); ibid. at 216 (Harlan, J., dissenting); "1962 Term," 96, 98; *Reed v. The Yaka*, 373 U.S. 410 (1963); *Italia Societa v. Oregon Stevedoring Co.*, 376 U.S. 315 (1964). Admiralty statistics are somewhat confused by the fact that for the 1962–63 term the *Harvard Law Review* classified two cases that raised admiralty issues under the heading "Private Litigation/Labor Relations."

22. *Department of Revenue v. James B. Beam Distilling Co.*, 377 U.S. 341 (1964); *Hostetter v. Idlewild Bon Voyage Liquor Corp.*, 377 U.S. 324, 333 (1964); *General Motors v. Washington*, 377 U.S. 436 (1964); *National Bellas Hess, Inc. v. Department of Revenue*, 386 U.S. 753 (1967).

23. *Powell v. McCormack*, 395 U.S. 486 (1969); ibid. at 503; Nowak and Rotunda, *Constitutional Law*, 125–28; *Baker v. Carr*, 369 U.S. 186 (1962); *United States v. Nixon*, 418 U.S. 683 (1974).

24. Fortas to Brennan, February 6, [1963], box 93, WJB; "Note: The Development of the Plenary Hearing Requirement in Federal Habeas Corpus for State Prisoners," 34 *Brooklyn Law Review* 247, at 247 (1968).

25. Theodore J. St. Antoine, "Judicial Valour and the Warren Court's Labor Decisions," 67 *Michigan Law Review*, 317, at 323 (1968); *NLRB v. Fruit & Vegetable Packers & Warehousemen Local 760*, 377 U.S. 58 (1964); *Food Employees Local 590 v. Logan Valley Plaza, Inc.*, 391 U.S. 308 (1968).

26. Kurland, *Politics*, 60–61; *Railroad Trainmen v. Terminal Co.*, 394 U.S. 369 (1969); St. Antoine, "Valour," 318–20; *Garner v. Teamsters Union*, 346 U.S. 485 (1953); *San Diego Building Trades Council v. Garmon*, 359 U.S. 236 (1959); *Street, Electric Railway & Motor Coach Employees Division 1287 v. Missouri*, 374 U.S. 74 (1963); *Linn v. Plant Guard Workers Local 14*, 383 U.S. 53 (1966); *United Workers v. Gibbs*, 383 U.S. 713 (1966); White, *Warren*, 285; Modjeska, "Labor," 533–34.

27. *Brotherhood of Railway and Steamship Clerks v. Florida East Coast Railway*, 384 U.S. 238 (1966); *American Shipbuilding Co. v. NLRB*, 380 U.S. 300 (1965); *NLRB v. Brown*, 380 U.S. 278 (1965); *Textile Workers v. Darlington Manufacturing Company*, 380 U.S. 263 (1965); conference notes attached to docket book entry for *Textile Workers Union of America v. Darlington Manufacturing Company*, box 411, WJB.

28. *NLRB v. Fruit & Vegetable Packers Union*, 377 U.S. 58 (1964); "1963 Term," 288; Modjeska, "Labor," 514, 496–98, 511–12; *Carey v. Westinghouse Electrical Corp.*, 375 U.S. 261 (1964); *John Wiley*

& Sons, Inc. v. Livingston, 376 U.S. 543 (1964); *Fiberboard Paper Products Corp. v. NLRB,* 379 U.S. 203 (1964); *United Mine Workers v. Pennington,* 381 U.S. 657 (1965); conference notes on *Pennington* attached to docket book entry, box 411, WJB; *Local Union No. 189, Amalgamated Meat Cutters v. Jewel Tea Co.,* 381 U.S. 676 (1965); *American Federation of Musicians v. Carroll,* 391 U.S. 99 (1968); *NLRB v. Gissel Packing Co.,* 395 U.S. 575 (1969); White, *Warren,* 291.

29. White, *Warren,* 291; Tushnet, *Constitutional Law,* 23; *Linn v. United Plant Guard Workers of America, Local 14,* 383 U.S. 53 (1966).

30. White, *Warren,* 295; Arnold, "Antitrust Laws," 3. No comparable statistics are available for the Warren Court's final three terms.

31. Modjeska, "Labor," 513; conference notes attached to docket book entry for *Local Union No. 189, etc. v. Jewel Tea Co.,* and conference notes attached to docket book entry for *United Mine Workers of America v. James M. Pennington, et al.,* both in box 411, WJB; 381 U.S. 697, 709–10 (Goldberg, J., concurring in *Jewel Tea* and dissenting in *Pennington);* at *Pennington,* 381 U.S. 665–66; *Local 189,* at *Amalgamated Meat Cutters,* 381 U.S. 690; *American Federation of Musicians v. Carroll,* 391 U.S. 99, 112–13 (1968); "1967 Term," 275.

32. Arnold, "Antitrust Laws," 4; *Pan American World Airways, Inc. v. United States,* 371 U.S. 296 (1963); *White Motor Co. v. United States,* 372 U.S. 253, 263, 261 (1963); *United States v. Arnold, Schwinn and Co.,* 388 U.S. 365 (1967); Kalman, *Fortas,* 267, 270–71.

33. *United States v. Philadelphia National Bank,* 374 U.S. 321 (1963); *United States v. First National Bank,* 376 U.S. 665 (1964); *United States v. Aluminum Co. of America,* 377 U.S. 271 (1964); *United States v. Continental Can Co.,* 378 U.S. 441 (1964); *United States v. El Paso Natural Gas Co.,* 376 U.S. 651 (1964); *United States v. Penn-Olin Chemical Co.,* 378 U.S. 158 (1964); *United States v. Grinnell Corp.,* 384 U.S. 563 (1966); *United States v. Von's Grocery Co.,* 384 U.S. 270 (1966); "1966 Term," 245; *United States v. Container Corp. of America,* 393 U.S. 333 (1969).

34. Arnold, "Antitrust Laws," 5; *FTC v. Sun Oil Co.,* 371 U.S. 505 (1963); "1962 Term," 173; *FTC v. Borden Co.,* 383 U.S. 637 (1966); *FTC v. Fred Meyer, Inc.,* 390 U.S. 341 (1968); White, *Warren,* 298; *FTC v. Consolidated Foods Corp.,* 380 U.S. 592 (1965); *FTC v. Procter & Gamble,* 386 U.S. 568 (1967); ibid. at 580; Kalman, *Fortas,* 267–68; *FTC v. Mary Carter Paint Co.,* 382 U.S. 46 (1965); *FTC v. Colgate-Palmolive Co.,* 380 U.S. 374 (1965).

35. Arnold, "Antitrust Laws," 5; *Silver v. New York Stock Exchange,* 373 U.S. 341, 365 (1963); *Simpson v. Union Oil Co.,* 377 U.S. 13 (1964); *Fortner Enterprises v. United States Steel Corp.,* 394 U.S. 495 (1969); White, *Warren,* 295.

36. Tushnet, "History," 3–4; Galloway, "Third Period," 773–74, 817; Archibald Cox, "Forward: Constitutional Adjudication and the Promotion of Human Rights," 80 *Harvard Law Review* 91, at 91 (1965); Richard E. Johnston, "Some Comparative Statistics on U.S. Chief Justice Courts," 9 *Rocky Mountain Social Science Journal* 89, at 92, 94–95 (1972); Kurland, *Politics,* 174.

37. Galloway, "Third Period," 807–13.

38. Ibid., 808.

39. Arthur S. Miller, "Social Justice and the Warren Court: A Preliminary Examination," 11 *Pepperdine Law Review* 473, at 486–87; Ronald S. Sheehan, "Governmental Litigants, Underdogs, and Civil Liberties: A Reassessment of a Trend in Supreme Court Decisionmaking," 45 *Western Political Quarterly* 27, at 29–32 (1992); Horwitz, *Warren Court,* xii, 11. The percentages presented in this paragraph are imprecise. For reasons of his own, Sheehan has done his calculations for a period that begins in 1953 and ends in 1970. Thus, they are for the Warren Court and about a year of the Burger Court.

40. Horwitz, *Warren Court,* 114–15.

11. THE END OF AN ERA

1. Tyrone Brown, "Clerking for the Chief Justice," in Schwartz, *Retrospective,* 276–77; Cray, *Chief Justice,* 494; Galloway, "Third Period," 803.

2. Cray, *Chief Justice*, 494–97; James R. Jones, "Memorandum for Record," June 13, 1968, Ex. PR 8–1/W, WHCF, LBJ; Warren to president, June 13, 1968, box 667, EW.

3. Warren to president, June 13, 1968, box 667, EW; "Chronology," undated, and Press Conference No. 128 of the President of the United States, 11:38 A.M., EDT, June 26, 1968, box 1, Chronology File, File Pertaining to Abe Fortas and Homer Thornberry, LBJ (hereafter cited as CF); Warren to John Massaro, December 10, 1973, box 667, EW; Newman, *Black*, 595–96; Ramsey Clark, "Memorandum for President Re: Vacancy in Position of Chief Justice," June 24, 1968, Ex. FG 535, WHCF, LBJ; "Memorandum for Larry Temple, Re: Fortas and Thornberry Nominations," December 20, 1968, box 3, CF; WHA, "Memo in re Retirement of Mr. Justice Minton," undated, box 357, EW; Warren Christopher, memorandum for Larry Temple, July 2, 1968, box 2, CF; John Massaro, "LBJ and the Fortas Nomination for Chief Justice," 97 *Political Science Quarterly* 603, at 605 (1982–83); Larry Temple, memorandum to president, box 2, CF; Kalman, *Fortas*, 328.

4. Cray, *Chief Justice*, 497; Bruce Murphy, *Fortas*, 270–71; Ramsey Clark to president, June 26, 1968, Ex. FG 535/A, WHCF, LBJ; Warren to Johnson, June 26, 1968, box 667, EW.

5. Warren to Johnson, June 26, 1968; Kalman, *Fortas*, 327–28; John Minor Wisdom to president, July 1, 1968, Ex. FG 535/A, WHCF, LBJ; Elbert Tuttle to Jacob Javits, July 2, 1968, and John R. Brown to James O. Eastland, July 10, 1968, both in box 2, CF; Bruce Murphy, *Fortas*, 316; Christopher, memorandum for Larry Temple.

6. Christopher, memorandum for Larry Temple; Albert E. Jenner Jr. to Ramsey Clark, June 26, 1968, box 1, CF.

7. Bruce Murphy, *Fortas*, 188, 200–207; VM, note to president, October 7, 1965, Abe Fortas folder, box 1, CF; Kalman, *Fortas*, 298–300, 306, 319, 322; Belknap, "Vietnam," 89, 98; Douglas, *Court Years*, 252.

8. Kalman, *Fortas*, 247–48, 328–32; Mike Mantos, memorandum for president, June 25, 1968, Ex. FG 535/A, WHCF, LBJ; ibid., 4:15 p.m.; Dirksen interview, 12–14; Bruce Murphy, *Fortas*, 315, 359; "Chronology"; Margaret McHugh to Warren, June 26, 1968, box 352, EW.

9. Kalman, *Fortas*, 217, 250, 261, 314–16, 3, 46, 271, 321–22, 334; Powe, *American Politics*, 464–70.

10. Gallup, *Poll*, 3:2147–48; Bruce Murphy, *Fortas*, 373–75; Kalman, *Fortas*, 335, 338, 340–41.

11. Kalman, *Fortas*, 340–41; Bruce Murphy, *Fortas*, 423–31; Senate Judiciary Committee, *Nominations of Abe Fortas and Homer Thornberry: Hearings before the Committee on the Judiciary*, 90th Cong., 2nd sess., July 11–23, 1968, 214–15, 218–19, 220, 900; Dennis Peterson to Black, June 5, 1968, box 402, HLB.

12. Kalman, *Fortas*, 342–43; Bruce Murphy, *Fortas*, 440–44; Senate Judiciary Committee, *Fortas and Thornberry Hearings*, 290, Christopher, memorandum for Larry Temple; Dirksen interview, 11–12; Mike Mantos, memorandum for president, September 16, 1968, Ex. FG 535/A, WHCF, LBJ.

13. Mantos, memorandum for president, September 16, 1968; Fortas to Warren, July 25, 1968, box 352, EW; Bruce Murphy, *Fortas*, 310–11, 496–504; Kalman, *Fortas*, 349–53; Christopher, memorandum for Larry Temple.

14. Senate, *Nomination of Abe Fortas*, 90th Cong., 2nd sess., 1968, Executive Report 8, 5; Kalman, *Fortas*, 355; Joe Califano, memorandum for president, September 11, 1968, and September 12, 1968, both in Ex. FG 535/A, WHCF, LBJ; *Washington Post and Times Herald*, September 6, 1968, box 127, Ramsey Clark Papers, LBJ; Pat Tucker, "Survey of U.S. Editorial Opinion," box 2, CF; Warren Christopher to Philip A. Hart, September 28, 1968, box 3, CF; *Cong. Record*, 90th Cong., 2nd sess. (October 1, 1968): 28,933.

15. Kalman, *Fortas*, 355; Abe Fortas to president, October 1, 1968, Ex. FG 535/A, WHCF, LBJ; Statement by President, October 2, 1968, box 3, CF.

16. "Norris Cotton Reports to You from the United States Senate," July 25, 1968, box 2, CF; Massaro, "Fortas Nomination," 620–21; Donald G. Tannenbaum, "Explaining Controversial Nominations: The Fortas Case Revisited," 17 *Presidential Studies Quarterly* 573, at 582 (1987); Cray, *Chief Justice,* 500; Laura Kalman, "Abe Fortas: Symbol of the Warren Court," in Tushnet, *Warren Court,* 164–65, 163; William M. Beaney, "The Warren Court and the Political Process," 67 *Michigan Law Review* 343, at 348–49 (1968); Frank Bogard to Douglas, March 16, 1967, box 352, EW.

17. Cray, *Chief Justice,* 355; DeVier Pierson, memorandum for president, October 3, 1968, and Ernest Gruening to president, October 2, 1968, both in Ex. FG 535, WHCF, LBJ.

18. Cray, *Chief Justice,* 504–5; White, *Warren,* 312.

19. *O'Callahan v. Parker,* 395 U.S. 258, 258, 272 (1969); ibid. at 274–84 (Harlan, J., dissenting); docket book entry, box 416, WJB; draft opinion by Harlan, April 8, 1969, draft dissent by Douglas, April 11, 1969, Harlan to Fortas, April 14, 1969, draft dissent by Douglas, May 14, 1969, draft opinion of the Court by Douglas, May 19, 1969, and Fortas to Harlan, April 11, 1969, all in box 417, WJB.

20. 50 U.S.C. app. § 456(j) (1990); *United States v. Seeger,* 380 U.S. 163, 165–66 (1965); conference notes attached to docket book entry, box 411, WJB; Cray, *Chief Justice,* 82; Belknap, "Vietnam," 123–24; Schwartz, *Super Chief,* 571; Harlan to Clark, February 8, 1965, box 493, JMH; 380 U.S. at 188 (Douglas, J., concurring). For Seeger's account of his case, see Peter Irons, *The Courage of Their Convictions: Sixteen Americans Who Fought Their Way to the Supreme Court* (New York: Free Press, 1988), 165–78.

21. Belknap, "Vietnam," 125–27; *Ostereich v. Selective Service System Local Board No. 11,* 393 U.S. 233 (1968); 50 U.S.C. app. § 456(g) (1990); *Ostereich v. Selective Service System Local Board No. 1,* 280 F. Supp. 78 (D. Wyo. 1968), *aff'd* 390 F.2d 100 (10th Cir. 1968); Military Selective Service Act of 1967, § 10(b)(3), 50 U.S.C. app. § 460(b)(3)(1990); 393 U.S. at 237; docket book entry, box 416, WJB; 393 U.S. at 243 n. 6 (Harlan, J., concurring).

22. Belknap, "Vietnam," 81–86, 97–101; Yarbrough, *Black,* 185; Newman, *Black,* 542.

23. Belknap, "Vietnam," 139–40; Cray, *Chief Justice,* 485; *Bond v. Floyd,* 385 U.S. 116, 137 (1966); ibid. at 136; docket book entry for *Bond v. Floyd,* box 414, WJB.

24. *Bond,* 385 U.S. at 124; Belknap, "Vietnam," 140, 129–30; Universal Military Service and Training Act, Pub. L. No. 89–157, § 12(b)(3), 79 Stat. 586 (1965); *O'Brien v. United States,* 376 F.2d 538 (1st Cir. 1967); "Brief for David Paul O'Brien, Respondent in No. 232 and Petitioner in No. 233," at 29, *United States v. O'Brien,* 391 U.S. 367 (1968); docket book entry and attached conference notes, box 415, WJB.

25. Belknap, "Vietnam," 131–34; Schwartz, *Super Chief,* 684; Cray, *Chief Justice,* 487; memorandum from LGS [Larry Simon] to Warren, undated, and preliminary circulation of concurring opinion by Harlan, May 1, 1968, both in box 625, EW.

26. *United States v. O'Brien,* 391 U.S. 367, 376–77, 377–82, 383–84 (1968); ibid. at 389–90 (Douglas, J., dissenting).

27. *Tinker v. Des Moines Independent Community School District,* 393 U.S. 503 (1969); Belknap, "Vietnam," 143–49; docket book entry and attached conference notes, box 416, WJB; conference notes, box 1430, WOD; 393 U.S. at 515, 513; ibid. at 514–15 (Stewart, J., concurring); ibid. at 515 (White, J., concurring); ibid. at 524 (Black, J., dissenting); Newman, *Black,* 592; 393 U.S. at 525 (Black, J., dissenting). For histories of the *Tinker* case, see John W. Johnson, *The Struggle for Student Rights: Tinker v. Des Moines and the 1960s* (Lawrence: University Press of Kansas, 1997), and Irons, *Courage,* 231–52.

28. *Street v. New York,* 394 U.S. 576, 577–79 (1969); docket book entry and attached conference notes, box 416, WJB; Cray, *Chief Justice,* 491–92; Kalman, *Fortas,* 282–86; AF, memorandum to the Conference, March 19, 1969, box 19, AF; 394 U.S. at 617 (Fortas, J., dissenting). Warren's statement to his clerks is quoted by Cray. He reports the vote as six to three, with

White and Black joining Warren in voting to affirm, but Brennan recorded White as voting to reverse, Douglas passing, and only Black supporting the Chief. See conference list, October 25, 1968, box 182, WJB. White devoted almost all of his dissenting opinion to faulting the majority's reasoning, before concluding without further explanation that if the Court were to find flag burning protected by the First Amendment, he would probably sustain such a conviction anyhow. 394 U.S. at 615 (White, J., dissenting).

29. *Gregory v. City of Chicago,* 394 U.S. 111 (1969); ibid. at 116–17 (Black, J., concurring); conference list, December 13, 1968, box 182, WJB; Schwartz, *Super Chief,* 735–36; 394 U.S. at 118, 114, 124–25 (Black, J., concurring); annotation by "Marty" on draft of Warren concurring opinion, box FL 7, AF; 394 U.S. at 947 (Black, J., concurring). Douglas joined Black's concurrence. Annotation.

30. *Watts v. United States,* 394 U.S. 705 (1969); Belknap, "Vietnam," 141–42; 394 U.S. at 708; ibid. at 711 (Fortas, J., dissenting); ibid. at 708 (Stewart, J., noting that he would have denied certiorari); note from HLB to Marshall, April 1, 1969, and note from Black to Marshall, April 4, 1969, both in box 56, TM.

31. *Gunn v. University Committee to End the War in Vietnam,* 289 F. Supp. 469 (W.D. Tex 1968), *appeal dismissed,* 399 U.S. 383 (1970); Schwartz, *Super Chief,* 737; Bernard Schwartz, "More Unpublished Warren Court Opinions," 1986 *Supreme Court Review* 317, at 390, 380, 389; Belknap, "Vietnam," 150–51.

32. Belknap, "Vietnam," 108–9; Douglas, *Court Years,* 152. For an extended discussion of the cases in which both the Warren and Burger Courts refused to pass on the legality of the Vietnam War, see Rodric B. Schoen, "A Strange Silence: Vietnam and the Supreme Court," 33 *Washburn Law Journal* 275 (1994).

33. Kalman, *Fortas,* 293–94; Larry Berman, *Lyndon Johnson's War: The Road to Stalemate in Vietnam* (New York: Norton, 1989), 87–88; Michal R. Belknap, "Constitutional Law as Creative Problem Solving: Could the Warren Court Have Ended the Vietnam War?" 36 *California Western Law Review* 99, at 104–5 (1999); Fortas memorandum quoted by Berman.

34. Belknap, "Vietnam," 90–96.

35. White, *Warren,* 306; Cray, *Chief Justice,* 483–84.

36. Currie, *Constitution,* 457; Schoen, "Strange Silence," 321, 318–20, 308–9; Belknap, "Vietnam," 118–19; Belknap, "Problem Solving," 113–16.

37. Galloway, "Third Period," 804; *Brandenburg v. Ohio,* 395 U.S. 444 (1969); Harry Kalven, *A Worthy Tradition: Freedom of Speech in America* (New York: Harper & Row, 1988), 123–24, 47; Samuel Walker, *In Defense of American Liberties: A History of the ACLU* (New York: Oxford University Press, 1990), 281.

38. *Wells v. Rockefeller,* 394 U.S. 542 (1969); *Kirkpatrick v. Preisler,* 394 U.S. 526 (1969); Schwartz, *Super Chief,* 752–53; *Kirkpatrick,* 394 U.S. at 530, 532; *Wells,* 394 U.S. at 549 (Harlan, J., dissenting); ibid. at 553 (White, J., dissenting); *Kirkpatrick,* 394 U.S. at 536 (Fortas, J., concurring).

39. *Kramer v. Union Free School District,* 395 U.S. 621 (1969); ibid. at 626–28; ibid. at 639–40 (Stewart, J., dissenting).

40. *Sniadach v. Family Finance Corp.,* 395 U.S. 337 (1969); Horwitz, *Warren Court,* xii; "1968 Term," 83, 114–15.

41. Tushnet, *Constitutional Law,* 96–97; Richard Funston, "The Double Standard of Constitutional Protection in the Era of the Welfare State," 90 *Political Science Quarterly* 261, at 269 (1975–76); Charles Reich, "The New Property," 73 *Yale Law Journal* 733 (1964); Charles Reich, "Individual Rights and Social Welfare: The Emerging Legal Issues," 74 *Yale Law Journal* 1245 (1965); Frank Michelman, "Forward: On Protecting the Poor Through the Fourteenth Amendment," 83 *Harvard Law Review* 7, at 9, 13, 11, 21, 42, 57 (1969); Kahn, *Constitutional Theory,* 51.

42. *Shapiro v. Thompson,* 394 U.S. 618 (1969); Gormley, *Cox,* 199; Schwartz, *Super Chief,* 725–28; docket book entry and attached conference notes, box 415, WJB; Schwartz, *Unpublished,* 315,

321–26, 329–41, 377–86; Brennan to Fortas, June 11, 1968, box 179, WJB. Schwartz erroneously reports the initial vote as six to three, when in fact Warren, Black, Harlan, Brennan, and White voted to reverse and Fortas, Douglas, Stewart, and Marshall to affirm.

43. Docket book entry, box 416, WJB; Schwartz, *Super Chief,* 728–30; handwritten notations on conference list for conference of Friday, October 25, 1968, box 403, HLB; Schwartz, *Unpublished,* 385; 394 U.S. at 627, 630, 634, 638; Brennan to Stewart, undated and never sent, box 184, WJB.

44. Schwartz, *Super Chief,* 330–32; Brennan to Douglas, Stewart, White, Fortas, and Marshall, March 25, 1969, and Fortas to Brennan, March 26, 1969, both in box 184, WJB; RHJG, note attached to March 28, 1969, circulation of Brennan's opinion, box 50, TM; 394 U.S. at 644; ibid. at 663–77, 658, 660, 662, 661 (Harlan, J., dissenting).

45. *Powell v. McCormack,* 266 F. Supp. 354 (D. D.C. 1967), *aff'd,* 395 F.2d 577 (D.C. Cir.) (1968), *aff'd* 395 U.S. 486 (1969); 395 U.S. at 550; Schwartz, *Super Chief,* 757–59; 395 U.S. at 559–60 (Stewart, J., dissenting); conference notes attached to docket book entry, box 416, WJB; 395 U.S. at 548–49; ibid. at 553 (Douglas, J., concurring).

46. "Comments on Powell v. McCormack," 17 *UCLA Law Review* 2, at 129, 191, 85, 87, 72 (1969).

47. Schwartz, *Super Chief,* 763.

48. *Alderman v. United States,* 394 U.S. 165 (1969); Warren, *Memoirs,* 333–41; Brennan, draft of his recollections of his interviews with Landau and cover note to Warren, March 18, 1969, box 348, EW; Alexander Charns, *Cloak and Gavel: FBI Wiretaps, Bugs, Informers, and the Supreme Court* (Urbana and Chicago: University of Illinois Press, 1992), 97–98.

49. Brennan, recollections; Douglas, *Court Years,* 260; Douglas, memorandum for files, box 1430, WOD; Warren, *Memoirs,* 341.

50. Brennan, memorandum to Black, et al., "re: Gift of Rifle to Chief Justice Earl Warren," May 7, 1969, and "re: Dinner for Chief Justice and Mrs. Warren," May 29, 1969, both in box 62, HLB. Bruce Murphy, *Fortas,* 195–200, 207–9; Kalman, *Fortas,* 359–60, 364.

51. Kalman, *Fortas,* 360–63, 366–71; AF, "Memorandum to Chief Justice Re: No. 1057—Wolfson v. United States," March 26, 1969, box 353, EW; Cray, *Chief Justice,* 508–10; Earl Warren to John Mitchell, May 14, 1969, box 503, EW.

52. Kalman, *Fortas,* 372–73; Walter R. Mansfield to Fortas, May 13, 1969, box 353, EW; Douglas, *Court Years,* 358–59; Bruce Murphy, *Fortas,* 570–71; Fortas to Warren, May 14, 1969, box 353, EW.

53. Kalman, *Fortas,* 374; Douglas, *Court Years,* 365–68; Douglas to Warren, October 31, 1966, box 352, EW; Judicial Conference of the United States, press release, June 10, 1969, box 59, HLB; "Statement by Chief Justice Warren," June 23, 1969, box 59, HLB.

54. Schwartz, *Super Chief,* 763–64; Herman Schwartz, "Warren Earl Burger," in Urofsky *Supreme Court Justices,* 69; Charles M. Lamb, "Chief Justice Warren E. Burger: A Conservative Chief for Conservative Times," in *The Burger Court,* ed. Charles M. Lamb and Stephen C. Halpern (Urbana and Chicago: University of Illinois Press, 1991), 130–32; Cray, *Chief Justice,* 513.

55. Schwartz, *Super Chief,* 764–65; "Retirement of Mr. Chief Justice Warren," 395 U.S. VII, at VII–VIII, IX, X, XI, XII (1969).

12. THE LEGACY OF THE WARREN COURT

1. Brennan, "Personal Remembrance," in Schwartz, *Retrospective,* 10; Kalman, *Liberalism,* 57.

2. Cray, *Chief Justice,* 414–19; Schwartz, *Super Chief,* 764–68; White, *Warren,* 316; Marshall interview, 18.

3. Cray, *Chief Justice,* 521–26; White, *Warren,* 325–26; Schwartz, *Super Chief,* 770–72.

4. White, *Judicial Tradition,* 423–24, 432–34; Currie, *Constitution,* 464; Tushnet, "History," 2–3, 33.

5. Sheehan, "Trends," 33; White, *Judicial Tradition*, 423; Lee Epstein and Joseph H. Kobylka, *The Supreme Court and Legal Change: Abortion and the Death Penalty* (Chapel Hill: University of North Carolina Press, 1992), 14, 20; Lamb and Halpern, *Burger Court*, 9–10; Albert W. Alschuler, "Failed Pragmatism: Reflections on the Burger Court," 100 *Harvard Law Review* 1436, at 1437 (1987); Earl Maltz, *The Chief Justiceship of Warren Burger, 1969–1986* (Columbia: University of South Carolina Press, 2000), 1.

6. Powe, *American Politics*, 486; Kurland, *Politics*, xvi–xviii, 204–5; Nelson, "Equality," 102; Bernard Schwartz, "Earl Warren as a Judge," 12 *Hastings Constitutional Law Quarterly* 179, at 179 (1985); Rosenberg, *Hollow Hope*, 304–5; Schwartz, *History*, 263. Fortas is quoted by Schwartz in the *Hastings* article.

7. Horwitz, "Jurisprudence," 610; Klarman, "Backlash Thesis," 81–84; Tushnet, "Significance of *Brown*," 173; Michael Klarman, "*Brown v. Board of Education:* Facts and Political Correctness," 80 *Virginia Law Review* 185, at 186 (1994); Gerald Rosenberg, "*Brown* is Dead! Long Live *Brown*! The Endless Attempt to Canonize a Case," 80 *Virginia Law Review* 161, at 162 (1994); Rosenberg, *Hollow Hope*, 156.

8. Rosenberg, *Hollow Hope*, 315–16, 317–21, 326, 331–33.

9. Ibid., 296–301; Tushnet, "History," 20; Kurland, *Politics*, 19.

10. Friedman, *Twentieth Century*, 312; Horwitz, *Warren Court*, 115; Lawrence M. Friedman, *Total Justice* (New York: Russell Sage Foundation, 1985), 107, 108, 120; Kahn, *Constitutional Theory*, 102–3.

11. White, *Judicial Tradition*, 318; Horwitz, "Pursuit," 8; Schwartz, *History*, 277, 276, 283; Walker, *Defense*, 300, 301, 305; Hall, *Mirror*, 309.

12. Schwartz, *History*, 284, 275; Kalman, *Liberalism*, 46–47; White, *Warren*, 248; David Luban, "The Warren Court and the Concept of Right," 34 *Harvard Civil Rights—Civil Liberties Law Review* 7, at 8 (1999).

13. Kurland, *Politics*, 172, xx, 190, 191, 194, 174; Kahn, *Constitutional Theory*, 33; White, "Jurist," 535, 539, 540.

14. White, "Jurist," 549; Anthony Lewis, "Foreword," in *The Burger Court: The Constitutional Counter-Revolution That Wasn't*, ed. Vincent Blasi (New Haven, Conn.: Yale University Press, 1983), ix; Vincent J. Blasi, "The Rootless Activism of the Burger Court," in Blasi, *Counter-Revolution*, 198; White, *Judicial Tradition*, 456.

15. Martin Shapiro, "The Courts, the Commentators—and the Search for Values," in Blasi, *Counter-Revolution*, 236; Kalman, *Liberalism*, 50–51, 92, 64–65; Ronald Dworkin, *Taking Rights Seriously*, 2nd ed. (Cambridge, Mass.: Harvard University Press, 1978), 136.

16. David M. O'Brien, *Storm Center: The Supreme Court in American Politics*, 2nd ed. (New York: Norton, 1990), 357–58, 410 n. 67.

17. Tushnet, *Constitutional Law*, 30; Kalman, *Liberalism*, 72–73, 84–85, 159.

18. Tushnet, "History," 1.

19. Kalman, *Liberalism*, 57; Parrish, "Warren," 1, 180.

20. Marshall interview, 18; Horwitz, *Warren Court*, 113; Tushnet, "History," 34; Powe, *American Politics*, 501.

Bibliography

PRIMARY SOURCES

Manuscript Collections

Dwight D. Eisenhower Presidential Library, Abilene, Kans.
Administration Series, Papers of Dwight D. Eisenhower as President (Ann Whitman File).
DDE Diaries Series, Papers of Dwight D. Eisenhower as President (Ann Whitman File).
William Rogers Papers
White House Central Files.

John F. Kennedy Presidential Library, Boston, Mass.
John F. Kennedy Papers, Papers of President Kennedy, President's Office Files, Special Correspondence.
Robert F. Kennedy Papers.
White House Central Files.

Library of Congress, Manuscript Division, Washington, D.C.
Earl Warren Papers.
Hugo L. Black Papers.
William J. Brennan, Jr. Papers.
Harold Burton Papers.
William O. Douglas Papers.
Robert Jackson Papers.
Thurgood Marshall Papers.

Lyndon Baines Johnson Presidential Library, Austin, Tex.
Ramsey Clark Papers.
File Pertaining to Abe Fortas and Homer Thornberry.
Office Files of John Macy.
White House Central Files.

Mudd Library, Princeton University, Princeton, N.J.
John Marshall Harlan Papers.

Stirling Library, Yale University, New Haven, Conn.
Abe Fortas Papers.

Tarlton Law Library, University of Texas Law School, Austin, Tex.
Tom C. Clark Papers.

Oral Histories
Dirksen, Everett. Interview by Joe B. Frantz. March 21, 1969. Tape 1. Transcript. LBJ Oral History Project, LBJ Library, Austin, Tex.

Dolan, Joseph F. Interview by Charles Morrissey. December 1, 1964. Transcript. John F. Kennedy Library Oral History Project, JFK Library, Boston, Mass.

Marshall, Thurgood. Interview by T. H. Baker. July 10, 1969. Transcript. LBJ Oral History Project, LBJ Library, Austin, Tex.

Mitchell, Clarence. Interview by Thomas H. Baker. April 30, 1969. Tape 2. Transcript. LBJ Oral History Project, LBJ Library, Austin Tex.

Weisel, Edwin, Jr. Interview by Joe B. Frantz. May 23, 1969. Transcript. LBJ Oral History Project, LBJ Library, Austin, Tex.

Congressional Hearings

U.S. Congress. House. Committee on the Judiciary. *Hearings on School Prayers before the House Committee on the Judiciary.* 88th Cong., 2nd sess., 1964.

U.S. Congress. Senate. Committee on the Judiciary. *Hearings on the Nomination of Thurgood Marshall. . . .* 90th Cong., 1st sess., 1967.

———. *Nominations of Abe Fortas and Homer Thornberry: Hearings before the Committee on the Judiciary.* 90th Cong., 2nd sess., July 11–23, 1968.

———. *Offerings on Prayer in Public Schools and Other Matters before the Senate Committee on the Judiciary.* 87th Cong., 2nd sess., 1962.

U.S. Congress. Senate. *Nomination of Abe Fortas.* 90th Cong., 2nd sess., 1968. Executive Report 8.

Published Primary Sources

Black, Hugo, Jr. *My Father: A Remembrance.* New York: Random House, 1975.

Brennan, William J., Jr. "A Personal Remembrance." In Schwartz, *Retrospective,* 8–11.

Brownell, Herbert. *Advising Ike: The Memoirs of Attorney General Brownell.* With John P. Burke. Lawrence: University Press of Kansas, 1993.

Clark, Tom C. "The Decisional Process of the Supreme Court." 50 *Cornell Law Quarterly* 385–93 (1965).

Douglas, William O. *The Court Years, 1939–1975: The Autobiography of William O. Douglas.* New York: Random House, 1980.

———. *The Douglas Letters: Selections from the Private Papers of Justice William O. Douglas.* Edited by Melvin I. Urofsky. Bethesda, Md.: Adler & Adler, 1987.

———. *Go East, Young Man: The Early Years: The Autobiography of William O. Douglas.* New York: Random House, 1974.

———. *A Living Bill of Rights.* Garden City, N.Y.: Doubleday, 1961.

———. "The Supreme Court and Its Case Load." 45 *Cornell Law Quarterly* 401 (1960).

Eisenhower, Dwight D. *The Eisenhower Diaries.* Edited by Robert H. Ferrell. New York: Norton, 1981.

———. *Ike's Letters to a Friend, 1941–1958.* Edited by Robert Griffith. Lawrence: University Press of Kansas, 1984.

———. *The White House Years: Mandate for Change, 1953–1956.* Garden City, N.Y.: Doubleday, 1963.

———. *The White House Years: Waging Peace 1956–1961.* Garden City, N.Y.: Doubleday, 1965.

Elman, Philip. "The Solicitor General's Office, Justice Frankfurter, and Civil Rights Litigation, 1946–1960: An Oral History." 100 *Harvard Law Review* 817–52 (1987).

Fortas, Abe. *Concerning Dissent and Civil Disobedience.* New York: New American Library, 1968.

Friedman, Leon, ed. *Argument: The Oral Argument before the Supreme Court in Brown v. Board of Education of Topeka, 1952–1955.* New York: Chelsea House, 1969.

Fry, Anita Roberts. "The Warren Tapes: Oral History and the Supreme Court." 1982 *Yearbook of the Supreme Court Historical Society* 10–22 (1982).

Goldberg, Arthur J. *Equal Justice: The Warren Era of the Supreme Court.* Evanston, Ill.: Northwestern University Press, 1971.

———. *The Evolving Constitution: Essays on the Bill of Rights and the U.S. Supreme Court.* Edited by Norman Dorsen. Middletown, Conn.: Wesleyan University Press, 1987.

———. "The Warren Court and Its Critics." 20 *Santa Clara Law Review* 831–39 (1980).

Hagerty, James C. *The Diary of James C. Hagerty: Eisenhower in Mid-Course 1954–1955.* Edited by Robert H. Ferrell. Bloomington: Indiana University Press, 1983.

Hand, Learned. *The Bill of Rights.* New York: Atheneum, 1968.

Hughes, Emmet John. *The Ordeal of Power: A Political Memoir of the Eisenhower Years.* New York: Atheneum, 1963.

Kurland, Philip B. *Mr. Justice Frankfurter and the Constitution.* Chicago: University of Chicago Press, 1971.

Kurland, Philip B., and Gerhard Casper, eds. *Landmark Briefs and Arguments of the Supreme Court of the United States.* Vol. 49A. Arlington, Va.: University Publications of America, 1975.

Marshall, Thurgood. *Thurgood Marshall: His Speeches, Writings, Arguments, Opinions, and Reminiscences.* Edited by Mark V. Tushnet. Chicago: Lawrence Hill Books, 2001.

Schwartz, Bernard. "More Unpublished Warren Court Opinions." 1986 *Supreme Court Review* 317–93.

———, ed. *The Unpublished Opinions of the Warren Court.* New York: Oxford University Press, 1985.

Thayer, James Bradley. "The Origin and Scope of the American Doctrine of Constitutional Law." 7 *Harvard Law Review* 129–56 (1893).

Warren, Earl. *The Memoirs of Earl Warren.* Garden City, N.Y.: Doubleday, 1977.

———. *The Public Papers of Chief Justice Earl Warren.* Edited by Henry M. Christman. New York: Simon & Schuster, 1974.

SECONDARY SOURCES

Books

Abraham, Henry J. *Justices, Presidents, and Senators: A History of the U.S. Supreme Court Appointments from Washington to Clinton.* Lanham, Md.: Rowman & Littlefield, 1999.

Abraham, Henry J., and Barbara J. Perry. *Freedom and the Court: Civil Rights and Civil Liberties in the United States.* 6th ed. New York: Oxford University Press, 1994.

Alley, Robert S. *School Prayer: The Court, the Congress, and the First Amendment.* Buffalo, N.Y.: Prometheus Books, 1994.

Baker, Gordon E. *The Reapportionment Revolution: Representation, Political Power, and the Supreme Court.* New York: Random House, 1967.

Baker, Leonard. *Brandeis and Frankfurter: A Dual Biography.* New York: Harper & Row, 1984.

Baker, Liva. *Miranda: Crime, Law and Politics.* New York: Atheneum, 1985.

Ball, Howard. *A Defiant Life: Thurgood Marshall and the Persistence of Racism in America.* New York: Crown Publishers, 1998.

———. *Hugo L. Black: Cold Steel Warrior.* New York: Oxford University Press, 1996.

———. *The Vision and the Dream of Justice Hugo L. Black: An Examination of a Judicial Philosophy.* University, Ala.: University of Alabama Press, 1975.

Ball, Howard, and Phillip J. Cooper. *Of Power and Right: Hugo Black, William O. Douglas and America's Constitutional Revolution.* New York: Oxford University Press, 1992.

Belknap, Michal R. *Cold War Political Justice: The Smith Act, the Communist Party, and American Civil Liberties.* Westport, Conn.: Greenwood Press, 1977.

———. *Federal Law and Southern Order: Racial Violence and Constitutional Conflict in the Post-Brown South.* Athens: University of Georgia Press, 1987.

Berger, Roaul. *Government by Judiciary: The Transformation of the Fourteenth Amendment.* Cambridge, Mass.: Harvard University Press, 1977.

Berman, Larry. *Lyndon Johnson's War: The Road to Stalemate in Vietnam.* New York: Norton, 1989.

Berry, Mary Frances. *Stability, Security, and Continuity: Mr. Justice Burton and Decision-Making in the Supreme Court 1945–1958*. Westport, Conn.: Greenwood Press, 1978.

Bland, Randall W. *Private Pressure on Public Law: The Legal Career of Justice Thurgood Marshall*. Port Washington, N.Y.: Kennikat Press, 1973.

Blasi, Vincent, ed. *The Burger Court: The Counter-Revolution That Wasn't*. New Haven, Conn.: Yale University Press, 1983.

Blum, John Morton. *Years of Discord: American Politics and Society, 1961–1974*. New York: Norton, 1991.

Bodenhamer, David J. *Fair Trial: Rights of the Accused in American History*. New York: Oxford University Press, 1992.

Bork, Robert H. *The Tempting of America: The Political Seduction of the Law*. New York: Free Press, 1990.

Burk, Robert F. *Dwight D. Eisenhower: Hero and Politician*. Boston: Twayne, 1986.

Casper, Jonathan D. *Lawyers before the Warren Court: Civil Liberties and Civil Rights, 1957–66*. Urbana: University of Illinois Press, 1972.

Caute, David. *The Great Fear: The Anti-Communist Purge under Truman and Eisenhower*. New York: Simon & Schuster, 1978.

Chafe, William H. *Changing Patterns in American Culture*. New York: Oxford University Press, 1977.

Charns, Alexander. *Cloak and Gavel: FBI Wiretaps, Bugs, Informers, and the Supreme Court*. Urbana and Chicago: University of Illinois Press, 1992.

Clark, Hunter R. *Justice Brennan: The Great Conciliator*. New York: Carol Publishing Group, 1995.

Cortner, Richard C. *The Apportionment Cases*. Knoxville: University of Tennessee Press, 1970.

———. *Civil Rights and Public Accommodations: The Heart of Atlanta and McClung Cases* Lawrence: University Press of Kansas, 2001.

———. *The Supreme Court and the Second Bill of Rights: The Fourteenth Amendment and the Nationalization of Civil Liberties*. Madison: University of Wisconsin Press, 1981.

Cottroll, Robert J., Raymond T. Diamond, and Leland B. Ware. *Brown v. Board of Education: Caste, Culture, and the Constitution*. Lawrence: University Press of Kansas, 2003.

Cox, Archibald. *The Warren Court: Constitutional Decision as an Instrument of Reform*. Cambridge, Mass.: Harvard University Press, 1968.

Cray, Ed. *Chief Justice: A Biography of Earl Warren*. New York: Simon & Schuster, 1997.

Currie, David P. *The Constitution in the Supreme Court: The Second Century 1888–1986*. Chicago: University of Chicago Press, 1990.

Cushman, Clare, and Melvin I. Urofsky, eds. *Black, White, and Brown: The Landmark School Desegregation Case in Retrospect*. Washington, D.C.: Supreme Court Historical Society, 2004.

DeGrazia, Edward. *Girls Lean Back Everywhere: The Law of Obscenity and the Assault on Genius*. New York: Random House, 1992.

Dixon, Robert G., Jr. *Democratic Representation: Reapportionment in Law and Politics*. New York: Oxford University Press, 1968.

Dolbeare, Kenneth M., and Phillip E. Hammond. *The School Prayer Decisions: From Court Policy to Local Practice*. Chicago: University of Chicago Press, 1971.

Drinan, Robert F. *Religion, Courts, and Public Policy*. New York: McGraw-Hill, 1963.

Dudziak, Mary. *Cold War Civil Rights: Race and the Image of American Democracy*. Princeton, N.J.: Princeton University Press, 2000.

Dunne, Gerald T. *Hugo Black and the Judicial Revolution*. New York: Simon & Schuster, 1977.

Dworkin, Ronald. *Taking Rights Seriously*. 2nd ed. Cambridge, Mass.: Harvard University Press, 1978.

Eisler, Kim Isaac. *A Justice for All: William J. Brennan Jr. and the Decisions That Transformed America*. New York: Simon & Schuster, 1993.

Epstein, Lee, and Joseph H. Kobylka. *The Supreme Court and Legal Change: Abortion and the Death Penalty*. Chapel Hill: University of North Carolina Press, 1992.

Ewald, William Bragg, Jr. *Eisenhower the President: Crucial Days, 1951–1960*. Englewood Cliffs, N.J.: Prentice Hall, 1981.

Fassett, John D. *New Deal Justice: The Life of Stanley Reed of Kentucky*. New York: Vantage, 1994.

Freyer, Tony Allen. *Hugo L. Black and the Dilemma of American Liberalism*. Glenview, Ill.: Scott, Foresman / Little, Brown, 1990.

———. *The Little Rock Crisis: A Constitutional Interpretation*. Westport, Conn.: Greenwood Press, 1984.

Fried, Richard M. *Nightmare in Red: The McCarthy Era in Perspective*. New York: Oxford University Press, 1990.

Friedman, Lawrence M. *American Law in the 20th Century*. New Haven, Conn.: Yale University Press, 2002.

———. *Crime and Punishment in American History*. New York: Basic Books, 1993.

———. *Total Justice*. New York: Russell Sage Foundation, 1985.

Friedman, Leon, and Fred L. Israel, eds. *The Justices of the United States Supreme Court: Their Lives and Major Opinions*. 3rd. ed. Vol. 4. New York and Philadelphia: Chelsea House, 1997.

Garraty, John A., and Mark C. Carnes, eds. *American National Biography*. New York: Oxford University Press, 1999.

Garrow, David J. *Liberty and Sexuality: The Right to Privacy and the Making of Roe v. Wade*. New York: Macmillan, 1994.

Gerhart, Eugene C. *America's Advocate: Robert H. Jackson*. Indianapolis and New York: Bobbs-Merrill, 1958.

Gilbert, James. *Another Chance: Postwar America, 1945–1968*. New York: Knopf, 1981.

Goldman, Roger. *Thurgood Marshall: Justice for All*. New York: Carroll & Graf, 1992.

Gormley, Ken. *Archibald Cox: Conscience of a Nation*. Reading, Mass.: Addison-Wesley, 1997.

Gugin, Linda C., and James E. St. Clair. *Sherman Minton: New Deal Senator, Cold War Justice*. Indianapolis: Indiana Historical Society, 1997.

Gunther, Gerald. *Learned Hand: The Man and the Judge*. New York: Knopf, 1994.

Hall, Kermit L. *The Magic Mirror: Law in American History*. New York: Oxford University Press, 1989.

Hamilton, Virginia Van der Veer. *Hugo Black: The Alabama Years*. Baton Rouge: Louisiana State University Press, 1972.

Hirsch, Harry N. *The Enigma of Felix Frankfurter*. New York: Basic Books, 1981.

Hockett, Jeffrey D. *New Deal Justice: The Constitutional Jurisprudence of Hugo L. Black, Felix Frankfurter, and Robert H. Jackson*. Lanham, Md.: Rowman & Littlefield, 1996.

Horwitz, Morton J. *The Transformation of American Law, 1870–1960: The Crisis of Legal Orthodoxy*. New York: Oxford University Press, 1992.

———. *The Warren Court and the Pursuit of Justice*. New York: Hill and Wang, 1998.

Huston, Luther A. *Pathway to Judgment: A Study of Earl Warren*. Philadelphia: Chilton Books, 1966.

Hutchinson, Dennis J. *The Man Who Once Was Whizzer White: A Portrait of Justice Byron R. White*. New York: Free Press, 1998.

Irons, Peter. *The Courage of Their Convictions: Sixteen Americans Who Fought Their Way to the Supreme Court*. New York: Free Press, 1988.

———. *Jim Crow's Children: The Broken Promise of the Brown Decision*. New York: Viking, 2002.

Johnson, John W. *The Struggle for Student Rights: Tinker v. Des Moines and the 1960s*. Lawrence: University Press of Kansas, 1997.

Kahn, Ronald. *The Supreme Court and Constitutional Theory, 1953–1993*. Lawrence: University Press of Kansas, 1994.

Kalman, Laura. *Abe Fortas: A Biography.* New Haven, Conn.: Yale University Press, 1990.

———. *The Strange Career of Legal Liberalism.* New Haven, Conn.: Yale University Press, 1996.

Kalven, Harry. *A Worthy Tradition: Freedom of Speech in America.* New York: Harper & Row, 1988.

Katz, Wilber G. *Religion and American Constitutions.* Evanston, Ill.: Northwestern University Press, 1964.

Kelly, Alfred H., and Winfred A. Harbison. *The American Constitution: Its Origins and Development.* 3rd ed. New York: Norton, 1976.

Kerber, Linda K. *No Constitutional Right to Be Ladies: Women and the Obligations of Citizenship.* New York: Hill and Wang, 1998.

Klarman, Michael J. *From Jim Crow to Civil Rights: The Supreme Court and the Struggle for Racial Equality.* New York: Oxford University Press, 2004.

Klehr, Harvey, and Ronald Radosh. *The Amerasia Spy Case: Prelude to McCarthyism.* Chapel Hill: University of North Carolina Press, 1996.

Kluger, Richard. *Simple Justice: The History of Brown v. Board of Education and Black America's Struggle for Equality.* Rev. ed. New York: Knopf, 2004.

Kurland, Philip B. *Politics, the Constitution, and the Warren Court.* Chicago: University of Chicago Press, 1970.

Kutler, Stanley I. *The American Inquisition: Justice and Injustice in the Cold War.* New York: Hill and Wang, 1982.

LaFave, Wayne, and Jerold H. Israel. *Criminal Procedure.* 2nd ed. St. Paul, Minn.: West Publishing Co., 1992.

Lamb, Charles M., and Stephen C. Halpern, eds. *The Burger Court: Political and Judicial Profiles.* Urbana and Chicago: University of Illinois Press, 1991.

Laubach, J. Herbert. *School Prayers: Congress, the Courts and the Public.* Washington, D.C.: Public Affairs Press, 1969.

Leahy, James E. *Supreme Court Justices Who Voted with the Government: Nine Who Favored the State Over Individual Rights.* Jefferson, N.C.: McFarland & Co., 1999.

Lee, R. Alton. *Dwight D. Eisenhower: Soldier and Statesman.* Chicago: Nelson-Hall, 1981.

Levy, Leonard W. *The Supreme Court under Earl Warren.* New York: Quadrangle Books, 1972.

Lewis, Anthony. *Gideon's Trumpet.* New York: Vintage Books, 1964.

———. *Make No Law: The Sullivan Case and the First Amendment.* New York: Random House, 1991.

Lytle, Clifford M. *The Warren Court & Its Critics.* Tucson: University of Arizona Press, 1968.

Lyon, Peter. *Eisenhower: Portrait of the Hero.* Boston: Little, Brown & Company, 1974.

Maltz, Earl. *The Chief Justiceship of Warren Burger, 1969–1986.* Columbia: University of South Carolina Press, 2000.

Matusow, Allen J. *The Unraveling of America: A History of Liberalism in the 1960s.* New York: Harper & Row, 1984.

McKay, Robert B. *Reapportionment: The Law and Politics of Equal Representation.* New York: Twentieth Century Fund, 1965.

Mendelson, Wallace. *Justices Black and Frankfurter: Conflict in the Court.* Chicago: University of Chicago Press, 1961.

Michelman, Frank I. *Brennan and Democracy.* Princeton, N.J.: Princeton University Press, 1999.

Miller, Loren. *The Petitioners: The Story of the Supreme Court of the United States and the Negro.* Cleveland and New York: World Publishing, 1966.

Miller, Richard Lawrence. *Whittaker: Struggles of a Supreme Court Justice.* Westport, Conn.: Greenwood Press, 2002.

Murphy, Bruce Allen. *Fortas: The Rise and Ruin of a Supreme Court Justice.* New York: Morrow, 1988.

———. *Wild Bill: The Legend and Life of William O. Douglas.* New York: Random House, 2003.

Murphy, Paul L. *The Constitution in Crisis Times 1918–1969.* New York: Harper & Row, 1972.

Murphy, Walter F. *Congress and the Court: A Case Study in the American Political Process.* Chicago: University of Chicago Press, 1962.

Newman, Roger K. *Hugo Black: A Biography.* New York: Pantheon Books, 1994.

Nieman, Donald. *Promises to Keep: African-Americans and the Constitutional Order, 1776 to the Present.* New York: Oxford University Press, 1991.

Nowak, John E., and Ronald D. Rotunda. *Constitutional Law.* 7th ed. St. Paul, Minn.: West Publishing, 2004.

O'Brien, David M. *Storm Center: The Supreme Court in American Politics.* 2nd edition. New York: Norton, 1990.

O'Neill, William. *Coming Apart: An Informal History of America in the 1960s.* New York: Quadrangle Books, 1971.

Pach, Chester J., Jr., and Elmo Richardson. *The Presidency of Dwight D. Eisenhower.* Rev. ed. Lawrence: University of Press Kansas, 1991.

Parmet, Herbert S. *Eisenhower and the American Crusades.* New York: Macmillan, 1972.

Parrish, Michael E. *Felix Frankfurter and His Times: The Reform Years.* New York: Free Press, 1982.

Patterson, James T. *Brown v. Board of Education: A Civil Rights Milestone and Its Troubled Legacy.* New York: Oxford University Press, 2001.

Pfeffer, Leo. *Church, State and Freedom.* Rev. ed. Boston: Beacon Press, 1967.

Polenberg, Richard. *One Nation Divisible: Class, Race and Ethnicity in the United States since 1938.* New York: Penguin, 1980.

Polsby, Nelson W., ed. *Reapportionment in the 1970s.* Berkeley and Los Angeles: University of California Press, 1971.

Powe, Lucas A., Jr. *The Warren Court and American Politics.* Cambridge, Mass.: Harvard University Press, 2000.

Pritchett, C. Herman. *The Political Offender and the Warren Court.* New York: Russell & Russell, 1967.

Rosenberg, Gerald N. *The Hollow Hope: Can Courts Bring about Social Change?* Chicago: University of Chicago Press, 1991.

Sabin, Arthur J. *In Calmer Times: The Supreme Court and Red Monday.* Philadelphia: University of Pennsylvania Press, 1999.

Schlesinger, Arthur M., Jr. *Robert Kennedy and His Times.* Boston: Houghton Mifflin, 1978.

———. *A Thousand Days: John F. Kennedy in the White House.* Boston: Houghton Mifflin, 1965.

Schrecker, Ellen. *Many Are the Crimes: McCarthyism in America.* Boston: Little, Brown, 1998.

Schwartz, Bernard. *A History of the Supreme Court.* New York: Oxford University Press, 1993.

———. *Super Chief: Earl Warren and His Supreme Court—A Judicial Biography.* New York: New York University Press, 1983.

———, ed. *The Warren Court: A Retrospective.* New York: Oxford University Press, 1996.

Schwartz, Bernard, and Stephan Lesher. *Inside the Warren Court.* Garden City, N.Y.: Doubleday, 1983.

Semonche, John E. *Keeping the Faith: A Cultural History of the U.S. Supreme Court.* Lanham, Md. Rowman and Littlefield, 1998.

Silverstein, Mark. *Constitutional Faiths: Felix Frankfurter, Hugo Black, and the Process of Judicial Decision Making.* Ithaca: Cornell University Press, 1984.

Simon, James F. *The Antagonists: Hugo Black, Felix Frankfurter and Civil Liberties in Modern America.* New York: Simon & Schuster, 1989.

———. *Independent Journey: The Life of William O. Douglas.* New York: Harper & Row, 1980.

Solinger, Rickie. *Wake Up Little Susie: Single Pregnancy and Race before Roe v. Wade.* New York & London: Routledge, 1992.

Sorauf, Frank J. *The Wall of Separation: The Constitutional Politics of Church and State*. Princeton, N.J.: Princeton University Press, 1976.

Stebenne, David L. *Arthur J. Goldberg: New Deal Liberal*. New York: Oxford University Press, 1996.

Tribe, Laurence H. *American Constitutional Law*. 2nd ed. Mineola, N.Y.: Foundation Press, 1988.

Tushnet, Mark V. *Making Civil Rights Law: Thurgood Marshall and the Supreme Court, 1936–1961*. New York: Oxford University Press, 1994.

———. *Making Constitutional Law: Thurgood Marshall and the Supreme Court, 1961–1991*. New York: Oxford University Press, 1997.

———. *The NAACP Legal Strategy against Segregated Education, 1925–1950*. Chapel Hill: University of North Carolina Press, 1987.

———, ed. *The Warren Court in Historical and Political Perspective*. Charlottesville and London: University of Virginia Press, 1993.

Urofsky, Melvin I. *Division and Discord: The Supreme Court under Stone and Vinson, 1941–1953*. Columbia: University of South Carolina Press, 1997.

———. *Felix Frankfurter: Judicial Restraint and Individual Liberties*. Boston: Twayne, 1991.

———, ed. *The Supreme Court Justices: A Biographical Dictionary*. New York: Garland, 1994.

Urofsky, Melvin I., and Paul Finkelman. *A March of Liberty: A Constitutional History of the United States*. 2nd edition. New York: Knopf, 2002.

Walker, Samuel. *In Defense of American Liberties: A History of the ACLU*. New York: Oxford University Press, 1990.

———. *Popular Justice: A History of American Criminal Justice*. New York: Oxford University Press, 1980.

White, G. Edward. *The American Judicial Tradition*. 2nd ed. New York: Oxford University Press, 1988.

———. *Earl Warren: A Public Life*. New York: Oxford University Press, 1982.

Williams, Juan. *Thurgood Marshall: American Revolutionary*. New York: Times Books, 1998.

Wolters, Raymond. *The Burden of Brown: Thirty Years of School Desegregation*. Knoxville: University of Tennessee Press, 1984.

Woodward, Bob, and Scott Armstrong. *The Brethren: Inside the Supreme Court*. New York: Simon & Schuster, 1979.

Wright, Charles Alan. *Law of Federal Courts*. 5th ed. St. Paul, Minn.: West Publishing Co., 1994.

Yarbrough, Tinsley E. *John Marshall Harlan: Great Dissenter of the Warren Court*. New York: Oxford University Press, 1992.

———. *Mr. Justice Black and His Critics*. Durham, N.C.: Duke University Press, 1988.

Articles and Book Chapters

Alschuler, Albert W. "Failed Pragmatism: Reflections on the Burger Court." 100 *Harvard Law Review* 1436–56 (1987).

Arenella, Peter. "Rethinking the Functions of Criminal Procedure: The Warren and Burger Courts' Competing Ideologies." 72 *Georgetown Law Journal* 175–248 (1983).

Arnold, Richard. "The Supreme Court and the Antitrust Laws, 1953–1967." 34 *Antitrust Journal* 2–20 (1967).

Arnold, Thurman. "Professor Hart's Theology." 73 *Harvard Law Review* 1298–1317 (1960).

Atkins, Burton M., and Terry Sloope. "The 'New' Hugo Black and the Warren Court." 18 *Polity* 621–37 (1986).

Atkinson, David N. "From New Deal Liberal to Supreme Court Conservative: The Metamorphosis of Justice Sherman Minton." 1975 *Washington University Law Quarterly* 361–94 (1975).

Auerbach, Carl A. "The Reapportionment Cases: One Person, One Vote—One Vote, One Value." 1964 *Supreme Court Review* 1–87.

Bair, Paul R. "Justice Clark, the Voice of the Past, and the Exclusionary Rule." 64 *Texas Law Review* 415–19 (1985).

Barnett, Helaine Meresman, Janis Meresman Goldman, and Jeffrey B. Morris. "A Lawyer's Lawyer, A Judge's Judge: Justice Potter Stewart and the Fourteenth Amendment." 51 *Cincinnati Law Review* 509–44 (1982).

Baum, Lawrence. "Measuring Policy Change in the U.S. Supreme Court." 82 *American Political Science Review* 905–12 (1988).

Beaney, William M. "Civil Liberties and Statutory Construction." 8 *Journal of Public Law* 66–80 (1959).

———. "The Warren Court and the Political Process." 67 *Michigan Law Review* 353–52 (1968).

Beaney, William M., and Edward N. Beiser. "Prayer and Politics: The Impact of *Engel* and *Schempp* on the Political Process." 13 *Journal of Public Law* 475–503 (1964).

Belknap, Michal R. "Constitutional Law as Creative Problem Solving: Could the Warren Court Have Ended the Vietnam War?" 36 *California Western Law Review* 99–124 (1999).

———. "God and the Warren Court: The Search for a Wholesome Neutrality." 9 *Seton Hall Constitutional Law Journal* 401–57 (1999).

———. "Tom C. Clark." In *American National Biography*. Edited by Garraty, 4:948–51. New York: Oxford University Press, 1998.

———. "The Warren Court and Equality." In *Constitutionalism and American Culture*. Edited by Sandra F. VanBurkleo, Kermit L. Hall, and Robert J. Kaczorowski, 211–39. Lawrence: University Press of Kansas, 2002.

———. "The Warren Court and the Vietnam War: The Limits of Legal Liberalism." 33 *Georgia Law Review* 65–154 (1998).

Benner, Laurence A. "Requiem for *Miranda:* The Rehnquist Court's Voluntariness Doctrine in Historical Perspective." 67 *Washington University Law Quarterly* 59–163 (1989).

Bickel, Alexander M. "The Original Understanding of the Fourteenth Amendment." 69 *Harvard Law Review* 1–65 (1955).

———. "The Supreme Court and Reapportionment." In Polsby, *1970s,* 57–74

Binion, Gayle. "Justice Potter Stewart: The Unpredictable Vote." 1992 *Journal of Supreme Court History* 99–108 (1992).

Birkby, Robert H. "The Supreme Court and the Bible Belt: Tennessee Reaction to the 'Schempp' Decision." In *Prayer in the Public Schools,* edited by Robert Sikorkie, 1:178–217. New York: Garland, 1993.

Black, Charles L., Jr. "The Lawfulness of the Segregation Decisions." 69 *Yale Law Journal* 420–30 (1960).

———. "The Unfinished Business of the Warren Court." 46 *Washington Law Review* 3–45 (1970).

Blasi, Vincent J. "The Rootless Activism of the Burger Court." In Blasi, *Counter-Revolution,* 198–217.

Boudin, Leonard B. "Involuntary Loss of American Nationality." 73 *Harvard Law Review* 1510–31 (1960).

Breen, Daniel I. "Stanley Forman Reed." In Urofsky, *Supreme Court Justices,* 367–72.

Brenner, Saul, Timothy M. Hagle, and Harold J. Spaeth. "The Defection of the Marginal Justice on the Warren Court." 42 *Western Political Quarterly* 409–25 (1989).

Brown, Tyrone. "Clerking for the Chief Justice." In Schwartz, *Retrospective,* 276–82.

Cahn, Edmund. "Jurisprudence." 30 *New York University Law Review* 150–69 (1955).

Carter, Robert L. "The Warren Court and Desegregation." 67 *Michigan Law Review* 237–48 (1968).

Cassell, Paul G. "*Miranda's* Social Costs: An Empirical Reassessment." 90 *Northwestern University Law Review* 387–499 (1996).

Cassell, Paul G., and Richard Fowles. "Handcuffing the Cops? A Thirty-Year Perspective on *Miranda*'s Harmful Effects on Law Enforcement." 50 *Stanford Law Review* 1055–1145 (1998).

Chernock, Gregory S. "The Clash of Two Worlds: Robert H. Jackson, Institutional Pragmatism, and *Brown*." 72 *Temple Law Review* 51–109 (1999).

"Comments on Powell v. McCormack." 17 *UCLA Law Review* 2–191 (1969).

Cox, Archibald. "Forward: Constitutional Adjudication and the Promotion of Human Rights." 80 *Harvard Law Review* 91–122 (1965).

Crain, Robert L., and Rita E. Mahard. "Desegregation and Black Achievement: A Review of the Research." 42 *Law and Contemporary Problems* 17–55 (1978).

Darbyshire, Glen M. "Clerking for Justice Marshall." 77 *ABA Journal* 48–51 (1991).

Defeis, Elizabeth. "Justice William J. Brennan, Jr." 16 *Seton Hall Law Review* 429–61 (1986).

Dixon, Robert G., Jr. "The Court, the People, and 'One Man, One Vote.'" In Polsby, *1970s*, 7–46.

———. "The Warren Court Crusade for the Holy Grail of 'One Man–One Vote.'" 1969 *Supreme Court Review* 219–79.

Doran, Dennis D. "Justice Tom Clark's Role in Mapp v. Ohio's Extension of the Exclusionary Rule to State Searches and Seizures." 52 *Case Western Reserve Law Review* 401–40 (2001).

Dudziak, Mary L. "The Limits of Good Faith: Desegregation in Topeka, Kansas, 1950–1956." 5 *Law and History Review* 351–91 (1987).

Dunne, Gerald T. "Justices Hugo Black and Robert Jackson: The Great Feud." 19 *Saint Louis University Law Journal* 465–87 (1975).

"Editorial: Religion Sponsored by the State." 4 *Journal of Church and State* 141–49 (1962).

Fassett, John B. "Mr. Justice Reed and Brown v. The Board of Education." 1986 *Yearbook of the Supreme Court Historical Society* 48–63 (1986).

Fisher, Joseph A. "The Becker Amendment: A Constitutional Trojan Horse." 11 *Journal of Church and State* 427–55 (1969).

Fiss, Owen. "Dombrowski." 86 *Yale Law Journal* 1103–64 (1977).

Freyer, Tony. "Hugo L. Black and the Warren Court in Retrospect." In Tushnet, *Warren Court*, 195–203.

Fried, Charles. "The Conservativism of Justice Harlan." 36 *New York Law School Law Review* 33–52 (1991).

Friedman, Leon. "Byron R. White." In Friedman and Israel, *Justices*, 4:1574–605.

Funston, Richard. "The Double Standard of Constitutional Protection in the Era of the Welfare State." 90 *Political Science Quarterly* 251–69 (1975–76).

Galloway, Russell W., Jr. "The Early Years of the Warren Court: Emergence of Judicial Liberalism (1953–1957)." 18 *Santa Clara Law Review* 609–40 (1978).

———. "The Second Period of the Warren Court: The Liberal Trend Abates (1957–1961)." 19 *Santa Clara Law Review* 947–84 (1979).

———. "The Third Period of the Warren Court: Liberal Dominance (1962–1969)." 20 *Santa Clara Law Review* 773–829 (1980).

Garrow, David J. "Hopelessly Hollow History: Revisionist Devaluing of *Brown v. Board of Education*." 80 *Virginia Law Review* 151–60 (1994).

Ginsburg, Ruth Bader. "Sexual Equality under the Fourteenth and Equal Rights Amendments." 1979 *Washington University Law Quarterly* 161–78 (1979).

Gordon, Charles. "The Citizen and the State: Power of Congress to Expatriate American Citizens." 53 *Georgetown Law Journal* 315–64 (1965).

Griswold, Erwin N. "Forward: Of Time and Attitudes—Professor Hart and Judge Arnold." 74 *Harvard Law Review* 81–94 (1960).

Gunter, Susan E. "Caryl Whittier Chessman." In *American National Biography*. Edited by Garraty, 4:790–91. New York: Oxford University Press, 1998.

Gunther, Gerald. "Forward, In Search of Evolving Doctrine on a Changing Court: A Model for a Newer Equal Protection." 86 *Harvard Law Review* 1–48 (1977).

Hagley, Judith A. "Massive Resistance—The Rhetoric and the Reality." 27 *New Mexico Law Review* 167–221 (1997).

Hall, Kermit L. "Justice Brennan and Cultural History: *New York Times v. Sullivan* and Its Times." 27 *California Western Law Review* 339–59 (1991).

Hart, Henry M. "Forward: The Time Chart of the Justices." 73 *Harvard Law Review* 84–105 (1959).

Heck, Edward V. "Justice Brennan and the Heyday of Warren Court Liberalism." 20 *Santa Clara Law Review* 841–87 (1980).

Hockett, Jeffrey D. "Justice Robert H. Jackson and Segregation: A Study of the Limitations and Proper Basis of Judicial Action." 1989 *Yearbook of the Supreme Court Historical Society* 52–67 (1989).

Horwitz, Morton J. "The Jurisprudence of Brown and the Dilemmas of Liberalism." 14 *Harvard Civil Rights-Civil Liberties Law Review* 599–613 (1979).

———. "The Warren Court: Rediscovering the Link Between Law and Culture." 55 *University of Chicago Law Review* 450–57 (1988).

———. "The Warren Court and the Pursuit of Justice." 50 *Washington and Lee Law Review* 5–13 (1993).

Howard, A. E. Dick. "The Road from 'Brown,'" 3 *Wilson Quarterly* 96–107 (1979).

Hutchinson, Dennis J. "The Black-Jackson Feud." 1968 *Supreme Court Review* 203–43.

———. "The Man Who Once Was Whizzer White." 103 *Yale Law Journal* 43–56 (1993).

———. "Robert H. Jackson, the Supreme Court, and the Nuremberg Trial." 1990 *Supreme Court Review* 257–99.

———. "Unanimity and Desegregation: Decisionmaking in the Supreme Court, 1948–1958." 68 *Georgetown Law Journal* 1–96 (1979).

Ides, Allan. "The Jurisprudence of Byron White." 103 *Yale Law Journal* 419–61 (1993).

Johnston, Richard E. "Some Comparative Statistics on U.S. Chief Justice Courts." 9 *Rocky Mountain Social Science Journal* 89–100 (1972).

Jones, John B., Jr. "Recent Developments in Federal Taxation." 16 *Tulane Tax Institute* 9–56 (1967).

Kahn, Michael A. "Shattering the Myth about President Eisenhower's Supreme Court Appointments." 22 *Presidential Studies Quarterly* 47–56 (1992).

Kalman, Laura. "Abe Fortas: Symbol of the Warren Court." In Tushnet, *Warren Court*, 155–68.

Kalven, Harry, Jr. "The New York Times Case: A Note on the Central Meaning of the First Amendment." 1964 *Supreme Court Review* 191–221.

———. "The Reasonable Man and the First Amendment: Hill, Butts, and Walker." 1967 *Supreme Court Review* 267–309.

———. "'Uninhibited, Robust, and Wide-Open'—A Note on Free Speech and the Warren Court." 67 *Michigan Law Review* 289–302 (1968).

Kamisar, Yale. "Can (Did) Congress Overrule *Miranda?*" 85 *Cornell Law Review* 883–955 (2000).

———. "The Warren Court and Criminal Justice." In Schwartz, *Retrospective*, 116–58.

Katz, Al. "Privacy and Pornography: Stanley v. Georgia." 1969 *Supreme Court Review* 203–17.

Kauper, Paul G. "Prayer, Public Schools and the Supreme Court." 61 *Michigan Law Review* 1032–68 (1963).

———. "The Warren Court: Religious Liberty and Church-State Relations." 67 *Michigan Law Review* 269–88 (1968).

Kauper, Thomas E. "The 'Warren Court' and the Antitrust Laws: Of Economics, Populism, and Cynicism." 67 *Michigan Law Review* 325–42 (1986).

Kelly, Alfred H. "The School Desegregation Case." In *Quarrels That Have Shaped the Constitution.* Edited by John Garraty, 2nd ed. 307–33. New York: Harper & Row, 1987.

Kirkendall, Richard. "Sherman Minton." In Friedman and Israel, *Justices.* 1361–72

Kitch, Edmund W. "Katz v. United States: The Limits of the Fourth Amendment." 1968 *Supreme Court Review* 133–52.

Klarman, Michael J. "Brown, Racial Change and the Civil Rights Movement." 80 *Virginia Law Review* 7–150 (1994).

———. "*Brown v. Board of Education:* Facts and Political Correctness." 80 *Virginia Law Review* 185–99 (1994).

———. "How Brown Changed Race Relations: The Backlash Thesis." 81 *Journal of American History* 81–108 (1994).

Krislov, Samuel. "From Ginzburg to Ginsberg: The Unhurried Children's Hour in Obscenity Litigation." 1968 *Supreme Court Review* 153–97.

Kurland, Philip B. "Of Church and State and the Supreme Court." 29 *University of Chicago Law Review* 1–96 (1961).

———. "Egalitarianism and the Warren Court." 68 *Michigan Law Review* 629–82 (1970).

———. "The Regents' Prayer Case: 'Full of Sound and Fury, Signifying . . .'" 1962 *Supreme Court Review* 1–33.

———. "Forward: Equal in Origin and Equal in Title to the Legislative and Executive Branches of the Government." 78 *Harvard Law Review* 143–75 (1964).

Lamb, Charles M. "Chief Justice Warren E. Burger: A Conservative Chief for Conservative Times." In Lamb and Halpern, *Burger Court,* 129–62.

Laycock, Douglas. "A Survey of Religious Liberty in the United States." 47 *Ohio State Law Journal* 409–51 (1986).

Leo, Richard A. "The Impact of Miranda Revisited." 86 *Journal of Criminal Law and Criminology* 621–92 (1996).

Lewis, Anthony. "Foreword." In Blasi, *Counter-Revolution,* vii–x.

Long, Edward R. "Earl Warren and the Politics of Anti-Communism." 51 *Pacific Historical Review* 51–70 (1982).

Luban, David. "The Warren Court and the Concept of Right." 34 *Harvard Civil Rights—Civil Liberties Law Review* 7–37 (1999).

Lund, Sister Candida. "The Sunday Closing Laws." In *The Third Branch of Government: 8 Cases in Constitutional Politics.* Edited by C. Herman Pritchett and Alan F. Westin, 275–308. New York: Harcourt, Brace & World, 1963.

MacKenzie, John P. "The Warren Court and the Press." 67 *Michigan Law Review* 303–16 (1968).

Marsel, Robert S. "The Constitutional Jurisprudence of Potter Stewart: Reflections on a Life of Public Service." 55 *Tennessee Law Review* 1–39 (1987).

———. "Mr. Justice Arthur J. Goldberg and the Death Penalty: A Memorandum to the Conference." 27 *South Texas Law Review* 467–92 (1986).

Mason, Alpheus Thomas. "Whence and Whither the Burger Court? Judicial Self-Restraint: A Beguiling Myth." 41 *Review of Politics* 3–37 (1979).

Massaro, John. "LBJ and the Fortas Nomination for Chief Justice." 97 *Political Science Quarterly* 603–21 (1982–83).

McCloskey, Robert G. "Forward: The Reapportionment Case." 76 *Harvard Law Review* 54–74 (1962).

McFeeley, Neil D. "A Change of Direction: Habeas Corpus from Warren to Burger." 32 *Western Political Quarterly* 174–88 (1985).

———. "The Supreme Court and the Federal System: Federalism from Warren to Burger." 8 *Publius* 5–36 (1978).

McGrath, C. Peter. "The Obscenity Cases: Grapes of Roth." 1966 *Supreme Court Review* 7–77.

McKay, Robert B. "Reapportionment: Success Story of the Warren Court." 67 *Michigan Law Review* 223–36 (1968).

McManamon, Mary Brigid. "Felix Frankfurter: The Architect of 'Our Federalism,'" 27 *Georgia Law Review* 697–788 (1993).

Mengler, Thomas M. "Public Relations in the Supreme Court: Justice Tom Clark's Opinion in the School Prayer Case." 6 *Constitutional Commentary* 331–49 (1989).

Michelman, Frank. "Forward: On Protecting the Poor Through the Fourteenth Amendment." 83 *Harvard Law Review* 7–59 (1969).

Miller, Arthur S. "Social Justice and the Warren Court: A Preliminary Examination." 11 *Pepperdine Law Review* 473–98 (1983–84).

Mills, Samuel A. "Parochiaid and the Abortion Decisions: Supreme Court Justice William J. Brennan, Jr. versus the U.S. Catholic Hierarchy." 31 *Journal of Church and State* 751–73 (1989).

Mitchell, John B. "What Went Wrong with the Warren Court's Conception of the Fourth Amendment?" 27 *New England Law Review* 35–59 (1992).

Modjeska, Lee. "Labor and the Warren Court." 8 *Industrial Relations Law Journal* 479–546 (1986).

Nelson, William E. "Byron R. White: A Liberal of 1960." In Tushnet, *Warren Court*, 139–54.

———. "The Changing Meaning of Equality in Twentieth-Century Constitutional Law." 52 *Washington and Lee Law Review* 3–103 (1995).

———. "Deference and the Limits to Deference in the Constitutional Jurisprudence of Justice Byron White." 58 *University of Colorado Law Review* 347–64 (1987).

Nesson, Charles. "The Harlan-Frankfurter Connection: An Aspect of Justice Harlan's Judicial Education." 36 *New York Law School Law Review* 179–97 (1991).

"Note: The Development of the Plenary Hearing Requirement in Federal Habeas Corpus for State Prisoners." 34 *Brooklyn Law Review* 247–68 (1968).

Palmer, Jan, and Saul Brenner. "Determinants of the Amount of Time Taken by the Vinson Court to Process Its Full-Opinion Cases." 1990 *Journal of Supreme Court History* 141–51 (1990).

Parrish, Michael E. "Earl Warren and the American Judicial Tradition." 1982 *American Bar Foundation Research Journal* 1179–88 (1982).

———. "Felix Frankfurter, the Progressive Tradition and the Warren Court." In Tushnet, *Warren Court*, 51–63.

Paulsen, Monrad. "The Sit-in Cases of 1964: 'But Answer Came There None.'" 1964 *Supreme Court Review* 137–70.

Perry, Barbara A. "Justice Hugo Black and the 'Wall of Separation Between Church and State.'" 31 *Journal of Church and State* 55–72 (1989).

Pfeffer, Leo. "The Becker Amendment." 6 *Journal of Church and State* 344–49 (1964).

———. "The New York Regents Prayer Case," 4 *Journal of Church and State* 150–58 (1962).

———. "The Schempp-Murray Decision on School Prayers and Bible Reading." 5 *Journal of Church and State* 165–75 (1963).

Pollak, Louis H. "Forward: Public Prayers in Public Schools." 77 *Harvard Law Review* 62–78 (1963).

———. "Racial Discrimination and Judicial Integrity: A Reply to Professor Wechsler." 108 *University of Pennsylvania Law Review* 1–34 (1959).

Post, Robert C. "Justice William J. Brennan and the Warren Court." 8 *Constitutional Commentary* 11–25 (1991).

———. "William J. Brennan and the Warren Court." In Tushnet, *Warren Court*, 123–36.

"Project: Federal Administrative Law Developments—1969." 1970 *Duke Law Journal* 67–246 (1970).

Rae, Douglas W. "Reapportionment and Political Democracy." In Polsby, *1970s*, 91–112.

Read, Frank T. "Judicial Evolution of the Law of School Integration Since *Brown v. Board of Education*." 39 *Law and Contemporary Problems* 7–49 (1975).

Redish, Martin H. "The Warren Court, the Burger Court and the First Amendment Overbreadth Doctrine." 78 *Northwestern University Law Review* 1031–70 (1983).

Redman, Barbara J. "Sabbatarian Accommodation in the Supreme Court." 33 *Journal of Church and State* 495–523 (1991).

Reich, Charles. "Individual Rights and Social Welfare: The Emerging Legal Issues." 74 *Yale Law Journal* 1245–57 (1965).

———. "The New Property." 73 *Yale Law Journal* 733–87 (1964).

Reid, Herbert O., Sr. "State of the Art: The Law and Education since 1954." 52 *Journal of Negro Education* 234–49 (1963).

Revesz, Richard L. "Thurgood Marshall's Struggle." 68 *New York University Law Review* 237–63 (1993).

Rodgers, Harrel R., Jr. "The Supreme Court and School Desegregation: Twenty Years Later." 89 *Political Science Quarterly* 751–77 (1974–75).

Rohr, Marc. "Communists and the First Amendment: The Shaping of Freedom of Advocacy in the Cold War Era." 28 *University of San Diego Law Review* 1–116 (1991).

Rosenberg, Gerald N. "*Brown* is Dead! Long Live *Brown*! The Endless Attempt to Canonize a Case." 80 *Virginia Law Review* 161–71 (1994).

St. Antoine, Theodore J. "Judicial Valour and the Warren Court's Labor Decisions." 67 *Michigan Law Review* 317–24 (1968).

Schoen, Rodric B. "A Strange Silence: Vietnam and the Supreme Court." 33 *Washburn Law Journal* 275–322 (1994).

Schoenfeld, Benjamin J. "Significant Administrative Law Decisions of the United States Supreme Court during the October 1962–1963 Term." 2 *Duquesne University Law Review* 47–76 (1963).

Schulhofer, Stephen J. "*Miranda*'s Practical Effect: Substantial Benefits and Vanishingly Small Social Costs." 90 *Northwestern University Law Review* 500–63 (1996).

———. "Reconsidering Miranda." 54 *University of Chicago Law Review* 435–61 (1987).

Schwartz, Bernard. "Chief Justice Rehnquist, Justice Jackson, and the *Brown* Case." 1986 *Supreme Court Review* 245–67.

———. "Earl Warren as a Judge." 12 *Hastings Constitutional Law Quarterly* 179–200 (1985).

———. "The Judicial Lives of Earl Warren." 15 *Suffolk University Law Review* 1–22 (1981).

Schwartz, Herman. "Warren Earl Burger." In Urofsky, *Supreme Court Justices*, 69–76.

Seidman, Louis Michael. "*Brown* and *Miranda*." 80 *California Law Review* 673–753 (1992).

Sexton, John. "The Warren Court and the Religious Clauses of the First Amendment." In Schwartz, *Retrospective*, 104–15.

Shapiro, Martin. "Father and Sons: The Courts, the Commentators—and the Search for Values." In Blasi, *Counter-Revolution*, 218–38.

———. "The Warren Court and Federal Tax Policy." 36 *Southern California Law Review* 208–28 (1963).

Sheehan, Reginald S. "Federal Agencies and the Supreme Court: An Analysis of Litigation Outcomes, 1953–1988." 20 *American Politics Quarterly* 478–500 (1992).

———. "Governmental Litigants, Underdogs, and Civil Liberties: A Reassessment of a Trend in Supreme Court Decisionmaking." 45 *Western Political Quarterly* 27–39 (1992).

Sheft, Mark A. "The End of the Smith Act Era: A Legal and Historical Analysis of *Scales v. United States*." 36 *American Journal of Legal History* 164–202 (1992).

Simon, James F. "William O. Douglas." In Schwartz, *Retrospective*, 211–23.

Smith, Rodney K. "Justice Potter Stewart: A Contemporary Jurist's View of Religious Liberty." 59 *North Dakota Law Review* 183–210 (1983).

Steamer, Robert J. "Contemporary Supreme Court Decisions on Civil Liberties." 92 *Political Science Quarterly* 425–42 (1977).

Steiker, Carol S. "Counter-Revolution in Constitutional Criminal Procedure? Two Audiences, Two Answers." 94 *Michigan Law Review* 2466–551 (1996).

Stone, Katherine Van Wezel. "The Post-War Paradigm in American Labor Law." 90 *Yale Law Journal* 1509–80 (1981).

Strossen, Nadine. "Freedom of Speech in the Warren Court." In Schwartz, *Retrospective*, 68–84.

"Symposium on the Fortieth Anniversary of Mapp v. Ohio." 52 *Case Western Law Review* 371–478 (2001).

Taggert, William A., and Matthew R. DeZee. "A Note on Substantive Access Doctrines in the U.S. Supreme Court: A Comparative Analysis of the Warren and Burger Courts." 38 *Western Political Quarterly* 84–93 (1985).

Tannenbaum, Donald G. "Explaining Controversial Nominations: The Fortas Case Revisited." 17 *Presidential Studies Quarterly* 573–86 (1987).

Thompson, Dennis L. "The Kennedy Court: Left and Right of Center." 26 *Western Political Quarterly* 263–79 (1973).

Tushnet, Mark. "The Significance of *Brown v. Board of Education*." 80 *Virginia Law Review* 173–84 (1994).

———. "The Warren Court as History: An Interpretation." In Tushnet, *The Warren Court*, 1–34.

———. "What Really Happened in Brown v. Board of Education." With Katya Lezin. 91 *Columbia Law Review* 1867–1930 (1991).

Ulmer, S. Sidney. "Governmental Litigants, Underdogs, and Civil Liberties in the Supreme Court: 1903–1968 Terms." 47 *Journal of Politics* 899–909 (1985).

Urofsky, Melvin I. "Conflict among the Brethren: Felix Frankfurter, William O. Douglas and the Clash of Personalities and Philosophies on the United States Supreme Court." 1988 *Duke Law Journal* 71–113 (1988).

———. "The Failure of Felix Frankfurter." 26 *University of Richmond Law Review* 175–212 (1991).

———. "William O. Douglas as a Common Law Judge." 1991 *Duke Law Journal* 133–59 (1991).

———. "William O. Douglas as Common-Law Judge." In Tushnet, *Warren Court*, 64–85.

Van den Haag, Ernest. "Social Science Testimony in the Desegregation Cases—A Reply to Professor Kenneth Clark." 6 *Villanova Law Review* 69–79 (1960).

Varat, Jonathan D. "Justice White and the Breadth and Allocation of Federal Authority." 58 *University of Colorado Law Review* 371–427 (1987).

Way, H. Frank, Jr. "Survey Research on Judicial Decisions: The Prayer and Bible Reading Cases." 21 *Western Political Quarterly* 189–205 (1968).

Wechsler, Herbert. "Toward Neutral Principles of Constitutional Law." 73 *Harvard Law Review* 1–35 (1959).

West, Ellis M. "Justice Tom Clark and American Church-State Law." 54 *Journal of Presbyterian History* 387–404 (1976).

White, G. Edward. "The Anti-Judge: William O. Douglas and the Ambiguities of Individuality." 74 *Virginia Law Review* 17–86 (1988).

———. "Earl Warren as Jurist." 67 *Virginia Law Review* 461–551 (1981).

———. "Earl Warren's Influence on the Warren Court." In Tushnet, *Warren Court*, 37–50.

———. "Warren Court." In *American Constitutional History*, edited by Leonard W. Levy, Kenneth L. Karst, and Dennis J. Mahoney, 279–93. New York: Macmillan, 1989.

Wright, J. Skelly. "The Federal Courts and the Nature and Quality of State Law." 13 *Wayne Law Review* 317–37 (1967).

Yarbrough, Tinsley E. "The Burger Court and Unspecified Rights: On Protecting Fundamental and Not-So-Fundamental 'Interests' Through a Flexible Conception of Equal Protection." 1977 *Duke Law Journal* 143–70 (1977).

Table of Cases

Index

389